TWELFTH EDITION

PROBATION AND PAROLE
Theory and Practice

Howard Abadinsky
St. John's University

PEARSON

Boston   Columbus   Indianapolis   New York   San Francisco   Upper Saddle River
Amsterdam   Cape Town   Dubai   London   Madrid   Milan   Munich   Paris   Montréal   Toronto
Delhi   Mexico City   Sao Paulo   Sydney   Hong Kong   Seoul   Singapore   Taipei   Tokyo

Editorial Director: Vernon Anthony
Executive Editor: Gary Bauer
Editorial Assistant: Lynda Cramer
Director of Marketing: David Gesell
Senior Marketing Manager: Mary Salzman
Senior Marketing Coordinator: Alicia Wozniak
Team Lead for Project Management: JoEllen Gohr
Production Project Manager: Jessica H. Sykes
Senior Operations Supervisor: Deidra Skahill
Senior Art Director: Diane Ernsberger
Cover Art: James Steidl/Shutterstock.com
Media Project Manager: April Cleland
Full-Service Project Management: George Jacob/Integra Software Services
Composition: Integra Software Services
Printer/Binder: Courier/Kendallville
Cover Printer: Lehigh-Phoenix Color/Hagerstown
Text Font: 10/12 Minion Pro

Library of Congress Cataloging-in-Publication Data

Abadinsky, Howard
  Probation and parole: theory and practice / Howard Abadinsky,
St. John's University.—Twelfth edition.
    pages cm
Includes bibliographical references and index.
ISBN-13: 978-0-13-348370-3
ISBN-10: 0-13-348370-3
1. Probation—United States.   2. Parole—United States.   I. Title.
HV9278.A2 2015
364.6'30973—dc23

                            2013042243

10 9 8 7 6 5 4 3 2 1

ISBN 10: 0-13-348370-3
ISBN 13: 978-0-13-348370-3

*Dedicated to the vital role of probation and
parole personnel throughout the United States and the
American Probation and Parole Association.*

Brief Contents

Contents

Chapter 9

Chapter 10

Chapter 11   Probation and Parole in Juvenile Justice   261

Preface

New to This Edition

- Each chapter opens with Learning Objectives
- Updates on statutory changes that impact probation and parole
- Updates on probation and parole-related statistics
- Updates on probation and parole research
- Extensive chapter summaries
- Extensive end-of-chapter review questions
- New example of the long-form presentence investigation report
- Changes and trends in community supervision
- Examination and analysis of current areas of controversy in probation and parole
- Re-organized and streamlined for ease of classroom use

The first edition of this book was written while I was a senior parole officer for the New York State Division of Parole. Since that time, new concepts (or sometimes simply buzzwords) have affected both the theory and practice of probation and parole. Some, such as *community-based corrections*, had a brief life, while the *justice model* and *determinate sentencing* had long-lasting effects, creating the need for *graduated sanctions* and *intermediate punishments*. The lexicon expanded to include *restorative justice, broken windows/community-based supervision, place-based supervision, evidence-based practice, offender reentry*, and, more recently, *motivational interviewing* and *cognitive-behavioral therapy*.

Political posturing and sound-bite polemics often replaced careful and thoughtful policy development and produced "truth-in-sentencing" (no parole or early release) and "three strikes and you're out" (life imprisonment on third felony conviction). "Tough on crime" and "war on drugs" encountered spending curbs and tax shortfalls. As a result, a new policy (buzzword?) has become popular: *justice reinvestment*, which is shifting funds away from prisons and toward community supervision. This edition deals with these issues.

This edition contains 12 chapters organized to enhance ease of classroom use. To remain at the cutting edge of the field, this edition continues to use current materials from juvenile and adult probation and parole agencies throughout the country. (Material whose source is not cited is from the appropriate agency.) Each chapter highlights key terms (which appear in the Glossary) and ends with a list of those key terms as well as relevant Internet sites; as in previous editions, review questions that conclude each chapter have been expanded. The instructor's resource guide available for this book provides a model curriculum and test questions.

The author would like to thank Editor Gary Bauer, Editorial Assistant Lynda Cramer, Production Editor Rex Davidson, Project Manager Lindsay Bethoney, copyeditor Indrani Samaddar and Project Manager George Jacob, for their dedication to this project, and reviewers for their thoughtful reviews and suggestions.

Instructor Supplements

MyTest and TestBank represent new standards in testing material. Whether you use a basic test bank document or generate questions electronically through MyTest, every question is linked to the text's learning objective, page number, and level of difficulty. This allows for quick reference in the text and an easy way to check the difficulty level and variety of your questions. MyTest can be accessed at www.PearsonMyTest.com.

PowerPoint Presentations. Our presentations offer clear, straightforward outlines and notes to use for class lectures or study materials. Photos, illustrations, charts, and tables from the book are included in the presentations when applicable.

Other supplements are:
• Instructor's Manual with Test Bank
• Test Item File for ingestion into an LMS, including Blackboard and WebCT.

To access supplementary materials online, instructors need to request an instructor access code. Go to **www.pearsonhighered.com/irc**, where you can register for an instructor access code. Within 48 hours after registering, you will receive a confirming email, including an instructor access code. Once you have received your code, go to the site and log on for full instructions on downloading the materials you wish to use.

Alternate Versions

eBooks. This text is also available in multiple eBook formats including Adobe Reader and *CourseSmart.* CourseSmart is an exciting new choice for students looking to save money. As an alternative to purchasing the printed textbook, students can purchase an electronic version of the same content. With a CourseSmart eTextbook, students can search the text, make notes online, print out reading assignments that incorporate lecture notes, and bookmark important passages for later review. For more information, or to purchase access to the *CourseSmart* eTextbook, visit **www.coursesmart.com**.

About the Author

Howard Abadinsky is professor of criminal justice at St. John's University. He was an inspector for the Cook County (IL) Sheriff's Office and a New York State parole officer and senior parole officer. A graduate of Queens College of the City University of New York, he has an M.S.W. from Fordham University and a Ph.D. from New York University. Dr. Abadinsky is the author of several books, including *Organized Crime*, 10th edition, and *Drug Use and Abuse*, 8th edition.

Howard Abadinsky welcomes comments about his work and can be reached at St. John's University, 8000 Utopia Parkway, Jamaica, NY 11439; abadinsh@stjohns.edu.

Caralyn Bishop-Abadinsky

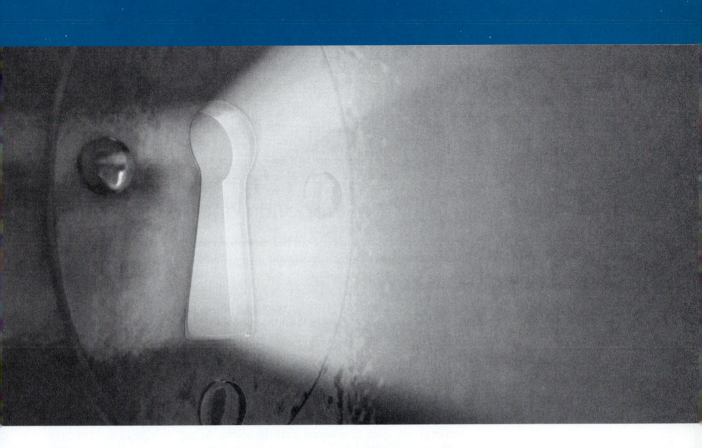

1 Probation and Parole in Criminal Justice

LEARNING OBJECTIVES

This chapter will enable the student to:

1 *Understand the contradictory goals and competing expectations of American criminal justice.*

2 *Explain why most convicted offenders are not imprisoned.*

3 *Discuss the impact of increases in the number of geriatric inmates.*

4 *Understand why reducing prison populations by keeping out or releasing early "nonviolent offenders" is a dubious policy.*

5 *Discuss why the system of criminal justice in the United States is not systematic.*

6 *Explain how the criminal law and its enforcement reflect distinctions in power.*

7 *Understand why prevention of recidivism is difficult to determine.*

8 *Distinguish the classical view from the positive view of crime and criminal behavior.*

Probation and parole are part of a uniquely American system of criminal justice in which contradictory goals and competing expectations are reconciled in a swirling cauldron of politics. Americans want greater protection from crime while insisting that these efforts do not impose significant tax dollar costs (DiIulio, 1993). Probation and parole are often made scapegoats for the impossibility of achieving these competing expectations.

▶ The "Why?" of Probation and Parole

Why be concerned with probation or parole? "If you do the crime, do the time." When a probationer or parolee commits a serious crime—killing a police officer or child, for example—that generates a great deal of media coverage, questions are raised about why this person was not in prison. Even a single case can result in changes that typically make sound politics but poor practice. For reasons of *justice* (punishment to fit the crime) or *cost* (too expensive to incarcerate all offenders in prison indefinitely), most convicted offenders are not imprisoned, and more than 90 percent of all imprisoned offenders are eventually released.

Convicted offenders can be placed on probation; incarcerated and released after completion of their entire sentence; and paroled or otherwise released early to supervision in the community. If laws are enacted that limit probation or increase the length of imprisonment by abolishing discretionary release (parole), for example, there must be corresponding increases in prison space to accommodate the results. As any shopper or grocery clerk knows, you can't get 10 pounds into a 5-pound bag. Against this reality is another: *Elected officials do not lose elections for supporting increased terms of imprisonment—but they are vulnerable when supporting tax increases that thereby become necessary.*

Compared with citizens of other industrialized nations, Americans tend to be more religious and entrepreneurial. We have more billionaires, we are the world leader in Nobel Prizes, and we send more people to universities—and prisons—than any other Western nation (Murphy, 2001). Over the past four decades, there has been a dramatic increase in the use of prisons to combat crime: Incarceration rates jumped by more than 700 percent since the 1970s (Henrichson and Delaney, 2012). The United States incarcerates a greater percentage of its population than any other country in the world (Schmitt, Warner, and Gupta, 2010; Walmsley, 2011). While the United States has an incarceration rate of about 625 per 100,000 residents (Carson and Golinell, 2013), our neighbor to the north has a rate of about 115; England has a rate of about 150; we do compete with Russia, which has a rate of about 575 (Walmsley, 2011). In the United States, there is wide variation by geography; southern states have many times the rate of states in New England.

There are in excess of 1.5 million prisoners in the United States at an annual cost of about $30,000 per inmate (Henrichson and Delaney, 2012). The cost of imprisonment, however, is typically underestimated because it leaves out many actual expenses such as fringe benefits for employees, which average more than 25 percent of salaries. And other state agencies pay many costs, including employee health insurance, pension contributions, and inmate hospital care, costs often overlooked when reporting prison spending (Henrichson and Delaney, 2012). The cost of building a new prison is about $250 million

(Washington State Institute for Public Policy, 2006). Although a state can float bonds to underwrite the cost of prison building, thereby amortizing the cost (which includes substantial interest) over a long period, operating costs such as staff salaries and benefits for retirees must be paid immediately out of the state's operating budget—it may be politically easier to build a prison than to staff and operate one. That can help explain why in recent years more than a dozen states have closed prisons.

Adding to prison costs are the problems of acquired immunodeficiency syndrome (AIDS), tuberculosis, hepatitis C, and the increasing number of geriatric offenders, often the result of "get tough" and **"three strikes and you're out"** (actually *in* for life) legislation. The increasing numbers of elderly inmates—the result of longer sentences and mandatory minimums, abolishing parole release, and "three strikes"—are adding extra burdens to the prison system. Florida, for example, housed less than 12,000 elderly inmates in 2006; in 2011, the number was more than 17,000. Between 1995 and 2010, the number of state and federal prisoners age 55 or older nearly quadrupled (increasing 282 percent), while the number of all prisoners grew by less than half (increasing 42 percent). In 2011, there were 124,400 prisoners age 55 or older (*Old Behind Bars*, 2012).

"Compared with their younger peers, older inmates have higher rates of both mild and serious health conditions, such as gross functional disabilities and impaired movement, mental illness, increased risk of major diseases, and a heightened need for assistance with daily living activities" (Chiu, 2010: 5). Because of lifestyle deficiencies, the average inmate is physiologically 10 years older than men who have never been incarcerated. Thus, 50 years is "senior inmate" status whose cost of incarceration is approximately three times that of a younger man (Harrison, 2006).

America's prisons have an increasing number of elderly inmates whose infirmities require wheelchairs and walkers, portable oxygen tanks, and hearing aids. They may be incontinent and without assistance, unable to dress or bathe. Some are suffering from dementia and Alzheimer's. Dental problems may be critical and require frequent periodontal work (*It's About Time,* 2010).

Tough-on-crime may be bad policy but good politics.

While there were about a million persons on probation and 220,000 persons on parole in 1979, there are currently about 5 million adults under some form of community supervision, more than 80 percent on probation. Incarceration costs about 12 times as much as probation and parole supervision. The extensive use of probation and parole is not based on some "liberal do-gooder," "hug-a-thug" notions, but on reality imposed by economics. In stark contrast to the amount spent on imprisonment, we spend relatively little on probation and parole, and informed observers argue that we are getting what we pay for.

The cost of imprisonment and, at times, the pressure of overcrowding leads to **front-door programs** such as intermediate punishments and **backdoor programs** such as "boot camp" prisons (discussed in Chapter 9) that either keep offenders from becoming inmates or lets them out early. Thus, although there was a steady decline in the percentage of inmates released by parole boards between 1980 and 2005, the percentage of prisoners being released from prisons to the community increased—despite building more than 200 prisons and hiring more than 100,000 additional correctional personnel (Glaze and Bonczar, 2006). Virginia, for example, abolished parole release in 1995 and the number of persons on probation more than doubled ("A Forecast," 2007). Interestingly, a study of inmates released in states that abolished parole revealed that they served seven months less than inmates released in states with parole (Petersilia, 2000b). Between 1995 and 2005, there was symmetry between the number of persons sent to prison and the number placed on probation: The percentage increase in the prison population was identical to the percentage increase in the probation population (Glaze and Bonczar, 2006).

For a decade, spending on prisons has been the fastest-growing or second-fastest-growing part of state budgets (competing with education). This increase was not the

Key Fact

The cost of imprisonment and, at times, the pressure of overcrowding lead to increased front- and backdoor programs.

natural consequence of spikes in crime, but "the result of policy choices that sent more people to prison and kept them there longer" (Pew Center on the States, 2009: 1). "For nearly three decades, most states have dealt with lawbreakers in two ways: lock more of them up for longer periods, and build more prisons to hold them. Now many governments, out of money and buried under mounting prison costs, are reversing those policies and practices" (Steinhauer, 2009: 1). As we will discuss in later chapters, offender treatment/rehabilitation has once again become fashionable (Byrne, 2009; Rosenfeld, 2009; Taxman, 2009).

If discretionary release—parole—is not an option (many states abolished their parole boards), then allowing inmates to earn "good time" (time off for good behavior) at a rate of half or more of their sentence becomes the most viable option, an option states adopted when they moved away from indeterminate sentencing (discussed in Chapter 4). However, so-called truth-in-sentencing laws limit this approach, permitting only small grants of good time—10 or 15 percent. Most states have enacted "three-strikes-and-you're-out" statutes, meaning lifetime imprisonment on a third- (or sometimes a second) felony conviction.[1] As these unreleasable inmates age, they become increasingly expensive wards of the state, requiring special housing—nursing homes surrounded by razor wire.

Key Fact

"Truth-in-sentencing" and "three-strikes-and-you're-out" laws have abolished parole and limited early release.

Economic crisis has brought into sharp focus the enormous cost of maintaining prisons. Some states that passed "three-strikes" laws have discovered loopholes allowing them to release inmates early. Those that still have parole boards have asked them to increase releases, whereas those without them are overhauling their sentencing laws. California, in the absence of a parole board, enacted a law permitting the release of "nonviolent" inmates without parole supervision (Archibold, 2010).

The release of nonviolent offenders is frequently offered as a way to reduce the prison population. However, as people who work in criminal justice recognize, the term "nonviolent" is disingenuous. Offenders who populate our criminal justice system are opportunists, not specialists—being convicted of a nonviolent crime does not indicate a nonviolent offender. Indeed, the most frequent conviction for a nonviolent offense is drug related. But the world of drugs is filled with violent people and violence that is often unreported. Burglary, a property crime, can turn into a violent crime when an offender encounters a homeowner. Is a robbery "violent" if the perpetrator uses a toy or unloaded gun? Is driving while intoxicated a nonviolent crime? What if a pedestrian or occupants of another vehicle are killed?

Key Fact

An offender convicted of a property crime is not necessarily a "nonviolent" criminal.

Getting lost in the often-simplistic approach to crime and criminals is any serious attention to the fate of persons released from prison: uneducated, unskilled, unemployed, with a criminal record that thwart job seeking, and now hardened by the prison experience.

THREE STRIKES IN CALIFORNIA

"It was sold to voters as a way of getting killers, rapists and child molesters off the streets for good." It snared a 55-year-old who is both retarded and mentally ill and who never committed a violent crime for receiving stolen property. In 2012, California revised their three-strikes law, which had been sending shoplifters and similar offenders to prison for life, to require that the third strike be for a serious or violent felony (Staples, 2012: 10).

---

[1]In 2003, the Supreme Court upheld the constitutionality of the "three strikes" laws (*Ewing v. California*, 538 U.S. 11; *Lockyer v. Andrade*, 538 U.S. 63).

About 70 percent are black or Latino; more than 60 percent are younger than 30 years of age; about 70 percent have not completed high school, and about 40 percent are unable to read; more than 20 percent are incarcerated for a drug offense, and most inmates have a history of substance abuse; about one-half grew up primarily in one-parent households; and many have been victims of neglect and/or child abuse. *In America's prisons are persons who are poorer, darker, younger, and less educated than the rest of the population.* That such persons return to crime and drugs is not surprising, and the wheels of criminal justice continue to spin, generating heat but not light.

▶ Criminal Justice in America

Criminal justice in America is an outgrowth of a fundamental distrust of government. Authority is divided between central (federal) and state governments, and at each level power is diffused further, shared by three branches—executive, legislative, judicial—in a system referred to as the "separation of powers." In each state, authority is shared by governments at the municipal, county, and state levels. Thus, policing is primarily a function of municipal government, whereas jails are usually administered by county government: County sheriffs run more than 80 percent of the nation's more than 3,000 jails. Probation may be a municipal, county, or state function, whereas prison and (usually) parole systems are the responsibility of state government, although in some states (e.g., Iowa and Oregon) parole and probation supervision is a function of the county or judicial district. There is also a separate federal system of criminal justice.

As those who work in criminal justice recognize, there is a lack of joint planning and budgeting, or even systematic consultation, among the various agencies responsible for criminal justice. The result is a system that is not systematic (Figure 1.1).

Although criminal justice agencies, whose members range from police to parole officers, are interdependent, they do not, *in toto*, constitute a system arranged so that its parts

> **Key Fact**
> The system of criminal justice in the United States is not systematic.

A CLOSER LOOK

Levels of Government	Branches of Government
Federal	Executive
State	Legislative
County	Judicial
Municipal	

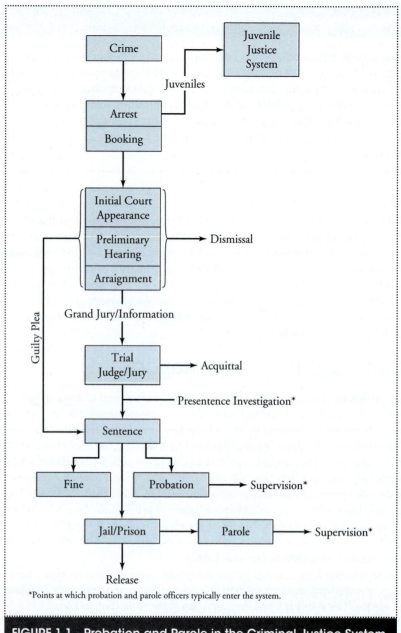

Crime

Juveniles → Juvenile Justice System

Arrest

Booking

Initial Court Appearance

Preliminary Hearing → Dismissal

Arraignment

Guilty Plea

Grand Jury/Information

Trial Judge/Jury → Acquittal

Presentence Investigation*

Sentence

Fine

Probation → Supervision*

Jail/Prison → Parole → Supervision*

Release

*Points at which probation and parole officers typically enter the system.

FIGURE 1.1   Probation and Parole in the Criminal Justice System

result in unity. Although the operations of criminal justice agencies lack any significant level of coordination, each affects the others. A disproportionate share of the criminal justice budget (about 42 percent) goes to the agency that has the most public visibility, the police (plus 6 percent for federal law enforcement). The courts, prosecutors, and public defenders receive about 22 percent; corrections receive about 29 percent. An additional 1 percent is allocated for miscellaneous functions (U.S. Department of Justice statistics). As a result, more persons are brought into the system by the heavily funded police than the rest of the system can handle adequately. Increasing the number of police officers, and thereby the total number of arrests, places further pressure on the rest of the system of criminal justice.

Because of their large caseloads, judges and prosecutors tend to concentrate on the speedy processing of cases. This, in turn, encourages "bargain justice," which frequently is neither a bargain nor just. When a probation agency is understaffed, judges tend to send marginal cases to prison instead of using probation. When prisons are underfunded and overcrowded, there is pressure on the parole board to accelerate the release of inmates, thereby overburdening parole supervision, which is also usually understaffed. Many states have abolished their parole boards, and while this may make political sense, it does not respond to the problem of prison overcrowding.

As pressure builds on prisons, usually the result of judicial scrutiny and financial considerations, prison officials are forced to release inmates without the benefit of the type of analyses a parole board usually provides. Some states are releasing inmates without the supervision usually provided by parole officers, leaving them adrift. In 2008, for example, 44 percent of high-risk and 27 percent of very high-risk offenders in Ohio were released without postrelease supervision (*Justice Reinvestment in Ohio*, 2011). In recent years, some of those retaining postprison supervision limit the use of incarceration as an option for some technical violators on parole (and probation). In North Carolina, individuals who fail to comply with their release conditions can be reincarcerated for no more than three months unless they commit a new crime or abscond.

To reduce prison overcrowding, California enacted legislation that requires parole violators to serve the remainder of their sentences in country jails. However, some county jails lack space, so violators remain at-large without supervision. Prison overcrowding also places pressure on the judicial system, and more persons are placed on probation as the revolving door of criminal justice continues to spin.

Probation and parole are linked to particular segments of the criminal justice system, and criminal justice is tied to a system of laws most frequently invoked against a distinct type of offender. Law reflects the need to protect the person, the property, and the norms of those who have the power to enact laws: The criminal law reflects power relations in society. Thus, the harmful activities of those with power are often not even defined as criminal (e.g., environmental violations) but may instead constitute only a civil wrong (e.g., the savings and loan debacle of the 1980s cost taxpayers an estimated $124 billion), or the perpetrators may receive taxpayer money from the government (e.g., the federal bailout that saved financial institutions whose reckless behavior facilitated economic catastrophe). When the criminal law is invoked, the results may represent distinctions in power; burglary prosecutions, for example, routinely invoke more significant penalties than do corporate

A CLOSER LOOK

RICH MAN, POOR MAN, CRIMINAL MAN

The United States is the most economically stratified of industrial nations the level of inequality exceeding that of any other industrialized nation (Stille, 2001). One percent of American households with net worth of at least $2.3 million each owns nearly 40 percent of the nation's wealth, while the top 20 percent of Americans have more than 80 percent of the country's worth, a figure higher than in other industrial nations (Bradsher, 1995a; Pérez-Peña, 1997). This inequality has continued to increase (Andrews, 2003).

A 1994 report for the Carnegie Foundation by a panel of prominent Americans revealed millions of children deprived of medical care, loving supervision, and intellectual stimulation, the result of parents overwhelmed by poverty. Many are subjected to child abuse and frequently witness random acts of violence (Chira, 1994), which means they are more likely to become juvenile delinquents and adult criminals (Widom, 1996; Widom and Maxfield, 2002). They become the pool from which the criminal justice system draws most of its clients.

crimes. For crimes committed by large corporations, the sole punishment often consists of warnings, consent decrees, or comparatively small fines. As the title of a book by Jeffrey Reiman (1998) notes, *The Rich Get Richer and the Poor Get Prison*.

▶ What is a Crime? Who Is a Criminal?

Quite simply, a *crime* is any violation of the criminal law, and a *criminal* is a person convicted of a crime. These definitions raise an important question: Is a person who violates the criminal law a "criminal" if he or she is not apprehended or convicted? Consider that most reported crimes do not result in an arrest and conviction. Furthermore, National Crime Victimization Surveys reveal that most crimes are simply not reported to the police. Thus, have probationers or parolees who are not arrested again been rehabilitated, or have they become infirm or more successful at avoiding detection? (Or have the police become either corrupt or less adept?) The issue of recidivism in probation and parole is critical, so the answer to this question has policy implications.

It is important for the study of probation and parole to consider who actually becomes identified as a criminal, since they are not representative of the U.S. population and tend to be clustered in particular sections of urban America—areas that are heavily policed—increasing the likelihood of arrest. Persons who have already been arrested become part of the official records ("usual suspects") of law enforcement agencies, increasing their susceptibility to further arrests, a fact of life with which all probation and parole personnel must deal. However, on average, only about one crime in four is cleared by an arrest. The result is prisons populated and repopulated by the least skillful criminals with multiple convictions.

▶ Early Responses to Crime

Early responses to criminal behavior ranged from the payment of fines to trial by combat, banishment, and death by torture. Lex talionis (an eye for an eye), a primitive system of vengeance, emerged and was passed down from generation to generation as each family, tribe, or society sought to preserve its own existence without recourse to a written code of laws. About 4,000 years ago, Hammurabi, king of Babylonia, authored a code inscribed on a block of diorite nearly 8 feet high and about 5 feet in circumference. Although in written form, his laws continued the harsh tradition of *lex talionis*—many crimes, including committing theft and harboring a runaway slave, were punishable by death (Harper, 1904).

Later, the Hebrews adopted the concept of an eye for an eye; however, this referred to financial compensation for the victim of a crime or negligence (there was no compensation for murder, which carried the death penalty), except for the "false witness," in which case "ye shall do unto him, as he had purposed to do unto his brother" (*Deuteronomy* 19: 19). A perpetrator who was unable to pay compensation was placed in involuntary servitude, a precursor to the concept of probation. The servitude could not last more than six years—release had to occur with the sabbatical year—and masters had rehabilitative obligations and responsibilities toward their charges. (Under the Code of Hammurabi, "If the thief has nothing wherewith to pay he shall be put to death" [Harper, 1904: 13].)

The Romans derided the use of restitution for criminal offenses and used the death penalty extensively in ways that have become etched in history. The fall of the Roman Empire resulted in there being little "rule of law" throughout Europe. When law was gradually restored, fines and restitution became important forms of punishment as monarchs sought funds to strengthen their military. Offenders who were unable to pay, however, were often enslaved or subjected to mutilation or death. A parallel issue in contemporary criminal justice, the extensive use of restitution and fees, is discussed in Chapters 2 and 10.

Trial by combat also flourished, in part because of the difficulty of proving criminal allegations. With the spread of Christianity, trial by combat was reserved for private accusations, whereas crimes prosecuted by the crown called for trial by ordeal, an appeal to divine power. A defendant who survived the ordeal (e.g., passing through fire) was ruled innocent. The unsuccessful defendant often received verdict and punishment simultaneously. Trial by ordeal was eventually replaced with *compurgation* ("wager of law"): The accused was required to gather 12 reputable persons who would swear to the defendant's innocence. Reputable persons, it was believed, would not swear falsely for fear of divine retribution. Compurgation eventually evolved into testimony under oath and trial by jury (Vold and Bernard, 1986). Throughout the Middle Ages in Europe, there was a continuation of the extensive use of torture to gain confessions, and public executions were often accompanied by torture, flaying, or the rack.

Despite biblical admonitions—"You shall not respect persons in judgment; ye shall hear the small and the great alike" (*Deuteronomy* 1: 17)—for many centuries disparity existed in the manner in which punishment was meted out, with the rich and influential receiving little or no punishment for offenses that resulted in torture and death for the less fortunate.

▶ Classicalism

The disparate practices of meting out justice were forcefully challenged in the eighteenth century with the advent of classicalism. **Classicalism** is an outgrowth of the European Enlightenment period of the eighteenth century (sometimes referred to as the "Age of Reason") whose adherents rejected spiritualism and religious explanations for criminal behavior. During this era, philosophers, such as Montesquieu (1689–1755) and Voltaire (1694–1778), spoke out against the French penal code and inhumane and inequitable punishments. Jean Rousseau (1712–1778) and Cesare Beccaria (1738–1794) argued for a radical concept of justice based on equality. At a time when laws and law enforcement were unjust and disparate and punishment was often brutal, they demanded justice based on equality and punishment that was humane and proportionate to the offense. This revolutionary doctrine—*equality*—influenced the American Revolution, with its declaration that "all men are created equal," and the French Revolution, whose National Assembly enacted a "Declaration of the Rights of Man and Citizen" (1789), which emphasized the equality of all citizens. The roots of this legal and political philosophy can be found in the concept of the social contract and natural rights.

> **Key Fact**
>
> Classicalism views human behavior as based on free will, a concept in law known as *mens rea*.

The **social contract** is a mythical state of affairs wherein each person agrees to a pact, the basic stipulation of which is that, all men being created equal, conditions of law are the same for all: "The social contract establishes among the citizens an equality of such character that each binds himself on the same terms as all the others, and is *thus* entitled to enjoy the same rights as all the others" (Rousseau [1762], 1954: 45). According to classical thought, by nature man is free and endowed with natural rights, a philosophical basis for the first 10 amendments to the U.S. Constitution, the Bill of Rights. According to John Locke (1632–1704), all men are by nature free, equal, and independent, and no one can be subjected to the political power of another without his or her own consent. These sentiments were incorporated into the U.S. Declaration of Independence as "all men are created equal" whose "governments are instituted among men, deriving their just powers from the consent of the governed."

The classical notion of the social contract stipulates that because all men are created equal, conditions of law are the same for all. Thus, Rousseau asserts, "One consents to die— if and when one becomes a murderer oneself—in order not to become a murderer's victim" (1954: 48). To be safe from crime, all people have consented to punishment if they resort to crime. This constitutes the greatest good for the greatest number; the social contract is rational and motivated by selfishness (Roshier, 1989).

Contrary to the manner in which law was being enforced, classical philosophers argued that law should respect neither rank nor station—all men are created equal—and punishment should be meted out with a perfect uniformity and in proportion to the offense. This premise was given impetus by Beccaria, who, in *An Essay on Crimes and Punishments* (1764; English edition, 1867), stated that laws should be drawn precisely and matched to punishment intended to be applied equally to all classes of men. The law, he argued, should stipulate a particular penalty for each specific crime, and judges should mete out identical sentences for each occurrence of the same offense (Maestro, 1973). This makes the administration of justice rational, whereas law is taken, uncritically, as given. Punishment has as its purpose deterrence and must be "the minimum possible in the given circumstances, proportionate to the crime, dictated by the laws" (Maestro, 1973: 33). The prosecution of defendants must be accomplished without resort to torture, common during this period. Not only is torture inhumane, but it is also highly unreliable for determining guilt. Unlike the position of Rousseau stated earlier, Beccaria opposed capital punishment.

According to the classical position, punishment is justified because offenders who violate the social contract are rational and endowed with **free will**. This concept, which has biblical origins (*Deuteronomy* 30: 15), holds that every person has the ability to distinguish and choose between right and wrong, between being law abiding and criminal; in other words, behavior that violates the law is a *rational choice* made by a person with free will—in legal terms, **mens rea**. However, there is evidence linking serious criminal behavior, that of psycho/sociopaths, to brain abnormalities (Haederle, 2010.)

The classical school argues that because humans tend toward *hedonism*—that is, they seek pleasure and avoid pain—they must be restrained, by fear of punishment, from pleasurable acts that are unlawful. Accordingly, the purpose of the criminal law is not simply *retribution* but also *deterrence*. In sum, the "individual is responsible for his actions and is equal, no matter what his rank, in the eyes of the law" (Taylor, Walton, and Young, 1973: 2).

Two additional requirements—*certainty* and *promptness*—round out the classical position. If law is to serve its deterrent purpose, the would-be violator must be in fear of the consequences. This element of fear requires certainty, whereas promptness, seemingly based on a primitive form of behaviorism (discussed in Chapter 6), is necessary to make a more lasting impression—connecting the deed to the punishment.

The classical approach supported the interests of a rising eighteenth-century commercial class that was demanding legal equality with the privileged noble class as well as protection from the economic-driven predations of the lower class. A contradiction remains between the defense of equality and the emphasis on maintenance of an unequal distribution of wealth and property. Crime could, indeed, be a rational response to severe differentiations in wealth and opportunity. Free will is an oversimplification because one's position in society determines the degree of choice with respect to committing crimes: "A system of classical justice of this order could only operate in a society where property was distributed equally," where each person has an equal stake in the system (Taylor, Walton, and Young, 1973: 6). It is irrational for a society, which in too many instances does not offer a feasible alternative to crime, to insist that criminal behavior is simply a matter of free will; the nature of our prison population for more than 200 years belies this claim. Nevertheless, as noted by Anatole France (1927: 91), "the law [based on classicalism], in its majestic equality, forbids both the poor man and the rich man to sleep under bridges, to beg in the streets, and to steal bread."

In sum, there are eight basic tenets of classicalism (Taylor, Walton, and Young, 1973):

1. Humans are rational.

2. All persons are created equal.

3. All persons have an equal stake in society and thus an equal stake in prevention of crime.

▼

4. Free will endows each person with the power to be law abiding or criminal.

5. People tend toward hedonism.

6. The purpose of punishment is deterrence.

7. Punishment must be meted out fairly, with absolute equality, and in proportion to the offense.

8. Punishment must be prompt and certain.

Classical theory is the basis of our legal system, its pictorial representation appearing on many courthouses and documents in the form of a woman—"Justice"—carrying scales and wearing a blindfold. The classical view provides the basis for determinate sentence discussed in Chapter 4.

▶ Neoclassicism

According to the classical position, punishment is justified because the offender who violates the social contract is rational, endowed with free will and, therefore, responsible for his or her actions no matter what the person's rank. The focus is on laws and the legal system, not on the nature of criminal motivation. In fact, under the U.S. system of justice, an explanation is not a justification unless it reaches the level of a (legal) compulsion, at which point the law does not blame the perpetrator—no *mens rea*. Classicalism provides the basis for a rational legal system that is relatively easy to administer, except for one annoying problem: Implementing a criminal code with perfect equality has proven elusive. This problem became apparent when the French Code of 1791 attempted to implement Beccaria's reforms. Equality and proportionality proved more difficult in practice than in theory, and the French increasingly added to the discretionary powers of judges in the form of neoclassicalism (Roshier, 1989).

Neoclassicalism maintains the basic belief in free will while paving the way for the entry of mitigation (and subsequently aggravation) into criminal justice by considering three areas:

1. Past criminal record

2. Insanity and retardation

3. Age

Punishment can be justified only if crime is freely chosen, intentional, and rational—that is, reasoned behavior: The neoclassicist revisions created an entrée for nonlegal experts—particularly psychiatrists and psychologists—into the courts (Taylor, Walton, and Young, 1973). These experts determine the presence of mitigation, and the system is able to continue to maintain a belief in free will. Allowing for the possibility of differences between offenders raises the specter of determinism, meaning that to varying degrees the offender's choices are limited, which is the basic premise of positivism.

▶ Positivism

Positivism, as formulated by Auguste Comte (1798–1857), refers to a method for examining and understanding social behavior. Comte argued that the methods and logical form of the natural sciences—the scientific method—are applicable to the study of man as a social being, producing the field of social sciences. Social phenomena, Comte insisted, must be studied and understood by observation, hypothesis, and experimentation in a new discipline he called *sociology*. Classical theory is based on philosophy and law, whereas the positivist view is based on empiricism in an effort to determine the cause of crime.

The positivist approach to the study of crime became known as *criminology*, a discipline whose early efforts are identified with Cesare Lombroso (1835–1909), a Venetian physician. In his *L'uomo delinquente* (*The Criminal Man*), first published in 1876, Lombroso argued that the criminal is a "primitive throwback" to earlier developmental stages through which noncriminal man had already passed—the influence of social Darwinism is obvious (Degler, 1991). Lombroso's research centered on physiological characteristics believed indicative of criminality, although his later work (published in 1911) noted the importance of environmental factors in causing crime (Lombroso, 1968). Instead of the classical emphasis on criminal behavior as rational, positivists tend to see it as a symptom of some form of pathology: biological, psychological, or social. (Positivist theories of crime are reviewed in Chapter 6.)

While Charles Darwin and Herbert Spencer were concerned with a general construct of human evolution and its effect on society, the criminal anthropology initiated by the work of Lombroso employed evolution to explain criminal behavior. Lombroso contributed to the study of crime by using, albeit in a rather imperfect way, the tools of science and shifting the field of inquiry from law and philosophy to empiricism. The positivist view places emphasis not on the crime but on the criminal. It contradicts the theory of free will for which positivists have substituted a chain of interrelated causes and, at its most extreme, a deterministic basis for criminal behavior: The criminal could not do otherwise. Because criminal behavior is the result of social and psychological, if not physiological, conditions over which the offender has little or no control, he or she is not culpable (in legal parlance, lacks *mens rea*), so punishment is inappropriate; however, because criminals do represent a threat to society, they must be "treated," "corrected," or "rehabilitated" (or according to early Lombrosians, separated from society, perhaps castrated or executed). In practice, the change in emphasis from punishment to correction

SOCIAL DARWINISM

The move toward using science to explain criminality received a major impetus from the work of Charles Darwin (1809–1882). Although his first book (Origin of Species, published in 1859) was concerned exclusively with nonhuman organisms, his second (Descent of Man, published in 1871) included the idea that humanity was shaped by the forces of natural selection. Darwin's thesis was advanced by the English philosopher Herbert Spencer (1820–1903), who coined the phrase "survival of the fittest," the credo for social Darwinism. Spencer (1961: 305) argued that "there can be no rational apprehension for the truths of Sociology until there has been reached a rational apprehension of the truths of Biology." According to Spencer (1961: 2), biology did not support help for the downtrodden: "As fast as they increase the provision for those who live without labor, so fast do they increase the number who live without labor; and that with an ever-increasing distribution of alms, there comes an ever-increasing outcry for more alms."

Darwin's theory of natural selection supplied the conceptual ammunition for an ideology (later labeled social Darwinism) that allayed the qualms of the rich about not helping the poor by telling them that the latter's sufferings were an inevitable price for societal advancement that could occur only through the struggle for existence ending in the survival of the fittest and the elimination of the unfit (Andreski, 1971). "If the unworthy are helped to increase, by shielding them from that mortality which their unworthiness would naturally entail, the effect is to produce, generation after generation, a greater unworthiness" (Spencer, 1961: 313). Spencer goes on to say, "Fostering the good-for-nothing at the expense of the good is an extreme cruelty. It is a deliberate storing-up of miseries for future generations. There is no greater curse to posterity than that of bequeathing them an increasing population of imbeciles and idlers and criminals" (1961: 314).

Are criminal justice policies and practices a twenty-first-century form of social Darwinism?

Classical View	Positivist View
Free will	Determinism
Choice	Cause
Punishment/deterrence	Treatment/incarceration

If, as the classical view argues, a person has free will and is rational, he or she will weigh the costs of committing (or not committing) a crime. The threat of sanctions is seen as an effort to tilt the weighing process away from crime. The classical approach would view enhancing education and job skills as increasing choice away from crime. Positivists would view this response as a treatment approach to deal with the causes of crime.

did not necessarily result in a less severe response to criminal offenders. Some modern critics contend that rehabilitation opened the door to a host of questionable schemes for dealing with offenders under the guise of "treatment" applied "for their own good." The American Friends Service Committee notes: "Retribution and revenge necessarily imply punishment, but it does not necessarily follow that punishment is eliminated under rehabilitative regimes" (1971: 20). The positivist view provides a basis for the indeterminate sentence and the juvenile court.

The views of the classical and positive schools are important because they transcend their own time and continue to influence contemporary issues in criminal justice. The question remains: Do we judge the crime or the criminal? This is a central question in the continuing debate over sentencing—definite versus indeterminate—discussed in Chapter 4. Probation and parole, it is often argued, emanate from a positivist response to criminal behavior, a view that is disputed in this book.

▶ U.S. System of Criminal Justice

Probation and parole are part of the U.S. system of criminal justice. The next section locates these two services within that system.

▶ Entering the System

Most crimes are not responded to by the criminal justice system because they have not been discovered by or reported to the police; when reported, most crimes are never solved. For the police to arrest a suspect, they must have a level of evidence known as probable cause. The Ohio Adult Parole Authority offers the following definition: "Reasonable grounds for suspicion supported by facts and circumstances sufficiently strong in themselves to lead a reasonably cautious person to believe that a person is guilty of a particular crime." Probable cause is also the level of evidence required to initiate a probation or parole violation (discussed in Chapter 8), and it is significantly less than that necessary to convict a defendant in a criminal trial (beyond a reasonable doubt).

When the police affect an arrest, the subject is transported to a holding facility, usually a police station equipped with cells—a "lockup." As opposed to a jail, a lockup is used on a temporary basis, for 24 to 48 hours. During this time, the suspect will be booked,

> **Key Fact**
>
> Levels of evidence range from probable cause to beyond a reasonable doubt.

photographed, and fingerprinted, and the police will request that formal charges be instituted by the prosecutor's office. A fingerprint check reveals whether the suspect has a previous arrest record, is wanted for other charges, or is on probation or parole.

▶ Pretrial Court Appearances

Depending on what time of day the arrest occurred and whether it happened on a weekday, weekend, or court holiday, the suspect may have to spend 24 hours or longer in the lockup before being transported to court. At the first appearance, the primary questions concern bail and legal representation. If a defendant is under probation or parole supervision, the bail decision is affected; for example, in some jurisdictions, a probation or parole warrant will be filed to preclude release on bail. If the subject is unable to provide bail or a probation/parole warrant is filed as a detainer, he or she will be kept in jail pending further court action. In many jurisdictions, probation or pretrial officers or other specialized court personnel will interview defendants with a view toward assisting the judge in making a bail decision. They may even provide supervision during the pretrial stage (discussed in Chapter 3).

▶ Pretrial Hearings

At pretrial hearings (sometimes referred to as an initial appearance, preliminary hearing, or arraignment), the official charges are read aloud, the need for counsel considered, and bail set or reviewed (if it has already been set at a bond hearing). Typically, these hearings last only a few minutes. If the case is a misdemeanor, it may be adjudicated at this time, often by a plea of guilty or dismissal of the charges on a motion by the prosecutor. If the charge constitutes a felony, a *probable cause hearing* is held to determine if the arresting officer had sufficient evidence—probable cause—to justify an arrest. This hearing takes the form of a short minitrial during which the prosecutor calls witnesses and the defense may cross-examine and call its own witnesses.

If the judge finds probable cause—evidence sufficient to cause a reasonable person to believe that the suspect committed a crime—the prosecutor files an *information* (details of the charges), which has the effect of bringing the case to trial. In some states, the prosecutor may avoid a probable cause hearing by presenting evidence directly to a *grand jury*—generally, 23 citizens who hear charges in secret. If they vote a *true bill*, the defendant stands *indicted* and the case proceeds to trial.

▶ Trials or Guilty Pleas

Few cases entering the criminal justice system actually result in a jury trial, an expensive and time-consuming luxury that most participants attempt to keep to a minimum. About 85 to 95 percent of all criminal convictions are the result of a guilty plea, and most guilty pleas are the result of a **plea bargain**, a widely condemned practice for disposing of cases that involves an exchange wherein the defendant agrees to waive his or her constitutional right to a jury trial, providing the prosecutor with a "win" and saving the court a great deal of time and effort; the defendant is rewarded for this behavior by receiving some form of leniency. (The impact of plea bargaining on probation is discussed in Chapter 3; its effect on parole in Chapter 4.) If plea negotiations fail to result in an agreement or if one side or the other refuses to bargain, the case is scheduled for trial. (For an extensive discussion of plea bargaining, see Abadinsky, 2008.)

The trial is an adversary proceeding in which both sides are represented by legal counsel and whose rules are enforced by a judge. To sustain a criminal charge, the prosecutor must prove the *actus reus* and *mens rea*. **Actus reus**, a wrongful act or deed, refers to the need to prove that a violation of the criminal law—a crime—actually occurred. The *actus reus* consists of a description of the criminal behavior and evidence that the accused acted accordingly. Robbery, for example, requires evidence that violence or the threat of violence was used by the accused to secure something of value to which he or she was not entitled. Mens rea, or "guilty mind," is a legal standard that refers to the question of *intent*: The prosecutor must be able to show that the defendant had a wrongful purpose—willfulness—in carrying out the *actus reus*, that the robbery, for example, was not a case of a young man playing a trick on his friend. The defendant is presumed innocent, and therefore defense counsel need not prove anything but will typically attempt to raise doubts about the evidence or other aspects of the prosecution's case.

Each side can subpoena witnesses to present testimony and can cross-examine adverse witnesses (Sixth Amendment). The defendant can take the stand on his or her own behalf; if the defendant prefers not to testify, he or she can maintain the Fifth Amendment privilege against self-incrimination. Defendants on probation or parole may be reluctant to testify because this would subject them to cross-examination and result in a disclosure of their criminal record to the jury. After lawyers for each side have introduced all their evidence, the judge instructs the jury on the principles of law applicable to the case. Every jury is told (charged by the judge) that the facts pointing to the guilt of the defendant must be established **beyond a reasonable doubt**, as opposed to the **preponderance of the evidence**, the standard in civil and some juvenile cases as well as probation and parole revocation hearings.

The jury now retires to deliberate in private. In most jurisdictions, the jury's decision for guilt or acquittal must be unanimous, or the result is called a *hung jury*. If the jury cannot reach a unanimous verdict, the jurors are discharged. If the prosecutor decides, the case must be tried a second time before a different jury. Except in some relatively rare instances when there are violations of both federal and state laws, the defendant who is acquitted cannot be tried again for the same charges, which would constitute *double jeopardy* (prohibited by the Fifth Amendment). If the jury finds the defendant guilty of one or more of the charges, the case moves to the sentencing stage, and the probation officer enters the case, usually for the first time. (In some jurisdictions, the probation officer is involved in gathering information—the *pre-plea investigation*—for the judge during plea bargaining.)

Key Fact

Plea bargaining affects sentencing and therefore impacts probation and parole.

▶ Sentences

After a verdict or plea of guilty, the judge decides on the sentence, although in some states the sentence is decided by the jury, particularly in cases of murder. The sentencing function reflects societal goals, which may be in conflict:

- *Retribution.* Punishment dimension (*lex talionis*, an eye for an eye, or just deserts) that expresses society's disapproval of criminal behavior
- *Incapacitation.* Reduces opportunity for further criminal behavior by imprisonment
- *Deterrence.* Belief that punishment will reduce the likelihood of future criminal behavior either by the particular offender (*individual/specific deterrence*) or by others in society who fear similar punishment (*general deterrence*)
- *Rehabilitation.* Belief that by providing services—social, psychological, educational, or vocational—an offender will be less likely to commit future crimes
- *Restitution.* Repayment by an offender to the victim or to society in money or services for the harm committed

Sentencing can be further complicated by concern for (Zawitz, 1988) the following:

- *Proportionality.* Punishment should be commensurate with the seriousness of the crime.
- *Equity.* Similar crimes should receive similar punishment.
- *Social debt.* Severity of punishment should consider the offender's prior criminal record.

These issues are discussed in subsequent chapters.

The trial judge sets a date for a sentencing hearing and in many jurisdictions will order a presentence investigation to be conducted by the probation department. A probation officer will search court records; examine other reports, such as psychiatric and school records; and interview the defendant, spouse, employer, arresting officer, and victim. Information from the presentence investigation will be presented in the form of a written presentence or probation report, which frequently contains the probation officer's sentencing recommendation. After reviewing the report, the judge conducts a sentencing hearing at which both defense and prosecution are allowed to make statements. The judge then imposes a sentence: fine, suspended sentence, probation, incarceration, or any combination thereof. A prison sentence may be determinate (classical) or indeterminate (positivist), depending on state law. The federal system uses only determinate sentencing.

A sentence of probation places the defendant, now a convict, under the supervision of a probation officer. A sentence of incarceration results in the defendant being sent to a jail (if convicted of a misdemeanor), usually for not more than one year, or to a state or federal prison (if convicted of a felony). In most jurisdictions, a parole board can release the defendant (now an inmate) before the expiration of his or her sentence. In other states and the federal system, the inmate can be released early as the result of accumulating time off for good behavior. Parolees and (in many states) persons released for good behavior—known as mandatory release—come under the supervision of a parole officer (the actual title varies from state to state).

▶ Appeals

Although the prosecutor cannot appeal an acquittal (Fifth Amendment), the defendant is free to appeal a guilty verdict in hopes of obtaining a reversal. The defendant can ask an appellate court to review the proceedings that culminated in his or her conviction. In fact,

American criminal justice is rather unique for the extensive postconviction review procedures to which a defendant is entitled. A prison inmate may petition the trial court for a new trial or take an appeal to the state's intermediate appellate court; if unsuccessful there, he or she can still appeal to the state court of last resort, and if unsuccessful in state court, he or she can petition the Supreme Court. The prisoner can also attack the conviction *collaterally*, that is, using indirect means, by way of a writ of *habeas corpus*, claiming that his or her constitutional rights were violated in some way by the state court conviction. Having exhausted direct and indirect appeals in state courts, the inmate can move over to the federal courts, claiming again that the conviction was unconstitutional, usually on grounds of the lack of due process.

The appellate court cannot act as a trial court, that is, receive new evidence concerning the facts already established at the original trial. It is limited to considering new theories or legal arguments regarding the law applicable to these facts or addressing procedural issues. The appellate court can uphold the verdict, overturn it, or order it reversed and remanded to the trial court for a new trial. The appellate court can also render decisions that affect other cases by setting a precedent or handing down a ruling that governs the actions of criminal justice officials; for example, in *Morrissey v. Brewer* the Supreme Court ruled that parolees are entitled to some basic forms of due process before they can be returned to prison for violation of parole (discussed in Chapter 8).

Summary

- American criminal justice has contradictory goals and competing expectations.
- For reasons of *justice* and *cost* most convicted offenders are not imprisoned.
- Among industrialized countries, the United States has the highest rate of incarceration.
- Southern states have the highest rates of incarceration.
- Increase in the number of geriatric inmates is a result of tough on crime laws such as "three-strikes-and-you're-out."
- Reducing prison populations by keeping out or releasing early "nonviolent offenders" is a dubious policy because conviction for a nonviolent crime is insufficient to identify a nonviolent offender.
- The system of criminal justice in the United States is not systematic.
- In the absence of a parole board, inmates are released without the benefit of the type of analyses a parole board usually provides.
- Some states have reacted to prison overcrowding by limiting the time a parole violator can serve.
- The criminal law and its enforcement reflect distinctions in power.
- Because most crime is not reported to the police, prevention of recidivism is difficult to determine.
- The classical view holds that people are endowed with free will and therefore deserve punishment for criminal behavior.
- Our legal system incorporates free will as *mens rea*.
- Classicalism argues for equal and proportionate punishment.
- Equality of punishment conflicts with economic inequality.
- Neoclassical recognizes diminished capacity as a mitigating factor.
- Positivism refers to a method for examining and understanding social behavior.

- Positivism provides a basis for rehabilitating criminals.
- Positivism conflicts with free will.
- Social Darwinism rejects punishing criminals but not imprisonment or execution for the protection of society.
- Classicalism and positivism are reflected in determinate versus indeterminate sentencing.
- There are different levels of evidence in criminal justice.
- A probation officer may be found during the pretrial or postconviction stage of criminal justice.

Key Terms

actus reus *15*

backdoor programs *3*

beyond a reasonable doubt *15*

classicalism *9*

determinism *11*

free will *10*

frontdoor programs *3*

level of government *5*

lex talionis *8*

mandatory release *16*

mens rea *10*

National Crime Victimization Surveys *8*

neoclassicalism *11*

plea bargain *15*

positivism *11*

preponderance of the evidence *15*

probable cause *13*

proportionality *11*

social contract *9*

social Darwinism *12*

"three strikes and you're out" *3*

truth-in-sentencing *4*

system that is not systematic *5*

Internet Connections

American Bar Association Criminal Justice links: **abanet.org/crimjust/links.html**

Council of State Governments: **csg.org**

General criminal justice links: **lawguru.com/ilawlib/96.htm**

Legal Resource Center: **crimelynx.com/research.html**

National Criminal Justice Reference Service: **ncjrs.org**

National Institute of Justice: **nij.gov**

U.S. Department of Justice links: **usdoj.gov/02organizations/02_1.html**

Vera Institute of Justice: **vera.org**

Review Questions

1. What are the contradictory goals and competing expectations of American criminal justice?
2. Most convicted offenders are not imprisoned. Why?
3. What region of the country has the highest rate of incarceration?
4. What is the relationship between "three-strikes-and-you're-out" laws and geriatric inmates?
5. Why is it difficult to identify a nonviolent offender?
6. Why is the system of criminal justice in the United States not systematic?

7. What problem results from abolishing a parole board?
8. How do the criminal law and its enforcement reflect power r elations?
9. Why is recidivism by persons on probation and parole difficult to determine?
10. What is the classical view of criminal behavior and punishment?
11. What is the relationship between free will and *mens rea*?
12. How does economic inequality diminish legal equality?
13. How does neoclassical differ from classicalism?
14. What is positivism and how does it influence criminal justice?
15. How does positivism contradict free will?
16. How does social Darwinism view criminals?
17. What is the relationship between classicalism and the determinate sentence?
18. What is the relationship between positivism and the indeterminate sentence?
19. What levels of evidence are relevant in probation and parole?
20. At what point in the criminal justice process can a probation officer be found?

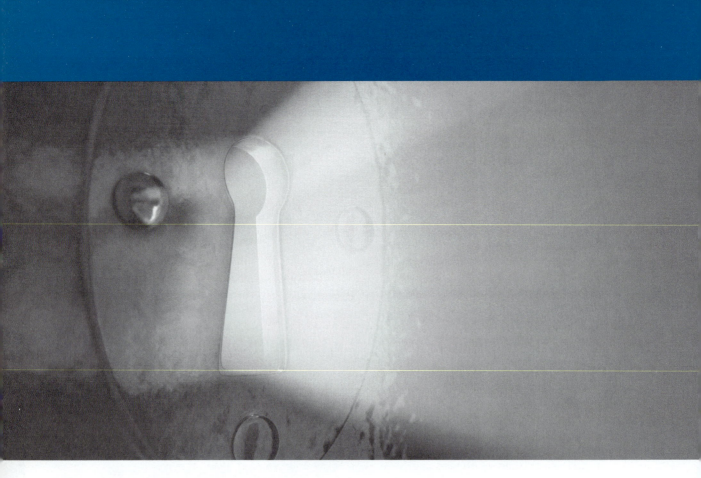

2 Probation History and Administration

LEARNING OBJECTIVES

This chapter will enable the student to:

1 *Distinguish the ways that probation may be administered.*

2 *Discuss how the juvenile court movement accelerated the spread of probation.*

3 *Describe the early history of probation and probation officers.*

4 *Distinguish arguments in favor of probation being in the judicial branch from being in the executive branch.*

5 *Understand the advantages of probation being administered on a state level or a county level.*

6 *Explain how the geographic area where the court is situated can affect the granting of probation.*

7 *Discuss conditions of probation.*

8 *Explain the use of community service in probation.*

Probation is the most common sentence in the United States whose administration may be under the auspices of the judiciary or an agency in the executive branch of government; in either event, a probation agency provides three basic services to the courts:

1. Presentence report
2. Community supervision
3. Juvenile services

Before examining these services and their administration, let us look at how and why probation developed in the United States.

► Early Probation and John Augustus

Although probation has antecedents that reach back to biblical times, its American history dates back to the nineteenth century. The concept of probation (from the Latin *probatio*, meaning period of proving) evolved out of the practice of *judicial reprieve*, used in English courts to serve as a temporary suspension of sentence to allow a defendant to appeal to the crown for a pardon. Although originally intended to be only a temporary postponement of punishment, it eventually developed into a *suspended sentence*, whereby punishment was never actually imposed. In the United States, the suspended sentence was used as early as 1830 in Boston and became widespread in U.S. courts, although there was no statutory authorization for such practice. At first, judges used "release on recognizance" or "bail" and simply failed to take further action. By the mid-nineteenth century, however, many courts were using a judicial reprieve to suspend sentences, and this posed a legal question.

"A judge had always had the power to suspend a sentence, if he felt for some reason that the trial had miscarried. But could judges suspend sentences wholesale, after trials that were scrupulously fair, simply to give the defendant a second chance?" (Friedman, 1973: 518). In 1894, this question was litigated in New York and the court determined that the power to suspend sentence was inherent in criminal courts *only* when this right had been granted by the legislature. In 1916, the U.S. Supreme Court, in a case (*Ex parte United States,* 242 U.S. 27) that affected only federal courts, ruled that judges did not have the discretionary authority to suspend a sentence. In its decision, however, the Court stated that Congress could authorize the temporary or indefinite suspension of sentence—a predecessor to probation statutes.

The term "probation" was applied by John Augustus to the practice of bailing offenders out of court, followed by a period of supervised living in the community. This pioneer of modern probation was born in Woburn, Massachusetts, and became a successful shoemaker in Boston. In 1852, a "Report of the Labors of John Augustus" was published at the request of his friends, and in it Augustus wrote: "I was in court one morning ... in which the man was charged with being a common drunkard. He told me that if he could be saved from the House of Correction, he never again would taste intoxicating liquors: I bailed him, by permission of the Court" (1972: 4–5). Thus began the work of the nation's first probation officer (PO), a volunteer who worked without pay.

Augustus's first experience with a drunkard led to an interest in helping others charged with the same offense. He would appear in court and offer to bail a defendant. If the judge agreed, which usually happened, the defendant would become Augustus's charge. The shoemaker would assist the offender in finding work or a residence; Augustus's own house was filled with people he had bailed. When the defendant returned to court, Augustus would report on his progress toward rehabilitation and recommend a disposition of the case, and these recommendations were usually accepted. During the first year of his efforts, Augustus assisted ten drunkards who, because of his work, received small fines instead of imprisonment. Later, he helped other types of offenders—young and old, men and women—and reported only ten absconders (persons who jumped bail or probation) out of 2,000 cases.

Augustus continued his work for 18 years and generally received support from judges as well as newspapers that reported on his efforts. Prosecutors, however, viewed him as an interloper who kept court calendars crowded by preventing cases from being disposed of quickly. Policemen and court clerks opposed his work because they received a fee for each case disposed of by a commitment to the House of Correction. As a result of his probation work, Augustus neglected his business and eventually experienced financial ruin; he required the help of friends for his support.

Several aspects of the system Augustus used remain basic parts of modern probation. Augustus thoroughly investigated each person he considered helping, including "the previous character of the person, his age and the influences by which in the future he would likely be surrounded" (1972: 34). Augustus not only supervised each defendant but also kept a careful case record for each that he submitted to the court. Augustus died in 1859, and until 1878 probation in Massachusetts continued to be the work of volunteers.

▶ Early Probation Statutes

After he died in 1859, supporters of John Augustus successfully lobbied the legislature, which in 1878 enacted the first probation statute, authorizing the mayor of Boston to hire a probation officer who would be supervised by the superintendent of police. For the first time, the position of probation officer was given official recognition as an arm of the court. The law authorized a PO to investigate cases and recommend probation for "such persons as may reasonably be expected to be reformed without punishment." Probation was made available in Boston to young and old, men and women, felons, as well as misdemeanants. In 1880, the legislature granted to all municipalities authority to employ probation officers, but few towns and villages did so. In 1891, the power to appoint POs was transferred to the lower courts, and each was required to employ a PO; in 1898, this requirement was extended to the superior courts. The second state to adopt a probation statute was Vermont, which in 1898 authorized the appointment of a PO by the courts in each county, each officer serving all the courts in a particular county.

Another New England state, Rhode Island, soon followed Vermont with a probation law that was novel—it placed restrictions on who could be granted probation, excluding persons convicted of treason, murder, robbery, arson, rape, and burglary. This practice violated a basic tenet of positivism: Judge the offender, not just the offense. The restrictive aspects of Rhode Island's probation law, however, were copied by other states. The Rhode Island probation law, which applied to children and adults, also introduced the concept of a state-administered probation system. A state agency, the Board of Charities and Correction, appointed a state probation officer and deputies, "at least one of whom should be a woman" (Glueck, 1933: 231).

In 1894, Maryland authorized its courts to suspend a sentence generally or for a specific time, and judges could "make such order to enforce terms as to costs, recognizance for appearance, or matters relating to the residence or conduct of the convicts as may be deemed proper." The courts of Baltimore began using agents of the Prisoner's Aid Society and later appointed salaried probation officers. In 1897, Missouri enacted a "bench parole law," which authorized courts to suspend sentences under certain conditions. The courts also appointed "parole officers," to carry out this probation ("bench parole") work (Glueck, 1933). In 1931, the Alabama legislature passed a law giving the judges power to suspend execution of sentences and place offenders on probation, but in 1935 this act was declared unconstitutional. Had it been constitutional, it would have done little more than authorize suspended sentences since in most cases there was no provision for investigation and supervision.

▶ Probation at the Turn of the Century

The juvenile court movement, which started in the Midwest and developed rapidly (discussed in Chapter 11), accelerated the spread of probation. In 1899, Illinois enacted the historic Juvenile Court Act, which authorized the world's first juvenile court. The law also provided for the hiring of probation officers to investigate cases referred by the courts but made no provision for their payment. (It was not until 1919 that the Illinois legislature enacted a law providing that counties pay the salaries and expenses of probation officers). At the end of the first year, there were six probation officers supported by the Juvenile Court Committee of the Chicago Women's Club; in addition, in each police district a police officer spent part of his time out of uniform performing the duties of a PO (Schultz, 1973).

In 1899, Minnesota enacted a law that authorized the appointment of county POs, but the granting of probation was limited to those younger than 18 years of age; 4 years later, this was changed to 21 years of age. In 1901, New York State enacted a probation law that was initially limited to those under 16 years of age and limited to certain cities, and authorized the appointment of salaried POs—until that year they were volunteers (Lindner and Savarese, 1984). In 1903, legislation authorized probation throughout the entire state and included children and adults.

In 1899, Colorado enacted a compulsory education law that enabled the development of a juvenile court using truant officers as POs. By 1925, probation was available for juveniles in every state (Glueck, 1933). In 1873, Michigan instituted a statewide system of juvenile probation officers named county agents. Volunteers at first, in 1875 county agents were paid $3 per case for their part-time work; for comparison, an American-born Detroit manufacturing worker at the time earned $457 a year (Hurl and Tucker, 1997). In 1908, Suffolk County on New York's Long Island appointed its first PO: "At the time, there was little appreciation of the value of probation, and the appointment was more in the nature of an experiment. As a part-time position, the probation officer had no office, and the probationers reported to him at his home, or by mail." The county appointed a full-time PO in 1919, and he was given a small office. Probation for juveniles was authorized in Pennsylvania in 1903 and extended to adults in 1909: Except for the offenses of murder, administering of poison, kidnapping, incest, sodomy, rape, assault with intent to rape, and arson or burglary of an inhabited dwelling, a judge could suspend the sentence and place the offender on probation.

In the early 1900s, federal probation officers were volunteers. In 1925, Congress enacted legislation establishing the Federal Probation System, and in 1929 the first paid U.S. probation officer was appointed under the Department of Justice. In 1939, probation administration was shifted to the newly created Administrative Office of the United States Courts where it remains.

Although Texas enacted the Suspended Sentence Act in 1913 to provide an alternative to incarceration, probation supervision of the convicted offender was not required until 1947. Probation for adults in Alabama did not begin until 1939, when the governor approved an enabling act giving the legislature power to authorize adult probation; before that, it had been held that courts did not have the inherent power to suspend sentences because it was deemed to be an encroachment on the executive power to pardon, commute, and reprieve. By 1956, probation was available for adults in every state (Task Force on Corrections, 1966).

The first directory of probation officers in the United States, published in 1907, identified 795 POs working mainly in the juvenile courts. Like the first PO in Illinois, many were volunteers, and some who were paid worked only part time. Training for POs was either limited or nonexistent, appointments were often based on considerations of political patronage, and salaries were typically low even when compared with those of unskilled laborers.

▶ Administration of Probation

Probation in the United States is administered by more than 2,000 separate agencies supervising in excess of 4 million adult offenders on probation for felonies and misdemeanors. In about three-fourths of the states, adult probation is located in the executive branch of state government (where it is typically combined with parole). For example, probation services in Georgia are provided by the Department of Corrections, which also manages all state correctional facilities, while the Board of Pardons and Paroles is responsible for discretionary release. In Pennsylvania, an independent state agency called the Board of Probation and Parole, in addition to its parole responsibilities, supervises probationers sentenced to less than two years when directed to do so by the courts; it also oversees county probation agencies. In Michigan, adult felony probation is the responsibility of the Department of Corrections, which also administers parole, whereas adult misdemeanor probation is the responsibility of district (limited jurisdiction) courts' probation departments. In Illinois, probation is a county-level responsibility that is part of the judicial branch, whereas in Iowa probation (and parole supervision) is the responsibility of the state's judicial districts, each of which encompasses several counties. In New York, each county as well as New York City has a probation department that is part of the executive branch of county/municipal government. In Massachusetts, probation is administered as a state executive branch agency. Although jails usually house persons convicted of misdemeanors, in response to a court order to reduce its prison population, in 2011, California began sending certain felony—for example, nonviolent—offenders to county jails instead of prison, with postincarceration supervision provided by county probation instead of state parole.

<aside>
Key Fact

Probation in the United States is administered by more than 2,000 separate agencies on the municipal, county, state, and federal levels in either the judicial or executive branch.
</aside>

PROBATION AND PAROLE ADMINISTRATION

"It is challenging to try to describe or discuss probation and parole in this country, not only because of the scope and scale of its operations, but also because of its structure and organization. The phrases 'probation and parole' [and] or 'community corrections' are used routinely and would imply a single or unified system. Nothing could be further from the truth. Probation and parole agencies are a fragmented, heterogeneous collection of organizations found at the federal, state, county, and municipal levels, housed in the judicial and executive branches" (Burrell, 2005: 1).

More than one-half of the agencies providing juvenile probation services are administered on the local level. Juvenile probation may be provided by a separate juvenile agency or a juvenile or family division of the same agency that administers adult probation, as is seen in Nassau County, New York. Fortunately, the administration of parole, which is discussed in Chapter 5, is less complex—usually one agency per state in the executive branch.

However, there are slight variations: In some states (e.g., Pennsylvania), persons paroled from a local jail come under the supervision of a *county* probation and parole department; in Oregon and Iowa, probation *and* parole supervision are at the county and judicial district levels. In 2011, to reduce the prison population—mandated by federal court order (affirmed by the Supreme Court, *Brown v. Plata*, No. 09-1233, 2011)—California transferred inmates convicted of low-level offenses to county jails where they can be released to supervision by county probation officers.

The administration of probation systems can be separated into six categories, and a state may have more than one system in operation:

1. ***Juvenile.*** Separate probation services for juveniles are administered on a county or municipal level or on a statewide basis.

2. ***Municipal.*** Independent probation units are administered by the lower courts or the municipality under state laws and guidelines.

3. ***County.*** Under laws and guidelines established by the state, a county operates its own probation agency.

4. ***State.*** One agency administers a central probation system providing services throughout the state.

5. ***State combined.*** Probation and parole services are administered on a statewide basis by one executive branch agency.

6. ***Federal.*** Probation is administered nationally as an arm of the courts, and federal probation officers also supervise parolees.

> **Key Fact**
>
> While most states combine probation and parole in one statewide agency, in the largest states they are separate.

Most states (about 60 percent) combine probation and parole in one statewide agency. However, in the largest states (e.g., California, Illinois, New York, and Texas), only parole is a state function, whereas the judiciary or executive branch on a county or municipal level administers probation. At the federal level, each of the 94 federal districts has a Chief U.S. Probation Officer who reports directly to the chief judge of the district, while the Administrative Office of the United States Courts provides national policies (Alexander and Van Benschoten, 2008).

Probation services in the executive branch can be part of state government under the office of the governor, county government under a chief executive officer, or municipal government under a mayor, as in New York City. Probation services may be part of a larger department of corrections, as in Georgia, or part of an independent probation and parole agency, as in Alabama and South Carolina. Probation services as part of the judicial branch of government usually place these services under the judges of the county, as in New Jersey:

> The judges of the County Court in each county, or a majority of them, acting jointly may appoint a *chief probation officer, [and] such men and women probation officers* as may be necessary. Probation officers and *volunteers in probation* shall be appointed with standards fixed by the Supreme Court. All *probation officers* and *volunteers in probation* shall be responsible to and under the supervision of the *Chief Probation Officer* of the county who shall be responsible to and under the supervision of the judge of the county court or, in counties having more than one judge of the county court, the county court judge designated by the Assistant Judge to be responsible for the administration of the *probation department* in the county in accordance with the applicable statutes, rules of the Supreme Court, and directives of the Chief Justice, the Administrative Director of the Courts, and the Assignment Judge of the county.

> **Key Fact**
>
> Probation may be administered on a municipal, county, or state basis, in either the judicial or executive branch.

There are also some variations. For example, Iowa is divided into eight judicial districts, each with a multicounty correctional department operating under a board of directors.

The board appoints a director who administers probation, parole, and related services that are funded and monitored by the Iowa Department of Corrections. In Texas, probation services are located in 120 Community Supervision and Corrections Departments, organized by the judges of each judicial district and funded by supervision fees and state aid. The Ohio Adult Parole Authority, in addition to parole services, provides probation services to 45 of the state's 88 counties. Although the 31 counties participating in the Minnesota Community Corrections Act (CCA) provide services to persons on probation, supervised release, or parole, the state provides these services to adult offenders in the remaining 56 counties. Juvenile probation and parole services in non-CCA counties are provided by county probation agents or by state agents under contract to the counties. In either case, the state pays up to 50 percent of the agent's salary.

Two basic issues arise in the administration of probation services:

1. Should probation be part of the judicial or executive branch of government?
2. Should probation be under municipal/county or state jurisdiction?

Those who support placement of probation services in the judicial branch offer the following advantages (Nelson, Ohmart, and Harlow, 1978):

- Probation is more responsive to the courts, to which it provides services, when administered by the judiciary.
- The relationship of probation staff to the courts creates an automatic feedback mechanism on the effectiveness of various dispositions.
- Courts will have greater awareness of the resources needed by the probation agency.
- Judges will have greater confidence in an agency for which they are responsible, allowing probation staff more discretion than they would allow members of an outside agency.
- If probation is administered on a statewide basis, it is usually incorporated into a department of corrections, and under such circumstances probation services might be assigned a lower priority than they would have as part of the judicial branch.

Those who oppose the placement of probation in the judiciary note the following disadvantages:

- Judges, trained in law and not administration, are not equipped to administer probation services.
- Under judicial control, services to persons on probation may receive a lower priority than services to the judge (e.g., presentence investigations).
- Probation staff may be assigned duties unrelated to probation.
- The courts are adjudicatory and regulative; they are not service-oriented bodies.

Placement in the executive branch has these features to recommend it:

- All other human services agencies are in the executive branch.
- All other corrections subsystems are located in the executive branch.
- With executive branch placement, program budgeting can be better coordinated, and an increased ability to negotiate fully in the resource allocation process becomes possible.
- A coordinated continuum of services to offenders and better use of probation personnel are facilitated.

E. Kim Nelson and her colleagues conclude:

When compared, these arguments tend to support placing probation in the executive branch. The potential for increased coordination in planning, better utilization of manpower and improved services to offenders cannot be dismissed. A state administered probation system has decided advantages over local administration. A total system planning approach to probation as a subsystem of corrections is needed. Such planning requires state leadership. Furthermore, implementation of planning strategies requires uniformity of standards, reporting, and evaluation as well as resource allocation. (1978: 92)

Mitchell Silverman (1994) points out, however, that state control typically means probation agencies administered by the state executive branch, with centralized administrators who are frequently far removed, both physically and intellectually, from the PO in the field. Often the central administrators have little knowledge and understanding of the important factors that are operating in the local community where the individual PO works. The distance has the potential of creating conflicts of interest when the state-level policy makers demand from the field worker one approach to clients while the local community, in which the PO and client live, demands another. Local administration enhances creativity by providing the capacity to adopt county-specific programs with shorter lines of decision making.

Probation administered by the judiciary (usually) on a county level promotes diversity. Innovative programming can be implemented more easily in a county agency because it has a shorter line of bureaucratic control than a statewide agency. A county agency can more quickly adapt to change, and the successful programs of one agency can be more easily adopted and unsuccessful programs avoided by probation departments in other counties. Those most familiar with the local community—its resources, attitudes, and politics—will be responsible for providing probation services, which can increase public confidence in the services provided by the agency. Although the judiciary is nominally responsible for the administration of probation, the day-to-day operations are in the hands of a professional administrator, the chief probation officer.

Conversely, county-level administration results in a great deal of undesirable variance between agencies. For example, the ratio of POs to clients may differ dramatically from one county to the other—a situation that would be less likely with a statewide agency. Because each county sets its own budget, probation staff cannot be shifted from a low-ratio county to a high-ratio county to equalize the services provided. Does the lack of uniformity in administering probation make justice less equitable statewide? This issue has led states with county-based probation systems to create statewide oversight agencies for better coordination and uniformity of probation. In Illinois, for example, the Probation Division of the Administrative Office of the Illinois Courts works to "improve the quality and quantity of probation and related court services throughout Illinois, provide more uniformity of organization, structure, and services, and increase the use of probation as a meaningful alternative punishment for nonviolent offenders. As part of these efforts, for example, the division promulgates regulations for the hiring and promotion of all probation personnel throughout the state."

The Texas Community Justice Assistance Division (formerly the Texas Adult Probation Commission) is responsible for establishing statewide standards and providing state aid to those local adult probation departments that choose to participate and are in compliance with the standards. As part of these efforts, the division has supported research and experimental probation programs throughout Texas. The agency has promulgated a "Code of Ethics for Texas Adult Probation Officers" and published standards for all phases of adult probation in Texas. For example, it has a policy on caseload size: "A caseload average within a department should be calculated by dividing the number of cases under direct

NEW YORK STATE DIVISION OF PROBATION AND CORRECTIONAL ALTERNATIVES

The New York State Division of Probation and Correctional Alternatives (DPCA) was established in 1985 to exercise general supervision over the operation of local probation agencies and the use of correctional alternative programs throughout the state. DPCA also administers a program of state aid funding for approved local probation services and for municipalities and private nonprofit agencies that have approved alternatives to incarceration service plans. These plans allow localities to maintain inmates in local correctional facilities more efficiently. The agency also funds designated demonstration and other specialized programs.

DPCA's mission is to promote and facilitate probation services and other community corrections programs through funding and oversight. These programs are generally designed to provide a continuum of sanctions, methods of supervision, and approaches to treatment that, when used individually or in combination, provide options to the judiciary and to the state's criminal justice system for the effective handling of offenders and juveniles in the community.

The director adopts and promulgates rules and regulations concerning methods and procedures used in the administration of local probation services and develops standards for the operation of alternatives to incarceration programs. The director also serves as the chairman of the New York State Probation Commission. The commission members, appointed by the governor, provide advice and consultation to the director on all matters relating to probation in the state.

supervision by the number of officers within the department devoting 80 percent or more of their time to direct case supervision. The average caseload of a probation officer in a department should not exceed 100 cases." Although the standards are not mandatory, the failure of a probation department to maintain them can result in a loss of the considerable funding provided by the state. All New York State probation directors are accountable to their respective chief county officials (executive branch) or, in the case of New York City, the mayor. Although administered locally, supervisory oversight of the administration of probation statewide is the responsibility of the New York State Division of Probation and Correctional Alternatives.

▶ Granting Probation

Most states have statutory restrictions on who may be granted probation in felony cases. Crimes such as murder, kidnapping, and rape usually preclude a sentence of probation, as do second- or third-felony convictions. In Texas, a defendant may elect to be sentenced by a jury but can thereby receive probation only if it is proved that he or she "has never before been convicted of a felony in this or any other state." In any event, no person in the Lone Star state is eligible to receive probation for a felony unless assessed a sentence of ten years or less by a judge or jury. In Georgia, a defendant who pleads guilty (or *nolo contendere*, "no contest") and who has never before been convicted of a felony can be placed on probation without the court entering a judgment of guilty. If the person successfully completes the terms of probation, he or she "shall not be considered to have a criminal conviction." In Michigan, those convicted of any crime except treason, criminal sexual conduct in the first degree, robbery while armed, and major controlled substance offenses can be granted probation.

> **Key Fact**
>
> Granting probation is limited by the seriousness of the offense and prior convictions.

When probation is a statutory alternative, judges differ in their approach to granting it. Although the recommendation of the probation department would be important—it is difficult to envision too many cases in which judges would grant probation against the recommendation of a probation officer—judges may also seek advice from the police and prosecutor. The geographic area where the court is situated may affect the granting of probation. Social and political attitudes in rural and urban jurisdictions can differ and thus affect the process, and when court calendars are crowded, as they are in many urban areas, plea bargaining is more likely to result in probation being granted. The pressing problem of jail and prison overcrowding also exerts influence: One research effort found that in the rural districts studied, many felons are placed on probation as the result of a plea bargain; another study found that in Tennessee this appeared to be directly related to the severe prison overcrowding experienced by that state (Champion, 1988a). The judge's feelings toward the particular offense or the offender may also enter into the sentencing decision. The many factors that determine whether a defendant is granted probation contribute to the continuing controversy over "differential punishment," a challenge to the classical approach to criminal justice.

However, some factors (to a greater or lesser extent) are considered in all cases relative to the granting of probation: the age and rehabilitation potential of the defendant; the defendant's criminal record, including indications of professional criminality, organized crime, and crimes of violence; the defendant's relationship with his or her family; any evidence of deviant behavior, such as drug abuse or sex offenses; and the attitude of the community toward the particular offense and the particular offender. Other questions may also be considered: Does the defendant's attitude toward the offense indicate genuine remorse? Was probation promised to the defendant to induce him or her to plead guilty? Will being placed on probation enable the defendant to provide the victim with restitution? Will being placed on probation enable the defendant to provide support and care for his or her family?

The sentencing judge must also consider the quality of service provided by a probation agency. Unfortunately, in too many jurisdictions, probation is nothing more than a suspending of sentence because little or no supervision is actually provided. Under such circumstances, a judge who might otherwise be inclined to place an offender on probation may instead impose a sentence of imprisonment. The cost to both the offender and the taxpayer is high—according to most estimates, imprisonment costs more than 12 times as much as probation. In many jurisdictions, a built-in incentive actually exists for sentences of imprisonment, even when probation is a feasible alternative. If probation services are funded by the county and the cost of prisons is always borne by the state, each defendant sent to prison instead of being placed on probation represents a savings to county government. A Florida study revealed a pattern of inappropriate sentencing in some counties apparently because they can save money by sending more offenders to state-funded prisons (Sever, 2000). This result can be, at least in part, overcome with a probation subsidy through which the state reimburses the county for offenders placed on probation instead of being sentenced to a state prison.

A CLOSER LOOK

OBJECTIVES OF PROBATION

- To provide public protection in keeping with the special duties of a probation officer
- To prepare the probationer for independent law-abiding living
- To provide an opportunity for full participation of the probationer in planning his or her activities in the community
- To identify, use, and create resources in the community to fulfill program needs of probationers

- To provide a system of differential supervision based on the classification and program needs of all probationers
- To conduct a cost-effective supervision program
- To provide restitution or reparation to victims of criminal acts whenever applicable

Source: New York State Code of Criminal Procedure.

► Conditions of Probation

Conditions of probation in different probation agencies tend to be similar (Figure 2.1). They typically exhort the probationer to live a law-abiding life, work, and support dependents. They require that the offender inform the PO of his or her residence and that permission be secured before leaving the jurisdiction of the court. Some require that the probationer obtain permission before getting married, applying for a motor vehicle license, or contracting any indebtedness. Many probation departments require that the offender pay a supervision fee, make restitution, or do community service as a condition of probation. Some probation and parole agencies require clients to carry an identification card at all times that reveals their supervision status and contains a telephone number for law enforcement agencies to use.

ASSOCIATION

Not knowingly associate with any person who is involved in criminal activity or who has been convicted of a felony without approval from the Probation Officer.

CHEMICAL ANALYSIS

Abstain from the illegal use, possession, control, delivery, production, manufacture or distribution of controlled substances and submit to tests of breath or body fluids to ensure compliance with the Probation Agreement.

CONDUCT

Obey all state, federal and municipal laws.

DNA

Comply with Utah Code Annotated by submitting an adequate DNA specimen, and, unless determination is made that there is no ability to pay, pay the required fee specified by statute.

EMPLOYMENT

Unless otherwise authorized by the Probation Officer; seek, obtain and maintain verifiable, lawful, full-time employment (32 hours per week minimum) as approved by the Probation Officer. Notify the Probation Officer of any change in my employment within 48 hours of the change.

REPORTING

Not abscond from probation supervision. Report as directed by the Department of Corrections.

RESIDENCE

Establish and reside at a residence of record and not change residence without first obtaining permission from the PROBATION Officer. Do not leave the state of Utah, even briefly, or any other state to which I am released or transferred without prior written permission from the Probation Officer.

SEARCHES

Permit Probation Officers to search my person, residence, vehicle or any other property under my control without a warrant at any time, day or night upon reasonable suspicion to ensure compliance with the conditions of the Probation Agreement.

FIGURE 2.1 Utah Standard Probation Conditions

SUPERVISION FEE

Agree to pay a supervision fee of $30 per month unless granted a waiver by the Department of Corrections.

TRUTHFULNESS

Be cooperative, compliant and truthful in all dealings with Adult Probation and Parole. If arrested, cited or questioned by a peace officer; notify the Probation Officer within 48 hours.

VISITS

Permit visits to my place of residence, my place of employment or elsewhere by officers of Adult Probation and Parole for the purpose of ensuring compliance with the conditions of the Probation Agreement. I will not interfere with this requirement by having vicious dogs, perimeter security doors, refusing to open the door, etc.

WEAPONS

Not possess, have under control, have in my custody or on the premises where residing any explosives, firearms or dangerous weapons. (Dangerous weapon is defined as any item that in the manner of its use or intended use is capable of causing death or serious bodily injury.) Exceptions to this condition may be made by the supervising agent and must be in writing. This waiver will only apply to individuals on probation for a misdemeanor and who have never been convicted of a felony.

Figure 2.1   (continued)

Conditions can generally be divided into two parts: **standard conditions**, which are applicable to all offenders and which typically involve restrictions on travel, association with other offenders, drug and alcohol use, employment, and residence, and **special conditions** which are tailored to the individual requirements of a particular offender. For example, persons with a history of sex offenses against children will be prohibited from areas where children typically congregate, such as playgrounds; persons with a history of alcohol abuse may be prohibited from using alcohol or being in facilities such as bars where alcohol is consumed. Some jurisdictions, for example, Pennsylvania and Missouri, require probationers and parolees to provide a DNA sample.

Although the Task Force on Corrections (1966: 34) observed more than four decades ago that "differential treatment requires that the rules [of probation] be tailored to the needs of the case and of the individual offender," this suggestion is often not put into practice. Probation agencies require a defendant to sign a standard form usually containing a variety of regulations that may or may not reflect the client's individual needs.

When **conditions of probation** are too restrictive or perhaps appear unreasonable or unrealistic, the PO is inclined to overlook their violation. This can result in the PO losing the respect of the probationer, making the supervision process difficult. The ABA (1970: 9) recommends that the conditions of probation be spelled out by the court at the time of sentencing and emphasizes that they should be appropriate for the offender.

The American Probation and Parole Association (APPA) recommends that the only condition that should be imposed on every person sentenced to probation is that the probationer lead a law-abiding life during the period of probation: "No other conditions should be required by statute, but the probation officer in making recommendations [in the PSI

> **Key Fact**
> When conditions of probation are too restrictive or perhaps appear unreasonable or unrealistic, the PO is inclined to overlook their violation.

report discussed in Chapter 3] should recommend additional conditions to fit the circumstances of each case." The APPA recommends that conditions "be reasonably related to the avoidance of further criminal behavior and not unduly restrictive of the probationer's liberty or incompatible with his freedom of religion. They should not be so vague or ambiguous as to give no real guidance."

The APPA suggests that conditions include the following:

1. Cooperating with the program of supervision

2. Meeting family responsibilities

3. Maintaining steady employment or engaging or refraining from engaging in a specific employment or occupation (e.g., a drug abuser prohibited from employment in a medical setting)

4. Pursuing prescribed educational or vocational training

5. When appropriate, undergoing medical or psychiatric treatment

6. Maintaining residence in a prescribed area or in a prescribed facility established for or available to persons on probation

7. Refraining from consorting with certain types of people (e.g., drug users) or frequenting certain types of places (e.g., where drug sales are being conducted)

8. Making restitution for the fruits of the crime, or making reparation for losses or damages caused thereby

9. Paying fines, restitution, reparation, or family support

10. Requiring the probationer to submit to search and seizure[1]

11. Requiring the probationer to submit to drug tests (e.g., urinalysis) as directed by the probation officer

▶ Fees

The Missouri Board of Probation and Parole is authorized to charge each offender on supervision a fee of up to $60 per month; the average fee is $30.00. Fees in other states generally range from $20 to $50, those on intensive supervision paying more. In West Virginia, parolees pay a monthly supervision fee of $40.00. In Pennsylvania, probation and parole clients must pay $25 per month unless the fee is waived; in Virginia, clients who are unable to pay the supervision fee may apply for an exemption; they need to prove unreasonable hardship based on insufficient monthly net income. In 1983, the Supreme Court (*Beardon v. Georgia*, 461 U.S. 660) ruled that probation cannot be revoked because of an inability to pay a fine and restitution as a condition of probation that is a result of indigence and not a refusal to pay. This point would appear to also apply to supervision fees. Indeed, even for willful refusal to pay, revoking supervision is rare, although offenders may be subjected to additional restrictions, such as a curfew, or extending supervision time. There is a bias by P/P officers against collection efforts—they typically view themselves more as *helpers* than *collectors*—although some agencies claim success in fee collection has enabled them to gain a significant level financial self-sufficiency. Their success is usually influenced by the category of offender: employed, high functioning offenders, for example, those on probation for DUI.

---

[1] Probation (and parole) officers have extraordinary authority to conduct warrantless searches of clients and items as well as places under their control (*Griffin v. Wisconsin*, 483 U.S. 868, 1987).

▶ Restitution

Restitution—an act of restoring, a condition of being restored, or the act of making good or giving an equivalent for some injury—is a popular condition of probation. Restitution is a court-ordered requirement for a convicted offender to compensate a victim for the financial losses resulting from his or her crime. In addition to paying court costs, fines, and fees, a probationer may be required to make restitution, that is, to pay a percentage of his or her income (as determined by the court) to the victim of the offense for any property damage or medical expenses sustained as a direct result of the commission of the offense. This concept has an ancient history: The Bible (*Exodus* 21, 22; *Leviticus* 5) orders restitution for theft, burglary, or robbery or a form of "community service"—indentured servitude—in the event the criminal has no means of providing restitution. Restitution fell out of favor when monarchs, seeking to centralize power, made crime a public (state) matter and directed payments (fines) away from the victim or his or her kin in favor of the crown. (Personal claims had to be brought in civil court.) Community service emerged as a modern sentencing option in Alameda County, California, in 1966, and the Minnesota Restitution Program was established in 1972. Persons convicted of property offenses were given the opportunity to reduce their jail sentence or avoid incarceration altogether if they secured employment and provided restitution to their victims. The idea soon spread to other states.

> **Key Fact**
>
> While the concept of restitution is appealing, offenders typically have little in the way of resources to compensate victims.

Douglas McDonald (1988: 2) notes that in addition to aiding victims, restitution and community service are animated by the belief that they may contribute to the rehabilitation of offenders: Disciplined work has long been considered reformative. In addition, offenders performing community service may acquire some employable skills, improved work habits, and a record of quasi-employment that may be longer than any job they've held before. Victim restitution, when it brings offenders and victims face-to-face, also forces offenders to see firsthand the consequences of their deeds and thus may encourage the development of greater social responsibility and maturity.

The Maricopa County (Arizona) Adult Probation Department has a unit for the collection of court-ordered payments made up of specially trained probation officers. The program offers a range of incentives and services to support offenders in complying with required restitution and graduated sanctions for noncompliance. Personal finance courses and employment readiness and placement services are available to offenders who need assistance in meeting their financial obligations. Failure to meet court-ordered financial obligations may result in mandatory participation in personal finance classes, referral to a collector, interception of tax refunds, and, ultimately, revocation of probation.

Texas is so committed to the concept of restitution that since 1983, based on models established in Georgia and Mississippi, it has operated restitution centers throughout the state. As a condition of probation, employable nonviolent felony offenders who would have otherwise been imprisoned can be sent to a restitution center for between 6 and 12 months, during which time the restitution center director attempts to secure employment for each new resident. The director also attempts to place each probationer as a worker in a community service project either during off-work hours (if the probationer is employed) or full-time (if the probationer is unable to find employment). The restitution facility, which is operated by probation staff, accommodates between 30 and 60 persons and is usually located in light industrial areas for access to employment.

The probationer's salary is submitted by the employer directly to the director of the restitution center. The director deducts the cost of food, housing, and supervision; support for the probationer's dependents; and restitution to the victim(s)—with the remainder, if any, going to the probationer upon release from the center. If a restitution center director determines that the probationer is knowingly or intentionally failing to seek employment, the director requests that the court having jurisdiction over the case revoke probation and transfer the probationer to the custody of the Texas Department of Corrections. If the judge determines that a resident has demonstrated an acceptance of responsibility, the court may order the resident released from the center. The first two months following release, the former resident is on intensive supervision before being transferred to a regular probation caseload.

▶ Community Service

Because relatively few offenders coming into the criminal justice system are in a position to provide meaningful financial restitution, the alternative of community service (work in the community to make reparation for the offense) has gained in popularity. In New Jersey, offenders sentenced to community service work without monetary compensation at public or private nonprofit agencies in the community. They usually perform their community service during the evenings and on weekends to complete their sentences: "The punitive aspect of a community service order is reflected in the imposition upon the time and freedom of offenders. While functioning in the traditional role as punishment, a community service order also directly benefits the public through the performance of services that may otherwise not be available" (Administrative Office of the Courts, n.d.: 11).

Community service in Georgia is seen as "an alternative sentencing option which is definitely punitive, yet is not perceived as being as harsh as incarceration, nor as lenient as

COMMUNITY SERVICE IN FEDERAL PROBATION

What is it?

A release condition that requires people on supervision to perform unpaid work for a civic or nonprofit organization, such as a public library, a soup kitchen, or a conservation program.

How does the court use it?

- As punishment, to restrict the personal liberty of people on supervision and require them to forfeit leisure time.
- As rehabilitation, to instill a work ethic and help people on supervision develop interests and skills.

The probation officer's duties

- Find agencies willing to work with people on supervision.
- Match people on supervision with suitable community service assignments.
- Visit the agency to monitor how community service is going and to resolve any problems.
- Take steps to control and correct the situation if people on supervision don't show up to do their com-

munity service; perform their community service assignment unsatisfactorily; behave unacceptably while performing community service; or otherwise fail to comply with their release conditions.

The probation officer's challenges

Not all people on supervision are suitable for community service, including those with.

- Drug or alcohol addiction.
- A history of assault or sexual offenses.
- Serious emotional or psychological problems.

What are the benefits?

- Requires people on supervision to give something back to society.
- Gives them an opportunity to get work experience, job skills, and references.
- Gives the community free labor and provides services that otherwise might not be available due to lack of funding.

▼

regular probation." In the state of Washington, compulsory service without compensation performed for the benefit of the community is available as an alternative to incarceration for certain nonviolent crimes. The Department of Corrections Division of Community Services solicits requests for personnel services from nonprofit or governmental agencies, and community service has included chore service, work in food banks, park and street cleanup, industrial oil removal, and recycling. The requesting agency is expected to do the following:

- Refrain from displacing a paid worker with an offender.
- Supply a description of the work site and tasks.
- Assign a supervisor for training and supervision of the offender.
- Provide working conditions for the offender equal to that of paid staff.
- Provide written verification of offender performance.

Similar programs exist in several states, including Georgia, Indiana, Kansas, Louisiana, Maryland, Minnesota, Ohio, Oregon, and Virginia. In Illinois and New Jersey, community service is used as an alternative for persons convicted of driving while intoxicated. In New Jersey, the community service program is the responsibility of the county probation department; although no offender is automatically disqualified for the community service alternative, the Administrative Office of the Courts recommends that persons suffering from chronic alcohol or drug abuse problems, persons convicted of arson or assaultive offenses, and those with previous convictions for certain sex offenses be excluded. In Georgia, community service is recommended for (but not limited to) persons convicted of traffic and ordinance violations and nonviolent, nondestructive misdemeanors and felonies. In other cases, "The judge may confer with the prosecutor, defense attorney, probation supervisor, community service officer, or other interested persons to determine if the community service program is appropriate for an offender." Typical placements in Georgia have included hospitals, the Red Cross, parks and recreation systems, senior citizen centers, and associations for the blind and deaf, and humane societies.

The Dauphin County (Pennsylvania) Adult Probation/Parole Department has a Community Resource Program in conjunction with the Harrisburg chapter of the American Red Cross. Clients placed at the Red Cross are regarded as volunteers (even though participation is a mandatory condition of the sentence of probation or county parole) and are provided with the same training, expectations, and benefits that any Red Cross volunteer receives. The Red Cross provides monthly evaluation reports. If work is satisfactory, a completion letter is given to the client and a copy to the P/P officer; unsatisfactory work results in a termination letter. Clients have served as first aid providers and assistants to an instructor of first aid courses and have conducted their own courses in first aid using multimedia systems; others serve in clerical, public relations, custodial, and research positions. Although no restrictions are placed on who may enter the program, clients have been nonviolent offenders.

Summary

- Probation may be under the auspices of the judiciary or an agency in the executive branch of government.
- The term "probation" was applied by John Augustus to the practice of bailing offenders out of court, followed by a period of supervised living in the community.
- Placing restrictions on who could be granted probation violated a basic tenet of positivism.

- The juvenile court movement accelerated the spread of probation.
- Early probation officers were often volunteers or poorly paid employees.
- Although most probation agencies are part of the executive branch where it is usually combined with parole, the most populous states separate probation and parole.
- There is disagreement over whether a probation agency should be in the judicial or executive branch and over whether it should be administered on a state or county level.
- The geographic area where the court is situated may affect the granting of probation.
- Through a probation subsidy the state reimburses the county for offenders placed on probation instead of being sentenced to a state prison.
- Conditions of probation can be divided into standard conditions and special conditions tailored to the individual requirements of a particular offender.
- Community service is an alternative to restitution when the offender has few assets or there is no specific victim, such as in a drug violation.

Key Terms

absconders *22*
community service *34*
conditions of probation *31*

plea bargaining *29*
probation subsidy *29*
special conditions *31*

standard conditions *31*
restitution *33*

Internet Connections

Administrative Office of the U.S. Courts: **uscourts.gov**

American Probation and Parole Association: **appa-net.org**

Federal Judicial Center: **fjc.gov**

Federal Probation and Pretrial Officers Association: **fppoa.org**

Nation's Court Directory: **courts.net**

National Center for State Courts: **ncsconline.org**

Probation agency links: **cppca.org/link**

State courts links: **doc.state.co.us/links.htm**

State Justice Institute: **statejustice.org**

Review Questions

1. How is probation administered?
2. What was the role of John Augustus in the development of probation?
3. How does placing restrictions on who could be granted probation violate a basic tenet of positivism?
4. In what branch of government are most probation agencies administered?
5. What are the arguments in favor of placing probation services in the judicial branch?
6. What are the arguments in favor of placing probation services in the executive branch?

7. What are the arguments over whether probation should be administered on a state or county level?

8. How can the geographic area where a court is situated affect the granting of probation?

9. How can a probation subsidy help reduce prison commitments?

10. How do standard conditions of probation differ from special conditions?

11. Why is community service used instead of restitution?

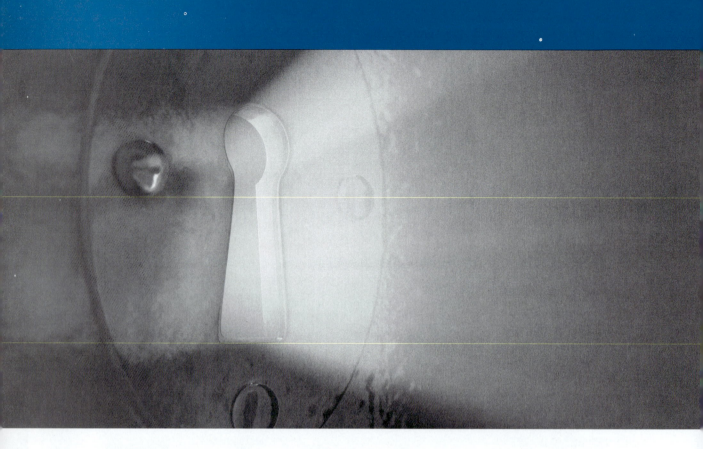

3 Pretrial Services, Sentencing, and the Presentence Report

LEARNING OBJECTIVES

This chapter will enable the student to:

1 *Understand the use of prediction scales that allow for determination of the risk posed by a defendant of failing to return to court or being arrested for a new crime.*

2 *Describe the disagreement over the most appropriate agency for providing pretrial supervision.*

3 *Discuss the presentence investigation report.*

4 *Identify the four basic purposes of a presentence investigation report.*

5 *Explain how a prior criminal record may affect the defendant's eligibility for probation.*

6 *Understand the use and purpose of sentencing guidelines.*

7 *Discuss how a preplea investigation has replaced the presentence investigation report in many jurisdictions.*

8 *Explain criticism of the presentence investigation report.*

This chapter will examine sentencing and the related issues of pretrial release, problem-solving courts, sentencing, and the presentence report.

▶ Pretrial Services

The Eighth Amendment of the Constitution prohibits excessive bail, but fails to define *excessive*. While a million-dollar bail may not be excessive for a large-scale drug dealer or corporate criminal, setting bail at $25 may be sufficient to keep a homeless defendant in custody until trial. Contemporary bail reform efforts can be traced back to a Vera Foundation project in New York City in 1961. In response to jail overcrowding, in a three-year experiment the Vera Foundation proved the feasibility and efficacy of a system of bail, based not on personal assets but on verified social criteria—a prediction scale.

Using objective criteria, a **prediction scale** allows for determination of the risk posed by a defendant of failing to return to court or being arrested for a new crime, while promoting a fundamental concept of American justice, equality, that is, treating similar defendants similarly. At this stage of criminal justice, the defendant is legally innocent. On a more practical level is the cost of jailing pretrial defendants. Prediction scales are actuarial-type instruments that rate defendants according to criminal history, education and employment record, family and marital history, companions, alcohol and drug problems, emotional and personal attributes, and attitude or orientation (e.g., supportive of crime and unfavorable toward convention). A total score recommends for or against release without the need to post bail and may also determine whether the defendant requires pretrial supervision, if available, provided by a probation department or an agency specifically created for this purpose, such as the Pretrial Services Agency (PSA) in Washington DC (Figure 3.1). The PSA interviews about 20,000 defendants a year and supervises more than 17,000 defendants and was among the first pretrial programs nationwide to offer defendant supervision based on varying levels of risk. Pretrial agencies may be housed in a probation department, the court, or sheriff's office. Most serve a local jurisdiction or a small cluster of local jurisdictions (Kim and Denver, 2011).

There is disagreement over the most appropriate agency for providing pretrial supervision. Probation agencies are a feature of all trial courts and thus readily available with personnel experienced in presentence investigations and community supervision of

---

AMERICAN BAR ASSOCIATION PRETRIAL RELEASE STANDARD 10-1

Every jurisdiction should establish a pretrial services agency or program to collect and present the necessary information, present risk assessments, and consistent with court policy, make release recommendations required by the judicial officer in making release decisions, including the defendant's eligibility for diversion, treatment, or other alternative adjudication programs, such as drug or other treatment courts. Pretrial services should also monitor, supervise and assist defendants released prior to trial, and to review the status and release eligibility of detained defendants for the court on an ongoing basis.

1. RESIDENCE
    (a) Length at present address
        • 6 months or less; undomiciled 2
        • Over 6 months to 1 year 1
        Over 1 year.. 0
    (b) Location of residency
        • Out of state or out of county... 2
        • County resident under 1 year 1
        • County resident over 1 year 0
    (c) Living with at present
        • Nonrelative, friend 2
        • Self 1
        • Relative (including spouse) 0
2. FAMILY IN AREA
    • Family out of state or county.. 2
    • Family in county 0
3. EMPLOYMENT/SCHOOL
    • Unemployed and/or not attending school.. 2
    • Inconsistent, sporadic, or part-time employment 1
    • Employed at least 20 hours per week or relatively stable employment
      the last year; homemaker; attends school regularly; disabled 0
4. PRIOR RECORD (past 10 years)
    (a) Felony convictions and delinquent adjudications
        • One or more prior convictions for class X
          or nonprobationable class I felony... 2
        • One or more prior convictions for a probationable offense 1
        • No prior felony convictions... 0
    (b) Prior record of misdemeanor, traffic, or local ordinance convictions
        • 2 or more misdemeanor convictions 2
        • 3 or more local ordinance and/or traffic convictions
          or 1 misdemeanor conviction (add 1 to score if DUI offense) 1
        • No misdemeanor, traffic, or local ordinance convictions................................. 0
    (c) Violent/assaultive convictions
        • One or more prior convictions for violent offenses 2
        • One or more prior misdemeanor or local ordinance
          convictions for violent offenses 1
        • No prior record of violent offenses 0
5. PENDING CHARGES
    • Pending felony.. 2
    • Pending misdemeanor/traffic/local ordinance 1
    • No pending charges 0
6. PREVIOUS FAILURE TO APPEAR (FTA)
    • One or more felony FTAs... 2
    • One or more misdemeanor/traffic ordinance FTAs.. 1
    • No prior FTAs... 0
7. PROBATION/PAROLE STATUS
    • Currently on probation or parole 2
    • Prior probation or parole 1
    • No prior probation or parole 0
8. SUBSTANCE USE
    • Regular, active use of drugs/alcohol 2
    • Occasional use of drugs/alcohol 1
    • No drug/alcohol use reported 0

TOTAL SCORE

RECOMMENDATION

0–9   = Release on recognizance
10–14 = Conditional release
15+   = Cash plus conditional release

FIGURE 3.1   Illinois Pretrial Recommendation Point Scale

offenders. However, as the American Probation and Parole Association (APPA) points out, the goals of pretrial services have a much more limited timeframe than probation services. "Their only legal charge is to monitor a defendant to reasonably assure his/her appearance in court and the safety of the community while his/her case is pending adjudication. In addition, given the different legal status of defendants, pretrial services officers may not discuss (and try to prevent the defendant from discussing) the current charge." Furthermore, probationers, "by the nature of their adjudicated status have had some of their rights either suspended or reduced, e.g., probable cause and a warrant may not be required for a search of probationer or his or her home. Rather reasonable grounds for the search is all that is required" (APPA, [2011], 15). One way to respond to this issue is by having a specialized unit whose probation officers are responsible only for PTR and/or retitling them as pretrial officers.

As with probation cases, PTR clients are required to abide by individual conditions that may include weekly contact with a probation assistant, referrals to community agencies, and continuance in school or employment. The PTR unit also provides a liaison function for the probation department and the courts. PTR staff appear at calendar calls to make PTR recommendations, dispense information on people placed on probation, and gather requests for presentence investigations.

In Baltimore, Pretrial Release Services provides supervision to defendants awaiting trial with specialized units for domestic violence, mental health, a priority unit for violent crimes, such as handgun violations or robbery, and a prostitution unit containing defendants who are typically at the highest risk of failure to appear. The prostitution diversion program is designed to provide intensive supervision and regular meetings with a social worker.

The Florida Department of Corrections operates a pretrial intervention program that diverts from prosecution any first-time defendants who are accused of third-degree felonies or misdemeanors; they must volunteer for the program and agree to abide by deferred prosecution conditions of supervision that include restitution and payment of supervision costs. The victim, prosecutor, and judge must also give consent. The subject is placed under the supervision of a correctional probation officer for a period that generally lasts from 90 days to six months. Those who complete the program successfully have their charges dismissed; those who fail are subject to prosecution for their original offense(s).

> **Key Fact**
>
> Many jurisdictions provide community supervision of pretrial defendants released without having to post bail/on their own recognizance.

The most extensive program using pretrial supervision is the Pretrial Services of the United States Courts. In 42 districts with large metropolitan areas, pretrial investigation and supervision are provided by pretrial services officers; in the rest, they are provided by U.S. probation officers. The officer submits a Pretrial Services Report, which includes the details of the alleged offense and the history and background of the defendant. Of particular importance is an assessment of the risk the defendant poses for nonappearance and for danger to the community. If the investigator determines that the defendant poses no risk of nonappearance or danger to the community, he or she recommends release without conditions, but if the officer determines that the defendant poses some risk of nonappearance or danger to the community, he or she recommends "the least restrictive conditions that would reasonably ensure the defendant's appearance and the safety of any other persons and the community" (Wolf, 1997: 20). Except that the defendant will not commit a crime, there are no general conditions; instead, they are tailored to the individual appearing before the court. Persons posing a reasonable level of risk are placed under supervision, and the officer monitors compliance with court-imposed conditions, such as home confinement with electronic monitoring, urinalysis, surrender of firearms and passports, and any curfew or in-person reports to the PTR office; home and employment visits are routine. Any violations of conditions are reported to the court and can lead to more restrictive conditions or a revocation of release.

The officer may also be called on to conduct diversion investigations for the U.S. attorney when that office is considering pretrial diversion instead of prosecution. If the person is diverted, the officer will provide supervision, which includes monitoring the conditions of the diversion agreement. Pretrial diversion is an alternative to prosecution that diverts the defendant to a program of supervision administered by the pretrial services officer. The U.S. attorney identifies candidates for diversion—persons who have not adopted a criminal lifestyle and who are likely to complete the program successfully. The pretrial services officer investigates the individual, recommends for or against placement, and recommends length of supervision and special conditions. Diversion is voluntary; the person may opt to stand trial instead. If the individual is placed in the program, a pretrial services officer supervises him or her, and if the person successfully completes supervision, the government declines prosecution and makes no record of the arrest.

U.S. pretrial service officers are the first court representatives defendants encounter after their arrest. In general, the officer's mission is to investigate defendants charged with a federal crime, recommend in a report to the court whether to release or detain defendants, and supervise the defendants who are released to the community while they await their day in court. At the core of the day-to-day work of officers is the hallowed principle of criminal law that the defendant is presumed innocent until proven guilty. Officers must balance this presumption with the reality that some persons—if not detained before their trial—are likely to flee or to threaten others. Defendants may pose danger to a person, such as by threatening a victim or a witness, or to the community, such as by engaging in criminal activity. The pretrial services officer's job is to identify persons who are likely to fail to appear or to be arrested if released, to recommend restrictive conditions that would reasonably ensure the defendant's appearance in court and the safety of the community, and to recommend pretrial detention when appropriate.

The officer conducts a pretrial services investigation, gathering and verifying important information about the defendant and the defendant's suitability for PTR. The investigation begins when the officer is first informed that a defendant has been arrested. The arresting or case agent calls the pretrial services office and, ideally, provides information about the defendant (e.g., name, date of birth, Social Security number, charges, circumstances surrounding the arrest, and location). Before interviewing the defendant, the officer runs a criminal history check and also, if possible, speaks to the assistant U.S. attorney about the defendant, the charges, and the government's position as to whether to release or detain the defendant. The purpose of the interview is to find out what the defendant has been doing, where the defendant has been living, and where the defendant has been working (or what the defendant's source of support is). What the officer learns from collateral sources—from other persons, documents, and online research—may verify what the defendant said, contradict it, or provide something more. The officer's research, for instance, may include contacting the defendant's family and associates to confirm background information, employers to verify employment, law enforcement agencies to obtain a criminal history, financial institutions to obtain bank or credit card statements, and the motor vehicle administration to check the defendant's license and registration.

Conducting the investigation in time for the defendant's initial appearance in court can be quite a challenge. Sometimes, the pretrial services officer must wait for the arresting agents to make the defendant available or for the U.S. marshals to finish processing the defendant. The defense counsel may be interviewing the defendant or may tell the defendant not to answer the officer's questions. The officer might have to wait for an interpreter or for an interview room. Sometimes, verifying information is hard because the defendant gives false information or a false identity or because persons able to verify information are not available. The interview may take place in the U.S. marshal's holding cell, the arresting law enforcement agency's office, the local jail, or the pretrial services office. During the interview, the officer talks to the defendant in private if possible, remains objective while interacting with the defendant, and explains that the information will be used to decide whether the defendant will be released or detained. The officer does not discuss the alleged offense or the defendant's guilt or innocence and does not give legal advice to the defendant or recommend an attorney.

When the investigation is complete, the officer prepares a report that helps the court make an informed release or detention decision. In preparing the pretrial services report, the officer addresses two basic questions: Is the defendant likely to stay out of trouble and come back to court? If not, what conditions should the court impose to increase that likelihood? The officer considers both danger and nonappearance factors before making a recommendation to the court to release or detain the defendant. For example, the offense with which the defendant is charged and the defendant's substance abuse history may present both danger and nonappearance considerations. Factors such as prior arrests and convictions or a history of violent behavior raise danger concerns; factors such as immigration status or ties to family and community may influence nonappearance. If no risk factors are evident, the officer recommends release on personal recognizance, but if risk factors exist the officer recommends either release with conditions or detention.

Release conditions are tailored to the individual defendant but always include a universal condition: that the defendant does not commit a federal, state, or local crime during the period of release. The officer may recommend (and the court may set) conditions to accomplish any number of goals, including prohibiting possession of weapons, contact with victims, or use of alcohol or drugs; restricting the defendant's freedom of movement or the people with whom the defendant associates; and requiring the defendant to seek or maintain employment, obtain education or training, or surrender a passport. If the defendant is likely to fail to appear, the officer may recommend a financial bond, which the defendant (or the defendant's family) forfeits if the defendant fails to appear in court as directed.

The pretrial services officer supervises offenders in the community to make sure that they comply with court-ordered conditions of release until they begin to serve their sentence, the charges are dismissed, or they are acquitted. They monitor defendants' compliance with their release conditions; manage risk; provide necessary services as ordered by the court, such as drug treatment; and inform the court and the U.S. attorney if the defendant violates the conditions. The officer selects appropriate supervision strategies and develops a supervision plan, which the officer modifies if the defendant's

A CLOSER LOOK

TYPICAL DAY FOR A PRETRIAL SERVICES OFFICER

Routine office activities for a pretrial services officer include meeting with defendants, discussing the release conditions, counseling defendants on drug abuse, encouraging them to maintain or seek employment, monitoring the submission of urine specimens, and reminding defendants of their next court date. Also, officers contact contract agencies to monitor attendance at drug treatment or mental health programs. In addition, officers speak with third-party custodians to ensure that defendants are abiding by release conditions. Another role of the pretrial services officer is to educate defendants on the court process. Sometimes defendants think every time they appear in court, they are going to jail. Pretrial services officers explain the

process—which may include a preliminary hearing, grand jury indictment, or arraignment—the role of the officer in preparing the presentence report, the sentencing hearing, and the possibility of self-surrender if a prison sentence is imposed. Knowing the process helps defendants alleviate some of their fears.

While completing routine paperwork, meeting with defendants, and handling phone calls, the pretrial services officer may receive a call that a new arrest has been made and the defendant needs to be interviewed in the marshal's cellblock. At that time, the officer stops what he or she is doing and proceeds to the cell block to interview the defendant, conduct an investigation, and prepare a report for the defendant's initial appearance (Wolf, 1997: 23).

circumstances change. The officer also carries out risk management activities to help ensure that the defendant complies with the release conditions: monitoring the defendant through personal contacts and phone calls with the defendant and others, including family members, employers, and treatment providers; meeting with the defendant in the pretrial services office and at the defendant's home and job; helping the defendant find employment; and helping the defendant find medical, legal, or social services.

▶ Presentence Report

An investigation before sentencing is the basis for a **presentence investigation report**, sometimes referred to as a probation report or PSI. After the conviction of a defendant and before the sentencing hearing, a judge may (depending on the circumstances and the statutes of the jurisdiction) order a PSI that traditionally has reflected a positivist view interest in the offender (not just the offense). It may be a short-form PSI (usually used in misdemeanor or less serious felony cases) or a long-form PSI (used in most felony cases). This chapter provides an example of the PSI report (Figure 3.3).

▶ Requiring a Presentence (PSI) Report

In some states, the law requires a PSI report for crimes punishable by more than one year of imprisonment; in others, the judge retains the discretion to order a report. In Michigan and New York, for example, a long-form report is required in all felony cases; in misdemeanor cases, the report is discretionary and, when done, is usually in the short form. In Utah, a PSI report is required for all felony and serious misdemeanors, and in Missouri and Nevada a PSI is mandatory in all felony cases unless the defendant waives the requirement—in which case, at the judge's discretion, a PSI may still be compiled. In Texas, no legal requirement exists that a PSI be prepared in each felony case, so the trial judge has the discretion to order a report or to sentence without one. In Illinois, "a defendant shall not be sentenced for a felony before a written presentence report of investigation is presented to and considered by the court," although this right is frequently waived by the defense counsel because a plea agreement has already been arranged (discussed later). In North Carolina, while a sentencing judge can order a PSI report, they are rare.

> **Key Fact**
>
> Jurisdictions differ on requiring a PSI report before sentencing; in some it is mandatory for felonies unless waived by the defendant; in others it is at the judge's discretion.

▶ Purposes of a PSI

The report has four basic purposes:

1. The primary purpose is to help the court make an appropriate sentencing decision. The report should help in deciding for or against probation, determining the conditions of probation or deciding among available institutions, and determining the appropriate length of sentence.

2. The PSI serves as the basis for a plan of probation or parole supervision and treatment. The report indicates the problem areas in the defendant's life, his or her capacity for using help, and the opportunities available in the community. During the investigation, the defendant usually begins to relate to the probation department, learning how probation officers (POs) work and gaining some understanding of the nature of the agency.

3. The PSI assists jail and prison personnel in their classification and treatment programs. Institutions are often dependent on the report when the inmate is first received, a time when little is known other than what is contained in commitment documents: conviction and sentence data. The PSI helps institutional staff

to understand and classify the offender; it can provide valuable information that will help in planning for the care, custody, and rehabilitation of the inmate. This includes everything from the type of custody required and the care of physical needs to the planning of the various phases of the institutional program.

Many institutions will have little, if any, background or social, medical, and psychological information other than that provided by the PSI report. This means that the report will have an effect on the way in which an inmate is viewed and approached by institutional personnel because they will take the word of the PO over that of the offender. The ideal report can give focus and initial direction to institutional authorities for treatment and training as well as care and management.

4. If the defendant is sentenced to a correctional institution, the report will eventually serve to furnish parole authorities with information pertinent to release planning and consideration for parole as well as determination of any special conditions of supervision.

Determining the financial condition of defendants has become important in preparing a PSI report. In the 1984 Criminal Fine Enforcement Act and the 1987 Criminal Fines Improvement Act, Congress cited the need to determine a defendant's ability to pay fines. Financial information is also necessary to assess the defendant's ability to make restitution and to pay any probation supervision fees, which are rather common. In the federal system, offenders must disclose to POs their assets and liabilities and the sources and amounts of their incomes and expenses. POs must then confirm these amounts by reviewing documentation provided by the offender. "Probation officers carefully review statements from savings and checking accounts including canceled checks, statements from stockbrokers, closing statements and appraisals from real estate transactions, sales and loan agreements on automobiles and other assets, credit card statements, and documentation on other consumer debt. The probation officer examines the supporting documentation to determine if it is consistent with the offender's financial statement" (Berg, 1997: 29).

All states, the District of Columbia, and the federal government have laws that provide for victim impact statements at sentencing and parole hearings. This may be accomplished in-person, by way of an interview, closed circuit TV, or a written statement. Some states include a separate **victim impact statement (VIS)** that is attached to the PSI and usually includes a "description of the harm in terms of financial, social, psychological, and physical consequences of the crime." The VIS may also include a statement concerning the victim's feelings about the crime, the offender, and the proposed sentence. The investigating officer in some states may also be required to provide offender information to a victim. In Indiana:

> The probation officer who interviewed a victim(s) and a witness(es) of a felony, as part of the presentence investigation, shall inform them of their right to receive from the Indiana Department of Corrections (IDOC) information regarding when the offender is to be discharged from prison; to be released on parole; is to have a parole release or violation hearing; has escaped; or is going into a temporary release program. The Probation Department shall provide the IDOC with the most recent list of addresses and/or phone numbers of victims no later than five days after receipt of the information from the victim(s). Victims may give the IDOC written notification that they do not wish to receive notification.

In the PSI, the PO attempts in the report to "focus light on the character and personality of the defendant, and to offer insight into his problems and needs, to help understand the world in which he lives, to learn about his relationships with people, and to discover salient factors that underlie the specific offense and conduct in general" and to "suggest alternatives in the rehabilitation process" (Division of Probation, 1974: 48). The report is not expected to show guilt or innocence, only to relate the facts that the PO has been able to gather during the course of the presentence investigation.

Key Fact

PSI reports often include information on offenders' financial status and a victim impact statement.

▶ Content of the Report

PSI reports should be flexible in format, reflecting a difference in the background of different offenders and making the best use of available resources and probation department capabilities. A full report should normally contain the following list of items (American Probation and Parole Association and the Administrative Office of the Illinois Courts):

1. **Legal data.** Arresting officer, victim, original charges filed, and summary of court action as well as complete description of offense and circumstances surrounding it (not limited to aspects developed for the record as part of the determination of guilt).

2. **Defendant statement.** Defendant's version of offense and his or her attitude.

3. **Codefendant(s).** Information about any codefendant(s), including age and court status.

4. **Victim statement.** Statement from victim and description of victim's status, impact on victim, losses suffered by victim, and restitution due to victim.

5. **Prior record.** Full description of offender's prior juvenile and/or criminal record (if any).

6. **Probation/parole.** Offender's prior adjustment and performance on probation, parole, or any other supervised sentence (if any).

7. **Education and employment.** Description of offender's educational background, present employment status, financial status, and capabilities.

8. **Military service.** Description of offender's military record (if applicable).

9. **Social history.** Information on offender's family relationships, marital status, dependents, interests and activities, residence history, and religious affiliations as well as reports from clinics, institutions, and other social agencies with which offender has been involved.

10. **Medical and mental status.** Offender's medical history and (if desirable) psychological or psychiatric report.

11. **Environments.** Information about environments to which offender might return or to which offender could be sent should probation be granted.

12. **Community resources.** Information about special resources available to assist offender, such as treatment centers, residential facilities, vocational training services, special educational facilities, rehabilitation programs of various institutions to which offender might be committed, special probation department programs, and other similar programs particularly relevant to offender's situation.

13. **Summary and analysis.** List of most significant aspects of report (special effort should be made in preparation of PSI reports not to burden the court with irrelevant and unconnected details).

14. **Recommendation.** Depending on the jurisdiction and or the sentencing judge's preference, the PO may offer a sentencing recommendation; particularly important when probation is being considered.

▶ Gathering Information

Information in the PSI is derived from persons and documents. Obviously, interview skills and the ability to locate, review, and interpret records and reports are crucial in preparing a PSI.

▶ Interviews

In probation and parole, much of the necessary information is received directly from people. Thus, report quality is often dependent on the interview skills of probation and parole personnel. In the PSI, a great deal of information is gained by interviewing the defendant: "Interviews shall be directed toward obtaining and clarifying relevant information and making observations of the defendant's/respondent's behavior, attitudes and character" (*New York State Code of Criminal Procedure*, 350.6–3ii). These interviews are conducted in all types of surroundings, from hot and noisy detention pens where dozens of people may be awaiting a court hearing to the relative quiet of the probation office.

A quiet, comfortable setting with a maximum of privacy is obviously the best environment for an interview because a place that lacks privacy or has numerous distractions will adversely affect the productivity of the interview. Sometimes interviews are conducted in the defendant's home, which provides an opportunity to observe the offender's home situation and adds an additional and sometimes vital dimension to the report. New York statutes advise: "Whenever possible, interviews with the defendant/respondent shall be at the probation office; however, visits to the defendant's/respondent's residence may be made when there is an indication that additional information will be obtained that is likely to influence the recommendation or court disposition."

The interview is an anxiety-producing situation for the defendant. Previous experiences in similar situations, such as questioning by the police, may have been unpleasant. The PO tries to lower anxiety by cordially introducing himself or herself and clearly explaining the purpose of the interview and the PSI report. This approach is especially important for the defendant who is not familiar with the criminal justice system in general and the court process in particular.

The PO may try to deal with matters of concern to the defendant. A male defendant may be engaged in a discussion of how his wife and dependents can secure public assistance in the event he is imprisoned. The PO might offer to write a letter of referral for his wife to take with her to the welfare department or other social agency that can provide assistance. Female offenders with children will need help in planning for their care in the event of a sentence of imprisonment. In some way, the officer must show genuine concern and interest in the defendant while being realistic enough to expect many answers and statements that will be self-serving. Because the PO's contact with the defendant is limited, the officer cannot expect to probe deeply into the defendant's personality.

Some defendants will be overtly hostile; others will mask their hostility or anxiety with wisecrack-type answers. The PO must control his or her temper and temperament—he or she is the professional and must never lose sight of that fact during an interview. In questioning, generalized queries (e.g., "What have you been doing?") should be avoided (lest the interviewer be told, "Nothin' much"). Questions should be specific but require an explanation rather than a simple yes or no answer. The PO must avoid putting answers in the defendant's mouth (e.g., "Did you quit that job because it was too difficult?").

When the PSI is complete, the defendant should be re-interviewed to give him or her an opportunity to refute certain information or clarify any aspect of the report that may be in conflict with other parts of the report. In addition to the defendant, the PO may interview the arresting officer, the victim, employers, and significant others in the defendant's environment, such as spouse, parents, siblings, teachers, and clergy. Some recommend interviewing the defense counsel and prosecutor (Storm, 1997).

> **Key Fact**
>
> Most of the information in a PSI report is gained from interviews.

► Records and Reports

The probation officer will be reviewing records and reports in the course of the PSI. The first is the arrest record of the defendant, referred to as a rap sheet. This record will take the form of an arrest sheet(s) of a law enforcement agency, such as the state police. Each rap sheet entry is usually the result of the subject being fingerprinted. The sheet typically contains numerous abbreviations that the PO must decipher if the record is to be useful (e.g., *Att Burg* for attempted burglary or *DUI* for driving under the influence). The arrest sheet does not describe the offense and may not even indicate whether it is a felony or misdemeanor; it simply contains the official charge (e.g., *Burg 2*). There is usually no mention of the premises that were burglarized or what (if anything) was taken. In addition, the sheet often omits the disposition of the arrest, so the officer may not be able to determine from the arrest report what happened to a particular case; therefore, it is often necessary to check court records or to contact out-of-state agencies to determine the disposition of a case.

The nature of the defendant's prior record is critical. The law usually provides for a harsher sentence if the defendant has one or more prior felony convictions. In addition, the defendant's eligibility for probation and a variety of treatment programs, such as drug rehabilitation, may be affected by a prior criminal record. Also there are the "three strikes and you're out" laws. The PO is especially interested in any information that may influence the sentence that was omitted during the trial, particularly any mitigating or aggravating circumstances, and information that can provide a different perspective on the case. The officer will review any previous PSI reports as well as reports of other correctional agencies that have had contact with the defendant, such as training schools, residential treatment centers, and prison and parole agencies. The PO may also be interested in reviewing the educational records of the defendant. With the high volume of substance-abusing defendants entering the criminal justice system, POs must review this dimension of each defendant and explore the appropriateness of a recommendation for substance abuse treatment.

If there are any medical, psychiatric, or psychological reports available, the PO will review and analyze them. To do this review, he or she must understand the nomenclature and the meaning of any tests used by medical and mental health professionals; these professionals often refer to the *Diagnostic and Statistical Manual of Mental Disorders* (referred to simply as DSM), so probation and parole agencies should have the latest copy available for their officers. The PO should make a judgment as to whether a psychiatric or psychological referral should be made during the PSI. Indiscriminate referrals to mental health or court-based clinics waste resources—a crime may be rational, and criminal behavior is not generally symptomatic of an internalized conflict. In cases in which symptoms of mental disorder are apparent and in those situations in which the offender may benefit from an exploration of his or her problems, a referral should be made. If no referral is made and a lack of psychiatric and psychological information exists, the PO should present his or her own observations concerning the defendant's intellectual capacity and personality (e.g., level of social functioning and contact with reality).

If the PO has received conflicting information about the defendant and is unable to reconcile the discrepancies, this difficulty should be pointed out in the report and not left up to the reader to discover (or, more likely, not discover). "The probation officer must also distinguish between facts and the inferences, or opinions, or conclusions based upon those facts" (Storm, 1997: 13).

Of crucial importance in any PSI report are the sections titled "Evaluative Summary" and "Recommendation" (although in some jurisdictions, a recommendation is not provided). In Nevada, statutes require the PSI to contain "a recommendation of a definite term of confinement or an amount of fine or both." Nothing should appear in either of these sections that is not supported by the rest of the report. The summary contains the highlights of the total report and should serve as a reminder to the reader of the information that has already been presented. The recommendation is a carefully thought-out statement, based on the officer's best professional judgment. It contains the alternatives that are available in the case and reflects the individualized attention that each case receives (Carter, 1966). The PO is in a unique position with respect to making a recommendation to the judge: "The officer has had an opportunity to observe the defendant in the community, not only from a legal-judicial, investigative perspective, but also from the viewpoint of a general lifestyle" (Carter, 1966: 41). To present a meaningful recommendation, the PO must have knowledge of the resources and programs that are available. An inexperienced PO may submit a recommendation for a treatment program that is not available either in the community or at a correctional institution.

One issue that the PO must decide is the recommendation for or against a sentence of probation. As noted earlier, in many jurisdictions a conviction for certain crimes or a previous felony conviction precludes a sentence of probation, so the PO must know the statutes of the jurisdiction. The officer must also weigh the potential danger the defendant poses to the community, evaluate the defendant's rehabilitative potential and ability to conform to probation regulations, and consider whether probation will be construed by the community as too lenient in view of the offense or by the defendant as "getting away with it."

> **Key Fact**
> Probation officers often make sentencing recommendations in the PSI, particularly for or against probation.

▶ PSI Process in Nevada

When a defendant pleads guilty, pleads *nolo contendere* (no contest), or is found guilty after trial, a date is scheduled for sentencing, usually 30 days away. The district attorney refers the case file to the Division of Parole and Probation—during this time an officer is assigned to the case—and he or she begins to research the offender's criminal history and records. Eventually, the defendant completes a preliminary questionnaire and is interviewed by the investigating officer.

Based on the interview and the questionnaire, the officer obtains information regarding the offender's social and environmental background, employment history, education, mental health and substance abuse problems, residential stability, support systems, finances, military experience, future goals, and feelings regarding the offense. The investigator must strive to be a perceptive listener and skilled interviewer who lends a keen ear and is attentive to attitudes, remorse, candor, and a cooperative spirit. It is important to remember that officers interview all types of people, including juveniles, first-time offenders, career criminals, members of organized crime, the mentally disturbed, substance abusers, and white-collar criminals. As one might assume, these people can be hostile, manipulative, and con-wise or they can be pleasant—their crimes notwithstanding.

The investigator must then begin to verify as much information as possible by contacting the victim, the police, and any other relevant persons and agencies. He or she then begins to formulate the report. Using sentencing guidelines that mix classical and positivist elements, the officer determines the probation success probability (positivist) and the length of sentence (classical). The report is dictated, typed, proofread, approved, and distributed. The officer's recommendation addresses the risks and needs of the offender, the community, and the victim. The report may recommend special conditions of probation appropriate for the offender and his or her criminal activity. Officers attend sentencing hearings and are called on to answer questions by the judge, district attorney, and defense counsel; recommendations, however, are disclosed only to the judge.

While hearsay (statements of a person other than the witness—third-party testimony) is generally inadmissible at trial because it cannot be subject to cross-examination, hearsay can be included in a PSI report. Jurisdictions vary on permitting suppressed (exclusionary rule) evidence to be included in a PSI report. In some jurisdictions the PO can be subjected to cross-examination; the more detrimental the information, the more likely the court will permit cross-examination.

▶ Short- and Long-Form PSI Reports

There are two basic types of PSI reports: short form and long form. The **short-form PSI** is usually less exhaustive and less time consuming and is typically done in misdemeanor and less serious felony cases. The *New York State Code of Criminal Procedure* states:

> The abbreviated investigation for short-form reports shall consist of the defendant's legal history and primarily current information with respect to: the circumstances attending the commission of the offense, family and social situation, employment and economic status, education and, when available, physical and mental conditions. Such investigation may also include any other matter which the probation department conducting the investigation deems relevant to the recommendation or court disposition and must include any matter directed by the court.

In cases of all felonies (or in some locations, only the more serious felonies), judges will order a **long-form PSI**. Figure 3.3 at the end of this chapter provides an example.

▶ Sentencing Guidelines and Mandatory Sentences

By 1994, every state had laws regarding **mandatory sentencing**, the latest being "three (and sometimes two) strikes and you're out" (actually *in* for life—the baseball metaphor accounting for at least some of its popularity). Some states require that the instant offense and the prior felonies be for violent crimes, whereas others permit consideration of juvenile adjudications for violent offenses.

A violent crime does not necessarily mean *violent* behavior on the part of an offender. For example, in New York residential burglary during the day is a "violent" offense even in the absence of the possession of a weapon or an encounter with an occupant. The same applies to the lookout during a street robbery or a battered woman who severely injures or kills her abuser. Offenders who are convicted of a violent crime in their youth become the subject of **mandatory sentencing** as adults even when the offense is nonviolent. Ironically, research reveals that violent offenders who are released from prison are much less likely to be convicted of a new offense than nonviolent inmates, particularly drug offenders. This raises questions about the strategy for reducing prison overcrowding by incarcerating only violent offenders. Although anecdotal, in the author's experience armed robbers were more likely to be aggressive about seeking and maintaining gainful employment than their nonviolent counterparts.

About 20 states and the federal government use **sentencing guidelines** primarily in an attempt to limit judicial discretion and reduce sentence disparity—a turn toward classicalism. In Minnesota, for example, sentencing guidelines were instituted in 1980 and are changed periodically (Figure 3.2). A judge is provided with a sentencing grid that considers the severity of the instant offense and the offender's prior criminal history—social and employment history is excluded. Departures from mandatory sentences derived from the grid are permitted only under limited circumstances. Probation officers (actually, state parole and probation agents) are responsible for completing the sentencing guidelines worksheet and calculating the presumed sentence; they no longer write PSI reports. Offenders serve two-thirds of their sentence in prison after which, assuming no disciplinary action, they are released to complete the remaining one-third under community supervision.

SENTENCING GUIDELINES GRID

Presumptive sentence lengths are in months. Italicized numbers within the grid denote the discretionary range within which a court may sentence without the sentence being deemed a departure. Offenders with stayed felony sentences may be subject to local confinement.

CRIMINAL HISTORY SCORE

SEVERITY LEVEL OF CONVICTION OFFENSE (Example offenses listed in italics)		0	1	2	3	4	5	6 or more
Murder, 2nd Degree (intentional murder; drive-by-shootings)	11	306 *261–367*	326 *278–391*	346 *295–415*	366 *312–439*	386 *329–463*	406 *346–480²*	426 *363–480²*
Murder, 3rd Degree Murder, 2nd Degree (unintentional murder)	10	150 *128–180*	165 *141–198*	180 *153–216*	195 *166–234*	210 *179–252*	225 *192–270*	240 *204–288*
Assault, 1st Degree Controlled Substance Crime, 1st Degree	9	86 *74–103*	98 *84–117*	110 *94–132*	122 *104–146*	134 *114–160*	146 *125–175*	158 *135–189*
Aggravated Robbery, 1st Degree Controlled Substance Crime, 2nd Degree	8	48 *41–57*	58 *50–69*	68 *58–81*	78 *67–93*	88 *75–105*	98 *84–117*	108 *92–129*
Felony DWI	7	**36**	**42**	**48**	54 *46–64*	60 *51–72*	66 *57–79*	72 *62–84²*
Controlled Substance Crime, 3rd Degree	6	**21**	**27**	**33**	39 *34–46*	45 *39–54*	51 *44–61*	57 *49–68*
Residential Burglary Simple Robbery	5	**18**	**23**	**28**	33 *29–39*	38 *33–45*	43 *37–51*	48 *41–57*
Nonresidential Burglary	4	**12¹**	**15**	**18**	**21**	24 *21–28*	27 *23–32*	30 *26–36*
Theft Crimes (Over $5,000)	3	**12¹**	**13**	**15**	**17**	19 *17–22*	21 *18–25*	23 *20–27*
Theft Crimes ($5,000 or less) Check Forgery ($251–$2,500)	2	**12¹**	**12¹**	**13**	**15**	**17**	**19**	21 *18–25*
Sale of Simulated Controlled Substance	1	**12¹**	**12¹**	**12¹**	**13**	**15**	**17**	19 *17–22*

☐ Presumptive commitment to state imprisonment. First-degree murder has a mandatory life sentence and is excluded from the Guidelines

▨ Presumptive stayed sentence; at the discretion of the court, up to one year of confinement and other non-jail sanctions can be imposed as conditions of probation. However, certain offenses in the shaded area of the Grid always carry a presumptive commitment to state prison.

¹ 12¹=One year and one day

²Minn. Stat. § 244.09 requires that the Guidelines provide a range for sentences that are presumptive commitment to state imprisonment of 15% lower and 20% higher than the fixed duration displayed, provided that the minimum sentence is not less than one year and one day and the maximum sentence is not more than the statutory maximum.

FIGURE 3.2 Minnesota Sentencing Guidelines

The Federal Sentencing Reform Act of 1984, which became effective in 1987, was designed to reduce sentence disparity and phase out parole release by 1992. The statute also generated a great deal of confusion and litigation—many judges oppose the legislation's sentencing guidelines that removed much judicial discretion. On January 18, 1989, however, the Supreme Court ruled that the 1987 sentencing rules, established by a commission created under the 1984 statute, were constitutional (*Mistretta v. United States*, 488 U.S. 361).

This ruling did not end the controversy: Appeals over guidelines interpretation have burdened appellate courts, and judges have been concerned about the lack of consideration given to such factors as age, education, and family ties for rendering sentencing decisions.

The commission established 43 offense levels and assigned each federal offense to one of the levels (e.g., murder scores 43 and blackmail scores 9). Judges must impose sentences according to these levels, adding to or subtracting from them based on factors such as the offender's age, prior record, use of a firearm, or cooperation with the prosecution. "Ordinarily, the judge must choose a sentence from within the guideline range unless the court identifies a factor that the Sentencing Commission failed to consider that should result in a different sentence. However, the judge must in all cases provide the reasons for the sentence. Sentences outside the guideline range are subject to review by the courts of appeals for an abuse of discretion, and all sentences can be reviewed for incorrect application of the relevant guidelines or law" (U.S. Sentencing Commission flier). The guidelines manual is thicker than this book, and hundreds of amendments have been added. Inmates can earn a maximum of 15 percent off their sentence for good behavior. In 2004, the Supreme Court declared unconstitutional a Washington State guidelines scheme based on the federal one, dooming that and other similar sentencing systems. The Court found that any factors increasing a criminal sentence, except prior convictions, must be proved beyond a reasonable doubt (*Blakely v. Washington*, 542 U.S. 296). In 2006, the Court ruled that sentencing guidelines were constitutional as advisory, but not as presumptive or required (*U.S. v. Booker*, 543 U.S. 220).

The 1984 law resulted in changes in the content and format of the PSI. Instead of preparing PSI reports focused on a positivist approach to the offender, the PO must dwell on the details of the offense and the offender's prior criminal history. A federal PO in Philadelphia pointed out that it is imperative "that every detail about offense and offenders be included when these reports are prepared. Otherwise, minor point fluctuations on either offense level or criminal history can make a significant difference of several years in time to be served by convicted offenders" (Marshall, 1989: 10).

In preparing the PSI report, "the probation officer sets out the details of the offense and the defendant's criminal history. The probation officer then applies the sentencing guidelines to those facts" (Adair and Slawsky, 1991: 60). To make a relevant sentencing recommendation, the PO must be familiar with any applicable sentencing guidelines and mandatory sentences in his or her jurisdiction and must study the case to determine whether there are valid grounds for a departure from the guidelines. "The presentence report has become more a legal document than a diagnostic tool, citing facts, statutes, and guidelines, justifying and supporting positions the guidelines treat as relevant in arriving at a sentencing range. The format and presentation of information [are] dominated by facts related to the offender's offense behavior and criminal history, the two primary factors establishing a defendant's sentencing range. Social and personal history information is reported, however, primarily to aid the court in choosing a point within the range, imposing conditions of release, and/or departures" (Denzlinger and Miller, 1991: 51). In some states, Kansas and Minnesota, for example, the report does not contain socioeconomic information about the offender, nor a sentencing recommendation.

▶ Plea Bargaining and the Preplea Investigation Report

Most court cases in the United States, criminal and civil, are settled not by trial but by negotiation (or dropping of the action). Nearly 90 percent of all federal criminal cases are resolved by guilty plea. In the criminal justice system, a negotiated settlement is referred to as a **plea bargain**—an *ad hoc* exchange between a defendant who agrees to plead guilty to a criminal charge and a prosecutor who (explicitly or implicitly) offers leniency in return. Plea bargaining is criticized both for providing criminals with excessive leniency and for coercing defendants to waive their constitutional rights to a trial. Its extensive use can be explained by the time it saves the prosecutor and the defense, as well as the certainty of outcome it offers to both. The influence of plea bargaining on parole and length of incarceration will be examined in Chapter 4.

The extensive use of plea bargaining has reduced the need for a PSI because the plea agreement may actually specify the sentence a defendant will receive. This is particularly true in jurisdictions with determinate sentencing (discussed in Chapter 4) that limit judicial discretion. Under such conditions, a presentence report would not serve any useful purpose at a sentencing hearing. Plea bargaining, however, has resulted in the use of a pretrial/preplea investigation (PPI) report. If prosecutor and defense counsel negotiate a plea agreement and the judge retains a great deal of discretion over the sentence to be imposed (which is the case in many states—see Chapter 4), the judge may request a pretrial investigation before agreeing to the negotiated plea. In Illinois, for example, for a simple burglary as a first offense, the judge has the discretion to sentence an offender to a term of 3, 4, or 5 years, all the way up to 14 years. In Cook County, which includes the city of Chicago, judges often require a PPI report before confirming a plea agreement; in fact, short-form pretrial reports are more frequent than PSI reports.

The practice of using a PPI report requires the defendant to agree to the investigation (*New York Code of Criminal Procedure*):

> The probation department shall conduct a pre-plea investigation only upon a court order and written authorization by the defendant, his attorney, the prosecuting attorney and the judge ordering the investigation. Such written authorization shall include statements that no probation department personnel will be called to testify regarding information acquired by the probation department, that information obtained by the probation department may not be used in a subsequent trial, and that this exemption does not apply to defense or prosecution material which may be included in the plea report.

Probation officers in Georgia are instructed: "If the defendant or his/her attorney refuses to sign the authorization, discontinue the investigation and report this fact to the court." In Ohio, a PPI cannot be conducted prior to a finding of guilty unless the defendant, on advice of counsel, has consented to allow the investigation to proceed before adjudication and unless adequate precautions are taken to ensure that information disclosed during the PPI does not come to the attention of the prosecution, the court, or the jury prior to adjudication. As in Georgia, refusal of the defendant, his or her attorney, or both to sign the waiver constitutes an end to the investigation.

▶ Confidentiality of the PSI Report

Some controversy exists concerning whether any or all the contents of a PSI report should be disclosed to the defendant or his or her attorney. The basic argument against disclosure is that sources of information must be protected or they will hesitate to provide information. Family members or employers may fear retribution from the defendant if they provide negative information; in addition, law enforcement agencies may be reluctant to provide confidential information if the defendant or the defendant's attorney will be privy to it.

The basic argument in favor of disclosure is to enable the defendant to contest information that he or she considers unfair and to be protected from the effects of unfounded information. Disclosure of the contents of the PSI is more likely to ensure that the information presented is more objective and accurate. The American Bar Association recommends that all information that adversely affects the defendant be discussed with the defendant or his or her attorney. The President's Commission on Law Enforcement and Administration of Justice stated that "in the absence of compelling reasons for nondisclosure of specific information,

Key Fact

Disclosure of PSI information enables the defendant to contest information that he or she considers unfair and to be protected from the effects of unfounded information, but disclosure may cause sources of information to dry up.

the defendant and his counsel should be permitted to examine the entire presentence report" (President's Commission on Law Enforcement and Administration of Justice, 1972: 356). The National Advisory Commission on Criminal Justice Standards and Goals recommended that the PSI be made available to the defense and the prosecution; the commission rejected the argument that sources of information will dry up: "(1) Those jurisdictions which have required disclosure have not experienced this phenomenon; and (2) more importantly, if the same evidence were given as testimony at trial, there would be no protection or confidentiality" (National Advisory Commission on Criminal Justice Standards and Goals, 1973: 189).

This has been based on the (presumed) neutrality/objectivity of the probation officer—he or she has no interest in punishment; by disposition and training, the PO is a helping, not a prosecutorial, agent. Thus, in the 1949 case of *Williams v. New York* (337 U.S. 241), the judge imposed a sentence of death based on information contained in the PSI report. The defendant had been convicted of murder, but the jury recommended life imprisonment. The PSI—to which the jury was not privy—revealed that Williams was a suspect in 30 burglaries. Although he had not been convicted of these crimes, the report indicated that he had confessed to some and had been identified as the perpetrator of others. The judge had referred to parts of the report, indicating that the defendant was a "menace to society."

Williams appealed the death sentence, arguing that the procedure violated due process of law "in that the sentence of death was based upon information supplied by witnesses with whom the accused had not been confronted and as to whom he had no opportunity for cross-examination or rebuttal." The Supreme Court rejected this argument:

> Under the practice of individualizing punishments, investigational techniques have been given an important role. Probation workers making reports of their investigations have not been trained to prosecute but to aid offenders. Their reports have been given high value by conscientious judges who want to sentence persons on the best available information rather than on guesswork and inadequate information. To deprive sentencing judges of this kind of information would undermine modern procedural policies that have been cautiously adopted throughout the nation after careful consideration and experimentation. We must recognize that most of the information now relied upon by judges to guide them in the intelligent imposition of sentences would be unavailable if information were restricted to that given in open court by witnesses subject to cross-examination. And the modern probation report draws on information concerning every aspect of a defendant's life. The types and extent of this information make totally impractical if not impossible open court testimony with cross-examination. Such procedure could endlessly delay criminal administration in a retrial of collateral issues.

Williams was executed.

In 1977, the Supreme Court (*Gardner v. Florida*, 430 U.S. 349) considered a case in which, like *Williams*, the sentencing judge rejected a jury recommendation for life imprisonment and imposed the death sentence. As in *Williams*, the PSI contained negative information to which the defendant was not privy. Unlike *Williams*, however, the sentencing judge did not refer to the parts of the PSI on which he relied and which would have afforded counsel an opportunity to contest. The Court vacated the sentence and remanded the case back to the trial court.

In the federal system, since 1983 the contents of the PSI have been disclosed to the defendant, his or her counsel, and the attorney for the government, and the 1984 Sentencing Reform Act "largely rejected the sentencing philosophy expressed in *Williams*" (Adair and Slawsky, 1991: 58). Under the federal system of sentencing guidelines, the contents of the report determine the parameters for imposing a sentence. As a result, the sentencing hearing has become increasingly hostile. In response to defense attorney objections, the PO "is obligated to review the objections, reinvestigate if necessary, reevaluate decisions made, and discuss the findings with counsel. Any unresolved objections must be summarized for the court in an addendum to the report. On occasion this process consumes more time than the preparation of the presentence report" (Denzlinger and Miller, 1991: 51).

In some jurisdictions, law or custom allows the defendant access to the report, whereas some states give the judge the option of disclosing the contents of the report. In Texas, for example, statutes require that the entire contents of the report be revealed to the defendant. However, a trend exists toward adopting the position previously used in the federal system. The PSI can be revealed to the defendant or counsel, but the *Rules of Criminal Procedure* exclude the probation officer's recommendation and any "diagnostic opinion [such as a psychiatric report] which might seriously disrupt a program of rehabilitation, sources of information obtained upon a promise of confidentiality, or any other information which, if disclosed, might result in harm, physical or otherwise, to the defendant or other persons." In Kansas, the PSI report, with the exception of the sections containing the official version, the defendant's version, victim comments, and psychological (including drug and alcohol) evaluations of the defendant, are public record. In Michigan, although the court must permit the prosecutor, the defendant's attorney, and the defendant an opportunity to review the report prior to sentencing, "the court may exempt from disclosure information or a diagnostic opinion which might seriously disrupt a program of rehabilitation or sources of information obtained on a promise of confidentiality.... Any information exempted from disclosure by the court must be specifically noted in the PSI and is subject to appellate review." In Ohio, "the Probation Department shall have the report completed no later than ten days prior to sentencing. When the report is completed, it shall be sent to the assigned judge and made available, at the probation department, for review by the defendant's attorney (or by the defendant if he is not represented by an attorney) and the prosecutor.... The report made available for review by the attorneys or the defendant shall reflect the fact that information, if any, has been deleted pursuant to Ohio statutes and the general categories of the deleted information shall also be noted."

There is also the issue of making the PSI available to victims. If the report is available to the defendant, the Pima County (AZ) Adult Probation Department makes the report, with certain confidential information excised, also available to victims.

▶ Criticism of the PSI Report

Some critics maintain that many judges do not even read the PSI report, whereas others carefully select passages critical of the defendant to justify their sentences. Judges may discount the report because of the hearsay nature of the information (Blumberg, 1970). Research reveals the types of inaccurate or misleading information found in the PSI reports of one state (Dickey, 1979: 33–34): "(1) rumors and suspicions that are reported without any factual explanations; (2) incomplete explanations of events that leave a misleading impression; (3) factual errors relating, usually, to the criminal record of the offender."

> Rumors and suspicions are often reported in presentence reports and identified as such. The report that the rumor exists may be accurate. What is objectionable is the fact that the subject of the rumor may cause the reader to give more weight to the rumor than it deserves, if any. If the rumor is without foundation, reference to it is particularly troubling.
>
> It is difficult to assess the impact of rumors, although they sometimes seem to directly affect correctional decisions. For example, one sex offender's presentence report contained the statement that the offender "was rumored to have killed his mother." This was referred to in several parole decisions before it was investigated. Upon inquiry, it was determined to the satisfaction of the parole board that the offender had been confined in another state at the time of his mother's death and had no connection to it.
>
> Some reports do not contain complete information and are therefore misleading. One inmate's PSI contained the statement that he "had been arrested for attempted first-degree murder after a bar fight. The charges were later dropped." Investigation showed that the reason the charges were dropped was that the inmate was actually the victim of an attack and not the aggressor. The other person involved was later charged with a crime for the attack.

The most frequently recurring factual problem with the reports is related to past offenses. The so-called FBI rap sheet (or yellow sheet) is part of the report. It contains a confounding listing of past offenses that is frequently repetitious (i.e., it reports the same offense more than once), but the repetitions are not identified. Past charges do not always contain their disposition, so the reader is never sure how many offenses there actually were which were dropped and why, what the facts underlying the charges and offenses were, and what the outcome was.

One observer is concerned with the enormous dependence on the PSI that he argues tends to make the PO, rather than the judge, the sentencer (Gaylin, 1974). Numerous studies have indicated a high correlation between the recommendation of the PO and the judge's sentence. For example, research by the American Justice Institute (1981), using samples from representative probation departments throughout the United States, found that recommendations for probation were adopted by the sentencing judge between 66 and 95 percent of the time. A study in Utah revealed that judges followed the recommendation 92 percent of the time (Norman and Wadman, 2000). A study of 1994 sentencing recommendations in Nevada revealed a concurrence rate of 97 percent when probation was recommended and 88 percent when the recommendation was imprisonment. A study in one Iowa judicial district (Campbell, McCoy, and Osigweh, 1990) revealed much less congruity—and in a surprising direction: In many cases, those recommended for incarceration (44 percent) were instead sentenced to probation or some lesser sanction, such as diversion or a fine. The researchers concluded that these decisions were probably the result of a plea bargain and a prosecutor's recommendation for a nonincarceration sentence.

One study examined the relationship between plea bargaining, the PO's recommendation, and the final disposition of cases in a large western county. In this county, after the defendant has accepted a "bargain" in exchange for a plea of guilty, the case is sent to the probation department for a PSI report. The researchers found a high correlation (93 percent) between the recommendation and the sentence (Kingsnorth and Rizzo, 1979); however, the PO may write in the PSI the recommendation that the PO believes will be well received by the judge. One observer suggests that the prosecutor often finds a way of communicating the plea bargain agreement to the probation department, and the latter responds with a conforming recommendation (Czajkoski, 1973). Conversely, in Wisconsin, "the prosecutor is often influenced by the recommendation in the report and the information underlying it. Some prosecutors frequently adopt the report's recommendations as their own recommendation to the court or use it as a benchmark in deciding on their recommendation. Sometimes a plea agreement will include the condition that the prosecutor will adopt the report's recommendation as his own" (Dickey, 1979: 30). In one county, the minutes of the plea bargaining session, including the details of the negotiated agreement, are sent to the probation department before the submission of the presentence report. "Probation officer concurrence with previously negotiated sentence agreements is a consequence, not of case characteristics, but of pressures emanating from the organizational structure of which the probation department is a part, namely the court system itself" (Kingsnorth and Rizzo, 1979: 9). These and other studies serve to remind us that the probation officer is simply one actor in a rather complex setting. How much influence the PO can exert may often depend on procedural or structural variables or perhaps on the officer's force of personality.

In many jurisdictions, the PO is overburdened with PSI reports and does not have the time to do an adequate investigation and prepare a (potentially) useful report. In courts in which the judge usually pays little or no attention to the contents of the report, the PO will not be inclined to pursue the necessary information and prepare well-written reports. Jonas Robitscher, an attorney and psychiatrist, believes that psychiatric reports and evaluations contained in the PSI often make the difference between probation, a short sentence, or a long sentence. However, he goes on to state: "Many of these reports and evaluations contain dynamic formulations about the cause of behavior based on as little as twenty minutes spent with the subject of the report" (Robitscher, 1980: 35).

<aside>
Key Fact

There is disagreement over the influence of a probation officer's sentencing recommendation.
</aside>

Walter Dickey found a most distressing problem related to the issue of erroneous information in the report:

> Even when an alleged error is challenged at sentencing and a contrary finding made, it does not necessarily follow that the report will be corrected. When a judge makes a finding of fact that is inconsistent with the presentence report, he usually states the finding in the record of the sentencing hearing.... Without more, this leaves the report itself uncorrected. The sentencing transcript is not made a part of the report; it is not attached to it. The oral finding does not signal anyone to amend the report or any of the copies of it. Subsequent users of the report, correctional and parole authorities, rely on the uncorrected report. Rarely is the report amended to reflect additional information or findings of fact inconsistent with it at sentencing. (1979: 35)

In Michigan, however, state law requires that "if the court finds that challenged information is inaccurate or irrelevant, that finding will be made part of the court record, and the inaccurate or irrelevant information must be stricken from the report prior to distribution." To improve the reliability of the report, the Massachusetts commissioner of probation provides the following standards:

- The PO should identify the sources of information in the report.
- The PO should make personal contact with informants or sources of information, when practicable, who can substantiate information. The PO should clearly state in the report those instances in which information has not been substantiated.
- The PO should obtain pertinent documentation, such as letters, clinical reports, school reports, and certified statements, when practicable. The PO should indicate when information in the report is supported by such documentation.
- Sources of information should be identified in most instances; however, this does not exclude from a report any relevant information from unnamed sources or informants with whom the PO has had personal contact. If a PO includes such information in an investigative report, the PO shall clearly indicate in the report that the information was obtained from sources or informants not being identified in this report.

Defendants are often dissatisfied with the role of their attorneys in the sentencing process (Dickey, 1979). Federal District Court Judge Irving Cooper (1977: 101) notes: "It is particularly distressing that many attorneys for the defense, who have proven themselves competent as to the facts and law in the case at trial… display on sentence hardly more than a faint glimmer as to who their clients really are as human beings."

> Another source of the sense of injustice is the belief that lawyers do not provide the court with positive information about the offender to supplement the presentence report that, it is frequently asserted, is incomplete. Sophisticated defendants realize that even the most forceful statements, if they are general, are of little value to their case. They recognize the importance of presenting the court with alternatives to confinement (i.e., job or school plan, place to live) if probation is sought or a specific statement of plans after release if a short period of confinement is the goal. These defendants are usually dissatisfied because they feel the court is forced to rely on an incomplete report because their lawyers did not provide the additional information. (Dickey, 1979: 36)

In response to this problem, the Legal Aid Society in New York City has used social workers to prepare sentencing memoranda for use by defense counsel at the sentencing hearing. In Buncombe County, North Carolina, I set up a similar effort using senior undergraduate students from Western Carolina University. The students worked for the public defender, providing PSI reports for use by defense counsel. Other profit and nonprofit agencies prepare PSI reports, and privately (for-profit) commissioned PSI reports have proliferated. This trend raises a serious question of equal justice because only those with the necessary financial resources can commission such a report.

PRE-SENTENCE INVESTIGATION

To: Honorable Judge Howard Mayne   **Date:** 09/25/11

From: Probation Officer Robert Hanson

Defendant: Paul Roe   **DOB:** 12/28/61   **POB:** Portar, VT

Address:

States Attorney: **DEFENSE ATTORNEY:**

Docket #:   11-CR-01520 Count 1

Offense: Sexual Assault – No Consent (fel)

Statute: VT 41.764

Penalty: *Imprisoned not less than 3 years and for a maximum term of life, and, in addition may be fined not more than $25,000.*

Docket #:   11-CR-01521 Count 2

Offense: Violation of Conditions of Release (mis)

Statute: VT 96.4

Penalty: *Imprisoned not more than 6 months or fined not more than $1,000 or both.*

Adjudication: Guilty (Jury)

Complaint:

DOCKET #278-6-10 CR COUNT 1

Sexual Assault – No Consent (fel)

In the County of Canton, at Highland, on or about January 1, 2010, Paul Roe engaged in a sexual act with another person and compelled the other person to participate in a sexual act without the consent of the other person in violation of VT 41.764.

DOCKET #11-CR-01521 COUNT 2

Violation of Conditions of Release (mis)

In the County of Canton, at Highland, on or about January 1, 2010, Paul Roe being subject to release conditions violated condition #37, in violation of VT 96.4.

ARREST SUMMARY

The affidavit, written by Officer Michael Brooke of the Highland Police Department, states that, on January 1, 2010, Roe or defendant had sexual intercourse with KB by placing

---

FIGURE 3.3 Long-Form PSI Report

his penis in her vagina against her consent. The incident occurred during a New Years Eve party at 90 Ithaca Street in Highland, VT. Roe consumed alcohol during the party. At the time, he was free on Conditions of Release from Lansbury District Court with regard to an open DUI #2 case, which included a condition not to possess or consume alcoholic beverages.

Officer Brooke became aware of the incident on April 2, 2010 when he received phone call from a woman who indicated that her daughter, AQ, witnessed a sexual assault in Highland on the morning of January 1, 2010. Officer interviewed AQ. She indicated that she had been visiting her friend, AX. People were drinking. At some point, another friend, KB, didn't feel well and went into a bedroom to go to sleep. Later, AQ observed Roe entering the bedroom, which belonged to her mother. "W" AQ indicated that Roe told her to "get the "F" out" and slammed the door on her. KB was still in the bedroom. AQ went to bed around 12:30 – 1 am. When she woke up in the morning she heard KB say "stop, please, you're hurting me." KB then exited the room and went into the bathroom. After exiting the bathroom, KB entered a different bedroom where she confided to AQ that Inmate had sex with her without her consent. She described going to bed fully dressed, and waking up without her pants or underwear.

Officer Brooke interviewed KB on May 25, 2010. KB advised that on New Years Eve, December 31, 2009. She was visiting her friend AX, who lived with her mother, and her mother's boyfriend KB stated that she consumed approximately 3 – 4 Screwdriver mixed drinks during the night. At some point she didn't feel well and went to lay down on the bed in the mother's bedroom. She was the only one in the room at that time. She stated she was completely dressed when she lay down. She woke up around dawn and was on her back and Roe was on top of her.

She realized that her pants and underwear had been removed. She stated Roe's penis was in her vagina. She stated that told him to "get off of me" and pushed him off. She went to the bathroom and it hurt when she urinated. She stated that she told AQ what happened and asked AQ to get her clothes the bed room. She left the house after getting dressed and did not go to the hospital that morning. She stated she did get tested for HIV and STD's once she got home.

Officer Brooke interviewed other people who attended the party. L stated that the morning after the party, KB told her that Inmate had raped her. She further indicated that during the party, Paul Roe told her he was turning 50 so he was getting drunk, and "getting a piece of ass" that night. L stated that Inmate drank approximately 20 beers and some champagne. W did not attend the party, but was a resident at 90 Ithaca St. in Highland. At some point she went home to get some things and noticed KB was asleep in W's bed. Inmate was also in the bedroom and J indicated she told Inmate to leave the bedroom. She said he left the room, and then she left the residence while KB was still asleep. J returned to the residence in the morning and KB seemed very upset. KB told J that Inmate had raped her W said that she spoke with Inmate and he denied having sex with KB. K. indicated that KB was at the party and Inmate had been hitting on her. According to A, KB was not responsive to Roe' advances. A said that everyone at the party told Inmate to leave KB alone. A said that KB texted her in the morning sometime between 6 – 7 am and stated that Inmate raped her.

Officer Brooke interviewed Paul Roe on June 1, 2010. He admitted being at a New Years Eve party at "Jeff's house" (90 Ithaca St. in Highland) twice during the night. He said he returned the second time around 2:30 am and, after drinking a 24 oz Heineken he'd gotten for his birthday, he lay down on the couch. Inmate said that KB called him into the bedroom. He indicated that KB initiated sex by putting her hand down his pants and touching his penis. He said they kissed and he touched her breasts. He then told KB he didn`t' want to have sex and he went to sleep. He said that KB was dressed, except for her pants being unbuttoned, when she got up to go to the bathroom in the morning.

Figure 3.3 (continued)

DEFENDANT'S STATEMENT:

Paul Roe advises that the testimony he provided during the trial is accurate and will serve as his statement.

VICTIM'S STATEMENT:

KB, who states she was 20 years old at the time of the offense, was interviewed via phone on 8/12/11. KB said the offense has impacted her in many ways.

Initially, she felt disbelief that such a thing could happen to her in the town where she grew up. She found herself stressed to the point she broke out in hives. She also felt a lot of shame, even though she knew it wasn't her fault. KB states she is still confused as to why she was so tired and disoriented the night of the offense; she does NOT attribute it to alcohol and states she has never felt that way before or since the offense occurred. She was embarrassed and kept it a secret from her family. She relates a lingering concern about the potential of retaliation from Inmate because of the trial; she worries, in particular, about family members who reside in the Highland area. She no longer enjoys socializing and has trust issues. She had to drop out of college as she could not focus on her studies. She tried counseling, but found it uncomfortable. She would like to try counseling again, but cannot afford it. She states that jail is the only resolution that makes sense to her in this matter. She would also like to see Paul Roe participate in sex offender programming.

PRIOR CONVICTION/SUPERVISION HISTORY

A. Juvenile Adjudication History: None reported.

B. Adult Conviction History:

Date:	Conviction:	Court:	Sentence:
2/2/2009	DUI#1	Lansbury	$400 fine
2/2/2009	DLS	Lansbury	$300 fine
2/12/2010	DUI #2	Lansbury	18m – 24m probation
2/12/2010	DLS #2	Lansbury	80 hrs Community Service
2/12/2010	Fraud - Credit Card	Lansbury	6m – 12m probation

*It should be noted that Record Checks were requested for the states of NH and MA, given defendant's reported ties to these states. No convictions were reported in either state.

C. Supervision History: Inmate has been supervised on probation since 2/12/2010. His former probation officer states that Inmate had some failures to report for supervision meetings and to her recollection, He did not follow through with his substance abuse evaluation and/or treatment requirements.

SOCIAL HISTORY

• *Family History:* Defendant Paul Roe is the middle of three children born of Lewis and Diane Roe. He was born in Porter, VT and was raised primarily in the Highland area. His parents were married for approximately 25 years. Defendant was approximately 15 years old when his older brother was killed in a car accident. Inmate's younger brother, has cerebral palsy and resides in Lansbury. Inmate's mother was killed in a head on collision in 2001. Lewis Roe confirmed this information.

Figure 3.3 (continued)

Defendant feels he had an average up-bringing: he reports his parents both worked to support the family and his father was the disciplinarian. He feels his parents were supportive of him and that his father is a good support for him now. He reports a satisfactory relationship with his brother Ronald.

- *Marital or Equivalent:* Inmate states he is not presently in a relationship, and reports no interest in having a romantic relationship until the present legal matter is resolved. He reports being married for approximately 4 years to G; they divorced in 1999 when his drug and alcohol use became too uncomfortable for G and she left. Roe indicates he got sober and he and G briefly resumed their relationship; their daughter S was born in 1996. Shortly thereafter, G left the relationship and has been the primary care-giver to S.

G communicated with this writer via phone on 8/11/11. She confirmed defendant's description of their marriage and marital problems. She states there is no visitation order in place for him to have contact with their twelve year old daughter S, nor is there a child support order. G reports that, in general, this arrangement – though not ideal – was tolerable over the years. Until recently, G (who lives in NH) would bring S to VT to visit with her father. She states she no longer feels comfortable with leaving S in his care. She attributes this primarily to defendant's failure to tell her, last summer, that he had a new DUI charge and had no driver's license; he allowed her to leave S with him for visits and he drove S around when he did not have a license. G indicated that the current sex offense case also weighs on her mind; this behavior is not something she would have anticipated from Paul.

Subsequent to his divorce from G, defendant was involved with a woman named K. They became engaged and moved to MA where he remained for about 3 years. The relationship did not work out and he eventually moved back to VT.

- *Residence:* Defendant resides with his father in Highland. It should be noted that the father said Paul will no longer be allowed to reside there after he is sentenced in this case.

- *Education:* Defendant attended P. S. 89 for his early education, and went on to Newtown High School. He states he completed "8th or 9th grade" and then left school to work and earn some money. He states that he was around 15 years old when his older brother, M, died in a car accident and this loss had a great impact on him. He didn't want to be at school. He described having behavior issues while in school, particularly acting out in the classroom, and reports receiving a number of detentions, but not being expelled. His father confirmed that Paul did not graduate high school and quit school in 8th or 9th grade. Father confirmed that defendant was a behavior issue when he was in school; he described a sense of relief when he finally quit school to work.

- *Employment:* Inmate has been employed by Countywide Waste for approximately 9 months. He is an equipment operator and reports earning $18 hr. His employer de-scribes him as a hard worker who is reliable and dedicated.

Prior to that, defendant was unemployed for approximately 71 weeks; he collected unemployment benefits during this time. He attributes the long period of unemployment to not having a driver's license (due to DUI #2), and to newly diagnosed medical issues (high blood pressure, high cholesterol, and pre-diabetes) which caused him a lot of stress.

Prior to that, defendant was employed as a truck driver for 8 months with M. He reports leaving the job because "he couldn't take the drug test due to medical issues." He states he was retaining water and couldn't urinate when asked to complete a drug test.

Figure 3.3 (continued)

Prior to that defendant was employed for a year with H. R. Kane. He reports being fired from that job due to missing work for medical reasons. He claims he had doctor's notes for the absences from work, but this did not impact the employer's decision to let him go. It should be noted that defendant is presently being supervised on probation for a conviction of "Credit Card Fraud:" after he was fired he continued to use a business credit card he'd been given by H.R. Kane when he was employed there. Inmate reports that he paid H. R. Kane full amount he owed them for this offense. The Restitution Unit confirmed that Inmate paid this balance ($581.31) in full in April of 2010.

Prior to working at H. R. Kane, Roe states he worked in Elmhurst, VT for 3 years as an equipment operator/laborer with a paving company.

Prior to that, defendant did some carpentry and construction work. He believed he was doing the work under the table, but at the end of the year the employer gave him a 1099 statement which indicated defendant had been working as a subcontractor; this incident resulted in defendant incurring tax debt with the IRS.

• *Financial:* Roe reports the following financial obligations: $400/per month to his father for rent and "around $50 per week in child support." He reports an outstanding debt for back taxes; he provided no dollar amount for this debt and reported no payment plan.

His father, confirmed that defendant pays $100 per week in rent. Mr. Roe said he feels defendant is not consistent about contributing to child support.

• *Military:* Defendant states he has never served in the military.

PHYSICAL AND MENTAL HEALTH STATUS

Defendant reports ongoing back problems (a degenerating disc in his neck) from a car accident in 1989. He also reports high blood pressure, high cholesterol, heartburn, and pre-diabetes. He is on medications for some of those conditions: He reports no mental health issues or treatment.

ALCOHOL/DRUG HISTORY

Defendant reports an extensive history of drug and alcohol abuse. He began using marijuana around the age of 15. When he was 18–19 years old he tried acid once or twice. He used LSD "a couple of times" in 1989–1990, and then began using cocaine after that. He indicates he hasn't used cocaine in about three and a half years. He states that at his worst, he used marijuana and alcohol on a daily basis, and used cocaine about once a week. He states that his drug of choice is alcohol, specifically Bud Light beer. He would normally drink 5-6 beers per day on average, and on pay day he would consume more by drinking a mixed drink of rum and coke. He states he hasn't consumed a drink since the night of the offense. He denies any current drug use, other than the medications prescribed by his doctor.

His father and ex-wife confirmed defendant's description of his substance abuse history. His father expressed concern that Paul continues to spend time with people who are "known drug users."

Per his current probation order, defendant is required to participate in a drug or alcohol screening and to follow the recommendations of his treatment provider. He said he had an evaluation prior to his sentencing date in that case, and that he was doing weekly sessions for a while but stopped attending because he ran out of money and

Figure 3.3 (continued)

had transportation issues. He submitted to a drug test, in compliance with his probation order, at the Lansbury probation office on 8/6/11; results were negative.

SEXUAL HISTORY

Defendant states he has never been sexually abused or victimized. He reports his first sexual experience (intercourse) occurred when he was 16 years of age with a girl who was two years older than him. He states he doesn't have or view pornography, nor has he ever had an interest in pornography because he finds it "degrading." Roe states he has always been interested in age appropriate females; as a teenage boy he was interested in teenage girls, and as an adult he is only interested in adult females. When asked, he states he is a "traditional" person when it comes to sex; no fetishes or interest in bondage, voyeurism, exhibitionism, rape, etc. He states that he is usually not the one to initiate sex, preferring to wait for his partner to do so. He states he is not currently in a sexual relationship with anyone. When in a relationship, average frequency of sexual activity is "a few times a week." He also states "I'm not a one night stand guy."

ASSESSMENTS

Before the Court is defendant Paul Roe, found guilty by trial of one count of Sexual Assault – No Consent and one count of Violation of Conditions of Release. He has a prior conviction history, but no prior record for crimes of a sexual nature. He is currently on probation supervision for DUI #2 and Fraud - Credit Card Use (more than $50).

Defendant's risk for general criminal re-offending was evaluated using the Level of Service Inventory-Revised (LSI-R). Based on his LSI-R score, his risk for general criminal recidivism is considered to be in the moderate range with a 48% probability for re-offense.

The Assessment for Sex Offender Risk was completed; the risk score was determined to be in the moderate - low range. The Static-99R was completed; his risk for sexual recidivism using this assessment instrument was determined to be in the low range. Overall, given his scores on these instruments, level of risk classifies him as a Level B offender for the purposes of incarcerated rehabilitation program placement.

According to the affidavit, the victim reports being "raped;" she described this as Inmate placing his penis in her vagina without her consent. According to Prosecutor, Michael Williams, these elements of the affidavit were upheld in trial, and are the basis of the guilty verdict. Roe denies these elements of the offense. When asked, he stated "It was consensual. I fingered her. I did not have sex with her."

For treatment purposes, defendant's denial of the elements of the offense for which he was found guilty makes him ineligible for both the incarcerated sex offender treatment program and the community based sex offender treatment program.

If an incarcerated offender is in denial of his offense, or refuses his designated treatment program, DOC will not recommend him for parole, and release planning will occur six (6) months prior to his maximum release date.

SUMMARY

Fifty nine year old Paul Roe was found guilty by jury trial of the felony offense of "Sexual Assault – No Consent." He denies the essential elements of this offense, particularly in his assertions that he had consent with the victim and that he did not put his penis in her vagina. Inmate is also found guilty of the misdemeanor offense of "Violation of Conditions of Release," which involves the consumption of alcohol. He admits to consuming alcoholic beverages when he was prohibited to do so per conditions of the

Figure 3.3 (continued)

Court.

Defendant is presently on probation supervision for DUI #2 and Fraud – Credit Card. He was sentenced in these cases on 2/12/10. The VT Restitution Unit confirms he paid his restitution in full on the case involving credit card fraud. A VT record check reveals convictions in 2009 for DUI #1 and DLS; no other criminal records were found.

Paul Roe is one of three children. He lost his brother to a car accident when defendant was in his teens; he lost his mother to a car accident in 1991. His remaining brother, P suffers from cerebral palsy and has been disabled since childhood. Defendant grew up in the Highland area, where he resided for most of his life, and he presently resides with his father in Highland. His father will not allow Inmate to continue to live there following sentencing in this case.

Defendant was married for approximately four years. By all accounts, the marriage ended due to his substance abuse issues. A daughter, now 12 years of age, was born of that relationship and she resides with her mother and step father in. There are no Court ordered child visitation or child support agreements in place. The mother of the child has expressed concern that defendant did not inform her when he incurred his second DUI and lost his license; according to her, Paul continued to drive their daughter during her visits with him.

Defendant self-reports substance abuse issues primarily with alcohol, but acknowledges a history of drug abuse as well. He reveals that substance abuse has impacted him: it cost him his marriage and resulted in criminal convictions. To date, it appears he has not followed through with probation conditions requiring him to participate in a substance abuse evaluation and to follow treatment recommendations. He did, however, pass a recent drug test.

Defendant has been employed by Countywide for approximately 9 months. According to his employer, he is considered a valued employee.

RECOMMENDATIONS

The Court has specifically requested a recommendation in this matter. The PSI was staffed with a quorum of corrections professionals.

Incarceration is recommended at this time. Given defendant's denial of the offense for which he was found guilty, he is not suitable for a probation recommendation or community supervision.

If incarcerated, he will be ineligible for incarcerated sex offender treatment programming. DOC policy is to not recommend a sex offender for community release until he has completed his incarcerated treatment program. If an offender is in denial of his offense or refuses his designated treatment program, DOC will not recommend him for parole and release planning will occur six (6) months prior to his maximum release date.

If incarcerated, and if he later takes responsibility for his offense, Paul Roe will be referred to the Level B incarcerated program at the Oranto State Correctional Facility. The length of program is typically twelve (12) months but may be as long as eighteen (18) months in duration. Treatment will not begin until defendant is within twelve to eighteen (12 – 18) months of his minimum release date. When Inmate completes treatment he will be eligible for community release and his treatment will continue in the DOC community-based treatment program.

Respectfully submitted,

PO

Figure 3.3   (continued)

Summary

- A prediction scale allows for determination of the risk posed by a defendant of failing to return to court or being arrested for a new crime.
- There is disagreement over the most appropriate agency for providing pretrial supervision.
- An investigation before sentencing is the basis for a presentence investigation report, sometimes referred to as a probation report or PSI.
- In some states, the law requires a PSI report for crimes punishable by more than one year of imprisonment; in others, the judge retains the discretion to order a report.
- The presentence report has four basic purposes.
- Information in the PSI is derived from persons and documents.
- A prior criminal record may affect the defendant's eligibility for probation and a variety of treatment programs, such as drug rehabilitation.
- Sentencing guidelines are an attempt to limit judicial discretion and reduce sentence disparity.
- The extensive use of plea bargaining has reduced the need for a PSI because the plea agreement may actually specify the sentence a defendant will receive.
- A judge may request a preplea investigation before agreeing to the negotiated plea.
- There is controversy over whether any or all the contents of a PSI report should be disclosed to the defendant or his or her attorney.
- The U.S. Supreme Court has consistently upheld the confidentiality of the PSI report.
- Some critics maintain that many judges do not even read the PSI report, whereas others carefully select passages critical of the defendant to justify their sentences.
- Some PSI reports do not contain complete information and are therefore misleading.

Key Terms

long-form PSI *50*

mandatory sentencing *50*

plea bargain *52*

preplea investigation *52*

prediction scale *39*

presentence investigation (PSI) report *44*

pretrial release *39*

sentencing guidelines *50*

short-form PSI *50*

victim impact statement (VIS) *45*

Internet Connection

National Association of Pretrial Services: **napsa.org**

National Criminal Justice Reference Service: **ncjrs.org**

Probation agency links: **cppca.org/link**

National Association of Drug Court Professionals: **nadcp.org**

Review Questions

1. What is the purpose of using a prediction scale in pretrial services?
2. What is the problem with having probation officers supervise defendants of pretrial release?
3. How does pretrial supervision differ from probation supervision?
4. What are the four basic purposes of the presentence report?
5. What are the thirteen categories of information in a presentence report?
6. What are the two purposes of sentencing guidelines?
7. How does plea bargaining affect the presentence report?
8. What is the purpose of a preplea investigation?
9. What is the controversy over PSI confidentiality?
10. What has Supreme Court ruled with respect to the confidentiality of the PSI report?
11. What are the criticisms of the PSI report?

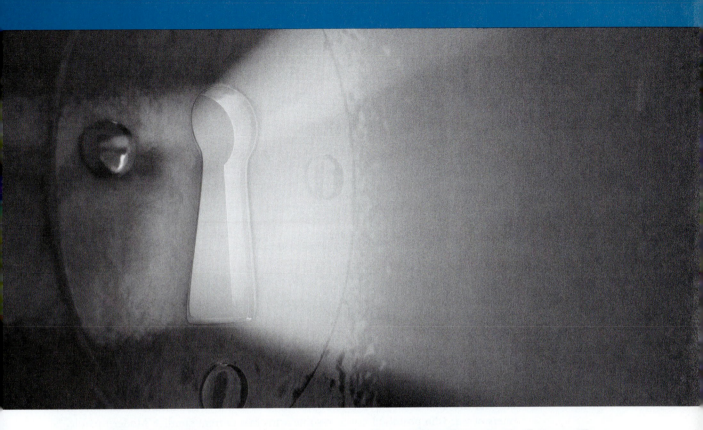

4 Parole and the Indeterminate Sentence

LEARNING OBJECTIVES

This chapter will enable the student to:

1 *Appreciate the history of parole.*

2 *Describe the connection between Zebulon Brockway, Elmira Reformatory, and the indeterminate sentence.*

3 *Discuss the connection between the Auburn system and the Great Depression, and the development of parole.*

4 *Explain the affect of World War II on the penological revolution that occurred in California.*

5 *Understand how the rebellion at Attica affected the indeterminate sentence and parole.*

6 *Describe the influence of Robert Martinson's "What Works?" on the indeterminate sentence and parole.*

7 *Distinguish between the views of the political left and right with respect to the indeterminate sentence and parole.*

8 *Explain why abolishing the indeterminate sentence and parole makes good politics but bad policy.*

9 *Describe the elements of an indeterminate sentence.*

10 *Discuss the different types of determinate sentence.*

11 *Understand how split sentencing reverses the normal sequence of probation, prison, and parole.*

12 *Explain how does split sentencing avoid the political liability inherent in discretionary release from prison.*

13 *Discuss how determinate sentencing shifts discretion away from judges and parole boards and toward the prosecutor.*

14 *Discuss how "normal crimes" and the "courtroom workgroup" help to control sentence disparity.*

15 *Describe how determinate sentencing ignores the role of the board in reducing sentence disparity.*

16 *Appreciate how governors dealt with prison overcrowding before the creation of parole boards.*

Parole, from the French *parol* referring to "word of honor," was a means of releasing prisoners of war who promised not to resume arms in a current conflict. Modern parole, "a period of conditional supervised release following a prison term," has several historical antecedents (Glaze, 2003: 5).

▶ Transportation of Laborers to America

In the early seventeenth century, a shortage of labor in colonial America led to the transporting of children—the indentured poor and delinquents—as well as pardoned criminals from England. At first, no specific conditions were imposed on those who received these pardons. However, after several of those pardoned evaded transportation or returned to England before the expiration of their term, certain restrictions were imposed. Around 1655, the form of pardons was amended to include specific conditions and provide for the nullification of the pardon if the recipient failed to abide by the conditions imposed.

During the early days of laborer transportation, the government paid a fee to contractors for each prisoner transported. Subsequently, this arrangement was changed, and the contractor was given what was called "property in service"—custody of the prisoner until the expiration of his full term. Once prisoners were delivered to the contractor, the government took no further interest in their welfare or behavior unless they violated the conditions of the pardon by returning to England prior to the expiration of their sentences.

When the pardoned felons arrived in the colonies, their services were sold to the highest bidder. The contractor then transferred the property-in-service agreement to the new master, and the felon was no longer referred to as a criminal but became an **indentured servant**.

These indentures bear a similarity to the procedure now followed by parole boards. Like the criminal *qua* indentured servant, a prisoner released on parole agrees in writing to accept certain conditions; a release form is signed by the prisoner and the parole board, and some of the conditions imposed today on parolees are similar to those included on the indenture agreement (New York State Division of Parole, 1953). The termination of the Revolutionary War ended transportation of laborers to America; and from then to 1879, England sent her convicts to Australia (Hughes, 1987).

▶ Maconochie and Norfolk Island

Torsten Erikkson refers to 1840 as the year in which "one of the most remarkable experiments in the history of penology was initiated" (1976: 81). In that year, Alexander Maconochie (1787–1860), a former naval officer, became superintendent of the remote British penal colony on Norfolk Island, about 930 miles northeast of Sidney, Australia, which was reserved for convicts who had committed crimes while in Australian or Tasmanian prisons. Maconochie set out a philosophy of punishment based on reforming the individual criminal: The convict was to be punished for the past and trained for the future. Because the amount of time needed to instill self-discipline and train a criminal could not be estimated in advance of sentencing, Maconochie advocated sentences that were open ended, what is known today as an **indeterminate sentence** . He set up a system of marks to be earned by each inmate based on good behavior; a sentence could not be terminated until a certain number of marks had been achieved. Norfolk housed the most dangerous felons, and riots occurred both before Maconochie arrived and after he left the island. His system, however, brought tranquility to the colony. Convicts passed through three stages on the way to release, each with an increasing amount of personal liberty; misbehavior moved an offender back to an earlier stage. Although Maconochie's experiment at Norfolk was successful from the standpoint of penology, he was opposed by authorities back in Australia who viewed him as "coddling criminals" while incurring extra costs on the government. Maconochie was relieved of his position in 1844 and returned to England, where in 1849 he became governor of a new prison; two years later, criticism of his approach as too lenient again led to his dismissal. Maconochie then embarked on a campaign for penal reform as a writer and speaker, and one of those he influenced was Walter Crofton.

▶ Crofton and the Irish System

In 1853, Parliament enacted the Penal Servitude Act, which enabled prisoners to be released—paroled—on a **ticket of leave** and supervised by the police. That same year, Sir Walter Crofton (1815–1897) was commissioned to investigate conditions in Irish prisons and in 1854 became director of the Irish prison system. Crofton was familiar with the work of Alexander Maconochie, and their views on the reformation of criminals were similar. The **Irish system** that Crofton established was based on Maconochie's work at Norfolk Island and consisted of four stages:

1. The first stage involved solitary confinement for nine months; during the first three months, the inmate was on reduced rations and was allowed no labor whatsoever. It was reasoned that after three months of forced idleness, even the laziest prisoner would long for something to do. He would then be given full rations, instructed in useful skills, and exposed to religious influences.

2. The convict was placed in a special prison to work with other inmates in the second stage, during which time he could earn marks to qualify for a transfer to the third stage.

3. This third stage involved transportation to an open institution where the convict, by evidencing signs of reformation, could earn release on a ticket of leave.

4. In the fourth stage, ticket-of-leave men were conditionally released and, in rural districts, supervised by the police; a civilian employee who had the title of inspector of released prisoners, however, supervised those residing in Dublin. He worked cooperatively with the police, but his responsibility was to secure employment for ticket-of-leave men. He required them to report at stated intervals, visited their homes every two weeks, and verified their employment—he was the forerunner of a modern parole officer.

▶ Parole Develops in the United States

A modified version of the Irish system was adopted in England, and Crofton's work was widely publicized in the United States. American supporters of the Irish system, however, did not believe that adoption of the ticket of leave would ever be accepted in the United States. Their attitude was apparently based on the belief that it would be un-American to place any person under the supervision of the police, and they did not believe that any other form of supervision would be effective. A letter written by Crofton in 1874, in reply to an inquiry sent to him by the secretary of the New York Prison Association, stressed that the police of Ireland were permitted to delegate competent persons in the community to act as custodians for ticket-of-leave men, and he suggested a similar system for the United States (New York State Division of Parole, 1953). These principles were first implemented in the Elmira Reformatory.

▶ Elmira Reformatory

In 1869, a reformatory was authorized for Elmira, New York, to receive male offenders between the ages of 16 and 30. The following year, the first convention of the American Prison Association met in Cincinnati. The noted Michigan penologist Zebulon R. Brockway presented a paper based on the Irish system, dealing with the idea of an indeterminate sentence and the possibilities of a system of parole. The prison reformers meeting in Cincinnati urged New York to adopt Brockway's proposal at Elmira. When the Elmira Reformatory opened in 1876, Brockway was appointed superintendent. Instead of the nineteenth-century penology of silence, obedience, and labor, Elmira's goal would be reform of the convict ("Elmira," 1998).

Brockway drafted a statute directing that young first offenders be sent to Elmira under an indeterminate sentence not to exceed the maximum term that was already in place for nonreformatory offenders. The actual release date was set by the board of managers based on institutional behavior: "After the inmate accumulated a certain number of marks based on institutional conduct and progress in academic or vocational training, and if the investigation of his assurance of employment was positive, he could be released" (New York State Division of Parole, 1984: 6). An entire building was set up as a trade school; by 1894, there was instruction in 34 trades ("Elmira," 1998). The system at Elmira "was designed to instill youthful offenders with the habits of order, discipline, and self-control and to mold obedient citizen-workers" (Pisciotta, 1994: 7–8). According to Brockway (1926: 111), this was a difficult task because the inmates "constitute a living antisocial human mass not easily resolved and brought into accord with the orderly life of a good community."

The Reverend Frederick Wines, a colleague of Brockway, described the principles on which the Elmira system was based (a clear manifestation of positivism):

> Criminals can be reformed; that reformation is the right of the convict and the duty of the State; that every prisoner must be individualized and given special treatment adapted to develop him to the point in which he is weak—physical, intellectual, or moral culture, in combination, but in varying proportions, according to the diagnosis of each case; that time must be given for the reformatory process to take effect, before allowing him to be sent away, uncured; that his cure is always facilitated by his cooperation, and often impossible without it. (1975: 230)

This cooperation was fostered by corporal punishment and the use of inmate classifications, according to which privileges were dispensed. Behavior judged to be "reformative" was rewarded by reclassification, which meant increased privileges, eventually leading to release on parole.

Brockway, reflecting the popularity of social Darwinism (discussed in Chapter 1) in his day, believed that his charges "belong to the grade of humanity that is inferior. The whole inmate population may be divided in this connection into two grades of inferiority—those whose defectiveness is apparent and others whose mental and moral defects are concealed under good (and sometimes quite brilliant) capabilities in given directions" (1926: 110). Despite its reform pretensions, Elmira had many problems:

> [It] was overcrowded, understaffed, and grossly mismanaged. Key treatment programs did not fulfill their stated goals and objectives. Violence, escapes, smuggling, theft, homosexuality, revolts, arson, and other forms of inmate resistance were serious problems. Inmates suffered extraordinarily harsh punishments—including severe whippings and months of solitary confinement in dark, cold dungeons—and deliberate psychological torture. Elmira was, quite simply, a brutal prison. (Pisciotta, 1994: 33–34)

Investigations led to charges against Brockway, but he succeeded in remaining superintendent until his retirement in 1900 ("Elmira," 1998).

On being admitted to Elmira, each inmate was placed in the second grade (of classification); six months of good conduct meant promotion to the first grade, but misbehavior could result in being placed in the third grade, from which the inmate would have to work his way back up. Continued good behavior in the first grade resulted in release—America's first parole system. Paroled inmates remained under the jurisdiction of reformatory authorities for an additional six months, during which the parolee was required to report on the first day of every month to his appointed guardian (from which parole officers evolved) as well as provide an account of his situation and conduct. Some believed that a longer period under supervision would be discouraging to the average parolee: "Inmates were released conditionally, subject to return if the Board believed there was actual or potential reversion to criminal behavior" (New York State Division of Parole, 1984: 6). However, no real attention was given to the training of prisoners for their future adjustment in the community, and both prison administrators and inmates soon accepted the idea that whether the inmate was reformed or unreformed, allowance of time for good behavior was automatic and release at the earliest possible date was a right rather than a privilege. After release, supervision was either nonexistent or totally inadequate, a deficiency also found in other states using parole release, such as Minnesota and Illinois (Pisciotta, 1992).

▶ Early Use of the Indeterminate Sentence and Parole

The Elmira system—which included military-style uniforms, marching, and discipline—was copied by reformatories in other states, such as the Massachusetts Reformatory at Concord, the Minnesota State Reformatory at St. Cloud, and the Illinois State Reformatory at Pontiac, and made applicable to all or part of the prison population in Pennsylvania and Michigan (Pisciotta, 1992; Wines, 1975). By 1880, 3 states had parole, and by 1889 the number had grown to 12. In 1893, Nebraska granted the governor the power to parole any inmates who had served the minimum time for the crimes for which they were convicted and, in 1911, established a three-member parole board. Alabama enacted a parole law in 1897, while Ohio and California had parole release statutes in place before the turn of the twentieth century (Zevitz and Takata, 1988). In Montana, the Board of Pardons and Parole was created in 1891 to provide pardon recommendations to the governor. In 1907, Montana authorized the State Board of Prison Commissioners—governor, secretary of state, and attorney general—to grant paroles; that same year, New York extended indeterminate sentencing and parole release to all first offenders, except those convicted of murder. On the heels of prison riots in 1930, New York established a full-time three-member parole board, transferring release decisions from the Department of Corrections, and created the Division of Parole to supervise parolees (Dressler, 1951). Georgia enacted legislation in 1908 that gave the Prison Commission authority to implement a system of "parole or conditional pardons"; however, there were no parole officers to provide supervision, so offenders were placed under supervision of an employer or sponsor. In 1938, the granting of parole was separated from gubernatorial authority and was given to an independent board; and by 1940, the state employed six parole officers.

A 1910 federal statute created parole boards in each federal prison, composed of the Superintendent of Prisons, the warden, and the prison physician Each had authority to parole prisoners from its own institution. Once out on parole, prisoners remained formally in the custody of the warden until the expiration of their term minus any good-time deductions. "A parole officer, appointed for each penitentiary, and the U.S. Marshals supervised the parolees" (Doherty 2013: 985). Federal parole was abolished in 1984.

In 1911, Minnesota enacted indeterminate sentencing for all felony offenders who could be kept under the jurisdiction of the Board of Control until they reached their maximum sentence. In 1913, Texas enacted an indeterminate sentence law and gave the governor power to issue paroles. A Board of Pardons and Paroles was established in 1929, but until 1947 only the governor could authorize parole release in the form of executive clemency; and until 1957, supervision was the work of volunteers. In 1915, Maryland created an Advisory Board of Parole, which recommended inmates for executive clemency whose supervision was the responsibility of the newly hired parole officers. In 1913, Massachusetts established the Commonwealth Board of Parole; before that, the commissioner of prisons and many correctional institutions conducted discharge or conditional release programs. Tennessee enacted indeterminate sentencing and parole in 1929; and in 1939, the North Dakota Pardon Board assumed the duties of a paroling authority. In 1909, Nevada expanded the authority of the Pardons Board to parole inmates who were required to report to the secretary of the board at least once a year. By 1939, only four states (Florida, Mississippi, South Carolina, and Virginia) did not have provisions for parole. Florida used the governor's authority to pardon inmates in an effort to keep down the cost of imprisonment—the governor and his cabinet often presided over more than 200 pardon applications in a day—but in 1941, the Florida Parole Commission was established. South Carolina began to use parole that same year, but it was not until 1949 that parole and pardon authority was removed from the governor and given to an independent parole board. Virginia established a parole system in 1942. By 1944, all 48 states had enacted parole legislation.

Although most states had a mechanism in place for parole release prior to 1929, the impetus for the expansion of the use of parole was the Great Depression and the related demise of the Auburn system.

▶ Auburn System

Auburn, New York, present-day population under 30,000, is 35 miles west of Syracuse. The prison at Auburn opened in 1819 and, as designed by its first agent, featured a center comprising tiers of cell blocks (each cell measured 7 by 3.5 feet and was 7 feet high) surrounded by a vacant area (the yard), with a high wall encircling the entire institution:

[The cells were] designed for separation by night only; the convicts were employed during the day in large workshops, in which, under the superintendency of Elam Lynds

Key Fact

Elmira Reformatory provided a model for the modern boot camp-style prison.

[1784–1855], formerly a captain in the army, the rule of absolute silence was enforced with unflinching sternness. Captain Lynds said that he regarded flogging as the most effective, and at the same time the most humane, of all punishments, since it did no injury to the prisoner's health and in no wise impaired his physical strength; he did not believe that a large prison could be governed without it. (Wines, 1975: 154)

No written regulations governed the use of the whip; guards were simply authorized to impose flogging—up to 39 lashes (the number has biblical roots)—when "absolutely necessary."

The **Auburn/New York system** divided its inmates into three classes: The most difficult inmates were placed in solitary, a less dangerous group spent part of the day in solitude and worked the rest of the time in groups, and the "least guilty" worked together throughout the day and were separated only at night when they returned to their individual cells. Solitary confinement played havoc on the psyche—inmates jumped off tiers, cut their veins, and smashed their heads against walls. Solitary confinement in Auburn was discontinued, except as punishment for violations of prison rules (Lewis, 1965).

New Yorkers believed that the complete isolation of prisoners from arrival to release, an essential feature of the **Pennsylvania system**, was inhumane, unnatural, and cruel. Far from reforming men, they believed that such absolute solitude resulted in insanity and despair. In addition, there was the issue, perhaps more pressing, of expense to the state. Inmates restricted to their cells 24 hours per day contributed nothing to the cost of their own confinement, so that in Pennsylvania the state had to provide all food, clothing, supplies, and materials to its prisoners. "If the prisoners were to learn the advantages and satisfactions of hard work and thrift, New York authorities believed, there could be no better way than to be compelled to work together in harmony. If such a system also offered the potential for inmates to grow and harvest their own vegetables, raise and butcher their own meat, make their own clothes, and manufacture other items for use or sale by the state, such a boon to the state's budget could not be reasonably ignored" (New York State Special Commission on Attica [Attica Commission], 1972: 8). "The prisons operated on the Auburn plan, in particular, were, most of them, notorious for the maltreatment of prisoners and for the excessive labor required of them in an attempt to meet the demand of legislators that prisons be self-supporting and even show a profit if possible" (Sellin, 1967: 21).

Under a **contract system**, convict labor was sold to private entrepreneurs who provided the necessary machinery, tools, raw materials, and (in some cases) supervisory staff. In many cases, the prison was built as a factory with walls around it. The use of convict labor often made Auburn-system prisons not only self-supporting institutions but also

> **Key Fact**
>
> A central feature of the Pennsylvania prison system was solitary confinement.

PENNSYLVANIA SYSTEM

The Pennsylvania system isolated each prisoner for the entire period of his confinement. Convicts ate, worked, and slept in individual cells. The convicted prisoner was to be kept totally separated from other prisoners. Prison staff, chaplains, officials of the Prison Society, and the Board of Inspectors provided guidance and role models. The Pennsylvania system proved expensive—the cost of constructing an institution for solitary confinement was staggering, and little profitable exploitation of inmate labor under such conditions could occur (McKelvey, 1972). As a result, most states patterned their prisons after the next great milestone in American prison history: Auburn.

profit-making enterprises throughout the nineteenth and twentieth centuries. Auburn Penitentiary balanced its books in 1829 and produced a profit in 1831 (Melossi and Pavarini, 1981).

Under the system developed by Captain Lynds, who became warden in 1822, prisoners worked in small, strictly supervised units in workshops or outdoors during the daytime and returned to individual cells at night. Dressed in grotesque and ridiculous-looking black-and-white-striped uniforms and caps, they marched in complete silence, worked in complete silence, and ate in complete silence: "A breach of this rule was punished by flogging. Discipline was extremely strict in all other respects. Inmates were required to keep their eyes downcast when walking" (Erikkson, 1976: 50).

Auburn developed the infamous lockstep shuffle: Inmates stood in line, with the right foot slightly behind the left, and outstretched the right arm, with the hand on the right shoulder of the man in front; they moved together in a shuffle, sliding the left foot forward, then bringing the right foot to its position just behind the left, then the left again, and then the right. Heads had to be turned toward the "keeper" so that lip movements could be detected (keepers also tiptoed shoeless up and down cell blocks to detect whispers). Citizens were encouraged to visit the prison, where for a small fee they could view the inmates, an act that was designed to cause further degradation. Prisoners were known only by number, and their reading matter was limited to a Bible ("Auburn Correctional Facility," 1998). Gustave de Beaumont and Alexis de Tocqueville[1] (1833–1964: 65) report on their visit to Auburn: "Nothing is heard in the whole prison but the steps of those who march, or the sounds proceeding from the workshops. But when the day is finished, and the prisoners have retired to their cells, the silence within these vast walls, which contain so many prisoners, is like that of death. We have often trod during night those monotonous and dumb galleries, where a lamp is always burning: we felt as if we traversed catacombs; there were a thousand living beings, and yet it was a desert solitude."

The administrators of Auburn believed that their most important task was the breaking of an inmate's spirit to drive him into a state of submission. Some had differences of opinion about what to do after the "breaking" process. One school of thought stressed deterrence as its goal and was determined to derive as much economic benefit from **inmate labor** as possible. Another school of thought held that rehabilitation was the ultimate goal and that, after breaking, inmates should be helped through education and religion so that they could return to society better persons (Lewis, 1965).

The Auburn system consisted of an unrelenting routine of silence, hard labor, moderate meals, and solitary evenings in individual cells six days per week: "Their labor is not interrupted until the hour of taking food. There is not a single instant given to recreation" (Beaumont and de Tocqueville, 1964: 65). On Sundays, when there was no work, inmates attended church—in silence—where they were addressed by the prison chaplain who stressed the American virtues of simple faith and hard work (Attica Commission, 1972). A Sunday school was established, and those not participating were locked in their cells and forced to stand until lights out ("Auburn Correctional Facility," 1998).

Auburn became the prototype for American prisons; it allowed for a factory contract system that could make profitable use of inmate labor. The concept of reformation gradually declined; by the end of the nineteenth century, rehabilitation had virtually disappeared— prisons were viewed simply as places to keep criminals incarcerated as cheaply as possible. This view was reflected even in the name of the warden's first assistant, the "principal

---

[1] Tocqueville and Beaumont were of Royal lineage in post-Revolutionary France and, thus, in danger of becoming victims of the swirling political waters of the time. They came up with an idea that would give them some respite: a study of American prisons. While they visited American prisons, the historical legacy of the trip is Tocqueville's classic *Democracy in America*.

keeper" (Attica Commission, 1972). Prisons became bleak and silent factories with labor pools of broken people disciplined with summary floggings.[2]

The contract system remained widespread until the Great Depression, which began in 1929 and ended with the onset of World War II. Vast unemployment led to federal legislation that effectively abolished the economic exploitation of convict labor: The Hawes-Cooper Act in 1929 and the Ashurst-Sumners Act in 1935 curtailed interstate commerce in goods produced with convict labor, and their constitutionality was upheld by the Supreme Court in 1936 (*Whitfield v. Ohio*, 297 U.S. 439).

The curtailing of convict labor had two long-ranging effects: It increased the cost of imprisonment and thus encouraged development of parole and forced prison officials to find other ways to deal with prison idleness—prisons initiated programs to train and educate their inmates. Curtailing convict labor was accompanied by prison overcrowding, the prohibitive cost of prison construction, and an outbreak of prison riots. A 1931 report by the National Commission on Law Observance and Law Enforcement described the overcrowding of America's prisons as "incredible"; Michigan, for example, had 78.6 percent more inmates than its original capacity; California, 62.2 percent; Ohio, 54.1 percent; and Oklahoma, 56.7 percent. In 1923, 81,959 inmates were in prison (74 per 100,000 population); in 1930, 120,496 (98 per 100,000 population); and in 1940, on the eve of World War II, 165,585 (125 per 100,000 population) (Cahalan, 1986). *Pressing economic conditions, not the press of prison reform, led to the popularity of parole release* as the following statistics for parole release indicate (Cahalan, 1986):

1923: 21,632

1926: 19,917

1930: 29,509

1936: 37,794

By 1935, more than 60,000 persons were on parole in the United States, although only six states had what was described as "suitable" parole systems (Prison Association of New York, 1936).

Before the Depression, parole systems stressed employment—criminals were idlers who needed the discipline of work—and depended on employers to monitor parolees. This was weakened by widespread unemployment during the Depression and, at the same time, the pressure to release more persons on parole (Simon, 1993). With World War II, industrial production increased, unemployment decreased, and parolees became eligible (for the first time since 1833) for military service. Before the war ended, every state had a parole system in place.

> **Key Fact**
>
> Most states had a mechanism in place for parole release prior to 1929, but the impetus for the expansion of parole was the Great Depression.

▶ Positivism and the Medical Model of Corrections

Despite its ravaging consequences, war can provide the impetus for many long-lasting social and scientific advances: With total mobilization, widespread unemployment ends, and improvements in manufacturing, communication, transportation, and medicine occur. During World War II, the United States experienced such important developments as the jet plane and the rocket, streptomycin, radar, sonar, and atomic energy. The war also provided psychologists with funds and an environment for extensive research and

---

[2] Although flogging was outlawed at Auburn in 1847, it was replaced by other gruesome punishments ("Auburn Correctional Facility," 1998).

experimentation (Herman, 1995). By the end of the war, the horizons of science appeared to be unlimited, and the influence of positivism reemerged in penology.

Toward the end of World War II, a penological revolution occurred in California, where former prosecutor Earl Warren (1891–1974) had been elected governor in the wake of a prison scandal. Under Warren's leadership, California reorganized its prison system according to the positivist ideal of individual reformation. The system was organized not for punishment but around rehabilitation. California would apply the methods of the behavioral sciences to *correct* criminal behavior.

To operationalize the new approach to penology, California implemented an extreme version of the indeterminate sentence: Judges would remand a criminal with an indefinite sentence to the California Adult (or Youth) Authority, which would determine his or her treatment needs through a process of classification and assign the convict-client to an appropriate facility—not a prison but a correctional institution. A convict would remain "under treatment"—incarcerated—until the Adult (or Youth) Authority determined that the client had been rehabilitated, at which time he or she would be paroled to a community-based treatment program, that is, supervision by a parole agent.

Prisons no longer existed in California; they became "correctional institutions." Guards became "correction officers," and wardens became "superintendents." New institutions—medium- and minimum-security correctional facilities—were built. Adult Authority clients could be moved from maximum- to medium- to minimum-security facilities and then to parole, or if their behavior required, they could be moved from parole supervision back into the institution for further "treatment in a secure setting."

▶ Medical Model of Corrections

This great faith in science occurred during a period of concern over the apparent rise in crime as measured by the *Uniform Crime Report*. The war had kept the wheels of industry spinning; unemployment did not exist. Suddenly, wartime production had ceased, and millions of young men who had been trained to kill and destroy (and who had done little else for several years) were returning from overseas. The vast allocation of societal resources in wartime had proved successful in the area of science, so perhaps a corresponding commitment of resources could prove successful in dealing with the problem of crime: a (scientific) "war on crime," based on the medical model.

The positive approach to crime and criminals seeks to explain and respond to criminal behavior in a manner not dependent on (classical) issues of law, philosophy, or theology. Instead, criminal behavior is to be examined using the principles and methods of science, much as physical illness is subjected to examination by the physician: "This new approach to criminal behavior stressed deviance as pathology. The criminal was not seen as 'bad' but as 'mad,' and he was to be given the benefit of the medical approach to madness. He should be helped to understand his unconscious motivation and to go through a process of psychoanalytic change" (Robitscher, 1980: 44). According to one author, "In its simplest (perhaps oversimplified) terms, the medical model as applied to corrections assumed the offender to be 'sick' (physically, mentally, and/or socially); his offense to be a manifestation or symptom of his illness, a cry for help" (MacNamara, 1977: 439). The medical metaphor extended to the postconviction process:

- Examination = presentence investigation report
- Diagnosis = classification
- Treatment = correctional program

According to the medical model as applied to corrections, the effects of a treatment program are subjected to review by the parole board, which determines whether the offender is sufficiently rehabilitated to be discharged from the correctional institution. A positive response means that treatment will continue on an outpatient basis in the form of parole supervision. The American Friends Service Committee (AFSC) sums up the rationale for this approach: "It rejects inherited concepts of criminal punishment as the payment of a debt owed to society, a debt proportioned to the magnitude of the offender's wrong. Instead it would save the offender through constructive measures of reformation, [and] protect society by keeping the offender locked up until the reformation is accomplished" (1971: 37).

The medical model is based on two questionable assumptions:

1. Criminals are "sick" and can thus benefit from treatment.
2. The behavioral sciences can provide the necessary treatment methods.

Although a paucity of systematic research supported this approach to criminal behavior, the medical model of corrections was adopted in most states—in theory, if not practice. William Parker argued that the theory never actually matched the practice: "The theory of rehabilitation has made some changes in the prison: terminology has changed, there are more programs, sweeping floors is now work therapy. The theory of rehabilitation has merely been imposed upon the theories of punishment and control" (1975: 26).

Into these correctional institutions came the *treaters*. New superintendents often had extensive education in the behavioral sciences, and their institutions employed teachers, social workers, psychologists, and psychiatrists to implement a rehabilitative regimen. Slowly but steadily, the California system was copied, at least in part, by all the other states and the federal system—prisons virtually disappeared from the United States. Parole and the indeterminate sentence became intertwined with the idea of corrections and a medical model approach to dealing with criminal behavior.

Despite the corrections revolution, prison officials remained preoccupied with management and security issues; most allocations for correctional institutions were for administration and security, leaving about 5 percent for items that could reasonably be labeled "rehabilitative." Providing such services has always been problematic. Correctional salaries are relatively low, and most prisons are located in rural areas, where land is relatively cheap and the prison provides important economic benefits to local residents,[3] but these areas are not particularly attractive to urban graduates trained in therapeutic disciplines.[4] Inadequate funding results in vocational training that is out-of-date and often of little use to inmates seeking employment based on skills developed in the correctional institution.

The problems encountered by the corrections approach were compounded by differences between corrections officers and the treaters. Older members of prison staff, particularly those responsible for prison security, were often resistant to the changes brought in by the treaters, which could be expected based on an examination of their differing backgrounds. Corrections officers were typically rural, white, Protestant, and socially and politically conservative, with (at best) a high school education; they tended to be poorly trained. The treaters tended to be reform-minded urban college graduates, many of whom were Catholics and Jews—and women.

Furthermore, the rhetoric did not match the reality. By the 1960s, the "correctional" expectations of prisons were not being fulfilled: "The spending of years in confined quarters, perhaps as small as eight by ten feet, in a setting dominated by a toilet and a possibly criminally-aggressive cellmate, can hardly be considered conducive to encourage socially acceptable behavior upon release" (Hahn, 1976: 6). The prison is what Erving Goffman

---

[3] A 1,200-bed prison requires about 200 construction workers and about 500 permanent positions.
[4] There is research indicating that prisons do not actually provide significant economic benefits to rural communities (King, Mauer, and Huling, 2004).

refers to as a total institution "a place of residence and work where a large number of like-situated individuals, cut off from the wider society for an appreciable period of time, together lead an enclosed, formally administered round of life" (1961: xiii). As such, these institutions have a tendency to mold persons into compliant and often shapeless forms to maintain discipline and a sound working order, or for less utilitarian reasons. The prison provides a dreary uniformity that leaves little room for self-assertion and decision making—the requisites for living in the free community. The corrections approach met with financial problems (i.e., a reluctance to expend tax dollars on inmates), and prisoners soured on rehabilitative programs that raised unrealistic expectations. "After prisoners were convinced that treatment programs did not work (by the appearance of persons who had participated fully in treatment programs streaming back to prison with new crimes or violations of parole), hope shaded to cynicism and then turned to bitterness" (Irwin, 1980: 63).

During the 1950s, prisoners were usually divided to the point of impotence: "The prisonization process, which had aligned the great majority of inmates against their keepers, had also divided them from one another, [blacks from whites, for example], making effective collaboration extremely difficult. Only a rumor of an excessively brutal incident or a report of revolts elsewhere could arouse a sense of community sufficient to support a riotous outbreak" (McKelvey, 1977: 323). However, there were such outbreaks during the 1950s in California, Louisiana, Massachusetts, Michigan, Missouri, New Jersey, Ohio, Pennsylvania, and Washington.

Into this environment came thousands of new African American and Latino inmates. During the 1950s, the number of blacks and Latinos committed annually to adult federal and state prisons increased from 17,200 to 28,500 (McKelvey, 1977), and this figure continued to grow during the 1960s and 1970s. Although white inmates could relate to their white keepers, young urban blacks and Hispanics found no such comfort. In 1954, the Supreme Court handed down its decision in *Brown v. Board of Education of Topeka, Kansas* (347 U.S. 483), which helped set off the civil rights revolution in the United States.[5]

Rising black consciousness occurring in the wider community took on more radical dimensions inside the prison. The Black Muslims emerged as a major separatist organization and confronted prison officials with demands based on religious freedom. The anti-Vietnam war movement and activities of radical groups, such as the Black Panthers and Students for a Democratic Society, stirred and politicized inmates, black and white. These inmates confronted correctional officials with demands often couched in Marxist terminology.

The traditional relationship between inmates and correctional officers, *rapprochement* based on private agreements or corrupt favoritism—inmate leaders allowed special privileges—started to come apart (Irwin, 1980). Inmates became increasingly militant in their refusal to cooperate with their keepers, and correction officials responded with repression that touched off violence in institutions throughout the United States, including riots at California's San Quentin in 1967 and Philadelphia's Holmesburg Prison in 1970. In 1968, correctional officers and police killed 6 inmates and wounded 68 others in quelling a riot at North Carolina's Central Prison. Correctional institutions simmered throughout the 1960s into 1971, when in September the focus of attention shifted to a small upstate New York town where the last of the Auburn-style prisons was built. The events at Attica would prove to be a turning point in corrections and the history of parole.

> **Key Fact**
> The racial makeup of prisons changed dramatically during the 1960s, and radical political movements on the outside impacted correctional institutions.

> **Key Fact**
> The 1971 events at Attica Prison were a turning point in corrections and the history of parole.

---

[5] In 1968 (*Lee v. Washington*, 390 U.S. 333), the Supreme Court ruled racial segregation in prisons unconstitutional.

▶ Attica Prison Uprising

The state prison at Attica, a town 30 miles east of Buffalo that in 1971 had a population of fewer than 3,000, was completed in 1931. It boasted of being the most secure, escape-proof prison ever built; at the time, it was also the most expensive prison ever built. Attica was a response to an outbreak of prison riots throughout the United States in the late 1920s. In 1929, Clinton Prison in Dannemora, New York, experienced a riot protesting overcrowded conditions; three inmates were killed. In that year, the prison at Auburn experienced a riot in July during which four inmates escaped and two others were killed; several guards were seriously injured and two were shot. In December, another riot ensued. Inmates with fire-arms took the warden, six guards, and a foreman hostage, and the principal keeper was shot and killed. The prison was retaken after eight prisoners were killed and seven employees injured. Three inmates were later executed for their role in the riot ("Auburn Correctional Facility," 1998).

Typical of prisons in New York and elsewhere, Attica was placed in a rural area where residents would accept the institution as a basis for employment and other economic ben-efits. On July 8, 1970, Attica (as well as the other maximum-security prisons in New York) received a name change. There were no more prisons in New York—in their places stood six maximum-security "correctional facilities." The prison wardens became "institutional super-intendents," the former principal keepers became "deputy superintendents," and the old-line prison guards awakened that morning to find themselves suddenly "corrections officers." "No one's job or essential duties changed, only his title" (Attica Commission, 1972: 18).

Fourteen months later, Attica Correctional Facility had more than 2,000 inmates who were locked in their cells for 12 to 16 hours per day being "rehabilitated" and who spent the remainder of the day with little to occupy their time. No gymnasium was available, and recreational opportunities were limited. Showers were available for most inmates—once a week. Meaningful rehabilitation programs were almost totally absent.

Most inmates were African Americans and Hispanics from the downstate New York area or upstate cities such as Buffalo, Syracuse, and Rochester. All but one (he was Puerto Rican) of the fewer-than 400 corrections officers were non-Hispanic whites drawn primar-ily from the communities surrounding Attica. Although the superintendent had a master's degree in correctional administration, correction officers who began their jobs between World War II and the late 1950s received no formal training. Those who started after that were given two weeks of training. They were expected to enforce the dozens of petty rules typical of correctional institutions and to relate in a meaningful way to inmates with whom they had little in common.

Attica had a large number of Black Muslims (members of the Nation of Islam) who had difficulty with a prison diet that was heavy with pork. Muslims also objected to the lack of ministers. Correctional officials would not allow the ministers, many of whom had prison records, into Attica. Black Muslims spent their recreation time in the yard engaging in wor-ship and highly disciplined physical exercise. The correctional staff, who never understood the Black Muslims, was quite fearful of this group who exhibited military-type discipline and remained aloof from both staff and other inmates.

> **Key Fact**
> The inmate uprising at Attica in 1971 led to a concerted attack on the corrections model and the indeterminate sentence.

As was typical of large correctional institutions, in Attica "popular conceptions of homosexual advances and assaults in prison were not exaggerated" (Attica Commission, 1972: 78). Correction officers were unable to protect inmates who were forced to resort to forms of self-protection, such as carrying a "shiv" (homemade knife), in violation of prison rules: "The irony was not lost on the inmates. They perceived themselves surrounded by high walls and gates, and tightly regimented by a myriad of written and unwritten rules; but when they needed protection, they often had to resort to the same skills that had brought many of them to Attica in the first place" (Attica Commission, 1972: 79).

During the summer of 1971, a number of peaceful protests by inmates over conditions at Attica occurred. Leaders of previously antagonistic inmate groups, such as the Young Lords (a Puerto Rican group) and the Black Panthers and Black Muslims, gained greater political awareness, submerged their differences, and joined with white inmates in a peaceful effort to effect changes at Attica. "Inmates had petitioned state correction officials to ease chronic overcrowding and censorship rules, and to improve conditions that limited them to one shower a week and one roll of toilet paper a month" (Haberman, 2000: 23). The new solidarity among inmates frightened officials. The superintendent responded by attempting to transfer the leaders as "troublemakers," but was prevented from doing so by the new Commissioner of the Department of Correctional Services Russell G. Oswald, who had been chairman of the New York State Board of Parole. Oswald met with inmate representatives at the prison but was called away on a personal emergency—his wife was seriously ill—before any agreement could be arranged.[6]

On September 8, 1971, when a correction officer attempted to discipline two inmates who appeared to be sparring, a confrontation ensued. The incident passed without any action on the part of the outnumbered staff. That evening, officers appeared and took the two inmates from their cells. A noisy protest ensued during the evening, and it was renewed when inmates gathered for breakfast on the morning of September 9. A melee broke out, corrections officers were taken hostage, and a riot quickly developed. Prison officials had no plan, nor had they been trained to deal with such an emergency. As a result, within 20 minutes inmates secured control of the four main cell blocks and seized 40 hostages. Corrections officers were beaten, and one died later as a result of his wounds. The Black Muslims, who had not taken part in the initial uprising, moved to protect the hostages who were used as a basis for negotiations. An inmate committee for that purpose was formed.

When he arrived back at Attica, Commissioner Oswald found the police were not prepared to retake the prison immediately. By the time sufficient forces had gathered, negotiations were already under way, and Oswald chose to continue them in an effort to avoid more bloodshed. At the request of the inmate committee, several outside observers, including reporters, lawyers, and politicians, were permitted to enter Attica. Although the negotiations were quite disorganized, Oswald agreed to most of the inmate demands for improved conditions at Attica. The negotiations broke down, however, over the issue of complete amnesty because one of the injured officers had died after the negotiations began. Governor Nelson Rockefeller ordered that the prison be retaken.

On the morning of September 13, in a poorly planned and uncoordinated nine-minute assault, heavily armed state police and corrections officers retook the prison. More than 2,000 rounds of ammunition were fired; 2 hostages were seriously injured by the inmates, and 10 hostages and 29 inmates were killed by state troopers and corrections officers (Wicker, 1975).

A number of official investigations occurred in the aftermath of the rebellion at Attica. In particular, rehabilitation, the parole board, and indeterminate sentencing were subjected to severe criticism. As Francis Cullen and Karen Gilbert point out, "Americans in the first half of the 1970s were faced with the prospect of an intractable crime rate and confronted with the reality—powerfully symbolized by Attica—that their prisons were both inhumane and grossly ineffective. In this context, a culprit was needed to take the blame, and a candidate was readily found. Rehabilitation would take the rap" (1982: 6). The medical model came under severe attack from both the right and left of the political spectrum.

---

[6]Oswald died in 1991, at age 82. His book *Attica: My Story* was published in 1972.

▶ Criticisms of the Medical Model

From its inception in California in 1944 under Governor Earl Warren, the medical model approach continued without serious opposition into the 1970s. Any opposition came primarily from the right of the political spectrum, as exemplified by the attacks of FBI Director John Edgar Hoover, who saw parole as "coddling" criminals, releasing them before they completed their sentences. During the 1970s, however, the attack on the medical model of corrections shifted to the political left.

In 1971, the Quaker-sponsored AFSC published the first comprehensive attack on the indeterminate sentence and parole. The AFSC noted that the indeterminate sentence and parole rested on the view that crime is a result of individual pathology and that it can best be "cured" by treating *individual* criminals. Such an approach, the AFSC noted, downgrades environmental factors, such as poverty, discrimination, and lack of employment opportunities. Furthermore, the committee argued that, even if the medical model approach is valid, the achievement level of the behavioral sciences does not offer a scientific basis for treatment.

Key Fact

The medical model approach to criminals began in California at the end of World War II and spread across the United States.

The work of the AFSC had only limited impact and no practical effect until 1974. In that year, sociologist Robert Martinson published a review of correctional treatment efforts titled "What Works?" to which he answered: Virtually nothing! "What Works?" (1974) was actually a synopsis of the research findings of Martinson, Douglas Lipton, and Judith Wilks; the complete work was published the following year. The three researchers surveyed 231 studies of correctional programs up until 1968, about which Martinson (1974: 25) concluded: "With few and isolated exceptions, the rehabilitative efforts that have been reported so far have had no appreciable effect on recidivism." Although the Martinson summary is more critical than the larger report, both lent credence to the arguments of the AFSC. In a review of the Lipton, Martinson, and Wilks (1975) research, a panel of the National Research Council concluded that it was "reasonably accurate and fair in the appraisal of the rehabilitation literature"; in fact, the panel concluded, Lipton and his colleagues "were, if anything, more likely to accept evidence in favor of rehabilitation than was justified" (Sechrest, White, and Brown, 1979: 31). "What Works" became a catchword for criticism of correctional treatment and parole.

According to Paul Gendreau and Robert Ross, however, the research examined by Martinson was dated; furthermore, substantial literature since 1968 (Martinson's cutoff date) demonstrated that "successful rehabilitation of offenders had been accomplished, and continued to be accomplished quite well" (1987: 350). In fact, "between 1973 and 1980 reductions in recidivism, sometimes as substantial as 80 percent, had been achieved in a considerable number of well-controlled studies. Effective programs were conducted in a variety of community and (to a lesser degree) institutional settings, involving predelinquents, hardcore adolescent offenders, and recidivistic adult offenders, including heroin addicts" (1987: 350–351). And, these results were not short lived: "Follow-up periods of at least two years were not uncommon, and several studies reported longer follow-ups" (1987: 351). The debate over correctional treatment effectiveness continued (e.g., Andrews et al., 1990; Lab and Cullen, 1990), with rigorous analysis indicating positive outcomes in a variety of studies.[7]

---

[7]His research notwithstanding, Martinson advocated prison treatment programming and was a strong supporter of parole, so much so that in 1977, the New York State Parole Officers Association presented him with a plaque in recognition of his efforts. What he saw as a misinterpretation of his work is believed to have led to his suicide in 1980.

► Alternative Models

Whatever the merits, criticism of the indeterminate sentence, the medical model of corrections, and the use of parole increased. David Fogel presented a justice model in which he criticized the unbridled discretion exercised by correctional officials, particularly parole boards, under the guise of "treatment":

> It is evident that correctional administrators have for too long operated with practical immunity in the backwashes of administrative law. They have been unmindful that the process of justice more strictly observed by the visible police and courts in relation to rights due the accused before and through adjudication must not stop when the convicted person is sentenced. The justice perspective demands accountability from all processors, even the "pure of heart." (1975: 192)

Instead of the often-hidden discretion exercised by parole boards, Fogel recommended both a return to flat time/determinate sentences, with procedural rules in law limiting sentencing discretion, and the elimination of parole boards and parole agencies. Furthermore, Fogel argued whatever "treatment" is offered in a prison should be voluntary and should in no way affect the release date of an inmate.

Andrew von Hirsch (1976) offered the concept of just deserts, according to which the punishment is to be commensurate with the seriousness of the crime—a return to the classical approach. "A specific penalty level must apply in all instances of lawbreaking which involves a given degree of harmfulness and culpability" (von Hirsch and Hanrahan, 1978: 4). Indeterminacy and parole would be replaced with a specific penalty for a specific offense.

The Twentieth Century Fund Task Force on Sentencing offered the presumptive sentence: Each category of crime would have a presumptive sentence "that should generally be imposed on typical first offenders who have committed the crime in the typical fashion" (1976: 20, italics deleted). For succeeding convictions or other aggravating circumstances, the judge could increase the presumptive sentence by a specific (albeit limited) percentage; mitigating circumstances could similarly reduce the presumptive sentence.

In sum, the basic thrust of these criticisms and proposals was to limit judicial discretion, eliminate the indeterminate sentence, and abolish the parole board. Here was an issue on which both the political left and right could agree—but for different reasons. Alfred Blumenstein notes:

> In the mid-1970s a striking consensus of the political left and the political right emerged in opposition to the indeterminate sentence. The political left was concerned over the excess of discretion in decisions about an individual's liberty and the excessive disparity that appeared in sentences in presumably similar cases. The political right appeared to be far more concerned about "leniency" than about disparity. They viewed the parole boards as excessively ready to release prisoners early and expressed shock that prisoners were back on the street on parole well before the maximum sentence. (1984: 130, edited)

Franklin Zimring and Gordon Hawkins (1995: 9) point out that this coalescing of otherwise divergent views "is a pretty reliable indication that some of the participants in the policy debate do not have a clear understanding of the practical implications of their stance."

As sentiments toward crime and criminals hardened, political changes generated by (often pandering) politicians led to "tough on crime" statutes that have further clogged our correctional facilities. "Sound-bite policy" replaced careful and thoughtful policy development. "Clearly, parole was an easy target for those looking for political opportunities," notes Barbara Krauth, and "the emotional appeal of an attack on the system that

Key Fact

Those on the left and right of the political spectrum opposed the corrections/medical model approach; both argued for limiting sentencing discretion and abolishing parole.

GOOD POLITICS CAN GENERATE BAD POLICY

The parole board is always vulnerable to criticism, and parole release often proves a tempting target for demagogic attack. After all, no one supports the release of a prison inmate who subsequently commits a heinous crime—the value of predictive hindsight. The issue, of course, is not if an inmate should be released but what mechanism will be used to make the release decision. Prisons are overcrowded, and virtually all inmates will eventually be released, facts usually overlooked in the focus on a particular crime or parolee. Nevertheless, governors in many states preferred to advocate abolishing parole than have to defend such a politically vulnerable system. Indeed, there is trend in favor of removing the term "parole" from the corrections lexicon.

released criminals to the streets may have benefited some political careers more than it actually addressed any of the complex problems of criminal justice" (1987: 52). By 1980, eight states had already adopted some form of determinate sentencing, including (in 1977) the pioneering state of California; the federal government and several other states have abolished the indeterminate sentence and parole release since that time, although a few have reintroduced the indeterminate sentence and parole supervision. The abolition of discretionary release—parole board—means that no distinction is made between inmates deserving early release and those who do not; there is an absence of any type of assessment to determine which inmates should be released prior to the expiration of their sentence and which inmates should be denied release. In states that have retained the indeterminate sentence, to be eligible for parole, an inmate prisoner must demonstrate that he or she has a job, or is likely to be able to secure employment, and a satisfactory residence. In the absence of discretionary release by a parole board, there is little, if any, pressure on prisoners to prepare for postrelease life (Visher and Travis, 2003).

> **Key Fact**
>
> Determinate and truth-in-sentencing laws have severely restricted discretionary/parole release.

States retaining discretionary parole release typically restrict eligibility. In Connecticut, offenders become eligible for parole release after serving 50 percent of their sentence, but those convicted of violent crimes after 85 percent. In Georgia, persons convicted of such serious crimes as rape and armed robbery must serve their entire sentence. In New York, violent offenders must serve 85 percent of their determinate sentence, after which they are subject to a court-imposed period of supervision of 1.5 to 5 years. In New Jersey, persons convicted of first- or second-degree violent crimes or burglary must serve 85 percent of their sentence, after which they remain under parole supervision for five years (first-degree crimes) or three years (second-degree crimes). There is also mandatory parole supervision for life for those convicted of certain violent or sex crimes.

The federal Sentencing Reform Act of 1984, which abolished the indeterminate sentence, was designed to reduce sentence disparity and phase out parole release by 1992. However,

ABOLISHING PAROLE RELEASE

"In the traditional parole model, one function of parole boards is to ensure that a prisoner is prepared for release, that he or she has a place to stay, a job or a solid job prospect, and the support of family and friends—in essence, a release plan that can be monitored by the parole officers supervising the released prisoner. Now, nearly three out of four released prisoners never see a parole board, so they may never be required to prepare a release plan" (Travis and Lawrence, 2002: 24).

the discretion lost by judges has been assumed by prosecutors, resulting in longer prison terms and an increasingly overcrowded federal prison system, and federal judges have been vociferous in their criticism of their lack of discretion in rendering sentencing decisions (Urbina, 2003). As the next section indicates, this scenario has often been repeated in state systems.

▶ Indeterminate Versus Determinate Sentencing

Under indeterminate sentencing, originally established as part of the Elmira system, a judge imposes a prison term that has both a minimum and a maximum length. For example, a defendant convicted of a class 3 felony could receive a sentence with a minimum of 3 years (written 3-0-0) and a maximum of 9 years (written 9-0-0); the actual release of the inmate (between 3-0-0/9-0-0) is determined by a parole board. In some states, such as New Jersey, the judge sets a maximum, and an inmate becomes eligible for parole release after serving one-third of the sentence. A provision is usually made for good-time credit, time deducted from the maximum sentence because of good institutional behavior, typically one-third of the sentence. For example, an inmate with a maximum sentence of 9-0-0 could accumulate up to 3-0-0 years of good time, thus being released after 6-0-0 years without the intervention of the parole board.

Under a system of indeterminate sentencing, persons convicted for the same class of offense could receive different sentences. For example, a first-degree robbery may carry a minimum sentence range of 2-0-0 to 6-0-0 and a maximum sentence range of 8-4-0 to 25-0-0. Even those who receive the same sentence, for example, 3-0-0 to 9-0-0, can be released (paroled) at different times: 3-0-0, or 4-0-0, or 5-0-0, all the way up to 9-0-0 (minus good time). Criticism of the indeterminate sentence has involved this differential treatment of persons convicted of similar crimes, which is contrary to the classical approach to criminal behavior: "Critics of the indeterminate sentence argued that the treatment model has never realized its lofty objectives in practice and that, given the nature of the correctional system, these goals never will be realized. Furthermore, they maintained that the indeterminate sentence has created a situation of gross sentencing disparity that no longer can be justified by referring to treatment goals" (Goodstein and Hepburn, 1985: 17).

"Indeterminate sentencing was ubiquitous, but when it lost credibility, no single approach replaced it. Every American jurisdiction has a crazy quilt of diverse and, in principle if not practice, irreconcilable elements" (Tonry, 2006: 1). In response to criticism of indeterminate sentencing and parole boards, a variety of so-called flat, definite, or **determinate sentence** schemes have been adopted. Although each requires the setting of a *specific* sentence—no minimum and maximum—these sentencing models differ according to the amount of discretion left to the judge:

• *Definite sentence/no discretion.* The legislature provides for a specific sentence for each level of offense. For example, all crimes that constitute a class 2 felony require the judge to impose a specific sentence—no deviations permitted. If a class 2 felony was punishable by imprisonment for 7 years, all judges would be required to sentence all defendants convicted of a class 2 felony to 7-0-0.

- *Definite sentence/wide discretion.* The legislature provides for a range of sentences for each level of offense. For example, a class 2 felony is punishable with a sentence between 3-0-0 and 7-0-0. Under this system, the judge retains discretion to sentence a class 2 offender to 3-0-0 or 4-0-0, all the way up to 7-0-0. The sentence imposed is definite—for a specific number of years—but the judge's discretion is wide.

- *Presumptive sentence/narrow discretion.* The legislature limits discretion to a narrow range of sentences for each level of offense; for each level, a presumed sentence exists from which the judge cannot deviate, except if aggravating or mitigating circumstances apply, and then in only a limited manner. For example, if a defendant is convicted of a class 2 felony, the judge could be required to set a sentence of 5-0-0. On a showing of aggravation by the prosecutor, the judge could increase the presumptive sentence to 6-0-0; on a showing of mitigation by the defense, the judge could decrease the presumptive sentence to 4-0-0. In some states (e.g., Minnesota), the presumed sentence is increased by a fixed amount based on the severity of any prior convictions (see Figure 3.2 in Chapter 3).

- *Presumptive sentence/wide discretion.* As in the presumptive sentence with narrow discretion, the legislature provides three possible terms for each class of felony. However, although each class has a presumptive sentence, the judge may decrease (for mitigation) or increase (for aggravation) by significantly fixed amounts; for example, a presumptive sentence of 12 years could be decreased to 6 years or increased to 16 years.

In 2007, the U.S. Supreme Court (*Cunningham v. California*, 549 U.S. 270) found the presumptive system used in California unconstitutional insofar as it allowed the judge to use a fact-finding process to decide which of three sentences to impose; *fact finding*, the Court noted, is reserved for juries.

Determinate sentencing systems usually include a provision for good time, ranging from 15 to 50 percent off the sentence, to promote prison discipline. A defendant sentenced to a determinate sentence of 5-0-0 in a system using 50 percent good time would be released (presuming good behavior) after 2-6-0. In practice, good time is deducted in advance when the offender is first received at the institution; misbehavior results in time being added. In some states, an inmate may be entitled to additional time off the sentence for exemplary performance: "meritorious good time" or "industrial good time." These grants of additional time off (which can be used to circumvent truth-in-sentencing laws) are usually the result of prison overcrowding in states without parole release but may also be used to reduce sentence minimums so that inmates can more quickly qualify for parole release.

Nationwide, more than half of prison releases are the result not of discretionary parole board decision making but of good time (mandatory release) provisions (Glaze, 2003). These mandatory releasees may be placed under the supervision of a parole officer and thus are often referred to as "parolees." Some states have discontinued postrelease supervision of "low-risk," usually "nonviolent," offenders. In the absence of discretionary release, the incentive for adequate funding of offender supervision is often absent—no one (the governor or parole board) can be held accountable for serious postrelease misconduct.

In place of parole, some states have substituted *split sentencing* that reverses the normal sequence of probation, prison, and parole. The offender is sentenced to a term of imprisonment and upon completion is released to *probation* supervision. Unlike parole, offenders do not serve terms of supervised release as a substitute for a portion of their sentences of imprisonment.

In Maine, the first state to abandon parole release (and parole supervision), postrelease supervision was reestablished by Maine's judges in the form of split sentences—"judicial

Key Fact

While they were advanced to promote equality of sentencing, some determinate sentencing schemes have not accomplished this goal.

Key Fact

In the absence of discretionary release, the incentive for adequate funding of offender supervision is often absent, as is offender interest in prison rehabilitation programs.

parole"—whereby offenders are sentenced to imprisonment followed by a period of probation supervision. As part of the 1984 Sentencing Reform Act, Congress eliminated parole release and authorized federal judges to impose a term of imprisonment followed by supervision by federal probation officers. In Virginia, which abolished parole release in 1995, about 80 percent of inmates have what is called *supervised probation* following incarceration. These schemes are politically safe since in the absence of discretionary release there is no accountability/blame should an offender recidivate. Knowing that they will be released automatically means inmates have no incentive to participate in rehabilitation programs.

▶ Determinate Sentences, Prosecutorial Discretion, and Disparate Justice

Although in theory the determinate sentence and sentencing guidelines (discussed in Chapter 3) were supposed to reduce unwarranted variation in sentencing and the amount of time served in prison, the practice has been otherwise. The "sentencing guidelines" effort to reign in sentencing disparity has not had notable success: "Study after study examining the effect of sentencing guidelines has indicated that these reforms have not provided convincing evidence that they eliminate unwarranted disparity" (Koons-Witt, 2009: 281). No state, for example, has adopted a determinate sentence without discretion, whereas several have adopted schemes with wide discretion. Thus, in Illinois, a defendant convicted of selling drugs as a first offense can receive a *determinate* sentence of anywhere from 4-0-0 all the way up to 30-0-0.

The issue of prosecutorial discretion presents the most obvious deficiency in the proposals set out by Fogel, von Hirsch, and others. This discretion is typically exercised privately, outside the scrutiny of official review, and affects sentencing more often and more significantly than does judicial discretion. Although a judge acting under a definite system with narrow discretion or a presumptive system with narrow discretion must apply a specific sentence for a particular class of crime, the prosecutor, using charging powers, determines the particular class of crime to charge and whether to move for aggravation or oppose a motion for mitigation.

"Legislatively mandated determinate sentencing has not proved to be a workable alternative to the traditional indeterminate system. Because uniform punishments assigned to each crime lead to unjust results in many cases, prosecutors and judges find ways to adjust the charges accordingly" (Wright, 1998: 4). In return for cooperation— a plea of guilty—the prosecutor can reduce the class of crime for which the offender will be charged and may also agree not to move for aggravation or accept mitigation offered by defense counsel. By manipulating the charging decision, the prosecutor (not the judge) can often determine the actual sentence. Thus, determinate sentencing can increase the ability of a prosecutor to plea bargain. In many instances, determinate sentencing merely shifts discretion away from judges and parole boards and toward the prosecution end of criminal justice; in other words, release decisions are being made at the front end rather than the back end of the system. Because the defendant's primary interest is in how much time he or she must actually serve, new laws limiting good time (under so-called truth-in-sentencing provisions) are now added to the plea-bargaining equation.

In 1984, when federal legislation established a guideline system that significantly reduced the sentencing discretion of judges, the prosecutor gained *de facto* sentencing power by determining the charges linked to specific sentences. Plea bargaining shifted from *sentence bargaining* to *charge bargaining* (Nasheri, 1998): "By assigning a narrow range of sentencing options to virtually every criminal violation and by giving judges only limited power to impose a sentence below that range, guideline systems have invested prosecutors with the power to dictate almost every sentence by choosing one set of charges over another" (Fisher, 2000: 1072).

John Kramer (2009) argues that the issue of sentencing disparity was not based on hard data—more rhetorical and political than research driven. He points out that the courts had already developed an environment that served to dampen sentencing disparities through a process known as the *going rate.* "Once the nature of the item is known, the posted price, the 'going rate,' prevails" (Eisenstein, Flemming, and Nardulli, 1988: 243). Although the guilty plea is most often a result of some form of exchange, the actual process may be so simple that it cannot be accurately described as "negotiation." David Sudnow (1965) explains such transactions by introducing the concept of normal crimes: those that have common features (the ways they usually occur, the characteristics of persons who commit them, as well as the typical victims) and can be classified as "normal." For example, a "normal burglary" involves a nonprofessional violator who is black or Latino, no weapons, low-priced items, little property damage, and a lower-class victim. However, possession of firearms, harm to the occupants, victims who are not lower class, and indications of professional criminality or organized crime, for example, would remove the incident from the category of "normal burglary." If the defense attorney and prosecutor agree that a burglary is a normal one, custom and precedent provide for a settlement without the need for negotiation. Although the statutes provide a penalty for each crime, judicial actors have established their own unwritten penalties for each "normal crime," which, because they mitigate statutory penalties, serve to encourage pleas of guilty and thus ensure a penalty for the perpetrator at a minimum expenditure of scarce legal resources. They also serve to control sentence disparity.

This procedure is made possible by the reality that "core members of the [court] community usually develop a common understanding of what penalties ought to be attached to which crimes and defendants" (Eisenstein, Flemming, and Nardulli, 1988: 203). "Through daily wrangling, court workers generally agree on a baseline, expected sentence for each category of crime" (McCoy, 1993: 55). During his research, Dean Champion found "considerable agreement among prosecutors concerning the going rate for various offenses" that facilitated plea bargain agreements (1989: 256–257).

The abolition of parole boards, a practical accomplishment of determinate sentencing schemes, ignores the role of the board in reducing the sentence disparity that the classicalists decry. Because the parole board reviews the sentences of all state prisoners, it is in a position to act as a panel for mediating disparate sentences for similar criminal behavior. In Nebraska, for example, the board of parole "serves as an 'equalizer.' Within the framework of the law, it attempts to produce equity and uniformity in the sentencing structure caused by the inherent disparity which understandably results from having ninety-three prosecuting offices and multiple judicial districts." The Georgia Board of Pardons and Paroles states that "the board's unique central position and authority allow it to reduce sentencing disparity. Excessive harshness is more readily reduced, but excessive leniency in the form of a too-light confinement sentence may be corrected partially by parole denial." Figure 4.1 provides a hypothetical example of the parole board as a sentencing review panel. "All parole boards, either implicitly or explicitly, serve the vital function of equalizing justice between judges, courts, and counties. Board members removed from the heat of trial are familiar with case practices in all jurisdictions and are able to apply a common statewide standard of justice. Left to their own devices, the…judges, district attorneys, defense counsel, juries, community temperament and the sophistication of defendants [produce] some very strange and disparate results" (Holt, 1995: 20).

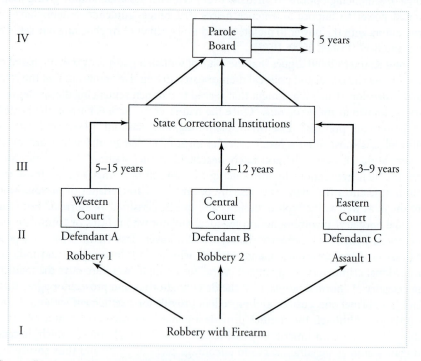

IV

Parole
Board

5 years

State Correctional Institutions

III   5–15 years   4–12 years   3–9 years

Western
Court

Central
Court

Eastern
Court

II   Defendant A   Defendant B   Defendant C

Robbery 1   Robbery 2   Assault 1

I   Robbery with Firearm

I   Three offenders, A, B, and C, all enter stores in different counties within the same state. They brandish loaded revolvers and steal several hundred dollars.

II Defendant A is processed in Western Court. Attempts at plea bargaining fail; he stands trial and is convicted of first-degree robbery.
Defendant B is processed in Central Court. He is allowed to plead guilty to second-degree robbery.
Defendant C is processed in Eastern Court. He is allowed to plead guilty to first-degree assault.

III Defendant A is sentenced to a minimum of 5 years and a maximum of 15 years in state prison.
Defendant B is sentenced to a minimum of 4 years and a maximum of 12 years in state prison.
Defendant C is sentenced to a minimum of 3 years and a maximum of 9 years in state prison.

IV The parole board, recognizing that the three defendants have committed the same criminal acts despite variations in the legal category of conviction (Robbery 1, Robbery 2, Assault 1), requires that each serve 5 years before being paroled.

Under a determinate sentencing scheme devoid of a parole board, the sentences for this hypothetical example would be as follows:

Defendant A would serve 8 years.
Defendant B would serve 6 years.
Defendant C would serve 4 years.

FIGURE 4.1 Parole Board as Sentencing Review Panel

▶ The "Why" of Parole

Some (AFSC, 1971; Fogel, 1975; MacNamara, 1977) presume that parole is based on a medical model or some humanitarian effort gone astray, but the history of prisons and parole in the United States underscores the fact that parole release has been used (and possibly abused) as a mechanism for maintaining prison discipline and reducing prison overcrowding. The parole board evolved out of the power of governors to issue pardons to selected convicts; before the creation of parole boards, governors often used their pardoning powers to relieve prison overcrowding. In the middle of the nineteenth century, pardons accounted for more than 40 percent of the releases from U.S. prisons (Hibbert, 1968). In Ohio, for example, whenever the state prison exceeded a certain number of inmates, the governor granted pardons to make room for new prisoners. In 1867, Nevada created a pardon board with the power to release inmates through commutation; and in 1909, the board's authority was expanded to include the parole of prisoners who were required to report to the governor's private secretary at least once per month. In 1898, Virginia passed an act permitting prisoners who had served half their sentence to file a petition with the governor who (upon the recommendation of the board of penitentiary directors) could grant a conditional pardon. The act was later amended—the word *parole* was substituted for pardon, and release authority was transferred from the governor to the penitentiary directors. As late as 1938, parole was simply a conditional pardon in many states.

In Florida, the pardon board often presided over as many as 200 pardon applications per day until the Parole and Probation Commission was established in 1941. In Utah, the Board of Pardons continues to have parole responsibilities, and the Alabama Board of Pardons and Paroles, established in 1939, has final authority on all pardons. The Vermont Parole Board was created in 1968; until that time, release from prison was by conditional pardon granted by the governor.

Blumenstein points out "one of the functions the parole agencies carried out during the period of indeterminate sentencing was serving as a 'safety valve' for crowded prisons. As prison populations began to approach or exceed the prison capacity, the parole board could simply lower the threshold of the degree of rehabilitation that warranted release" (1984: 131). The clear use of parole as a safety valve for prison population control is highlighted by the Texas experience. Faced with overcrowding during the 1980s, Texas simply increased parole releases: "In 1983, about 40 percent of inmates were released on parole after their first hearing. By the end of the decade, this had increased to nearly 80 percent" (Kelly and Ekland-Olson, 1991: 604). In 1980, with 15,257 prison admissions, the parole board released 5,660 inmates; in 1991, when prison admissions reached more than 37,000, the parole board released more than 31,000 inmates—an increase of more than 400 percent (Bodapati, Marquardt, and Cuvelier, 1993). A similar situation occurred in Georgia where, in 1980, 14,000 inmates were in prison; a decade later there were 44,000 prisoners, and county jails were backing up with prisoners sentenced to state prison. A class-action lawsuit—which state officials believed they would lose—was initiated. In response, the parole board accelerated the parole release of thousands of inmates (for which the board was labeled "soft on crime"). Nationally, increases in the prison population result in even greater increases in the parolee population.

In many states using determinate sentencing, the same release function is being carried out by prison officials using good-time or "special release" provisions. However, prison officials lack the information, time, or expertise to make rational release decisions—a reason why parole boards developed. Those who see parole as simply a rehabilitative device have bought the *rhetoric* but not the *reality*—parole is more realistically understood as "risk management." Corrections officials in several states that have abolished the indeterminate sentence have (by necessity caused by overcrowding) become *de facto* parole boards. In Delaware, which abolished parole release (but not the parole board) in 1989, the Department of Correction may apply to the parole board for a modification of the inmate's sentence. The board then holds a hearing for the purpose of providing a recommendation to the sentencing judge. In Florida, as the result of overcrowding (and a federal lawsuit), the parole board was reconstituted as the Control Release Authority to act under the state's determinate sentencing laws in essentially the same capacity as it had under indeterminate sentencing—*a change in name but not the game.*

Parole is a method for encouraging inmates to avoid institutional disciplinary infractions and to participate in institutional programs while incarcerated. "In addition to helping the department of corrections maintain order and security in the prisons, parole provides a powerful incentive for the inmate to develop pro-social personal goals and strengths and to become motivated for law-abiding behavior" (*State Parole Board Annual Report 2005*, 2006: 3). And, research indicates that inmates participating in prison rehabilitation programs have lower rates of postrelease recidivism than similar inmates who do not (Texas Department of Criminal Justice, 2011). Ilyana Kuziemko (2013) found that a 1998 policy change in Georgia requiring serious offenders to complete at least 90 percent of their sentence—virtually eliminating the possibility of early parole release—led to a significant increase in disciplinary infractions, a decrease in participation in prison rehabilitation programs, and substantial a substantial increase in recidivism.

David Greenberg and Drew Humphries (1980) argue that the forces of the political right co-opted the issues of sentencing reform and abolition of parole and were successful in implementing changes that are increasing the length of time served by offenders, now without the possibility of parole release, in a prison atmosphere devoid of any rehabilitative component. In a strong defense of the medical/rehabilitative model, Cullen and Gilbert (1982: xxix) state: "Whatever its failings, criminal justice rehabilitation has thus persisted as a rationale for caring for offender needs and not for making the wayward suffer. Without its humanizing influence, the history of American corrections would be even bleaker than is now the case."

A relevant question is now at issue: Do we entrust the decrease of prison populations; reduction of sentencing disparity; and risk management of criminal offenders to judges, prison officials, or parole boards? A review of the history that led to the establishment of parole in the first instance argues for this discretion to be the responsibility of a professional parole board.

> **Key Fact**
>
> Most inmates will eventually be released; the question is: "Who will make the release decision?"

Summary

- The transporting of pardoned criminals from England to colonial America was an historical antecedent of modern parole.

- Alexander Maconochie (1787–1860), superintendent of the British penal colony on Norfolk Island, set out a philosophy of punishment based on reforming the individual criminal with sentences that were open ended, what is known today as an indeterminate sentence.

- The "Irish System" of Walter Crofton was a direct influence on the establishment of parole release and community supervision in the United States.

- Zebulon Brockway established an indeterminate sentence system at Elmira Reformatory.

- A central feature of the Auburn system was the exploitation of inmate labor to control the cost of imprisonment.

- Federal laws enacted during the Great Depression ended the financial exploitation of inmate labor.

- Toward the end of World War II, a penological revolution occurred in California that reorganized its prison system according to the positivist ideal of individual reformation.

- In the aftermath of the rebellion at Attica, rehabilitation, the parole board, and indeterminate sentencing were subjected to severe criticism.

- In 1974, Robert Martinson published a review of correctional treatment efforts titled "What Works?" to which he answered: Virtually nothing!

- "What Works?" led to attacks on the indeterminate sentence and parole and the eventual adoption of determinate sentencing in many states.
- The political left and right favored proposals to limit judicial discretion, eliminate the indeterminate sentence, and abolish the parole board, but for different reasons.
- Abolishing the indeterminate sentence and parole makes good politics but bad policy.
- Under indeterminate sentencing a judge imposes a prison term that has both a minimum and a maximum length, with release determined by a parole board.
- The different types of determinate sentence are distinguished by the amount of discretion enjoyed by a sentencing judge.
- While advanced to promote equality of sentencing, determinate sentencing schemes have not accomplished this goal.
- In place of parole, some states have substituted *split sentencing* that reverses the normal sequence of probation, prison, and parole.
- Split sentencing avoids the political liability inherent in discretionary release from prison.
- Determinate sentencing shifts discretion away from judges and parole boards and toward the prosecutor.
- "Normal crimes" and the "courtroom workgroup" control sentence disparity.
- Determinate sentencing ignores the role of the board in reducing sentence disparity.
- Before the creation of parole boards, governors often used their pardoning powers to relieve prison overcrowding.

Key Terms

Auburn/New York system *73*
contract system *73*
courtroom workgroup *61*
determinate sentence *84*
indentured servant *68*
indeterminate sentence *69*
inmate labor *74*

Irish system *69*
just deserts *82*
justice model *82*
medical model *76*
Pennsylvania system *87*
parole board *76*
plea bargain *86*

positivism *76*
presumptive sentence *82*
reformatory *70*
split sentencing *85*
ticket of leave *69*
total institution *78*
truth in sentencing *85*

Internet Connections

American Probation and Parole Association: **www.appa-net.org**

Corrections news/topics: **corrections.com**

Parole boards: **crimelynx.com**

Parole boards and departments of correction: **crime-guide4all.com**

Review Questions

1. Why is the transporting of pardoned criminals from England to colonial America an historical antecedent for modern parole?
2. What was the innovation set out by Alexander Maconochie that was a forerunner of modern parole release?
3. What were the elements in Walter Crofton's "Irish System" that influenced the establishment of parole release and community supervision in the United States?
4. What was the Elmira system and its relationship to parole?
5. What was the connection between the Great Depression that began in 1929 and the expansion of parole?
6. What was the essential feature of the Auburn system that controlled the cost of imprisonment?
7. What caused the demise of the Auburn system?
8. What are the characteristics of the Medical Model of corrections?
9. What are criticisms of the Medical Model?
10. How did the inmate uprising at Attica affect parole?
11. How did Robert Martinson's "What Works" affect parole?
12. Why does abolishing the indeterminate sentence and parole make good politics but bad policy?
13. What are the elements of an indeterminate sentence?
14. What distinguishes the different types of determinate sentence?
15. Why has the determinate sentence not achieved the goal of sentencing equality?
16. How does *split sentencing* reverse the normal sequence of probation, prison, and parole?
17. Why is split sentencing politically safe?
18. How does determinate sentencing shift discretion?
19. How do "normal crimes" and the "courtroom workgroup" control sentence disparity?
20. What is the role of the parole board in reducing sentence disparity?

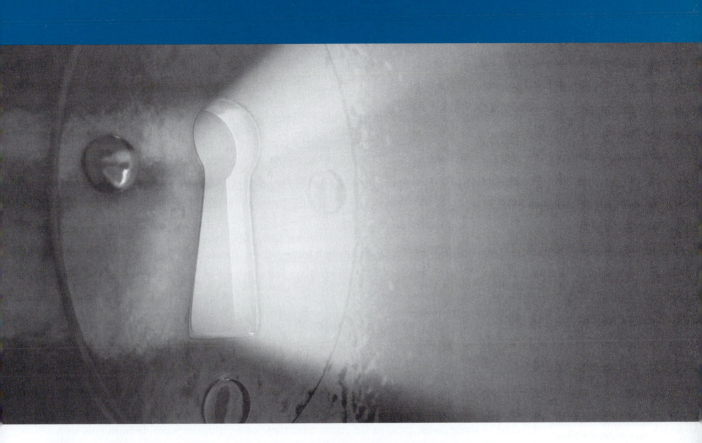

5 Parole Administration and Services

LEARNING OBJECTIVES

This chapter will enable the student to:

1 *Identify the three basic services provided by a parole agency.*

2 *Explain the administration of parole services.*

3 *Discuss the two basic models for administering parole.*

4 *Understand how states that do not have a parole board release inmates early.*

5 *Discuss the qualifications for parole board members and how they are chosen.*

6 *Appreciate Supreme Court decisions with respect to parole release.*

7 Explain how parole board guidelines typically go well beyond the medical/rehabilitative model.

8 Understand how parole board guidelines make the release decision process intelligible.

9 State the primary responsibility of institutional parole staff.

10 Appreciate why probation and parole regulations in different agencies tend to be similar.

11 Explain why an inmate has no liberty interest, *but a parolee does.*

12 Appreciate that parole board members do not have total immunity.

13 Discuss the executive clemency role of parole boards.

A parole agency can provide three basic services: parole release, parole supervision, and executive clemency. For administrative purposes, these can be classified into three categories:

1. Institutional services
2. Field services
3. Executive clemency

> **Key Fact**
>
> The administration of parole is less complex than that of probation because parole services are usually administered centrally on a statewide basis.

The administration of parole is less complex than that of probation because parole services are usually administered centrally on a statewide basis. In Oregon, however, county probation/parole officers supervise all felons on probation or parole/postprison supervision. And in some states, local jurisdictions have their own city/county parole from jails with supervision provided by *probation* officers.

▶ Administration of Parole Services

There are two basic models for administering parole:

> **Key Fact**
>
> Parole can be administered independently or as part of a department that administers prisons, with or without being combined with probation.

1. **Independent model.** In the independent model, a parole board is responsible for making release and revocation determinations and for supervising persons released on parole (and good time); it is independent of any other state agency.

2. **Consolidated model.** In the consolidated model, the parole board is an autonomous panel within a department that also administers correctional institutions. The board makes release and revocation decisions, but supervision of persons released on parole (and good time) is under the direction of the commissioner of corrections.

In both models, probation services are sometimes combined with parole services in a single statewide agency.

The Task Force on Corrections (1966) summarized arguments for the independent model:

- The parole board is in the best position to promote the idea of parole and to generate public support and acceptance. Because the board is often held accountable (by the public, news media, public officials) for parole failures, it should be responsible for supervising parolees.

- The parole board in direct control of administering parole services can more effectively evaluate and adjust the system.
- Supervision by the parole board and its officers properly divorces parole release and parolees from the correctional institution.
- An independent parole board in charge of its own services is in the best position to present its own budget request to the legislature.

The Task Force on Corrections (1966) also summarized arguments for including both parole services and institutions in a single department of corrections:

- The correctional process is a continuum; all staff, institutional and parole, should be under a single administration rather than be divided, with both resultant competition for public funds and friction between policies.
- A consolidated correctional department has the advantage of consistent administration, including staff selection and supervision.
- Parole boards are ineffective in performing administrative functions. Their major focus should be on case decisions, not on day-to-day field operations.
- Community-based programs partway between institutions and parole, such as work release, can best be handled by a single centralized administration.

Critics contend that the independent model tends to be indifferent or insensitive to institutional programs and that the parole board in this model places undue stress on variables outside the institution. Conversely, critics of the consolidated model argue that the parole board will be under pressure to stress institutional factors in making parole decisions, although these are of dubious value in making a parole prognosis.

▶ Mandatory or Conditional Release

Conditional release (sometimes referred to as "mandatory release") is the term used to describe inmates released on good time. In such cases, either the parole board has denied them parole release or the state does not have a parole board. Inmates in most states are eligible for good time; that is, they can accumulate days, months, and years off their maximum sentence by avoiding institutional infractions and/or participating in prison programs. In Connecticut, inmates serving a sentence of two years or less are eligible to be released after serving 50 percent of their sentence, after which parole officers supervise them.

In addition, some states have meritorious good time for exemplary behavior and emergency good-time provisions to reduce the prison population in cases of severe overcrowding. In states using indeterminate sentences and parole boards, good time can usually be accumulated at the rate of 10 days per month—one-third off the maximum sentence. In some of these states, good time may also be subtracted from the minimum sentence, making the inmate eligible for parole before the minimum sentence has actually been served.

In states using determinate sentencing, good time usually amounts to one day off for every day served. Those with truth-in-sentencing laws have reduced this to 15 percent of the sentence (although in cases of severe prison overcrowding, it can be increased by any number of schemes). In New York, where determinate sentencing is now the rule for most offenders, they must serve at least six-sevenths of the sentence (unless prison overcrowding demands otherwise) after which they must begin serving a period of court-imposed postrelease supervision of one and a half to five years. States that have abolished discretionary release by a parole board usually retain supervision requirements for at least some offenders released on good time.

> **Key Fact**
>
> Conditional/mandatory release is based on accumulation of good time and is devoid of (parole board) discretion.

In some of these states, decisions regarding good time and revocation of conditional release are the responsibility of a variety of boards: In California, it is the Board of Prison Terms; in Illinois, it is the Prisoner Review Board; and in Missouri, the Board of Probation and Parole was placed in the Department of Corrections and Human Services, where it deals with questions of good time and supervision revocation. In Minnesota, where the parole board has been abolished, supervision of conditional releasees is the responsibility of the commissioner of corrections, who delegates this authority to the executive director of adult release. The Florida Conditional Release Program requires postprison supervision for inmates who are sentenced for certain violent crimes and have served a prior felony commitment or who are sentenced as a habitual offender, violent habitual offender, violent career criminal, or sexual predator. Conditional release supervision by correctional probation officers is for a period of time equal to the good (called "gain") time they received in prison. These offenders are subject to conditions of supervision set by the Florida Parole Commission, and supervision can be revoked and the releasee returned to prison if the commission determines that a violation of supervision has occurred.

These (nonparole) boards are also responsible for making parole decisions for persons imprisoned under indeterminate sentencing statutes that have since been repealed and for persons serving "life sentences." Some also serve as a pardons board, considering requests for the granting of executive clemency. In California, as in most states, the Department of Corrections is responsible "for deducting good time credit from the sentence and for establishing procedures to deny good time credit." If good time is denied to an inmate, the person can appeal through department appeals procedures. A final department appeal can be submitted for review to the Board of Prison Terms, which conducts a hearing on the matter. In Illinois, the Prisoner Review Board has broader responsibilities:

> Panels of at least 3 members [the board has 10 members] hear and decide cases brought by the Department of Corrections against prisoners in custody of the Department for alleged violation of Department rules with respect to good conduct credits…in which the Department seeks to revoke good conduct credits, if the amount of time at issue exceeds 30 days or when, during any 12-month period, the cumulative amount of credit revoked exceeds 30 days. However, the Board is not empowered to review the Department's decision with respect to the loss of 30 days of good conduct credit for any prisoner or to increase any penalty beyond the length requested by the Department…Upon recommendation of the Department the Board restores good conduct credit previously revoked.

▶ Parole Boards

As in most states, the governor appoints the nine members of the Pennsylvania Board of Probation and Parole and they serve 6-year terms; the five members of the Georgia Board of Pardons and Paroles and the seven members of the Arkansas Board of Parole serve 7-year terms; in New Jersey, the board consists of a chairperson, 14 associate members assigned to panels to review adult and young offender cases, 2 associates assigned to a panel to review juvenile offender cases, and 3 alternate associate members, who serve 6-year terms. The Texas Board of Pardons and Paroles has 18 members who serve 5-year terms; the five members of the Alaska Board of Parole serve 5-year terms. In Connecticut, the chairperson and 2 vice chairpersons serve full-time for 4-year terms; the other 12 members serve part-time for 4-year terms. The Iowa Board of Parole consists of five members; the chairperson and vice chairperson serve full-time, while the three other members are on a per diem basis. The Montana State Board of Pardons and Parole is composed of 12 members appointed by the governor for staggered 4-year terms. The South Carolina Board of Paroles and Pardons is composed of seven members appointed by the governor, one from

PAROLE IN MICHIGAN

The Michigan Parole Board consists of 15 full-time noncivil service employees appointed by the Director of the Department of Corrections. The parole board gains jurisdiction of a case when a prisoner serving a nonlife sentence has served his or her minimum sentence, less any good time or disciplinary credits the prisoner may have earned. (In most cases the minimum sentence is set by the judge and the maximum by statute.)

The parole board is divided into three-member panels. The decision whether to grant or deny parole is made by majority vote of a parole board panel. (All cases involving a life sentence must be decided by a majority vote of the full parole board.) If the panel denies parole, a date is selected for the next parole board review.

Parole board members conduct prisoner interviews throughout facilities in Michigan. Each facility visit is for 3 to 4 days, and a typical interview lasts 15 to 20 minutes. During the interview, the parole board questions the prisoner about the nature of the offense and whether the prisoner accepts appropriate responsibility for his or her prior criminal record, as well as his or her behavior and adjustment while in prison, participation in programming, and mental health and substance abuse history.

The factors considered by the parole board in making parole decisions include the parole guidelines score. The parole guidelines score, mandatory for all prisoners eligible to be considered for parole, is a numerical scoring system designed to assist in applying objective criteria to any decision made by the parole board. Information used to calculate the parole guidelines score is the prisoner's current offense, prior criminal record, institutional conduct and program performance, age, mental status, and statistical risk. Michigan law and departmental policy allow parole to be granted without interview if the prisoner's parole guidelines score falls in the high guidelines, provided the prisoner is not serving time for a crime involving a sex offense or a death.

each of the state's six congressional districts and the seventh in an at-large capacity. They serve six-year staggered terms. In Utah, the Board of Corrections appoints the three members of the Board of Pardons for six-year terms. In South Dakota, the Board of Pardons and Paroles has nine members, three appointed by the governor, three by the attorney general, and three by the state supreme court, who serve terms of four years.

Parole boards have been criticized because members may lack relevant background or education. Specific professional qualifications are required for board members in only a few states. Maryland requires "at least a B.A. or B.S. degree in one of the social or behavioral sciences or related fields…[and] at least three (3) years experience in a responsible criminal justice or juvenile justice position, or equivalent experience in a relevant profession such as law or clinical practice." In Vermont, the governor "shall appoint as members persons who have knowledge of and experience in correctional treatment, crime prevention or related fields, and shall give consideration, as far as practicable, to geographic representation to reduce necessary travel to the various parole interview centers of the state." In Iowa, the board must contain one minority group member, one attorney knowledgeable in correctional procedures and issues, and one person with a master's degree in social work or a counseling-related discipline who is knowledgeable in corrections. Pennsylvania requires members of the Board of Probation and Parole to have at least six years of professional experience in parole, probation, social work or related areas (including one year in a supervisory or administrative capacity) and a bachelor's degree.

The role of patronage politics in the selection of parole board members is similar to that of many other responsible government positions, although the relatively low salary and extensive travel requirements tend to make parole board membership less attractive to those with other opportunities for political appointments.

Several months before an offender's parole eligibility review date, an institutional parole officer interviews the inmate. The parole officer prepares a case summary that includes the facts of the inmate's offense; other relevant information such as assaultive behavior or the use of narcotics; personal history; assignments, adjustment, and disciplinary record while in prison; physical and mental condition; and a summary of positive and negative factors.

As the inmate's parole eligibility review date approaches, a parole board panel reviews the case. The offender may be interviewed by one of the members of this panel before the panel votes. For most offenders, the panel will consist of three members of the board, and two of the three panelists must vote for parole

before it can be granted. A few categories of offenders may be paroled only with a two-thirds majority vote of the entire 18-member board.

Parole panel members look at the circumstances and seriousness of the offense; any prior prison commitments; relevant input from victims, family members, and trial officials; the prisoner's adjustment and attitude in prison; the offender's release plan; and factors such as alcohol or drug use, violent or assaultive behavior, deviant sexual behavior, use of a weapon in an offense, institutional adjustment, and emotional stability. Based on the entirety of the available information, the parole panel then determines whether the offender deserves the privilege of parole.

Key Fact

In some states, a panel of parole board members will interview eligible inmates; in others, a parole examiner interviews inmates and reports to the board with a recommendation.

▶ Parole Board Hearings

Typically, from one to three parole board members briefly interview an inmate who is eligible for parole, and they usually hold release hearings in the state's prisons. In Maryland, these hearings are open to the media as well as victims or their designees; in Iowa, the board uses a two-way fiber-optic system for interviews conducted from the board's conference room. The members of the board panel will have available a case folder prepared by an institutional parole officer (or correctional staff person) containing information about each inmate: the presentence investigation report; institutional reports relative to education, training, treatment, physical and psychological examinations, and misconduct; and a release plan, that is, residence, employment, in the event that parole is granted.

In some states, this aspect of parole release is handled by parole examiners who interview the inmate and report back to the board with a recommendation; some states do not conduct hearings or interviews—decisions are made on the basis of written reports. The Pennsylvania Board of Probation and Parole uses a panel of two, a board member and a hearing examiner, to consider the release of a nonviolent offender. Violent offenders are considered by a panel of two board members—in the event of a tie, the chairperson selects an additional member—while certain sex offenders and those convicted of murder require a majority of the board. In Colorado, the manner in which the parole hearing is conducted depends on the seriousness of the inmate's offense. For violent crimes or for inmates with a history of violence, two board members may conduct an initial hearing and submit their recommendation to the seven-member board (four affirmative votes are required for parole release). A single board member may hear nonviolent cases, which can be face-to-face or by telephone; if the decision is to grant parole, an additional board member must agree. In Oklahoma, the Pardon and Parole Board sends a recommendation to the governor who, with the exception of low-level offenses, must sign off on release decisions.

According to David Stanley, the parole hearing is of dubious value: "It is a traumatic experience for the inmate, and parole board members are subjected to the rigors of holding hearings far away from home, with hours spent in travel and in prisons" (1976: 42). Furthermore, Stanley report "hearings are of little use in finding out whether the inmate is likely to succeed on parole." He argues that a strong case can be made for abolishing parole

PRESUMPTIVE PAROLE IN NEW JERSEY

An inmate *shall* be released on parole at the time of parole eligibility unless it is demonstrated by a preponderance of the evidence that the inmate has failed to cooperate in his or her own rehabilitation or that there is a reasonable expectation that the inmate will violate conditions of parole if released on parole.

hearings: In cases where the information in the file and the board's own precedents plainly show that parole must surely be granted or denied, the hearing is a charade. And in those cases where the outcome is not so obvious it is a proceeding in which the inmate is at a great disadvantage and in which he has reason to say anything that will help his chances for parole. The atmosphere at such a hearing is full of tension and latent hostility. Under these circumstances the hearing is an ineffective way to elicit information, evaluate character traits, and give advice, all of which parole boards try to do" (1976: 43).

One way to deal with some of these issues is to permit the inmate to have representation at the hearing. The National Advisory Commission on Criminal Justice Standards and Goals believes that representation helps promote a feeling of fairness and enables an inmate to communicate better and thus participate more fully in the hearing, stating that "representation can also contribute to opening the correctional system, particularly the parole process, to public scrutiny" (1973: 403). The commission makes note of the fact that representation at parole hearings may be considered "annoying" to parole officials—there is fear that the hearing may take the form of an adversary proceeding—but adds that "these inconveniences seem a small price for the prospective gains" (1973: 403).

In Missouri, inmates may have a person of their choice—other than another inmate—at the hearing. This person may offer a statement on behalf of the inmate, ask questions, and provide additional information that may be requested by the parole panel. In Montana, "offenders who appear for parole hearings may have a representative, including an attorney, present with them." The Hawaii Paroling Authority not only permits representation at its release hearings but also offers inmates the right to appointed counsel if they cannot afford to hire an attorney; however, this is unusual, and most jurisdictions do not permit representation at parole hearings. In Pennsylvania, "as the interview is not an adversarial process, the Board does not permit counsel representation at these interviews." In 1979, the U.S. Supreme Court (*Greenholtz v. Inmates*, 442 U.S. 1) ruled that the Constitution does not require that an inmate be given the opportunity to participate in parole board hearings (or to be informed of the reasons for denial of parole). However, Stanley (1976: 43) concludes that, given the present parole system, hearings are necessary as an expression of our national tradition and culture: "A man has his day in court before he is convicted and sentenced. In all sorts of situations we feel outraged if a person is not even confronted with the evidence before something adverse is done to him. In the hearing the prisoner is at least given a chance to state his case, correct erroneous statements, and impress the board with his determination (real or alleged) to reform."

> **Key Fact**
> In most states, inmates are not permitted to be represented at parole release hearings.

► Victim Participation

Most states permit victims or their next of kin to appear before the parole board, and others permit written statements to be considered at the parole hearing. In Nevada, for example, state law "provides that victims of crimes may attend meetings of the Nevada Board of Parole Commissioners. The parole board will provide notice of pending parole hearings if the victim of crime provides the board with a current address and requests such notice." In Pennsylvania, "at the time public notice is given that an inmate is being considered for parole, the board shall also notify any victim or nearest relative who has previously contacted the board of the availability to provide a statement for inclusion in the parole report or to present testimony for inclusion at the parole hearing." And the victim statement relative to physical, psychological, or economic harm is confidential and privileged.

In Alabama, "Victims of violent crimes and families of children who have been abused are notified prior to an inmate's being considered for parole by the Board. The victim's right to be present at the Parole Hearing and to express their concerns in person and in writing to the Board is provided by law." In Connecticut, victims are notified of pending hearings and advised of their right to appear and testify. In Iowa, victims can use the state's two-way fiber-optic communications system to address the board from a site near their residence. New Jersey requires the county prosecutor to notify any victim injured as a result of a crime of the first or second degree, or the nearest relative of a murder victim, of the opportunity to present a statement to be included with the parole reports considered at the parole hearing or to testify before the parole board concerning harm at the time of the parole hearing. Many states include a **victim impact statement** (VIS) as part of the documentation considered by the parole board. While most parole boards invite victims to attend the parole hearing, there are less hearings and victim's rights are thereby less meaningful (Travis and Petersillia, 2001).

"Community corrections agencies have made significant strides in engaging crime victims and those who serve them throughout the correctional process. Many probation agencies have designated victim assistance personnel or have assigned victim services to officers as a collateral duty; nearly all paroling authorities have victim assistance staff who help victims through the parole hearing and parole supervision processes" (American Probation and Parole Association, n.d. [2012]: 2).

The Massachusetts Victims Services Unit provides a wide array of support services to victims who have been certified to receive information regarding offenders by the Criminal

> **Key Fact**
>
> Parole boards typically provide for input by victims through either a personal appearance or the submission of a statement.

VICTIM RIGHTS IN NEW JERSEY

Crime victims have the right to participate in the parole process. Whenever a person is convicted of a first- or second-degree crime, the prosecutor must notify the victim or nearest relative of a murder victim in writing of their right to testify before the parole board prior to the inmate's parole consideration. At the time of parole eligibility, the victim will be invited to submit a written statement or appear personally to testify to a Senior Hearing Officer of the board.

If the victim elects to present testimony in person, a hearing will be scheduled for that purpose. Every effort will be made to accommodate the victim in scheduling the hearing. Most hearings will take place at the parole board's Office of Victim Services but in special situations such as where the victim is physically disabled it may be possible to conduct the hearing elsewhere.

The statement or testimony of the victim should include the following:

- Explanation of the continuing nature and extent of any physical, psychological, or emotional harm or trauma suffered
- The extent of any loss of earnings or ability to work suffered
- The continuing effect of the crime upon the victim's family
- Any other information that would help the parole board determine the likelihood of the inmate committing a new crime, or requiring additional conditions of supervision

The Hearing Officer prepares a report that becomes a permanent part of the inmate's file. Victim statements or testimony are deemed confidential, and will only be used by the State Parole Board. The victim will not confront the inmate in person.

History Systems Board. The unit's staff acts as the parole board's representative in addressing and advancing victim/witness issues by collecting victim/witness input for board consideration, providing timely notifications of parole hearing dates and hearing results, providing information about parole and criminal offender record information, assisting citizens in completing impact statements, directing referrals to other criminal justice or social services agencies for collateral assistance, and heightening the community's level of awareness regarding victim/witness issues through both the media and direct contact.

In Pennsylvania, the Office of Victim Assistance is charged with keeping victims apprised of the status of the inmate and assists in preparing oral or written testimony by registered victims before the parole board. Staff will also refer victims for community services and provide training for correctional, probation, and parole staff on victim issues. In Montana, "If a victim/witness wants to present testimony to the Board members considering an offender's case, arrangements are made for their admittance into the correctional facility where the hearing will be held. Upon request, the Board's Victim Services Specialist accompanies them to the prison. The Victim Services Specialist is there to help the victim/witness understand the process and to answer any questions the victim/witness may have. When a disposition has been rendered in the offender's case, the Victim Services Specialist, upon request, contacts the victim/witness with the hearing results and again answers any questions that may arise." In Montana, board hearings are open to the public.

▶ Parole Board Guidelines

Parole boards usually consider the crime, the length of time served, and the inmate's age, prior criminal history, abuse of alcohol or drugs, and institutional record. Some parole boards may request a recommendation from the prosecutor. All will certainly consider opposition to an inmate's parole from the police and the news media. A study of parole decisions in Massachusetts (Luther, 1995) found that the election of a "law and order" governor caused the board (whose membership remained almost unchanged) to decrease parole release rates, particularly for high-security inmates for whom they were virtually eliminated. The widespread use of parole guidelines has reduced the importance of general criteria.

As criticism of parole and parole boards began to mount in the 1970s, the U.S. Board of Parole engaged a group of researchers to develop a model for improved decision making. In particular, the board was interested in a means of reducing disparity and making the decision-making process intelligible (and defensible) to both inmates and the public. The researchers derived a set of variables they saw as fairly representative of those used by board members in making decisions—the most salient being the seriousness of the offense and the parole prognosis. They also conducted a two-year study of 2,500 federal parolees and uncovered a variety of "success factors," which they reduced to seven variables. The combined variables for severity of offense and parole prognosis were arranged in the form of a grid to determine the actual length of imprisonment.

Parole board guidelines typically go well beyond the *medical/rehabilitative model* on which the indeterminate sentence is often presumed to be based. Indeed, satisfactory progress in those institutional programs that are "rehabilitative" may not even affect the parole decision. Good institutional behavior is *expected*, not rewarded, although poor behavior can be punished with denial of parole. In fact, the institutional adjustment of an offender has never been an accurate guide for predicting postinstitutional behavior (Dolan, Lunden, and Barberet, 1987); some evidence exists that certain offenders (e.g., substance abusers and professional criminals) often perform well while in prison, but back in the community they tend to recidivate. In effect, the use of guidelines whose primary focus is *just deserts* is a form of deferred sentencing. Some critics claim that no justification exists for deferring sentence (the term of imprisonment) and that it creates problems by adding to the offender's uncertainty. Others argue that the parole board is relatively free of the "heat" that certain crimes and criminals can generate. The board does not typically operate with the same high visibility of a court; unlike a sentencing judge, the parole board is not normally under the gaze of the community and news media. These observers stress that the parole board, using guidelines, is better equipped to make a rational decision commensurate with just deserts than is a sentencing judge. The possibility of parole release also serves as an incentive for inmates to control their behavior and take advantage of rehabilitative programming.

Guidelines used by state parole boards consider the seriousness of the present offense and prior criminal history; most also consider rehabilitative items and parole prognosis. For example, the Georgia Board of Pardons and Paroles, in a mix of the classical and positive views, states: "Justice demands that punishment should be tailored to fit both the offense and the offender." A board hearing examiner identifies an inmate's crime severity level from a table of offenses ranked in seven levels from lowest to highest in severity (the higher the severity, the longer the time the inmate will be recommended to serve). Then the hearing examiner calculates the inmate's parole success likelihood by adding weighted factors with proven predictive value from the inmate's criminal and social history. A history of factors such as prior imprisonment, parole or probation failure, illegal drug use or possession, and joblessness would increase the risk of paroling the inmate and cause him or her to be recommended for longer confinement. The parole board may go beyond the guideline range in the event of mitigating or aggravating circumstances, but the detailed reason for such decisions must be provided to the inmate in writing.

▶ Institutional Parole Services

The primary responsibility of institutional parole staff is preparation of reports on inmates for the parole board. Staff may also help inmates secure furloughs, work release, or halfway house placement and may assist with personal problems ranging from matters relating to spouse and children to questions of a technical or legal nature.

Under ideal conditions, when an offender is first received at an institution, a member of the parole staff interviews him or her. The results of the interview, psychiatric and psychological tests, and the information in the presentence report are then used to help plan an institutional program for the inmate. Parole staff periodically update the material with additional information and discuss release plans with inmates and request the field staff to visit and interview family members and prospective employers. When an inmate is ready to meet the parole board, staff provide a report on the inmate that includes an evaluation of changes made since the offender was first received at the prison. The report may also contain a completed parole guidelines form and a recommendation if requested by the board.

Institutional parole staff may also hold group meetings with new inmates to orient them about parole; these group sessions are then followed by individual interviews. At preparole group sessions, parole staff attempts to lower anxiety about meeting the board or hearing examiners. When an inmate has been granted parole or becomes

INSTITUTIONAL PAROLE OFFICER, CONNECTICUT

In correctional institutions, the parole officer performs case management and counseling activities for an assigned group of inmates; meets with and interviews inmates who are eligible for parole consideration; reviews Department of Correction files and retrieves data relevant to offense and sentencing information; verifies parole eligibility and discharge dates; obtains information and verifies inmates' involvement in rehabilitative programs; provides inmates with information regarding parole process; conducts administrative reviews of cases and makes disposition recommendations to Board of Parole in accordance with agency criteria; coordinates attendance of victim and inmate families at Board of Parole hearings; ensures completeness of inmates' files; attends Board of Parole hearings and serves as administrative hearing officer; presents case documentation to board members; answers questions from board members regarding case files; takes notes at Board hearings, records official minutes, processes disposition of board hearings; and processes violation of parole cases.

eligible for conditional release, he or she will meet with a parole staff member for a final discussion.

In some jurisdictions, institutional parole staff is responsible for notifying victims and local law enforcement agencies of the impending release of certain offenders. Some states require that when an offender is released, the police in the area where the parolee is to reside or where the crime occurred be notified. In some instances, the parolee must register in person with the local law enforcement agency. Institutional parole staff must determine the probable disposition of any warrants lodged against an inmate. When appropriate, the staff arrange for an out-of-state program under the Interstate Compact (discussed in Chapter 10). In some states, nonparole institutional staff members perform the same or similar functions as institutional parole officers; these persons sometimes have the title of *correctional counselor*; in North Dakota, they are institutional case managers.

Field service staff who usually operate out of district offices located throughout the state conduct investigations requested by institutional staff relative to parole release programs. Field staff may also be involved in a variety of special programs, such as work release and furloughs. In New York, some field officers are assigned to correctional facilities to supervise Temporary Release participants—inmates permitted by the corrections department to work, attend school, provide community service, and reestablish family ties (furloughs).

▶ Parole Conditions

Probation and parole regulations in different agencies tend to be similar (Figures 5.1 and 5.2). They typically exhort the offender to live a law-abiding life, work, and support dependents. They require that the offender inform the P/P officer of his or her residence and that permission be secured before leaving the jurisdiction of the court. Some require that the probationer/parolee obtain permission before getting married, applying for a motor vehicle license, or contracting any indebtedness. Some agencies require clients to carry an identification card at all times that reveals their supervision status and contains a telephone number for law enforcement agencies to use. Many departments require that the offender pay a supervision fee, make restitution, or do community service as a condition (discussed in Chapter 2).

Key Fact

Parole conditions are similar throughout most jurisdictions and are also similar or identical to probation regulations. Conditions can generally be grouped into standard conditions and special conditions.

1. I will proceed directly to the area to which I have been released and, within 24 hours of my release, make my arrival report to that office of the Division of Parole unless other instructions are designated on my release agreement.

2. I will make office and/or written reports as directed.

3. I will not leave the State of New York or any other state to which I am released or transferred, or any area defined in writing by my Parole Officer without permission.

4. I will permit my Parole Officer to visit me at my residence and/or place of employment and I will permit the search and inspection of my person, residence, and property. I will discuss any proposed changes in my residence, employment, or program status with my Parole Officer. I understand that I have an immediate and continuing duty to notify my Parole Officer of any changes in my residence, employment, or program status when circumstances beyond my control make prior discussion impossible.

5. I will reply promptly, fully, and truthfully to any inquiry of, or communication by my Parole Officer or other representative of the Division of Parole.

6. I will notify my Parole Officer immediately any time I am in contact with, or arrested by, any law enforcement agency. I understand that I have a continuing duty to notify my Parole Officer of such contact or arrest.

7. I will not be in the company of, or fraternize with any person I know to have a criminal record or whom I know to have been adjudicated a Youthful Offender, except for accidental encounters in public places, work, school, or in any other instance with the permission of my Parole Officer.

8. I will not behave in such manner as to violate the provisions of any law to which I am subject, which provides for a penalty of imprisonment, nor will my behavior threaten the safety or wellbeing of myself or others.

9. I will not own, possess, or purchase any shotgun, rifle, or firearm of any type without the written permission of my Parole Officer. I will not own, possess, or purchase any deadly weapon as defined in the Penal Law or any dangerous knife, dirk, razor, stiletto, or imitation pistol. In addition, I will not own, possess or purchase any instrument readily capable of causing physical injury without a satisfactory explanation for ownership, possession or purchase.

10. In the event that I leave the jurisdiction of the State of New York, I hereby waive my right to resist extradition to the State of New York from any state in the Union and from any territory or country outside the United States. This waiver shall be in full force and effect until I am discharged from Parole or Conditional Release. I fully understand that I have the right under the Constitution of the United States and under law to contest any effort to extradite me from another state and return me to New York, and I freely and knowingly waive this right as a condition of my Parole or Conditional Release.

11. I will not use or possess any drug paraphernalia or use or possess any controlled substance without proper medical authorization.

12. Special Conditions: (as specified by the Board of Parole, Parole Officer or other authorized representative).

13. I will fully comply with the instructions of my Parole Officer and obey such special additional written conditions as he/she, a member of the Board of Parole, or an authorized representative of the Division of Parole, may impose.

FIGURE 5.1 New York State Conditions of Parole

Name of Offender _____ DOC Number: _____

The Indiana Parole Board hereby imposes the following stipulations upon the parole of the above referenced offender. The stipulations outlined below are effective from the date the offender receives notice through the facility release coordinator or a parole officer. Only those stipulations checked apply

_____ 1. You shall have no contact with _____ or his/her family. "Contact" means face-to-face, telephone, electronic, correspondence, or via third parties.

_____ 2. You must attend, participate, and successfully complete the VOA Zero Tolerance Program. This program includes electronic monitoring and residential treatment.

_____ 3. You shall submit to a substance abuse evaluation and follow all recommendations.

_____ 4. You shall submit to a mental health evaluation and follow all recommendations.

_____ 5. You shall not use, consume, or possess illegal controlled substances, alcohol, or beverages containing alcohol.

_____ 6. You shall not frequent or be present at any establishment whose main business purpose is the selling, distribution, serving, drinking of alcoholic beverages, or illegal controlled substances.

_____ 7. You must not travel to, through or be present _____ without prior, written approval of your parole officer. Your parole officer shall not give you written approval without first consulting with the Parole Board.

_____ 8. You shall attend, participate and successfully complete anger management counseling/treatment.

_____ 9. You shall attend, participate and successfully complete the residential program at _____.

_____ 10. You must participate in and successfully complete _____.

_____ 11. Intensive Supervision.

_____ 12. You shall attend, participate and successfully complete the residential treatment program at Salvation Army Adult Rehabilitation Center.

_____ 13. Other:

FIGURE 5.2   Special Condition of Parole, Indiana

▶ Legal Decisions Affecting the Parole Board

In 1970, the U.S. Court of Appeals for the Second District considered the case of *Menechino v. Oswald* (430 F.2d 403). Joseph Menechino (a "jailhouse lawyer") was serving a 20-year-to-life sentence in New York for murder in the second degree.

He was paroled in 1963 and returned to prison as a parole violator 16 months later. Subsequently, he appeared before the board of parole and admitted consorting with persons having criminal records and giving misleading information to his PO. Two years later, Menechino appeared before the board for a reparole hearing and parole was denied. He brought a court action claiming that his rights were violated by the absence of legal counsel at both his revocation and parole release hearings. The court ruled:

- A parole proceeding is nonadversarial in nature because both parties, the board and the inmate, have the same concern—rehabilitation.

Key Fact

An imprisoned offender has no *liberty interest*, but a parolee does.

- Parole release hearings are not fact-finding determinations because the board makes a determination based on numerous tangible and intangible factors.

- The inmate has "no present private interest" to be protected (he has no **liberty interest**) because he is already imprisoned—has nothing to lose—and this "interest" is required before due process is applicable.

The court further stated, "It is questionable whether a board of parole is even required to hold a hearing on the question of whether a prisoner should be released on parole." Relative to the question of parole revocation, however, the court advised that a minimum of procedural due process should be provided because at this stage a parolee has a present private interest in the possible loss of conditional freedom.

In 1979, the U.S. Supreme Court reversed a court of appeals decision in a class action brought by inmates of the Nebraska Penal and Correctional Complex in *Greenholtz v. Inmates of Nebraska Penal and Correctional Complex* (442 U.S. 1, 1979). The inmates claimed that they had been unconstitutionally denied parole release by the board of parole, but the Court ruled:

- A convicted inmate has no constitutional right to be released before the expiration of his or her lawful sentence.

- Although a state may establish a parole release system, it has no constitutional obligation to do so. According to Nebraska law, at least once a year initial parole hearings must be held for every inmate, regardless of parole eligibility. At the initial hearing, the board examines the inmate's total record and provides an informal hearing during which the inmate can present statements and documents in support of a claim for release.

- If the board determines from the record and hearing that the inmate is a likely candidate for release, a final hearing is scheduled. However, the Nebraska law provides that the board "shall order an inmate's release unless in the final hearing, the board concludes that inmate's release should be deferred for at least one of four specified reasons."

This procedure is a somewhat unusual, possibly peculiar to the state of Nebraska, and Rolando del Carmen points out that it amounts to a "state-law created liberty interest," an expectation of being granted parole release (1985: 50). As noted earlier, whenever this liberty interest exists, some minimum due process is required. Del Carmen and Paul Louis conclude that "an inmate does not have a constitutional right to be released on parole, nor does he or she enjoy any constitutional right in the parole release process. In more succinct language, the parole board can do just about anything it pleases [with respect to release], and whatever it says and does prevails because it enjoys immense discretion" (1988: 20). Although parole boards are not constitutionally required to provide reasons for denying release, parole guidelines often provide inmates with such documentation.

Key Fact

Inmates have no *liberty interest* and thus no right to parole, so due process is not required at parole release hearing.

▶ Parole Board Liability

Although state agencies are generally exempt from liability for their governmental activities unless sovereign immunity is waived, immunity ordinarily is unavailable to individual state officers who are sued. Therefore, members of a state parole board may be sued as individuals.

In a unanimous decision (*Martinez v. California*, 444 U.S. 277, 1980), the Supreme Court affirmed the constitutionality of statutory provisions that provide parole officials with **immunity** from tort claims. In this instance, Thomas, a parolee convicted of attempted rape, tortured and murdered 15-year-old Mary Martinez five months after his release from prison. Thomas had been labeled as not amenable to treatment, and the sentencing court recommended that he not be paroled. Nevertheless, after serving five years of a 1- to 200-year sentence, Thomas was paroled. The deceased girl's parents argued that in releasing Thomas, parole authorities subjected their daughter to deprivation of her life without due process of law.

Justice Stevens, delivering the opinion for the Court, stated, "We cannot accept the contention that this statute deprives Thomas' (a paroled offender) victim of her life without due process of law because it condoned a parole decision that led indirectly to her death. The statute neither authorized nor immunized the deliberate killing of any human being. This statute merely provides a defense to potential state tort law liability. At most, the availability of such a defense may have encouraged members of the parole board to take somewhat greater risks of recidivism in exercising their authority to release prisoners than they otherwise might. But the basic risk that repeat offenses may occur is always present in any parole system." But because parole boards act only in a *quasi*-judicial capacity, they do not enjoy the total immunity conferred on judges. Justice Stevens pointed this out that in this decision: "We need not and do not decide that a parole official could never be deemed to 'deprive' someone of life by action taken in connection with a prisoner on parole."

> **Key Fact**
> Parole board members do not have the total immunity enjoyed by judges.

▶ Executive Clemency

All states and the federal government (Article II, Section 2, of the Constitution) have provisions for **executive clemency** (reprieve, commutation, pardon). In 31 states and the federal government, the chief executive holds the final clemency power; and in most of these states, the parole board or a clemency board appointed by the governor investigates clemency applications at the request of the governor. In some states, clemency authority is vested entirely in a special board, usually a board of pardons and paroles. In South Carolina, the Board of Paroles and Pardons can issue a pardon by a vote of at least two-thirds of its members. In North Dakota, there is a pardon advisory board made up of the attorney general, two members of the parole board, and two gubernatorial appointees, but the Board of Pardons in Pennsylvania is completely separate from the parole board. Some states conduct formal hearings, and the governor generally must report annually to the legislature on all clemencies granted.

> **Key Fact**
> Executive clemency consists of the reprieve, the commutation, and the pardon.

A **reprieve** is a *temporary* suspension of the execution of sentence. As noted in Chapter 2, probation developed (in part) out of the judicial reprieve. Its use today is limited and usually concerns cases in which capital punishment has been ordered. In such cases, a governor or the president of the United States can grant a reprieve—a stay of execution—to provide more time for legal action or other deliberations.

In Georgia, the Board of Pardons and Paroles may grant a reprieve lasting a few hours or a few days to an inmate so that he or she may visit a critically ill member of the family or attend the funeral of an immediate member of the family. A reprieve may also be granted in Georgia when it is shown that an inmate is suffering from a definable illness for which necessary treatment is available only outside the state prison system. An inmate granted a reprieve has the reprieve period credited to the sentence if he or she does not violate any of its conditions.

A **commutation** is a modification of sentence to the benefit of an offender. Commutation has been used when an inmate provided some assistance to the prison staff, sometimes during prison riots. Commutation may also be granted to inmates with a severe illness, such as cancer or AIDS. The laws governing commutation differ from state to state. In New York, an inmate sentenced to more than one year who has served at least one-half of the minimum period of imprisonment and who is not otherwise eligible for release or parole may have his or her sentence commuted by the governor. In Georgia, the Board of Pardons and Paroles will consider commuting a sentence when it receives substantial evidence that the sentence is excessive, illegal, unconstitutional, or void; evidence that justice would be served by a commutation; and evidence that commutation would be in the best interests of society and the inmate. The board may also consider commutation of sentences of death after all other legal remedies have been exhausted; a person whose death sentence has been commuted by the board cannot be pardoned or paroled before serving 25 years. In Maryland, correctional personnel identify candidates who meet criteria established by the governor's office for commutation, and their names are submitted to the parole board for a recommendation to the governor.

A **pardon** means that an individual is fully forgiven from all the legal consequences of his or her crime and conviction—direct and collateral—including the punishment, whether imprisonment, fine, or whatever penalty is provided for by law. Following the American Revolution, it was necessary to find a new basis for the pardoning power to replace the English theory that it resided in the king as the fountainhead of justice and mercy. This new basis was found in the theory that the power to issue a **pardon** was a sovereign power, inherent in the state but not necessarily inherent in the chief executive or in any branch of government. Because the people were the ultimate sovereign, the power resided in them, and they could provide for its exercise through any agency of government they deemed proper. Although historically the executive would seem the most natural agency with which to entrust this power, the attitude of the American people after the Revolution did not lead to this conclusion. The struggle with the mother country had left them suspicious of the chief executive. This conflict was natural enough because the royal governor was not usually sympathetic to the colonists (the champion of the people was usually the lower house of the legislature). Not surprisingly, the early constitutions that replaced the colonial charters tended to place restrictions on the governor's power in many respects, including the power to pardon: Only five states left this power with the governor alone; six, including the newly admitted state of Vermont, provided that the governor could pardon only with the consent of the executive council; Georgia deprived the governor of the pardoning power entirely, giving him only power to reprieve until the meeting of the assembly, which could then make such disposition of the matter as it saw fit; and Connecticut and Rhode Island continued to function under their colonial charters, by which the pardoning power was exercised by the general assembly.

By the time the federal Constitution was written, however, opinion had begun to swing back toward placing greater power in the hands of the governor. The framers of the Constitution gave the pardoning power to the president without any limitations as to its exercise or supervision by any other official or agency, and President George Washington was the first to exercise this power in 1795 (when he granted amnesty to participants in the so-called Whiskey Rebellion). The executive councils that several states had set up as a means of preventing too much power from being vested in one person began to lose favor about the same time, and several states began abolishing them, giving the power to the governor. Toward the end of the nineteenth century, an overwhelming movement occurred to give the governor some assistance in this task by providing an advisory pardon officer or pardon board. Some states set up pardon boards not merely to advise the governor but to actually exercise pardoning power, although the governor was a member, if not the controlling member, of the board (U.S. Attorney General, 1939). As noted in Chapter 4, the pardon has been used historically in the United States as a form of "parole." As the indeterminate sentence came into use, pardon boards, originally established to advise the governor with respect to release, began to act independently, developing into parole boards. Despite widespread use of parole, however, the power of pardon has continued. In South Carolina, the Board of Paroles and Pardons can issue a pardon by a vote of at least two-thirds of its members. In Utah, the Board of Pardons, an independent state agency, has rather extraordinary powers. This three-member body serves as a board of parole, deciding when and under what conditions persons convicted and serving sentences should be released from imprisonment; in addition, the board can commute sentences of death, reduce terms of imprisonment, and completely terminate an offender's sentence, regardless of whether he or she is an inmate or on parole. The board also has absolute pardoning authority for the state and can forgive the sentence and restore civil rights, although this power is rarely exercised. In Utah, executive clemency is usually limited to deciding on the granting of relief from disabilities, a limited pardon that restores certain civil and political rights, such as the right to apply to vote (the local board of registrars makes final decisions) and to hold certain licenses. To be considered for such a pardon, a person discharged from prison without parole must wait two years, parolees wait five years under supervision or two years after discharge, and probationers wait two years after discharge from supervision. The pardon report, which is prepared by state probation and parole officers, is exhaustive and allows the board to determine whether the applicant has become a law-abiding person and a useful citizen in the community.

In California, the Board of Prison Terms investigates all pardon petitions from persons who have been free of criminal conduct for 9.5 years since discharge from probation, parole, or custody. In Maryland, a pardon requires at least five years of exemplary crime-free behavior following release from incarceration and after expiration of any parole supervision. Pardon requests are received by the parole board, which investigates and makes a recommendation to the governor. A governor's pardon restores citizenship rights to the person who has demonstrated a high standard of constructive behavior following conviction for an offense. Pardon applications are considered only after an offender has been discharged from probation or parole for at least 10 years and has not engaged in further criminal conduct. The 10-year rule may be waived in truly exceptional circumstances if the applicant can demonstrate an earlier need for the pardon.

The basis for a pardon may vary in different states, but the pardon is not used extensively anywhere. In New York, the only basis for a pardon is new evidence indicating that the person did not commit the offense for which he or she was convicted. In Florida, a pardon is a declaration of record that a person is relieved from the legal consequences of a particular conviction; as in New York, a pardon will be granted only to a person who proves his or her innocence of the crime for which convicted. Florida also has a *first-offender pardon*, which carries no implication of innocence and may be granted to an actual first offender. This pardon restores civil and political rights and removes legal disabilities resulting from the conviction. A *10-year pardon* works the same way and may be granted offenders who have had no further convictions for 10 years after completing his or her sentence. In Georgia, a pardon is a declaration of record by the board that a person is relieved from the legal consequences of a particular conviction; it restores civil and political rights and removes all legal disabilities resulting from the conviction. A pardon may be granted in two instances: First, a pardon may be granted when a person proves his or her innocence of the crime for which he or she was convicted under Georgia law; second, a pardon that does not imply innocence may be granted to an applicant who has completed his or her full sentence obligation, including any probated sentence and paying any fine, and who has thereafter completed five years without any criminal involvement (the five-year waiting period may be waived if it is shown to be detrimental to the applicant's livelihood by delaying his or her qualifying for employment in a chosen profession). The president of the United States typically grants hundreds of pardons (to persons convicted in federal court).

In Texas, executive clemency is the power of the governor to grant a full or conditional pardon, a full pardon based on innocence, a commutation of sentence, a remission of a fine or forfeiture resulting from a criminal conviction, an emergency medical reprieve, or a 30-day reprieve of execution. In accordance with the Texas Constitution, the governor may grant executive clemency only on the recommendation of the Board of Pardons and Paroles. The board is limited to recommending clemency and to setting minimal eligibility requirements for clemency applicants.

> **Key Fact**
>
> Most chief executives have the power of executive clemency whose exercise usually involves a recommendation from the parole board.

A full pardon restores certain citizenship rights forfeited by law as the result of a criminal conviction, such as the right to vote, the right to serve on a jury, and the right to hold public office. In Texas and many other states, voting rights are automatically restored upon completion a felony sentence, even without a pardon In Montana, with the exception of jury duty, upon termination of state supervision, the person is restored civil rights and full citizenship. A full pardon will remove barriers to some (but not all) types of employment and professional licensing—licenses are granted at the discretion of the state licensing boards of each profession. A pardon will not restore eligibility to become a licensed peace officer in Texas.

Summary

- A parole agency can provide three basic services: parole release, parole supervision, and executive clemency.
- Parole services are usually administered centrally on a statewide basis.
- There are two basic models for administering parole: independent and consolidated.
- The independent model may be indifferent to institutional programs, while under the consolidated model the parole board may be under pressure to stress institutional factors in making parole decisions.
- In states that do not have a parole board, inmates can be released early on good time allowances.
- In most states that have parole boards, the governor chooses members.
- Qualifications for parole board members vary from state to state. In some states, a panel of parole board members will interview eligible inmates; in others, a parole examiner interviews inmates and reports to the board with a recommendation.
- The Supreme Court has ruled that inmates are not entitled to representation at parole release hearings—they have no *liberty interest.*
- Most states permit victims or their next of kin to appear before the parole board, and others permit written statements to be considered at the parole hearing.
- Parole board guidelines typically go well beyond the *medical/rehabilitative model* on which the indeterminate sentence is often presumed to be based.
- Parole board guidelines make the release decision process intelligible.
- The primary responsibility of institutional parole staff is preparation of reports on inmates for the parole board.
- Probation and parole regulations in different agencies tend to be similar and typically exhort the offender to live a law-abiding life, work, and support dependents.
- While an inmate has no *liberty interest*, a parolee does.
- Parole board members do not have the total immunity enjoyed by judges.
- Executive clemency consists of the reprieve, the commutation, and the pardon.
- The parole board has a role in executive clemency.

Key Terms

commutation *107*
conditional release *95*
consolidated model *94*
executive clemency *107*
field services *94*

good time *95*
immunity *106*
independent model *94*
institutional services *94*
liberty interest *106*

pardon *108*
parole board guidelines *101*
reprieve *107*
victim impact statement *100*

Internet Connections

American Probation and Parole Association: **appa-net.org**

National Institute of Corrections: **nicic.org**

Parole board links: **crimelynx.com**

Review Questions

1. What are the three basic services provided by a parole agency?
2. Why is the administration of parole less complex than that of probation?
3. How do the two basic models for administering parole differ?
4. What are the criticisms of each of the models for administering parole?
5. How are parole board members selected?
6. What has the Supreme Court ruled with respect to inmate representation at parole release hearings?
7. What is the primary purpose of parole guidelines?
8. What is the primary responsibility of institutional parole staff?
9. What are the typical conditions of parole?
10. How does the liberty interest of a parolee differ from that of inmate?
11. How does the legal immunity of judges differ from that of parole board members?
12. What is the role of a parole board in executive clemency?

Research has revealed that interventions "based on punishment and deterrence appeared to increase criminal recidivism (most often equated with re-arrest within 12 months after intervention); whereas therapeutic approaches based on counseling, skill building and multiple services had the greatest impact in reducing further criminal behavior."

—Patrick M. Clark, 2011: 1

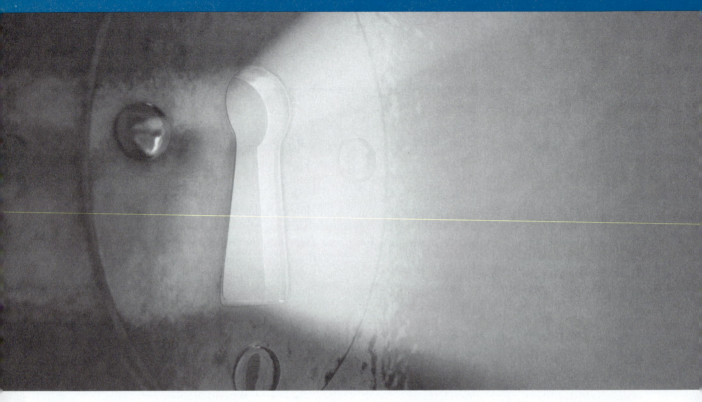

6 Treatment Theory and Practice

LEARNING OBJECTIVES

This chapter will enable the student to:

1 *Distinguish between theories of crime that emphasize nature or nurture.*

2 *Understand psychoanalytic theory and the importance of the unconscious in human behavior.*

3 *Discuss stages of psychosexual development and their association with types deviant/criminal behavior.*

4 *Explain how the id, ego, and superego are connected to criminal behavior.*

5 *Distinguish between the medical model contemporary and social work.*

6 *Understand Motivational Interviewing and how it differs from other therapeutic approaches.*

7 *Discuss behavior modification and cognitive behavior therapy and how they are applied in probation and parole.*

8 *State the basic premise of Reality Therapy.*

9 *Appreciate how the reality therapist works with offenders.*

10 *Describe how group work differs from the one-to-one situation of social casework.*

11 *Appreciate how the theory of anomie offers the probation/parole officer practical suggestions for responding to the real problems encountered in practice?*

12 *Discuss how the theory of differential association is expressed in probation/parole regulations.*

13 *Explain the theory of Neutralization.*

14 *Discuss how differential opportunity theory integrates anomie with differential association.*

15 *State how social control theory links criminal behavior with weak connections to conventional society.*

16 *Explain the theory of drift and its policy implications.*

17 *Appreciate the implications of labeling.*

Probation and parole (P/P) have traditionally been viewed as having two primary goals—protection of the community and rehabilitation of the offender. Of course, the two are not incompatible: Rehabilitation of the offender improves community safety. During the "Nothing Works" decades—late 1970s to the early twenty-first century—rehabilitation was discounted in favor of "just deserts," and gradually control at the expense of treatment became prominent in P/P. In the second decade of the twenty-first century, offender treatment is once again fashionable.

Some modes of treatment are more easily applied than others to P/P practice. Some methods require more training than most P/P officers have received, and their use may require an expenditure of time that is not realistic in most P/P agencies. In practice, P/P officers use a variety of techniques, tailoring them to different clients. Effective supervision is based on sound theoretical principles, yet rehabilitative services tend to be atheoretical (Russell, Latessa, and Travis, 2005). P/P officers often use techniques without understanding the theoretical basis or even recognizing them as part of a particular mode of rehabilitation—"flying by the seat of the pants" is often characteristic of P/P. Nevertheless, most P/P officers, even when they do not provide extensive direct treatment, refer clients to programs for such problems as substance abuse, pedophilia, unemployment, and mental illness. Knowledge of various modalities, therefore, is important in P/P. Treatment, no matter the discipline, requires both theoretical knowledge and sound principles applied to specific cases. Being knowledgeable about both theory and therapy enables the P/P officer to make appropriate referrals, understand treatment reports, and better relate to rehabilitation professionals. Those with sufficient training can provide direct treatment.

Key Fact

Some methods of treatment require more training than most P/P officers have received, and their use may require an expenditure of time that is not realistic in most P/P agencies.

Key Fact

Being knowledgeable about both theory and therapy enables the P/P officer to make appropriate referrals, understand treatment reports, and better relate to rehabilitation professionals.

NATURE VERSUS NURTURE

Theories of crime can be distinguished by how the authors or supporters conceive of the nature of human behavior. Prominent in any discussion of human behavior is the *nature versus nurture* controversy. Both sides address the same question: What is the dominant force shaping human behavior? Supporters of the *nature* position answer that behavior can best be explained by genetic, biological, or other properties inherent in the individual. In short, human behavior is largely inherited. Conversely, proponents of the *nurture* position look to the social environment for the causal factors; that is, human behavior is largely the product of social interaction.

▶ What Is a Theory

A theory is part of an explanation—a statement about the relationship between two classes of phenomena that permits us to better understand our environment, which helps to explain events by organizing them in the world so that they can be placed in perspective. A theory also explains the causes of past events and predicts when, where, and how future events will occur. "A theory consists of a set of assumptions; concepts regarding events, situations, individuals, and groups; and propositions that describe the interrelationships among the various assumptions and concepts" (Binder and Geis, 1983: 3).

Theories are abstract, a necessary dimension if they are to be applied to more than one specific set of circumstances, facts, or observations. We cannot determine the cause of particular criminal behavior based on a satisfactory explanation for a single case; however, if enough individual cases fit into the same explanation, we can develop a theory and test it against future cases of criminal behavior. The ability to predict is a measure of a theory's validity. Validity requires testing, and any theory that cannot be tested—and, therefore, disproved—is not (according to scientific principles) a theory. A purported cause of crime that does not permit testing, therefore, has more in common with theology than criminology—it lacks scientific merit.

There are three basic theoretical models for treatment in P/P:

1. Psychoanalytic theory
2. Reality therapy
3. Behavior/learning theory

▶ Psychoanalytic Theory

Psychoanalytic theory refers to a body of work fathered by Sigmund Freud (1856–1939). Over the years, the theory has undergone change, although Freud's basic contribution, his exposition of the importance of phenomena of the unconscious in human behavior, remains: Personality is strongly influenced by determinants in the unconscious that develop early in life. Rather than being driven by reason, that is, rational thought, human behavior is largely controlled of our unconscious. Simply put, this concept argues that the most important determinants of our behavior are not available to our conscious thought (Cloninger, 2013). These determinants evolve during the stages of psychological development.

Freud postulated unconscious processes in the stages of psychological development that, although not directly observable, were inferred from case studies with patients. He divided mental phenomena into three groups:

1. *Conscious.* Contents of a person's thoughts at any given time

2. *Preconscious.* Thoughts and memories that can easily be called into conscious awareness

3. *Unconscious.* Repressed feelings and experiences that can be made conscious only with great difficulty

"The unconscious is essentially dynamic and capable of profoundly affecting conscious ideational or emotional life without the individual's being aware of this influence" (Healy, Bronner, and Bowers, 1930: 24). Unconscious feelings and experiences are related to normal stages of psychosexual development through which each person passes on the way to adulthood (psychosexual maturity). Memories of these stages of psychosexual development are repressed and, therefore, unconscious—not part of conscious or preconscious memory—yet they drive behavior and serve as a source of anxiety and guilt, the basis for psychoneurosis and psychosis. The stages overlap, and transition from one to the other is gradual, the time spans being approximate:

1. *Oral stage.* During the oral stage (birth to 18 months), the mouth, lips, and tongue are the predominant organs of pleasure for the infant. In the normal infant, the source of pleasure becomes associated with the touch and warmth of the parent, who gratifies oral needs. When this is lacking, deviant behavior, particularly drug and alcohol abuse, is to be expected in the adult. Drugs and alcohol serve as a substitute for maternal attachment; in adults, drug abuse is seen as a regression to an unfulfilled oral stage. The infant actually enters the world a "criminal," that is, unsocialized and devoid of self-control.

2. *Anal stage.* In the anal stage (18 months to 3 years), the anus becomes the most important site of erotic interest and gratification. Pleasure is closely connected to the retention and expulsion of feces as well as the bodily processes involved and the feces themselves. During this stage, the only partially socialized child acts out rather destructive urges, breaking toys or even injuring living organisms such as insects or small animals. A great deal of psychopathology in the adult, including violent behavior and sociopathological personality disorders, is traced to disruptions during this stage.

3. *Genital stage.* Erotic interest becomes associated with the genitals during the genital stage (3 to 5 years) and in normal persons is maintained by them thereafter. During this period of life, the child experiences *Oedipus* (in boys) and *Electra* (in girls) *wishes* in the form of fantasies of incest with the parent of the opposite sex. The healthy child must relinquish the dependent paternal/maternal attachment and deal with the feelings of sadness that result. Sexual problems, such as pedophilia, are linked to this stage when the adult remains fixated on a parent and is not attracted to adults of the opposite sex. Drug and alcohol abuse are also traced to failures during this stage of development (see Abadinsky, 2013).

4. *Latent stage.* In the latent stage (6 to 13 years), there is a lessening of interest in sexual organs, as well as an expanded relationship with playmates of the same sex and age.

5. *Adolescence-adulthood stage.* A reawakening of genital interest and awareness occurs at the adolescence–adulthood stage. The incestuous wish is repressed and emerges in terms of mature (adult) sexuality.

> **Key Fact**
>
> According to psychoanalytic theory, id, ego, and superego explain human behavior.

When a person is passing through the first three stages of psychosexual development, the mind simultaneously undergoes the development of three psychic phenomena:

1. *Id.* The id is a mass of powerful drives that seeks discharge or gratification—it is asocial and devoid of values and logical processes. Constituting wishes, urges, and psychic tensions, according to Freud (1933: 104), the id is "a cauldron of seething excitement," seeking pleasure and avoiding pain. The id is the driving force of the personality; and from birth until about 7 months of age, it is the total psychic apparatus.

2. *Ego.* Through contact with the reality around them and the influence of training, infants modify their expressions of id drives. This development of the ego is prag-

matic and permits maximum gratification with a minimum of difficulty in the form of environmental restrictions—learning from experience. Without the ego to act as a restraining influence, the id would destroy the person through its blind striving to gratify instincts in complete disregard for reality. As a result of disturbances in psychosexual development, a person may remain at the ego level of development: "The child remains asocial or behaves as if he had become social without having made actual adjustment to the demands of society" (Aichhorn, 1963: 4), which requires a healthy superego. Feelings of rage and aggression associated with the anal stage lurk in the background awaiting an opportunity to break through to satisfaction.

3. *Superego.* Often viewed as a conscience-type mechanism, the **superego** exercises a criticizing power, a sense of morality over the ego: "It represents the whole demands of morality, and we see all at once that our moral sense of guilt is the expression of tension between the ego [which strives to discharge id drives] and the super-ego" (Freud, 1933: 88). A healthy superego is the result of identification with parents—the superego is an internalized parent—that is accomplished during the genital stage of psychosexual development. In Freud's words, "The role which the super-ego undertakes later in life is at first played by external power, by parental authority" (1933: 89). "The super-ego then supports the ego in controlling the instinctive [id] impulses" (Smart, 1970: 45).

A delicate balance is maintained by unconscious forces as a person experiences various sociocultural and biological aspects of existence. When the balance is upset, the psyche passes from the normal to the psychoneurotic or the psychotic (mental illness). The fact that a thin line exists between the normal and the neurotic and between the neurotic and the psychotic is basic to psychoanalytic theory. In fact, only a difference of degree separates the "normal" and the "abnormal": The degree to which there is a malfunctioning in psychic apparatus is the degree to which a person is "abnormal" or "sick," that is, socially dysfunctional.

► Crime and the Superego

"[The] psychoanalytic theory of crime causation does not make the usual distinction between behavior as such and criminal action" (Falk, 1966: 1). The distinction is a legal one; that is, crime is behavior defined by a society as illegal. Antisocial behavior is seen as a neurotic manifestation whose origin can be traced back to early stages of development: "There is no fundamental difference between the neurotic criminal and all those socially harmless representatives of the group of neurotic characters; the difference lies merely in the external fact that the neurotic lawbreaker chooses a form of acting out his impulses which is socially harmful or simply illegal" (Alexander and Staub, 1956: 106).

According to August Aichhorn (1963: 221), "The superego takes its form and content from identifications which result from the child's effort to emulate the parent. It is evolved not only because the parent loves the child but also because the child fears the parent's demands." However, Freud (1933: 92) states that "the superego does not attain to full strength and development if the overcoming of the Oedipus [in males] complex has not been completely successful."

The superego keeps primitive (oral and anal) id impulses from being acted on. Persons with an **antisocial personality disorder** suffer from a poorly developed superego (psychopaths or sociopaths) and are restrained only by the ego, which alone cannot exercise adequate control over id impulses. Such persons experience little or no guilt as a result of engaging in socially harmful behavior. They are characterized by a combination of antisocial behavior and emotional detachment (Black, 1999), a lack of remorse for their actions and a lack of empathy for their victims.

At the other extreme are persons whose superego (internal parental voice) is destructive. Their superego is overwhelming and cannot distinguish between *thinking about* and *doing* bad deeds. Unresolved conflicts of earlier development and id impulses that are normally repressed or dealt with through other secondary processes (such as reaction formation or sublimation) create a severe sense of (unconscious) guilt. This guilt is experienced (at the unconscious level) as a compulsive need to be punished. To alleviate this (unconscious) guilt, the actor is impelled toward committing acts for which punishment is virtually certain. Delinquents of this type are the victims of their own morality (Aichhorn, 1963). Persons employed in the criminal justice system often see cases in which the crime committed was so poorly planned and executed that it would appear that the perpetrator *wished* to be caught. The FBI catches between 40 and 50 bank robbers per year who write their note demanding money on the back of a deposit slip for their own checking accounts (Martin, 1995).

In sum, much criminal behavior is related to the superego function, which is a result of an actor's relationship to parents (or parental figures) during early developmental years. Parental deprivation through absence, lack of affection, or inconsistent discipline stifles the proper development of the superego. Parental influence is thus weakened by deprivation during childhood development, so in adulthood the actor is unable to adequately control aggressive, hostile, or antisocial urges. Overly rigid or punitive parents, conversely, can lead to the creation of a superego that is rigid and punitive, for which the actor seeks punishment as a way of alleviating unconscious "guilt."

A P/P officer must be able to distinguish those offenders with an inadequate superego from those with a punitive one. With the latter, attempts to deter criminal behavior through the application of threats may actually have an opposite effect; with the former, the P/P officer may need to act in a parental role to substitute for a poorly developed superego.

▶ Psychoanalytic Treatment

Psychic disorders are treated by psychoanalysis or one of its variants, such as psychotherapy. According to Freud, psychoanalysis "aims at encouraging the patient to give up the repressions belonging to his or her early life and to replace them with more psychically mature reactions. To achieve this goal, a psychoanalyst attempts to get the patient "to recollect certain experiences and the emotions called up by them which he has at the moment forgotten" (Reiff, 1963: 274). To the psychoanalyst, present symptoms are tied to repressed material of early life—the primary stages of psychosexual development. The symptoms will disappear when the repressed material is exposed under psychoanalytic treatment.

Today, most psychoanalytically oriented therapists practice a variety of approaches (such as ego psychology whose focus is more immediate) rather than classical Freudian analysis (Nietzel et al., 2003), and psychoanalysis is not used in P/P because it requires highly trained and thus expensive practitioners, treatment takes many years, and it needs a level of verbal ability in patients beyond that of most persons on P/P. In fact, psychoanalytically oriented therapists may underestimate how difficult it is to verbalize experience, even for otherwise verbal patients (Omer and London, 1988). Instead of psychoanalysis, psychoanalytic theory has traditionally been applied in P/P through the use of social casework.

> **Key Fact**
>
> In P/P, psychoanalytic theory has traditionally been applied through the use of social casework.

▶ Social Casework

Social work has its roots in charity work and **social casework**—the supplying of concrete services to persons in need—solving problems rather than changing personalities. Mary Richmond (1917), whose colleagues included many physicians, presented the practice of **social work** as including (nonpsychoanalytic) psychological and sociological aspects of a person's behavior. She also set the groundwork for what is sometimes referred to as the **medical model** of therapy, dealing with nonphysiological problems through the method of *study*, *diagnosis*, and *treatment*.

In the years following World War I, social work was characterized by practice based primarily on the psychoanalytic perspective and the medical model (Miley, O'Melia, and DuBois, 2013). During the 1930s, some American physicians began to use psychoanalytic treatment, and social workers adopted this "talking cure"—one that did not require medical training—to their own practice (Specht, 1990). Psychoanalytic theory was still central to social work education when this writer received his master's of social work degree in 1970. In contrast to the medical model that "searches the past to detect when, why, and how client systems went wrong," the focus of contemporary social work is on the present to discover resources that clients can employ to take charge of their future (Miley, O'Melia, and DuBois, 2013: 78).

Social casework is one of the basic specialties of social work: "An art in which knowledge of the science of human relations and skills in relationship are used to mobilize capacities in the individual and resources in the community appropriate for better adjustment between the client and all or any part of his total environment" (Bowers, 1950: 127). Social casework "can be defined essentially as the development of a relationship between worker and client, within a problem-solving context, and coordinated with the appropriate use of community resources" (Brennan et al., 1986: 342). The purpose of social casework is the solution of problems that block or minimize the effectiveness of the individual in various social roles (Skidmore, Thackeray, and Farley, 1988), for example that of a parent or employee, expected of the mature adult.

As Freudian thought had its impact on social work, caseworkers began examining the client's feelings and attitudes to understand and "cope with some of the unreasonable forces that held him in their grip" (Perlman, 1971: 76). The client's behavior is conceived as purposeful and determined, but some of the determinants are unconscious. Casework was thus expanded to include work with psychological and social or environmental stress and adopted the open listening style of relationship—even the notion of relationship is grounded in Freudian thought (Payne, 1997). It is the therapeutic relationship that serves as a medium for facilitating change: The caseworker helps clients maintain constructive reality-based relationships, solve problems, and achieve adequate and satisfying independent social functioning within the client's existing personality structure (Torgerson, 1962). To accomplish this task, social workers use encouragement and moral support, persuasion and suggestion, training and advice, comfort and reassurance, together with reeducation and some sort of guidance (Casius, 1954).

Although social casework borrowed much of its theory from Freud, it avoided the psychoanalytical goal of trying to effect personality changes. Instead, a more immediate and pragmatic version of the Freudian model was adopted, helping people "perform in their appropriate social roles by providing information and knowledge, social support, social skills, and opportunity" (Specht, 1990: 354). Twenty-first-century social casework, while recognizing the influence of early development, social environments, and traumatic events, generally focuses on immediate concerns and addresses maladaptive behaviors and adverse conditions that perpetuate problems in current functioning (Borden, 2000). Whereas the medical model searches the past to detect problems in the present, contemporary social work—while not discounting

> **Key Fact**
>
> Social casework focuses on problems that block or minimize the effectiveness of an individual to carry out expected social roles.

> **Key Fact**
>
> Psychoanalysis searches the past to detect problems in the present, while social casework explores the present for client strengths and resources that can promote effective social functioning.

ADVICE TO WEST VIRGINIA PROBATION AND PAROLE OFFICERS

The offender must be approached as an individual. In seeking to rehabilitate the offender, the probation and parole officer must avoid the temptation to create someone in their own image. An effective treatment plan recognizes that there are vast differences in cultural backgrounds, moral values, and personal lifestyles. Probation and parole does not seek to destroy the offender's identity, but rather to help him or her express his or her individuality in creative ways as he or she progresses toward personal and social maturity.

the importance of the developmental past—explores the present for client strengths and resources that can promote effective social functioning (Miley, O'Melia, and DuBois, 2013)

The importance of social casework in P/P practice (sometimes called *forensic* social work) goes beyond theory and into the skills and training that schools of social work provide. These include "an extension and refinement of information on how to interview, how to obtain facts about the client's background, how to identify and distinguish surface from underlying problems, what community resources exist, and how to refer" (Wilensky and Lebeaux, 1958: 288–89). "The knowledge base developed for social casework is eclectic, interdisciplinary, tentative at best, complex and often subjective" (Johnson and Yanca, 2007: 42). The newer approaches borrow from ego psychology, emphasizing coping and social functioning. In place of the medical model terms "study," "diagnosis," and "treatment," modern social casework adopted the terms "assessment," "planning," and "action" (Johnson and Yanca, 2007):

- *Assessment.* Collection and analysis of relevant information on which to base a plan
- *Planning.* Thoughts about and organization of facts into a meaningful goal-oriented explanation for action
- *Action.* Implementation of the plan

▶ Assessment

Assessment determines the nature of the client's current situation, resulting in a written report (variously called a psychosocial study, intake report, or social history, among other nomenclature). The assessment involves gathering information from documents and through interviews with persons familiar with the offender as well as the client himself or herself. It provides the "here and now" and how it got that way. More complex and significant than data collection, assessment incorporates the tasks of deciding which data to seek and how to organize it (Bisman, 2000). Assessment includes identifying strengths and resources that exist within the client and his or her environment (Johnson and Yanca, 2007). "When assessment is complete, the social worker should be able to describe the problem or situation accurately and identify what needs to be changed to improve the client's situation" (Sheafor, Horejsi, and Horejsi, 2000: 301).

▶ The Focus of Assessment Is on Gathering Information

During this phase, client interviews provide the basis for a relationship between the client and the P/P officer that is central to the casework process. As Wayne Scott (2008) notes, correctional treatment is relationship driven, and high-quality interpersonal relationships are characterized by respect, concern, hopefulness, and enthusiasm. To accomplish this, the

---

A CLOSER LOOK

SOCIAL WORK PRINCIPLES

A cardinal principle of social work is belief in the value and worth of every person—respecting him or her as an individual without approving of all of the client's behavior. The dignity and respect that flow as a consequence of this principle allow the worker "to care about the client as a human being even though he may find things about the client he does not like" (Johnson and Yanca, 2007: 178).

worker must be what Gordon Hamilton calls "a person of genuine warmth" (1967: 28). Using face-to-face interviews, the worker conveys acceptance and understanding. Walter Friedlander notes that "caseworkers communicate their respect for and acceptance of the client as a person whose decisions about his own living situation are almost always his own to make" (1958: 22). The caseworker seeks to understand the client's press and stress: "People are affected by *press* from the environment and by *stress* from conflicts within themselves" (Payne, 1997: 80).

Caseworkers know that the way they communicate will have an effect on clients' perceptions of them and the worker–client relationship. Therefore, they must be cognizant of the way they greet clients; the way they use tone of voice, facial expressions, and posture; and the way they express themselves verbally. In P/P practice, workers who exude authority, who are curt, and who emphasize the enforcement aspect of their position will encounter difficulties in establishing a sound casework relationship.

Caseworkers engage clients in the helping process and make certain judgments about clients' motivation—how much they want to change and how willing they are to contribute to bringing about change. Workers recognize that a client brings attitudes and preconceptions about being on probation or parole. The P/P client is fearful, or at least realistically on guard, because he or she recognizes the power of the P/P officer.

An anxious client will be resistant to a caseworker's efforts; and in the mandated setting that is P/P practice, a P/P officer can easily raise a client's anxiety level, thus increasing resistance, including "evasive, angry, and uncooperative behaviors" (Hutchinson, 1987: 591). Psychoanalytic theory also posits **resistance** that is unconscious. P/P clients frequently have a negative impression of all authority figures, a perception usually based on experiences with parents, school officials, police officers, court officials, training schools, or prisons. In addition, a client may have a low self-image, a severe superego, or a chronically high anxiety level. The result will be resistance. The worker must not become defensive about client resistance or take negative behavior personally. Wayne Scott (2008: 27) points out that P/P officers "work with individuals who have violated societal norms, who are often verbally aggressive and lack interpersonal boundaries, and who can actively sabotage the very professional relationships charged with aiding and rehabilitating them." And yet, to be effective, P/P officers "must consistently take the high road in response to these predictable relational assaults."

To lessen resistance, workers may discuss the client's feelings about being on P/P, allowing him or her to vent some feelings and anxiety. This approach will also enable workers to clarify any misconceptions that clients have about P/P supervision. Elizabeth Hutchinson (1987: 592) suggests "letting it all hang out": "It is essential for the social worker to make early acknowledgement of client reluctance toward the mandated transactions and to validate such reluctance as understandable. This makes the issue explicit rather than latent and assures the client of the acceptability of his or her feelings as well as the genuineness of the social worker."

The client's motivation can also be influenced by the psychoanalytical concept of **transference**: He or she may view the worker as a friendly parent or as an authoritarian and demanding mother or father. The worker can be influenced by **countertransference** because he or she may view the client as a childlike figure; if the worker is a great deal younger than the client, the former may view the latter as a parent or older sibling.

The caseworker prepares a psychosocial study of the client. In non-P/P agencies, workers often stress the importance of early childhood development and experiences with a view toward applying a psychoanalytic explanation to the client's behavior. This practice is not usual in P/P settings, where "the unique constellation of social, psychological, and biological determinants of the client's current stressful situation" is more relevant and appropriate to analyze (Friedlander, 1958: 47). In P/P practice, the primary focus of assessment is on the present or the recent past.

The P/P officer seeks information that will provide an indication of the client's view of his or her present situation, is concerned with the client's plans for improving the situation, and weighs the sincerity and intensity of the latter's commitment to change. During the assessment phase, "particular attention needs to be given to assessing client strengths [because this] builds hopefulness and uncovers possibilities for dealing with the problem" (Sheafor, Horejsi, and Horejsi, 2000: 304). When the caseworker interprets the situation as needing to fix something that is wrong, it gives him or her the status of "expert" with the expectation that the worker will bring about change rather than the client: "The real work must be done by the client; otherwise it either does not get done or the change is temporary" (Johnson and Yanca, 2007: 61). The caseworker reviews the client's relationship with his or her family and evaluates the impact of the client's current situation. While engaged in study, the worker must also be aware of the cultural, racial, and ethnic factors that influence a client.

In P/P, material from the unconscious is not sought; but with clients who are mentally ill, material that in the better-functioning person is normally repressed may be brought to the fore. In such situations, the worker must direct his or her efforts toward keeping the client in touch with reality and should usually avoid exploring the normally repressed material.

▶ Planning

The planning phase converts the assessment content into a goal statement that describes the desired results (Johnson and Yanca, 2007). Helen Perlman (1957: 168–69) suggests what this phase of casework involves:

- Nature of the problem and goals sought by the client
- Nature of the person who bears the problem (his or her social and psychological situation and functioning) and who needs help with the problem
- Nature and purpose of the agency and kind of help it can offer or make available

In discussing the origin of the client's malfunctioning, Perlman refers to "this history of his development as a problem-encountering, problem-solving human being" and notes that this can provide the worker with an understanding of the client's present difficulties and the probable extent of his or her ability to cope with them (1957: 176). For a plan to be complete, psychological testing or a psychiatric evaluation may be necessary. The results of a clinical examination will indicate whether the client is in need of any special therapy (e.g., whether he or she is psychotic) or medication (e.g., for ADHD). In many instances a psychological or psychiatric report will not be available, so the P/P worker must make the determination whether an evaluation will be of enough help in planning to justify the expense.

"[The evaluation] plan considers both process and outcomes by specifying intermediate objectives as well as end goals" (Johnson, 1998: 294). Anticipating difficulties that may be encountered, the plan needs to be flexible and effective. In P/P, the plan provides a basis for holding the offender accountable for his or her efforts toward achieving a productive and law-abiding lifestyle.

▶ Action

The action phase involves activity designed to bring about change in a systematic way (Johnson and Yanca, 2007). During this stage, the relationship between worker and client enables the P/P officer to use his or her influence. It is a basic concept in social work that the client has the right to **self-determination**; the "Code of Ethics" of the National Association Social Workers emphasizes client freedom: The worker has no right to impose his or her goals. Obviously, the authority inherent in the P/P officer's role necessarily limits self-determination; for example, the P/P officer may be bound by statute or agency regulation to make decisions about the client's living situation. Dale Hardman (1960: 250) states that "authority conflict is a major causative factor in delinquency," a proposition that is widely accepted in correctional social work, so helping the offender come to grips with the reality of authority is a basic goal treatment in P/P. The client's relationship with a P/P worker is often the only positive experience he or she has ever had in dealing with an authority figure. "Many clients' involvement with the law expresses a need for control they cannot themselves provide. If used with respect and care, the authority of the court can be invoked by the forensic social worker to strengthen the client's weak motive to get treatment and to improve impulse control" (Brennan et al., 1986: 345).

Social caseworkers in other than correctional settings must also deal with the reality of their authority. They require clients to keep appointments, provide personal information, and pay fees—usually under the threat (implied or expressed) of denying the client the help or service the client is asking for. Workers in child welfare agencies may even be required to remove children from their parents or guardians in neglect or child abuse cases. In addition, because of the impact of an agency setting or the phenomenon of transference, the caseworker is always an authority figure. The concept and the use of authority and the limits placed on self-determination by reality are not alien to the practice of social casework, but "unwilling clients often do not see the need for service, do not believe help is possible, or have difficulty in developing a relationship with the worker" (Johnson and Yanca, 2007: 160).

The plan for intervention in social casework will use procedures that, it is hoped, will move the client toward the goal of enhancing the ability to function within the realities placed on him or her by society in general, and the client's present P/P status in particular. Three basic techniques are involved: change in the environment, ego support, and clarification.

> **Key Fact**
>
> Social casework adopted three terms for the helping process: assessment, planning, and action.

Change in the Environment

Effecting a change in the environment may involve obtaining needed resources if these are available from the agency or locating other agencies that can provide them. Research using a randomized experimental design found that increasing offender employment, expanding offender social support systems, and facilitating access to services and programming in the community significantly reduces recidivism (Minnesota Department of Corrections, 2010).

In effecting a change in the environment, the worker may assume a mediator or advocate role when the client is unable to secure a service that he or she needs and to which he or she is entitled. In P/P practice, this role is common; as advocates, P/P officers act as intermediaries between clients and agencies and may function as spokespersons for clients needing to deal with the bureaucratic maze of governmental agencies (Miley, O'Melia, and DuBois, 2013). The technique is used by the juvenile P/P officer who is seeking placement for a youngster in a foster home, group home, or residential treatment center and by the aftercare worker who is trying to place a juvenile back in public school after a stay at a juvenile institution. The P/P worker may have to intervene on behalf of clients who require assistance from a welfare department or may help a client to secure a civil service position or a necessary license/certificate to enter a particular trade or profession.

The P/P worker may help his or her client by talking to an employer or school official while helping the client to modify behavior relative to problems encountered at work or school. Many P/P clients have had few positive work or school experiences, and their difficulty with authority extends to employers and teachers. By using role play, reflection, and suggestion, the worker tries to modify the client's behavior, at least to the degree required for continued employment or schooling.

While being of direct assistance when necessary, the P/P officer should promote independence on the part of the client. The worker realizes that he or she is not continually available, and treatment is rarely indefinite. *The worker should not do anything for the client that the client is capable of doing for himself or herself.*

Ego Support

The use of **ego support** entails efforts by the worker to sustain the client through expressions of interest, sympathy, and confidence. The worker, through the use of his or her relationship with the client, promotes or discourages behavior according to whether the behavior is consistent with the goals of treatment. The P/P worker also encourages the client to vent and deals with any anxiety that may inhibit functioning.

The worker imparts a feeling of confidence in the client's ability to deal with problems, makes suggestions about the client's contemplated actions, and indicates approval or suggests alternatives relative to steps that the client has already taken. The officer may, at the very least, provide a willing and sympathetic ear to a troubled and lonely client—it is not unusual for the P/P officer to be the only person available to an offender to whom he or she can relate and talk. When the relationship is a good one, the client cannot help but view the officer as a friend.

The officer is also supportive of the client's family, parents, or spouse. In P/P practice, home visits are a usual part of the responsibilities. During the home visit, the worker has an opportunity to observe the client's environment directly, and this firsthand information adds another dimension to the worker's knowledge of the client. As a parole officer, I always asked clients to take me on a tour of their residence, a practice that had both treatment and law enforcement relevance.

The knowledge that a client lives in substandard housing or in a high-delinquency area is easy for the P/P officer to incorporate into his or her working methodology, but the concept is an intellectual one. A home visit provides direct information about the smell of urine in the hall, roaches, broken fixtures, and substandard bathroom facilities as well as housing that is hot in the summer and cold in the winter; a home visit also enables the officer to experience the presence of drug addicts huddling in a hallway, waiting for their connection. The worker is able to see, hear, and smell the environment in which a client is forced to live and thus understand the hostility and frustration that fill the life of many P/P clients almost from the time they are born.

By working directly with parents or a spouse, in addition to working with the client, the P/P officer broadens his or her delivery of help to the client. The worker can make referrals for the client's children when special aid is necessary—indeed, he or she can intervene on behalf of the client in the role of mediator/advocate to get services for any family member. The P/P officer can assist with marital problems (marital discord is an acute problem in many parole cases when a client has been incarcerated for many years). The worker may try to deal with the problem directly or may provide a referral to a specialized agency for the client and spouse. For example, it is not unusual for a distraught wife to call the P/P officer to complain about her husband. Sometimes she is merely seeking some way of venting her feelings; at other times, the situation may be more serious (e.g., she may have been subjected to physical abuse).

When a client is living with parents, the worker strives to involve them in the treatment effort, which is often difficult. The client may be the perennial black sheep in a large family or may come from a family that also has other members on probation, in prison, or on parole. This may dissipate the family's energy and resources and directly affect their ability and willingness to help the client.

Clarification

According to Florence Hollis (1950), clarification is sometimes called counseling because it usually accompanies other forms of rehabilitation in casework practice. Clarification includes providing information that will help a client to see what steps he or she should take in various situations. The worker, for example, may help the client weigh the issues and alternatives to provide a better picture on which to base a decision. Hollis notes that the client "may also be helped to become more aware of his own feelings, desires and attitudes" (1950: 418–19).

The client is encouraged to explain what is bothering him or her. If the problem is external, verbalizing it may be relatively easy; if the difficulty is internally caused, however, it may go deep and provoke anxiety. This difficulty will cause resistance, and the P/P officer will need great skill to secure enough information about the problem to be able to be of assistance. In response to the information, the worker may provide a direct interpretation to the client; more often, the P/P officer will ask questions and make suggestions designed to help the client to think out the problem more clearly and to deal with it in a realistic manner.

In the quest for evidence-based practices, P/P has been exploring an approach to counseling that has a great deal of research support and which has become prevalent in clinical psychology: *motivational interviewing*.[1] Karla Miley, Michael O'Melia, and Brenda DuBois (2013) state that motivational interviewing "provides tools for social workers to enhance a client's commitment to change."

▶ Motivational Interviewing

Motivational interviewing (MI) is "a style of communicating that helps people explore and resolve ambivalence about changing specific, maladaptive behaviors" (Bogue and Nandi, 2012: 1). MI was developed during the early 1980s by psychologists William Miller and Stephen Rollnick (2002) as a result of clinical experience with problem drinkers. Essentially atheoretical, MI is not a "school" of psychotherapy or a comprehensive approach to treatment; rather, it is a method for "assessing a specific problem when a person may need to make a behavior or lifestyle change and is reluctant or ambivalent about doing so" (Miller and Rollnick, 2009: 136). MI combines the supportive and empathic client-centered counseling style of Carl Rogers (1951) with a consciously directive method for resolving ambivalence in the direction of change. "It involves the conscious and disciplined use of specific communication principles and strategies to evoke the person's own motivations for change" (Miller and Rollnick, 2009: 135).

Motivational interviewing is particularly useful when working with resistive offenders, "an alternative to a counseling style largely characterized by confrontation and polarization between clients and agents" (Bogue and Nandi, 2012: 1). Replacing authoritarian approaches with techniques that include reflecting, rather than reacting to, resistant statements, helps clients improve communication effectiveness by providing them with feedback about perceived resistance, and exploring the offender's natural ambivalence about changing behavior. P/P workers are encouraged to use "communication strategies that values a client's perspective, that helps build a working relationship with the client, and that" provides a practical and valuable alternative to escalating the use of authority and control" (Bogue and Nandi, 2012: 3).

Clients are conflicted between wanting to change their behavior and the costs involved in doing so.

> Attempting to directly persuade a client to change will be ineffective because it entails taking one side of the conflict that the client is already experiencing. The result is that the client may adopt the opposite stance, arguing against the need for change, thereby resulting in increased resistance and a reduction in the likelihood of change. Instead, motivational interviewing allows the client to overtly express their ambivalence in order to guide them to a satisfactory resolution of their conflicting motivations with the aim of triggering appropriate behavioral changes…It is not the counselor's function to directly persuade or coerce the client to change. Rather it is the client's responsibility to decide for themselves whether or

---

[1] A Google search for MI produced 385,000 entries.

not to change and how best to go about it. The counselor's role in the process is to help the client locate and clarify their motivation for change, providing information and support and offering alternative perspectives on the problem behavior and potential ways of changing. (Markland, Ryan, Tobin, and Rollnick, 2005: 813)

Acknowledging that people tend to become more committed to that which they hear themselves defend, MI explores the client's own arguments for change. The interviewer seeks to evoke this "change talk"—expressions of the client's desire, ability, reasons, and need for change—and responds with reflective listening. "Clients thus hear themselves explaining their own motivations for change, and hear them reflected again by the counselor. Furthermore, the counselor offers periodic summaries of change talk that the client has offered, a kind of bouquet composed of the client's own self-motivational statements" (Hettema, Steele, and Miller, 2005: 92).

MI is "guided by the notion that motivation to change should not be imposed from without, in the form of counselor arguments for change, but elicited from within the client" (Rollnick and Allison, 2004: 105). Autonomy is promoted by avoiding confrontation and coercion, by exploring behavioral options, by developing the discrepancy between the client's current behavior and how they would like to be so that they present the arguments for change themselves, and by encouraging clients to choose their preferred courses of action (Markland, Ryan, Tobin, and Rollnck, 2005: 822). MI follows five basic principles (Walters, Clark, Gingerich, and Meltzer, 2007):

1. **Express empathy.** Empathy is about good rapport and a positive working environment. It is an attempt to understand the client's mindset, even though the counselor may not agree with his or her point of view. Empathy also involves an effort to draw out concerns and reasons for change from the client. In MI, "empathy is not 'feeling sorry' for offenders nor agreeing with their point of view. Rather, accurate empathy involves a sincere attempt to listen to and understand the offender's point of view" (Alexander, VanBenshoten, and Waltersd, 2008: 63).

2. **Avoid argument and direct confrontation.** When a client is unsure or unwilling to change, trying to convince the client that he or she has a problem could precipitate even more resistance (Center for Substance Abuse Treatment, 2005).

3. **Roll with resistance.** It is normal to have mixed feelings when thinking about change. Therefore, the counselor does not argue with the client—arguments can easily degenerate into a power struggle (Center for Substance Abuse Treatment, 2005). Rolling with resistance means finding other ways to respond when the client challenges the need for change.

4. **Develop discrepancy.** Discrepancy is the feeling that one's current behavior is out of sync with one's goals or values. Rather than telling the client why he or she should change, the counselor asks questions and makes statements to help the client identify his or her own reasons for change. "This involves exploring the pros and cons of the client's current behaviors and of changes to current behaviors, within a supportive and accepting atmosphere, in order to generate or intensify an awareness of the discrepancy between the client's current behaviors and his or her broader goals and values" (Markland, Ryan, Tobin, and Rollnck, 2005: 814).

5. **Support self-efficacy.** A person is more likely to follow through with behavior he or she believes has been freely chosen. Therefore, the counselor remains optimistic, reminds the client of personal strengths and past successes, affirms all efforts toward change, and expresses support for a person's belief in his or her ability to change.

By emphasizing respect, optimism, and choice, MI differs from confrontational approaches by engaging in patient listening while looking for ways to guide the

- MI is a client-centered, directive approach that emphasizes listening and looking for ways to direct the interaction toward positive talk.

- Mixed feelings, hesitancy, and even arguments against change are a normal part of the change process.

- Aggressive confrontation pushes offenders backward in the change process.

- MI facilitates change by reducing levels of resistance, raising discrepancy, and increasing positive change talk.

- The best interaction is one in which the offender gives the reasons for change.

- Identifying and calling attention to an offender's ambivalence can help him determine whether his behavior is in conflict with other personal values.

- Talk about desire, ability, reasons, and need leads to commitment talk, which, in turn, predicts behavior change.

Source: Walters, Clark, Gingerich, and Meltzer (2007: 28).

interaction toward positive talk. In MI the client does most of the talking; "The more the officer is talking, the less opportunity there is for the probationer [or parolee] to talk and think about change" (Clark, Walters, and Melzter, 2006: 40). When faced with resistance, the P/P officer avoids becoming argumentative and, instead, encourages the client to develop solutions to the problems they have expressed. However, many/most P/P clients are not articulate or even verbal. And using MI may require more time than the average P/P officer can devote to each client. Melissa Alexander, Scott VanBenschotem, and Scott Walters (2008: 65) state that MI is intended as an additional tool for officers to use as they provide supervision and services to offenders. And they note, "MI is not a replacement for everything officers currently use nor is it appropriate for all situations."

The complexity of motivational interviewing is a practical challenge in training persons in the methodology. "Competency in the MI style is achieved through long-term training that involves skill practice and feedback" (Alexander, VanBenschoten, and Walters, 2008: 62). Agencies in search of rapid training engage in time-limited, one- or two-day, workshops that may erroneously convince staff that they have learned the method. There is also a plethora of MI self-study programs. However, "proficiency in MI is not readily developed through self-study or by attending a workshop, but typically requires practice with feedback and coaching over time" (Miller and Rose, 2009: 135). As with any complex clinical skill, "it is unreasonable to expect that a one-shot workshop will establish enduring competence" (Miller et al., 2004: 1060). And Rollnick and Miller (1995: 1) note that "some approaches being delivered under the name of motivational interviewing bear little resemblance to our understanding of its essence and indeed in some cases directly violate what we regard to be central characteristics."

MI is popular in P/P; the New York State Division of Parole, for example, "has adopted Motivational Interviewing methods in its casework practice." While MI has strong empirical support in areas relevant to probation and parole supervision, such as preparing clients to engage in alcohol and drug treatment programs, there is a paucity of research on the efficacy of MI in P/P settings. A study that examined the effectiveness of MI training on probation officer skill and subsequent probationer outcome found that that while probation officers can be taught to use MI in standardized probation interactions, such skills were not linked to positive probation outcome. In comparison to a control group, the MI training program improved officer skill, but after controlling for baseline characteristics, probationer outcome did not vary by training, nor did officer MI competence predict outcome (Walters et al., 2010).

MINT is an international organization of trainers in motivational interviewing that emerged in 1997 among people trained by William R. Miller and Stephen Rollnick. Members come from diverse backgrounds, and their central interest is in improving the quality and effectiveness of counseling and consultations given to clients about behavior change.

MINT members have to complete a three- or four-day workshop designed to teach them the training methods, techniques, and spirit of the MI approach. In order to encourage good practice standards, MINT membership is limited to trainers who have completed a training workshop for new MI trainers recognized by the MINT.

▶ Learning Theory and Behavior Modification

To better understand learning theory and behavior modification, one may place the various modes of treatment related to P/P practice on a continuum represented by a straight horizontal line. Acceptance of psychoanalytic theory is on the extreme left of this line and rejection on the extreme right. Social casework would be at the left of center; reality therapy (discussed later) is toward the right of center, while behavior modification is firmly on the extreme right of this imaginary line.

Behavior modification, the therapeutic application of **learning theory** (that all behavior is shaped by its consequences), emanated from the science laboratory and experimental psychology, rejects psychoanalytic theory as an unscientific basis for an even more unscientific mode of rehabilitation. B. F. Skinner (1904–1990), America's foremost behaviorist, argued that analytically oriented therapists "rely too much on inferences they make about what is supposedly going on inside their patients, and too little on direct observation of what they do" (Goleman, 1987: 18). "If a client's aggressive behavior has been rewarded, at least part of the time, no further explanation in terms of internal needs is necessary; the client has simply learned to behave aggressively" (Nietzel et al., 2003: 47).

Behaviorists take pride in displaying and subjecting their methods and results to rigorous scientific analysis. Behavior modification proceeds on the theory that all forms of behavior are the result of learning responses to certain stimuli. "Disturbed" behavior, for example, is a matter of learning responses that are inappropriate (London, 1964). The behaviorist contends—and has been able to prove—that animal behavior, human and otherwise, can be modified through the proper application of behaviorist principles.

Behavior is "*strengthened* by its consequences, and for that reason the consequences themselves are called 'reinforcers' " (Skinner, 1972: 40). When some aspect of (animal or human) behavior is followed by a reward, this action is a **reinforcer**, and it makes it more likely that the action will be repeated. "Reinforcers are types of consequences that strengthen a behavior" (Baldwin and Baldwin, 1998: 42). The reward is called **positive reinforcement**. If the probability of a behavior goes up after the *removal* of a stimulus, then **negative reinforcement** has occurred: "A negative reinforcer strengthens any behavior that reduces or terminates it" (Skinner, 1972: 47). For example, the negative reinforcement that occurs when a heroin addict fails to ingest enough heroin—withdrawal symptoms—strengthens drug-seeking behavior; as opposed to negative reinforcement, *punishment* (e.g., imprisonment) suppresses the frequency of an operant (e.g., heroin use). "Punishment either takes away something an organism wants or gives it something it does not want" (Hergenhahn and Olson, 1999: 289). While punishment is frequently used interchangeably with negative reinforcement, the two are quite different: "*Punishment* is when the *onset* of a stimulus decreases the frequency of behavior" (Oltmanns and Emery, 2010: 32). Thus, according to Skinner (1972), punished behavior such as crime is likely to reappear after the punitive contingencies are withdrawn. These applications form the basis for **operant conditioning**, conditioning that follows positive and negative reinforcers.

> **Key Fact**
> Behavior modification proceeds on the theory that all forms of behavior are the result of learning responses to certain stimuli—behavior is strengthened by its consequences.

> **Key Fact**
> Operant conditioning involves positive and negative reinforcement.

Antisocial behavior is merely the result of learning directly from others (e.g., peers) or the failure to learn how to discriminate between competing norms, both lawful and unlawful, because of inappropriate reinforcement. When conforming behavior is not adequately reinforced, an actor can more easily be influenced by competing, albeit antisocial, sources of positive reinforcement (e.g., money and excitement from criminal behavior). To be effective for learning, however, reinforcement must follow rather closely the behavior that is to be influenced: "Generally, operant conditioning is most likely to occur when reinforcers and punishers follow immediately after an operant" (Baldwin and Baldwin, 1998: 89). Offenders have problematic reinforcement contingencies and often engage in behavior that provides an immediate payoff but has negative long-term consequences. If criminal behavior is almost always rewarding, significant but intermittent punishment is unlikely to suppress it.

The behaviorist stresses client analysis to discover the variables that are reinforcing and then attempts to discover the situational demands and emotions that are related to the behavior. The analysis deals with the day-to-day functioning of the subject in order to discern the cause (independent variables) of the maladaptive behavior (dependent variables). The therapist attempts to elicit specific descriptions of actual events that constitute a problem—functional analysis—so that he or she can evaluate which components of the situation are amenable to change by behavioral techniques (Nietzel et al., 2003). Whenever possible, the specific description is based on direct observations or interviews with the client and/or significant others (e.g., parents or spouse) and a review of any relevant records. Maladaptive behavior is analyzed in terms of intensity and frequency and is often presented in the form of graphs.

The therapist teaches the client to conduct his or her own functional analysis for subsequent self-produced modification of the environmental contingencies that are reinforcing the maladaptive behavior. The functional analysis can be combined with self-monitoring techniques. A highly motivated client maintains a daily log of the specific problem—for example, lack of temper control—and records the number of times that he or she exhibits the specific manifestations of a lack of temper control. Although this technique can be combined with other forms of therapy, alone it seems to have the power to modify behavior because it increases awareness and makes the response sequence less automatic. This may provide the opportunity for the person to suppress the response or engage in some incompatible behavior. In addition, self-monitoring may encourage the person to reward or punish himself or herself depending on whether appropriate gains have been made. Investigators have shown that self-reinforcing statements, such as "I am doing well," are important in maintaining a behavior. "A recording system which facilitates this process undoubtedly will be effective in helping people to change their own behavior as well" (Bootzin, 1975: 11).

▶ Cognitive Behavioral Therapy (CBT)

The need for timely reinforcement makes operant conditioning difficult to apply in P/P practice. Stimulants (such as cocaine) and depressants (such as heroin), for example, are powerful reinforcers that can provide instant gratification and relieve the psychological stress that frequently drives drug use. Competing with this reality in many cases is difficult and often impossible. However, in contrast to Skinner, Albert Bandura argues that in humans "outcomes resulting from actions need not necessarily occur instantly," because as opposed to lower animals, people "can cognitively bridge delays between behavior and subsequent reinforcers without impairing the efficacy of incentive operations" (1974: 862). Cognition refers to covert verbalizations and/or imagery frequently referred to as *believing*, *thinking*, and *expecting* (Martin and Pear, 2011).

The cognitive position, which has become dominant in psychology (Craske, 2010)—and which has been found to reduce recidivism (Aos, Miller, and Drake, 2006; P. Clark, 2011; Lipsey, Chapman, and Landenberger, 2001; Pearson et al., 2002; Wilson, Bouffard, and MacKenzie, 2005)—maintains that it is necessary to look to thoughts, memory, language, and beliefs. The emphasis is on inner rather than environmental determinants of behavior (Hollin, 1990).

Bandura (1974) argues that to ignore the influence of covert reinforcement in the regulation of behavior is to deny a uniquely human capacity. According to the cognitive view, a human being is an active participant in his or her operant conditioning processes—the individual determines what is and what is not reinforcing. For example, to become a drug abuser, one must *learn* that ingesting certain chemicals is desirable (Abadinsky, 2014); in other words, human behavior is complex and reinforcement often abstract. Humans have a unique capacity to use abstractions, or symbols, that can serve as important reinforcers, such as the medals and trophies dear to any amateur athlete. Behavior can be learned vicariously through observation without obvious reinforcement (Nietzel et al., 2003). Self-reinforcement in humans may take on many tangible or symbolic dimensions. In reality therapy (discussed in a later section in this chapter), praise and encouragement are dispensed by the therapist; in correctional settings, the positive reinforcements are often privileges dispensed through secondary reinforces or *tokens* that can be redeemed for tangible items such as chocolate bars or television time (Gendreau, Listwan, and Kuhns, 2011).

Cognitive-based therapy flows from the belief that "defective or maladaptive cognitions can cause emotional and behavioral disorders" (Martin and Pear, 2011: 341).

"Cognitive therapists believe that psychological problems stem from faulty learning, making incorrect assumptions as the result of inadequate or incorrect information and not being able to adequately distinguish between imagination and reality" (Hansen, 2008:43).

The offender is suffering from faulty thinking patterns and lacks that level of social competence necessary to cope adequately with a variety of situational demands. "Their behavior may be guided by dysfunctional assumptions about how one should behave, for example, 'you have to punish people for messing with you or they won't respect you,' 'you have to rebel against authority or they will break you'" (Lipsey, Chapman, and Landenberger, 2001: 145). "Cognitive behavioral interventions (CBI) are based on the simple principle that thinking (an internal behavior) controls overt actions (external behavior). The focus is on coping and problem-solving skills. Therefore, through CBI programs (or curricula), offenders learn new skills and new ways of thinking that can lead to changes in their behavior and actions, and ultimately affect their criminal conduct" (*Cognitive Behavioral Interventions*, 2001: 4).

"Cognitive Behavioral Therapy is not a single method of psychotherapy. Rather, CBT is an umbrella term for therapies with many similarities" (Hansen, 2008: 43) designed to correct dysfunctional and criminogenic thinking patterns. "Clients are not only taught more positive behaviors to replace their old ways of getting through life, they are also shown how to be more attuned to the thought processes that led them to choose negative actions in the past" (Morris Thigpen in Foreword to Milkman and Wanberg, 2007: vii). CBT is a short-term, problem-oriented approach whose "goal is to teach offenders to manage their own behavior by engaging in processes that develop self-control, making them responsible for and in charge of their actions no matter how stressful the situation" (North Carolina Division of Community Corrections, 2005: 7).

Since people can monitor and change their cognitive activity—"think crime"—and resulting behavior—"do crime"—the therapeutic process begins with an assessment of positive and negative aspects of their behavior. The assessment includes a focus on the social, physical, and emotional environments in which the behavior occurs. After the assessment, the role of the therapist is to enable the person to deal with cues that trigger problem behavior in a manner that avoids resorting to illegal activity, with the patient's own report of the negative aspects (e.g., arrest, incarceration) serving as a motivator for adopting more positive coping strategies (Donovan, 1988). Negative reinforcement in the form of avoidance strategies serves to prevent the occurrence of influences that trigger criminal behavior. CBT uses role play, graduated rehearsal, and practice.

A popular group approach in P/P entails the application of cognitive behavior theory (discussed earlier) and is known as **cognitive skills training (CST)**; some call it *problem-solving therapy* (PST). This approach views criminal behavior not as the symptom of some disorder, but as the result of a combination of social and economic situations and behavioral factors, the result of inadequate socialization. Basic to this approach is a belief that conventional prosocial thinking and behavior can be taught, that offenders can learn to anticipate the consequences of their actions and consider alternate courses of action. Thus, a low social intelligence involves offenders who have deficits in the ability to envision the consequences of their behavior and are unable to use means–ends reasoning to achieve their goals. Operating at the ego level of development, they are unable to place themselves in someone else's position or understand another's behavior. The CST approach is based on a belief that "individuals can be taught to be better problem-solving thinkers" (Husband and Platt, 1993: 34).

CST "emphasizes the importance of problem-solving skills that can be applied to a variety of problem situations. These include skills such as awareness of interpersonal problems, defining problems, causal thinking, consequential or alternative thinking, means-ends thinking, and perspective-taking" (Husband and Platt, 1993: 33). Training is designed to modify impulsive, egocentric, illogical, and rigid thinking and to teach offenders to think—consider the consequences—before acting.

Packaged programs such as "Aggression Replacement Therapy," "Reasoning for Change," and "Thinking for Change," involve 20–30 sessions sometimes lasting up to 20 weeks (P. Clark, 2011). P/P officers who receive relevant training can conduct CBT sessions. Generally, 40 two-hour sessions with audiovisual presentations, role play, behavior rehearsal, and reasoning exercises are offered. With 6 to 10 offenders, the therapist—called a *coach*—leads the group in problem solving, anger management, negotiation skills, value enhancement, critical reasoning, creative thinking, planning, and decision making. A focus is placed on enabling offenders to think in terms of options/alternatives to gain greater control over their own lives. Exercises ask offenders to respond to dilemmas, target skills, apply the skills and techniques, and then return to the group to discuss the experience.

Some problems in implementing CST include the use of groups that require a specific starting and completion date, which is complicated by offenders being placed on supervision and completing supervision at different times. Also, P/P officers may not be comfortable in the role of a coach and may resist training. Research into a program in New York City (Greenlight Reentry) that used the CST approach with prerelease inmates and parolees found no benefits (Wilson and Davis, 2006). However, observers question the manner in which the program was implemented (Marlowe, 2006; Rhine, Mawhorr, and Parks, 2006).

Another CBT approach, *moral reconation therapy* (MRT), used by P/P agencies ranging from Arkansas to the state of Washington, is designed to promote positive lifestyle changes—*reconation* refers to a redirecting of decision making to higher standards of moral reasoning. This group approach is led by a facilitator trained in MRT, its philosophy, and its method. Participants are chosen based both on a perceived willingness to change current lifestyles and on a shared problem such as substance abuse or sex offenses. There are reading and homework assignments. Group members are asked to briefly look at their past to gain insight into choices they have made and the specific motivations behind these choices; then they take an in-depth look at what makes up their life situation and how they are spending their time. Participants are encouraged to set goals and break these down into achievable steps. Research into CRT in Washington State (Burnett, 2007), in agreement with other studies into CRT, revealed that participants experienced significantly less recidivism.

► Other Behavior Modification Systems

Behavior modification can also use **aversive therapy** in which the therapist specifies in advance an unpleasant event that will occur if the subject performs an undesirable behavior. Drug antagonists, for example, can render the use of alcohol or other substances ineffective (lack of positive reinforcement) or extremely unpleasant (negative reinforcement or punishment). Disulfiram (Antabuse), metronidazole, or chlorpropamide can serve this purpose for alcohol abusers. Antabuse—the best known of these substances—disrupts the metabolism of alcohol in the liver, producing a severe reaction that includes stomach and head pain, nausea, and vomiting. A substance that has the appearance and smell of cocaine and even produces a numbing effect but is not psychoactive is used in conjunction with an aversive chemical, one that induces vomiting, for example. In voluntary patients, electric shocks may be self-administered whenever a craving for the chemical arises. Alternatively, verbal aversion techniques may be used when a patient is asked to imagine strongly aversive stimuli (usually vomiting) in association with imaginal drug-related cues, scenes, or behaviors. Similar procedures can be used with sex offenders such as pedophiles by associating erotic feelings toward children with an unpleasant consequence.

Other behavioral therapies use biofeedback and relaxation training, and sometimes assertiveness training, to prepare drug abusers to cope better with the stress and anxiety believed linked to drug use. Researchers have found that certain environmental cues can serve as triggers to activate drug cravings (Dole, 1980). When desensitization is used, "patients are usually first relaxed, then given repeated exposure to a graded hierarchy of anxiety-producing stimuli (real or imaginal)" to provide a form of immunity (Childress, McLellan, and O'Brien, 1985: 957).

► Reality Therapy

Reality therapy (RT) was developed as a mode of treatment by William Glasser while he was a psychiatrist at the Ventura School, an institution for the treatment of older adolescent girls who had been unsuccessful on probation. It is probably the easiest of the three modes of rehabilitation to describe, and simplicity has been a major reason for its popularity in P/P practice. Glasser's book *Reality Therapy* (originally published in 1965), which contains only 166 pages, describes RT as a method "that leads all patients toward reality, toward grappling successfully with the tangible aspects of the real world" (1975: 6). As opposed to RT, "conventional therapy goals do not include client responsibility or personal actions as primary" (Bersani, 1989: 177). RT attempts to teach people a better way of fulfilling their needs and taking responsibility for themselves and their behavior—reality therapy stresses accountability.

> **Key Fact**
>
> Simplicity has been a major reason for the popularity of reality therapy in P/P practice.

Although Glasser accepts the developmental theories of psychoanalytic theory, he rejects them as a sound basis for treatment: "It is wishful thinking to believe that a man will give up a phobia once he understands either its origins or the current representation of its origin in the transference relationship" (1975: 53). Glasser believes that "conventional treatment depends far too much on the ability of the patient to change his attitude and ultimately his behavior through gaining insight into his unconscious conflicts and inadequacies" (1975: 51). The reality therapist denies the claims of psychoanalytic theorists that cure depends on the recovery of traumatic early memories that have been repressed. The ability of psychoanalysis to cure persons, states Melitta Schmideberg (1975), a psychiatrist whose mother (Melanie Klein) was eminent in the field of psychoanalysis, has never been clinically substantiated. "The goal of reality therapy [in contrast to psychoanalytical approaches] is neither insight about underlying causes of problems nor resolution of unconscious conflicts. Rather, the desired outcome is a change in behavior resulting in need satisfaction and greater happiness" (Wubbolding, 2000: 10).

Various mental problems, Glasser argues, are merely symptomatic illnesses that have no presently known medical cause and that act as companions for the lonely people who *choose* them. The behaviors or symptoms are actually chosen by the person from a lifetime of experiences residing in the subconscious. In place of conventional treatment, the reality therapist proposes first substituting the term "irresponsible" for mental health labels (e.g., neurotic, personality disorder, and psychotic). A "healthy" person is called *responsible*, and the task of the therapist is to help an irresponsible person to become responsible. Furthermore, notes Schmideberg, the psychoanalytic approach of "dwelling on the past encourages the patient to forget his present problems, which is a relief at times, but often—undesirably—the patient feels that after having produced so many interesting memories, he is now entitled to rest on his laurels and make no effort to change his attitude or plans for the future" (1975: 29). This diverts attention from the client's current problem(s), which is a reality that should be dealt with directly.

Glasser argues that conventional treatment does not deal with whether a client's behavior is right or wrong in terms of morality or law but "contends that once the patient is able to resolve his conflicts and get over his mental illness, he will be able to behave correctly" (1975: 56). Societal realities, however, particularly in P/P practice, require direct interventions with a client, with the therapist not accepting "wrong" behavior.

"Reality therapy is based upon the belief that all of us are born with at least two built-in psychological needs: (1) the need to belong and be loved and (2) the need for gaining self-worth and recognition" (Glasser, 1980: 48). According to Glasser, people with serious behavior problems lack the proper involvement with someone; and lacking this involvement, they are unable to satisfy their needs." According to the William Glasser Institute website, "Unsatisfactory or non-existent connections with people we need are the source of almost all human problems, thus the goal of reality therapy is to help people reconnect." Therefore, to be a helping person, the therapist must enable the client to gain involvement, first with the worker and then with others. The traditional therapist maintains a professional objectivity or distance, whereas the reality therapist strives for strong feelings between worker and client. This type of relationship is necessary if the therapist is to have an impact on the client's behavior. The therapist, although always accepting of the client, firmly rejects irresponsible behavior and can then teach the client better ways of behaving.

To accomplish this reeducation, the P/P worker must know about the client's reality—the way he or she lives and his or her environment, aspirations, and *total reality*. Reality is always influenced by culture, ethnic and racial group, economic class, and intelligence. The worker must be willing to listen open-mindedly and learn about the client (Schmideberg, 1975). While observing, the counselor develops a relationship with the client, a relationship that can lead to responsible behavior. Alluding to the fact that RT does not always work, Glasser states that the fault is with the therapist who is unable to become involved in a meaningful way with the client; however, mandated correctional clients may avoid counseling because of their difficulties with intimacy (Harris and Watkins, 1987). For many people, it feels safer to reject someone trying to help them than to risk accepting that help, only to be disappointed. Such clients try to create physical and emotional distance in relationships. Paradoxically, a warm and empathetic counselor is often met with barriers to bonding in the therapeutic relationship, and too much pursuit of the client to bring about intimacy only intensifies the client's anxiety.

Glasser expresses a great deal of support for the work of P/P officers, although he cautions persons in corrections, as well as other fields, against the use of punishment: "For many delinquents," he notes, "punishment serves as a source of involvement. They receive attention through delinquent behavior, if only that of the police, court, probation counselor, and prison [workers].... A failing person rationalizes the punishment as a reason for the anger that caused him to be hostile" (1976: 95).

> **Key Fact**
>
> The reality therapist, although always accepting of the client, firmly rejects irresponsible behavior and helps the client to act responsibly.

Like behavior modification, RT is symptom oriented. The P/P client is in treatment because he or she has caused society to take action as a result of his or her behavior. If the P/P worker can remove the symptoms and make the client responsible, that will satisfy society and relieve client anxiety caused by fear of being incarcerated.

Schmideberg (1975: 24) states that for a delinquent symptom to disappear, it is usually necessary for the person to accomplish three interrelated tasks:

1. Face it fully with all of its implications and consequences.
2. Decide to stop it and consider the factors that precipitate it.
3. Make a definite effort to stop it.

She maintains that a general and nondirective method is not likely to change symptoms that the client may find satisfying (e.g., drugs to the addict, excitement and money to the robber, or forced sex to the rapist). Reality therapists "ask clients to do more than merely describe their behavior, their wants, their perceptions, their level of commitment, or their plans. They ask clients to make judgments about them," as if they were looking in a mirror (Wubbolding, 2000: 111). RT requires that clients evaluate their actions.

> **Key Fact**
>
> Like behavior modification, reality therapy is symptom oriented.

Richard Rachin (1974) states that the reality therapist seeks to help the client act responsibly. As opposed to someone taking the more distant approach of social casework, the reality therapist becomes emotionally involved—warm, tough, interested, and a sensitive human being who genuinely gives a damn and demonstrates it. RT is concerned only with behavior that can be tried and tested on a reality basis, and only with the problems of the present. And the reality therapist is not interested in uncovering underlying motivations or drives; rather, he or she concentrates on helping the person act in a manner that will help meet his or her needs responsibly. While the reality therapist praises responsible behavior and provides recognition for positive accomplishment, he or she offers no crying towel. Sympathy can indicate that the worker lacks confidence in the client's ability to act responsibly.

RT flows easily from the P/P officer's need to hold an offender accountable for his or her behavior. Some maintain that the value emphasis in RT coincides with the paternalistic and perhaps authoritarian attitudes of some P/P officers. Carl Bersani states that "Glasser's writings do not provide a systematic methodology for clearly separating the moral standards of the counselor from that of the client" (1989: 188). Although Glasser does not deal with theory and RT is practice oriented, the theoretical underpinnings are close to those in behavior modification. Instead of manipulating the environment or using tangible reinforcers, the therapist develops a close relationship with the client and uses praise or concern as positive and negative reinforcers. For this method to be effective, the counselor needs to be a genuinely warm and sympathetic person who can easily relate to persons who have often committed very unpleasant acts and whose personalities may leave a great deal to be desired—no easy task. Thus, although training someone in the use of RT may be relatively easy, success requires qualities of personality that are not part of the basic qualifications for becoming a P/P officer.

In more recent books, Glasser (1998, 2000) acknowledges that his earlier work did not present a theoretical foundation for RT, and he offers **choice theory**, which replaces "the term responsibility with the more explicit idea that we choose all our behavior because we can't be anything but responsible for all that we choose to do" (2000: 227). "Choice theory provides an explanation for human behavior and how the human mind functions and thus serves as a basis for the delivery system reality therapy" (Wubbolding, 2011: 15).

Glasser argues that people *choose* problematic behavior as their best effort to deal with a present unsatisfying relationship or, worse, no relationships at all. According to choice theory, "significant conscious behaviors that have anything to do directly with satisfying basic needs [love/belonging, freedom, fun, power, and survival] are chosen" (Glasser, 1998: 71). Therefore, "you are either the beneficiary of your own good choices or the victim of your own bad choices" (1998: 77). To the person whose behavior is destructive or inimical to his or her interests, Glasser states: "You are choosing what you are doing, but you are capable of choosing something better" (1998: 77).

Nevertheless, RT remains practice based, and not theory based, "to teach clients how to act and think more effectively so they can better satisfy their needs," with the objective of guiding people in the direction of actually doing something about their problems (Glasser, 2000: 67). While remaining nonjudgmental and noncoercive, the goal of RT is to help clients "*make specific, workable plans* to reconnect with the people they need, and then follow through on what was planned by helping them evaluate their progress" (William Glasser Institute website).

▶ Group Work

Group work provides a therapeutic milieu wherein individuals agree to help one another; in contrast with the therapist in casework, the group is the agency of help. According to Allan Brown, the basic operating premise of social group work is that "groups of people with similar needs can be a source of mutual support, mutual aid and problem solving" (1986: 10); probationers/parolees discover in the group that they are not alone with their problems and that others share similar difficulties (Morgan and Winterowd, 2002). In the group, "every member is a potential helper" (Brown, 1986: 11). Helen Northern states that one of the advantages of the use of groups "is that stimulation toward improvement arises from a network of interpersonal influences in which all members participate" (1969: 52). The theory underlying the use of the group is that the impact provided by peer interaction is more powerful than worker–client reactions within the one-to-one situation of social casework. Furthermore, groups "help members realize that they are not alone with their problems" (Toseland and Rivas, 1998: 17). They can instill hope and impart information through a shared interaction, and their members promote the learning of basic social skills. The group serves a cathartic function: Members can experience and express feelings in a safe and confidential environment (Gladding, 1999). "Truth and conflicts are brought to the surface, and participants are guided to examine and grapple with all of the positions and options involved" (Drumm, 2006: 20).

In P/P, groups consist of members who share a common status, in this case legally determined. Groups in P/P may also be organized on the basis of age or around a common problem, such as substance abuse. The group is a mutual aid society in which members are given an opportunity to share experiences and assist each other with problems in a safe, controlled environment. The group helps to confirm for each member the fact that others share similar problems—"they are in the same boat"—thus reducing the sense of isolation. With the help of the group worker, members are able to share a sense of purpose and develop a commitment to helping each other through patterns of group interaction: "As members offer solutions to common problems, make supportive comments, and share in the skill development of fellow members by participating in group exercises, they become committed to helping each other" (Shaffer and Galinsky, 1987: 26).

The group can reduce the anxiety of having to report alone to a P/P officer; collaboration tends to offset the more direct authority of the one-to-one situation and to lower the impact of sociocultural differences between client and P/P worker. As Gisela Konopka (1983: 93) points out, "In a group members support each other; they are not alone in the face of authority." In a group, she notes, the offender is surrounded by equals; he or she is not a client, but a *member*, an arrangement that permits "feelings of identification that are impossible to achieve on an individual basis with even the most accepting social caseworker" (1983: 97). In P/P, groups are typically open ended because members enter and leave—complete their sentence or violate supervision—at various intervals. Group work requires a level of skill and training not widely available in social work in general and P/P practice in particular.

Psychological theories and methods of rehabilitation have been examined; the next section looks at some sociological theories that have application to P/P practice.

▶ Sociological Theory

Psychological theory attempts to identify causes of criminal behavior within the individual actor and to treat the causes accordingly. Sociological theory places crime in a social context, adding to our understanding of individual offenders. The following sections briefly review sociological theories relevant to P/P practice.

▶ Anomie

The concept of **anomie**, derived from the Greek meaning "lack of law," was developed by the French sociologist Emile Durkheim (1858–1917) to explain variations in suicide rates. In 1938, Robert Merton "Americanized" the concept of anomie, which became part of what are often called **strain theories**. Merton argues that no other society is as close to the United States in considering economic success as an absolute value. Furthermore, he argues, in the United States "the pressure of prestige-bearing success tends to eliminate the effective social constraint over the means employed to this end. The 'end-justifies-the-means' doctrine becomes a guiding tenet for action when the cultural structure unduly exalts the end and the social organization unduly limits possible recourse to approved means" (Merton, 1938: 681). "The desire to make money without regard to the means in which one sets about doing it is symptomatic of the malintegration at the heart of American society" (Taylor, Walton, and Young, 1973: 93).

According to Merton, anomie results when people are confronted by the contradiction between goals and means—*strain*. They "become estranged from a society that promises them in principle what they are denied in reality [economic opportunity]," so despite numerous success stories—the poor boy from humble origins who becomes rich and famous—"we know that in this same society that proclaims the right, and even the duty, of lofty aspirations for all, men do not have equal access to the opportunity structure" (Merton, 1964: 218). This point is particularly true of the most disadvantaged segments of our population who become the clients of our probation, prison, and parole systems.

How do persons respond to the anomic condition? Most simply scale down their aspirations and conform to conventional social norms. Some rebel, rejecting the conventional social structure and seek, instead, to establish a "new social order" by utilizing political action or by establishing alternative lifestyles. Two responses, retreatism and innovation, are of particular interest for P/P practice.

Retreatism means that all attempts to reach conventional social goals are abandoned in favor of a deviant adaptation—a "retreat" to alcohol and drug abuse. Time and energy are now expended to reach an attainable goal: getting "high." **Innovation** is a term used by Merton to describe the adoption of illegitimate means to gain success. Societal goals of success have been incorporated and accepted, but the person finds access to legitimate means for becoming successful limited; anomie results, and the person seeks alternatives such as professional and organized crime. Crime is viewed as a basically utilitarian adaptation to the anomic situation. Thus, with the innovation response, the ends justify the means; with retreatism, the ends ("getting high") are sufficiently reduced to make the means readily accessible.

Merton assumes a consensus and commitment to "American values"—an attitude fixated on moneymaking pervades our society. This assumption does not account for nonutilitarian deviance or the class-linked dynamics of criminal behavior. More recent versions of strain theory have expanded the goals of American youth to include such short-term variables as popularity with the opposite sex, good school grades, and athletic achievements. This enlargement would explain conditions of strain experienced by middle-class youth because these goals are not necessarily class linked. For adults, the failure to achieve expected goals causes strain that in some persons leads to anger, resentment, and rage—emotional states that can lead to criminal behavior (Agnew, 1992). Robert Agnew (1992) suggests that social justice or equity might be at the root of strain; in this case, a sense of being dealt with unfairly—adversity is blamed on others—and not simply an inability to reach goals, results in strain.

What does the theory of anomie offer the P/P officer and the real problems of his or her practice? One consideration has to do with aspirations. Offenders often have unrealistic goals: Their aspirations surpass their ability. In such cases, if anomie is to be avoided, the P/P officer must help the client to make a realistic assessment of the situation and then to assist him or her with achieving goals that are both constructive and reality based. Each client should be encouraged to achieve the limits of his or her ability, and the officer has, accordingly, a responsibility to see that barriers such as discrimination do not block client's goals. In such instances, the P/P officer must assume an advocacy role by making use of agencies responsible for enforcing equal opportunity laws.

▶ Differential Association

As proposed by Edwin Sutherland (1883–1950), **differential association** explains how criminal behavior is transmitted (not how it originates). According to Sutherland (1973), criminal behavior is learned, and the principal part of learning criminal behavior occurs within intimate groups based on the degree of intensity, frequency, and duration of the association. The person learns, in addition to the techniques of committing crime, the drives, attitudes, and rationalizations that add up to a favorable precondition to criminal behavior. Most criminal and noncriminal behaviors have the same goal—securing economic and personal status—but differential association accounts for the difference in selecting criminal or noncriminal methods for achieving the goal. The process of learning criminal behavior by association with criminal and anticriminal patterns involves all the mechanisms that are involved in any other learning (Boy Scouts and gangsters learn behavior in the same manner).

In sum, criminal behavior results from the strength or intensity of criminal associations and is the result of an accumulative learning process. A pictorial portrayal of differential association can easily be conceived in terms of a balanced scale that starts out level: On each side are the various accumulated weights of criminal and noncriminal associations; and at some theoretical point, criminal activity will tip the scale with an excess of criminal associations over noncriminal or prosocial ones.

What import does this theory have for P/P practice? P/P regulations usually contain prohibitions against certain associations. A person on P/P is usually cautioned against associating with others similarly situated, a recommendation that can easily be seen as a practical attempt to respond to the theory of differential association. In addition, the P/P officer can provide exposure to prosocial associations, an exposure whose influence conceivably can help to balance our theoretical scale. The officer can assist the client by encouraging and helping him or her secure association with community, charitable, religious, athletic, fraternal, and other such organizations.

> **Key Fact**
>
> Differential association is experienced in P/P regulations by the prohibition against associating with criminal companions.

▶ Neutralization

Gresham Sykes and David Matza (1957) refer to a social psychological mechanism—**neutralization**—that permits a delinquent to accept the social norms of the wider society and, at the same time, violate these norms. Sykes and Matza maintain that the delinquent actually retains his or her belief in the legitimacy of official middle-class norms: "The juvenile delinquent frequently recognizes both the legitimacy of the dominant social order and its moral rightness" (1957: 664). They argue that "if there existed in fact a delinquent subculture such that the delinquent viewed his illegal behavior as morally correct, we could reasonably suppose that he would exhibit no feelings of guilt or shame at detection or confinement. Instead, the major reaction would tend in the direction of indignation or a sense of martyrdom." However, the authors note, many delinquents do, indeed, experience a sense of guilt, "and its outward expression is not to be dismissed as a purely manipulative gesture to appease those in authority" (1957: 664–65).

Sykes and Matza (1957: 666) postulate that "the delinquent does not necessarily regard those who abide by the legal rules as wrong or immoral." Furthermore, many delinquents are probably not totally immune from the demands for conformity made by the dominant social order. Therefore, "the juvenile delinquent would appear to be at least partially committed to the dominant social order in that he frequently exhibits guilt or shame when he violates its proscriptions, accords approval to certain conforming figures, and distinguishes between appropriate and inappropriate targets for his deviance" (Sykes and Matza, 1957: 666). They conclude that "the delinquent represents not a radical opposition to law-abiding society but something like an apologetic failure, often more sinned against than sinning in his own eyes" (1957: 667).

By using various techniques of neutralization, delinquents are able to avoid guilt feelings for their actions—contend that rules are merely qualified guidelines limited to time, place, and person conditions. This line of reasoning is in accord with the legal code that requires *mens rea*, criminal intent, to be present for penal sanctions to be imposed. Delinquents justify their actions in a form that, although not valid to the larger society, is valid for them. Sykes and Matza (1957) present five types of neutralization:

1. *Denial of responsibility.* Rationalization that delinquency was not their fault (e.g., they were simply victims of circumstances)
2. *Denial of injury.* Premise that nobody got hurt (e.g., just a prank was involved, or the insurance company will cover the damage)
3. *Denial of the victim.* Belief that the victim deserved to be hurt
4. *Condemnation of the condemners.* Focus on the weakness and motives of those in authority or judgment (e.g., police, school officials, and judges are corrupt or hate kids)
5. *Appeal to higher loyalties.* Belief in the necessity of their action for friends, family, neighborhood, and so on

P/P officers, in the course of a presentence investigation or P/P supervision, often encounter these sentiments, or variants of them. Sykes and Matza caution against dismissing them as merely postaction rationalizations because they indicate a genuine commitment to societal norms and a basis for treatment.

▶ Differential or Limited Opportunity

Richard Cloward and Lloyd Ohlin (1960) integrate anomie with differential association to explain how delinquent subcultures arise, develop various law-violating ways of life, and persist or change over time. They distinguish among three types of delinquent subcultures that are a result of anomie and differential association:

1. *Criminal subculture.* Gang activities devoted to utilitarian criminal pursuits (e.g., racketeering)
2. *Conflict subculture.* Gang activities devoted to violence and destructive acting out as a way of gaining status
3. *Retreatist subculture.* Activities in which drug abuse is the primary focus

> **Key Fact**
>
> Neutralization explains how a delinquent can both accept and violate societal norms.

Each of these subcultural adaptations arises out of a different set of social circumstances or opportunities. Cloward and Ohlin state that the dilemma of many lower-class people is that they are unable to locate alternative avenues to success or goals: "Delinquent subcultures, we believe, represent specialized modes of adaptation to this problem of adjustment" (1960: 107). The criminal and conflict subcultures provide illegal avenues, while the retreatist "anticipates defeat and now seeks to escape from the burden of the future" (1960: 107). Criminal behavior is not viewed as an individual endeavor but as part of a collective adaptation. Cloward and Ohlin note that "many lower-class adolescents experience desperation born of the certainty that their position in the economic structure is relatively fixed and immutable—a desperation made all the more poignant by their exposure to a cultural ideology in which failure to orient oneself upward is regarded as a moral defect and failure to become mobile as proof of it" (1960: 106–107).

The turn toward alternative means of success is to be understood in terms of this socio-psychological phenomenon. However, Cloward and Ohlin also point out that illegitimate means of success, like legitimate means, are not equally distributed throughout society: "Having decided that he 'can't make it legitimately,' he cannot simply choose among an array of illegitimate means, all equally available to him" (1960: 145). Thus, for the average lower-class adolescent, a career in **professional** or **organized crime** (Abadinsky, 1983, 2013; Sutherland, 1972) can be as difficult to attain as any lucrative career in the legitimate sphere of society.

This difficulty warns the P/P officer of the need to be able to differentiate persons involved in "professional" and "organized" criminality from the more frequent offender who has only limited skills and contacts. Professional and organized criminals are usually not good candidates for the rehabilitative efforts of P/P agencies because such persons are not likely to give up criminal skills and status, which were achieved only after a considerable expenditure of time and effort, for a conventional and law-abiding lifestyle. In these cases, the investigative and control (not the therapeutic) skills of the P/P officer must be used.

▶ Social Control Theory

If, as control theorists generally assume, most persons are sufficiently motivated by the potential rewards to commit criminal acts, why do only a few engage in criminal behavior? According to **social control theory**, "Delinquent acts result when an individual's bond to society is weak or broken" (Hirschi, 1969: 16). The strength of this bond is determined by internal and external restraints; in other words, internal and external restraints determine whether we move in the direction of crime or law-abiding behavior.

Internal restraints include what psychoanalytic theory refers to as the superego; they provide a sense of guilt. As noted earlier, dysfunction during early stages of childhood development or parental influences that are not normative can result in an adult who is devoid of prosocial internal constraints; some refer to this as psychopathology or sociopathology, or they apply the diagnostic term "antisocial personality disorder"[2] (Black, 1999). There is evidence tying sociopathy to a central nervous system/brain defect (Haederle, 2010). Whether they are conceived in terms of psychology or sociology, internal constraints are linked to the influence of the family (Hirschi, 1969), an influence that can be supported or weakened by the presence or absence of significant external restraints, such as the P/P officer.

External restraints include social disapproval linked to public shame or social ostracism and fear of punishment. People are typically deterred from criminal behavior by the possibility of being caught and the punishment that can result, ranging from public shame to imprisonment (and in extreme cases, capital punishment). The strength of official deterrence—force of law—is measured according to two dimensions: risk and reward.

---

[2] Diagnostic categories are found in the *Diagnostic and Statistical Manual* (DSM) published by the American Psychiatric Association.

Risk involves the ability of the criminal justice system to detect, apprehend, and convict the offender, and the amount of risk is weighed against the potential rewards. Both risk and reward, however, are relative to one's socioeconomic situation: The less one has to lose, the greater is the willingness to engage in risk. In the words of a Bob Dylan song (*Like a Rolling Stone*), "When you ain't got nothin', you got nothin' to lose." And, the greater the reward, the greater is the willingness to engage in risk. This theory explains why persons in deprived economic circumstances would be more willing to engage in certain criminal behavior. However, the potential rewards and a perception of relatively low risk may also explain why persons in more advantaged economic circumstances would engage in remunerative criminal behavior, such as corporate crime. According to Gary Becker (1968: 176), "A person commits an offense if the expected utility to him exceeds the utility he could get by using his time and resources at other activities." Becker argues that "a useful theory of criminal behavior can dispense with special theories of anomie, psychological inadequacies, or inheritance of special traits and simply extend the economist's usual analysis of choice" (1968: 40).

Instead of conforming to conventional norms, some persons, through differential association, organize their behavior according to the norms of a delinquent or criminal group with which they identify or to which they belong. This affiliation is most likely to occur in environments characterized by relative social disorganization, where familial and communal controls are ineffective in exerting a conforming influence. The increasing number of children living below the poverty level intertwined with a collapse of many inner-city families has created "America's new orphans" (Gross, 1992)—data clearly associates poverty with juvenile crime (Snyder and Sickmund, 2006). Conforming prosocial behavior may be dependent on the ability of the P/P officer to carefully monitor the client combined with a realistic threat of punishment. From the casework dimension, the P/P officer may offer the client an opportunity to repair weak or broken bonds and thereby move the client in the direction of conventional behavior.

P/P officers cannot affect offenders' environment that research has determined is associated with recidivism: "The neighborhood where an individual returns for supervision is an important factor in the success of his or her supervision. Offenders who return to neighborhoods that are seen as impoverished and transient have higher failure rates" (Rhodes et al., 2013: 18).

▶ Drift

Does the juvenile delinquent move on to become an adult criminal, or does the youngster mature and become a conforming member of society? This process of gradually maturing and becoming law abiding is referred to as **drift**. David Matza (1964: 59) views the delinquent's lifestyle as not fully committed: "He drifts between criminal and conventional action." Matza denies the portrayal of a juvenile delinquent as a person committed to an oppositional culture; instead, the delinquent reveals a basic ambivalence toward his or her behavior. Matza believes that juveniles are less alienated than others in society, and that most of the time delinquents behave in a noncriminal manner: "The image of the delinquent I wish to convey is one of drift; an actor neither compelled nor committed to deeds nor freely choosing them; neither different in any single fundamental sense from the law abiding, nor the same; conforming to certain traditions in American life while partially unreceptive to other more conventional traditions" (1964: 28).

Although Matza does not contradict the idea of a delinquent subculture, he finds that the subculture is not a binding force on its members: "Loyalty is a basic issue in the subculture of delinquency partially because its adherents are so regularly disloyal. They regularly abandon the company at the age of remission for more conventional pursuits" (1964: 28). The "age of remission" is a time when adolescent antisocial behavior is abandoned in favor of adult prosocial or conventional behavior. The crime-prone years for young men are roughly ages 15 to 25, with remission occurring after age 25. Matza's theory has important

> **Key Fact**
> Participants in delinquent subcultures typically exit with the onset of adulthood, unless justice system intervention is an impediment.

policy implications: Justice system intervention can stigmatize—label—a juvenile, thereby blocking entry into a conventional lifestyle as he or she matures into adulthood.

▶ Labeling

A stigma, sometimes referred to in terms of labeling (also called *societal reaction theory*), is the concern of a sociological perspective known as *symbolic interactionism*:

> Symbolic interactionists suggest that categories which individuals use to render the world meaningful, and even the experience of self, are structured by socially acquired definitions. They argue that individuals, in reaction to group rewards and sanctions, gradually internalize group expectations. These internalized social definitions allow people to evaluate their own behavior from the standpoint of the group and in doing so provide a lens through which to view oneself as a social object. (Quadagno and Antonio, 1975: 33)

The focus is not on the behavior of any social actor (person) but on the way that behavior or actor is viewed by others (e.g., society). The societal reaction labels—stigmatizes—the actor, which results in a damaged self-image, a deviant identity, and a host of negative social expectations. Think about the societal reaction to the terms *mentally ill*, *ex-convict*, and *parolee*. Furthermore, some argue, the damaged self-image and its ramifications can result in a self-fulfilling prophesy. Edwin Schur (1973: 124) notes that "once an individual has been branded as a wrongdoer, it becomes extremely difficult for him to shed that new identity." The ex-convict finds it difficult to secure employment, increasing the attraction of further criminal activity. According to Edwin Lemert, the labeled deviant reorganizes his or her behavior in accordance with the societal reaction and "begins to employ his deviant behavior, or role based on it, as a means of defense, attack, or adjustment to the overt and covert problems created by the consequent societal reaction to him" (1951: 76)—"If you got the name, mind as well play the game." Lemert has termed this process "secondary deviation," which is evidenced by deviants seeking to associate with others like themselves. The negative influence of the delinquent label is viewed as so detrimental to future conduct that Schur (1973) argues for *radical nonintervention*: The focus should be on avoiding the movement of adolescents into the official agencies of social control.

The P/P officer is constantly faced with the dynamics of labeling as clients encounter difficulty in returning to school, securing employment, obtaining housing, and making friends because of the stigma (label) inherent in the terms "probationer" and "parolee." The label results in a negative self-image, whereby the offender's view of himself or herself is that of an inferior and unworthy person. In such a condition, he or she may seek the companionship of others similarly situated and may engage in further antisocial activities in an effort to strike back at the society that is responsible for the labeling.

Key Fact

Labeling results in a damaged self-image, a deviant identity, and a host of negative social expectations.

A CLOSER LOOK

VALUE OF A BAD REPUTATION

"In fact, far from stigmatizing, prison evidently confers status in some neighborhoods. Jerome Skolnick…found that for drug dealers in California, imprisonment confers a certain elevated 'home boy' status, especially for gang members for whom prison and prison gangs can be an alternative site of loyalty. And according to the California Youth Authority, inmates steal state-issued prison clothing for the same reason. Wearing it when they return to the community lets everyone know they have done 'hard time'" (Petersilia, 1995: 23). And a "bad rep" can provide advantages in criminal subcultures (Abadinsky, 2013).

Summary

- Theories are abstract explanations about the relationship between two classes of phenomena.
- Theories of crime can be distinguished by explanations that emphasize nature or nurture.
- Psychoanalytic theory emphasizes the importance of the unconscious in human behavior.
- Memories of stages of psychosexual development although unconscious, drive conscious behavior.
- Each stage of psychosexual development is associated with types of deviant/criminal behavior.
- When a person is passing through the first three stages of psychosexual development, the mind simultaneously undergoes the development of three psychic phenomena: id, ego, and superego.
- Both a weak and an overactive superego can explain criminal behavior.
- Most psychoanalytically oriented therapists practice a variety of approaches whose focus is more immediate than classical Freudian analysis.
- Whereas the medical model searches the past to detect problems in the present, contemporary social work explores the present for client strengths and resources that can promote effective social functioning.
- Contemporary social work emphasizes coping and social functioning and in place of the medical model terms "study," "diagnosis," and "treatment," adopted the terms "assessment," "planning," and "action."
- Motivational interviewing (MI) is a style of communicating that helps people explore and resolve ambivalence about changing specific, maladaptive behaviors.
- MI differs from confrontational approaches by engaging in patient listening while looking for ways to guide the interaction toward positive talk. In MI the client does most of the talking.
- The central view of behavior modification is that all behavior is shaped by its consequences.
- Behavior modification applies operant conditioning, positive and negative reinforcement.
- Cognitive behavior therapy seeks to correct faulty thinking that can result in criminal behavior.
- Behavior modification can use aversive therapy.
- Cognitive behavior therapy is often applied in P/P through the use of cognitive skills training.
- Reality therapy stresses accountability.
- The reality therapist strives for strong feelings between worker and client.
- The theory underlying the use of the group is that the impact provided by peer interaction is more powerful than worker–client reactions within the one-to-one situation of social casework.
- The theory of anomie offers the P/P officer practical suggestions for responding to the real problems encountered in practice.
- The theory of differential association is expressed in P/P regulations containing prohibitions against certain associations.

- The theory of neutralization explains how a delinquent can both accept and violate societal norms.
- Differential opportunity theory integrates anomie with differential association.
- Social control theory links criminal behavior with weak connections to conventional society.
- The theory of drift notes that most youngsters mature out of delinquency.
- Labeling theory argues that once an individual has been branded as a wrongdoer, it becomes extremely difficult to shed that identity.

Key Terms

anal stage *115*

anomie *135*

antisocial personality disorder *116*

aversive therapy *131*

behavior modification *127*

choice theory *133*

cognitive behavioral therapy *128*

cognitive skills training (CST) *130*

countertransference *120*

differential association *136*

drift *139*

ego *115*

ego support *123*

genital stage *115*

group work *134*

id *115*

innovation *135*

labeling *140*

learning theory *127*

medical model *117*

motivational interviewing *124*

negative reinforcement *127*

neutralization *136*

operant conditioning *127*

oral stage *115*

organized crime *138*

positive reinforcement *127*

psychoanalytic theory *114*

reality therapy (RT) *131*

reinforcer *127*

resistance *120*

retreatism *135*

self-determination *121*

social casework *117*

social work *117*

social control theory *138*

strain theories *135*

superego *116*

theory *114*

transference *120*

unconscious *114*

Internet Connections

Academy of Criminal Justice Sciences: **acjs.org**

American Psychological Association: **apa.org**

American Society of Criminology: **asc41.com**

Glasser Institute on Reality Therapy: **wglasser.com**

Center for Reality Therapy: **realitytherapywub.com**

Motivational Interviewing: **motivationalinterview.org**

National Association of Social Workers: **naswdc.org**

National Organization of Forensic Social Work: **nofsw.org**

Reality Therapy links: **socc.ie/~wgii/address.htm**

Review Questions

1. What are the elements that characterize a theory?
2. What distinguishes theories that emphasize nature from those that emphasize nurture?
3. According to psychoanalytic theory, what is the unconscious?
4. What types of deviant/criminal behavior are associated with each stage of psychosexual development?
5. How can both a weak and an overactive superego explain criminal behavior?
6. Why is psychoanalysis not used in P/P?
7. How is the approach of contemporary social casework different from that of the medical model?
8. How does motivational interviewing differ from approaches using persuasion?
9. What is the central belief of behavior modification?
10. What is operant conditioning?
11. How does cognitive behavior therapy attempt to change behavior?
12. How is cognitive skills training applied in P/P?
13. What is aversive therapy?
14. How does reality therapy differ from other types of treatment?
15. What are the advantages of group work?
16. What suggestions does the theory of anomie offer the P/P officer?
17. How is the theory of differential association expressed in P/P regulations?
18. What insight into delinquent behavior is offered by the theory of neutralization?
19. What insight does differential opportunity theory offer the P/P officer?
20. According to social control theory why do youngsters engage in delinquent behavior?
21. With respect to juvenile delinquency, what does the theory of drift suggest?
22. What are the implications of labeling theory for P/P?

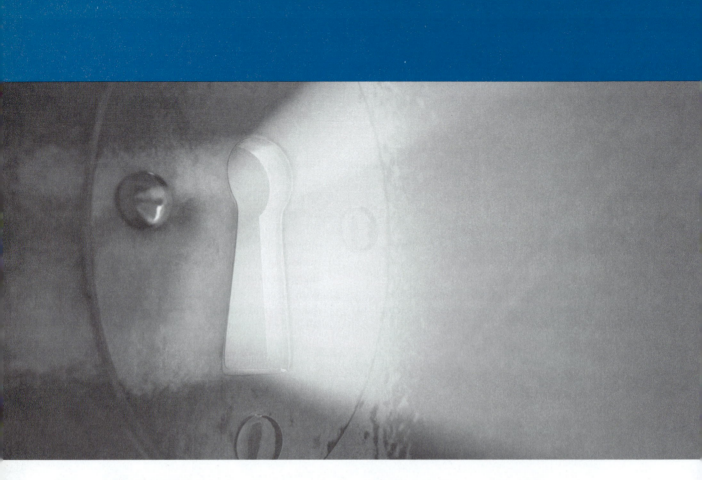

7 Probation and Parole Officers

LEARNING OBJECTIVES

This chapter will enable the student to:

1 *Describe the qualifications for probation/parole (P/P) officer entry-level positions.*

2 *State how P/P officers spend their working time.*

3 *Discuss the three systems are used to select P/P officers.*

4 *Group probation and parole agencies by model: control, social services, and combined.*

5 *Appreciate the roles of P/P officers related to these models.*

6 *Discuss the role of a P/P officer as enforcer.*

7 *Explain the controversy over P/P officers being armed and responsible for arresting violators.*

⑧ *Appreciate the extraordinary powers of P/P officers with respect to search and seizure.*

⑨ *Discuss the absolute immunity from liability enjoyed by probation officers when they prepare a presentence investigation report.*

⑩ *Distinguish the four volunteer models in P/P.*

This chapter examines the qualifications, roles, and responsibilities of the approximately 75,000 probation and parole (P/P) officers in the United States as well as the use of volunteers.

▶ Qualifications and Qualities

There are a few minimum requirements for entry-level positions across probation and parole jurisdictions: absence of a conviction for a felony and certain serious misdemeanors, such as perjury and domestic violence; possession of a state driver's license; minimum age, generally 21; U.S. citizenship; and physical qualifications, which vary. Note that probation and parole titles also vary. For example, Michigan state juvenile probation officers are called juvenile justice specialists and require a bachelor's degree (BA) in social science and two years of relevant experience. Juvenile probation officers with Maricopa County, Arizona, must possess a bachelor's degree and excellent communication (written and oral) skills. They must have the ability to establish and maintain working relationships with other employees, probationers, and the public and have the ability to prioritize/organize as well as plan and manage multiple assignments efficiently and effectively.

In Florida, correctional probation officers must possess a bachelor's degree and complete basic recruit training. South Carolina probation and parole agents must possess a BA, take a reading comprehension and vocabulary test, complete the Basic Law Enforcement Training Program, and undergo on-the-job training. Indiana parole agents require a BA in criminology, criminal justice, law enforcement, or social work or a related area, and one-year full-time experience in correctional counseling; criminology; parole/probation work, law enforcement, or social work or a related area; full-time experience in protective services may substitute for the required education on a year-for-year basis. Candidates must complete basic training at the Correctional Training Academy. West Virginia probation and parole officers require a BA in business administration, public administration, management, political science, industrial relations, organizational behavior, psychology, sociology, criminal justice, corrections, or social work or closely related field. To carry a firearm, P/P officers must complete a psychological evaluation and meet annual training requirements established through the West Virginia.

Corrections Academy

New York State parole officer candidates must possess a master's degree or a BA and three years of social service experience and successfully complete a rigorous eight-week training program that includes supervision skills and firearms proficiency. New York's Onondaga County requires probation officer candidates to possess a BA and two years of counseling or casework; or a master's degree in social work, education, administration, law, sociology, psychology, criminology, or a closely related field. Candidates are required to successfully complete the N.Y. State requirements for firearms training and carry a firearm on duty. Georgia parole officers are required to have a BA and pass a complete background check, which includes a psychological test, to determine their job competency. Soon after they are hired, officers attend the Basic Training Program, a six-week package of instruction at the Georgia Police Training Center. Included are classes and hands-on training in report writing, interpersonal communications, cultural diversity, arrest procedures, lifesaving techniques, and firearms training and certification. Every year officers return for more training in the form of 40 hours of agency-mandated in-service training.

New Jersey parole officer recruit requirements include a BA and passage of a civil service examination. Recruits complete a 24-week Police Training Commission course that includes arrest procedures, investigation techniques, parolee supervision, and other law enforcement subjects including unarmed defensive tactics and firearms training. After graduation, they assist Senior Parole Officers in the performance of parolee supervision duties for a one-year probationary period. During this probationary period, the recruit works under the close supervision of an officer mentor or as a member of a group to receive on-the-job training and instruction. Texas parole officers require a BA with major coursework in criminal justice, counseling, social work, psychology, sociology, or a related field. Pima County, Arizona, probation officers must have a BA, preferably in behavioral science, and one-year of related experience, such as counseling. The county also employs surveillance officers who aid probation officers to monitor offenders; they require an associate degree or 63 credits in a relevant field or two-years of experience in an agency that deals with offenders or a social services, teaching, or coaching position. Candidates for probation and parole officer positions in Missouri are graded on the basis of relevant experience (40 percent) and a written exam (60 percent) whose knowledge areas include interviewing, basic human behavior, basic computer skills, report writing, security and safety. North Dakota requires Parole and Probation Officers to possess a bachelor's degree with a major in a behavioral science, eligibility to be licensed as a peace officer, and three years of work experience directly interacting with offenders in a correctional, law enforcement, or social work setting.

The qualities generally considered desirable for P/P officers can be divided into four categories:

1. *Basic knowledge.* A P/P officer should have a working understanding of psychology, sociology, criminal statutes, police operations, and court and correctional systems. In some jurisdictions, particularly federal probation, an increase in the number of white-collar offenders referred for a presentence investigation or under supervision requires officers with knowledge of the Internet, securities, accounting, and banking.

2. *Individual characteristics.* A P/P officer needs the ability to relate to all offenders and to deal with their sometimes subtle or overt hostility, to exercise authority in an appropriate manner, to work well with other staff members, to organize work properly, and to prepare written reports in a coherent and timely manner.

3. *P/P agency.* The P/P officer must be willing to accept the responsibilities engendered by working for a public agency that handles offenders and to enforce its rules and adhere to its regulations.

4. *Other agencies.* The P/P officer has to be able to deal effectively with many kinds of agencies and persons, usually divided into criminal justice (police, prosecutors, judges, and correctional officials) and social services (treatment, welfare, employment, and educational agencies). These agencies often have varying attitudes toward offenders who must be handled appropriately.

The standards for New Jersey parole officers include:

- Knowledge of the economic, social, emotional, and other problems of paroled persons and of the reactions to be expected of such persons

- Ability to read, interpret, and apply information on the laws of New Jersey relevant to probation, parole, the operation of law enforcement agencies, and the courts

▼

- Ability to read and interpret information on the theory of modern social casework, penology, sociology, and criminology
- Ability to function as a peace officer for the detection, apprehension, arrest, and conviction of offenders
- Ability to recognize and evaluate potentially dangerous situations involving parolees and to exercise caution and independent judgment in the handling of these circumstances
- Ability to assist with the work involved in supervising persons on parole who may be of varied ethnic and social backgrounds, who may possess varied levels of intellectual comprehension and English ability, and who may be antagonistic and/or emotionally disturbed
- Ability to visit and speak with businesspersons, employers, judges, clergy, police officers, school officials, and representatives of health, welfare, civic, and business organizations to enlist their cooperation in plans for the rehabilitation of parolees and, as required, to collect information for future action
- Ability to conduct interviews of prospective parolees and investigations of parole violations
- Ability to set appropriate payment schedules to collect court-imposed revenue obligations concomitant with the capability to pay, to coordinate the efforts necessary to collect payments in default, and to maintain records thereon
- Ability to plan and work constructively with parolees in the areas of improved family life, steady employment, and wholesome personal and neighborhood associates
- Ability to be proficient in the care, use, and security of firearms and other restrain/defense equipment
- Ability to apprehend and arrest parole violators
- Ability to investigate and evaluate the living conditions of parolees
- Ability to prepare correspondence; clear, sound, accurate, and informative case histories; summaries; and other reports concerning parole matters containing findings, conclusions, and recommendations
- Ability to maintain essential records and files

▶ The Tasks and Hiring of Probation/Parole Officers

P/P officers spend their working time writing reports, visiting and interviewing clients, making referrals, and talking to persons in and out of the criminal justice system. The ten tasks and responsibilities of a Los Angeles probation officer are typical:

1. **Monitoring and enforcing compliance.** Monitoring probationers' adherence to the terms of probation, detecting violations, and enforcing compliance. Reviewing relevant probation conditions, such as employment, residence, treatment, and payments. Contacting probationers with appropriate frequency, including home or school visits and drug tests. Conducting regular and thorough discussions with parents, relatives, and school officials to check on probationers' conduct and compliance. Setting goals for probationers' treatment or conduct, and monitoring progress. Being alert to signs of problems, anticipating and preventing such problems when possible.

2. *Investigating.* Gathering and learning all relevant case and background information. Obtaining and reviewing appropriate department records, probation files, District Attorney's files, rap sheets, Juvenile Hall logs, police reports, chronological records, and so on. Gaining a working knowledge of information in all probationers' files and living situation, including the nature of offenses, prior criminal records, family living situation, and evidence of the quality of environment.

3. *Analyzing and making recommendations.* Synthesizing and evaluating all relevant information in reaching decisions and recommendations. Making appropriate decisions and recommendations regarding detention, placement, sentencing, payments, terms and conditions of probation, degree of monitoring and supervision required, and release/revocation. Giving appropriate weight and consideration to all relevant factors in reaching conclusions.

4. *Report writing and documentation.* Writing reports (e.g., detention, fitness, presentence, disposition), correspondence, and other documents/reports related to intake, progress, detention/release, which are clear, complete, accurate, and concise. Adhering to legal and departmental guidelines regarding all paperwork and documentation requirements and keeping appropriate and accurate records of field and other work activities.

5. *Handling emergencies.* Taking appropriate actions in emergency or crisis situations (e.g., injuries, escapes, fires, physical fights, and attacks upon staff). Using sound judgment and following proper procedures in using physical force or restraints, enlisting and providing appropriate assistance, and rendering appropriate first aid.

6. *Interacting/communicating with probationers.* Clearly conveying the terms of probation to probationers, including their rights, responsibilities, the nature of probation violations, and the consequences for committing violations. Gaining probationers' cooperation and respect through professionalism, answering questions, providing support and counseling, and offering guidance as appropriate regarding meeting the conditions of probation (e.g., school attendance, urinalysis testing, employment, housing, transportation, treatment, payment schedules).

7. *Interacting/communicating with nonprobationers.* Appropriately and effectively working with affected parties such as parents/guardians, victims, witnesses, employers, and teachers. Interviewing family, school officials, and so on regarding probationers' history, character, and conduct. Providing all necessary information to affected parties regarding court or hearing dates and relevant legal procedures, in a timely and effective manner. Providing warnings to others of potential problems, threats, or dangers. Counseling and assisting victims and family members as appropriate.

8. *Working with probation staff and other agencies.* Working effectively and professionally with coworkers and with external departments, agencies, and institutions. Informing police of law violations by probationers and assisting in their investigations. Keeping law enforcement, other probation officers, and other correctional and governmental agencies informed when necessary. Referring probationers to medical, mental health, social service, and educational institutions, as needed.

9. *Working with the justice system.* Filing accurate, complete, and timely legal reports, affidavits, warrant requests, petitions, memoranda, and so on with the courts. Adhering to filing and court appearance procedures and deadlines. Demonstrating professionalism and effectiveness in providing testimony, participating in detention hearings, recommending sentencing, and in all other interactions with judges, the District Attorney's office, and defense attorneys. Maintaining cooperative relationships with attorneys, judges, and court staff. Maintaining current knowledge of case law and sentencing precedents.

The job of a parole officer, a dynamic blend of social work and law enforcement that is equal parts science and art, is among the most demanding of any profession in the field of public safety. A parole officer's day may begin shortly after dawn with a visit to a releasee's home before they leave for work and may end near midnight with postwork visits, curfew checks, or late-night surveillance. Home visits may entail as much time spent with the releasee's family as with the releasee. Required additional visits include the releasee's place of employment and any programs in which the releasee is participating. Parole officers also work closely with federal, state, and local law enforcement agencies, sharing intelligence about neighborhood crime trends and patterns, working on special operations, and collaborating in the apprehension of parole violators and releasees suspected of new crimes.

10. *Performing physically demanding work.* Working with physical skill sufficient to handle emergency situations such as medical emergencies; defending oneself; and pursuing, disarming, subduing, and restraining probationers.

A process similar to that used to select most public employees is typically used to select P/P officers. One of three systems—the merit system, the appointment system, and a combined system—is generally employed:

1. *Merit system.* Under the merit system, applicants who meet the minimum qualifications for the position are required to pass a competitive written examination. Persons who score at or above the minimum passing grade are placed on a ranked list; from this list, candidates are selected, generally in the order of their rank. The merit system was developed to remove public employment from political patronage. Critics argue, however, that a written examination cannot determine who will be a good P/P officer. In some systems, such as Connecticut, applicants are graded on the basis of their education and employment background.

2. *Appointment system.* Under the appointment system, applicants who meet minimum requirements are hired on the basis of an evaluation by the agency. Applicants do not take a written examination, although agency representatives usually interview them. This system provides agency officials with the greatest amount of flexibility; it also has a history of being used for political purposes.

> **Key Fact**
>
> P/P officers spend their working time writing reports, visiting and interviewing clients, making referrals, and talking to persons in and out of the criminal justice system.

1. *Following Written Directions:* Apply a set of rules to determine the correct action or solution for a problem.

2. *Problem Solving:* Evaluate a set of facts and draw logical conclusions.

3. *Reading Comprehension:* Read a passage and answer questions that require identifying facts, interpreting information, and drawing conclusions.

4. *Writing Clearly:* Recognize writing that avoids ambiguous or erroneous communication.

5. *Writing Detail:* Evaluate written information to determine if it provides a useful description of people or events.

6. *Accuracy with Forms and Coded Information:* Check the accuracy of information coded in report forms compared to a written summary; and compare coded information to a brief list of information to determine if the coded information matches items on the list.

7. *Work Attitudes:* Test items designed to measure attitudes about work-related situations and behavior.

3. *Combined system.* The **combined system** involves elements of both the merit and appointment systems. Applicants are first screened through a qualifying examination. Those who receive a passing grade are placed on a list from which candidates are selected, usually after an interview with agency representatives.

▶ Agency Models and P/P Officer Roles

Probation and parole agencies can be grouped by model: control, social services, and combined. Most P/P agencies would be located somewhere in the middle of this continuum, with probation agencies typically found on the right of the combined model and parole agencies on the left. Although it would not be unusual to find many social services model agencies, particularly in probation, the *control* model would not be found anywhere in its pure form, although specific programs—such as electronic monitoring and intensive supervision (discussed in Chapter 10)—may be based on a control model.

In a combined model agency, officers integrate their control or community protection role with their social services role while maintaining flexibility to stress one over the other in an individualized response to each case. For example, a young offender under supervision for joyriding in a stolen car will receive a different response than an experienced offender who is associated with organized criminal activity. In P/P treatment, officers adapt those methods that are useful to their practice while sacrificing the rest (sometimes cynically) on the altar of reality. Support for combining the social services and the control functions comes from Elizabeth Hutchinson (1987), who argues that social workers should avoid sending out other people to carry out coercive actions.

Georgia Parole Officers (PO)

Charged with the task of protecting Georgia's citizens by assisting with the reintegration of the inmate back into the community and returning to prison those who fail, an officer is, on the one hand, a counselor and mentor and, on the other hand, a law enforcement officer and a prosecutor. In the course of one day, a PO may participate in the arrest of a parole violator; help another get a job; counsel a family dispute; interview an inmate or his family; assist in obtaining treatment for a substance abuser; testify at a parole revocation hearing; and make an assortment of contacts with parolees, their families, and their employers. Every day, POs travel Georgia's city streets and rural back roads, in many cases areas that are potentially dangerous, to monitor parolee compliance with the conditions of parole and to help them break with their criminal past. Being a PO means being accessible around the clock, with after-hours calls from parolees, anxious families, and law enforcement always a possibility. As certified peace officers, they are frequently called on to assist in emergency situations, such as floods and tornadoes. Still, many POs find the time to volunteer for community projects, school programs, church activities, and an assortment of other events that they know will positively impact the quality of their hometown life. Georgia's POs work every day to intervene with and to successfully bring about change in others who had until that point been unable to abide by the rules of society.

Multnomah County (Portland, Oregon) Probation/Parole Officers

The Multnomah County Department of Community Justice promotes public safety and strives to reduce recidivism among juvenile delinquents and adult offenders through a balance of supervision, services, and sanctions. Officers provide counseling, case management, and supervision of adult clients on formal P/P. They identify individual needs of clients; assess clients' immediate functional and dysfunctional patterns; work with community agencies to develop and implement individual and family treatment plans; and counsel clients on how to comply with their P/P conditions, legal obligations, and other requirements of the court. P/P officers counsel clients on the consequences of noncompliance, develop time frames to assist clients in meeting goals and court-ordered conditions, and monitor clients' compliance through reviewing provider agency reports and by making unannounced visits to clients' residence or place of employment. They develop individual supervision plans to enhance clients' compliance with probation or parole conditions; they conduct searches and seize evidence as authorized; and they may arrest, detain, search, handcuff, and transport clients. They must maintain a chronological record of all contacts and an ongoing evaluation of clients' progress. P/P officers also prepare pre- and postsentence investigation reports for the court.

► Probation/Parole Officers as Treatment Agents

Chapter 6 reviewed a variety of approaches to treatment. However, requirements for P/P officer positions (discussed earlier in this chapter) are often a bachelor's degree, hardly adequate to provide the background (let alone the skills) for carrying out a sophisticated treatment role. Shelle Dietrich (1979: 15) points out that "the probation officer usually has not received extensive specialized training for the function of change agent; that is, the function of being competent to facilitate another person's changing his behavior, attitude, affect, or personality style." Generally, the P/P officer is not educated or trained to be a treatment agent: "It is an unrealistic expectation of probation [and parole] officers to expect themselves to be competent in an area for which they have not received adequate training" (Dietrich, 1979: 15).

In a review of the literature purporting to advise P/P officers whose background is otherwise deficient on how to become effective change agents, Dietrich (1979: 16–19) found it simplistic and at times potentially harmful to the client. Thus, she argues, professional intrusion is often advocated in areas for which the P/P officer lacks training. Cynically, she proposes, "Why not go ahead and prescribe medications, prepare legal documents, or write an insurance plan for the probationer?" (1979: 17). Dietrich cautions: "And what about the probationer? Certainly, his position in relation to the probation officer is a vulnerable one. Shouldn't the probationer be protected from being the involuntary patient of an unlicensed and untrained person, even if the person's intentions are the most purely humanistic?" (1979: 18).

Dietrich raises two other related issues:

1. Is the therapeutic enterprise possible in a P/P setting?
2. Given a positive response to this question, is it realistic to expect the delivery of treatment in P/P where caseloads usually average between 80 and 100?

She argues that even if the P/P officer "were optimally skillful in such therapeutic endeavors," without the full promise of confidentiality (impossible in a P/P setting), full and open discussion—the basis for a therapeutic relationship—is not possible (1979: 18).

Key Fact

The P/P officer is expected to be a treatment agent, although preparation for this role may be limited (if not deficient).

Dietrich is using a rather narrow definition of *therapy*, however, and within that definition she is correct in saying that therapy is not possible in a P/P setting. This author believes that therapy is more usefully defined here as the purposeful use of self to improve the social and psychological functioning of a client; defined in that way, therapy is possible within the confidentiality limitations of a P/P agency. Therapy, however, is *not* possible, given the lack of adequate education and training and the (usually) excessive caseloads encountered in P/P practice. Accordingly, some propose that treatment should take the form of the P/P officer acting as broker or advocate.

▶ Probation/Parole Officers as Brokers and Advocates

The provision of necessary services in P/P practice often requires that the P/P officer act as a broker and/or an advocate. Private and public agencies may view the P/P client as undesirable or even undeserving, and welfare, mental health, and educational agencies may see the client as threatening. Their responses to a client's needs may lead to frustration, and a frustrated client who reacts in a manner that does indeed appear threatening—frustration control is often a problem with P/P clientele—becomes a self-fulfilling prophecy.

Eric Carlson and Evalyn Parks see the broker role in P/P as almost diametrically opposed to the treatment approach because the P/P officer "is not concerned primarily with understanding or changing the behavior of the probationer, but rather with assessing the concrete needs of the individual and arranging for the probationers to receive services that directly address these needs" (1979: 120). The officer functions as a manager or broker of resources and social services available from other agencies. "It is the task of the probation officer to assess the service needs of the probationer, locate the social service agency which addresses those needs as its primary function, to refer the probationer to the appropriate agency, and to follow up referrals to make sure that the probationer actually received the services" (1979: 120–21).

▶ Probation and Parole Officers as Law Enforcement Agents

The most controversial role of a P/P officer is that of enforcer, and during the past two decades "there seems little doubt that probation and parole work has moved away from a general embracing of offender assistance [social services] models into a solid marriage with control, compliance, and punishment models of community supervision" (Castellano, 1997: 22). In many jurisdictions, particularly in high-crime urban areas, the police/sheriff is either unwilling or unable to provide sufficient warrant enforcement services. If the P/P agency does not enforce its own warrants, they often go unattended; the potential danger to the public is obvious as hundreds (or in larger jurisdictions, thousands) of warrants go unenforced. Warrants turned over to outside agencies are occasionally used to force P/P violators into becoming informants, and P/P agencies usually have rules against clients serving as informants. As more and more P/P agencies move in the direction of a control model of supervision, arrest (peace officer) powers and the carrying of firearms by P/P officers became increasingly common.

In practice, P/P agency policy with respect to firearms generally falls into one of three categories: (1) Officers are not peace (law enforcement) officers, for example, Maryland and Michigan. (2) Officers are peace officers and the carrying of firearms on duty is optional, for example, correctional probation officers in Virginia and probation officers in Maricopa County, Arizona. (3) Officers are peace officers required to carry firearms on duty, for

HAZARDS OF PAROLE SUPERVISION

The very nature of supervising offenders subjects P/P officers to potentially hazardous events on a routine basis. Fortunately, not every officer has had a bad or harrowing experience, but many have. On one occasion, New York State Parole Officer Tom Brancato was strangled almost to the point of unconsciousness in a remote wooded area where he stopped to see his parolee at work. This surprise attack occurred after Officer Brancato had asked the parolee to have a seat in his car. As soon as they were seated, the parolee reached over, grabbed Officer Brancato by the throat, and began choking him. Wedged between the bucket seats of his Volkswagen, the officer's right arm and gun were pinned beneath him. After considerable effort, he managed to get his gun with his left hand and stick the barrel in the parolee's ear. Case closed.

In 2009, a registered sex offender with a history of violence was making a routine office visit to his parole officer in Jamaica, New York. When she sought to search his backpack, the parolee drew a knife and attempted to take the officer hostage. She struggled to free herself from the parolee, and when he refused to drop the knife, the parolee was shot and killed by two backup parole officers.

example, probation and parole officers in Nevada, and parole officers in New Jersey, and parole and probation officers in North Dakota. The line between peace officers and civilians has blurred as many states have "shall issue" statutes requiring that civilians who meet relevant criteria, such as no criminal history, be issued a permit to carry a concealed handgun. A few states, such as Vermont, allow adult residents without a criminal conviction to carry a concealed firearm without the need for a permit. Some agencies, for example Missouri, while permitting their P/P officers to be armed, except in emergencies, do not allow officers to participate in arrest activities.

▶ Should P/P Officers Make Arrests and Carry Firearms?

In 1975, while still a parole officer, I answered with a resounding "Yes." Four decades later, I find myself still in agreement with the legendary New York parole chief David Dressler (1951: 152), who wrote: "I am convinced a parole system worth its salt has to make its own arrests." Although some (typically nonpractitioner) observers bemoan the existence of a role conflict in P/P or an incompatibility between control and treatment, this author never experienced such conflicts in practice, nor did his colleagues in New York. Indeed, given the nature of P/P clientele, sound treatment demands the use of appropriate methods of control—offenders under supervision often engage in behavior that is self-destructive and dangerous to the community. As a trained social worker, I found that the application of casework principles was enhanced by the legal powers inherent in P/P settings. Indeed, if role conflict is inherent in P/P practice, as Todd Clear and Edward Latessa (1989: 2) note, such is the nature of many professional positions, but "among other professions, role conflict is seldom seen as a justification for eviscerating the profession of a few less salient tasks; rather, it is felt that the 'true' professional finds a way of integrating various role expectations, balancing them and weighing the appropriateness of various expressions of the roles."

Misunderstanding of the control/enforcement role vis-à-vis the social services role is highlighted by Norval Morris and Michael Tonry, who argue that "there is no way in which effective, regular, but unpredictable urine testing to ensure that the convicted offender is drug free can be made other than as a police-type function" (1990: 185). As a trained social

> **Key Fact**
>
> Controversy continues over whether or not P/P officers should be armed and responsible for arresting P/P violators or whether this should be left to the police.

PAROLE OFFICERS, FIREARMS, AND PUBLIC SAFETY

Colorado parole officers on a routine evening home visit in Denver found that their client was not at home, but his sister permitted the officers to check the premises. Inside his closet, the officers found a pistol. As they were removing the weapon, the parolee arrived and was met by the officers in front of the house. Informed that he was to be taken into custody, the parolee bolted and ran behind the house with the officers in pursuit.

Suddenly, he halted, drew a handgun, and aimed at the officers, who fatally shot the parolee.

In 2008, a Colorado parole officer in Denver was making a routine visit when inside a hallway he encountered a man he knew was wanted for some robberies. The suspect refused to follow the parole officer's orders and produced a weapon, at which time he was shot and killed by the officer.

worker, I disagree: Preventing drug abuse—the purpose of drug testing—is to the client's advantage; testing enhances the ego function of the offender, strengthening resolve to avoid harmful substances. Indeed, the client can demur when under pressure from drug-using associates: "Can't man; got to report to my PO and he'll check me out." This approach is sound social work.

As a private citizen with a working knowledge of P/P, I have certain concerns about personal safety—that of my family, friends, and neighbors. From this (I believe typical) layperson's perspective, I evaluate a P/P agency by providing some examples. During the course of an office or home visit, a P/P officer may discover that a client is using heroin or cocaine. If the offender is unemployed, the drug habit is probably financed by criminal activities, so the client is a clear and present danger to himself or herself and to the community. A P/P agency whose officers cannot immediately (and safely) arrest such a person is not providing an adequate level of client service or community protection. P/P agencies also supervise offenders who have been involved in sex offenses against children, vehicular homicide as a result of intoxication, burglary, and armed robbery. A P/P agency whose officers are not responsible for expeditious enforcement of prohibitions—through investigation and arrest—against frequenting children's play areas, drinking and driving, and carrying tools for forced entry, or who cannot investigate money sources or a lifestyle that cannot be supported by the offender's employment status, is not providing the minimum acceptable level of community safety.

Furthermore, the adult (and frequently the juvenile) P/P client is often a serious law violator who has proved to be a potential danger to the community. Many have been involved in crimes of violence, and the public and elected officials expect that probationers

FIREARMS AND SELF-DEFENSE

In 1993, in a change of policy, the Florida legislature authorized correctional probation officers (CPOs) to carry firearms. Subsequently, a CPO made a routine field visit to a client's home. Unknown to the officer, the client had expressed his intention to kill the CPO in retaliation for the arrest of the offender's brother for technical violations (the brother was returned to prison). After the officer completed his visit and was driving away from the home, he was shot twice and lost control of his car, which struck a tree. The offender continued to advance toward the car, but the officer was able to draw his weapon and return fire, striking the offender three times and saving his own life (Papy, 1997).

and parolees, if they are to remain in the community, will be under the scrutiny of P/P authorities. This scrutiny is why the law of most jurisdictions empowers P/P agencies with law enforcement responsibilities. However, the question is often raised whether the P/P officer should be the law enforcer or merely the treatment agent or broker.

Do arrest powers and the carrying of a firearm interfere with the P/P officer's ability to form a casework relationship with which to provide treatment? I am of the opinion that they do not. Indeed, because of P/P officers' relationships with their clients, in delinquency situations they are able to effect an arrest without the tension and hostility that often accompany arrests made by other law enforcement officers (who have no relationship with the client). In fact, whether the P/P officer actually makes the arrest, the client knows that the P/P officer initiated the warrant action.

In my many years of parole work, I posed the following question to clients: "I know that you are determined not to get into trouble, so this is a hypothetical question. If you violate parole, would you prefer the police, or would you rather that I came to arrest you?" Typically, stories about being badly treated by the police ensued before they generally responded, "If I gotta go back to prison, you come to get me, please."

In Massachusetts, when it was decided that unarmed POs from the Dorchester Division of the District Court would make unannounced home visits at night, they required police escorts—poor social work practice on at least two levels: First, it draws attention to the client, violating confidentiality; second, it conveys a (perhaps unintended) message that the client is too dangerous to visit without a police escort, which may actually enhance the prestige of a gang-involved youth. Having a police officer present during a home visit places in jeopardy the casework relationship between the supervising officer and the client. In a potentially serious breach of confidentiality, the police officer can be privy to discussions of matters such as the client's medical status (e.g., HIV/AIDS) and his or her relationship with a spouse and children.

Nevertheless, the "Massachusetts model" has been extended to Boston and other jurisdictions. In Jackson County, Oregon, teams of probation officers and Medford police officers conducted what a daily newspaper (Conrad, 2009) referred to as an "early morning sweep"—visits to the residences of 27 probationers. "Project Spotlight," housed at Sam Houston State University in Huntsville, Texas, promotes police officer–probation officer teams to provide intensive supervision and surveillance, including evening, early morning, and weekend visits to the homes and communities of probationers. In Washington, D.C., the P/P status of clients is flagrantly displayed by community supervision officers

IN THE FIELD

Georgia Parole Officer Joje Wilson-Gibbs turns into East Lake Meadows, a housing project just inside Atlanta city limits, and notes that the surroundings are particularly lively for so early an hour. Throughout the warren of circling streets sprawl barrack-like apartments, several tattooed with graffiti and one encircled by a flower garden. A gray-bearded old man crouches in the corner of his stoop; two carloads of young men pass while slowly inspecting the sedate blue sedan driven by the parole officer.

Wilson-Gibbs is checking on her parolee, but it's not him she fears. Like most parole officers, the unpredictability of the environment most concerns her. Next to her on the seat is a bulky purse, on which is perched a can of pepper spray and in which is concealed a .38-caliber revolver. "I don't want to use my gun in a real-life situation," she says. "I don't want to use pepper spray, either, but I feel better knowing I'm trained and can react with these weapons if I'm in a life-threatening situation. All sorts of things add up to a sense of security for me—including having good tires on a reliable car that won't leave you stranded."

OKLAHOMA P/P OFFICERS

Two Oklahoma P/P officers were interviewing a client in his apartment when someone entered and directed their attention to a man standing nearby who was arguing with a woman—he was holding an assault rifle. The officers approached from behind, drew their weapons, identified themselves, and ordered the man to drop his weapon. The man glanced back at the officers, who continued to shout for him to drop his weapon. He suddenly moved his hand to the weapon, turned, and pointed it at the officers, one of whom fired a fatal shot into the man's chest (Thornton, 2003).

and uniformed police officers who use marked police vehicles to conduct accountability tours—joint visits with offenders in the community—throughout the city. In some jurisdictions, such as Redmond, Washington, and Ogden City, Utah, police officers are authorized to make parolee home visits. For more than a decade, I made routine evening, early morning, and weekend visits to parolees in New York, as did my colleagues, without unduly displaying my parole officer status or needing to be escorted by police officers.

P/P clients are potentially dangerous and usually reside in high-crime neighborhoods, reason enough to be armed. This facet of parole work was dramatically revealed while I was a parole officer in New York. My colleague, 32-year-old Donald Sutherland, attempted to arrest a parole violator on the street and was shot to death. The parolee was subdued at the scene by other parole officers. After being convicted of murder, the parolee escaped from prison and eluded law officers for several weeks (on one occasion after an exchange of gunfire). He was finally killed after refusing to surrender to a combined force of city and state police and parole officers.

During my career as a parole officer, I admit to being concerned about entering certain areas, walking certain streets, and entering the buildings of some neighborhoods. But, I never felt threatened by any of my clients; quite the reverse. Many were (I believe genuinely) solicitous of my safety, providing warnings about events in the area that could prove dangerous and/or insisting on escorting me to my car. It was not unusual for men whose behavior in the past had been dangerous to others to nevertheless have rapport with *their* PO.

Although carrying a firearm does not guarantee safety, a person with a firearm may discourage attacks by carrying himself or herself more confidently than others who might be selected for victimization. Knowing that P/P officers are routinely carrying firearms has a deterrent value. Indeed, many *unarmed* P/P officers (perhaps unknowingly) gain a degree of safety because they are perceived as police officers or are believed to be armed.

▶ Probation and Parole Officers' Powers of Search and Seizure

There has been a shift in the sympathy displayed by courts regarding the rights of prisoners and those under supervision in the criminal justice system (Jermstad, 2002). This is highlighted by the interpretation of the Fourth Amendment's protection against unreasonable searches and seizures as applied to probationers and parolees. Persons on probation and parole sign conditions of supervision that routinely permit a warrantless search of their property and person. In 1987, the Supreme Court held (*Griffin v. Wisconsin* 107 S. Ct. 3164) that the special needs attendant to supervising probationers justified a warrantless search based on "reasonable grounds," that is, evidence less than the search warrant standard of probable cause.

In 1998, in another 5–4 decision, the Court ruled that evidence seized by parole officers without a search warrant, which would be barred at a criminal trial by the exclusionary rule, could be used at a parole violation hearing. In this case (*Pennsylvania Board of Probation and Parole v. Scott*, 524 U.S. 357, 1998), Keith Scott had been serving a 10- to 20-year sentence for third-degree murder when he signed a parole agreement that stipulated: "I expressly consent to the search of my person, property and residence, without a warrant by agents of the Pennsylvania Board of Probation and Parole. Any items in [*sic*] the possession of which constitutes a violation of parole/reparole shall be subject to seizure, and may be used as evidence in the parole revocation process." After receiving information that Scott had violated his parole by possessing firearms, consuming alcohol, and assaulting a coworker, parole officers obtained an arrest warrant and arrested him at a diner. They then went to his residence where they commenced a search without asking for or receiving permission from Scott's mother, who owned the residence; they found five firearms in Scott's room. The Pennsylvania Supreme Court held that Scott's Fourth Amendment protection was not waived by his signing of the parole agreement; furthermore, the court ruled that the exclusionary rule applies to parole violation hearings. The U.S. Supreme Court, in overruling the Pennsylvania court, stated:

> In most cases the State is willing to extend parole only because it is able to condition it on compliance with certain requirements. The State thus has an "overwhelming interest" in ensuring that a parolee complies with those requirements and is returned to prison if he fails to do so. The exclusion of evidence establishing a parole violation hampers the State's ability to ensure compliance with these conditions by permitting the parolee to avoid the consequences of his noncompliance.

The Court noted that the usually adversarial relationship between a criminal suspect and police is not a characteristic of the parole officer/parolee relationship: "Their relationship is more supervisory than adversarial."

In 2001, this time in a unanimous decision (*United States v. Knights*, 122 S. Ct. 587), the Supreme Court expanded the *Scott* decision, ruling that a probationer's residence can be subjected to a warrantless search based on "reasonable suspicion." This does not violate the Fourth Amendment, the Court ruled, even when the search (in this case by sheriff's officers) is for "investigatory" rather than probation purposes. A California court's sentencing order (rules of probation) "included the condition that Knights [the probationer] submit to search at any time, with or without a search or arrest warrant or reasonable cause, by any probation or law enforcement officer." Knights was "unambiguously informed of the search condition"; thus, his "reasonable expectation of privacy was significantly diminished." This condition, the Court stated, furthers the two primary goals of probation: rehabilitating the client and protecting society from future criminal violations. The Court concluded that "the very assumption of probation is that the probationer is more likely than others to violate the law," so the state "may justifiably focus on probationers in a way that it does not on the ordinary citizen." Todd Jermstad states, "It is clear from the context and tone of this opinion that the Supreme Court's overall expectation of probation was to be much more oriented toward law enforcement than serving the needs of probationers" (2002: 15).

In 2006, the Court ruled 6–3 (*Samson v. California*, 547 U.S. 843) that the Fourth Amendment does not prohibit a police officer from conducting a suspicionless search of a parolee. The Court noted "parolees, who are on the 'continuum' of state-imposed punishments, have fewer expectations of privacy than probationers, because parole is more akin to imprisonment than probation is." And California requires every prisoner eligible for release on state parole to agree in writing to be subject to search or seizure by a parole officer or other peace officer with or without a search warrant and with or without cause. The search of parolee Donald Samson by a police officer resulted in finding methamphetamine for which he was convicted and sentenced to seven years imprisonment.

▶ Legal Liability of Probation/Parole Officers

In addition to agency disciplinary sanctions that range from a written reprimand to dismissal, probation and parole officers can be held liable under state law, civil and criminal; they are not mutually exclusive. Civilly, they can be held liable for a tortuous act that causes damage to the person or property of another or for violating a state civil rights statute. Criminally, they can be held liable under penal code provisions designed for public officers who acting under color of his or her office subjects someone to mistreatment, such as unlawful detention or sexual harassment. Like any other person, they can also be liable for violation of state criminal law.

Under federal law, P/P officers can be held liable both civilly and criminally for acting under color of law—misuse of authority—to deny a person of rights, privileges, or immunities secured by the Constitution and laws. If there are threats of or actual bodily injury, penalties include fines and long terms of imprisonment. If two or more persons are involved, they can be prosecuted for conspiracy to commit these unlawful acts. They can also be tried for the same acts in both state and federal courts, prohibitions against double jeopardy not with standing because state and federal courts are different jurisdictions (Lyons and Jermstad, 2013).

P/P officers have generally been successful in avoiding **legal liability** for actions performed in the course of their duties. Although state (but not municipal or county) agencies are generally exempt from liability for their governmental activities unless waived, immunity ordinarily is unavailable to state officers who can be sued as individuals. Immunity for probation officers is often dependent on the agencies for which they work and the nature of the functions they perform, but in general they merely have qualified immunity (as opposed to the absolute immunity enjoyed by judges). Probation officers who are employees of the court and who work under court supervision, while they do not enjoy the same absolute immunity of judges, are vested with judicial immunity for some acts, such as preparing and submitting a presentence report in a criminal case, because they are performing a quasi-judicial function (del Carmen et al., 2001).

P/P officers may be vulnerable to civil liability for such wrongs as negligence and failure to warn. **Negligence**, the most common form of tort action, refers to a failure to exercise that degree of care which a person of ordinary prudence would exercise under similar circumstances or conduct that creates an undue risk of harm to others. There are three elements in a negligence action:

> **Key Fact**
>
> Although P/P officials may be sued as individuals, generally they have been successful in avoiding legal liability for actions performed in the course of their duties.

1. A legal duty is owed to the plaintiff.

2. There is a violation of that duty by an act or omission to act, which constitutes a breach of that duty.

3. That act or omission was the proximate cause for the injury or damage suffered by the plaintiff.

Although no definitive Supreme Court decision exists concerning the liability of probation and parole officers for a **failure to warn** in the supervision process, state and federal cases have established liability for crimes committed by parolees under their supervision within a narrow set of circumstances. Case law has established a duty to warn third persons when there is a "special relationship" between certain types of professionals and a person under their care. This duty to warn arises because of the professional's training and expertise, which place the professional in a good position to predict that the person presents a reasonably foreseeable risk of harm to a particular third person. This "special relationship" could be seen in the relationship between a P/P officer and an offender under the officer's supervision. The P/P officer, in some situations, could be in a position to predict that the offender presents a reasonably foreseeable risk of harm to a particular third person.

In a leading federal case in the area of the failure to warn, *Reiser v. District of Columbia* (563 F.2d 462, 1977), a federal court ruled that because of the special relationship between a parole officer and parolee with a history of brutal violence against women, appropriate warnings to employers and other persons foreseeably at risk were required. In this case, the parolee used his position as an apartment building custodian to gain access to a woman's apartment, where he murdered her. The court held the agency liable.

The common element in these circumstances, note Rolando del Carmen and Paul Louis, is the rather unclear concept of a "special duty" on the part of the P/P officer:

> For this "special duty" to be relevant, there must be a *reasonably foreseeable risk* which exists when the circumstances of the relationship between the parolee and a third party suggest that the parolee may engage in criminal or antisocial conduct related to his or her past conduct. This, in turn, results from a combination of three factors: (a) the parolee's job; (b) his or her prior criminal background and conduct; and (c) the type of crime for which he or she was convicted. For example, it is reasonably foreseeable that a parolee convicted of child sexual assault would commit a similar act if employed in a childcare center, but not if employed as a janitor on a college campus. (1988: 37; emphasis in original)

▶ Volunteers in Probation/Parole

Probation in the United States originated with **volunteers**. Keith J. Leenhouts, judge of the Royal Oak, Michigan, municipal court, reactivated the tradition in 1959. In that city, the municipal (misdemeanor) court probation department was staffed entirely by volunteers. Through the efforts of Judge Leenhouts, a national organization, Volunteers in Prevention, Probation, and Prisons, Inc. (VIP), was formed. VIP merged with the National Council on Crime and Delinquency in 1972; in 1983, it reverted to independent status.

There are four volunteer models (Carlson and Parks, 1979: 237):

1. *One-to-one model.* On a one-to-one basis, volunteers seek to obtain the trust and confidence of P/P clients and help them maintain their existence, clarify their role in society, and plan for the future.

2. *Supervision model.* Working as a case aide to a P/P officer, the volunteer provides services to several clients at the direction of the officer.

3. *Professional model.* The volunteer is a professional or semiprofessional in his or her field (e.g., teacher and mechanic) who provides specialized services to several clients, such as literacy help or automotive skills training.

4. *Administrative model.* The volunteer assists with P/P administrative functions and interacts only indirectly with clients.

The primary approach of Judge Leenhouts and VIP is mentoring the juvenile and misdemeanor court clients. This venue is seen as critical because the "vast majority of all crimes and offenses are tried in these courts...[and] it is estimated that as many as 80 percent of all felonies are committed by persons who first are convicted of a misdemeanor or juvenile offense" (Reeves, 2003: v). Therefore, according to Bob Reeves, "there is no better place to identify and divert a (usually) young apprehended offender from a life punctuated with habitual criminal activity" (2003: v). Mentors typically work with youths sentenced to probation, spending time that features recreation and education.

Some P/P agencies and staff members are critical of the use of volunteers. They may view the efforts of volunteers as interference with their prerogatives or may be concerned about sharing information with volunteers because of the confidential aspect of P/P practice. Chris Eskridge and Eric Carlson (1979) report that in some agencies the regular P/P workers see volunteers as a threat to their jobs. Some P/P officers resent the fact that volunteers are able to play the "good guy," while they have control and enforcement functions. Some complain of volunteers acting as advocates for the offender in opposition to regular P/P work.

Because volunteers are not paid, they need to derive some satisfaction from their efforts. Satisfaction results when a level of success exists; and to be successful, volunteers require adequate training and supervision. In other words, the successful use of volunteers is not "cost free"; staff is required for the training, coordination, and supervision of volunteers. If additional staff members are not to be employed for these tasks, the agency has to take away from the working time of regular P/P agency personnel. Eskridge and Carlson (1979) report that lack of success in volunteer programs is a function of management operations rather than the volunteer concept. Faulty management includes the inability to assign volunteers expeditiously, inadequate volunteer training, poor supervision or support for volunteers, and lack of communication.

Los Angeles County Reserve Deputy Probation Officer Program

Reserve deputy probation officers are deputized volunteers who complete a training course and a subsequent on-the-job training period; for specialized assignments, they may be required to complete additional training. Reserve probation officers work on weekdays, weekends, or evenings for a minimum of 16 hours per month. Under the direct supervision of regular officers, they provide support services and aid in the investigation and supervision of juveniles and adults. They assist in field offices, juvenile halls and camps. Other counties in California, such as San Diego, also use reserve deputy probation officers.

New Jersey Volunteers in Parole Program

As a component of the New Jersey Bureau of Parole, the Volunteers in Parole Program is designed to provide help through a pool of individuals from the community. These individuals are qualified and willing to assist bureau personnel in serving the varied needs of its many diverse clients. The following volunteer categories reflect the service needs of the Bureau of Parole while showing the scope of ways in which volunteers provide valuable assistance:

Parole officer aide. He or she helps the parole officer with various investigations and assists as officer of the day for routine office interviews; however, involvement with law enforcement activities is prohibited.

Professional aide. He or she is a member of a profession offering specific services on an as-needed basis.

Administrative aide. He or she works in a district office in an administrative or clerical capacity.

Student intern. He or she assumes the same role as the parole officer aide while a student from one of the various colleges and universities that provide internships within the bureau as part of a cooperative arrangement.

South Carolina Department of Probation, Parole, and Pardon Services

South Carolina offers a variety of volunteer opportunities:

Job developers. These volunteers help offenders find employment and learn new job skills. They aid the offender's job search and provide pointers on interviews, demeanor, and job conflicts. They also make referrals to employment agencies and develop a job bank for offenders.

Community sponsors. These sponsors are matched with offenders to develop a relationship of guidance, support, and motivation. They assist offenders with obtaining support and rehabilitative services. Through recreation, conversation, and other activities, the volunteer provides a positive role model.

Court assistants. These volunteers aid the department with such tasks as processing offenders placed on probation, investigating and collecting information, reviewing information with offenders, and monitoring other court activity.

Agent/team assistants. These assistants help P/P agents by monitoring and meeting the needs of offenders, which include maintaining contacts with service and referral agencies, law enforcement agencies, court offices, family members, and employers.

Missouri Board of Probation and Parole

Volunteers are used by the Missouri Board of Probation and Parole on a one-to-one basis to increase the services available to P/P clients. As P/P aides, they are provided with training in reality therapy (discussed in Chapter 6) and are expected to influence behavior by setting an example while being patient listeners. The volunteer helps the client develop and carry out realistic plans, provides advice and encouragement, and may offer concrete assistance by helping the client secure employment. They can opt for serving as reparation board members who assist in the implementation of restorative justice programs (discussed in Chapter 10).

There are also volunteer positions available with juvenile probation:

- *Mentor.* A mentor develops a long-term stable relationship with a juvenile probationer (a one-year commitment).
- *Probation officer assistant.* This assistant works in close cooperation with the assigned probation officer, providing supervision, maintaining case records, and being available for court appearances with the juvenile.
- *Sole sanction restitution.* This volunteer monitors a large number of cases with court-ordered consequences to ensure that court orders are followed and restitution payments are made.
- *Victim services case manager.* This volunteer manager contacts victims to answer questions regarding victims' rights in the court process and to verify losses.

> **Key Fact**
>
> Volunteers in P/P can fill various roles, from clerical duties to direct services.

Summary

- Minimum qualifications for P/P officer entry-level positions usually include a bachelor's degree.
- P/P officers spend their working time writing reports, visiting and interviewing clients, making referrals, and talking to persons in and out of the criminal justice system.

- Three systems are used to select P/P officers.
- Probation and parole agencies can be grouped by model: control, social services, and combined.
- The roles of P/P officers are related to these models.
- The most controversial role of a P/P officer is that of enforcer.
- Controversy continues over whether or not P/P officers should be armed and responsible for arresting P/P violators or whether this should be left to the police.
- P/P officers have extraordinary powers of search and seizure.
- When probation officers prepare and submit a presentence investigation report, they enjoy absolute immunity from liability.
- There are four volunteer models in P/P.

Key Terms

appointment system *149*
broker *152*
combined system *150*
control model *150*

failure to warn *158*
legal liability *158*
merit system *149*
negligence *158*

probable cause *156*
reasonable expectation of privacy 157
social services model *150*
volunteers *159*

Internet Connections

American Probation and Parole Association: **appa-net.org**

Criminal justice links: **faculty.ncwc.edu/toconnor**

Probation agency links: **cppca.org/10_links.shtml**

Volunteers in Prevention, Probation, and Prisons: **vipmentoring.org**

Review Questions

1. What are the three systems used to select P/P officers?
2. What are the three models of P/P agencies?
3. How is P/P officer role related to the P/P agency?
4. What is the most controversial role of P/P officers? Why?
5. What is the broker and advocate role of a P/P officer?
6. What are the extraordinary search and seizure powers of P/P officers?
7. When do probation officers enjoy absolute immunity from liability?
8. What are four volunteer models in P/P?

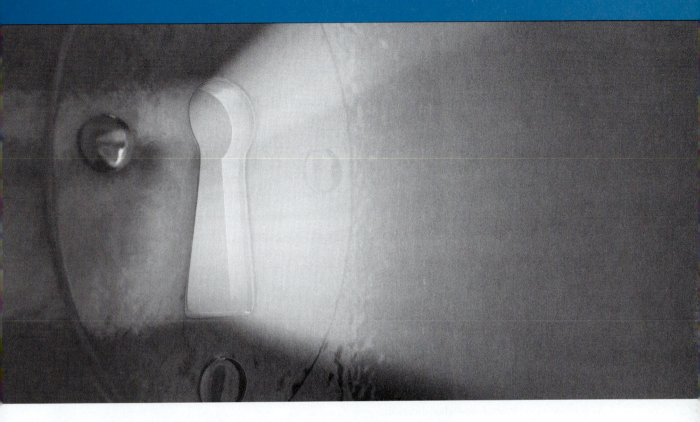

8 Probation and Parole Supervision

LEARNING OBJECTIVES

This chapter will enable the student to:

1 *Understand classification in probation/parole (P/P).*

2 *Explain the risk/needs assessment.*

3 *Distinguish between assigning cases on a caseload and workload basis.*

4 *Appreciate how parolees differ from probationers.*

5 *Describe place-based supervision.*

6 *Understand why the initial interview in P/P practice is considered a crucial time in the supervision process.*

7 *Discuss the relationship between criminality and unemployment.*

8 *State how the length of P/P supervision is determined.*

9 *Understand the implications of supervision-for-life provisions for certain offenders.*

10 *Identify the methods for responding to a supervision violation in probation and parole.*

11 *Discuss the two types of P/P violation.*

12 *Distinguish between the standard of evidence of a P/P violation from that of a criminal prosecution.*

13 *Explain how "Street time" in probation differs from that in parole.*

14 *Discuss the Supreme Court decisions of Gagnon and Morissey.*

15 *Understand the exclusionary rule, diminished expectation of privacy, and liberty interest in P/P.*

Probation and parole (P/P) supervision begins soon after an offender is placed on probation or released from a correctional facility. Within 24 to 48 hours they report in-person to a probation and parole office for an initial interview and assignment to a P/P officer caseload. Although probation and parole supervision across agencies may differ in the details, there are commonly shared concerns: that the offender will recidivate (particularly when the nature of the recidivism generates media coverage) and that personnel resources are insufficient to meet the service needs of clients and the safety concerns of the community. In this chapter, we begin our examination of the supervision process with a method for dealing with the problem of insufficient resources—classification.

▶ Classification in Probation and Parole

Prisons have traditionally classified inmates on the basis of the security needs of the institution and the physical limitations or handicaps (if any) of the prisoner. With the advent of the corrections model, **classification** was expanded to include items relevant to rehabilitation programs offered by the correctional department in its various facilities. The de-emphasis of the corrections model has, correspondingly, lessened the importance of institutional classification (at least for rehabilitation). However, classification has become widespread in P/P, primarily for **caseload management**.

During the 1970s, P/P administrators came to the realization that their resources would never be sufficient to even approach the service needs of their clientele and that the typical P/P officer approximated agency objectives (protection of the community and rehabilitation of the offender) through the use of an unofficial and unarticulated classification system:

> Because not all offenders require the same level of supervision or exhibit the same problems, most experienced probation and parole agents utilize an intuitive system of classifying offenders into differential treatment or surveillance modes, usually based on their judgments of client needs and their perception of the client's potential for continued unlawful behavior. It seems reasonable to assume that without this type of caseload management,

successes would diminish and failures increase.... [But] this untested, highly individualized approach does not provide information necessary to rationally deploy staff and other resources. (Baird, Heinz, and Bemus, 1982: 36)

"The nation's parole and probation departments are struggling to find the balance between dwindling financial resources and ensuring the lowest possible risk to communities" (Ritter n.d. 1).

Enter the **risk/needs assessment** that measures an offender's criminal risk factors and specific needs that, if addressed, will reduce the likelihood of future criminal behavior. "Tools consist of a set of questions that guide face-to-face interviews with offenders, probing behaviors and attitudes that research show are related to criminal reoffending," usually supplemented with an official records check (*Risk/Needs Assessment 101*: 2).

Risk assessments gauge static and dynamic factors that influence whether a person will recidivate by committing a new offense or violating the terms of P/P. Risk assessment tools vary somewhat in the types of questions presented and how well they differentiate among individuals with a high versus a low probability of recidivating. The primary *static predictors* whether someone will reoffend are as follows: (1) current age, (2) past criminal history, (3) age at first arrest, and (4) type of crime committed.

"Researchers have found seven *dynamic risk factors* that predict recidivism among individuals under community supervision.

1. Anti-social personality pattern (e.g., antagonism, impulsivity, risk-taking)
2. Pro-criminal attitude (e.g., negative expressions about the law)
3. Anti-social associates
4. Poor use of leisure/recreational time
5. Substance use
6. Problematic circumstances at home (e.g., neglect or abuse, homelessness)
7. Problematic circumstances at school or work (e.g., limited education, unemployment)"
   (Clement, Schwarzfeld, and M. Thompson, 2011: 14)

A study of predicted risk in federal probation revealed that of those classified as "lowest risk" 2 percent were arrested for a new crime during their period under community supervision, while those categorized as "highest risk" had a new arrest rate of 34 percent (Rhodes et al., 2013).

During the late 1970s and early 1980s, the use of formal classification in P/P expanded greatly. This movement was led by the state of Wisconsin, which in 1975 received funding from the Law Enforcement Assistance Administration for a Case Classification/Staff Deployment Project. After four years, a **risk/needs assessment** was designed, implemented, and evaluated statewide.

The system developed in Wisconsin was adopted by the National Institute of Corrections and, subsequently, by many other P/P jurisdictions. The basic strengths of the risk/needs assessment system are its completeness, simplicity, and utility to management—indeed, classification for supervision is basically a management tool. Although variations exist between jurisdictions, all risk/needs classification schemes quantify variables along two dimensions:

> **Key Fact**
>
> The risk/needs classification system used in P/P is for caseload management.

1. Degree to which the offender presents a *risk* of recidivism (commit a new offense)
2. Degree to which the offender has *needs* and requires assistance from the P/P agency

Taken together, these two dimensions allow for a prognostication that has implications for the level of supervision required and thus for caseload management and deployment of personnel.

▼

The system tested in Wisconsin demonstrated its effectiveness in predicting success or failure in completing P/P terms. In a sample of 8,250 clients, the percentage of individuals who were rated low risk and whose probation or parole was later revoked was 3 percent; of the cases rated high risk, 37 percent were revoked. A more recent evaluation found overclassification of the high-risk population—93 percent of parolees—due to the weight given to assaultive offenses, although this factor is not predictive of recidivism (Eisenberg, Bryl, and Fabelo, 2009). Other jurisdictions have also tested the system. The Los Angeles Probation Department found that the risk scale (in comparison with intuitive judgments by probation officers) did well in predicting which cases would be successful and which would not; the needs scale, however, was found to have almost no predictive value (Program Services Office, 1983). Massachusetts found that using a variation of the Wisconsin instrument, half the clients classified as "maximum" risk were subsequently recidivists compared with 36 percent of those classified as "moderate" and 17 percent of those classified as "minimum." (Brown, 1984); and a risk scale used in Ohio that classified offenders as low, medium, and high risk was successful in predicting the likelihood recidivism (Latessa et al., 2010). In Philadelphia, a successful forecasting method (Random Forest Modeling) "allowed the [probation] agency to stratify offenders by the risk they pose, to tailor supervision requirements, to focus resources in accordance with policy directives, and to balance caseload sizes in the face of budgetary constraints" (Barnes and Hyatt, 2012: 11).

The instruments typically used by P/P agencies require the officer to place a number in a box that corresponds with the case record or the officer's assessment for each of the risk assessment variables, adds up the score, and records that in a box labeled "Total." He or she then proceeds to do the same for the needs assessment variables. Afterward, the two final scores are compared; whichever is higher (risk or needs) determines the level of supervision—*reduced*, *regular*, *close*, and *intensive*. (In some jurisdictions, only three levels of supervision exist: minimum, medium, and maximum.) Some flexibility is possible because the procedures provide for an override if, after completing the assessment, there is a compelling reason to raise or lower the grade of supervision. Typically, after a case is classified along the risk/needs dimension, it is assigned to a P/P officer according to a predetermined workload distribution.

Using a risk/needs instrument to determine the level of supervision encounters the reality of an urban environment in which many offenders are clustered in particular neighborhoods.

Supervising a workload in which offenders are in relative proximity is more easily accomplished than a similar workload spread over a wide area. If P/P officers are supervising risk-homogeneous workloads, they may be traversing the same neighborhoods, each visiting offenders with a particular risk level, thereby impacting on agency efficiency.

A CLOSER LOOK

LEVEL SERVICE INVENTORY–REVISED (LSI-R)

The LSI-R is a popular classification system developed in Canada for matching offenders to levels of probation supervision. According to its publisher (MHS.com), the inventory "is a quantitative survey of offender attributers and their situations relevant to level of supervision and treatment decisions." An actuarial predictive scale with 54 items, the LSI-R combines the risk of reoffending and the needs assessment using factors such as age, previous convictions, alcohol and drug use, and attitudes/ orientations. The assessment relies heavily on an interview with the offender. Problem areas are scored and the total number of problem points determines the level of risk of reoffending, which is then matched to appropriate levels of supervision and services. The overall predictive value of the LSI-R has been demonstrated in a number of studies (Holsinger, Lowenkamp, and Latessa, 2006; Lowenkamp, Lovins, and Latessa, 2009), but others reveal a lack of significant predictive value (e.g., Simourd, 2006).

Supervision Levels in Georgia

The P/P officer interviews a new client; and with the help of the presentence report, institutional reports (for parolees), and other relevant documents, he or she fills out a risk/needs instrument that attaches a numerical value to factor, for example, age at first conviction, substance abuse, and criminal history. A total is derived from the scoring of information on the instrument and is plugged into a particular level of supervision; typically, a reassessment is performed every six months. Because clients with a higher level of supervision require a greater expenditure of P/P officer time, equity is determined based not simply on **caseload** (the total number of clients supervised) but on **workload** (the anticipated amount of time each case will demand). This quantification allows for the easy use of computers, which can determine the need for more P/P officers in a particular jurisdiction (or if additional officers are not economically feasible, a corresponding reduction in the amount of supervisory time devoted to each case).

Each case is placed in one of six levels of supervision:

1. *Administrative.* No standard of supervision is required for this classification. Probationers who have absconded, who are serving a prison sentence on a new offense and have not been revoked on the present offense, and who are receiving no direct supervision per court approval should be classified as *administrative.*

2. *Minimum (nondirect supervision).* Mailed-in change of address or employment; monthly payment of fine, restitution, and court costs; and monthly telephone contact with probationer.

3. *Minimum (direct supervision).* Monthly telephone contact and quarterly face-to-face contact.

4. *Medium.* Monthly telephone contact, quarterly face-to-face contact, and one field contact or collateral contact quarterly.

5. *High.* Two monthly face-to-face contacts, monthly field contact, and monthly collateral contact.

6. *Maximum.* Four monthly face-to-face contacts, two monthly field contacts, and two monthly collateral contacts.

The use of the minimum or administrative supervision classification for active cases is troubling since these offenders will not be given an opportunity to develop a personal relationship with a P/P officer: "Clearly, processes of interpersonal change based on offender identification with the change agent and the internalization of new values will not transpire" (Castellano, 1997: 24). Some states, California, for example, are releasing inmates to "non-revocable parole," meaning they will not be supervised.

Travis County, Texas

The risk/needs assessment matrix used by Travis County allows the department to separate probationers into three supervision tiers, ranging from those who are relatively stable (at the low end) to those who demonstrate criminal thinking and orientation (on the high end). Probationers who score lower in both criminogenic risk and need receive fewer interventions. The expectation is that these probationers will comply with the rules without much need for supervisory involvement. Officers make sure these probationers know the rules they have to follow, address any issues with which they may need assistance, and conduct follow-up reporting. These probationers are placed on a "low-risk caseload" with minimal contact requirements. Officers have greater tolerance for minor violations, such as failure to report a change in employment or to report the completion of a GED class.

For the mid-range probationers, the strategies include more reporting requirements and more intensive treatment interventions. Individuals with the highest risk and need are subject to the most restrictive and intense supervision, including field visits, surveillance, and low tolerance for any violations (Fabelo, Nagy, and Prins, 2011).

▶ Supervision Process in Probation and Parole

The supervision process in probation and parole, which are handled by the same agency in most states, is similar, if not identical. However, parolees (by definition) have been imprisoned, and imprisonment generally reflects the severity of the offense and the criminal history of the offender. Therefore, parolees are generally considered a greater danger to the community than are probationers. Furthermore, given the lack of adequate educational and training resources in prison, most parolees leave the institution without the literacy and job skills necessary for employment. Nancy La Vigne and her colleagues (2008: 2) note that "without access to food, clothing, shelter, transportation, personal identification, and other key necessities, former inmates may see no other option than to return to illegal activities in order to meet their needs." And yet, "these basic necessities represent some of the most overlooked needs of any returning prisoner" (2008: 8). If the state does not provide postincarceration supervision, the releasee may find himself or herself without a critical source of information and guidance. And there is the issue of housing: "When individuals are released from prisons or jails, the ability to access safe and secure housing within the community is crucial to their successful reentry…. Yet, in most jurisdictions to which individuals return after incarceration, accessible and affordable housing is in exceedingly short supply" (Cortes and Rogers, 2010: vii).

Parolees differ from probationers as a result of their prison experiences. The changeover from prison life to community living requires a major readjustment. In prison, inmates' lives are rigidly controlled: They are told when to sleep, when to eat, when to work, and when to have recreation. When they are released into the community, they must adjust to managing their own lives. This may be compounded by police harassment, particularly in smaller communities. Social agencies often do not recognize parolees' needs and somehow believe that they should be receiving assistance from the parole agency. Unfortunately, most parole (and probation) agencies are extremely limited in their ability to deliver tangible services. This fact, coupled with the usual lack of employable skills, often makes parolees a burden on their families, worsening what may have been an already difficult family situation. This is particularly the case with female offenders (discussed in Chapter 10).

> **Key Fact**
>
> While parolees are generally more serious offenders than probationers, the supervision process is similar, and in many agencies officers supervise both.

Parolees have told this author that even so minor an experience as taking a bus ride can be traumatic to a newly released offender—several stated they were not aware of the required fare and exact change and had a feeling that everyone on the bus, especially the driver, recognized that they had just been released from prison. Being in prison also isolated them from normal social contacts with members of the opposite sex. They were self-conscious and often believed that because of the way they looked at women, everyone would realize that they had been in prison. Parolees must "unlearn" prison habits and acquire new patterns of behavior if readjustment is to be accomplished quickly. They are frequently subjected to social rejection because of their status and usually lack the necessary connections and economic resources that are effective in dealing with crisis situations.

▶ Case Assignment

The supervision process begins when the offender is placed on the caseload/workload of a P/P officer. This aspect of supervision, case assignment, can be accomplished in a variety of ways, depending on the practice used by the particular agency and the scope of its jurisdiction. In agencies that have statewide jurisdiction (such as most parole agencies), district/area offices are located throughout the state and each office covers a specific geographic area. County probation agencies, depending on the size of the county, may also have (sub) offices scattered throughout the jurisdiction. Some P/P agencies are offering services through neighborhood centers, a decentralization that parallels community policing efforts in many communities, or P/P officers may work out of police substations. **Place-based supervision** entails P/P agencies operating satellite offices 24/7 that are physically located in communities with high concentrations of offenders under supervision. For example, while Michigan has about 1 in 61 adults under some form of correctional control, in a group of blocks around Brewer Park, on the East Side of Detroit, it is 1 in 16 (Pew Center on the States, 2009). Officers assigned to these offices become familiar with the area, fostering relationships with local resources and improving public safety through ongoing relationships with police officers assigned to the same neighborhood. The approach also makes it easier for clients who do not have to leave their neighborhoods to visit the P/P office, and it improves the efficiency of P/P officers whose reduced travel time allows greater interaction with clients.

Offenders on probation or parole are directed to report to the office responsible for the area in which they (intend to) reside. At the P/P office, they will be assigned to a caseload either on a totally random basis or according to the specific area in which they plan to reside. Caseloads incorporating geographic considerations are advantageous insofar as they limit the travel time involved in supervising the offender; each officer also gains greater familiarity with his or her territory and the social and law enforcement agencies therein (not to mention places to eat and clean washrooms), which can enhance the supervision process. In more rural areas, where travel will be extensive, caseloads will be smaller than in urban areas where offenders are usually clustered in certain areas of the city. In the caseload assignment process, the agency typically attempts to achieve parity by keeping the size of caseloads roughly equal. In Beaumont County, Texas, juveniles on probation are placed on caseloads according to their home schools, which allow one officer to see all of his or her clients by making one stop and fosters ongoing relationships with school personnel.

Offenders are also assigned to specialized caseloads (discussed in Chapter 10) by virtue of a salient characteristic, such as a history of drug abuse or mental illness. Another model uses classification schemes (discussed earlier); quantitative weights are assigned to each case based on the level of supervision indicated by each case (e.g., risk/needs classification), and workloads are balanced by maintaining ongoing comparative statistics for P/P officers assigned to field supervision. In Texas, the Department of Criminal Justice probation guidelines require assignment of cases to probation officers in "such a manner as to promote public protection through offender supervision and the attainment of a 100 point workload" for each officer using the following weights:

Level I. This classification is calculated as 4.0 workload points and extends the most restrictive nonresidential supervision to these offenders.

Level II. This classification is calculated as 2.5 workload points and extends a heightened level of supervision to these offenders.

Level III. This classification is calculated as 1.33 workload points and extends a moderate level of supervision to these offenders.

Level IV. This classification is calculated as 1 workload point and extends a minimum level of supervision to these offenders.

> **Key Fact**
>
> An offender may be assigned to a caseload or workload based on his or her residence and/or a salient characteristic, such as a substance abuse problem.

► Initial Interview

The initial interview in P/P practice is considered a crucial time in the supervision process. The first meeting between the client and the P/P officer usually occurs in the P/P office and is a time of apprehension and anxiety: The officer "represents a power that can, and does, limit his freedom" because the offender is in the office *involuntarily* in a situation "where two individuals are joined by legal force in a counseling … relationship" (Arcaya, 1973: 58–59). The offender encounters the P/P officer for the first time with a mixture of fear, weariness, and defiance: "Particularly difficult is the non-voluntary nature of the probationer; this individual places a premium on the skills of the PO who must counter resistance with patience, persistence, and good will" (Strong, 1981: 12).

The sizing-up process at the time of the initial interview works both ways. The P/P officer is meeting a stranger who is usually known only through information in the case record and/or presentence investigation report. Although the record may say a great deal about the offender's background, it may not accurately reflect his or her current attitude toward P/P supervision. How will the client deal with current problems? Will the probationer or parolee follow regulations? Will he or she abscond from supervision if pressured or frustrated? Will the officer be responsible for having a warrant issued and having the offender sent to prison? Will this be, instead, an easy case with a minimum number of problems?

The client is asking similar questions: Will the P/P officer give me a difficult time? Will my officer be rigid about every minor rule? Is he or she quick to seek delinquency action? Does the officer have the knowledge and ability to help me secure employment, training, education, and a place to live?

> **Key Fact**
>
> The initial interview in P/P practice is considered a crucial time in the supervision process.

During an initial interview, the officer explains the P/P rules, answering questions while attempting to set realistic standards for a client. Several necessary directives for clients are usually emphasized:

- Make in-person, telephone, or mailed reports.
- Keep the P/P officer informed of current place of residence.
- Seek and maintain lawful employment.
- Avoid unlawful behavior and report contacts with law enforcement officers.

When a particular problem arises, an offender drinking excessively, for example, he or she may be directed to refrain from using any intoxicating beverages; an offender with a drug problem may be directed to enter a treatment program.

At the other end of the risk/needs spectrum, offenders requiring minimal supervision may "report" to a kiosk instead of a P/P officer. In New York City, there are kiosks in probation offices that allow an offender to check in and update his or her records, a process that takes a few minutes (National Research Council, 2008: 33):

> To begin a session, the probationer is asked to select one of four supported languages (English, Spanish, Russian and Mandarin Chinese). The probationer is then asked to provide a **P**ersonal **I**dentification **N**umber (PIN, assigned to them during their initial registration). Their identity is confirmed through the use of a biometric hand scan. Once the probationer has been successfully identified, they are presented with a screen that contains their image, pedigree information, and their Maximum Expiration Date. The probationer is then asked to verify and update various information, such as their home and mailing addresses, employment, school information, re-arrest and emergency contact details by walking them through a series of questions. Based on the probationer's responses, reporting compliance and other mitigating circumstances, various alerts are generated and are instantly viewable by kiosk attendants, probation officers and other supporting staff. Kiosk attendants, probation officers, and other staff follow up with direct contact with the probationer to resolve alerts. Once resolved, the specific solution is recorded by the application to be used in future reporting and investigation. At the end of the probationer's session, their next reporting date is calculated and a receipt is provided to the probationer. This receipt contains anything pertinent to the session and a graphical calendar instructs the probationer when to report next. Several kiosks can be employed and in use at a time. Live monitoring tools allow staff to stay current with the activity occurring at any time.

The P/P officer explains that he or she will be visiting the offender's residence periodically. Officers may offer clients assistance with employment or other problems. Some clients need financial assistance because one of the immediate problems encountered by a newly released parolee is finances—the money that an inmate receives on release, *gate money*, is usually inadequate for even immediate housing and food needs. This problem continues, despite research indicating that support payments to just-released prisoners reduce recidivism (Berk, Lenihan, and Rossi, 1980). A parolee may have some funds as a result of prison work, but wages are well below that received on the outside, and some jurisdictions require that any funds possessed by an inmate be used to help pay for his or her incarceration.

Upon release from prison, most offenders will live with family. When relatives are unable or unwilling to provide a residence, parole officers face a dilemma: Private market rental is often closed to their clients either because they lack sufficient funds or because landlords are unwilling to rent to people with criminal records; and public housing often prohibits those with a criminal history based on limited federal exclusions and the generally much broader local restrictions. "Even when people who have been in prison or jail are not excluded systematically and receive financial assistance (for example, through housing choice vouchers), affordable units are frequently so scarce relative to need that the options are, effectively, unavailable" (Cortes and Rogers, 2010: vii). "At a time when so many people who have had no contact with the criminal justice system lack affordable housing, it can be difficult to garner support for appropriate housing options for the recently incarcerated" (2010: viii). Yet, lack of a residence makes securing employment, difficult even in the best of times, almost impossible, and, as will be discussed later, there is evidence of a relationship between employment and recidivism.

An additional issue in placing parolees are statutes requiring notification of local officials and sometimes neighbors when certain offenders plan to live in their community (more than 35 states currently have such legislation). In some highly publicized cases, officials have been unable to provide housing for sex offenders, particularly when their crimes involved children or violence (discussed in Chapter 10).

Initial Parole Interview in New York

As the name implies, this is the first major interview between the parole officer responsible for the supervision of the case and the newly released parolee. It is at this time that the officer initiates a counseling or casework relationship with the parolee. Because the parole officer is endeavoring to establish this relationship with individuals whose knowledge of and acceptance of parole vary to a great degree, the interview must be planned and handled with casework skills. There are those whose attitudes toward parole are based on prejudice, doubt, and fear brought about by rumors. With this group, only patience and skill will overcome the hostility and resistance to a working relationship.

This is the interview on which the planning for future supervision of the parolee will be based, so it is important that the parole officer prepare for it by studying all the pertinent information contained in the case folder. It is also important that this interview be well planned, unhurried, and without interference, if possible, because it is the key to the future of the case.

The parole officer undertakes the initial interview with four major objectives in mind:

1. Establish a casework relationship with the parolee.
2. Secure the parolee's participation in an analysis of his or her problems.
3. Make constructive suggestions that will give the parolee "something to do" toward beginning the overall parole program.
4. Leave the parolee with some positive assurance of what there is to look forward to as the parole period progresses.

▶ Content of Initial Interview

At this time, the parolee's physical appearance should be updated from the time of his arrival report, with any particular changes such as mode of dress and attitude noted. It should be borne in mind that an individual's habit of dress and mannerisms often offer nonverbal communication that can tell much about how a person regards himself or herself. (From time to time during the parolee's period of supervision, the officer should note whether there are any significant changes in the parolee's mode of dress and mannerisms, as these may signal changes in the parolee's self-image or adjustment pattern.)

In conducting an initial interview, the officer is expected to encourage the parolee's participation in discussion of his or her problems and goals. This discussion should be based on information contained in the parolee's folder, other available knowledge about the parolee, and the parolee's input. There should be a discussion of the parole program. Both the residence and employment aspects of the program should be carefully reviewed to ascertain that they are as approved, and the officer should take pains to fill in any information regarding the residence and employment that may otherwise be missing in the reports.

Care should be exercised to make sure that any questions or concerns the parolee has regarding the program are addressed. The parole officer should ensure that the parolee understands the employment program; if necessary, arrangements should be made for the parolee to report to the employer. The parolee's prompt reporting to a prospective employer or employment program is, of course, a necessity. The parolee's actual employment or participation in employment program should be verified as soon as possible.

If the parolee has no specific employment or an alternative program, he or she should report promptly to any party or agency that may have offered approved assistance in securing employment. If no such program has been previously established, the officer must assist the parolee during the initial interview to devise a plan for seeking employment. If possible, the parole officer may provide the parolee with referrals to potential employers or parties who might assist the parolee in securing employment. Information should be provided to the parolee concerning the provisions for early discharge as well as possible eligibility for a Certificate of Relief from Disabilities that removes legal bars imposed as a result of conviction of the crime or crimes.

The officer should make every attempt to determine whether the parolee has any questions, reservations, or misconceptions concerning his or her relationship with parole and the conditions of parole. This should be done in such a manner as to assure the client that the officer is ready and willing to assist him or her in a constructive manner with the problems that might arise during the time on parole.

Before concluding the initial interview, the parolee should be clearly told why office reports are necessary and helpful and should also understand when, where, and with what frequency to report to his or her parole officer. If the parolee is to report to the officer at a different location, he or she should be given the address of that location and the time to report. The officer should give the parolee an official business card, writing the parolee's name on the front and reporting instructions on the back; the parolee is to be clearly informed that if he or she is unable to make a scheduled report, the officer must be contacted in advance for permission to miss a scheduled report and to obtain an alternative appointment.

The parole officer should note the parolee's attitude toward the officer and the interview, and the officer should include a description of the parolee's attitudes, interpretation of these attitudes, and his or her basis for such interpretation.

The initial interview is the foundation on which the relationship between the parolee, the parole officer, and the parole system is established. The way it is conducted and its content are highly important to that relationship; it is also important, from both a casework and a legal perspective, that what transpired during the initial interview be clearly and promptly recorded in the parole case folder. In summarizing the initial interview, the parole officer should report any immediate problems the parolee has and any long-range problems that are anticipated. In making this assessment, the officer should also indicate what immediate intervention on the parolee's behalf has been undertaken or is contemplated, what immediate and obtainable goals have been established for (or preferably with) the parolee, and what long-range plans for the parolee are being considered.

Supervision Planning Process: U.S. Probation

The supervision planning process is designed to create a strategy-based plan of action to address specific issues. This process requires that all supervision activities, including personal contacts, be structured to ensure compliance with the conditions of supervision, protect the community, and provide for correctional treatment. The linking of supervision activities to what is necessary to fulfill relevant statutory responsibilities in each case is intended to provide for efficient and effective use of the officer's time.

This process does not de-emphasize the importance of personal contact with the offender but recognizes that the quality of supervision depends on what is accomplished by a particular activity rather than its frequency. The measure of success of the supervision program is the degree to which the offender conforms to the conditions of supervision, identified supervision issues are resolved, and officer intervention is timely and appropriate.

Supervision planning begins with an initial assessment period during which the officer will obtain and evaluate information regarding the conditions of release, the degree and kind of risk the offender poses to the community, and the characteristics and conditions of the offender that indicate the need for correctional treatment. Based on the information gathered, the officer will identify as supervision issues those specific conditions of supervision and case problems that require direct action by the officer during the period and then select the supervision strategies necessary to address those issues.

The plan will be reviewed by a supervisor and, when approved, implemented. The officer is responsible for accomplishing those supervision activities selected as being necessary to enforce the conditions, control risks, and provide the correctional treatment for as long as the supervision issue is relevant.

Montgomery County (Ohio) Adult Probation Department Probation Orientation Program

Each probationer is expected to attend one probation orientation program within the first 30 days of placement under supervision (at least two orientation programs are presented each month). Probationers often have a personal view of what probation is all about, as influenced by their own assigned probation officer or fellow probationers. Often they believe that there is a difference between officers—the way officers handle their probation cases in terms of service to the client, police tactics, use of special conditions of probation, and so on.

The orientation programs are meant to give each client a clearer understanding of the official probation process and, more important, to introduce them to the services that are available to them through the Community Resource Division of the Adult Probation Department. It is further hoped that the orientation program schedule will allow each client to participate in an orientation session before the formulation of case plans. With the background of the orientation program, the probationer should have more of an opportunity to discuss with the probation officer the types of needs and concerns that he or she personally has that can be addressed by programs within the department or that are directly or indirectly supported by it. It is also an opportunity to convey to the new probationers that they can have an active part in the development of programming within the department.

▶ Ongoing Supervision

Offenders are usually relieved to be out of the office after their first visit but generally leave with mixed feelings. If the officer has been warm, concerned, and helpful, positive feelings will predominate; but if the officer was not sensitive to the attitude conveyed and did not evince a feeling of acceptance, negative feelings will predominate. Claude Mangrum (1972: 48) notes that "there is nothing necessarily incompatible between

BENEFITS OF HOME/FIELD VISITS (ILLINOIS DIVISION OF PROBATION)

1. The probation officer (PO) can verify the probationer's address.

2. Visiting the home helps the PO better understand the probationer.

3. The PO becomes aware of neighborhood resources available to help the probationer.

4. The PO sees the probationer in a natural environment.

5. There is an opportunity to involve other family members in the supervision plan.

6. Home visitation can improve the relationship between the PO and the probationer.

7. Surprise visits can catch the probationer off guard and serve as a deterrent to criminal behavior.

8. The probationer sees the PO as a human being.

9. Field supervision improves the agency's public image.

10. Increased community visibility enhances the relationship with police and other agencies.

warmth and acceptance and firm enforcement of the laws of the land. We must take whatever corrective measures are necessary, but these must not permit us to demean the dignity of the individual."

During periodic visits to the client's residence, the P/P officer should try to spend enough time to be able to relate to the client and the client's family. The home visit provides an opportunity to meet family members and interpret the role of the P/P agency to them, and the worker should leave a business card and invite inquiries for information or help. The home visit also provides an opportunity to ensure that spouse or child abuse is not a problem. Does a spouse or child(ren) have any noticeable bruises and/or are clothes being worn that may be an effort to cover bruises? If there is a child(ren) residing there, a discussion of the type of food normally served is appropriate. If the response appears vague, the officer should ask to see what and where the food is stored. The officer should ask to be shown around the residence and, if relevant, the premises and record the physical layout.

REALITIES OF PROBATION/PAROLE SUPERVISION

In my career as a N.Y. state parole officer assigned to New York City there remain scents I cannot dispel: the powerful odor of jail disinfectant, the sickening smell of urine in hallways, and the mix of odors in many crowded apartments.

Recognizing that P/P clientele often reside in substandard housing shared with a spouse and children is an academic exercise unless accompanied by the reality of home visits. The SRO—single-room occupancy—home to many released inmates is hot in the summer and cold in the winter. Visits may require stepping over intoxicated bodies in hallways without lights—a flashlight is an essential tool for a PO—and walking past clusters of drug users—unpleasant and potentially dangerous.

What to do when approaching a residence with a cluster of young men outside passing around a bottle—ignore them and enter the hallway that may be darkened? While "in my day" there were no cell phones, I did enjoy the advantage of being 6'1," armed, and a muscular 200-plus pounds—a powerful deterrent to would-be miscreants. But the danger in some neighborhoods is so apparent that visiting in pairs is routine.

Knowing that at the end of my workday I would be returning to my comfortable apartment in a pleasant neighborhood enabled me to endure some of the realities of supervision; most of my clients enjoyed no such reality. Returning home after a day in the field one thought would always race through my mind: There for but the grace of G-d....

HOME VISITS BY COLORADO PAROLE OFFICERS (POs)

Home visits are conducted to do the following:

- Confirm parolees' residence
- Identify conditions in which parolees live and potential problems that may exist
- Acquaint POs with parolees' household relationships
- Provide POs with opportunities to enforce conditions of supervision, issue lawful directives, advise and counsel parolees
- Provide POs with opportunities to scrutinize parolees' residence for contraband
- Provide POs with opportunities to collect urine specimens from parolees
- Address any other purpose deemed appropriate for case supervision

When visiting the home, it is incumbent on the officer to try to protect the confidentiality inherent in each case. Officers do not advertise their business or draw unnecessary attention to the visit to a client's home. Florida advises its correctional probation officers: "In order to help maintain the confidentiality of the probation/parole status of offenders under supervision, unmarked vehicles shall be used by officers. Correspondence shall be sent in envelopes that do not contain references to the Department of Corrections or Probation/Parole Services. Notes left at an offender's residence should be done with discretion to avoid broadcasting the status of the offender to others who may have access to the note." In many cases, neighbors know the client's P/P status and the officer may be a familiar figure in the neighborhood.

The accompanying excerpt from a case record shows how increased understanding of an offender caused a change in the direction of treatment and also reveals the value of home visits as a means of gaining new insights into an offender's situation. The second excerpt describes an interview with an offender in jail to indicate how the officer approached a hostile and uncooperative offender. The officer guides the interview to avoid futile and repetitious rationalizations and also explores to find some area in which he or she and the offender can work constructively together.

Peter, aged 18, has been on probation for two months. He was accorded youthful offender treatment following indictment for an assault during which he threatened to, but did not use, a knife. During the course of our contact, he has been on a weekly reporting schedule. I have concentrated on trying to help him get work. He has conformed in rather surly fashion and has never volunteered to discuss any of his problems. He lives at home with his mother, a divorcee, and an older brother, who is a conforming person who did well in school, has regular employment, and generally does everything he should, thereby winning the mother's approval.

Recently, Peter was arrested for drunk and disorderly conduct. He pleaded guilty and received a 30-day jail sentence, which he is just beginning to serve. The arresting officer's report indicated that he was assaultive and that it required three policemen to get him to the station. I visited him at the jail to obtain information for a violation report to be submitted to the court for action regarding his probation status. When I explained this, Peter went into what threatened to be a long harangue against the police and everyone connected with the current offense. He was in jail, he said, only

QUARTERLY SUMMARY

03/09/11 Office report: 6 P.M.

03/23/12 Failed to report.

03/30/12 Home visit: 3 P.M. Mother and aunt seen.

04/06/12 Failed to report. Notice sent, giving 48 hours to report.

04/09/12 Reported: 7 P.M.

04/13/12 Failed to report.

04/20/12 Home visit: 8 P.M. Offender and aunt seen.

04/27/12 Reported: 6:15 P.M.

05/02/12 Contact made with Community Settlement.

05/11/12 Reported: 3 P.M.

05/25/12 Reported: 11 P.M.

During March and April, attempts were made to get the offender to look for work. Early in March, he reported that he had a temporary job as a truck driver's helper and believed that because of this he did not have to report. I corrected this idea and emphasized the importance of keeping his appointments. He had little to say but seemed amenable to conforming. The failure to report in April was excused because of illness.

During home visits, his mother reported that the offender is keeping reasonable hours. She informed me that he spends most of his spare time at the Community Settlement and recently won a trophy for basketball. His aunt, a single woman who lives in the home, takes an active interest in him. She said that the offender is really very shy and needs special attention, which she tries to give him because the mother has little time to spare from the younger children. The aunt has accompanied him to the State Employment Office, where he has been trying to obtain work; however, as he is unskilled, he has few opportunities. Such protectiveness seems inappropriate for a 19-year-old youth.

I called the Community Settlement and talked with the director, Mr. Apt. He is very much interested in the offender but told me confidentially that he is afraid the subject might be getting into a neighborhood gang that is beginning to form. He has noticed that when the offender leaves the settlement, he often joins other young men, some of whom have been in trouble. The settlement has an employment service for members and will try to help the offender obtain employment. When the offender reported, I suggested that he apply at the settlement employment service. The next day, Mr. Apt telephoned. The offender had been referred to a job in a downtown warehouse. He returned to the settlement in tears. He was so frightened that he had been unable to apply. He does not think he could do such work, although it is simple unskilled labor. Mr. Apt thinks that the offender needs psychiatric attention, but this may be the first time the offender has tried to seek work by himself.

At the time of the last report, the offender discussed some of his fears about work. He speaks warmly of the personnel at the settlement but talks somewhat resentfully of his mother and aunt, who "keep nagging" him about work. It is planned to try to encourage this offender by building his self-esteem, giving recognition to his success in settlement activities, and planning visits when he is at home to deal with him directly rather than with relatives. The possibility of psychiatric referral will be explored.

because his girlfriend's father objected to him and was trying to keep him from dating her. I stated briefly and flatly what I knew about his present situation and noted that his own conduct was the reason for his being here. I asked him to tell me something about his girl, but he cut this off by saying that she and her family had moved to get the girl away from him, and he would not be seeing her any more. I asked what he had been assigned to do in jail. He replied that he was just washing dishes and it was a bore, and everyone here was a jerk. Had his family visited him? His mother had, but not his brother. I wondered how he got along with his brother. As if I had turned on a faucet, the story of his resentment toward his brother gushed out. He recalled things that had happened when he was only about six years old and revealed that he is conscious of his jealousy over the mother's favoritism.

CASE NOTES

Jones, Herbert L.
CASE # 01-CF-566

10/26/11. Defendant sentenced this date to three years' probation; sentenced to credit for time served in jail; fined $300.00 plus costs; ordered to pay $825.00 in restitution to Ace Awning; and ordered to be evaluated by and cooperate with recommended alcohol treatment.

Intake interview conducted by Officer John Miller this date. Conditions read, explained, and signed by defendant in acknowledgment. PSI information reviewed with defendant; no information update. Defendant ordered to contact Sauk River Alcohol Center by 10/31/11 to obtain an appointment for the evaluation. Defendant to report again to this officer at 10:30 A.M., 11/09/11, to continue intake process.

Summary of Subject's Background

Herb is 22, a high school graduate, single, and currently unemployed. His last employer Rydrox Corp. will consider him for rehire, but there were some attendance problems that may keep him from getting a job there at this time.

Herb was previously on probation in this county for misdemeanor theft and supervised by this officer. He reported regularly and paid all his monies but did not seem motivated to make any change in his life. Besides the prior theft, Herb has also been on unsupervised probation for DUI and on Conditional Discharge for Illegal Possession of Alcohol, speeding, and a muffler violation.

Herb has never received any type of counseling. He has no apparent mental health or physical problems. He clearly has a substance abuse problem. He has been drinking since age 14 and using marijuana since 16; he admits to getting drunk twice per week and going to taverns every Friday and Saturday night. He likes to "party" and does not seem to do much else with his leisure time. Herb's father is a recovering alcoholic and attends Alcoholics Anonymous (AA). Both parents had previously been seen by this officer as enablers of Herb's drinking problems. However, with this last arrest, they decided not to bond him out; this is seen as a realization by them that it was time to stop "taking care of him."

10/27/11. Letter sent to Dennis Goodman, Ace Awning, re: court order for restitution. It should be noted that Ace Awning has been paid by the insurance company, but because the court order says to pay them, they will have to work out reimbursement with the insurance company (see file).

10/27/11. Referral letter sent to Sauk River Alcohol/Drug Center (see file).

10/28/11. Received statement of costs owed from Circuit Clerk's office: $161.87. Financial sheet updated.

10/29/11. Sauk River Alcohol/Drug Center called. Herb called yesterday for an appointment. He will see Dr. Kim Carter for evaluation on 11/11/08.

11/09/11. Herb failed to keep his appointment as scheduled for this date.

11/10/11. Failure to report letter sent to Herb; rescheduled for 3:30 on 11/16/06.

11/12/11. Herb called to explain that he'd missed his appointment because his grandmother in Oswald, Illinois, fell and broke her hip; he went to visit her at the hospital. Spoke with mother by telephone, and she confirmed this.

11/16/11, 6 P.M. Herb reported as scheduled. He was advised of the court costs he owed. Herb kept his appointment for alcohol evaluation. Said Dr. Carter was "OK," but her tests and questions were "really stupid." He's to see her again on 11/18/11.

Began discussions with Herb about what changes he believes he needs to make in his life to stay out of trouble. The main thing he wants to do is find a job. His parents say he can continue to live with them; but once he goes to work this time, he will have to pay them for room and board plus pay them back for the car payments they have been making for him. Herb says he'll probably look for his own apartment. He will need to learn some better financial habits if he is going to live on his own, pay the court-ordered monies, and pay back his parents. Herb seems to understand that he will have to cooperate with alcohol treatment if recommended. Right now he doesn't believe it will be, since he does not see his usage as a problem. He does report that he has "only" been out drinking once since his release from jail. He thinks this proves that he does not have a drinking problem. Herb is to report again on 11/23/11, after his appointment with Dr. Carter. His case will be assessed by that time, and we will begin the initial case planning.

11/18/11, 7:30 P.M. Unannounced home visit. Herb and both parents were at home. Reminded Herb of his appointment with Dr. Carter and this PO. He has been job hunting, but it doesn't look like Rydrox will rehire him at this time. They flat out asked him whether he was still running around with the same people and drinking. He's pretty upset at them for not believing him when he said drinking was not a problem. His parents say it is going better at home. They confirmed that he has been home most nights but were aware of the one night that he did go out drinking. His girlfriend has been coming over to the house frequently, and parents feel she's getting on him about his friends, the drinking, and the partying.

11/19/11. Case assessment. Scored "Max" on RISK and a "High Medium" on NEEDS. Identified problem areas are financial management, employment, alcohol usage, drug usage, companions, and attitude toward supervision. Herb will be supervised at the MAXIMUM level.

11/23/11. Phoned Lynnville Police to conduct a record check. They show no police contact; Sgt. Ron Peters said he hasn't seen Herb out and about lately, but his friends are still doing their share of partying.

11/24/11, 10 P.M. Herb reported as scheduled. He said that Dr. Carter had recommended he attend alcohol education classes and that he sees her for individual counseling every other week. He's not happy about this but decided it would be better than going back to jail. Herb starts class next Monday, and the next appointment with Dr. Carter is 12/02/11. Officer will verify information.

Herb continues to reside with his parents and remains unemployed. He has not gone job hunting since he was turned down at Rydrox. He sees employment as the biggest thing to accomplish, while this office, in addition to the need for seeking employment, stressed the need to comply with alcohol treatment and discontinue usage.

▶ Offender Employment

Conventional wisdom—often a poor basis for drawing conclusions—argues that a poor economic climate and unemployment drives criminal behavior and that unemployment as a negative social experience generates stress-induced aggression against persons and more rational crimes against property. However, research into the connection between the economy, unemployment, and crime is inconclusive (Carlson and Michalowski, 1997; Krisberg, Guzman, and Vuong, 2009). One study found that although employment did not reduce recidivism, it did delay reincarceration (Tripodi, Kim, and Bender, 2010).

> The central assumption in the crime-employment argument is that employment is a resiliency factor that would keep individuals from engaging in criminal conduct because of the economic and affective benefits of employment and the high risks of crime and punishment. Some researchers have argued that employment may be, for an undefined percentage of cases, a risk factor—that is, employment increases stress and unhappiness and leads some to abandon employment for illegal pursuits or to add illegal pursuits to legal employment. (Krienert and Fleisher, 2004: 40)

Indeed, one research effort found that juveniles who were gainfully employed had a *greater* chance of involvement in delinquency (Cullen, Williams, and Wright, 1997).

Definitions of unemployment present difficulties: Does it include only those who were unemployed and are now looking for full-time or part-time employment? Official unemployment figures cannot include those (usually young inner-city males) who are not part of Labor Department statistics because they fail to qualify for unemployment insurance or sign up for help in finding a job. We know many offenders were, in fact, employed at the time of their arrest, but in what is referred to as the secondary labor market—dead-end jobs having no real advancement potential and paying the minimum or near minimum wage. "A growing body of literature, however, suggests that the quality of the work may be more important than the simple existence of a job in the employment-crime relationship" (Henderson, 2004: 84). Under such conditions, explanations of crime may fit the classical model: a rational response to one's financial condition. Criminal involvement by persons in the secondary job market could also be explained by social control theory (discussed in Chapter 6): little stake in conforming behavior. In other words, persons who value their employment would be reluctant to engage in behavior that could jeopardize it. "This would suggest that simply forcing former inmates to obtain a job, particularly low paying unskilled employment, upon release may not be enough to prevent them from coming back to prison" (Henderson, 2004: 92). However, a national work experiment found that participants aged 27 and older were more likely to desist from crime even when provided with marginal employment; for younger participants, there was no affect (Laub and Sampon, 2008).

There are additional problems with the employment–crime hypothesis:

> The observed relationship between criminality and unemployment has been explained in different ways. Some researchers have proposed that there is a *causal relationship* between unemployment and crime, while analysts have agreed that unemployment and recidivism are highly correlated only because each is associated with another factor (e.g., the influence of family members or a decision to "go straight"), which induced widespread behavioral change. Whatever the explanation, unemployment and recidivism are often closely related. (Toborg et al., 1978: 2)

Thus, the variable *employment* may not be the cause of the variable *go straight*, but both variables may actually be dependent on the (independent) variable *motivation*. In other words, whatever it is that motivates an offender to seek and maintain gainful employment (the P/P officer?) also tends to motivate that offender to avoid criminal behavior.

In fact, "there are few studies that demonstrate a direct causal relationship between current employment service practices and recidivism rates" (Duran et al., 2013: 2).

Nevertheless, securing and maintaining of employment and training for employment have been considered crucial aspects of P/P supervision. In addition to providing economic rewards, employment also enhances the self-worth and image of the client. "Employment can make a strong contribution to recidivism-reduction efforts because it refocuses individuals' time and efforts on prosocial activities, making them less likely to engage in riskier behaviors and to associate with people who do" (Duran et al., 2013: 2). However, parolees

CENTER FOR EMPLOYMENT OPPORTUNITIES (CEO)

Created as a demonstration project in the 1970s, CEO is an independent nonprofit organization that offers a highly structured, job-focused "second chance" to people released from New York State prisons and jails. The program involves seven structured steps to sustainable employment. Each participant begins the program by completing an orientation, intensive four-day "Life Skills" training workshop and initial meeting with their job counselor for an in-depth skills assessment. Participants are then put to work immediately on day-labor work crews. The crews are paid for by city and state agencies and involve a variety of assignments, including providing custodial services to government buildings, maintaining nature trails, painting classrooms, and cleaning up roadways. The program pays the crew members minimum wage at the end of each work day. While the participants are employed through this program, they continue to work with CEO staff on job readiness and eventual placement in full-time unsubsidized employment. CEO specializes in finding jobs in customer service, food industries, manufacturing, office support, and semi-skilled trades. CEO also provides a range of postplacement support services for a minimum of 12 months, and has developed an expansive employment network with government agencies and a number of private sector employers.

Research into CEO revealed lower recidivism in those offenders at highest risk, although it did not show an effect on increases on unsubsidized employment. (Zweig, Yahner, and Redcross, 2011)

Surveys show that many employers are not fundamentally worried about a repeat crime on their premises or a negligent hiring lawsuit. Rather, they are worried that ex-offenders will not be good employees. And, based on employment records of ex-offenders, they have a right to be worried. Most ex-offenders have simply never demonstrated that they can commit to hold a job day in and day out for a substantial period of time. As a result, the single most important thing that any ex-offender can do for long-term success is to get and keep one job for a significant period of time (possibly one year). Once the offender learns he can do it, he will actually start to learn new coping skills that help him maintain his new identity as a desistor. And once the ex-offender has demonstrated the ability to stick with something over the long haul, other employers will be more willing to hire him. In other words, better job opportunities await the ex-offender if and only if he can demonstrate—to himself and to others—the ability to work successfully for a period approaching one year. (Bushway, 2003:13)

and probationers "who are often undereducated and with few skills learn that finding work is problematical and frustrating" (Davidoff-Kroop, 1983: 1). The employment problem for parolees is often a great deal more difficult than for probationers. The parolee has been separated from employment and community contacts, usually for at least 18 months and often longer. The prison environment offers little help. More than three decades ago, the Comptroller General of the United States (1979: 46) reported that federal and state prison systems have been deficient in their approach to training and educating inmates for employment. In view of the punitive shift in corrections, no reason exists to believe that the situation has gotten better since that report was published—20 years after the Comptroller General's report, there were more than 1,231,000 persons in state prisons, but only about 185,000 were receiving job training and job-related education (Shilton, 2000).

In assisting clients with employment, officers make direct referrals to particular employers if they have the necessary contacts, or they may refer clients to other agencies, such as state employment services. Officers may have to provide guidance and counseling concerning some of the basic aspects of securing employment, items that for middle-class persons are usually taken for granted. For example, officers will emphasize the need to be on time for interviews (in fact, the need to arrive early). They will help to fill out applications or help the client prepare for this aspect of the job search. Some officers may use role playing to accustom clients to job interview situations and discuss the importance of good grooming and appropriate clothes for an interview.

> **Key Fact**
>
> Offender employment is often seen as the key to P/P success, but lack of skills, a criminal record, and often a lack of job commitment are significant impediments.

▶ Stigma of a Criminal Record

One critical aspect of employment for ex-offenders is the question of revealing their record. I allowed my clients to decide for themselves; however, I did provide guidance by discussing the experiences of other clients relative to this issue. Many clients reported that their candor resulted in not securing employment, but others reported that some employers were interested in providing them with an opportunity "to make it." Unfortunately, many (if not most) employers will not hire an ex-offender if any alternative exists. A survey of 3,000 employers in four major metropolitan areas revealed that two-thirds would not knowingly hire an ex-prisoner (Kachnowski, 2005).

All states have statutes barring convicted felons from certain types of employment, in law enforcement, for example. There are about two-dozen categories of jobs for which certain criminal convictions serve as an absolute bar, most under state law, some under federal law. With a couple of exceptions, these are lifetime prohibitions. Some offenders are required by law or P/P agency policy to reveal their records when applying for certain jobs, government positions, for example, while banks, hospitals, and other sensitive areas of employment may also require disclosure. Certainly, allowing an offender with a history of drug abuse to work in a hospital or similar situation would not be advisable, especially if the employer did not know of the person's record. In recent years there has been a major effort to "ban the box," that part of an employment application that asks if the person has ever been arrested/convicted. More than 40 cities and counties have taken steps to remove barriers to employment for qualified workers with criminal records, specifically by removing conviction history questions from job applications known as "ban the box" (National Employment Law Project, 2012).

Many states make criminal conviction records available to the public, selling them in digital form to private Internet services, thereby allowing employers to easily screen prospective hires. The Kansas Bureau of Investigation, for example, has placed all of its criminal history records for the past 65 years on the Internet, which businesses and individuals can access for a fee of $17.50 for each record retrieved, and most of the inquiries come from employers doing background checks. Even records that have been ordered expunged by the courts may remain in commercial databases, affecting a person's employment, housing, and ability to secure loans and mortgages (Liptak, 2006). The implications are troubling: Access to such records allows employers to deny employment to otherwise qualified ex-offenders, rendering the probationer or parolee virtually unemployable. Dee Wallace and Laura Wyckoff (n.d.) recommend that offenders obtain their rap sheets to check for errors and to be prepared for prospective employers who will conduct a criminal background check: Offenders can be fired for lying if their disclosures conflict with the record, even if discrepancies were unintentional.

Richard Schwartz and Jerome Skolnick (1962) studied the effects of a criminal record on the employment opportunities of unskilled workers. Four employment folders were prepared, which were the same in all respects except for the criminal record of the applicant:

1. One of the folders indicated that the applicant had been convicted and sentenced for assault.
2. Another noted that he had been tried for assault and acquitted.
3. The next again showed that he was tried for assault and acquitted, but it contained a letter from the judge certifying the finding of not guilty.
4. One folder made no mention of any criminal record.

The study involved 100 employers who were divided into units of 25, with each group being shown one of the four folders on the mistaken belief that they were actually considering a real job applicant:

- Of the employers shown the "no record" folder, 36 percent gave positive responses.
- Of the employers shown the "acquittal" folder with the judge's letter, 24 percent expressed an interest in the application.

A CLOSER LOOK

THE BIG QUESTION

An employment training instructor for ex-inmates in New York City has to deal with "the Big Question": "You don't check 'yes.' You don't check 'no.' You don't leave it blank. You put down 'Wish to discuss during interview.' Answering 'yes' or leaving it blank almost guarantees rejection. Answering 'no' is lying and grounds for dismissal" (Ken Guggenheim, 1998 "Biggest Question Awaits After Prison." *Chicago Tribune* (March 11): Sec. 5: 8).

▼

- Of the employers shown the "acquittal" folder without the judge's letter, 12 percent expressed an interest in the applicant.
- Of the employers shown the "conviction" folder, only 4 percent expressed interest in the applicant.

Because most persons on P/P are unskilled, the ramifications of these findings are obvious. In addition, "legal precedent established under 'negligent hiring law' explicitly states that employees must demonstrate 'reasonable care' in the selection of employees or the employer may be held liable for acts of violence or loss of property caused by an employee against a customer or fellow employee." Legal considerations, therefore, exercise a negative incentive to employ ex-offenders (Pager, 2006: 511).

A study (Pager, 2003; Pager and Western, 2009) to test the effect of a "negative credential" impact of a criminal record on employment opportunity used four 23-year-old college students, two white and two black. They applied for 350 entry-level positions requiring no education greater than high school and no previous experience. The four rotated presenting themselves as having a felony conviction for possession of drugs with intent to sell. The research revealed that race plays a dominant role in shaping employment opportunity that is equal to or greater than the impact of a criminal record and "the negative effect of a criminal conviction is substantially larger for blacks than for whites" (2009: 4): 34 percent of white applicants without a criminal record got callbacks, as opposed to 17 percent of whites with a record; among blacks without a criminal record, only 14 percent received callbacks, compared with 5 percent with a record.

One extensive research effort revealed that "in terms of employer willingness to hire ex-offenders, fewer than 40 percent of all employers claim that they would definitely or probably hire ex-offenders into their most recently filled noncollege job. This figure stands in sharp contrast to their general willingness to hire other groups of workers that are commonly stigmatized, such as welfare recipients, applicants with a GED instead of high school diploma, or applicants with spotty work histories" (Holzer, Raphael, and Stoll, 2002: 4).

In an effort to minimize the legal harm caused by a criminal record, some states have removed various statutory restrictions on gaining licenses necessary for employment, and a few have even enacted "fair employment" laws for ex-offenders. New York, for example, prohibits the denial of employment or license because of a conviction unless there is a "direct relationship" between the conviction and the specific employment or license or it involves an "unreasonable risk" to persons or property. A direct relationship requires a showing that the nature of the criminal conduct for which the person was convicted has a direct bearing on the fitness or ability to carry out duties or responsibilities related to the employment or license. The statute requires that a public or private employer provide, on request, a written statement setting forth the reasons for a denial of license or employment and provides for enforcement by the New York State Commission on Human Rights.

A New York prison inmate, abandoned as an infant and raised in foster homes, spent hundreds of hours learning to be a barber. When he was paroled, however, he was denied a state barber's license because he lacked "good moral character," as evidenced by his robbery conviction. For years he fought unsuccessfully for his license, finally succumbing to AIDS at age 40 (Haberman, 2005). In 2008, a law was enacted that prohibits the state from denying a barber's license simply because of the applicant's criminal record.

Title VII of the Civil Rights Act of 1964 and guidelines set by the Equal Employment Opportunity Commission (EEOC) pursuant to that law require that when an employer takes into account an individual's conviction, the screening policy must be "job related." The EEOC has ruled that an absolute bar to employment based on the mere fact that an individual has a conviction record is unlawful under Title VII. Enforcement, however, has been sporadic (*Employing Your Mission*, 2009). A few states have laws protecting the formerly incarcerated from job discrimination by private employers. "Most of these laws require that a decision to deny a job due to a criminal conviction record be based on a business necessity or public safety concern" (*Employing Your Mission*, 2009: 4).

The Federal Bonding Program, which is administered through state employment services agencies, has a long-standing program that provides bonding for probationers and parolees without any cost to either the employee or the employer. Devah Pager (2006) recommends an extension of this approach: government offering a cost-free insurance and/or limiting the liability of employers who employ ex-offenders.

While this is anecdotal, while I was a parole officer, I found that offenders who committed violent crimes (e.g., armed robbers) were more aggressive and successful at finding and maintaining satisfactory employment than those who were "sneaks" (e.g., burglars). And my impressions are supported by research that reveals those incarcerated for violent offenses are more likely to desist from crime—permanent abstention—than those convicted of drug and property crimes (Rosenfeld, Petersilia, and Visher, 2008). A study of parolees in Massachusetts found that property offenders had the highest rate (57 percent) of recidivism (Kohl et al., 2008). This raises questions about the strategy of releasing nonviolent offenders in order to reduce the prison population.

While I was a parole officer, there were employers who had such positive experiences with parolees that they sought them out for employment. Hiring a parolee meant the employer had someone to complain to if there were problems and the employee had a strong incentive to do a good job. Employers understood that parolees had more to lose— a minor theft by a parolee could cause his or her return to prison—whereas a regular employee has no corresponding concern because prosecution is unlikely. And I remember "Jake," a physically imposing parolee with a history of violence, who was able to get a service station job for the graveyard (midnight to 8 A.M.) shift. When a patron opened his jacket to reveal a revolver and demanded money, Jake explained his situation. He simply couldn't hand over the money without a fight because no one would believe him. Jake explained that there was not enough cash in the register to risk a murder rap and informed the would-be robber that if he reached for his gun and the first shot did not kill him, Jake would take him apart. The man thought for few seconds, closed his jacket, walked back to his car, and drove off. Jake took down the license plate number and called the police—the car had been stolen. Like many parolees I supervised, Jake was grateful for the opportunity to prove himself trustworthy.

▶ Relief From Disabilities

Attached to felony convictions are a variety of civil disabilities, and states vary in the method and extent to which they provide relief from disabilities incurred by probationers and parolees. Some states have adopted automatic restoration procedures on satisfactory completion of P/P supervision; many states also have statutes designed to restore forfeited rights, although they may be subjected to restrictive interpretation in licensing and occupational areas. In Georgia, the right to vote is automatically restored to offenders who have completed their sentences, and the Georgia Board of Pardons and Paroles automatically considers restoring civil and political rights to parolees upon discharge from supervision. Pardon is another method, although its use is generally limited: Some states, such as Missouri, have limited forms of pardon that restore certain rights (discussed in Chapter 7); in New York, the judiciary and parole board have the power to restore certain rights through the granting of a "relief from disabilities."

With respect to voting rights, 48 states deny prisoners the right to vote, whereas 13 states ban some felons either conditionally or permanently from voting. For instance, Arizona and Maryland permanently ban twice-convicted felons from voting, whereas Delaware bans felons from voting until five years after they have completed their sentences.

There are 7 states that impose lifetime disenfranchisement on anyone convicted of a felony; 22 states permit felons on probation to vote ("Court Orders Trial on Ban of Voting by Felons," 2003; Lewin, 1998; Sengupta, 2000; Zielbauer, 2001).

Lifetime disenfranchisement has an ugly history dating back to the years after the Civil War—it was part of a legal strategy to keep the vote from emancipated African Americans in the states of the Confederacy. When the Reconstruction Congress compelled each Confederate state to grant black men the franchise in 1868, Florida responded by denying any individual convicted of a felony or larceny the right to vote, thereby disenfranchising many blacks because such persons were overwhelmingly African American. Throughout the South, poll taxes and literacy tests were also enacted as an attempt to minimize the effect of emancipation. Although the Supreme Court eventually abolished these archaic practices, felon disenfranchisement remains constitutional (Eisenkraft, 2001).

▶ Length of Supervision

The length of probation terms varies from state to state. The ABA recommends that the term should be two years for a misdemeanor conviction and five years for a felony. Some states, such as Michigan, have followed this recommendation. In Illinois, it is four years for the more serious felonies and 30 months for other felonies; for a misdemeanor, it is one year. In Texas, "the court may fix the period of probation without regard to the term of punishment assessed, but in no event may the period of probation be greater than 10 years or less than the minimum prescribed for the offense for which the defendant was convicted." In 2007, Texas enacted a law setting the maximum probation sentence for nonaggravated offenses at five years unless the department can show just cause for keeping someone under supervision. In the federal system, termination for a misdemeanor may occur at any time and for a felony after one year.

Some states authorize early termination of probation without actually having statutory guidelines as to when it is to be exercised. In most states, however, statutes provide for the termination of probation and the discharge of the offender from supervision before the end of the term. This allows the judge some needed flexibility because it is difficult to determine, at the time of sentencing, how long the term should actually be. In Texas, for example, "at any time, after the defendant has satisfactorily completed one-third of the original probationary period or 2 years of probation, whichever is the lesser, the period of probation may be reduced or terminated by the court." In Illinois, "the court may at any time terminate probation...if warranted by the conduct of the offender and the ends of justice." In Oklahoma, probation supervision "shall not normally exceed two years unless it is determined [that] the interests of the public and the probationer would be best served by an extended period of supervision not to exceed the length of the original sentence." In Virginia, probation may be terminated for cases placed on supervision for two years or more after serving one-half of the term or three years, whichever comes first. In Arizona, probation officers may file petitions for early termination after over half the probation period has been served. In some states, Arizona and Maryland, for example, persons under community supervision for less serious offenses can receive 20 days off for every 30 days of good behavior.

The length of time an offender must spend on parole/conditional release supervision is governed by the length of the sentence and the laws of the state where he or she was convicted. In Oregon, a conditional releasee "is subject to a period of supervision similar to parole, not to exceed six months or the maximum date, whichever comes first." In Indiana, persons are to be discharged no later than one year after conditional release, whereas in Illinois the length of supervision for a conditional releasee varies from one to three years, depending on the class of crime for which the offender was convicted. In California, for

> **Key Fact**
>
> Length of probation supervision may be fixed, such as five years for a felony, or be as long as what a sentence of imprisonment would require.

> **Key Fact**
>
> Length of probation supervision may be shortened by the court in response to exemplary probationer performance or high caseloads.

persons sentenced under a life sentence, the maximum period (including time under parole supervision and time under revocation status) cannot exceed seven years; for persons sentenced under a nonlife sentence, the maximum period (including time under supervision and time under revocation status) cannot exceed four years. In Ohio, those convicted of serious felonies must be under supervision for three to five years. For less serious felonies, supervision up to three years is discretionary with the parole board, which may reduce the term. In Missouri, after the releasee has three years of successful supervision, the parole board may discharge an offender from parole or conditional release. Some states, for example, New Jersey, have supervision-for-life statutes for certain offenders, usually those convicted of sex offenses.

In most states, a parolee/releasee can be discharged before the expiration of a sentence or a mandated period of supervision. In California, based on satisfactory performance, a nonlife releasee can be discharged from supervision after one year and a lifer after three years. In Kentucky, a parolee can request a final discharge from parole after the expiration of 24 months, but those serving a life sentence must wait five years. The Hawaii Paroling Authority can issue a discharge whenever "the parolee has demonstrated for a sustained period of time that the parolee is unlikely to commit another crime and the parolee's discharge is compatible with public safety"; and in any event, parolees under supervision for at least five years "shall be brought before the Paroling Authority for purposes of consideration for final discharge." In Alaska, the board may discharge a parolee after he or she has successfully completed two years of supervision; in Oklahoma, active supervision of parolees will not normally exceed three years. In Alabama, however, "early termination in parole cases may be accomplished only by means of a Pardon, which will be considered after a subject has served five years under supervision." The same board that is responsible for parole in Alabama, the Board of Pardons and Paroles, has the power to grant pardons. In Vermont, "although the Board may terminate parole supervision at any time, it will normally consider termination only after successful completion of one half of the maximum parole term."

▶ Violation of Probation/Parole Supervision

Although the procedures involved in probation and parole violations are similar, there are distinctions. Probation supervision is within the purview of the courts, while parole supervision is an administrative function devoid of a court connection. Thus, revoking probation is a decision made by a judge, while revoking parole is the responsibility of a parole board. In both, there are two types of violation:

1. *Technical violation.* When any condition of probation/parole (discussed in Chapters 2 and 5) has been violated, a **technical violation** exists.

2. *New offense violation.* When a violation involves a new crime, it is a nontechnical or new offense violation.

In practice, new offense violations often involve technical violations. A violation that involves an arrest for robbery with a firearm, for example, also constitutes a technical violation of the condition prohibiting possession of a weapon.

The agency response to a violation is a matter of considerable discretion. For example, in Philadelphia, the Adult Probation Department advises its probation officers: "Minor violations of probation/[county] parole do not necessarily need to be brought to the attention of the sentencing Judge, but may be handled between the PO and the P/P (probationer/parolee) if such violations are not repeated and do not develop into a pattern." Several P/P agencies provide for a structured, measured response to violations. In Utah, this includes a point system, based on the offender's history and the present violation, that determines the level of the violation—minimum, medium, maximum—and each level provides a choice of responses, such as a reprimand or more restrictive conditions (e.g., curfew, residential drug treatment, incarceration).

In many jurisdictions (e.g., Allen County, Pennsylvania, and New York), the PO has the authority to "discuss the alleged violation(s) with the probationer and inform him that repeated or more serious violation(s) will be dealt with by the court." In New York, if the behavior continues but a formal violation of probation is not necessary, "the court shall be informed of the alleged violation(s) and the department's action to date...[and] a recommendation may be made to the court requesting that the court require that the probationer appear before it ... for a judicial reprimand."

To minimize the number of violations filed with the court, probation officers in Marion County, Indiana, are encouraged to use administrative hearings to address instances where a formal violation of probation is not yet warranted but the probationer is exhibiting some behavior that could lead to a more serious violation. The PO notifies the probationer in writing of the date, time, and reasons for the hearing, which is attended by the probationer, the PO, and the PO's supervisor. At the conclusion, the three participants sign a hearing report, which can include a modification of the conditions of probation. A failure to appear results in the filing of a violation of probation request for a warrant.

Because violations of probation and parole are contributing factors to prison over-crowding, P/P agencies have been using violation of supervision management strategies to avoid incarcerating clients who are in violation of their conditions of supervision. Typically, these strategies involve graduated sanctions ranging from intensive supervision, to a halfway house placement, to a brief period of incarceration (Burke, 2006; Cox and Bantley, 2005). Pennsylvania has reduced the number of parolees returned to prison for technical violations, particularly substance abuse violators in need of treatment, by establishing a Violation Center in each of the state's parole regions. Located within secure portions of community corrections centers, each center can accommodate between 25 and 75 offenders for a period of 90 days. The Iowa Violation Program (IVP) provides an intermediate sanction for P/P violators who would otherwise be admitted to the prison system. They are assigned to the program at revocation hearings on the recommendation of the P/P officer. IVP has 60 beds at the Women's Reformatory and 100 beds at the Release Center. At each facility, participants are segregated from the general population and have treatment staff assigned solely to the program. Those who successfully complete the 60-day residential program are returned to community supervision to complete their probation or parole term.

<aside>
Key Fact

Probation and parole violation may be nontechnical, for committing a new crime, and/or technical, for violating the rules of supervision.
</aside>

▶ Violation of Probation Process

Although the actual procedures differ from jurisdiction to jurisdiction, typically the probation officer confers with his or her superiors; if a violation is considered serious enough, a notice will be filed with the court. The case will then be placed on the court calendar, and the probationer will be given a copy of the alleged violations and directed to appear for a preliminary or probable cause hearing. In some jurisdictions, an official other than a judge conducts this hearing. In other jurisdictions such as Texas, "A probationer is not entitled to a preliminary hearing or examining trial to determine whether there is probable cause to proceed to a revocation hearing"; in cases of violation, the case goes directly before a judge for a revocation hearing. (A probable cause hearing is necessary only if the probationer is to be held in custody pending the revocation hearing.) In any event, if a probationer fails to respond to a notice or summons to appear for a hearing, the judge will usually issue a warrant. A probationer may also waive the right to a preliminary hearing.

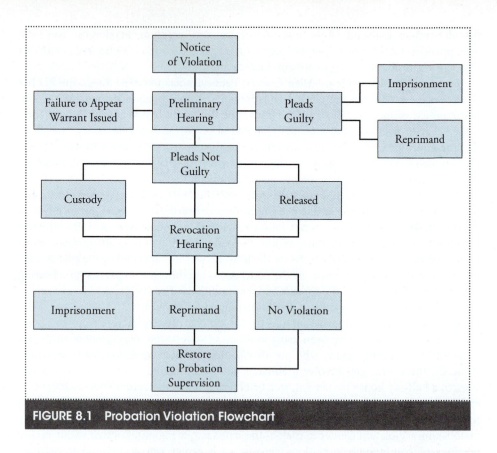

FIGURE 8.1 Probation Violation Flowchart

The flowchart in Figure 8.1 indicates the possibilities presented at each stage of the probation revocation process. At the preliminary hearing, the probationer can deny the charges of probation violation or plead guilty to them. If the plea is "guilty," the judge may deal with the case at once; if the probationer denies the charges, the judge will decide whether there is sufficient (probable) cause to believe that probation was violated (in order to remand the probationer to custody), and a revocation hearing is scheduled. The judge may remand the probationer to custody pending the hearing or may release him or her on bail or on his or her own recognizance. The probation department will subsequently prepare a violation of probation report. "The report shall contain a summary of the probationer's supervision activities to date, and the alleged facts which would be sufficient, if proven, to establish any violation(s) of probation occurred" (*New York State Code of Criminal Procedure*). Rather than a narrow legal document, the violation of probation report contains information about the probationer's behavior under supervision—for example, employment record—and is presented to the judge prior to the revocation hearing.

Revocation Hearing

At the revocation hearing, the probationer will have an opportunity to testify and present witnesses. An attorney may be present to represent the probationer (according to the provisions outlined in the *Mempa* and *Gagnon* decisions discussed later in this chapter), and in some jurisdictions it is common for the defense attorney and the prosecutor to plea-bargain in probation revocation proceedings as they do when new criminal charges are filed. If the judge finds no or only minor violations, the probationer is restored to supervision; but if the judge sustains any of the charges brought by the probation department, the probationer can be reprimanded and restored to supervision, or probation can be revoked and imprisonment ordered. In most cases, the defendant is actually sentenced at the time of conviction, but the imposition of sentence is suspended in favor of probation. Less frequently, the defendant is placed directly on probation without being sentenced. In the latter case, if the violation charge is sustained, the judge can revoke probation and sentence the probationer to a term of imprisonment; the sentence, however, must be in accord with the penalty provided by law for the crime for which the probationer was originally convicted.

While proof of guilt in a criminal trial must be **beyond a reasonable doubt**, at a probation revocation hearing it need not be greater than by a **preponderance of the evidence**, a lower standard used in civil cases. In a criminal trial, the testimony of an accomplice usually requires **corroboration**—supportive evidence—but no such requirement exists for revocation hearings. Evidence that would not ordinarily be admitted in a criminal trial, such as hearsay testimony, can be entered into evidence at a revocation hearing. When the judge renders a decision on the charges, he or she can consider only the evidence presented at the hearing. When making a decision as to the disposition of a probationer found in violation, the judge can consider many items, such as employment record, relationship to spouse and children, and efforts at drug treatment. The range of options after a finding of "guilty" has been increasing as states seek to avoid the traditional two-dimensional outcomes—prison or continued supervision—that

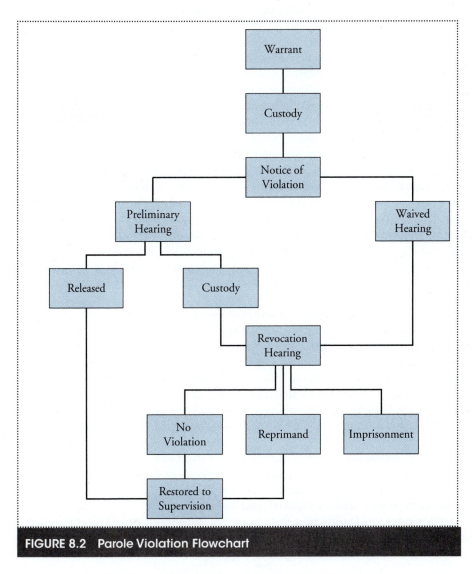

FIGURE 8.2 Parole Violation Flowchart

can affect prison overcrowding or (at the other extreme) undermine the supervision process. Responses now include short terms in a local jail or halfway house, electronic monitoring, intensive supervision, or some combination thereof (discussed in Chapter 9).

▶ Violation of Parole Supervision

As in probation, in parole there are two types of violation: technical and new offense. In either event, the violation process begins when a parole officer (PO), who may also be called a probation and parole officer, parole agent, correctional program officer, or probation/parole supervisor, becomes aware of a violation. The PO can usually take steps short of a formal violation of parole. The Alaska Division of Community Corrections advises: "If the violation is a conditions violation, it does not require any notification to the Parole Board. You, as the Parole Officer, can verbally make the parolee aware of the violation and issue a verbal warning." The Alaska parole officer can also issue a written reprimand and "hold these charges in abeyance should there be any future violations," or the officer can impose more restrictive conditions, but the parolee must agree: "If the parolee does not agree to the new condition, a preliminary hearing must be held within 15 days of the imposition of the condition."

In most agencies, after discussing the situation with a supervisor, a decision is made as to whether there is **probable cause** (evidence needed to determine that a violation has probably occurred) relative to the issuance of a warrant. This stage has the greatest amount of variance among agencies. In Pennsylvania, parole agents can use an "order to detain for 48 hours" in lieu of a warrant when circumstances require it. A similar situation obtains in New York, where field parole officers carry a 24-hour detainer warrant. Thus, in Pennsylvania and New York, a parole agent/officer who becomes aware of a serious violation of parole while in the field can summarily take the violator into custody and receive telephone authorization for the use of the order to detain or a 24-hour detainer warrant. (These temporary detainers must be replaced by a warrant: in Pennsylvania, within 48 hours; in New York, within 24 hours.) When I was a parole officer in New York, it was not unusual to unexpectedly encounter parolees who were in serious violation of the conditions of their release: those heavily involved in abusing heroin (and engaging in criminal acts to support the habit); those prohibited from the use of alcohol (because of the dangerous nature of their behavior while under the influence) in an intoxicated state; or child sex offenders found in the company of children. I could take such persons into custody immediately and subsequently (at a jail or police station) receive telephone authorization for a detainer warrant. In the opinion of this writer, agencies that do not provide their officers with this authority endanger public safety. In jurisdictions that are rather conservative about issuing violation warrants, the process may be time consuming and involve a written request to the board of parole (Figure 8.2).

In Oregon, in lieu of a summary arrest, the parole officer may issue a citation requiring the parolee/releasee to appear for a violation hearing. This citation is authorized when the person has violated a condition of supervision, but the nature of the violation does not jeopardize the safety of the general public, and the person, if left undetained, is not likely to flee. In Iowa, a PO having probable cause to believe that any person released on parole has violated the conditions of parole may arrest such person, or he or she may make a complaint before a magistrate, charging such violation; and if it appears from such complaint … that there is probable cause to believe that such person has violated the terms of parole, the magistrate shall issue a warrant for the arrest of such person. In either event, the violator must be taken before a magistrate for consideration of release on bail—"bail is discretionary with the magistrate and is not a matter of right" in Iowa. Most jurisdictions do not permit a parole violator to be released on bail.

In Wisconsin, in lieu of an arrest or warrant issuance, a parole agent's immediate supervisor can order the alleged violator to appear for a case review: "The focus of case review is threefold: to determine whether there is probable cause to believe there was a violation of the rules or conditions of probation or parole, to determine whether, if there is probable cause, it makes correctional sense to revoke, and to determine whether the client should remain in custody during revocation proceedings." Although this case review has many of the characteristics of a preliminary hearing (to be discussed shortly), the review is both more broadly focused—it can consider issues relating to supervision adjustment—and less formal: It is hoped by making the proceedings less formal and adversary, the client, the client's attorney, the agent, and the agent's supervisor can frankly discuss the issues in an atmosphere that focuses attention on the most important issues as noted earlier. Because parole violators are a contributing factor to prison overcrowding, agencies have been using graduated sanctions ranging from intensive supervision, a halfway house placement, to a brief period of incarceration, in place of revocation and imprisonment.

Preliminary Hearing

If a parolee/conditional releasee has been arrested pursuant to a violation warrant or if the offender is in custody for a new offense and a violation warrant has been filed as a detainer, the PO will provide him or her with a notice of a preliminary hearing and a list of the alleged violations. The purpose of the preliminary hearing is to determine whether probable cause exists to establish that the offender has committed one or more acts that constitute a violation of the conditions of release.

This hearing is required if the offender is to be detained on a warrant pending a revocation hearing; furthermore, the hearing is required within 15 days of the time the warrant was executed by arrest or was filed as a detainer. If no warrant has been issued—the subject is not being held in custody by parole authorities—but the offender has been summoned to appear for a revocation hearing, a preliminary hearing is not necessary. (About half-dozen states do not use a preliminary hearing.) The offender may also waive the right to a preliminary hearing.

At the preliminary hearing, the parolee/conditional releasee will have an opportunity to challenge the alleged violations and (a limited right) to confront and cross-examine adverse witnesses, including the parole officer, and to present evidence on his or her own behalf. Legal counsel can represent the offender, although the state is not constitutionally required to provide an attorney. In some states, attorneys are not permitted at the preliminary hearing. In Missouri, for example, "as the preliminary hearing is an informal review to establish probable cause only, attorneys do not have a role to play in this particular process. Generally, any request to have an attorney present shall be denied. The only exception shall be when the hearing officer has reason to believe that the offender is incapable of understanding the proceedings."

As opposed to the rules of evidence in the criminal process, hearsay is admissible at preliminary hearings (although hearsay is not used alone to determine probable cause). The hearing officer who presides is usually an attorney regularly employed for this purpose by the agency; however, any agency employee who is not directly involved in the case may fulfill this role. As a senior (supervisory) parole officer in New York, for example, I served as a hearing officer when personnel normally fulfilling this function were unavailable. Because

A CLOSER LOOK

PROBABLE CAUSE, WYOMING

Probable cause is defined as the state of facts that would lead a person of ordinary caution or prudence to believe and conscientiously entertain a strong suspicion of an individual's violation of the terms of parole or conditional release. It is a determination that the allegations of the violations are not frivolous but present a substantial and easily recognizable question that is worthy of consideration by the parole board.

this hearing is a relatively minimal and informal inquiry, the hearing officer need not hear all the allegations for a finding of probable cause (Figure 8.3).

If the hearing officer determines that evidence sufficient to make a finding of probable cause has not been presented, the parolee/conditional releasee will be restored to supervision. If probable cause is found, the offender will be held in custody pending a revocation hearing (Figure 8.3). Before the revocation hearing, the PO will prepare a parole violation report for use at the hearing.

STATE OF NEVADA BOARD OF PAROLE

SUMMARY OF PRELIMINARY INQUIRY HEARING

RE: Blackstone, John L.
File No. L82-001
Criminal Case No. 28001

The above-named subject appeared for a Preliminary Inquiry on July 19, 2009, at the hour of 2:20 P.M. at the Carson City Jail.

RIGHTS VERIFIED

Hearing Officer Sally Gomez inquired of defendant Blackstone if he had received copies of the Violation Report dated July 6, 2009, and the "Notice of Preliminary Inquiry Hearing" form listing his rights per the Morrissey and Scarpelli decisions. Blackstone replied that he had both documents and had read them. He also indicated that he fully understood the charges and his rights during the violation process as explained in the form. It is noted that Blackstone retained as private counsel for this hearing Michael Smith, Esq., of Carson City. Blackstone says he is satisfied with counsel and the time for preparing the defense case. With the indication that Mr. Blackstone fully understands his rights in this matter, we will proceed with the hearing.

VIOLATION CASE

Parole and Probation Officer James Richards read in part the Violation Report dated July 6, 2009, which indicates that Mr. Blackstone is charged with violation of Rule 9 of the Parole Agreement, WEAPONS. It was read that Blackstone was found in possession of a snub-nose .38 pistol by Police Sergeant John Brown in the After Hours Bar, 111 N. Carson Street, City of Carson, Nevada, at about 11:00 P.M. on July 4, 2009. Blackstone had shown the weapon to another customer of the bar, a Mr. William Mundy, allegedly stating to Mundy: "Sucker, I'm going to blow you apart if you keep bugging me tonight." Mundy left the bar and phoned the police to complain of the threat from Blackstone. Sgt. Brown arrived at the bar with several officers and asked Blackstone about the alleged weapon. Blackstone admitted to having an unloaded revolver in his jacket pocket, and Sgt. Brown removed same without incident. Blackstone was then placed under arrest for "assault" and an "ex-felon in possession of a firearm." He was transported to the Carson County Jail and booked. Parole Officer Richards placed a Hold for Parole Violation Investigation on Blackstone the following day, July 5, 2009, at about 10:00 A.M.

Officer Richards called William Mundy as his first witness. Mundy told how Blackstone had come into the bar and sat next to him at the counter. Mundy tried to engage Blackstone in some friendly conversation, but Blackstone told him to "shut up and to quit bugging him" or he'd "blow his body apart," showing Mundy a small pistol taken from his jacket pocket. Mundy says that he immediately left the bar and called the police, complaining of the incident and asking that the police arrest Blackstone. Mundy identified John L. Blackstone as the person who threatened him in the After Hours Bar on July 4, 2009. Mundy was dismissed after the defense had no questions of him.

Officer Richards called his second witness, Sgt. John Brown of the Carson City Police Department, to testify in this case. Brown related that he was dispatched to the After Hours Bar at about 10:55 P.M. on July 4, 2009, to investigate a citizen's complaint of a man with a gun making threats in the bar to shoot him. On arrival, Brown said he was met by Mr. Mundy at the entrance of the bar and that Mundy pointed Mr. Blackstone out for him in the crowded bar. The officer approached Blackstone and asked him if he was carrying a weapon in his jacket pocket; Brown said that Blackstone informed him that he had an unloaded pistol in his right-hand jacket pocket. Sgt. Brown then

FIGURE 8.3 Summary of a Nevada Preliminary Hearing

removed the weapon from Blackstone's right jacket pocket and found that it was empty of shells. Sgt. Brown directed Blackstone to step outside the bar with him. Sgt. Brown advised Blackstone that he was being placed under arrest for "simple assault" on the complaint of Mr. William Mundy and that he would have to come to the jail for booking but could post bail that evening. Blackstone went along to the jail without incident.

On arrival at the jail, the head jailer told Sgt. Brown that Mr. Blackstone was a parolee and should also be booked for the felony charge of "ex-felon with a firearm." Thus, he was so booked. Sgt. Brown was dismissed after the defense offered no cross-examination.

Officer Richards rested his prosecution case, noting that Blackstone has one felony charge of "Felon in Possession of Firearm" pending in Carson Justice Court. A preliminary hearing has been set for July 30, 2009, on the case. The weapon was not present at this hearing but listed as in the evidence locker of the Carson City Police.

DEFENSE CASE

Attorney for the accused Blackstone stated that he would decline to present any evidence or statements at this time regarding the possession of the weapon as the case was a felony charge awaiting disposition in Justice Court. However, attorney Smith did offer a defense witness, Gary Jones, to tell of the alleged threats in the bar. Jones was called into the hearing room and related he was sitting near the counter at a small table next to John Blackstone and Mundy at about 10:30 on July 4, 2009. Mundy, Jones explained, was "pretty drunk" and kept slapping Blackstone on the back, calling him "pal" and "buddy," and so on. Blackstone told Mundy to leave him alone and Mundy got mad and left the bar in a "huff," Jones testified. A short time later, Jones testified, police officers took Blackstone out of the bar and that is the last time he saw Blackstone until today. Attorney Smith suggested that Blackstone did not threaten Mundy in the manner alleged by Mundy. Hearing Officer Gomez asked Jones if he saw Blackstone take anything out of his jacket pocket and show it to Mundy. Jones replied, "no." Richards asked Jones if he could have missed seeing Blackstone show Mundy the gun and say he was going to "blow him apart." Jones was hesitant but said he was pretty sure; because of the back slapping, he was watching the incident pretty closely, wondering what Mundy was going to do next.

Attorney Smith closed the defense, advising Blackstone not to make any statements to the hearing officer until the Justice Court case was held.

FINDINGS

Having considered the evidence presented in this case by both the charging officer and the defendant, this hearing officer finds that probable cause exists to continue detention on the charge of violation of parole rule #9, WEAPONS. The hearing officer has determined that probable cause exists to continue detention pending your formal revocation hearing before the Board of Parole. You are duly notified that at the formal revocation hearing the Board of Parole has the discretion to review and act on all charges that were presented at this preliminary inquiry. With no further evidence to be heard, this hearing will be closed at 3:40 P.M., July 19, 2009.

Respectfully submitted,

Sally Gomez
Hearing Officer

FIGURE 8.3 (continued)

Revocation Hearing

A revocation hearing is similar to and takes place within 90 days of a preliminary hearing, except that it is comprehensive and the violator is entitled to counsel. The purpose of the revocation hearing is to determine whether the violation of parole/conditional release is serious enough to revoke supervision and return the offender to prison or whether some less drastic response is sufficient.

In addition to considering the allegations of parole violation, the revocation hearing will consider information about the offender's adjustment to supervision with respect to making timely reports, maintaining employment/education, supporting dependents, and

> **Key Fact**
>
> A revocation hearing is similar to a preliminary hearing but more comprehensive and the purpose is to determine whether the violation of parole is serious enough to return the offender to prison.

other critical elements of the supervision process. In most jurisdictions, the revocation hearing is presided over by one or more members of the parole board; in other states, it is the responsibility of hearing officers to make recommendations to the parole board for or against revocation. In Iowa, revocation hearings are conducted via two-way fiber-optic communications from the board's conference room; if the board votes against revocation, the offender is restored to supervision. In New York, revocation hearings are held before administrative law judges, attorneys appointed by the parole board, and they have the power to render final decisions.

▶ Street Time

Key Fact

Time under supervision (street time) is usually not deducted from the time owed by a probation violator.

A defendant is convicted of burglary and sentenced to 3.5 years' imprisonment (written 3-6-0: 3 years, 6 months, 0 days). His sentence is suspended in favor of probation. The probationer spends 1 year (1-0-0) under supervision and then violates the conditions of probation in an important respect. After a revocation hearing, the judge revokes probation and orders the probationer to begin serving the 3-6-0 sentence in prison. Must the offender serve a maximum of 3-6-0 in prison, or is the 1-0-0 year of probation supervision, so-called street time, to be subtracted from the 3-6-0 sentence?

The answer to this question varies from state to state. Some states do not recognize the time spent under supervision as time served against the sentence unless the full probationary term is successfully completed, a minority of states provide street time credit for probation violations not involving the commission of a new crime, and others leave it to the discretion of the judge. In the federal system, street time is not granted for those under any type of community supervision.

If parole/conditional release is revoked, how much time must the parolee must serve in prison. This also varies from jurisdiction to jurisdiction. In Pennsylvania and New York, a parolee receives credit for the time spent under supervision (street time) before the violation, so an inmate who is paroled after serving two years of a four-year sentence is required to be on parole for two years, the remainder of the sentence. If, after one year, the parolee violates parole and is returned to prison, he or she will have to serve only the one-year remaining on the sentence. However, in a state that does not give credit for street time, this same parolee would be required to serve two years in prison; the one year of satisfactory time on parole would not be credited against the four-year sentence in the event of a parole violation that results in being returned to prison. In Pennsylvania, if the parole violation is the result of a conviction for a new crime, the Board of Probation and Parole is prohibited from granting street time.

In California, counties are responsible for the incarceration of certain low-level felony offenders with postrelease supervision provided by probation officers. Offenders whose (county) parole is revoked can serve no longer than 180 days in the county jail, and those who do not violate supervision are discharged from supervision after six months. State parolees returned to prison for a technical violation can be confined for a maximum of twelve months. During the time they are awaiting case disposition, they receive day-for-day credit, so on average parole violators spend only slightly more than four months in custody—they quickly learn that violating parole does not carry serious consequences. But it does tax the resources of the police and parole officials who have to reprocess same individuals over and over again (Grattet et al., 2009). In Oregon, the maximum term for a technical violation of probation is 60 days; for a violation of postrelease supervision, the maximum is 90 days. In Washington, technical violators can serve no more than 60 days, and Louisiana provides a cap of 90 days for a first technical violation. Nevada's pardon board utilizes a cap of six months. In North Carolina, reincarceration time ranges from four to nine months (five years for sex offenders). A favorite offender saying expresses the lack of deterrent value of these limitations: "I can do that kind of time standing on my head." While the specter of short-term incarceration can generate fear in many, street-tough urban youth may have a different reaction. For them it can provide an opportunity for socializing, reacquainting with old friends, making new friends, and networking for enhanced criminal opportunities.

In several states, the supervision of technical violators is not subject to revocation—nonrevocable parole (NRP). A study in California found that while NRP did not contribute meaningfully to arrest activity, it contributed to reducing prison crowding (Council of State Governments Justice Center, 2013).

▶ Legal Issues in Probation and Parole Supervision

As the least democratic of our three branches of government, the judiciary—particularly the federal courts and, especially, the U.S. Supreme Court—can decide cases in a manner that may be politically unpopular. It can champion the legal rights of persons who (1) do not represent a significant bloc of votes or a source of campaign funding or (2) cannot generate a great deal of media attention, sympathy, or public support. Thus, in 1966 the Supreme Court rendered the famous *Miranda* decision (*Miranda v. Arizona*, 384 U.S. 436), which mandated that police suspects be informed of certain rights (to remain silent, to have counsel) before any questioning. The following year, in another Arizona case, the Supreme Court rendered the *Gault* decision, which gave important rights to juveniles (discussed in Chapter 11). That same year, the *Mempa* decision gave probationers the right to counsel in certain instances of probation violation.

Legal decisions that affect probation usually affect parole and vice versa. For example, the *Gagnon* on probation violation used the *Morrissey* that concerned parole violation, as a precedent. The basis for these decisions has been the constitutional concern for **due process** contained in the Fourth through Eighth Amendments. The Fourteenth Amendment, which was adopted in 1868 to protect newly freed slaves, applied these amendments to the states: "No state shall make or enforce any law which shall abridge the privileges or immunities of citizens of the United States; nor shall any State deprive any person of life, liberty, or property, without due process of law." However, the courts did not uniformly apply the Fourteenth Amendment to all constitutional guarantees. In 1961, the Supreme Court decided the case of *Mapp v. Ohio* (367 U.S. 643): Evidence (pornographic materials) seized by the police in violation of the Fourth Amendment could not be admitted into evidence in a *state* trial (such evidence was already inadmissible in *federal* trials since 1914). This decision provided a basis for the so-called **exclusionary rule**, which does *not* apply to probation or parole violation proceedings—evidence seized in violation of the Fourth Amendment can generally be used in a probation or parole violation hearing (*Pennsylvania Board. of Probation and Parole v. Scott*, 524 U.S. 357, 1998).

▶ Case Law and Conditions of Probation and Parole

In general, courts can impose any conditions of probation reasonably related to rehabilitation of the offender (e.g., to undergo drug treatment or avoid areas where a great deal of drug trafficking is known to occur), or protection of the community (e.g., avoid the possession of any weapons.) The state has a compelling interest in setting limits on the behavior of probationers; therefore, the Fourth Amendment notwithstanding, probationers have a **diminished expectation of privacy**. Thus, an offender with a history of drug addiction can be required to submit to periodic urinalysis as a condition of probation. Probationers can be required to report in person and to answer all reasonable inquiries by the PO, the Fifth Amendment right to remain silent notwithstanding, although the probationer need not incriminate himself or herself. If the offender is not in custody, the PO does not have to recite "Miranda rights." While a probationer can be compelled to answer questions under threat of revocation, answers are not admissible in criminal proceedings. If there is no coercion, the probationer must specifically invoke the privilege to remain silent, or incriminating responses may be used against him or her (*Minnesota v. Murphy,* 104 S.Ct. 1136, 1984).

In 1982, the U.S. Court of Appeals for the Fifth Circuit reviewed a case involving the First Amendment (*Owens v. Kelley,* 681 F.2d 1362). The plaintiff (probationer) claimed that a probation condition requiring him to participate in a program called "Emotional Maturity Instruction" violated his First Amendment freedom of religion because of the religious content of the course. The court stated that a "condition of probation which requires the probationer to adopt religion or to adopt any particular religion would be unconstitutional.... It follows that a condition of probation which requires the probationer to submit himself to a course advocating the adoption of religion or a particular religion also transgresses the First Amendment."

Owens also challenged a probation condition that required him to "submit to and cooperate with a lie detector test ... whenever so directed by the Probation Supervisor [title of probation officers in Georgia] or any other law enforcement officer." The probationer claimed that this condition violated his Fifth Amendment privilege against compelled self-incrimination. The court of appeals rejected this claim: "The condition on its face does not impinge upon Owens' Fifth Amendment rights. The condition does not stipulate that Owens must answer incriminating questions. If any question is asked during [the lie detector] examination which Owens believes requires an incriminating answer he is free to assert his Fifth Amendment privilege, and nothing in the probation condition suggests otherwise."

<aside>
</aside>

▶ Probation and Parole Violation and Case Law

Under our system of justice, the amount of due process—literally procedures required before adverse consequences can be imposed—is directly related to what is at risk. Persons accused of a crime are at risk of losing their liberty or even their life. Accordingly, they are afforded all of the due process rights granted by the Constitution, including the right to remain silent, to be represented by counsel, to cross-examine adverse witnesses, to have a jury trial, and to require a finding of guilt be based on the legal standard of beyond a reasonable doubt. At the other extreme are prison inmates who, having little at risk, have virtually no due process rights; for example, they can be transferred from one facility in to another without a hearing. What about persons on probation or parole accused of violating conditions of supervision?

> On a scale of zero to ten:
> **person accused of a crime (10) ....probationer/parolee (?) ....prison inmate (0)**

In 1967, the Supreme Court ruled (*Mempa v. Rhay,* 389 U.S. 128) that under certain conditions a probationer is entitled to be represented by counsel at a revocation hearing. In 1959, Jerry Mempa entered a plea of guilty to the charge of joyriding in a stolen car in the state of Washington. Imposition of sentence was deferred, and Mempa was placed on probation for 2 years on the condition that he spend 30 days in the county jail. About four months later, the Spokane County prosecutor moved to have Mempa's probation revoked on the grounds that he had been involved in a burglary while on probation. Mempa, who was 17 years old then, was not represented by counsel at his revocation hearing, nor was he asked whether he wanted to have counsel appointed for him.

At the hearing, Mempa was asked whether it was true that he had been involved in the alleged burglary, and he answered in the affirmative. A PO testified without cross-examination that according to his information Mempa had been involved in the burglary and had previously denied participation in it. Without asking the probationer whether he had any evidence to present or any statement to make, Mempa's probation was revoked, and he was sentenced to 10 years' imprisonment. The judge added that he would recommend to the parole board that Mempa be required to serve only one year.

In a companion case considered by the Supreme Court, William Earl Walkling was placed on probation (for burglary), with imposition of sentence deferred. At a subsequent revocation hearing, Walkling informed the court that he had retained an attorney. When the attorney did not arrive on time, the court proceeded with the hearing, at which a PO presented hearsay testimony to the effect that the probationer had committed 14 separate acts of forgery and grand larceny. The court revoked probation and imposed a sentence of 15 years. No record was kept of the proceeding. The *Walkling* case was consolidated with the *Mempa* case by the Supreme Court.

The Supreme Court noted that previously it had held that the right to counsel is not confined merely to representation during a trial, stating that counsel is required at *every* stage of a criminal proceeding when substantial rights of an accused criminal may be affected, and sentencing is one of these critical stages. In *Mempa*, the Court stated that counsel could aid in marshaling facts, introducing evidence of mitigating circumstances, and in general assisting the defendant in presenting his or her case with respect to sentence. The Court ruled that some rights could be lost if counsel were not present at a sentencing hearing, and "we decide here that a lawyer must be afforded at this proceeding whether it is labeled a revocation of probation or a deferred sentencing." The importance of the *Mempa* case goes beyond the limited finding made by the Court—it was the first time that the Supreme Court had ruled in favor of the rights of a person on probation.

Until 1970, parole agencies operated without any interference from the judiciary, but this policy changed when the New York Court of Appeals handed down a decision (*Menechino v. Warden*, 27 N.Y.2d 376, 318) that granted parolees the right to counsel and the right to call their own witnesses at parole revocation hearings for the first time. Although the decision applied only to New York, it indicated the direction in which the courts would rule in future decisions and provided a precedent for the U.S. Supreme Court.

In 1972 (*Morrissey v. Brewer*, 408 U.S. 471), the Supreme Court stipulated that the amount of due process rights to which a person is constitutionally entitled is directly related to the potential loss that can result. The greatest amount of potential loss is clearly in a criminal case, where total liberty may be forfeited creating a liberty interest. Thus, the criminal process represents the extreme end of the due process continuum. Located somewhere at the other extreme would be the due process rights of a student to challenge a course grade. Where are probation and parole located along this due process continuum?

Morrissey v. Brewer marked the beginning of the U.S. Supreme Court's involvement with parole revocation procedures. The issue in this case was whether the due process clause of the Fourteenth Amendment required that a state afford a person the opportunity to be heard before revoking parole. Morrissey was charged with the false drawing of checks in 1967 in Iowa. After pleading guilty, he was sentenced to seven years in prison but was paroled from the Iowa State Penitentiary in June 1968, only seven months later. Morrissey, at the direction of his PO, was arrested in his hometown as a parole violator and held in a local jail. One week after review of the PO's written report, the Iowa Board of Parole revoked Morrissey's parole, and he was returned to prison. He had received no hearing before the revocation decision.

Morrissey violated the conditions of his parole by buying a car under an assumed name and operating it without the permission of his PO; he also gave false information to the police and an insurance company concerning his address after a minor traffic accident.

Besides these violations, Morrissey also obtained credit under an assumed name and failed to report his residence to his PO. According to the parole report, Morrissey could not explain adequately any of these technical violations of parole regulations.

Also considered in the *Morrissey* case was the petition of Booher, a convicted forger who had been returned to prison in Iowa by the Board of Parole without a hearing. Booher had admitted the technical violations of parole charges to his PO when taken into custody.

The Supreme Court considered all arguments that sought to keep the judiciary out of parole matters, and it rejected the "privilege" concept of parole as no longer feasible. The Court pointed out that parole is an established variation of imprisonment of convicted criminals—it occurs with too much regularity to be simply a "privilege": "It is hardly useful any longer to try to deal with this problem in terms of whether the parolee's liberty is a 'right' or a 'privilege.' By whatever name the liberty is valuable and must be seen within the protection of the Fourteenth Amendment. Its termination calls for some orderly process however informal."

The Court pointed out that parole revocation does not occur in just a few isolated cases—it has been estimated that 35 to 40 percent of all parolees are subjected to revocation and return to prison. The Court went on to state that, with the numbers involved, protection of parolees' rights was necessary. The Court noted, however, limitations on a parolee's rights:

> We begin with the proposition that the revocation of parole is not part of the criminal prosecution and thus the full panoply of rights due to the defendant in such a proceeding does not apply to parole revocation. Supervision is not directly by the court but by an administrative agency which sometimes is an arm of the court and sometimes of the executive. Revocation deprives an individual not of absolute liberty to which every citizen is entitled but only the conditional liberty properly dependent on observance of special parole restrictions.

The Supreme Court held: "Society thus has an interest in not having parole revoked because of erroneous information or because of an erroneous evaluation of the need to revoke parole, given the breach of parole regulations."

In *Morrissey*, the Supreme Court viewed parole revocation as a two-stage process: (1) the arrest of the parolee and a preliminary hearing and (2) the revocation hearing. Because a significant time lapse usually occurred between the arrest and revocation hearing, the Court established an interim process for all parole violators, a hearing before the final or revocation hearing: "Such an inquiry should be seen in the nature of a preliminary hearing to determine whether there is probable cause or reasonable grounds to believe that the arrested parolee had committed acts which would constitute a violation of parole conditions."

The Court specified that the hearing officer conducting this preliminary hearing need not be a member of the parole board, only someone who is not involved in the case; that the parolee should be given notice of the hearing; and that the purpose is to determine whether there is probable cause to believe that the parolee has violated a condition of parole. On the request of the parolee, persons who have given adverse information on which parole violation is based are to be made available for questioning in the parolee's presence. Based on this information presented before the hearing officer, a determination should be made whether a reason exists to warrant the parolee's continued detention (pending a revocation hearing). The Court stated that "no interest would be served by formalism in this process; informality will not lessen the utility of this inquiry in redressing the risk of error." In reference to the revocation hearing, the Court stated: "The parolee must have an opportunity to be heard and to show if he can that he did not violate the conditions or if he did, that circumstances in mitigation suggest the violation does not warrant revocation. The revocation hearing must be tendered within a reasonable time after the parolee is taken into custody. A lapse of two months as the state suggests occurs in some cases would not appear to be unreasonable."

The Court also suggested minimum requirements of due process for the revocation hearing: Our task is limited to deciding the minimum requirements of due process. They include (1) written notice of the claimed violation of parole; (2) disclosures to the parolee of evidence against him; (3) opportunity to be heard in person and to present witnesses and documentary evidence; (4) the right to confront and cross-examine adverse witnesses (unless the hearing officer specifically finds good cause for not allowing confrontation); (5) "neutral and detached" hearing body such as a traditional parole board, members of which need not be judicial officers or lawyers; and (6) a written statement by the fact finders as to the evidence relied on and reasons for revoking parole.

The Supreme Court left open the question of counsel: "We do not reach or decide the question whether the parolee is entitled to the assistance of retained or to appointed counsel if he is indigent."

In 1973, the Court rendered a similar decision in the case of a probation violation, *Gagnon v. Scarpelli* (411 U.S. 778). In 1965, Gerald Scarpelli pleaded guilty to a charge of armed robbery and was sentenced to 15 years' imprisonment, but the sentence was suspended and he was placed on probation for 7 years. The probationer was given permission to reside in Illinois (under the Interstate Compact discussed in Chapter 10), where he was placed under the supervision of the Cook County Adult Probation Department. Shortly afterward, Scarpelli was arrested in a Chicago suburb with a codefendant and charged with burglary. The following month, his probation was revoked, and Scarpelli was incarcerated in the Wisconsin Reformatory to begin serving the 15 years to which he had originally been sentenced; at no time was he afforded a hearing. Scarpelli appealed.

> **Key Fact**
>
> The controlling case in probation violation, *Gagnon v. Scarpelli,* found that probationers have a liberty interest and are thus entitled to diminished due process rights.

Scarpelli was released on parole in Wisconsin, at which time his appeal reached the U.S. Supreme Court. He claimed that revocation of probation without a hearing and counsel was a denial of due process. The Court ruled that, in legal jargon, Scarpelli had a liberty interest: "Probation revocation, like parole revocation, is not a stage of a criminal prosecution, but does result in a loss of liberty. Accordingly, we hold that a probationer, like a parolee, is entitled to a preliminary and a final revocation hearing under the conditions specified in *Morrissey v. Brewer,* supra." In other words, as noted in a 1982 state of Texas decision (*Rogers v. State*, 640 S.W.2d 248), liberty on probation, although indeterminate, "includes many of the core values of unqualified liberty, such as freedom to be with family and friends, freedom to form other enduring attachments of normal life, freedom to be gainfully employed, and freedom to function as a responsible and self-reliant person."

In *Gagnon*, the Supreme Court held that a probationer is entitled to:

- A notice of the alleged violations
- A preliminary hearing to decide whether there is sufficient (probable) cause to believe that probation was violated (to remand the probationer to custody)
- A revocation hearing ("a somewhat more comprehensive hearing prior to the making of the final revocation decision")

At these hearings, the Court ruled that the probationer will have the opportunity to appear and to present witnesses and evidence on his or her own behalf as well as a conditional right to confront adverse witnesses. With respect to the right to counsel, the Court was ambiguous: "We...find no justification for a new inflexible constitutional rule with respect to the requirement of counsel. We think, rather, that the decision as to the need for counsel must be made on a case-by-case basis." In practice, however, probationers have been afforded the right to privately engaged or appointed counsel at probation revocation hearings.

Summary

- Classification in P/P is primarily for caseload management.
- The risk/needs assessment measures an offender's criminal risk factors and specific needs that, if addressed, will reduce the likelihood of future criminal behavior.
- The risk/needs assessment determines the level of offender supervision.
- Assigning cases on a workload basis is based on the anticipated amount of time each case will demand.
- While parolees are generally more serious offenders than probationers, the supervision process is similar, and in many agencies officers supervise both.
- Parolees differ from probationers as a result of their prison experiences and often encounter problems with housing.
- Place-based supervision entails P/P agencies operating satellite offices 24/7 that are physically located in communities with high concentrations of offenders under supervision.
- The initial interview in P/P practice is considered a crucial time in the supervision process.
- Persons who value their employment would be reluctant to engage in behavior that could jeopardize it.
- The observed relationship between criminality and unemployment has been explained in different ways.
- Most employers will not knowingly hire a probationer or parolee whose criminal record is often available on the Internet.
- Probationers and parolees suffer from many legal disabilities as the result of a felony conviction.
- Length of P/P supervision may be fixed or be as long as what a sentence of imprisonment would require.
- States provide for the termination of probation and the discharge of the offender from supervision before the end of the term.
- Terms of postprison supervision vary, but they typically provide for discharge before the expiration of the sentence.
- Some states have supervision-for-life provisions for certain offenders.
- Revoking probation is a decision made by a judge, while revoking parole is the responsibility of a parole board. In both, there are two types of violation.
- Violations of probation and parole are contributing factors to prison overcrowding, so P/P agencies use strategies to avoid incarcerating clients who are in violation of their conditions of supervision.
- Violation of probation involves the judiciary; violation of parole is an administrative process.
- The standard of evidence of a P/P violation differs from that of a criminal prosecution.
- "Street time" in probation differs from that in parole.
- Two Supreme Court decisions provide some due process rights to those accused of probation (*Gagnon*) and parole (*Morissey*) violation.
- The exclusionary rule does not apply to probation or parole violation hearings.
- Persons on P/P have a diminished expectation of privacy.
- Persons on P/P have a limited liberty interest.

Key Terms

Internet Connections

American Probation and Parole Association: **appa.org**

Center for Community Corrections: **communitycorrectionsworks.org**

Criminal justice links: **faculty.ncwc.edu/toconnor**

International Community Corrections Association:.**iccaweb.org**

Officer.Com Corrections Resources: **officer.com/correct.htm**

Probation and parole links: **talkjustice.com/links.asp?453053932**

Probation agency links: **cppca.org**

Review Questions

1. What is the primary purpose of classification in P/P?
2. What does the risk/needs assessment measure?
3. What is the difference between assigning cases on a workload rather than a caseload basis?
4. What problems are likely to be encountered by parolees but not probationers?
5. What is place-based supervision?
6. Why is the initial interview so important in P/P?
7. What is usually discussed during an initial interview?
8. What are the problems in explaining the relationship between criminality and employment?
9. What has research revealed with respect to a criminal record and the ability to secure employment?
10. What legal disabilities result from a felony conviction?
11. Who determines if a probationer is to be discharged from supervision before the expiration of his or her sentence?
12. Who determines if a parolee is to be discharged from supervision before the expiration of his or her sentence?
13. What are the two types of P/P violation?
14. What are the strategies used by P/P agencies to avoid sending supervision violators to prison?
15. What are the steps in the violation of P/P process?
16. How does the standard of evidence in P/P violations differ from that of a criminal prosecution?
17. How is "street time" determined?
18. What did the Supreme Court rule in the *Gagnon* and *Morrissey* decisions?
19. What has the Supreme Court ruled with respect to P/P violation hearings and the exclusionary rule?
20. Why do persons on P/P have a diminished expectation of privacy?
21. What is the connection between due process and a liberty interest?

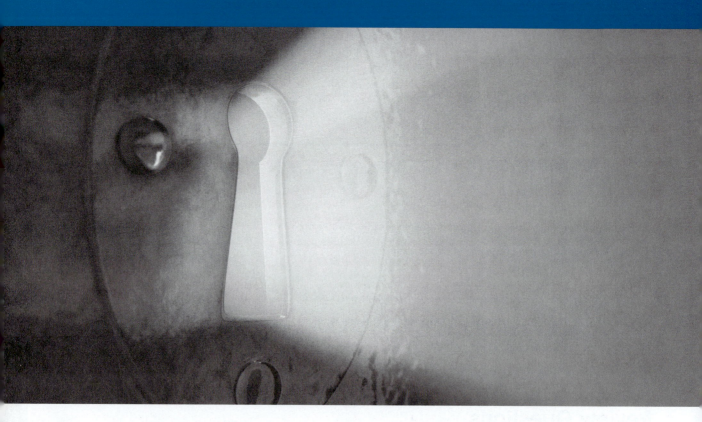

9 Intermediate Punishments

LEARNING OBJECTIVES

This chapter will enable the student to:

1. *Understand the stated and actual purpose for intermediate punishments.*

2. *Discuss standards for determining if a program of supervision is "intensive."*

3. *Describe the results of research into intensive supervision.*

4. *Explain why diversion from prison by using by intensive supervision requires assignment after a sentence of imprisonment.*

5. *Discuss the irony of releasing serious offenders with inadequate or no supervision, while nonviolent offenders are placed on intensive supervision.*

6. *Understand the advantages and drawbacks of GPS tracking in probation and parole.*

7 *Discuss the advantages and problems of halfway houses.*

8 *Explain the use of day reporting centers for probationers and parolees.*

9 *Describe criticism of shock incarceration ("boot camps").*

The stated explanation for **intermediate punishments** is a classical emphasis on matching the sanction to the offense, while the actual purpose is to reduce incarceration. The trend in favor of classicalism—just deserts and determinate sentencing—has been intertwined with the reality of jail and prison overcrowding. Widespread support for punishment and deterrence through greater use of incarceration—for example, "truth-in-sentencing," "three-strikes-and-you're-out"—has encountered serious financial limitations. Judges have been unwilling to permit conditions of incarceration that violate the Eighth Amendment's prohibition against cruel and unusual punishment, thereby increasing the cost of a policy of punishment by way of incarceration. In response, officials have scrambled to create alternative systems that satisfy a public/political appetite for punishment while limiting the financial costs involved.

Intermediate punishments are also used to expand the response to probation and parole (P/P) violators: "In the past, officials had two sanctions for violators—either to continue supervision (perhaps with modest changes in conditions) or to revoke and imprison the violator. Often the choice of options was either too lenient or too harsh for the circumstances of the violation" (Parent et al., 1994: 13). In response to the critical role in prison overcrowding played by P/P violators—parole violators account for about one-third of all prison admissions—many jurisdictions are instead using intermediate punishments for P/P violations.

▶ Intensive Supervision

If one can judge by the amount of agency literature and research efforts, **intensive supervision** has become the most popular program in P/P. Early versions of intensive supervision were based on the premise that increased client contact would enhance rehabilitation while affording greater client control. Current programs are usually a means of easing the burden of prison overcrowding. The Colorado Department of Corrections notes that its intensive supervision program "expands prison capacity by requiring participation of selected offenders who would otherwise be incarcerated in departmental facilities." In any event, by 1990 jurisdictions in all 50 states had instituted a community-based sanction called *intensive probation/parole supervision* (Petersilia and Turner, 1991). This chapter will use IPS to indicate intensive supervision of both probationers and parolees.

In probation, IPS is usually viewed as an alternative to incarceration; in other words, persons who are placed on IPS are supposed to be those offenders who, in the absence of intensive supervision, would have been sentenced to imprisonment. In parole, intensive supervision is viewed as risk management—allowing a high-risk inmate to be paroled but under the most restrictive of circumstances. Thus, although intensive supervision is invariably more costly than regular supervision, the costs "are compared not with the costs of normal supervision but rather with the costs of incarceration" (Bennett, 1988: 298). In Pima County, Arizona, for example, standard probation costs slightly more than $3 a day, while the cost of intensive supervision is slightly more than $18 a day; in

Maricopa County, Arizona, standard probation costs less than $5 a day, while the cost of intensive supervision is more than $22 a day. But, the cost of imprisonment in Arizona is about $62 a day.

Pima County IPS uses teams consisting of a probation officer (PO) and a surveillance officer. The PO is responsible for developing a case plan and coordinates the surveillance officer's activities to ensure that the team provides day and night, weekday and weekend, monitoring. Both officers are armed and conduct unannounced early morning and late evening home visits.

IPS can be classified into those types that stress diversion and those that stress enhancement:

- **Diversion** is commonly referred to as a "front-door" program because its goal is to limit the number of offenders entering prison. Prison diversion programs generally identify incoming lower-risk inmates to participate in IPS as a substitute for a prison term.

- **Enhancement** programs generally select already-sentenced probationers and parolees and subject them to closer supervision in the community rather than regular P/P. People placed on IPS-enhanced P/P have shown evidence of failure under routine supervision or have committed offenses deemed to be too serious for supervision on routine caseloads (Petersilia and Turner, 1993).

Intensive supervision actually takes many shapes. In Texas, for example, IPS involves an experienced probation officer whose maximum caseload does not exceed 40. In Suffolk County, New York, IPS clients are required to attend a day reporting center (discussed later) where they pass through four program phases before being placed on regular supervision.

Georgia Intensive Probation Supervision

In 1982, faced with the reality of prison overcrowding, the Department of Offender Rehabilitation inaugurated IPS. Although this plan began as a pilot program, IPS became a routine method of keeping down prison commitments. In addition to seeking to divert offenders from prison, the program attempts to accomplish the goal of punishment. IPS provides close community supervision to selected offenders who normally would have entered prison if it were not for the existence of the program: "The IPS team, composed of an experienced PO and a Surveillance Officer, supervises a maximum caseload of twenty-five (25) offenders [or two Surveillance Officers and 40 cases] who present no unacceptable risk to the community in which they are supervised. The caseload consists primarily of nonviolent felony offenders who have been convicted of property offenses."

Georgia IPS skims off low-risk offenders—persons who are nonviolent property and drug- and alcohol-related offenders—for the program, although most have been sentenced to imprisonment. An analysis of the program revealed that as a result of IPS, the percentage of offenders sentenced to prison decreased and the number of probationers increased. Furthermore, the "kinds of offenders diverted were more similar to prison inmates than to regular probationers, suggesting that the program selected the most suitable offenders" (Erwin and Bennett, 1987: 2). However, Georgia traditionally incarcerates many offenders for nonviolent offenses, including driving with a suspended driver's license. The IPS program may be diverting offenders from prison, but there is a serious question of why such persons are being sentenced to imprisonment in the first place.

Texas Intensive Supervision Program

Created in 1981 to deal with a prison crisis, the Texas ISP attempts to divert selected felony offenders by offering an alternative to incarceration. For these offenders, intensive supervision is a condition of probation. In most Texas probation departments, ISP caseloads do not exceed 40, and the officers are specially selected and trained for the assignment. In some Texas jurisdictions, however, the officers supervise a mixed ISP and regular caseload. Whenever this occurs, the mixed caseloads may comprise no more than 125 regular probationers before officers receive the first ISP case, and then they must be reduced by 5 regular cases each time a new ISP case is assigned to the caseload. Either of the cases is received directly from the court after sentencing, or they involve persons facing probation revocation and shock probationers (discussed later in this chapter).

Using a risk/needs assessment classification (discussed in Chapter 8), the IPS officer develops a supervision plan that outlines behavioral objectives to be met by the offender within specific time frames. By contracting with various community resources, the IPS officer negotiates for the exact type of services needed for each client. A formal reassessment occurs every 90 days. Typically, an IPS client remains under intensive supervision for one year or less and is then transferred to regular supervision. However, the court may amend the terms of probation to continue the offender under intensive supervision for an additional year; in rare or exceptional cases, the period may last beyond two years.

Texas also has a superintensive supervision program called *surveillance probation*. It is reserved for offenders whose regular probation has been revoked and those who are sentenced to shock probation; it can also be a special judicially imposed condition pursuant to a grant of probation. Each offender remains in the program for 90 days, although an extension can be granted during which time two officers (who supervise no more than 20 cases) maintain a minimum of five contacts per week, three of which are in person. There is a mandatory curfew and frequent drug and alcohol testing.

> **Key Fact**
>
> There is an absence of standards for determining whether a P/P program of supervision is indeed "intensive."

▶ Research Findings on Intensive Supervision

Before examining the effectiveness of intensive supervision, we should note that the establishment of IPS programming was not based on careful research and evaluation but was simply a response—perhaps ill-conceived—to jail and prison overcrowding (Clear, Flynn, and Shapiro, 1987). Indeed, policy implications of evaluative research into IPS may be irrelevant: "If the results are negative…then these findings will be viewed as support for both the continued use of incapacitation and the development of even more' intrusive, surveillance-oriented community control programs" (Byrne, 1990: 8). In fact, although evidence of the effectiveness of IPS is wanting, the program has been a public relations success (Clear and Hardyman, 1990).

Intensive supervision is usually accomplished by severely reducing caseload size for each officer on the assumption that this will lead to increased contact between the officer and the client and/or any significant others (such as spouse or parents) and that this increased contact will improve service delivery and control, thus reducing recidivism. Some programs, however, have had difficulty achieving *intensity*: "While it may be inconceivable for intensive supervision to occur in caseloads that exceed some finite number, such as fifty persons, it is certainly conceivable that much smaller caseloads might not result in significant levels of intensity" (Clear and Hardyman, 1990: 44). Two researchers claim that intensive supervision does indeed increase case contacts, often by 50 percent or more, and the amount of time spent in contact also increases significantly. However, the difference between spending one-half hour per month with a client and spending an hour per month is, relatively speaking, an extremely small difference considering the magnitude of the treatment and service provision task which the PO is trying to accomplish (Carlson and Parks, 1979).

In one Tennessee county, a comparison between a sample of regular and intensively supervised probationers over a three-year period revealed significant differences in recidivism: 25.8 percent of the regular probationers had new felony arrests, whereas the rate for the IPS sample was 8 percent. The results for technical violations were the reverse: 60 percent of the IPS participants and 34 percent of the regular probationers (Burrow, Joseph, and Whitehead, 2001). Perhaps IPS was successful in screening out—by way of technical violations—those probationers most likely to reoffend.

Intensive supervision for drug offenders on probation in seven cities (Atlanta, Georgia; Des Moines, Iowa; Macon, Georgia; Santa Fe, New Mexico; Seattle, Washington; Waycross, Georgia; and Winchester, Virginia) did not appear to impact recidivism. Another study revealed no significant differences between the arrest rates for IPS participants and a control group receiving regular supervision during a 12-month period (Petersilia, Turner, and Deschenes, 1992), and similar findings were reported in a study of IPS programs in 14 cities (Petersilia and Turner, 1993). As noted by the researchers, however, drawing conclusions from recidivism statistics can be misleading because recidivism could be a feature of the intensity of the supervision—IPS could increase the probability of new criminal activity being *discovered* (this issue is discussed in Chapter 10).

California

Research into the effectiveness of intensive supervision dates back to 1953 when California conducted "probably the most extensively controlled experiment in American correctional history" (Glaser, 1969: 311). The California Special Intensive Parole Unit experiment ran from 1953 until 1964, during which time caseload sizes were varied from 15 to 35. In addition, research was conducted into the impact of increased supervision on particular risk classes of offender. A positive outcome occurred only with those parolees classified as "lower-middle risk"—they had significantly fewer violations. In a review of this research, however, Robert Martinson (1974) found that the successful cases were concentrated in northern California, where agents were more apt than agents in southern California to cite both the experimental subjects and the controls for violating parole. The limited success, Martinson argues, was not due to the intensive nature of supervision but was the result of a realistic threat of reimprisonment. A problem also exists with using parole violation as a criterion for success because of what researchers refer to as the **halo effect**: a tendency on the part of P/P officers to tolerate greater levels of misbehavior than is usual to prove the experiment is successful.

Later research into California IPS was conducted in three counties. Cases were randomly assigned from a pool of high-risk offenders (HROs) on probation to IPS caseloads of 40 (Contra Costa), 19 (Ventura), and 33 (Los Angeles) or control caseloads that averaged 150 to 300 offenders. After six months, IPS clients received more intensive supervision: two to three times the usual number of contacts. About 30 percent of the IPS cases had a technical violation, a much higher rate than the control caseloads; however, no statistically significant difference existed between new arrest rates for IPS and control cases. The research revealed that intensive supervision in these counties did not affect the rate of new arrests: IPS failed to enhance the rehabilitative or control function of supervision (Petersilia and Turner, 1990). The researchers conclude: "When compared with routine probationers, the ISP participants, with few exceptions, had similar rates of technical violations and new arrests" (Petersilia and Turner, 1991: 9).

Research on a Los Angeles Probation Department IPS program involving gang-member drug offenders also had disappointing results. Although caseloads were small— 33 as opposed to 300—the supervision that resulted was hardly intensive, and home visits

Key Fact

Research into intensive supervision has produced mixed results, with no clear indication that the process is successful in meeting its goals.

were infrequent (Agopian, 1990). *Calling* a program "intensive" by reducing caseload size is obviously not the same as *providing* intensive supervision.

Georgia

Research in Georgia has produced mixed results for the concept of intensive supervision. As noted earlier, IPS probationers are under the joint supervision of a probation officer and a surveillance officer in caseloads that do not exceed 25. One comparison of outcomes for 542 IPS probationers and a matched sample of 752 regular probationers revealed that 13.7 percent of the IPS group had their probation revoked for new crimes (none for violent crimes), whereas 10.2 percent was the figure for the control sample. The IPS group had a higher rate of technical violations (11.8 percent) than the control sample (6.5 percent)—which the researchers argue is to be expected considering the intensive supervision—and there was little difference in the absconder rate: 2.2 percent for the IPS participants, 2.4 percent for the control sample. A second study of the program revealed that 18.5 percent of the IPS probationers and 24.0 percent of the regular probationers were convicted of new crimes. However, 42.3 percent of prison releasees during the same period were convicted of new offenses, and "59.4 percent of the IPS cases were more similar to those incarcerated than to those placed on probation" (Erwin and Bennett, 1987: 4; also Erwin, 1984).

According to Joan Petersilia (1988a), several states adopted IPS programming based on the apparent success of the Georgia program. However, she cautions, judges in Georgia (like those in many southern states) tend toward the punitive, imposing more sentences of imprisonment and for longer terms than elsewhere. Thus, there is a greater pool of IPS prospects—nonviolent offenders—than would be expected outside of the South in general, and Georgia in particular. In fact, when it comes to the risk of new criminal behavior, IPS clients are not markedly different from the regular probation population in Georgia. The basic claims of IPS in Georgia with respect to cost-effectiveness, diversion of offenders, and improved public safety "are not supported by the available research evidence" (Clear, Flynn, and Shapiro, 1987: 35). In fact, "a convincing argument can be presented that the Georgia evaluation actually demonstrates the opposite" (Byrne, Lurigio, and Baird, 1989: 27).

The Georgia ISP probation officer is supposed to provide typical professional casework services, whereas the probation surveillance officer (with less education, training, and salary) provides "24 hour surveillance capability through day, night, and weekend visits and telephone contacts." Surveillance officers, however, developed greater rapport with clients and their families than did probation officers. The surveillance officer had more direct contact with, and was more easily accessible to, the client and his or her family:

> One of the most interesting findings of the IPS evaluation is the near impossibility of separating treatment from enforcement. The Georgia design places the PO in charge of case management, treatment and counseling services, and court-related activities. Surveillance Officers, who usually have law enforcement or correctional backgrounds, have primary responsibility for frequently visiting the home unannounced, checking curfews, performing drug and alcohol tests using portable equipment, and checking arrest records weekly. The Surveillance Officer becomes well acquainted with the family and is often present in critical situations. Both the Probation and Surveillance Officers report a great deal of overlap of functions and even a reversal of their roles. (Erwin and Bennett, 1987: 6)

In practice, the surveillance officer was doing the work of a professional probation officer, while the latter's role was either redundant or reduced to that of a paper-pushing case analyst.

New York

Research conducted by the New York State Division of Parole (Collier, 1980) indicates that intensive supervision can have a modest effect on violent felony offenders. In 1978, the legislature provided funding for the supervision of violent felony offenders. In 1979, all released inmates who had been convicted of a violent felony (crimes ranging from robbery to arson, with most being imprisoned for robbery) were placed in intensive units whose officers supervised no more than 35 cases: 97 percent were male; the median age was 27.3; blacks constituted 57.5 percent, whites 23 percent, and Hispanics 19.5 percent; 62 percent completed less than the twelfth grade; and 80 percent were unskilled laborers. Interestingly, two-thirds of this group had little or no prior criminal history.

After one year of research (ending March 31, 1980), the 1,905 violent felony offenders released in 1979 and placed under intensive supervision were compared with 1,732 of the same population released in 1978 to regular supervision:

- 12.6 percent of the (1978) controls and 1.8 percent of the (1979) intensives were returned to prison for a new offense.
- 3.3 percent of the controls and 4.0 percent of the intensives were returned to prison for technical violations of parole.
- 5.0 percent of the controls and 3.4 percent of the intensives absconded from supervision.
- 6.5 percent of the controls and 3.9 percent of the intensives had parole violation or court hearings pending.

Ohio

Funded by a state probation subsidy program, the Lucas County Incarceration Diversion Unit (IDU) consisted of four probation officers, each with a caseload maximum of 25 (with the exception of the supervisor, who is assigned 15). The IDU probationers were compared with a group of shock probationers under regular supervision. (The study did not indicate the size of regular shock probation caseloads.) The researchers found that the IDU officers recorded almost four times as many client contacts, and more social services were provided to their clients. However, no statistically significant differences with respect to recidivism occurred; the IDU group did have significantly fewer technical violations, which the researchers conclude was the result of a realistic fear of being sent to prison because of the nature of IDU supervision and strict violation practices. (An alternative hypothesis would raise questions about the quality of the supervision.) The researchers conclude that their study "should provide a word of caution to officials seeking ways to limit incarceration rates" by using intensive supervision (Latessa and Vito, 1988: 327).

The Lucas County Intensive Supervision Unit (ISU) was designed to divert nonviolent felony offenders who had already been committed to a Department of Youth Services (DYS) facility because DYS facilities were under pressure from overcrowding. The program excluded youth whose instant offense involved drugs, use of a weapon, or victim injury. Research compared ISU youngsters to similar youth committed to a DYS facility and then paroled. The supervision provided by ISU was indeed intensive, with respect to both control and rehabilitative services, but no significant difference in recidivism occurred: It was rather high for both—almost 50 percent of both groups were reinstitutionalized within the 18-month period of the research. However, there was a potential savings: The annual cost of ISU per client was more than $6,000, as contrasted with more than $32,000 for incarceration (Wiebush, 1993).

A study in Montgomery County (Dayton), Ohio, compared matched samples from IPS units (with 25 cases per officer) and regular units (caseload size not indicated). The research revealed that 11.7 percent of the intensive supervision cases ended with a felony conviction, against 3.8 percent for regular supervision, and that 1.2 percent of the intensive cases were incarcerated for misdemeanors, as opposed to 6.2 percent of the regular cases. Interestingly, the IPS officers, on average, made less than one face-to-face contact per month with their clients in the clients' homes—hardly an *intensive* level of supervision (Noonan and Latessa, 1987).

A study of IPS in the rural Ohio county of Clermont noted that implementing a special supervision program in rural areas is difficult because of long travel times to reach clients, making unannounced visits problematic. The researchers found that persons assigned to IPS were clearly higher risk than those on regular caseloads, but they were unable to determine whether these were prison-bound cases. As might be expected if supervision is indeed intensive, the IPS clients had a higher rate of technical violations: 39 percent (IPS) versus 24 percent (regular). "[However,] there were no significant differences in the number of felony arrests, convictions, or completion rates of probation. A high percentage of both groups were classified as successful" (Haas and Latessa, 1995: 168).

Washington State

The stated objective of the Washington State Adult Corrections Division intensive program was to save tax dollars by removing low-risk offenders from the state's prisons—persons released into the program had on average served less than three months in prison. A total of 289 were placed under the intensive supervision of an officer whose caseload did not exceed 20. At the end of one year, it was determined whether the individual's behavior warranted a conditional discharge from supervision or supervision by a regular probation officer.

To evaluate the program, a matched historical sample (102) was selected as the control group. Random assignment was ruled out because of "equal treatment under the law considerations." The control group was made up of inmates who were paroled at the same time as those selected for early release and intensive supervision; however, the control group subjects were released after having served normal sentences to a probation officer who supervised an average caseload of 73. A person in the control group was selected on the basis of the same criteria as those in the test group, with the following three results (Fallen et al., 1981):

1. After one year of supervision, 19 percent of the test (IPS) group had been arrested or convicted for new (nontraffic) offenses, whereas the figure for control cases was 40 percent.

2. The IPS officers showed a strong tendency to invoke delinquency action. After one year, 42 percent of the test group had been cited for technical parole violations as opposed to 24 percent for the control group.

3. The one-year revocation rate for the IPS group was 17 percent; for the control group, it was 6.1 percent (the average for general supervision in Washington is 15 percent).

Fallon and colleagues (1981) speculate on explanations for their findings:

- Intensive parolees were less likely to commit new offenses because of the fear of detection produced by increased supervision.

- By brief incarceration, intensive parolees received the initial "shock value" of prison but were not in long enough to learn the "skills" or adopt the "values" of the incarcerated criminal population.

- Because many intensive parolees received formal technical violations, these served as effective warnings that undesirable behavior would not be tolerated.

- Because many intensive parolees were revoked for technical violations only, this may have screened out those disposed to commit new offenses.

Wisconsin

In 1984, the Wisconsin Division of Corrections established an experimental IPS program for high-risk offenders, with 30 offenders (later increased to 40) supervised by two-agent teams in two locations. The research did not indicate the caseload for non-IPS parole agents. Experienced agents screened all new cases in their areas and selected only high-risk offenders as clients. To qualify as a high-risk offender, the client required a history of assaultive behavior; other distinguishing characteristics included a lengthy criminal record, poor prison adjustment record, and poor attitude toward community supervision, as well as an unwillingness to participate in drug and alcohol abuse programs or mental health programs.

As part of intensive supervision, specialized rules were tailored for each offender; these restricted certain associations, use of motor vehicles, and evening hours: "The general tactic is to establish rules which restrict behavior(s) associated with a past criminal pattern" (Wagner, 1989: 23). Offenders were required to provide a weekly schedule indicating where they would be at any given time. Each client registered with the local police, submitting a photograph, fingerprints, handwriting sample, past offense history, and current address. The police were expected to assist in the offender monitoring process. Parole agents made at least four in-person contacts each month, including two visits (scheduled and unscheduled) to the offender's residence. Frequent collateral visits with police, employers, landlords, and associates occurred. In at least one case, school officials and parent association members were informed of the release of a child sex offender so that they could aid in the surveillance process.

The high-risk offender group under IPS was compared with a matched sample that received regular supervision. The results were dramatic: After one year, only 3 percent of the IPS parolees had been convicted of a felony; it was 27 percent for the control group. The statistics for parole violation provide at least a partial explanation for these differences because only 12 percent of the control group were returned to prison for parole violations, whereas the number was 40 percent for the IPS group. A researcher for the state of Wisconsin concludes that "the IPS program suppresses criminal behavior by preempting it" (Wagner, 1989: 26). The research does not indicate how many of the remaining IPS clients successfully completed their entire supervision period.

Reducing probation officer caseloads can reduce criminal recidivism when delivered in a setting where probation officers apply evidence-based practices (EBP). Funded by the National Institute of Justice, researchers found that lowering probation officer caseloads in Oklahoma reduced recidivism when evidence-based practices were implemented (Jalbert and Rhodes, 2012). Research in Colorado and Iowa revealed, similarly, that lowering the caseloads of probation officers trained to apply EBP (discussed in Chapter 12) reduced recidivism. The combination of training and reduced caseloads enabled POs to identify the treatment needs of their clients and to focus resources on those most in need (Jalbert et al., 2011; Jalbert and Rhodes, 2012). Thus, in Polk County, Iowa, which includes the city of Des Moines, intensive probation supervision (caseload size reduced from 50 to 30) with higher-risk offenders (as determined by risk scores) reduced recidivism significantly. Evidence "suggests that intensive control strategies can be effective if they are focused on the appropriate offenders and if they are balanced with rehabilitative strategies" (Jalbert et al., 2010: 236).

▶ Discussion

To evaluate IPS, we need to examine the two premises on which it is based.

Premise One

IPS will divert offenders who would otherwise be incarcerated. In any number of jurisdictions, this goal is not being accomplished. A study in Tennessee, for example, revealed that although some offenders were being diverted away from prison, many more IPS clients would have normally been sentenced to regular probation (Whitehead, Miller, and Myers, 1995). Judges continued to send probation-eligible offenders to prison while using IPS for those who would be sentenced to probation in any event. A study of IPS in Colorado found no significant differences between cases recommended for IPS and those not recommended, leading researchers to conclude that this program "may not be one of prison-diversion as the state guidelines proclaim" (Reichel and Sudbrack, 1994: 57).

For the diversion goal to be accomplished, cases need to be assigned to IPS *after* a sentence of imprisonment. Only after conviction, sentence, and remand to jail pending transportation to prison should the IPS screening officer review the case and, if appropriate, submit a recommendation for resentencing. Cases not intercepted should proceed to prison. With respect to parole, parole boards often assign cases to intensive supervision that would have been granted parole even in the absence of an intensive program. If intensive supervision is to serve the goal of reducing the prison population, it should be reserved for cases that have been denied parole. A screening officer (e.g., institutional parole officer) should review the case *after* parole has been denied and, if appropriate, submit a recommendation for reconsideration of parole with intensive supervision.

In sum, many (if not most) intensive supervision programs are not actually diverting offenders—they are simply providing judges and parole boards with an additional supervision option that is not being used in lieu of prison (although this may not have the effect of lowering prison commitments, it certainly has merits of its own). Many IPS programs appear to be accepting those offenders who are not at high risk and who probably should have been on regular probation in the first instance. In some counties, the probation department routinely recommends inappropriate cases for IPS. This serves two intertwined purposes: First, it ensures that the IPS program will deliver "good stats"; second, it helps keep down regular caseloads by shifting some cases to probation officers funded by special state allocations (and the continuation of these allocations is dependent on "good stats").

However, intensive supervision for inappropriate cases unnecessarily increases the cost of probation and may be harmful to the client: "Behavioral scientists have long speculated that the addition of strains and controls to a human system can, at some time, result in a reaction that is contrary to the direction of the controls" (Clear and Hardyman, 1990: 55). According to the labeling perspective (discussed in Chapter 6), an offender inappropriately identified as "high risk" by virtue of IPS status may indeed assume that role and organize his or her behavior accordingly, so subjecting low-risk offenders to intensive supervision may lead to more—not less—trouble with the law (Altschuler and Armstrong, 1994). Indeed, research reveals that inappropriate placement of offenders on intensive supervision can have adverse consequences: "Providing intensive services and supervision to low-risk offenders does little to change their likelihood of recidivism and, worse, occasionally increases it" (Lowenkamp, Lemke, and Latessa, 2008: 2).

An additional problem involves offenders who believe that intensive supervision is as punitive as imprisonment: "In many states, given the option of serving prison terms or participating in IPS, many offenders have chosen prison" (Petersilia, 1990: 23; emphasis

> **Key Fact**
>
> To ensure that diversion from prison is accomplished, cases need to be assigned to IPS *after* a sentence of imprisonment.

deleted). Petersilia points out that for many/most serious offenders, imprisonment and the stigma that can result are not the frightening phenomena that they are for the community at large: "For many offenders, it may seem preferable to get that short stay in prison over rather than spend five times as long in an IPS" (1990: 25; also Petersilia and Deschenes, 1994). Under these circumstances, in order for intensive supervision to work, it may be necessary to offer it as an option for much more serious offenders than are now being subjected to IPS.

In sum, large amounts of scarce resources are being allocated to less serious offenders, whereas more dangerous offenders are released to the community under parole supervision that is often inadequate because of lack of funding (Clear, Flynn, and Shapiro, 1987) and some states have discontinued postprison community supervision. It is the worst "Alice in Wonderland" situation when serious offenders are released from prison with inadequate or no supervision, while nonviolent offenders are placed on IPS.

This irrational approach to crime and justice is exemplified by a 1988 Texas Adult Probation Commission study. IPS cases were compared with offenders eligible for probation but sentenced to imprisonment and offenders not eligible for probation and sentenced to imprisonment using the "risk" part of the Texas Risk/Needs Assessment form. Following are the mean scores:

Intensive probation supervision	20.10
Eligible for probation but incarcerated	18.93
Ineligible for a sentence of probation	26.26

In other words, although the IPS program was apparently diverting offenders from prison (a risk mean of 20.10), there were less serious risks (risk mean of 18.93) imprisoned, and the high-risk offenders (risk mean 26.26) who were imprisoned will be released to parole supervision that is not intensive. There was a similar situation in Illinois when the state funded intensive probation supervision programs while laying off 60 percent of the state's parole agents.

Alan Schuman (1989: 29) argues that the "IPS concept actually depicts local communities' original image of how probation services should operate. IPS provides the type of comprehensive surveillance services, restitution payments, drug testing and treatment, employment verification, and networking with other community services that should be expected of all probation agencies that are adequately funded." Gerald Buck (1989: 66) argues that intensive supervision "*is* probation practiced as it was originally intended to be. Other probation programs are a sham that ought not be called probation supervision" (emphasis in original).

Premise Two

More of whatever it is that the P/P agency does with routine cases will have a salutary effect on cases at greater risk. Although several research studies have challenged this premise, a strong (if unproven) belief regarding P/P is that *more is better*. I want to dwell on the question *more of what?* The implication of intensive supervision—the bait that hooks funding from elected officials—is that offenders will be closely monitored, be under surveillance, and be made to fear detection for any violations they might be inclined to commit. Arthur Lurigio and Joan Petersilia note "an important assumption of IPS programs is that close supervision should increase the probability of detecting and arresting offenders who are not deterred by the program and who continue to commit crimes. Speedy revocation to custody results in incapacitation, and, because IPS participants are encouraged to be employed and to attend counseling sessions, reha-bilitation *may* occur. However, newer IPS programs are designed to boost offenders' perceptions of the effectiveness of the system in detecting and punishing their criminal behavior" (1992: 9).

P/P officers are portrayed as making unannounced contacts with offenders, whom they are monitoring around-the-clock, ready to take immediate action to prevent any danger to the community. For agencies whose officers are armed and trained in law enforcement, this approach is a natural extension of the services they are already pro-viding; agencies in which officers do not have adequate law enforcement training or authority, however, cannot live up to the image of *intensive*. Indeed, agencies that adopt a meaningful form of intensive supervision—one that does indeed increase unannounced face-to-face in-field contacts—but fail to equip and train their officers accordingly, place these officers in danger. When I worked as a parole officer in New York, unannounced visits found parolees with firearms left on the dresser, large amounts of heroin and drug paraphernalia on the kitchen table, and other potentially dangerous situations. The neighborhoods in which most clients live are high-crime areas, which can be particularly hazardous at night.

IPS programs are typically set up outside the traditional supervision structure. Clients and officers are handpicked; the latter receive special training and sometimes salary increases, and they report to their own supervisory chain of command. This hierarchy can affect general agency morale, because the IPS unit receives a disproportionate share of resources and attention. In some agencies, only IPS officers are authorized to carry fire-arms, and they are viewed as "elite." These special units experience strong pressure to dem-onstrate results:

> This is one reason why these programs often seem to be encased in an atmosphere of caution—they are very vulnerable to errors. Based on a rationale of effective offender con-trol, and in contrast to seemingly more lenient traditional probation methods, the idea of intensive probation can be seriously damaged by even one publicized incident of serious cli-ent failure, such as a violent crime. Therefore, despite the control rhetoric, program officials seem to bend over backward to avoid the riskiest clients and to resist giving accepted clients many chances to violate probation. (Clear, Flynn, and Shapiro, 1987: 42)

This accounts for the relatively high rate of probation violations in most IPS programs.

When I was a parole officer in New York, each caseload had some cases designated "intensive" by the parole board, and they required at least one face-to-face unannounced home visit and four in-person office visits each month. Cases were subjected to more supervisory review, and there was less latitude—in the event of a technical violation of the rules, such offenders were more likely to be taken into custody and returned to prison. New York State parole officers are required to carry firearms while on duty, so this system avoids the elitism that has apparently reared its head in at least some P/P agencies with IPS programs.

There is also a problem inherent in evaluating IPS effectiveness. Random assignment of high-risk cases between the IPS and routine caseloads fails to account for the classification and unofficial intensive supervision typically carried out by P/P officers. When confronted with unmanageable caseloads, P/P officers identify those cases with greatest risks/needs and devote most of their quality time working with these clients (at the expense of most other cases, which receive little more than "paper" attention). Thus, experimental model research is often comparing IPS with quasi-IPS. Recidivism rates may vary according to the ability of the police, the skill of perpetrators, and the cooperation between P/P agencies and law enforcement agencies. Ironically, IPS may "fail" (statistically) by being "successful":

While criminals are arrested for relatively few of the crimes they commit, should they recidivate, the greater scrutiny given to those on intensive supervision increases their risk of detection.

► Electronic Monitoring

Electronic monitoring (EM) is used in conjunction with a variety of programs, such as home detention instead of jail for defendants awaiting trial and DUI offenders. The first system of EM system monitored the location of parolees, mental patients, and volunteers in Massachusetts from 1964 through 1970. Although interest in EM of offenders always existed, until the crisis in prison overcrowding, "market conditions were never attractive enough to make the technology commercially available" (Przybylski, 1988: 1). Reputedly inspired by a "Spiderman" comic strip, Albuquerque District Court Judge Jack Love asked Michael Goss to develop a device suitable to monitor probation curfews. The "Gosslink" was first attached to the ankle of a 30-year-old probation violator for a 1-month period starting in 1983. Judge Love subsequently sentenced four other offenders to monitored home confinement.

Meanwhile, a Monroe County, Florida, judge tried a new EM system with 12 offenders over a 6-month period; they served house confinement sentences ranging from 2 days to 4 months. As a result, the state of Florida incorporated electronic home confinement in the Correctional Reform Act of 1983, and the following year a pilot program was initiated in Palm Beach County for misdemeanants, mostly drunken drivers. By 1988, EM was being used in 33 states for 2,277 offenders: "Most of those monitored were sentenced offenders on probation or parole, participating in a program of intensive supervision in the community" (Schmidt, 1989: 2).

The technology for monitoring offenders in the community has expanded as have the firms that offer the devices. This chapter will examine the most popular devices.

► Continuously Signaling Systems

Two primary types of continuously signaling systems are available: those that use telephone or cell phone lines and those that use a radiolike transmitter and receiver. One system uses telephone lines or cellular wireless communication and requires the offender to wear a battery-powered moisture-, water-, and shockproof transmitter that is about the size of a pack of cigarettes and weighs about 6 ounces. The device is securely fastened by riveted plastic straps just above the ankle; once strapped on, it can only be removed by stretching or by cutting the straps in a manner easily detected by visual inspection. Some versions provide an immediate electronic alert if the band is subjected to tampering. A circuit board contained in the transmitter has an individually calibrated unique identification code. The transmitter emits a signal at regular intervals with a range of about 100 to 150 feet. The signal is monitored by a receiver connected to a 110-volt outlet and a standard telephone jack installed in the residence (or a cell phone unit for those not having access to a basic phone line at home or in a halfway house). The receiver automatically dials a central computer and describes the time the person goes beyond the range of the signal or returns within range and automatically dials the computer when it has been subjected to tampering. If the dialer is disconnected or loses its source of power (e.g., by a power outage), the message is stored until such time as power is restored; at that time, a delayed message describing the time of each activity is sent to the computer.

Simpler continuously signaling systems consist of a transmitter and a portable receiver. The transmitter, which is strapped to the offender's ankle or wrist or worn around the neck, emits a radio signal that travels about one city block. When within 200 to 800 feet of an offender's ankle or wrist transmitter—and sometimes more than 1,000 feet depending on the location and the use of special antennas—the device can detect the radio signals of the transmitter. It can also determine the tamper status and battery status of the transmitter. By driving past the offender's residence, place of employment, or treatment center, the P/P officer using a handheld portable receiver can verify the offender's presence.

▶ Programmed Contact Systems

A programmed contact system usually relies on the telephone and computerized voice identification—individuals have unique voiceprints just as they have distinctive fingerprints. The computer records the offender's voice and is then programmed to call him or her at home random times and request that a series of words or phrases be repeated; they are then matched with the earlier recording to verify the offender's presence. In the event of a failure to answer the telephone or a voice verification failure, the computer reports a monitoring infraction. Another system requires the offender to wear a pager that is beeped on a random basis, after which he or she is required to call a toll-free number. The caller's voice is verified against an original voiceprint, and the telephone number from which the call is being placed is captured. If the voice does not match that of the offender, or the offender is not calling from home, the officer is notified by page within minutes.

▶ Global Positioning System

Taking advantage of satellite-based technology, agencies are using a global positioning system (GPS). Orbiting about 12,000 miles above earth, 24 government satellites transmit precise time and position to receivers that pick up signals from multiple satellites simultaneously. A monitoring station determines location by calculating the time it takes the signal to reach the receiver, accurately plotting the receiver's position within a few feet. Passive GPS provides information regarding the whereabouts of an offender during the previous 24-hour period. The information is collected throughout the day and transmitted via landline telephone to a main computer that downloads the information. Active GPS provides constant tracking of an offender's location and is typically used with sex offenders to create customized exclusion zones, such as schools and children's play areas. The computer can be programmed to send an alert any time the offender enters an exclusion zone or leaves an inclusion zone at the wrong time. If an alert registers, it is then possible to follow the offender's movements to determine whether he is clearly violating his restrictions or has accidentally gone in the wrong zone temporarily. Real-time tracking allows P/P officers to respond to the offender's exact location (Crowe et al., 2002).

A GPS requires the offender to wear a transmitter similar to the EM system's ankle bracelet.

A GPS cannot track inside buildings or other enclosed areas and is limited to areas with good-quality cell phone coverage. Furthermore, officials are not stationed at computer terminals tracking the movement of offenders in real time; tracking software records movements and possible violations of restrictions, for example, entering a forbidden zone such as a children's playground. Responding to violations in a timely manner requires personnel available 24/7. The cost of GPS equipment is about $10 a day and generates large amounts of data that must be processed on a daily basis. It is not unusual for the system to generate a false positive, as when an offender is on a bus that passes through an exclusion zone (Downing, 2006). GPS tracking of high-risk offenders, such as gang members and sex offenders—sometimes legislatively mandated—is labor intensive and, therefore, imposes personnel costs on P/P agency (DeMichele and Payne, 2005). Despite cost, GPS proved effective with sex offenders in California; those monitored with GPS had significantly lower recidivism than similar offenders under regular parole supervision (Gies et al., 2012).

▶ Alcohol Monitoring

Alcohol monitoring systems are used primarily as a response to the problem of intoxicated driving that causes about 13,000 fatalities annually. One type of device, a hand-held ignition-interlock device (IID), is typically attached to a vehicle's dashboard and connected to the ignition and uses fuel-cell technology to measure the concentration of alcohol in a person's breadth. The driver breathes into the device; and if the blood alcohol content (BAC) is higher than a set level, usually 0.04 percent, the vehicle will not start. While the car is in use, the IID requires additional breadth samples at random intervals to keep running. If a reading is not provided, or if there is sufficient alcohol on the driver's breadth, the horn will honk and the lights will flash on and off until the engine is turned off. The unit maintains a sealed log of BAC tests, so tampering can be detected. Installation of the IID costs about $200, and rental and maintenance costs are about $150 monthly, a cost usually borne by the offender. Some jurisdictions, New Mexico, for example, have created a special fund to finance the cost for low-income offenders. The IID can be circumvented by an intoxicated driver using another vehicle (Cook and Gearing, 2009).

The Secure Continuous Remote Alcohol Monitor (SCRAM) consists of a cell phone-size device worn on the ankle that detects a BAC as low as 0.02 and a modem that transmits the information to a monitoring agency (and probation officer). Costs are about $12 day in addition to installation and maintenance fees. False positives can be generated as a result of some baked goods that can cause the body to produce its own alcohol (Markel, 2009). This device is particularly useful for ensuring compliance by offenders who are prohibited from *any* use of alcohol because of the nature of their behavior while under the influence. It is not unusual in P/P to encounter persons who, while they conform to social norms when sober, act out in a reckless or violent manner when under the influence of alcohol.

▶ Discussion

Considering the cost of imprisonment, the appeal of EM is easy to understand. However, startup costs for EM are high. To offset these costs, offenders can be required to pay supervision fees and/or pay for the cost of installing the monitoring, a practice that raises important ethical and legal issues. Should an offender who is otherwise qualified be denied access to the program—and thereby face incarceration—because he or she lacks the ability to pay. If the answer is "no," how far should the government go in providing the financing? Candidates for electronic home confinement are often low-risk offenders who, in many jurisdictions, would be candidates for regular probation. Thus, the program may actually be adding to the cost of supervision without affecting the problem of jail/prison overcrowding. The use of EM for intoxicated drivers devoid of relevant alcohol abuse treatment will endanger the public when monitoring ceases at the end of a sentence of probation.

Researchers found that the electronic surveillance programs they examined have not affected jail or prison commitments in any noticeable manner. Persons selected for EM are typically from social and economic circumstances that, in any event, would predict a positive outcome. "There is little evaluative evidence to indicate that EM has proved to be a success, however that term is defined" (Cohen, 2007: 37). There is also concern over the impact of such programming on P/P officers: "Are these professionals going to see their relationships to offenders change from helping agents to surveillance agents?" (Ball, Huff, and Lilly, 1988: 97). During 1992, as the popularity of EM grew, news stories began to appear with some frequency detailing the inadequacies of controlling offender behavior through electronic means. The articles highlighted several problems:

- Offenders committed crimes after taking off the device; some even committed crimes while still wearing it.
- Failure to replace older devices with more advanced technology resulted in a failure to monitor offenders adequately.
- Personnel were not always available to respond quickly to tampering or other violations of the conditions of EM.

EM does not prevent crime: "Despite the growing popularity of electronic supervision tools—especially GPS tracking of sex offenders—the bulk of research fails to find a significant crime reduction benefit from using electronic supervision" (DeMichele and Payne, 2005: 60).

Instead, EM is designed to assist in curfew and location management. However, enforcement is dependent on having sufficient personnel monitoring the equipment and personnel being dispatched to check into reported violations, such as the New Jersey Electronic Monitoring Response Team of parole officer that operates 24/7 and is also available to provide emergency backup for field officers.

Research in Florida revealed that offenders and probation officers "were almost unanimous in their belief that the visibility of the monitoring systems makes it much more difficult for offenders to obtain and keep a job. Offenders told stories of job interviews taking on a different tenor as soon as an interviewer noticed the devices. GPS require an offender to wear an ankle bracelet that communicates with a larger device that they must carry or wear. It is a distinctive piece of equipment that can be noticed by others.

Sometimes the systems would issue an alarm because the signal had been lost when offenders were inside a building. They would then have to take a break from work and walk outside, often for 15 minutes, before the signal was reestablished. This did not please employers. Some offenders reported they had been fired or asked to leave a job because of electronic monitoring" (*Electronic Monitoring Reduce Recidivism*, 2011: 2).

> **Key Fact**
> EM does not prevent crime; it is designed simply to assist in curfew and location management.

▶ Halfway Houses/Residential Reentry Centers

Halfway Houses (places where offenders can work and pay rent while they participate in counseling and/or job training) have a long history. "The concept of halfway houses was introduced in 1817 by the Massachusetts Prison Commission. This group recommended the establishment of temporary homes for destitute released offenders as a measure to reduce recidivism" (Rosenblum and Whitcomb, 1978: 9). "It is intended to afford a temporary shelter in this building, if they choose to accept it, to such discharged convicts as may have conducted themselves well in prison at a cheap rate, and have a chance to occupy themselves in their trade, until some opportunity offers a placing of themselves where they can gain an honest livelihood in society. A refuge of this kind, to this destitute class, would be found perhaps humane and politic" (Commonwealth of Massachusetts Legislative Document, Senate No. 2, 1830).

"The name *halfway house* itself suggests its position in the corrections world: halfway-in, a more structured environment than P/P; halfway-out, a less structured environment than institutions. A halfway-in house represents the last step before incarceration for probationers and parolees facing revocation." A halfway-out house provides services to pre-releasees and parolees leaving institutions. Halfway houses also offer a residential alternative to jail or outright release for accused offenders awaiting trial or convicted offenders awaiting sentencing (Thalheimer, 1975: 1).

> **Key Fact**
>
> Halfway houses are an effective means of providing housing and services but often face community opposition.

Victor Goetting notes that "it is accepted that these facilities are based on sound correctional theory; in order to ultimately place a person in society successfully that person should not be any further removed from that society than is necessary" (1974: 27). When used in conjunction with prison or training school release programs, the halfway house provides (1) assistance with obtaining employment, (2) an increased ability to use community resources, and (3) needed support during the difficult initial release period (Griggs and McCune, 1972). The various types of halfway houses operated by public and private agencies and groups can be divided basically into those that provide bed, board, and some help with employment and those that provide a full range of services, including treatment—residential reentry centers. A halfway house may be primarily for released inmates, for parolees, or for probationers as an alternative to imprisonment. Halfway houses may be used for probationers or parolees who violate their conditions of supervision but not seriously enough to cause them to be imprisoned. "Residential reentry centers facilitate the community reintegration of formerly incarcerated persons through the provision of a multiplicity of residential, employment, treatment, advocacy, support, and family reunification services that are expected to build the capacities and competencies necessary for successful community living" (Rutgers Center for Behavioral Health and Criminal Justice Research [hereafter Rutgers Center], 2013: 1).

The major difficulty with opening and maintaining a halfway house is community reaction. A Lou Harris poll, for example, found that 77 percent of the representative U.S. sample favored the halfway house concept, but 50 percent would not want one in *their* neighborhood, and only 22 percent believed that people in *their* neighborhood would favor a halfway house being located there. As a consequence, it is not uncommon for people to be released to residential reentry centers (RRC) "located 30 to 100 miles from their home locations. While at the RRC, they may secure jobs and treatment services in these areas but once released from the RRC, they return to their home communities where they have no jobs or connections to treatment services but have family and perhaps parenting responsibilities" (Rutgers Center 3). Experts stress the importance of getting community support for the project before opening a halfway house. Among some of the strategies used in gaining support is the formation of an advisory board made up of influential community people. Community residents may be placed on the board of directors and hired as staff for the facility (*In Our Backyard*, 2009).

▶ Shock Probation/Parole/Incarceration

In addition to community-based intermediate punishments that have been discussed, some jurisdictions use short-term incarceration that "shocks" the offender while saving prison space.

Shock probation/parole was pioneered by the state of Ohio, which enacted legislation in 1965 permitting the early release from prison of convicted felons on either probation (within 30 to 120 days of imprisonment) or parole (within 6 months of imprisonment). Since that time, other states (e.g., Idaho, Indiana, Kentucky, Maine, North Carolina, and Texas) have adopted similar statutes. Shock probation was authorized by the Texas legislature in 1977 as a rehabilitation technique in which an offender is given a sample of jail/prison and then placed on probation for the remainder of the sentence.

How can you get tough on crime while bringing down the cost of imprisonment? In 1983, the states of Georgia and Oklahoma, in an effort to deal with their problems of prison overcrowding, devised shock incarceration often referred to as "**boot camp**." A shock incarceration (SI) program involves short stays of imprisonment—3 to 6 months—combined with shaved heads, marching, close-order drills, exercise, and harassment by corrections officers/drill instructors during 12-hour days. No television, radio, or telephone privileges are available. The boot camp resembles its military counterpart—a Spartan regimen of rigorous discipline and exercise. It is of historical interest to note that the use of military discipline was standard in New York's Elmira Reformatory well into the twentieth century—"reinventing the wheel" is symptomatic of American penology. By the end of 1988, 11 states had initiated similar programs; except for New York and Michigan, all in the South. By 1992, state-operated SI programs for adult offenders were available in 25 states (MacKenzie and Souryal, 1994). The number of boot camps has declined "due to moderate to negative evaluation results, media attention to the negative impact of shock incarceration programs, and increased government funding for rehabilitation focused sanctions" (Austin and Chapman, 2009: 4). Contemporary boot camps often feature a modified SI approach.

Doris MacKenzie et al. (1995: 327) state that most boot camps "are designed for young offenders convicted of nonviolent crimes who do not have a prior history of imprisonment." They point out that although "all boot camp prisons use military basic training as a model, they differ considerably in other aspects. For example, some programs select participants from a pool of prisoners sentenced to a traditional sentence of incarceration. Other programs receive inmates directly from the sentencing court" (MacKenzie et al., 1995: 328).

Because of the physical nature of the program, candidates have typically been required to be in good health. In 1998, the Supreme Court ruled that an otherwise eligible candidate could not be denied the boot camp alternative because of a history of hypertension; the plaintiff's rejection was ruled a violation of the 1990 Americans with Disabilities Act (*Pennsylvania Department of Corrections v. Yeskey*, 524 U.S. 206).

The New York program was authorized by the legislature in 1987 as a way of easing overcrowding. Successful SI graduates are typically released nine months before their parole

BOOT CAMP FOR YOUNG OFFENDERS—HISTORICAL ANTECEDENT

According to Colonel Vincent M. Masten (1896–1924), a military instructor at Elmira Reformatory, "As part of the institutional regime, they [inmates] are advisedly ordered for supreme military test as to all-around steadiness, which embraces everything a soldier should do, or leave undone; everything from the strictest of undivided attention under command, to execution that exemplifies the highest order of muscular reaction to command, of which constantly improving stature is a component exaction" (Allen, 1926: 378).

BOOT CAMP

"Perhaps no other intermediate sanction or prison alternative has captured more attention from the public or policy makers than the boot camp prison. Its combination of punitiveness, visual appeal, and, in the view of some, rehabilitative value seems to offer everything to everyone frustrated with crime committed by young adults, especially males. The idea underlying boot camps is based on simple common sense: give a young rebel a sound three or four month-long thrashing and some firm discipline and that youth will see the evil of his/her way, become an adult, and sin no more" (Jones and Ross, 1997: 147).

eligibility date. The parole division's "Aftershock" program in New York City provides comprehensive services, which are designed to maintain the motivation and discipline the parolee has demonstrated before release, for the parolee's first six months on the street. Shock parolees are supervised at a ratio of 25 to 1.

By 1991, New York had the largest SI program in the country and estimated that for every 100 SI inmates released, the state saved $1.94 million that would otherwise be expended for care and custody, plus capital costs associated with the need for greater institutional space. The daily per-inmate expense for SI, however, exceeds that of medium-security facilities or camps. The relatively high cost may be linked to the services provided at New York's SI camps—the state rejects the "boot camp" label because that belies the therapeutic environment the program strives to achieve.

More than 40 percent of SI inmate time is spent on treatment and education: 12 hours of academic education, drug and alcohol treatment, prerelease counseling, and decision-making classes (Clark, Aziz, and MacKenzie, 1994; *Seventh Annual Shock* Legislative Report, 1995). The Willard Drug Treatment Campus is staffed by corrections and parole personnel, and features a quasi-boot camp environment in which residents participate in daily physical fitness regimens and abide by military standards of bearing, behavior, and dress. Willard is licensed by the Office of Alcoholism and Substance Abuse and must meet standards regarding the number of hours spent in therapy, educational and vocational development, and individual growth activities. The residents are parole violators involved in substance abuse and offenders judicially sanctioned—sent directly to parole supervision by the court for a drug conviction and required to complete the 90-day Willard program. Aftercare includes continuing substance abuse treatment for six months through contract agencies.

> **Key Fact**
>
> Shock incarceration/ boot camps stress brief periods of incarceration under physically and psychologically demanding conditions.

The idea behind SI "is to break the prisoners down, strip them of their street identity, and then systematically build them up by providing discipline and self-control" (Spencer, 1987: Sec. 3: 1). Offenders must be young (usually 17 to 35 years old) and in good health and must volunteer for the program—dropouts return to complete their sentences of imprisonment, and many drop out (Parent, 1988). New York SI uses a recycling program for inmates who are removed for disciplinary reasons and for those who are in danger of being removed for unsatisfactory adjustment. It consists of being sent back for refresher training, during which their behavior is closely monitored. Success in recycling leads to being integrated into an existing platoon that will graduate at a date closest to the time owed by the inmate. Inmates who do not perform well after two weeks in recycling are removed from the program and returned to prison.

The Pennsylvania Motivational Boot Camp allows inmates under the age of 35 to serve a reduced six-month sentence. The program is designed to instill discipline and structure through regimented 16-hour days consisting of work and program activities. A typical day begins at 5:30 A.M. with reveille, followed by an hour of physical training. The remainder of the day is tightly scheduled with educational and rehabilitative counseling and work. Offenders who have not graduated from high school attend mandatory education classes, while those who have a diploma are assigned to work duties. In-house research has found that the camp does not lower recidivism (Kempinen, 2011).

Michigan's Special Alterative Incarceration Program operates a site near Ann Arbor that houses approximately 425 residents and relies on a quasi-boot camp approach: drill and physical exercise, but also a curriculum designed to prepare a person for reentry. During the 90-day program residents are involved in financial planning, cognitive behavioral-based "Thinking Matters" classes, supervised work, and aid in obtaining their GED (Austin and Chapman, 2009).

▶ Discussion

Critics of the SI approach argue that it has not proven to have any salutary effect on postincarceration behavior and that even short-term imprisonment exposes the offender to the destructive effects of institutionalization, disrupts his or her life in the community, and further stigmatizes the offender for having been imprisoned. Furthermore, many SI inmates are released without receiving relevant education or having developed employment skills. No doubt exists that these programs do release strong, healthy, unemployed young men into the community after only a brief term of incarceration. However, in an Oklahoma study, SI graduates returned to prison at a higher rate than did other inmates; in Alabama, boot camp residents, who were first-time nonviolent offenders, had a recidivism rate slightly worse than that of a comparative group of regular inmates (Burns and Vito, 1995). A Georgia study found no difference in return rates between SI and regular inmates (Parent, 1989). In Texas, SI appears to do more harm than good, since within four years of release almost 62 percent of boot camp graduates are serving a traditional prison sentence (Anderson, Dyson, and Lee, 1997). Pennsylvania incorporated rehabilitative programming into its six-month boot camp for high-risk adult offenders, but outcome research failed to show any postrelease benefits when compared to similar offenders released from prison (Kempinen and Kurlychek, 2003). MacKenzie and her colleagues (2001: 2) conclude that "in general, no significant differences have been found for either adults or juveniles when recidivism rates of boot camp participants have been compared with others receiving more traditional correctional options."

A CLOSER LOOK

"TOUGH LOVE"

At age 14, Gina was in boot camp for a series of petty thefts. The overweight youngster was with 15 other girls on a mandatory 2.6-mile jog at about 6:30 A.M. when she began to lag behind. Two counselors shouted for her to catch up. About 500 feet from the finish, Gina collapsed. Counselors called to her to stop faking. After being examined by a staff nurse, Gina struggled to her feet and began walking to the air-conditioned cottage when she collapsed again. Believing she was faking "again," the staff did nothing. By the time she was transported to a hospital, Gina was dead from heatstroke (Selcraig, 2000). After the death of a 14-year-old boy who was beaten by guards, Florida closed the state's four boot camps (Sexton, 2006).

A study of the program in Louisiana found no evidence that SI reduces recidivism. There were no significant differences in recidivism between SI inmates and either parolees from traditional prisons or probationers. All had recidivism rates of approximately 30 percent during their first year of community supervision (MacKenzie, Shaw, and Souryal, 1992).

A New York in-house research effort revealed that 23 percent of shock parolees were returned to prison within one year of their release compared with 28 percent of a comparison group (Office of Policy Analysis and Information, 1989). In a 1992 New York effort, SI graduates in New York were compared with parolees who matched the SI criteria but who were committed to prison before the establishment of the program (pre-SI) and with parolees who had been removed from the program (removals), as well as with a group who met the SI criteria but did not enter the program (considered). SI graduates were more likely than the comparison groups to be drug offenders with longer maximum sentences. (Those with shorter sentences were less likely to volunteer for SI and more likely to drop out.) After all, subjects were out for at least one year, the following rates of return to prison for violations were recorded:

	Total	Percentage of Violations-Technical	Percentage of Violations-Criminal
SI	1,641	7	7
Pre-SI	1,418	11	8
Removals	1,662	11	9
Considered	366	11	11

After 24 months, SI parolees continued to have lower rates of return to prison for technical and new arrest violations than those of any of the comparison groups (although many of the comparison group members had already been discharged from parole supervision). The New York researchers conclude that SI parolees are more likely to be successful than are comparison group parolees after the completion of 12, 18, and 24 months' time, despite having spent considerably less time in a state prison. A subsequent in-house study (*Seventh Annual Shock Legislative Report,* 1995) revealed that shock parolees are generally more likely, or just as likely, to be successful as a similar comparison group. SI was found particularly effective for young drug offenders.

A boot camp program (IMPACT) was created in North Carolina in 1989. To be eligible, offenders must be aged 16 to 25 and physically fit; they cannot have previously served more than 120 days in an adult correctional facility for convictions of misdemeanors and non-serious felonies. Participants stay for 90 days of drilling, marching, and exercising, which can be extended to 120 days in the event of disciplinary problems, after which they are released to probation supervision. Those without high school diplomas receive educational services, and 70 percent who take the equivalency test receive their general equivalency diploma (GED).

Researchers compared IMPACT graduates with a similar group on probation who had not gone through boot camp. They found that while other similar studies reported little or no differences, in North Carolina, *boot camp participation was significantly associated with rearrest.* They note that while SI aims to instill pride and responsibility, the boot camp graduates must now bear the stigma of being an "ex-con," a significant barrier to gainful employment (Jones and Ross, 1997). Similar results were found in a Cleveland, Ohio, boot camp program where 72 percent of the graduates recidivated, as opposed to 50 percent of a control group released from Ohio DYS facilities (Peters, Thomas, and Zamberlan, 1997).

Boot camps were established without "rigorous, controlled experiments to test the components of that model, perhaps through a series of pilot tests to determine what worked, with whom, and why. Instead, they were created full-blown, with a mixed bag of programmatic components, usually determined by the jurisdiction, the resources, and especially the ideological perspective of those doing the creating" (Finckenauer, 2005: 205).

Boot camp programs are in place to save prison or juvenile institutional resources; an offender sent to a shock program avoids long-term incarceration. This assumes that in the absence of such programming, the offender would have been incarcerated and not placed on probation. A study in Florida found that candidates for SI were selected from among those sentenced to traditional incarceration, but they tended to be those who were less serious offenders (Sechrest, 1989). In Georgia, however, SI was used by judges as part of probation sentences. In Alabama, boot camp is part of the discretionary sentencing power of a judge and is sometimes the result of a plea bargain agreement (Burns, 1993). In Arizona, which established its program in 1988, research found that only some of the inmates in boot camp were diverted from prison and that "the rest would have been placed on regular probation or intensive probation" (Palumbo and Peterson, 1994: 8).

Although SI might not meet the needs of rehabilitation and community safety, it appears to meet the short-term needs of political officials who can boast of "doing something" about crime and criminals. Dale Parent found that SI was given to "the very offenders who would likely have been given nonconfinement sentences if SI were not available—thus using more, not less, prison space"—referred to as "net widening" (1989: 12).

An element of absurdity exists in the prison as boot camp approach, particularly in light of the fact that the military has drastically changed the way it trains recruits, no longer using abusive or degrading methods: "While the military has reduced the harshness of its training, boot-camp prisons have embraced an outdated version of military basic training" (Jacoby et al., 1994: 32).

"The very idea of using physically and verbally aggressive tactics in an effort to 'train' people to act in a prosocial manner is fraught with contradiction" (Morash and Rucker, 1990: 214). Such programs run the risk of turning out young men who are more aggressive and hostile than they would have been under routine imprisonment: "The irony in emphasizing an aggressive model of masculinity in a correctional setting is that these very characteristics may explain criminality" (Morash and Rucker, 1990: 216).

A cynic might argue that the boot camp approach is simply a scam for gaining public acquiescence to the (otherwise politically unacceptable) early discharge of inmates. Two researchers posit a grim possibility—"the effect of boot camp is that it will be effective for those who will subsequently put their lessons of discipline and organization to use in street gangs and drug distribution networks" (Feeley and Simon, 1992: 464). "Based on a vague, if not unstated, theory of crime and an absurd theory of behavioral change ('offenders need to be broken down'—through a good deal of humiliation and threats—and then 'built back up'), boot camps could not possibly have 'worked'" (Latessa, Cullen, and Gendreau, 2002: 44).

Others note that after boot camp, military personnel enter a structured, stable environment that provides for their basic needs of food, shelter, clothing, employment, and health care, a situation very different from the environment to which most SI subjects will return (Mathias and Mathews, 1991). MacKenzie (1994: 65) concludes: "If the core components of boot camps (military atmosphere, drill, hard labor, physical training) reduced recidivism, we would have expected that the boot camp releasees in all states would do better than the offenders in the comparison groups. This did not happen. The military atmosphere does not appear to reduce recidivism." Based on 10 years of data, researchers found that boot camp participants experienced positive short-term changes in attitude and behaviors and also had better problem-solving and coping skills—but with few exceptions, these positive changes did not lead to reduced recidivism. Those boot camps that produced lower recidivism rates offered more treatment services, had longer sessions, and included more intensive postrelease supervision. However, not all programs with these features had successful results. The length of stay in boot camps— usually from 90 to 120 days—is too brief to realistically affect recidivism, and there is typically insufficient preparation for reentry into the community. Many boot camps provide little or no postrelease programming to prepare graduates to lead productive lives (Parent, 2003). Based on an analysis of the research, MacKenzie (2006) concludes that there is no evidence that boot camps are effective in reducing the recidivism of juveniles or adults.

In 1994, Connecticut closed the nation's first boot camp for juveniles run by the National Guard after an investigation revealed gang activity, drug use, and violence (Johnson, 1994). Other states, faced with scandals (e.g., beatings of young inmates) and poor result statistics, have done the same (Blair, 2000).

▶ Day Reporting Center

The day reporting center concept originated in Great Britain, a response to less serious but chronic offenders who lacked basic skills and were often dependent on drugs or alcohol. The British experience led Connecticut and Massachusetts in 1986 to set up **day reporting centers** (DRCs), whose purposes are "to heighten control and surveillance of offenders placed on community supervision, to increase offender access to treatment programs and services, to give officials more proportional and certain sanctions to be used for less serious probation or parole violations, or to reduce prison or jail crowding" (Parent, 1990: 9). In fact, DRC programs "are typically implemented to alleviate prison crowding and save correctional costs" (Steiner and Butler, 2013: 154). And for this to occur, persons assigned to DRC must be those who otherwise would be incarcerated.

In Georgia, the Department of Corrections operates 13 Day Reporting Centers throughout the state. Centers provide intensive substance abuse treatment for up to 100 offenders sentenced by the Courts or who have not responded to more traditional supervision and treatment efforts. Failure at a DRC results in revocation proceedings against the offender. Although the cost is more than field probation, a DRC it is only a fraction of the cost of providing a residential alternative.

The program includes components such as substance abuse counseling, cognitive restructuring, adult basic education, employment enhancement, intensive supervision, and community service. An aftercare component follows the on-site programming. Offenders assigned to the program are required to be employed as soon as they have completed the initial orientation, assessment, diagnostics, and programming.

New Jersey employs the DRC as an alternative to incarceration for technical parole violators or those with a DRC stipulation as a condition of parole release. "The philosophical foundation of the program derives from the belief that at any given time there are a number of individuals incarcerated who could safely be paroled, provided they participate in a highly structured assessment driven program." While offenders are in the program, they are supervised by parole officers assigned to the DRC. Offenders report to the centers frequently (usually once or even twice a day), and treatment services are usually provided on-site either by the public or private agency running the program or by other human services agencies whose staff work at the site: life skills training; job skills training; job search counseling; individual, group, and family counseling; and educational sessions that include GED.

The DRC operates 7 days a week, and offenders generally participate for 90 days, after which they are assigned to a regular supervision caseload. Typically, offenders must be on the DRC premises 18 hours per week during the program's most intensive phase. An offender usually checks in at the DRC early each morning and briefly talks with a counselor before going to work; after work, offenders often return to the DRC for an evening group counseling session. When not in the DRC, they are monitored by tele-phone calls to their job sites, homes, or other locations where they are supposed to be. Offenders fill out a daily itinerary that helps to keep track of their whereabouts in the community. (A study [Bulman, 2013] of day reporting centers in New Jersey found par-ticipants had higher rates of recidivism than a matched sample of parolees on traditional supervision.)

The Chicago DRC targets high-risk parolees, such as those with two or more prior incarcerations, or who have served a sentence of 10 or more years, or are 25 years old or younger sentenced for a violent crime, returning to neighborhoods on the city's Southside. Parolees assigned to report to the DRC must do so within 24 hours of release.

There are four levels of supervision: Each participant begins at the most intensive level and works toward less intensive levels as he or she moves through the program. They are assigned an individual case manager who meets with them at least once a week (and, in some cases, up to seven days a week).

They undergo an extensive assessment upon entering the program that helps the case manager develop an individualized treatment and education plan. Parolees may be assigned up to three separate rehabilitation activities per week, including substance abuse education and treatment, adult basic education, GED preparation, parenting and family reintegration support group, anger management, employment skills training, and career development counseling. Case managers prepare monthly reports for parole officers on parolees' prog-ress in meeting the goals of their reentry plan. Progression through the DRC is individually paced and based on the parolee's compliance with the requirements at each level of supervi-sion. For instance, a parolee cannot move to a reduced level of supervision until he/she has been drug free for 30 days.

In 1990, the Social Services Department of the District of Columbia Superior Court, which administers probation services, established the P/P Resource Center (PPRC) to pro-vide a structured nonresidential program for high-risk offenders with a history of drug abuse. This DRC is located at an independent site, separate from routine P/P operations, in the northeast section of the nation's capitol. The PPRC has P/P officers who are certi-fied addiction counselors (CACs) as full-time staff members. Professional staff includes employees from appropriate federal government agencies assigned to provide on-site direct services or referrals. Staff work on varying shifts to provide comprehensive monitor-ing of PPRC clients and maintenance of center operations. The project also contracts for additional services from the private sector.

The PPRC program consists of three distinct phases: assessment, treatment, and continuing care. A caseload management approach is employed and coordinated with staff from other participating agencies. The P/P officers/CACs monitor and supervise program participants throughout the treatment and continuing care phases. The assessment phase begins with a series of diagnostic services: intake interviews and medical and psychiatric or psychological screening. In the second phase, drug treatment strategies, education, counseling, support services delivery, and various supervision activities are tailored to meet the identified needs of each client. This includes a range of community sanctions such as curfew, home detention, and electronic surveillance. The continuing care phase carries over into existing P/P supervision programs where participants are assigned to other P/P officers who are CACs. These officers provide long-term treatment and supervision throughout the remainder of the court-imposed sentence.

The Adult Probation Department of Maricopa County, Arizona, has three DRCs for nonviolent offenders during the final 60 days of their jail sentence. The participant follows an hour-by-hour schedule of courses offered at the DRC and other community-based agencies and/or participates in a job search program until employed. Participants with employment follow daily schedules; when not participating in work or programs, participants are required to remain at home, where they are monitored by probation and surveillance officers. After completing the program, participants continue under standard supervision or IPS. A failure to complete the program results in reincarceration.

New Jersey employs the DRC as an alternative to incarceration for technical parole violators or those with a DRC stipulation as a condition of parole release. "The philosophical foundation of the program derives from the belief that at any given time there are a number of individuals incarcerated who could safely be paroled, provided they participate in a highly structured assessment driven program." While offenders are in the program, they are supervised by parole officers assigned to the DRC. Offenders report to the centers frequently (usually once or even twice a day), and treatment services are usually provided on-site either by the public or private agency running the program or by other human services agencies whose staff work at the site: life skills training; job skills training; job search counseling; individual, group, and family counseling; and educational sessions that include GED.

The DRC operates 7 days a week, and offenders generally participate for 90 days, after which they are assigned to a regular supervision caseload. Typically, offenders must be on the DRC premises 18 hours per week during the program's most intensive phase. An offender usually checks in at the DRC early each morning and briefly talks with a counselor before going to work; after work, offenders often return to the DRC for an evening group counseling session. When not in the DRC, they are monitored by telephone calls to their job sites, homes, or other locations where they are supposed to be. Offenders fill out a daily itinerary that helps to keep track of their whereabouts in the community.

Medium- and high-risk parolees in New Jersey randomly assigned to DRC did no better, and in some instances worse, than similar non-DRC parolees (Boyle et al., 2013). The research does not indicate "why," although Grant Duwe (2013) speculates that service delivery—primarily employment services—may have been inadequate, or the length of time in DRC may have been too short (Steiner and Butler, 2013). Duwe notes that in Minnesota, the DRC program revealed significantly improved employment rates and correspondingly decreased recidivism. Benjamin Steiner and H. Daniel Butler (2013) state that parolees in the New Jersey research were not in fact "high-risk," but rather low/medium to medium-risk parole violators for whom intensive services were unnecessary and possibly counterproductive.

Summary

- The actual purpose for intermediate punishments is to reduce incarceration.
- Intensive supervision is more costly than regular supervision, but considerably less than the cost of incarceration.
- There is an absence of standards for determining whether a P/P program of supervision is indeed "intensive."
- Research into intensive supervision has produced mixed results, with no clear indication that the process is successful in meeting its goals.
- A problem exists with using parole violation as a criterion for success because of the "halo effect."
- Reducing caseloads can reduce criminal recidivism when delivered in a setting where evidence-based practices are used.
- For diversion from prison to be accomplished by intensive supervision, cases need to be assigned to *after* a sentence of imprisonment.
- Otherwise, serious offenders may be released from prison with inadequate or no supervision, while nonviolent offenders are placed on intensive supervision.
- A GPS cannot track inside buildings or other enclosed areas and is limited to areas with good-quality cell phone coverage, and responding to violations in a timely manner requires personnel available 24/7.
- For offenders with an alcohol problem, there are devices that prevent a vehicle from starting if a certain blood-alcohol content (BAC) is revealed; other devices worn on the ankle transmit BAC data on a continuous basis.
- Halfway houses are an effective means of providing housing and services but often face community opposition.
- There is considerable criticism of shock incarceration ("boot camps").
- Day reporting centers are used as an alternative to incarceration for P/P violators and can provide a variety of services for probationers and parolees.

Key Terms

boot camp *219*
continuously signaling
   systems *214*
day reporting centers *224*
diversion *204*

electronic monitoring *214*
global positioning systems *215*
halfway houses *217*
"halo effect" *206*
intensive supervision *203*

intermediate punishments *203*
programmed contact system *215*
residential reentry centers *218*
shock incarceration *219*
shock probation/parole *219*

Internet Connections

American Correctional Association: **corrections.com/aca/index**

American Probation and Parole Association: **www.appa-net.org**

Center for Community Corrections: **communitycorrectionsworks.org**

International Community Corrections Association **iccaweb.org**

National Institute of Corrections: **nicic.org**

Review Questions

1. What is the actual purpose of intermediate punishments?
2. How is intensive supervision an alternative to incarceration?
3. What are the standards for determining whether a P/P program of supervision is "intensive"?
4. What has research on intensive P/P supervision determined?
5. In P/P supervision research, what is the "halo effect"?
6. How do evidence-based practices affect intensive supervision?
7. For intensive supervision to be effective, why do cases need to be assigned after a sentence of imprisonment or after parole release had been denied?
8. What are the problems and limitations of using GPS to monitor offenders?
9. What devices are used to monitor offenders with an alcohol problem?
10. What is the biggest problem confronting a half-way houses?
11. How does shock probation differ from shock parole?
12. What are the features of that shock incarceration?
13. What is the idea behind shock incarceration?
14. What are the criticisms of shock incarceration?
15. What is the purpose of a day reporting center?

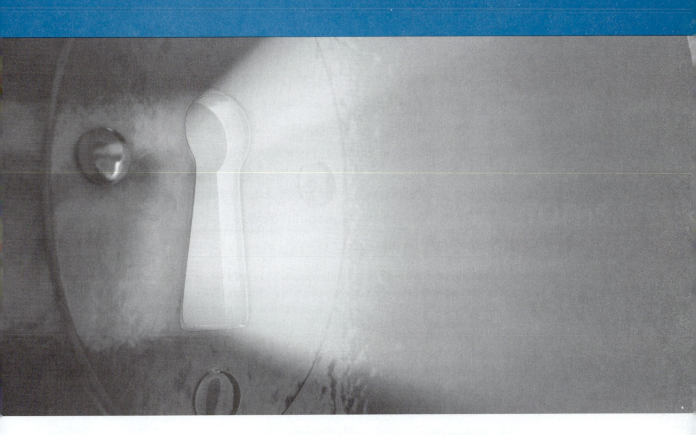

10 Special Issues and Programs in Probation and Parole

LEARNING OBJECTIVES

This chapter will enable the student to:

1 *Understand substance abuse among the probation/parole (P/P) population.*

2 *Explain why cocaine detoxification presents serious problems not encountered in heroin withdrawal.*

3 *Discuss why heroin addicts may undergo detoxification with no intention of discontinuing drug use.*

4 *Appreciate the use of methadone to treat addicts.*

5 *Understand how behavior modification is used with drug antagonists.*

6 *Discuss the use of the therapeutic community in drug treatment.*

7 Appreciate criticism of chemical dependency programs.

8 Understand the Alcoholics Anonymous self-help group approach.

9 Describe the problems and limitations of drug testing.

10 Understand the problems associated with HIV/AIDS among the P/P population.

11 Discuss supervision of sex offenders on P/P.

12 Explain the role of P/P in restorative justice.

13 Appreciate the lack of resources for female offenders.

14 Understand the importance of supervising "driving under the influence" offenders.

15 Explain the purposes and procedures used of the interstate compact.

16 Discuss the use of neighborhood-based offices for P/P supervision.

It has long been recognized that offenders with certain salient characteristics could benefit from the services of a specialist—a probation and parole (P/P) officer who, as a result of education, training, and experience, is in a better position to provide social services and control functions. Many P/P agencies have specialized units or specialists for particular offenders:

- Substance abusers
- HIV/AIDS offenders
- Sex offenders
- Driving while intoxicated (DWI) offenders
- Developmentally challenged offenders

We will examine the problems posed by these special problem offenders and the specialized caseloads organized in response. Then, we will review special issues and programs in P/P supervision.

▶ Substance Abusers

Substance abuse is the single most frequently encountered problem across P/P populations. "Substance abuse increases the obstacles facing returning offenders to communities. Offenders with substance abuse problems have an uphill battle to find employment, meet familial and childcare responsibilities, and actively participate in treatment" (Lowe and DeMichele, 2010: 3).

Substance abuse treatment typically begins with detoxification with or without the assistance of drugs (e.g., the antihypertension drug clonidine, which relieves many of the symptoms of heroin withdrawal). Cocaine detoxification presents serious problems because of the patient's craving for the substance and the extreme depression during the early days of abstinence, which can lead to suicide. Medication (e.g., antidepressants) may be needed by those who are suicide risks during the post–cocaine "crash," characterized by a lack of energy and an inability to feel pleasure. Those who exhibit transient psychotic or severe delusional states and paranoid reactions from excessive cocaine also require medication. Immediate withdrawal from heroin and cocaine can be accomplished without

▼

using other chemicals, although the patient may feel quite uncomfortable; detoxification from sedatives can lead to seizures and cardiac arrest and therefore must be accomplished by gradually decreasing dosages.

The use of chemicals to facilitate drug withdrawal can serve to attract drug abusers into treatment and increases the probability that they will complete detoxification. However, at least with respect to heroin abusers, the use of chemical aids has some troubling aspects. Addicts may enter treatment when their habit is too expensive to support, and they have to work quite hard simply to prevent the onset of withdrawal symptoms, while a high level of tolerance to heroin reduces the sought-after high. Tolerance, the progressive ability of the body to adapt to the effects of a drug used at regular and frequent intervals, makes heroin less effective; higher doses are required to produce the same effect. Under such conditions, addiction is no longer fun: "Then he enters a detoxification ward and is comfortably withdrawn from heroin. Detoxification is made so easy, compared to 'cold turkey,' that addicts are not confronted with negatively reinforcing pharmacological and physiological aspects of addiction" (Bellis, 1981: 139). Detoxification reduces the addict's tolerance so that the "high" can be enjoyed once again at an affordable price. P/P officers should not be surprised "when addicts leave the detoxification ward and inject heroin within a few minutes or hours" (Bellis, 1981: 140).

Some drug treatment programs use chemicals as the primary treatment or as a supplement to (or in conjunction with) some other form of treatment. Scientists have developed a number of heroin antagonists, substances that block or counteract the effects of opiates. These substances bind with opiate receptor sites, thereby preventing stimulation, or displace an opiate already at the site (see Abadinsky, 2014, for a discussion). Antagonists, however, often have unpleasant side effects.

<aside>
Key Fact

Substance abuse is the single most frequently encountered problem across P/P populations.
</aside>

▶ Methadone Treatment

Certain synthetic substances—agonists—have a chemical makeup similar to that of opioids. The most widely used agonist, methadone, which is a wholly synthetic narcotic, produces virtually the same analgesic and sedative effects as heroin and is no less addictive; however, methadone can be administered orally, its effects last longer, and the high it produces is less dramatic compared to that produced by the shorter-acting opiates such as heroin. Whereas the effects of heroin wear off in 2 to 3 hours, the effects of oral methadone continue for 12 to 24 hours. Methadone can be prepared in a way that makes it difficult to inject, rendering it less likely to be diverted into the black market.

Naloxone is recommended for testing for opiate dependence (Narcon test) before admission to a methadone program (Judson and Goldstein, 1986). It has no effect on the nondependent person but causes immediate signs of heroin withdrawal in the opiate-dependent person. The substance is administered to people who are seeking methadone because such people might not be opioid dependent or might have only minimal dependence: "Treatment of these addicts with methadone raises important ethical and legal questions in view of the likelihood of producing physical dependence in previously nondependent persons" (Peachey and Lei, 1988: 200). According to federal regulations, admission to methadone treatment is restricted to people who have been addicted to heroin for at least one year. The typical methadone program begins with a period of inpatient care during which low doses of the drug are substituted for heroin (the patient is not informed of the dosage he or she receives). The methadone is usually mixed with orange juice, which helps reduce its bitter taste, and is consumed in front of a nurse. Slow increases in dosage reduce the high, which disappears once significant tolerance develops. Addicts subsequently report daily on an outpatient basis and are given take-home doses for weekends. Patients usually provide a urine specimen before they are given methadone. As they progress, less than daily pickups are permitted. Although methadone impacts the high, which usually lasts several hours, it does not affect the euphoric "rush" (which lasts about 10 seconds). Thus, methadone patients (even those at high daily doses) may continue abusing heroin and other drugs—in fact, cocaine is a major drug of abuse among methadone patients.

Buprenorphine (pronounced byoo-pre-NOR-feen), marketed under the brand name Suboxone, is chemically an opioid but is only mildly addictive. Because buprenorphine is only a partial agonist, it yields the same effects but with less intensity than heroin or methadone. Since it is a partial agonist, buprenorphine exhibits ceiling effects—increasing the dose only has effects to a certain level. Partial agonists usually have greater safety profiles than full agonists because they are less likely to cause respiratory depression, the major toxic effect of opiate drugs (Jones, 2004).

Another benefit of buprenorphine is that the withdrawal syndrome is (at worst) mild to moderate and can often be managed without administration of narcotics. Addicts being maintained on high doses of methadone, on the other hand, will go through withdrawal symptoms if suddenly switched to buprenorphine (Pérez-Peña, 2003). However, since it is a partial agonist, "in severely addicted people, it may not provide enough opiate agonist activity to treat them adequately" (Mann, 2004: 8).

In 2002, the Federal Drug Administration announced the approval of buprenorphine and buprenorphine-naloxone (partial opiate agonist with an opiate blocker) under the brand name Subutex. When taken orally, buprenorphine-naloxone does not produce euphoria; if it is injected, it makes the user feel sick—naloxone causes an immediate withdrawal syndrome in opioid addicts. It only needs to be taken over 1 to 3 days. As a result of the Drug Addiction Treatment Act of 2000, these drugs can be dispensed in a doctor's office instead of a clinic and are subject to the same restrictions on quantities as methadone. This has the added benefit of not having addicts associating at clinics while they await their methadone. Legislation enacted in 2005 allows each qualified doctor within a group medical practice to prescribe Suboxone up to the individual physician limit of 30 patients. Group medical practices include large institutions such as hospitals and health maintenance organizations, many of which have numerous doctors certified to treat opioid dependence.

The National Institute on Drug Abuse was instrumental in developing naltrexone hydrochloride, a long-acting orally administered narcotic antagonist first synthesized in 1965 and marketed in tablet form as Trexan by DuPont. This nonaddicting drug defeats the effects of opiates by occupying their receptor sites in the brain. It also displaces any agonists that are present, causing severe precipitated withdrawal in people who are opioid dependent. Naltrexone users often suffer from nausea and vomiting; less common side effects include headache, anxiety or depression, low energy, skin rashes, and decreased alertness. Taken in large doses, naltrexone can cause liver damage. Discontinuing naltrexone will not cause withdrawal symptoms, but the drug does not ease the craving for heroin (Batki et al., 2005). In 1995, the Food and Drug Administration (FDA) approved naltrexone to prevent alcohol relapse by alcohol-dependent patients; and under the brand names ReVia and Depade, naltrexone is marketed for use in treating alcoholism.

▶ Behavior Modification

Some treatment programs use behavior modification (discussed in Chapter 6) as the primary method. The strength of psychoactive substances as positive reinforcers and the negative reinforcement associated with abstinence provides conditioned responses that can explain the key difficulty in treating drug abusers: finding reinforcers that can successfully compete with these substances. As noted in Chapter 6, according to the principles of operant conditioning, for behavior modification to be effective, reinforcement must follow immediately after the behavior is exhibited; instant gratification is what makes drug use so reinforcing and why it is difficult to use behavior modification techniques with chronic drug users.

Behavior modification can be used with drug antagonists to render opiates or other substances ineffective (i.e., lacking in positive reinforcement). Disulfiram (Antabuse), metronidazole, or chlorpropamide can serve this purpose for alcohol abusers. Antabuse, the best known of these substances, disrupts the liver's metabolism, producing a severe reaction that includes stomach and head pain, extreme nausea, and vomiting. (Milder reactions can be triggered by any number of products that contain alcohol, such as cough medicine, mouthwash, or even skin creams.) In 1990, a patent was granted for a substance that has the appearance and smell of cocaine and that even produces a numbing effect but is not psychoactive. The substance is used in conjunction with aversive stimuli.

In voluntary patients, aversive stimuli may be used; for example, electric shocks may be self-administered whenever a craving for the chemical arises. Some researchers report that the use of chemical or electrical stimuli has not proven effective in producing a conditioned aversion in drug abusers, while success has been reported with verbal aversion techniques in which "a patient is asked to *imagine* strongly aversive stimuli (usually vomiting) in association with imaginal drug-related cues, scenes, and/or behavior" (Childress, McLellan, and O'Brien, 1985: 951). Thus, *imagined* aversive stimuli may be superior to *real* aversive stimuli with the drug dependent (although this appears to run contrary to a great deal of research in operant conditioning). In any event, "aversive counterconditioning is not a substitute for support for life-enhancing behavior [but] suppresses the undesirable behavior while other modalities support positive alternatives" (Frawley and Smith, 1990: 21).

Other behavioral therapies use biofeedback and relaxation training, and sometimes assertiveness training, to prepare drug abusers to better cope with the stress and anxiety believed linked to drug use. Researchers have found that certain environmental cues activate drug cravings. These are countered by desensitization treatment: "Patients are usually first relaxed, then given repeated exposure to a graded hierarchy of anxiety-producing stimuli (real or imaginal)" to provide a form of immunity (Childress, McLennan, and O'Brien, 1985: 957).

As noted in Chapter 6, social learning theory, a variant of behaviorism, views people as active participants in their operant conditioning processes who determine what is and what is not reinforcing. The drug abuser is seen as lacking the level of social competence necessary to cope adequately with a variety of situational demands. In using operant conditioning with drug abusers, social learning theory stresses patient analysis to discover the variables that are reinforcing. The therapist attempts to discover the situational demands and their related negative emotions that are related to the patient's drug use. Treatment begins with an assessment of the positive and negative aspects of drug use and a self-report on the type, amount, and frequency of drugs used. The assessment includes a focus on the social, physical, and emotional environments in which drug use occurs. After the assessment, the role of the therapist is to enable the patient to deal with triggering behavior so that it does not lead to drug use, with the patient's own report of the negative aspects of drug use serving as a motivator for adopting more positive coping strategies (Donovan, 1988).

A cognitive approach developed by Anna Rose Childress (1993) first conducts a study to develop a set of cues that trigger drug cravings. Patients are then taught methods of combating the urges, including using a planned delay before acting on a craving, having an alternative behavior planned for this delay period, and using systematic relaxation to counter drug arousal. Other techniques include listening to a recording of positive/negative craving consequences that instructs the addict to list the three most negative consequences of relapsing into drugs and the three most positive consequences of not acting on cravings. Negative imagery is used to encourage patients to remember their worst period of addiction—a type of scare tactic.

▶ Therapeutic Community

The therapeutic community (TC) is a generic term for residential, self-help, drug-free treatment programs that have some common characteristics, including concepts adopted from Alcoholics Anonymous (AA): "There is no such thing as an ex-addict, only an addict who is not using at the moment; the emphasis on mutual support and aid; the distrust of mental-health professionals; and the concept of continual confession and catharsis. However, the TC has extended these notions to include the concept of a live-in community with a rigid structure of day-to-day behavior and a complex system of punishment and rewards" (DeLong, 1972: 190–91).

According to George De Leon, a considerable number of TC clients have "never acquired conventional lifestyles. Vocational and educational deficits are marked; mainstream values either are missing or unpursued. Most often, these clients emerge from a socially disadvantaged sector where drug abuse is more a social response than a psychological disturbance. Their TC experience can be termed *habilitation*—the development of a socially productive, conventional lifestyle for the first time in their lives" (De Leon, 1994: 19).

"TC programs reflect a view of the drug abuse client as having a social deficit and requiring social treatment. This social treatment may be characterized as an organized effort to resocialize the client, with the community as an agent of personal change" (Tims, Jainchill, and De Leon, 1994: 2). The primary aims are global changes in lifestyle reflecting abstinence from illicit substances, elimination of antisocial activity, increased employability, and prosocial attitudes and values. The TC becomes a surrogate family and a communal support group for dealing with alienation and the drug abuse that derives from it. Its purpose, notes Mitchell Rosenthal (1973), is to strengthen ego functioning. Therapy, except for the time spent asleep, is total. James DeLong (1972) notes that there is a quasi-evangelistic quality to the "TC movement." The residences are often similar to the communes that were popular during the late 1950s and 1960s counterculture movement, except they generally have a strict hierarchy and insist on rigid adherence to norms even more stringent than those of the proverbial middle class.

A prominent feature of the TC has been the stiff entry requirement: a devastating initial interview that tests an applicant's motivation by focusing on his or her inadequacies and lack of success. Successful applicants must invest completely in the program, which encourages the resident to identify with the former addicts who work in the program and become resocialized into a drug-free existence. The new resident is isolated from all outside contacts, including family and friends. The withdrawal process is accomplished without drugs but with the support of other residents. Once withdrawal has been accomplished, a program of positive and negative reinforcement is implemented. The resident is assigned menial work projects, such as cleaning toilets, but is given an opportunity to earn more prestigious assignments and greater freedom through conformity with the program. Transgressions are punished by public humiliation—reprimands, shaved heads, or signs indicating the nature of the violation. Those who leave, relapse, and return are required to wear a sign announcing their situation. Shame and guilt are constantly exploited to force the addict to conform and to change his or her view of drugs (Platt and Labate, 1976). There is little privacy. Drug use, physical violence, and sexual activity between residents— who are to relate to one another as family—are punished with expulsion.

Residents are kept busy in a highly structured environment that offers little time for idleness or boredom. "A typical day begins at 7 A.M. and ends at 11 P.M., and includes morning and evening house meetings, job assignments, groups, seminars, scheduled personal time, recreation, and individual counseling. As employment is considered an important element of successful participation in society, work is a distinctive component of the TC model. In the TC, all activities and interpersonal and social interactions are considered important opportunities to facilitate individual change" (*Therapeutic Community*, 2002: 5).

Residents are expected to be active in all aspects of the TC program. Failing to do so becomes the subject of criticism at the encounter session, a central feature of the therapeutic process. The encounter is a relatively unstructured, leaderless group session in which members focus on a particular resident (who occupies the "hot seat") and bombard him or her with criticisms about attitude and behavior. The target is encouraged to fight back—verbally—although the goal of such sessions is to destroy the rationalizations and defenses that help perpetuate irresponsible thought patterns and behavior—a resocialization process. "The style of the encounter, with its abrasive attacks and its permitted verbal violence,... is designed to encourage the spewing out of pent-up hostility and anger, to force the patient to confront his maladaptive emotional response and behavior patterns." (Rosenthal, 1973: 91).

The TC is an exciting, friendly, and highly moral—almost utopian—environment (Waldorf, 1973). However, it is not for all abusers: "Severe disturbances may be exacerbated by the TC regimen and may have an adverse effect not only on the disturbed client but also on the treatment environment and the progress of others in the treatment population. Also unsuitable for treatment are candidates whose drug involvement is of so limited a nature as to require a less rigorous intervention or who—despite the deleterious effects of drug abuse—are able to function with the help of a positive support network (e.g., family or significant others)" (Rosenthal, 1984: 55).

TCs have been established in prisons in New York, California, and a number of other states. Inmates selected for the program are recruited at state correctional facilities and housed in units segregated from the general population, although they eat and attend morning activities with other prisoners. The program typically lasts from 6 to 9 months and is staffed by graduates of community TCs and by ex-offenders with prison experience who act as role models demonstrating successful rehabilitation. Upon release, prison TC graduates are encouraged to become part of the extensive community-based TC network.

▶ Chemical Dependency Programs

During the last several decades, the number of programs to treat substance abusers has increased. Some are profit making and others are nonprofit; many call themselves "therapeutic communities," although they differ dramatically from the TCs already discussed. These programs typically share a number of variables: They do a great deal of outreach—most employ a marketing person—and often advertise for clients likely to have health insurance, such as employed alcohol and cocaine abusers as opposed to heroin addicts, because the costs can run more than $500 per day for inpatient care. Many chemical dependency programs are located in a health care facility, which typically increases the cost of treatment. The treatment approach usually includes individual and group counseling, and the model tends to be eclectic rather than doctrinal. The treatment orientation of these programs is varied but mainly reflects a mix of traditional mental health and 12-step perspectives (discussed in the next section). They offer a variety of services, including education, nutrition, relaxation training, recreation, counseling or psychotherapy, psychopharmacological adjuncts, and self-help groups.

The typical program is a 3- to 6-week intensive and highly structured inpatient regimen. Patient care begins with a psychiatric and psychosocial evaluation and then follows a general education-oriented program track of daily lectures plus two to three meetings per week in small task-oriented groups. The educational component teaches about the disease concept of dependence, focusing on the harmful medical and psychosocial effects of illicit drugs and excessive alcohol consumption. "There is also an individual prescriptive track for each client, meetings about once per week with a 'focal counselor,' and appointments with other professionals if medical, psychiatric, or family services are needed"

(Gerstein and Harwood, 1990: 171). Aftercare services are typically meager, so many programs simply refer a patient to an AA or Narcotics Anonymous (NA) group.

▶ Alcoholics and Narcotics Anonymous

Alcoholics Anonymous is a fellowship founded by Robert ("Dr. Bob") Holbrook Smith (1879–1950), a physician and alcoholic, and William ("Bill W.") Wilson (1895–1971), a financial investigator and alcoholic. Bill W. helped Dr. Bob become abstinent, and the two recognized that success in helping alcoholics was not to be found in preaching abstinence but rather in belonging to a fellowship where each alcoholic simply relates his or her story of drunkenness and conversion to a nonalcoholic lifestyle. The "listening" was as important as the "telling." The group became known as Alcoholics Anonymous, after the title of Wilson's 1939 book that AA members often refer to as "The Big Book" (it was quite bulky when originally published). Wilson, who died in 1971, was supported by the substantial royalties the book eventually generated. His wife, who was a nonalcoholic, established Al-Anon, patterned on the AA model, for the family members of alcoholics (Pace, 1988). There are now similar groups for the family and friends of cocaine users—Co-Anon.

AA is the original twelve-step program and requires an act of surrender—an acknowledgment of being an alcoholic and of the destructiveness that results—a bearing of witness, and an acknowledgment of a higher power. While AA is nondenominational, there is a strong repent of your sins–type revivalism—groups begin or end their meetings holding hands in a circle and reciting the Lord's Prayer (Robertson, 1988) or the Serenity Prayer: "God grant me the serenity to accept the things I cannot change; courage to change the things I can; and wisdom to know the difference" (DuPont and McGovern, 1994: 27). As in Protestant revival meetings, the alcoholic/sinner seeks salvation through personal testimony, public contrition, and submission to a higher authority (Delbanco and Delbanco, 1995; Peele, 1985). AA also provides "an important social network through which members learn appropriate behavior and coping skills in drinking situations and become involved in various (nondrinking) leisure activities with other recovering alcoholics" (McElrath, 1995: 314).

AA recognizes the potency of shared honesty and mutual vulnerability openly acknowledged, and the AA group supports each member in his or her effort to remain alcohol free. "Maintenance of sobriety depends on our sharing of our experiences, strength and hope with

A CLOSER LOOK

AA ALTERNATIVES

The "spiritual" dimension of AA and its insistence on a disease model of alcoholism—alcoholics cannot help themselves—have encountered opposition and led to the establishment of alternative groups, such as Rational Recovery (RR) and Secular Organization for Sobriety. Although it is a voluntary self-help group in the AA mode, RR rejects the twelve-step approach as fostering dependency and instead argues that alcoholic participants are not powerless but fully capable of overcoming their addiction (Hall, 1990). According to RR, alcoholism is not a disease but an individual shortcoming. Their approach emphasizes taking personal responsibility for behavior ("Clean and Sober—And Agnostic," 1991).

RR uses "The Big Plan," a commitment never to drink again. It focuses on planning to prevent relapses and attempting to gain insight into how self-defeating beliefs encourage drinking behavior. Various strategies are discussed to deal with high-risk situations where temptations may run high (Galaif and Sussman, 1995). There are also groups that reject the total abstinence proviso of AA and instead emphasize sobriety—drinking in moderation—such as Moderation Management (MM) (Marriott, 1995). MM is designed for persons who want to limit, rather than eliminate, their drinking (Foderaro, 1995).

▼

each other, thus helping to identify and understand the nature of our disease" (AA literature). The AA conceptual model is that alcoholism is a disease, a controllable disability that cannot be cured—thus, there are no ex-alcoholics, merely recovering alcoholics. AA members are encouraged to accept the belief that they are powerless over alcohol, that they cannot control their intake, and that total abstinence is required. New members are advised to obtain a sponsor who has remained abstinent and who will help the initiate work through the 12 steps that are the essence of the AA program. Those who are successful, "twelfth steppers," carry the AA message and program to other alcoholics—they become "missionaries" for AA.

> AA and groups based on the AA approach] attempt to instill the substitution of more adaptive attitudes to replace habitual dysfunctional ones. The extreme use of denial and projection of responsibility for chemical dependency onto other people, circumstances, or conditions outside oneself is an example of a target behavior strongly challenged in the substance abuse self-help group. The familiar opening statement of "I'm an alcoholic and/or drug addict" epitomizes the concrete representation that defense mechanisms of projection and denial run counter to the group culture and norms. (Spitz, 1987: 160)

The basic AA unit is the local group, which is autonomous except in matters affecting other AA groups or the fellowship as a whole: "No group has powers over its members and instead of officers with authority, groups rotate leadership" (AA literature). A secretary chosen by the members plans the meetings and sets the agenda; in most local groups, the position is rotated every six months. There are no entry requirements or dues—"the hat is passed" at most meetings to defray costs. Because of their fear of losing employment, recovering alcoholics were often unwilling to admit their problem in front of others, so strict anonymity became part of the AA approach.

Because many AA groups are less than accepting of persons addicted to substances other than alcohol—Bill Wilson was opposed to allowing heroin addicts to become part of AA—there are separate groups for drug abusers based on the 12-step approach, such as NA and Cocaine Anonymous (CA).

The AA approach has been criticized because of its emphasis on total abstinence and its lack of research support: "The erstwhile abstainer who, for whatever reason, takes a drink may in effect be induced to go on a spree by the belief that this is inevitable. Spree drinking could also be induced by the fact that status in AA is correlated with length of sobriety. Years of sobriety with their attendant symbols and status can be obliterated by one slip, so the social cost of a single drink is as great as the cost of an all-out binge" (Ogborne and Glaser, 1985: 176). Some 12-step groups "do not consider members 'clean and sober' when they are using any psychoactive medication. Cases of adverse treatment consequences, even suicide, have resulted from well-meaning 12-step members dissuading individuals from taking prescribed medications" (DuPont and McGovern, 1994: 56).

▶ Drug Testing

P/P officers routinely test clients for drug use—most frequently those with a history of substance abuse. There has been a proliferation of instant testing devices that are relatively inexpensive. They require securing a urine sample, which is intrusive: The subject must be under close observation when producing a sample in order to prevent tampering, for example, drug-free urine delivered through a prosthetic penis. Devices and chemicals for defeating urine testing are widely available over the Internet. Typically, when there is a positive finding, unless there is corroboration, such as needle marks or an admission, a sample will be sent to a laboratory for confirmation. Sloppy recording procedures and/ or failure to maintain careful controls over the chain of custody of the specimen can also produce serious test errors.

Some agencies use saliva tests that are less intrusive and particularly useful in the field. There is also a sweat patch test, in which a Band-Aid-like patch is attached to the skin to collect sweat for up to seven days and subsequently lab tested for drug residue. If the patch is removed, it cannot be reattached. However, drug molecules from clothes or other people can penetrate the patch and trigger a false positive (Hawkins, 2002).

At best, drug testing can only determine that the subject has used a drug recently; it cannot determine when or how much. Tests cannot discern the casual user from a chronic one. There are also complications inherent in collecting, storing, and shipping urine samples. There is also the problem of the nonmedical use of prescription drugs and so-called designer drugs, substances that do not have a readily available or economically feasible method of detection.

▶ Offenders with Tuberculosis, Hepatitis C, and HIV/AIDS

Adding to the numerous safety and health problems endemic to prisons and thus parolees are those presented by several infectious diseases, in particular, tuberculosis, hepatitis C, and HIV/AIDS. An editorial in the *New York Times* (May 17, 2004: 20) noted that "drug-resistant strains of tuberculosis, easily transmitted in tight spaces, have become a common problem. Illegal drugs ferried in by prison employees—and used by inmates who share needles—have made prison a high-risk setting for HIV infection and most recently liver-destroying hepatitis C.... By failing to confront public health problems in prison, the country could be setting itself up for new epidemics down the line."

Tuberculosis (TB) is a deadly disease, and according to the Center for Disease Control one-third of the world's population is infected with TB; more than 10,000 cases were reported in the United States in 2011. TB bacteria are put into the air when a person infected with TB of the lungs or throat coughs, sneezes, speaks, or sings. The bacteria can float in the air for several hours depending on the environment.

> Prisons and jails, like other congregate facilities, are high-risk settings for the spread of tuberculosis infection. Living conditions are invariably crowded, and many buildings have antiquated systems with poor ventilation and air circulation. Inmates are already more susceptible to TB infection and TB disease because of factors associated with their high-risk lifestyles and inadequate access to health care services, as well as increased prevalence of HIV/AIDS among them. Finally, the appearance of multidrug resistant tuberculosis raises the threat of an often-untreatable disease spreading in a closely confined population. (Hammett, Harrold, and Epstein, 1994: xi)

Drug- and multidrug resistant TB cannot be effectively treated using conventional TB drugs. Those weakened by AIDS are at particular risk for new drug-resistant strains of TB, but all inmates and corrections personnel are at risk from this contagious disease. Approximately 12,000 inmates with TB are released each year (Butterfield, 2003b). "Not only do inmate populations contain concentrations of persons at risk for both TB and HIV, but the facilities themselves are high-risk settings for TB transmission because of crowded conditions and poor ventilation" (Crawford, 1994: 31). The Centers for Disease Control and Prevention has guidelines for isolating persons with active TB; however, in a prison setting, these are expensive to implement, and most prisons have inadequate methods for dealing with TB.

Hepatitis C, an often-fatal liver disease, is spread primarily through contact with human blood and sexual contact and is prevalent among intravenous drug users.

An estimated 4 million Americans have the disease. About 1.5 million inmates with the disease are released each year (Butterfield, 2003b). Carriers often have no symptoms, and the disease can progress undetected for years, silently destroying the liver. Although most state prisons do not require hepatitis C testing for inmates—it is expensive—the number of those with the disease has been estimated by health officials to be about 20 percent of the prison population. Treatment requires the use of drugs at a per-patient cost of about $10,000 to $20,000 per year; advanced cases can be cured only with a liver transplant. In 2001, New York was treating 95 infected inmates at a cost of $6 million per year. There is concern in the medical community that hepatitis C will spread as infected inmates are released into the community, and there is also concern about the safety of prison workers,

AIDS and its precursor, human immunodeficiency virus (HIV), were first identified in the United States in 1981. Today about one in six AIDS patients has spent time in an American prison or jail. Intravenous drug users and male homosexuals have been identified as primary groups at risk for the disease, and prisons house many intravenous drug users and inmates who resort to homosexual practices in the absence of available female partners. AIDS also spreads in prison through rape, a rather widespread problem officials appear unwilling or unable to curtail (Lewin, 2001a). Inmates frequently sport prison tattoos, and the sharing of primitive tattoo needles is also a source of infection. The number of HIV positive state and federal inmates is about 22,000 persons, but most states do not test all inmates. According to the Center for Disease Control, the rate of confirmed AIDS cases in correctional facilities is about two-and-a-half times that of the general population.

Although some P/P officers may have personal concerns, the manner in which the disease is transmitted places them at low risk. (The primary risk occurs during a search of clients who could have a contaminated hypodermic needle on their person.) Difficult questions concern enforcement of rules and confidentiality. Offenders who are sexually active place their partners in jeopardy. Can the client be required to refrain from unprotected sexual activity? How would this rule be enforced? Should the spouse or sex partner(s) be informed of the client's condition? If so, how is this to be accomplished? These are serious public safety and liability issues with which P/P agencies are struggling—a conflict between a "duty to warn" and "breach of confidentially."

Missouri P/P officers are instructed to guard the confidentiality of HIV/AIDS information and no mention is to be made in the official case record. However, the "probation and parole officer will use language to the effect that the offender is experiencing significant medical difficulties." HIV/AIDS information is placed in a letter-size manila envelope marked: "CONFIDENTIAL/DO NOT RELEASE." This envelope is removed before allowing those without a need to know to carry out their job functions to review the case folder.

The Illinois Department of Corrections offers (voluntary) HIV testing to all inmates upon intake and release to the community. Probation officers in Kansas are advised that "when staff become aware a specific offender is HIV-positive, disclosure without the subject's informed consent may be a violation of the offender's right to privacy. In special cases where there is evidence suggesting ongoing high-risk behavior that might result in the infection of a third party, the right to privacy may be outweighed by a duty to warn possible victims. In such cases, staff should be encouraged to seek supervisory and legal assistance on a case by case basis." Probation officers and parole agents in California are warned that willful or negligent disclosure of HIV information by a peace officer is a misdemeanor. When it becomes known that a probationer or parolee has tested positive for HIV or AIDS and has not informed his or her spouse, the supervising officer may request that the chief medical officer of the parolee's releasing institution, or the physician treating the spouse or probationer/parolee, inform the spouse. In such cases, the supervising officer shall seek to

> **Key Fact**
>
> The rate of HIV/AIDS is higher in the offender population than the general population and presents challenges to prison and community supervision officials.

ensure that counseling is provided to the spouse by the person providing the information to the spouse.

In New York, medical information, including HIV/AIDS, "will not be disclosed within or outside the Division of Parole without written consent of the protected individual." However, a parole officer can request that an application be made for a court order permitting disclosure when there is a significant risk of HIV transmission and the parolee refuses to inform a person(s) at risk. The Division of Parole provides individuals and households with whom an inmate proposes to live with HIV/AIDS information regardless of his or her HIV/AIDS status.

In Multnomah County, Oregon, confidentiality rules determine how client information is to be recorded. Offenders who refuse to sign releases will have their HIV-related issues, such as an inability to work, recorded in a manner that does not disclose their status, for example, "This offender is unable to meet the probation condition of obtaining employment for he is under doctor's orders to not work until further notice," and "HIV infected clients who are known to be engaging in activities that put others at risk of HIV infection will be counseled to stop those activities. If such activities continue, the client may be reported to the County Health Officer." The Alabama Board of Pardons and Paroles requires infected inmates to sign a statement of "commitment to a course of personal conduct which maximizes his/her efforts to prevent any risk of transmission of the infection to others." If the board believes that the inmate is not prepared to live up to these conditions, it will deny parole. The board also imposes special conditions to protect the parolee's family or coresidents. A failure to abide by these conditions can result in parole being revoked. Some agencies have formed special units or designated officers as HIV/AIDS specialists.

▶ New York State Division of Parole AIDS Caseloads

The Division of Parole in New York established specialized AIDS caseloads. The need for specialized assistance was increased by a law passed in 1992 that permits the parole board to release certain terminally ill inmates before their parole eligibility date—many of these candidates have AIDS. Parolees often experience difficulties with the community reintegration process, and AIDS is an additional complicating factor. The specialist parole officers participate in ongoing training regarding the illness and its management, and each supervises no more than 20 clients, permitting time to visit clients and arrange contracts with service providers or negotiate with service agencies. About 20 percent clients are hospitalized during some point each month, and many others are on nonreport status because of their physical condition; caseload attrition through death is extraordinarily high, which can have a serious impact on officer morale.

Parole officers' activities resemble those typically provided by medical social workers, including aid with securing Social Security, public assistance, and Medicaid. The parole officer works with the client's family, providing support and information under trying circumstances. In many cases, he or she must arrange for housing for clients who lack family resources. Home visits are often accomplished in teams that facilitate working with families and parolees. The visits are considerably longer than those for parole officers with routine caseloads. Some parole officers utilize group methods with their clients. Despite their medical condition, some HIV clients manage to get involved with serious criminal activity and are returned to prison. Because of the problem of HIV-infected clients who also suffer from tuberculosis, parole officers take special precautions to reduce the possibility of infection.

▶ Sex Offenders

The category of sex offender represents a number of different types of offenders, ranging from a 19-year-old who had consensual sex with a 16-year-old to the sexual predator who stalks children in parks and playgrounds (Jenuwine, Simmons, and Swies, 2003). Although child sexual abuse is a serious and widespread problem in the United States, P/P agencies had been slow to respond adequately to this type of offender when he (they are overwhelmingly male) is on a supervision caseload. Indeed, child sexual offenders often ended up on probation because of the extreme level of prison overcrowding (Lurigio, Jones, and Smith, 1995)[1] or received probation as a result of a plea agreement stemming from weakness in evidence or the desire to avoid putting children through the trauma of a trial (Stalans, 2004). In New York State, for example, probation is the most common sentence for sex offenders (N.Y. State Division of Probation and Correctional Alternatives, 2006). Today, virtually all P/P agencies pay special attention to sex offenders.

Sex offenders, particularly those who prey on children, present significant risk factors to the community and supervision problems for the P/P agency. Trauma inflicted on young victims and resulting community outrage pose problems not typically encountered

Key Fact

The category of sex offender represents a number of different types of offenders, but those who prey on children present significant risk factors to the community and supervision problems for the P/P officer.

SHOULD SEX OFFENDERS BE PAROLED?

Except for those sentenced to life without parole, sex offenders will be released either automatically (mandatory release) after they serve their prison sentences (minus any "good time") or by discretionary release, for example parole. The primary difference between these two methods of release highlights the potential negative implications of mandatory release for sex offenders who have little incentive to participate in specialized treatment or other risk-reducing programs and services while incarcerated.

In contrast, the leverage of a discretionary release system provides paroling authorities the opportunity to facilitate successful sex offender reentry by encouraging or requiring offenders to participate in specialized services in order to be considered for early release. This is a particularly valuable tool because the evidence indicates that sex offenders who receive well-designed and appropriate prison-based treatment recidivate at lower rates than those who do not receive, as do sex offenders who, once released from prison, participate in specialized community-based sex offender treatment

while under supervision upon return to the community. (Center for Sex Offender Management [CSOM], 2007: 7; citations deleted)

"The 'stranger danger' notion of offending (upon which much sex crime legislation is based) may not reflect the empirical reality that most sex crimes (85%) are committed by individuals known to the victim" (Mercado et al., 2013: 4-5).

Research into the Sex Offender Treatment Program of the Alaska Department of Corrections revealed that inmates "who were in treatment tended to last longer in the community without re-offense. Those who completed all stages of treatment through the advanced stage had a zero-re-offense rate for sexual offenses. This included sexual assault offenders (rapists) who generally tend to re-offend more quickly and at a higher rate" (Mander et al., 1996: 2). A study of sex offenders in New Jersey found that those who received prison-based treatment recidivated (25%) at a rate of less than half compared to those who did not receive treatment (51.7%). However, over a 6.5-year period reconviction rates for sex offenses were 5 percent for both groups (Mercado et al., 2013).

---

[1]Although the U.S. Supreme Court has ruled the practice constitutional (*Seling v. Young*, 531 U.S. 250, 2001), statutes allowing violent sex offenders to be kept in custody beyond their sentence have encountered severe financing problems associated with the cost of providing medical and legal professionals required in such cases (Davey and Goodnough, 2007a, 2007b; Parsons, 1998).

with other types of offenders. This has been highlighted by the passage of registration statutes in virtually every state. Enacted in 1994, the Jacob Wetterling Act—named after Jacob Wetterling, an 11-year-old boy who was kidnapped in 1989—requires all states to establish stringent registration programs for sex offenders. In 1994, seven-year-old Megan Kanka was raped and murdered in New Jersey by a convicted sex offender who had been living across the street. In response to interest and concern over this incident and other recent sex crimes involving child victims, Congress passed Megan's Law in 1996, requiring all 50 states to develop procedures to notify communities where released sex offenders will be residing. Research reveals that community notification laws have no effect on sex reoffending rates (Tewksbury, Jennings, and Zgoba, 2012; Zgoba, Veysey, and Delessandro 2010).

In 2006, Congress passed the Adam Walsh Child Protection and Safety Act, which sets forth specific responsibilities for the U.S. Department of Justice in identifying, arresting, and prosecuting individuals convicted of criminal offenses against minors, individuals convicted of sexually violent offenses, and individuals who are designated as sexually violent predators who have failed to register or update a registration. The statute makes it a federal felony punishable by 10 years imprisonment for sex offenders who fail to register to travel interstate.

Registration is designed to deter potential offenders while providing law enforcement agencies with a registry to aid their investigations. In addition, most states have enacted notification statutes that either make information about sex offenders available on request to individuals and organizations or authorize or require P/P agencies, law enforcement agencies, or prosecutor offices to disseminate information to the community at large. For example, the Missouri Highway Patrol operates a toll-free telephone number in order to disseminate information on registered sex offenders as well as a Web page on registered sex offenders that is open to the public.

These laws pose problems for P/P officers who must help offenders deal with potential vigilantism as well as the stigma that presents a significant barrier to housing and employment. In 2009, for example, 70 Florida postprison probationers were living under a Miami highway because no facility would provide them with housing and they were unable to find a residence sufficiently distant from a school to satisfy state law. They included an 83-year-old deaf man and another who was wheelchair bound. The air in the encampment reeked of human excrement since there was no running water or sewage system (Skipp and Campo-Flores, 2009). In 2009, a group of homeless sex offenders was living in a camp in the woods behind an office park in Marietta, Georgia—a site that does not violate the many living restrictions that the state's sex offender law imposes—when they were ordered out by the Cobb County Sheriff (Associated Press, 2009; Pickel, 2009).

Sex offenders must be prevented from employment where they would have access to potential victims, so unnecessary impediments present frustrations that can impact on the offender's behavior. When the result is absconding, they remain at large without any monitoring.

Sexual assault that is most profound in its traumatic implications involves a violation of trust that occurs when, as in most sexual assault victimizations, offenders are known to victims. "Trauma and length and level of recovery seem linked to trust violation more than to many other factors. Thus, what might be regarded by some as a relatively minor type of sexual assault (e.g., 'just fondling') can be extremely traumatic to a victim who trusted the perpetrator" (English, Pullen, and Jones, 1997: 1). Most victims of sex crimes are known to the offender and a majority by someone known to them or their family. Approximately 60 percent of boys and 80 percent of girls who are sexually victimized are abused by someone known to them or their family—relatives, babysitters, persons in authority over the child, or persons who supervise children (CSOM, 2001a).

SEX OFFENDER RECIDIVISM

Sex offenders are not a homogeneous group, and their rates of reoffending differ. They have a wide variety of racial, ethnic, and socioeconomic backgrounds; the majority of them do not have extensive criminal histories or "traditional" criminal lifestyles; and they differ significantly in age (Gilligan and Talbot, 2000). Studies indicate that for child molesters, the recidivism rate is between 13 and 20 percent, and for rapists, 19 percent. Individual characteristics further distinguish rates of sexual reoffending. One study found that offenders whose female victims were not relatives had a recidivism rate of 18 percent, whereas for male victims the rate was 35 percent. Of course, these statistics can only account for offenders who were convicted—many sex offenses are never even reported (CSOM, 2001a).

An Oregon study confirmed that unlike other offenders who tend to "age out" of their criminal behavior as they grow older, many sex offenders continue to abuse throughout their lifetimes. The study revealed that sex offenders frequently score in the low range on traditional correctional risk assessment instruments because these instruments do not address many of the areas that are indicators of risk for sex offenders

(Gilligan and Talbot, 2000). A study of sex offenders released in 1994 revealed that 3.5 percent were reconvicted of a sex crime within three years. Within the first three years following release from prison, 3.3 percent of the released child molesters were rearrested for another sex crime against a child (Langan and Durose, 2003).

In fact, adult sex offenders have relatively low sex offense recidivism rates. A study of sex offenders released from prison in 1994 shows that 5.3 percent of them were rearrested for a new sex crime after being at risk three years. Similarly, a study of Delaware adult sex offenders, released from prison in 2001, found 3.8 percent were rearrested for a new sex crime after being at risk three years. In a very extensive recidivism study in Ohio, 8 percent of sex offenders released from prison returned to prison for a new sex offense after being at risk 10 years. However, sentenced juvenile sex offenders have a recidivism rate about 10 times higher than their adult sex offender prison counterparts (Weidlein-Crist and O'Connell, Jr., 2008). Of course, "many sex offenses go unreported, and so there is a large variety of offenders who have not been caught, and victims who have not come forward" (2008: 51).

Although practitioners use terms such as "manipulative," "secretive," "devious," and "deceptive," to describe sex offenders, "a set of characteristics (e.g., physical, mental, psychological, personality, emotional) that is common to all sex offenders has not been identified. Because of the diversity in the demographic and social makeup of those who commit sexual offenses, a profile of a 'typical' sex offender does not exist, although the vast majority of sex offenders are male" (M. Carter and Morris, 2007: 6).

Because of the sensitivity of this offender class, the focus of sex offender supervision is usually *containment*: Preventing recidivism is the single goal, and the client is the community. As part of this approach, sex offenders may be subjected to periodic **polygraph** examinations. "Use of the polygraph with sex offenders under community supervision can serve to help the probationer overcome denial, aid in developing treatment plans, be a deterrent for sexual reoffending and assist in monitoring compliance with the conditions of supervision" (N.Y. State Division of Probation and Correctional Alternatives, 2009: 1). Under a 2005 law, all sex offenders under lifetime parole supervision in New Jersey are subject to at least one annual polygraph test. "Exams are conducted by parole officers who completed their polygraph training and are from other districts so that parolee has no previous contact or relationship with polygrapher" (Tubman-Carbone, 2009: 2). While the result of a polygraph examination cannot be used as evidence of a P/P violation or a new crime, it can provide the basis for further investigation. Evidence of deception, while not a violation per se, can result in the imposition of increased levels of supervision, such as more frequent reporting and electronic monitoring.

Rules of supervision can include avoiding places where children can be expected to congregate or be present; not having contact with persons under 18; maintaining a driving log containing mileage, time of departure and arrival, time of return, routes traveled, and passenger names; and not possessing or viewing any sexually oriented media—printed, video, audio, telephonic, electronic—relevant to the deviant behavior pattern. And these rules are enforced by unannounced home visits and surveillance activities. In Cook County, Illinois, probation officers in their Adult Sex Offender Program report that many offenders "have expressed the view that their POs serve as an external conscience" and that the intensive supervision program "serves to constantly remind each probationer of the consequences for re-offense" (Jenuwine, Simmons, and Swies, 2003: 22).

Sex offenders, particularly those whose victims are children, have prohibitions with respect to what can be accessed on their computers. Monitoring computer use is thus a critical aspect of the supervision process and is aided by *Field Search*, a free software tool developed by the National Institute of Justice. Downloaded on a flash drive, the program enables nontechnical P/P officers to efficiently scan the offender's computer, PC or Mac, and create a detailed report of their findings. The P/P officer brings the software on a flash drive to the offender's residence and runs it on the suspect computer for about 30 minutes. *Field Search* automatically retrieves Internet histories from popular browsers whose results are displayed in an easy-to-read format that includes the date and time each website was visited. Results can be sorted in a number of ways to help the officer understand an offender's surfing patterns.

Items are selected for inclusion in the report by a single mouse click, and images also can be easily seized to removable media. Officers also can choose to search free space for deleted history records. The software can scan specific folders as opposed to scanning the entire hard drive, delivering quicker, targeted results. The keyword search reveals such things as pornographic materials and stories or the victim's name. *Field Search* has a built-in report function: Once items are selected for inclusion, the report is automatically created and each item's associated path and date/time stamp is included in the report. *Field Search* can export data to spreadsheets for further analysis. The final report can be exported to a flash drive for the officer to review in the office.

Research (Gilligan and Talbot, 2000) indicates that specialized sex offender caseloads provide these clear advantages for supervision staff:

- Staff gain expertise and training related to sex offender management.
- Specialized caseloads ensure that sex offenders, who might have become "lost" on nonspecialized caseloads because of their seemingly compliant nature, are supervised intensively.
- Staff can establish rapport with sex offenders in order to encourage them to talk openly about their thoughts and activities.
- Feelings of camaraderie and support are promoted among officers who maintain these caseloads, which reduce secondary trauma.
- There is increased agencywide consistency in sex offender supervision practices.

Hunt County (Texas) Sex Offender Unit

The Hunt County (Texas) Probation Department's Sex Offender Accountability Program (SOAP) is a specialized caseload monitoring sexual abusers' compliance with conditions of supervision. SOAP uses a team comprising a probation officer, sex offender therapist, and polygraph examiner. The probation officer, accompanied by a peace officer for security reasons, makes random checks of offenders' home environments to discuss special issues and monitor their surroundings for warning signs of risk.

Sex offenders must adhere to the 18 standard conditions of supervision common to all felony offenders, which include refraining from criminal conduct, drug/alcohol use, and association with felons; reporting to the probation officer as directed; and submitting to drug testing. In addition, sex offenders are required to attend and participate in sex offender treatment with a registered treatment provider. These treatment groups typically meet once per week.

The offender must submit to and pay for polygraph testing. These examinations may be required every 6 to 12 months. There is some variation in probation conditions regarding contact with children: Most offenders are initially prohibited from any contact with children, although some offenders are permitted to have supervised contact with their biological children; but as an offender participates and progresses in sex offender treatment, his conditions may be modified gradually to allow more supervised contact with children. An offender cannot reside near a school or daycare center and cannot go to places where children are known to congregate.

SOAP offenders are prohibited from viewing or purchasing pornography or going to sexually oriented businesses. They are typically restricted from accessing the Internet. Texas law allows the judge placing an offender on probation to order him to serve time in the local jail (up to 180 days) as a condition of supervision, an option often used by the Hunt County Courts. Electronic monitoring and home curfews are also options the court may use.

Sex offenders in the program are ordered by the court to submit a blood sample, which is sent to the crime lab in Austin, and a DNA record is made. The DNA database is used to assist in the investigation of unsolved crimes.

Maricopa County (Arizona) Sex Offender Program

In 1987, the Arizona legislature passed a law mandating lifetime probation for sex offenders convicted of crimes against children. The Maricopa County Adult Probation Department's response includes intensive supervision, subsidized treatment and assessment, and services for victims and their families. Maricopa County is a mostly urban jurisdiction, with more than 2.5 million people living in a metropolitan area that includes Phoenix and Scottsdale. Approximately two-thirds of the state's population reside within the county.

Assessment involves the use of psychological testing as well as **plethysmography**, which electronically measures an offender's penile arousal to various audiovisual stimuli. The instrument, similar to a blood pressure gauge, is attached to the offender's penis and measures the arousal, recording changes in penile tumescence, when different types of deviant and nondeviant stimuli are presented. Along with the plethysmograph, a polygraph is used to secure a complete sexual history and to periodically monitor compliance with probation regulations.

Offenders begin their probation terms by participating in 45 classroom hours on sexuality and sexual deviation. They are placed in treatment groups that usually use a cognitive behavior approach and that can last from 18 months to 2 years or (in some cases) longer. Those with the means are expected to pay for the therapy. Offenders are subject to a curfew and may not operate a motor vehicle without the consent of their probation officer.

The supervision units consist of 21 specialized probation officers, whose average caseload is 53 offenders, and 10 surveillance officers, each of whom works with 2 probation officers and thus averages about 100 offenders. Probation officers supervise offenders' progress in dealing with behavioral and life issues and their compliance with program conditions. Surveillance officers make random field visits, particularly evening and weekend visits, and work closely with the other officers.

New Haven (Connecticut) Sex Offender Intensive Supervision Unit

The city of New Haven, Connecticut, has a population of about 150,000. It is a diverse urban area and the home of Yale University but is one of the poorest cities in the nation. The Sex Offender Intensive Supervision Unit is a cooperative effort of the Office of Adult Probation (OAP), a statewide agency housed within the judicial branch, and the Center for the Treatment of Problem Sexual Behavior (CTPSB), a private nonprofit community-based treatment program that operates statewide. The unit supervises high-risk adult sex offenders (aged 16 and older) identified through risk assessment by probation and treatment staff. All offenders on the caseload have been convicted of a sex offense and are under the legal supervision of a probation officer.

The team consists of a lead probation officer, four more probation officers, three treatment providers from CTPSB, and a victim advocate from Connecticut Sexual Assault Crisis Services whose position is funded by OAP and is housed primarily within the New Haven Probation Office. Three probation officers supervise a maximum of 25 high-risk offenders each. These officers are responsible for 24-hour supervision, 7 days per week; are highly mobile and very proactive; are in contact with the offenders on their caseload nearly every day; routinely make unannounced home visits (including evenings, weekends, and holidays); maintain communication with family members, friends, and employers; assess the appropriateness of offenders' residence and employment; search for at-risk behaviors (including evidence of contact or potential contact with children, pornography, illegal substances or alcohol, and Internet use); and collaborate with local law enforcement.

The fourth probation officer is a Relapse Prevention Specialist and has a maximum caseload of 50 offenders. As offenders progress in treatment, they transition from specialized Intensive Supervision to the Relapse Prevention caseload, based on time in treatment, stable behavior, and active engagement in the treatment process. The Relapse Prevention caseload provides heightened but less intense monitoring. Offenders move toward incorporation in nonspecialized "regular" high-risk supervision (maximum caseload of 75). The Relapse Prevention Officer receives specialized training, collaborates with treatment providers, and co-faciitates groups.

The CTPSB treatment staff provides assessment and treatment, and they often accompany probation officers on home visits. Treatment staff use a psychopathy checklist, a psychological survey, and a risk assessment instrument based on current research. Offenders are accepted for treatment if the nature of their offense and their history indicate they would benefit from treatment. Offenders who are assessed as having psychopathic personalities (this is very uncommon) are often refused treatment because such offenders may pose greater risks with treatment. Generally, an offender's evaluation determines the type of treatment received.

Treatment staff is responsible for group therapy provided to offenders. Most offenders begin with an introductory group (the "cognitive lab"), which provides treatment orientation and expectations and lasts about 14 weeks. Treatment draws on cognitive behavior approaches and includes cognitive restructuring, victim empathy training, sexual education, and relapse prevention training. CTPSB offers special bilingual groups and groups for people with developmental disabilities as well as a "family seminar" before family reunification. Whenever possible, rapists, child molesters, and exhibitionists/voyeurs are assigned to separate specialized groups. A portion of the offenders also receives specialized medication to control their impulses and behavior.

Treatment proceeds toward realization of 14 goals, categorized as immediate, intermediate, and extended. The first immediate goal is acceptance of responsibility for the sexual offense. The final goal is to "learn about, and utilize, a Relapse Prevention Strategy and an Offense Prevention Plan." Length of time in treatment depends on the individual's progress because treatment is considered open ended; it ranges from 1 to 7 years.

A victim advocate supports supervision activities by accompanying probation officers on home and field visits, attending case review meetings, and leading the victim empathy component of treatment groups. He or she initiates contact with the victim and/or the victim's family and maintains that contact as long as necessary. The advocate provides information and raises concerns to probation officers and treatment staff throughout the supervision process, provides referrals for counseling and other services, obtains background information from all probation files on each individual supervised by the unit, and also gathers information from victims or significant others and family members about an offender's behavior as part of supervision.

Notification is provided to victims, victims' parents or guardians (as appropriate), the police, the offender's immediate family members, other occupants of the offender's residence, and treatment providers. For the highest-risk cases, including most unit cases, the team may decide to include notification to neighbors, local schools, employers, and organizations with which the offender is involved. Notification is a probation responsibility but often involves both the probation officer and the victim advocate. Notification is also regarded as an important opportunity for public education about sex offenders. The advocate and/or the officers hold public meetings in advance of notification when possible.

▶ Female Offenders

"The correctional system has historically been male-dominated. Not only [is] the structure of prison settings, the rules, the operating procedures, and the treatment programs largely based on the needs of males, but research studying the effectiveness of programs is also based on male subjects. Correctional systems frequently can assign male inmates to programs based on the individual rehabilitative or treatment needs of the offender, the severity of the crime the offender committed, and/or the security risk of the offender. Female offenders are not offered these same considerations" (Shearer, 2003: 46). Because they are less likely to be considered high risk—to have committed personal rather than property or "victimless" offenses—they are less likely to receive needed attention and may even be viewed as burdensome or inconvenient because of their high level of needs.

Women offenders are most likely to have committed crimes associated with poverty: property, drug, and vice offenses. "Given the poverty-crime link, it is unlikely that the female crime rate will decrease unless the factors which contribute to the poverty of women are addressed" (Scroggins and Malley, 2010: 147). They "often suffer from trauma and victimization, and officers may feel uncomfortable with or incapable of dealing with these issues and unsure of their ability to secure appropriate resources in the community" (Sydney, 2006b: 37).

Although women make up a smaller proportion of the prison population, their incarceration rate has actually outpaced men's and the number of women under community supervision has reached an all-time high (Opsal, 2010; Scroggins and Malley, 2010). Females represent about 24 percent of the probation population and 13 percent of parolees, and most are single mothers with minor children. They "are disproportionately low income women of color who are undereducated and unskilled, with sporadic employment histories" (Bloom, Owen, and Covington, 2003: 2; Scroggins and Malley, 2010) and they "enter the criminal justice system with a host of unique medical, psychological, and financial problems" (Chesney-Lind, 1997: 170). In Georgia, for example, 99 percent of female parolees are mothers with more than two children. For women who have primary child-care responsibilities, participating in community service, attending treatment sessions,

▼

or even reporting to their probation/parole officer requires making childcare arrangements (Sydney, 2006b). While female offenders often have extensive social services needs, the limited resources of probation/parole agencies are focused on controlling the behavior and movement of offenders (Schram et al., 2006).

Tara Opsal (2010: 310) reports that although men and women have many similar challenges upon release from prison, women face unique circumstances: They are more likely to have to deal with remnants of their drug abuse and reuniting with their children. "Compared to men, female offenders are less likely to be able to amass family support on the outside and more likely both to establish relationships on the outside with ex-offenders ·or recovering drug users as well as to deal with mental health issues."

Because the majority of women in the correctional system are mothers, a major consideration for these women is reunification with their children (Bloom, Owen, and Covington, 2003). Thus, "engaging the family, particularly her children, in the recovery process can promote successful outcomes for a woman" (Bloom and McDiarmid, 2001: 11). Women who commit crime often do so under the influence of their male partners (Scroggins and Malley, 2010). Female probationers and parolees frequently require protection from abusive partners.

"Although relationships with others (family, friends, partners) are often the impetus to criminal involvement, these relationships may also support offenders' success in community corrections" (Sydney, 2006b: 34). However, P/P conditions prohibit associating with other offenders, and female offenders will likely have significant others with a criminal history. Thus, this prohibition may have to be adjusted in specific cases. When male P/P officers supervise female offenders, there is concern with the possibility of compromising situations, real or feigned.

▶ Driving While Intoxicated (DWI)

Intoxicated drivers kill many more people than those who commit deliberate homicide. Annually, there are about 1.5 million arrests for intoxicated driving; about one-third are repeat offenders. However, unless there is a fatality, offenders are typically released back into the community. As a result, about a half-million DWI offenders are on probation and many larger departments have specialized DWI units.

In Nassau County (Long Island), New York, the DWI unit is provided with a list of DWI defendants for whom presentence investigation (PSI) reports have been requested by the court. Each case is computer checked for a prior criminal record, outstanding warrants, and any motor vehicle record. Cases with multiple DWI arrests are flagged, and their names are entered into a prescreening log, which is used by the unit supervisor to monitor DWI court activity in anticipation of future screening and assignment to probation supervision. This information is then sent to the probation officer assigned to conduct the PSI.

When the case is flagged by the DWI unit, the PSI officer sends it to the mental health unit, where a consultant determines whether the defendant is a candidate for the county's drug and alcohol abuse agency and also makes a recommendation regarding therapy that will accompany the final PSI report sent to the sentencing judge. The judge revokes the defendant's motor vehicle license at this time (six months for misdemeanors and one year for felonies), and the case is submitted for DWI unit screening.

Each unit officer maintains a caseload of no more than 30 DWI probationers in a designated area of the county (which is updated periodically in order to conform better to the distribution of DWI clientele). DWI supervision requires the offender to report weekly to a designated agency where he or she completes a 10-week alcohol education program and a 24-week closed group therapy session program; the group sessions are co-led by a

▼

probation officer and an alcohol counselor. Individual counseling is made available on an as-needed basis. Clients are subjected to random alcohol testing, and a positive reading can result in a variety of sanctions. On completion of the agency program, the client is encouraged to participate in an AA program (discussed earlier). The client is required to report in person to the probation officer, and the officer makes periodic home visits. When an offender successfully completes the program, a letter is sent to the Department of Motor Vehicles indicating that the subject is no longer prohibited from obtaining a driver's license.

The Cook County, Illinois, Adult Probation Department has an enhanced DUI probation supervision unit for female offenders who have a prior DUI conviction, are sentenced for a DUI misdemeanor, and are classified as in need of intensive treatment needs. The majority of those supervised by the unit have been sentenced to probation for 12 to 18 months. During this period, the program focuses on providing enhanced levels of individualized supervision that includes substance abuse treatment. As a result of its specialized nature, additional training of its program staff, and a reduced caseworkers–client ratio, probation officers are able to provide clients with individualized, gender-specific supervision and assistance. As part of the treatment aftercare, the majority of program clientele attend 14 weekly group meetings each lasting approximately 90 minutes. If participants miss two consecutive group sessions, their lack of attendance is viewed as a violation of their conditions of supervision (Armstrong, Burruss, and Henderson, 2007).

The Pima County (AZ) Adult Probation Department has an "Aggravated DUI Caseload" for probation-eligible repeat DUI offenders with a problematic score on assessment screening. Offenders are referred to the Aggravated DUI Caseload through a plea deal or as part of the presentence investigation. They typically remain on the specialized caseload for 10 to 12 months. They must adhere to a curfew, are prohibited from any alcohol use, and subject to random drug and alcohol testing. Each probationer must conform to a treatment plan that results from screening by a state-licensed provider. They also are required to complete 60 hours of community restitution work and attend a MADD/Victim Impact presentation.

▶ Developmentally Challenged

The offender who is developmentally challenged presents supervision problems not typically found with other types of cases. Without specialized training and given the myriad of problems caused by rather large caseloads, P/P officers are often unable to meet the needs of these clients—hence the logic of specialized caseloads. Intelligence quotient (IQ) in P/P is determined by a standardized test administered by a clinical psychologist. In general, those whose scores fall below 70 are diagnosed as in need of special services.

Compared with the size of regular caseloads (usually more than 200), the Cuyahoga County (Ohio) Mentally Retarded Offender Unit averages between 55 and 65 probationers. Clients have a tested IQ of 75 or less, and the level of supervision for each offender is determined by a risk/needs classification: extended (mail contact only), low, medium, high, and super high. The unit has a clinical director who is a licensed psychologist. Each case is evaluated by a probation officer and the clinical director, and probationers are then referred for appropriate services. An interdisciplinary team—representatives from public and private services and advocacy groups specializing in mental retardation as well as public welfare agencies—aids in case planning for each probationer.

The rules and regulations of probation have been drafted in a form more easily understood by this population, and probation violation hearings are conducted in a manner more likely to be understood by the offender. Probation officers spend a great deal of time securing services for their clients (many social services agencies are reluctant to aid retarded offenders, both out of fear and due to the difficulties such clients present due to their disabilities).

The Erie County (Pennsylvania) Adult Probation/Parole and Mental Health/Mental Retardation Offices jointly fund a Special Probation Services unit, which provides County Court of Common Pleas judges with alternatives to incarceration for offenders who are mentally retarded—persons with a full-scale IQ score of 74 and below. The program offers the structure and support of the criminal justice system simultaneously with the expertise of mental retardation services. The P/P officer is responsible for monitoring and enforcing the P/P conditions, while the case manager is responsible for coordinating community services to meet the individual's needs.

In addition, the unit monitors defendants released under pretrial conditions. The case manager serves on an interdisciplinary evaluation committee, which screens pretrial defendants for program eligibility. A judge can elect to release the qualified offender into the community under the supervision of the Special Probation Services pending case disposition. A representative from the unit is on an interdisciplinary team that screens and reviews case histories of newly incarcerated inmates in the Erie County Prison. Persons suspected of being mentally impaired are further evaluated to determine whether they are mentally retarded and eligible for services. In addition, referrals are taken from Adult Probation and other agencies.

▶ Crime Victims and Restorative Justice

Our system of criminal justice is an outgrowth of the historical emergence of the state as the dominant power in modern times whereby crime is perceived as an act against the state. "This approach has led to the gross neglect of individual victims, who have been seen as passive entities, have been almost completely locked out from any decision making in the justice proceedings, and often have not been compensated for the harm that occurred to them" (Niemeyer and Shichor, 1996: 3). Emerging during the 1970s as part of the victim's movement, restorative justice (RJ) "views crime as a violation of one person by another, rather than against the state" (Maloney and Umbreit, 1995: 43).

RJ is the guiding philosophical framework for a paradigm that seeks to promote maximum involvement of the victim, the offender, and the community (Bazemore and Maloney, 1994). Instead of simply punishing those who commit crimes—*retributive justice*—the focus is on allowing the offender an opportunity to make amends to his or her victim (Crowe, 1998; Wright, 1991; Zehr and Mika, 1998).

> The depersonalized mechanisms of corrections fail to deliver the message to the offender that by his/her actions he/she has harmed another human being, and that part of the offender's habilitation or rehabilitation should be geared toward making the victim whole again. The evolution of the criminal justice system in this country has resulted in a de-emphasis on the responsibility of the offender toward the victim(s) of his/her wrongful acts. Professionalization and abstract proceduralism ... hinder the reintegration of offenders into law-abiding society. (Sinclair, 1994: 16)

Punishment (retributive justice) has "counterdeterrent effects on offenders, including stigmatization, humiliation, and isolation, that may minimize prospects for regaining self-respect and the respect of the community" (Bazemore and Umbreit, 1994: 300), while the treatment response provides little in the way of a message that the offender has harmed someone and should take action to repair damages to the victim. RJ offers an alternate way to look at the response to crime and criminal behavior beyond the traditional treatment versus punishment. Instead of advocating more or better treatment or greater punishment, RJ seeks systemwide change, a philosophical framework in which the victim is at the center: "While probation and parole place a plethora of educational, counseling and social services at the disposal of the offender, little is done to reach out to crime victims with services they may desperately need" (Sinclair, 1994: 15). RJ argues not only that it is necessary to bring the victim back into the criminal justice system but also that all parties—victim, offender, and community—should be included in the response to crime.

In targeting only offenders for intervention, notes Gordon Bazemore, both the surveillance and the individual treatment models ignore two primary "clients" or constituents of community corrections—victims and the community—and offer weak choices to criminal justice decision makers, placing the victim and offender in passive roles, but by "holding the offender accountable and responsible—RJ does not simply seek to punish and reintegrate the offender back into the community" (1994: 19). Some offenders need incarceration, and RJ does not substitute for that need. The offender must take responsibility and perform actions to restore that which he or she destroyed—damage to the victim and loss of a sense of security to the community. Instead of rehabilitation, RJ seeks competency development—beyond simply trying to get the offender to give up crime—by providing life skills so that he or she can give back to the victim and community. P/P agencies are in a unique position to implement RJ because of their long-term relationships with offenders (Sinclair, 1994).

RJ can be accomplished by means of victim–offender mediation through which the parties are given a human face: "Facing the person they violated is not easy for most offenders. While it is often an uncomfortable position for offenders, they are given the equally unusual opportunity to display a more human dimension to their character. For many, the opportunity to express remorse in a very direct and personal fashion is important. The mediation process allows victims and offenders to deal with each other as people, oftentimes from the same neighborhood, rather than as stereotypes and objects" (Umbreit, 1994: 9).

The Victim/Offender Reconciliation Program (VORP) is a sentencing alternative popular in a number of communities, including Orange County, California, where it is sponsored by the St. Vincent De Paul Center. VORP handles both juvenile and adult criminal cases often referred by the probation department. Mediators are trained volunteers who receive cases from a case manager, make the initial call to the offender, and meet with that person and his or her parents. If the offender is willing to participate, the mediator calls the victim and arranges a joint meeting during which each tells his or her story, expresses feelings, and discusses what might be done to make things right. After an agreement is

---

A CLOSER LOOK

MESSAGE TO CRIME VICTIMS IN MONTGOMERY COUNTY, OHIO

As the victim of a crime, you have the unique opportunity, if you choose, to become more involved in the justice process as it involves the crime committed against you. The Montgomery County Common Pleas Court makes it possible for victims and offenders to meet in safe and secure settings for the purpose of resolving issues related to the offense.

What if you could meet and talk to the person who committed the crime? What if a neutral third person—a mediator—was in the room to help you talk freely and safely? What if you tell the offender how the crime affected you and others, and what if you worked

out an agreement that seemed fair to you and helped make things right? That is possible when victims and offenders meet.

If property has been lost and restitution is owed, a victim has the opportunity to tell the offender how much is owed and then to work out a repayment agreement. Experience has shown that offenders are more likely to complete their obligations when they "put a face on the crime" and are held accountable for their behavior. It is also important to know that offenders who meet with their victims and reach an agreement are less likely to reoffend.

reached, a contract is drafted and the case returned to the VORP office where a staff person follows up on the execution of the agreed-upon conditions.

In meetings that last about an hour, victims typically ask, "Why me?" or "Were you watching us?" or "Do you have any idea what this has done to me/us/our family?" This process is believed to hold offenders more directly accountable for their actions—they must listen to the human side of the injuries they have caused and must begin to take some responsibility for repairing the damage they caused. In some cases, that might also include offering genuine expressions of remorse (Gehm, 1998).

Victims are most likely to participate in cases involving minor personal crimes and least likely to participate when they are victims of serious personal crime; perpetrators are least likely to agree to participate when convicted of minor personal crimes. Noncompliance with contracts is rare (Niemeyer and Shichor, 1996), and P/P officers are in a position to insist on participation and compliance with contracts.

Although this approach appears appropriate for less serious crimes and offenders, particularly when a prior relationship exists between victim and offender, with more serious crimes and more hardened criminals, RJ appears difficult. When either victim or offender is unwilling to participate or when the offense is too heinous or the suffering too severe, the offender meets with other victims (often through victim advocate organizations) rather than his or her own victim(s) as a step toward assuming responsibility (Zehr, 1990). In some programs, victim–offender discussion occurs through video or written dialogue.

RJ has proven so popular in some jurisdictions that entire systems have been redesigned (Levrant et al., 1999). Minnesota began using RJ in the early 1990s and has an RJ representative and committee of staff and offenders working together on RJ issues in each state correctional facility. Although RJ programs are now quite common at the state and local levels in the United States, they handle mostly property offenses and minor assaults by juveniles (Dzur and Wertheimer, 2002).

In 1994, the Idaho legislature adopted the restorative justice model for its newly created Department of Juvenile Corrections. In Kootenai County, the juvenile probation department uses a trained professional to mediate sessions between victims and offenders. "Through mediation, the victims ask their offenders questions they have struggled to understand, such as: 'Why would you want to harm me or my property? What made you target me over others? How can I be sure that you won't do this again? Should I be afraid of you?'" The department also arranges for restitution and/or community service. "Kids are learning that if caught, they can't just show up at juvenile court, pay a fine and call it a day" (Crowley, 1998: 10).

Begun in 1995, reparative probation, which is Vermont's statewide approach to restorative justice, requires probationers convicted of minor crimes to meet with one of 67 Reparative Citizen Boards made up of volunteers. Typically a board is composed of five or six citizens assisted by a department of corrections staff member. Meetings take place in public libraries, community centers, town halls, or police stations; while meetings are open to the public, attendance by uninvolved persons is not common.

After establishing guilt, courts follow a two-track system: "risk management" for violent and other felony offenders thought to be likely recidivists and the "reparative program" for nonviolent offenders. Reparative probation is part of the reparative program track, and Citizen Reparation Boards (CRBs) typically use sanctions such as community service, victim reparation, and formal and informal apologies. Judges sentence offenders directly to the reparative probation program. If the offender accepts, after sentencing by the court, the reparative services unit (what was previously called a probation agency) conducts an orientation and intake session with the offender to explain the reparative probation program and gathers information about the crime, the offender's history, and the extent of damages or injuries caused. A meeting before a CRB is scheduled, and a reparative team of correctional staff and volunteers prepares an information packet for the CRB that includes the probation order, offense information, criminal record, and any available victim information. This team is also responsible for processing paperwork, identifying and contacting victims, monitoring offender compliance with CRB decisions, and recruiting volunteers for CRB membership.

Offenders are called up, one by one, to answer board members' questions and to determine the requirements for successful completion of the program or to check in with the board. If victims or other affected parties are in attendance—something that happens only in a minority of cases—they are invited to sit in with the board and interact with the offender. An average reparative board session with a single offender lasts between a half-hour and an hour; meetings are usually scheduled at the end of the workday.

At the first meeting, the board deliberates, sometimes in private but frequently with the offender present, on the tasks it will require of the offender, usually allowing the offender 90 days to complete them, but sometimes asking the offender to return after a month or two as a progress check. At the end of the 90-day period, there is a closure meeting where offenders who have successfully completed their tasks are congratulated. The board can return offenders to court for resentencing if they fail to complete their tasks. While one-on-one victim-offender mediation is not a part of the Vermont program, the program does seek to involve victims at board meetings. However, Vermont Department of Corrections staff, in contact with victim advocates, have had to do a good deal of work to get victims involved in CRBs—either in dealing with their own case or in serving on a victim impact panel (Dzur and Wertheimer, 2002; Kurki, 1999; Olson and Dzur, 2003).

Some observers urge caution in adopting the RJ model. They note that liberals and conservatives also supported determinate sentencing:

> The restorative justice movement is reminiscent of the determinate sentencing movement of the 1970s. Both restorative justice and determinate sentencing emerged from contrasting ideologies posited by liberals and conservatives.... Liberals sought to limit discretion and create sentencing practices that were fairer while conservatives supported determinate sentencing as a means of controlling crime with harsher sentences that would deter crime and incapacitate criminals. But the conservative view prevailed. RJ, instead of reducing crime through reconciliation, could simply become another variation of the "get tough on crime" approach. This is particularly troubling because RJ programs typically target low-risk offenders. (Levrant et al., 1999: 7)

▶ Community Justice

Community justice refers to a method of crime reduction and crime prevention based on partnerships within communities. Some refer to the approach as "environmental corrections" (e.g., Cullen, Williams, and Wright, 2002); others use the metaphor of **broken windows supervision** to emphasize this linkage between law enforcement and the community (e.g., Reinventing Probation Council [RPC], 2000; Rhine, 2002) that was first applied to policing (Wilson and Kelling, 1982). Whatever the term, the model stresses that P/P "must move well beyond the management of individual caseloads and engage the community in the business of community supervision" (Rhine, 2002: 39). This neighborhood-based supervision abandons the traditional 9 to 5, Monday through Friday, approach typical of many P/P agency operations; instead, offenders who are deemed a potential threat to community safety are subject to surveillance and control by officers who have available a continuum of both sanctions and treatments designed to maintain public safety and to hold offenders accountable for all violating behaviors

> **Key Fact**
>
> Community or "broken windows" justice uses neighborhood-based offices for proactive offender supervision and incorporates close working relationships with the police.

(Rhine, 2002; RPC, 2000). There is proactive pursuit of absconders as part of a program of offender accountability.

The focus is on crime fighting policies that "emphasize proactive, problem-solving practices intended to prevent, control, reduce and repair crime's harm" and that "create and contribute to healthy, safe, vibrant and just communities and to improve citizens' quality of life" (RPC, 2000: 16). Regardless of the name, notes Joan Petersilia (2003), the key components of this approach are the same: It is a "full-service" model that stresses "activist supervision" by strengthening linkages with law enforcement and the community. Officers aggressively patrol those neighborhoods of urban America with high concentrations of high-risk offenders—areas characterized by poverty and minority populations (Travis, Davis, and Lawrence, 2012). Working out of local offices—community centers, municipal offices, public housing projects, police precincts, mental health centers, and local storefronts—they deliberately maintain a high profile, interacting with the police, human services agencies, community groups, and businesspeople. In Bell and Lampasas Counties in Texas, high-risk offenders are visited by P/Ps wearing official uniform jackets and shirts and driving marked department vehicles (Jermstad, 2002). "By widening the community net, [P/P officers] reduce the anonymity that offenders all too often enjoy while they are under supervision" (RPC, 2000: 21). Supervision officers attend neighborhood meetings and participate in local crime prevention activities. They facilitate the formation of task forces that include representatives from human services and the religious community, in addition to law enforcement, for the purpose of joint staffing and shared accountability for curtailing crime.

Many of Connecticut's towns and cities have adopted community policing as a law enforcement strategy. Partnerships have been formed with several of Connecticut's largest cities to incorporate parole officers into their community policing programs. As a result, many parole-related activities are based in neighborhood substations, where caseloads can be assigned geographically to coincide with these local precincts. In addition, parole officers often team up with local police on routine patrols. These partnerships reaffirm the link between parole and law enforcement and increase the efficiency of parole supervision by enhancing the parole officer's knowledge of neighborhood crime concerns while enhancing the police officer's knowledge of Connecticut's parole system.

Community supervision officers can be an important source of intelligence for the police, and police/parole officer collaboration can be important for the control of crime. When I was state parole officer, New York City was divided into territories for purposes of supervision with boundaries drawn to coincide with those of specific police precincts. Parole officers visited detective units in their territory to exchange information about parolees residing in their district. Police aided the supervision process by reporting offenders observed violating conditions of parole that were not criminal per se, associating with known criminals, for example. Parole officers aided the police, for example, by reviewing modus operandi and descriptions of perpetrators for leads in solving specific crimes. Probation and parole officers are recipients of information from clients and their families that can be of use to the police.

To promote interagency cooperation and understanding, P/P and law enforcement agencies may have personnel assigned a liaison role, and P/P representatives make presentations at police training facilities or at patrol roll call. There may be regular meetings between staff from law enforcement and P/P agencies on matters of mutual interest. In some jurisdictions, P/P officers have offices in police precincts and police officers are assigned to P/P offices.

Obvious benefits also have potential drawbacks: use of P/P clients as informants, encouraging them to interact with active criminals in violation of supervision rules; or the use of P/P authority by police to conduct warrantless searches that can undermine the rehabilitation role of P/P (Jannetta and Lachman, 2011).

▼

▶ Project HOPE

Hawaii's Opportunity Probation with Enforcement (HOPE) began in 2004 and has been widely acclaimed and copied in other jurisdictions. HOPE begins when a sentencing judge warns offenders enrolled in the program that any supervision violations will result in an immediate, brief jail stay—swift and certain punishment. The program enrolls more than 1,500 substance-abusing probationers who are subjected to close monitoring, for example, randomized drug testing six times a month, and swift reaction to every detected violation: The probationer is taken into custody by deputy sheriffs and the PO submits a motion for probation modification, a two-page, fill-in-the-blanks form that is faxed to a judge. Courtroom proceedings average less than seven minutes and are typically done in a group rather than individually. Sanctions are brief periods in jail: a few days for the first violation, escalating with each subsequent violation. Mandated treatment is imposed only on high-violation offenders. The program cost is about $1,400 a year above the cost of routine probation, but the cost is more than paid for by reduced incarceration (Hawken and Kleiman, 2009). Outcome research in Hawaii and several experimental sites revealed outstanding results: 55 percent less likely to be arrested for a new crime than control groups.

HOPE success is limited to substance abusers, "low hanging fruit" whose violations are relatively easy to detect during an office visit. Swift and certain punishment for persons convicted of crimes such as burglary, sex offenses, and the gang involved, requires field monitoring and investigation, and an ability to expeditiously respond to detected violations. Absconders from the program, about 10 percent of HOPE probationers, typically remain at-large until arrested for a new crime: Probation (and parole) officers in Hawaii are not peace officers, and law enforcement agencies show little interest in expending resources for HOPE warrant enforcement (Dooley, 2011).

▶ The Probation Officer and Problem-Solving Courts

In the adult criminal justice system, the probation officer has generally had a secondary role; this changed with the growth of problem-solving courts (PSC). The common element of these nonadversarial courts is ongoing judicial involvement with a rehabilitative focus and collaboration between judge, prosecutor, defense counsel, and probation officer. While the judge retains power over the final disposition, the PO is typically the only court employee with rehabilitation-relevant education, training, and experience (Rudes and Portillo, 2012). Indeed, a quasi-social service role for a judge involves areas beyond their competence, a criticism of PSC. While there are about a dozen types of PSC, the most prevalent is the drug court.

▶ Drug Court

When the "war on drugs" policy of the 1980s (see Abadinsky, 2014) exacerbated already-overcrowded prisons and court dockets, new methods were devised to divert drug abusers from the criminal justice process and into treatment (Gebelein, 2000). Judges increasingly made participation in drug treatment a condition of probation, as did parole boards. In 1989, treatment and punishment were melded in the form of a specialized "drug court" in Miami, Florida (Boldt, 1998). This high-volume court expanded traditional drug-defendant diversion programs by offering a year or more of court-run treatment; defendants who complete this option have their criminal cases dismissed. Between 1991 and 1993, Miami influenced officials in more than twenty other jurisdictions to establish drug courts (*The Drug Court Movement*, 1995). The 1994 Crime Act provides federal funding to establish or expand drug courts, and by the end of 1999 they were available in almost every state. In 1994, the National Association of Drug Court Professionals (NADCP) was formed by about a half-dozen judges; five years later, its annual training meeting drew 3,000 participants (Gebelein, 2000). Today, there are about 2,500 drug courts.

Drug Court is a special docket or calendar in which a judge serves as the leader of an interdisciplinary team. Participants are drug- and alcohol-dependent defendants charged with drug-related offenses such as possession of a controlled substance, or other offenses that are determined to have been caused or influenced by their drug use. They remain under court supervision for 12 to 18 months, although some participants may need more time to satisfy the criteria for program completion.

Participants undergo random drug and alcohol testing and attend regular status hearings in court, during which the judge reviews their progress and may impose a range of positive or negative consequences ranging from praise to brief jail detention.

Program completion is referred to as "graduation," and there is a graduation ceremony that resembles that of public school. To graduate, "participants must demonstrate continuous abstinence from drugs and alcohol for a substantial period of time (often six months or longer), satisfy treatment and supervision conditions, pay applicable fines or fees, and complete community service or make restitution to victims" (Huddleston and Marlowe, 2011: 7).

Drug courts may be *preplea* in which defendants enter the program as part of a pretrial diversion agreement with the understanding that charges will be dropped after successful completion. Program failure can result in resuming case processing. As a condition of entry into a drug court program *postplea* requires a defendant to plead guilty. This can be held in abeyance and vacated upon successful program completion.

▶ Interstate Compacts

The federal Crime Control Consent Act of 1934 authorized two or more states to enter into **interstate compacts**, agreements for cooperative efforts and mutual assistance in the prevention of crime. Pursuant to this legislation, in 1937 a group of states signed the Interstate Compact for the Supervision of Probationers and Parolees, which enabled them to serve as each other's agents in the supervision of persons on P/P. Before the establishment of the compact, thousands of convicted felons were permitted to leave the state of conviction with no verified or approved plan of residence and employment in the receiving state. On occasion, dangerous criminals were released by states and permitted (sometimes forced into "internal exile" or "sundown probation or parole") to enter other states without any provision for supervision or even the knowledge of any official body in the receiving state.

By 1951, all 48 (and now all 50) states and the District of Columbia, Puerto Rico, and the Virgin Islands were signatories of the compact. In 1998, the National Institute of Corrections, following several public hearings and discussion among state officials and corrections policy experts, revised the compact to reflect a modern administrative structure with modern data collection and information sharing system. By 2002, the new Interstate Compact for Adult Offender Supervision reached its threshold of 35 states, and later that year the first meeting of the new Interstate Commission took place with more than 45 states and territories represented.

The compact provides a system whereby a person under supervision can leave the state of conviction—the **sending state**—and proceed to another state for employment, family, or health reasons, and at the same time it guarantees that the **receiving state** will provide supervision of the offender. The state of original jurisdiction (where the

INTERSTATE COMPACT FOR ADULT OFFENDER SUPERVISION

It is the purpose of this compact and the Interstate Commission created under this compact, through means of joint and cooperative action among the compacting states, to provide the framework for the promotion of public safety and protect the rights of victims through the control and regulation of the interstate movement of offenders in the community; to provide for the effective tracking, supervision, and rehabilitation of these offenders by the sending and receiving states; and to equitably distribute the costs, benefits, and obligations of the compact among the compacting states.

In addition, this compact will create an Interstate Commission that will establish uniform procedures to manage the movement between states of adults placed under community supervision and released to the community under the jurisdiction of courts, paroling authorities, corrections, or other criminal justice agencies that will adopt rules to achieve the purpose of this compact; ensure an opportunity for input and timely notice to victims and to jurisdictions where defined offenders are authorized to travel or to relocate across state lines; establish a system of uniform data collection, access to information on active cases by authorized criminal justice officials, and regular reporting of compact activities to heads of state councils, state executive, judicial, and legislative branches and criminal justice administrators; monitor compliance with rules governing interstate movement of offenders and initiate interventions to address and correct noncompliance; and coordinate training and education regarding regulations of interstate movement of offenders for officials involved in that activity.

The compacting states recognize that there is no right of any offender to live in another state and that duly accredited officers of a sending state may at all times enter a receiving state and there apprehend and retake any offender under supervision subject to the provisions of this compact and by-laws and rules adopted under the compact.

---

offender was convicted) retains authority over the probationer or parolee and is kept advised of his or her whereabouts and activities by the receiving state. The compact also provides for P/P violators to be returned without the need to resort to time-consuming extradition procedures. Because it is based on a federal statute and governed by the substantive law of contracts, the interstate compact supersedes state law. (The U.S. Supreme Court has never ruled on the constitutionality of the compact, having denied *certiorari* whenever the issue has been raised.) The Interstate Commission reports that in 2012 there were more than 115,000 offenders under supervision on an interstate compact transfer.

The compact provides a systematic method for supervision purposes for the receiving state to verify and approve a plan of residence and employment or education before a probationer or parolee is permitted to enter the state. After a probationer or parolee is accepted for supervision by the receiving state, the latter sends quarterly "progress and conduct" reports to the sending state.

The compact also regulates interstate travel by probationers and parolees. Each state issues a travel pass, a copy of which is sent to the interstate administrator, who notifies the receiving state of the impending visit. The Association of Administrators of the Interstate formed in 1946, now known as the Interstate Commission for Adult Offender Supervision (ICAOS), has a designated commissioner from each state who is that state's compact administrator. The ICAOS meets at least once per year, prepares uniform reports and procedures, and attempts to reconcile any difficulties that have arisen with respect to the compact.

Some problems remain. One is the difference in P/P administration. Parole is an executive function with statewide procedures, so interstate activities are centralized through a

> **Key Fact**
> The interstate compact provides for the orderly visit or transfer of an offender from one state to another.

compact administrator in each state. Probation, however, can be administered on a county basis and may lack statewide coordination. The local autonomy that often exists in the judicial branch can cause difficulties in using and administering the pact in probation cases; in such cases, the probation officer of the sending state may need to make direct contact and arrangements with the court of the receiving jurisdiction.

States sometimes allow probationers or parolees to go to a receiving state under the guise of a visit when the offender's intentions are to stay permanently. The receiving state is then contacted by the sending state to investigate "with a view toward accepting supervision." The receiving state is faced with a *fait accompli*. These types of situations may make a receiving state reluctant to accept future cases from a particular sending state, a situation that needs to be reconciled at the compact administrator's (ICAOS) meeting.

Another problem results from different approaches to supervision in various states. One state may exercise close control and require strict enforcement of the conditions of probation or parole, while another state may be more flexible or may simply be incapable of close supervision and control because of the size of its caseloads. When a "strict" state notifies a "permissive" sending state that one of its probationers or parolees is in violation, the sending state may not consider it serious and may leave the offender in the receiving state with a request that it continue supervision. In some cases, the sending state may simply not want to incur the expense of transporting the violator back to one of its state prisons, which are probably overcrowded anyway. The receiving state has two options: continue to supervise an offender it considers in violation or discontinue supervision and leave the offender without any controls at all. At its 2010 meeting, ICAOS passed an amendment requiring sending states to retake all violent offenders who were in violation of the rules of P/P supervision. "As a result, some jurisdictions are terminating supervision to avoid the cost of retaking the offender. This is particularly troubling given the often violent and non-compliant nature of the offenders in question" (ICAOS, 2012: 13).

The **Interstate Compact for Juveniles** (ICJ) governs interstate matters pertaining to juvenile delinquents and **status offenders**—persons whose behavior would not be a criminal offense if they were adults, such as habitual truants and runaways. The Compact on the Placement of Children covers interstate transfers of dependent or neglected youth. As of 2012, 49 states and the District of Columbia are signatories of the ICJ.

In addition to providing for cooperative supervision, the ICJ provides for the return of juvenile P/P absconders and escapees as well as runaways without the need for formal extradition. The Interstate Commission for Juveniles is responsible for developing rules and regulations that govern the administration of the compact, and they are binding on the states. The annual number of cases involving interstate juvenile matters exceeds 20,000.

In contrast to the compact for adults, the juvenile compact has mandatory and discretionary cases. Thus, the receiving state must accept supervision whenever a juvenile will be returning to his or her legal parents or guardians and has no custodial parent or legal guardian remaining in the sending state, and each state must accept its own residents. Other cases are discretionary. When supervision has been arranged, the sending state retains jurisdiction and the receiving state becomes the agent of the sending state. Because of variations in state laws regarding juveniles, a person who is a juvenile in one state may be considered an adult in another. The compact overcomes this problem by applying the law of the state from which the juvenile has run away or from which he or she was sent for supervision: If a person is a juvenile under law in his or her home state, he or she is a juvenile to all member states. And the receiving state may not treat transferred juveniles any differently than it would treat its own juvenile.

▼

Summary

- Substance abuse is the single most frequently encountered problem across P/P populations.
- Cocaine detoxification presents serious problems because of the patient's craving for the substance and the extreme depression during the early days of abstinence.
- Heroin addicts may undergo detoxification simply to reduce their tolerance and thus the cost of drug use.
- Methadone is used to treat addicts because it can be administered orally, its effects last longer, and the high it produces is less dramatic compared to that produced by heroin.
- Behavior modification can be used with drug antagonists, such as Antabuse, for alcohol abusers.
- The therapeutic community is a residential, self-help, drug-free treatment program.
- Chemical dependency programs are inpatient, costly, focused on persons having medical insurance, and provide little or no aftercare.
- Alcoholics Anonymous is a self-help group approach that requires acknowledgment of being an alcoholic.
- Drug testing cannot discern the casual user from a chronic one, and there are complications inherent in collecting, storing, and shipping urine samples.
- HIV/AIDS is higher among the P/P population than general public, and confidentiality requirements can place P/P officers in a quandary.
- There are a number of different types of sex offenders, but those who prey on children present significant risk factors to the community and supervision problems for the P/P officer.
- Females are generally high-need/low-risk offenders less likely to receive needed attention.
- Intoxicated drivers kill many more people than those who commit deliberate homicide.
- Restorative justice changes the focus of criminal justice from perpetrator to victim.
- Community justice uses neighborhood-based offices for proactive offender supervision.
- The interstate compact provides for the orderly visit or transfer of an offender from one state to another.

Key Terms

agonists *231*
Antabuse *233*
antagonists *231*
aversive stimuli *233*
behavior modification *232*
"broken windows" supervision *253*
buprenorphine *232*
chemical dependency programs *235*

community justice *253*
detoxification *230*
interstate compact *256*
methadone *231*
naltrexone *232*
plethysmography *245*
polygraph *243*
receiving state *256*

restitution *252*
restorative justice *250*
sending state *256*
status offender *258*
therapeutic community *234*
tolerance *231*
twelve-step program *236*

Internet Connections

Addictions page: **well.com/user/woa**

Alcoholics Anonymous: **alcoholics-anonymous.org**

American Probation and Parole Association: **www.appa-net.org**

Center for Community Corrections: **communitycorrectionsworks.org**

Center for Sex Offender Management: **csom.org**

Federal Resource Center on Children and Families of the Incarcerated: **fcnetwork.org**

International Community Corrections Association: **iccaweb.org**

Interstate Commission for Adult Offender Supervision: **interstatecompact.org**

Interstate Commission for Juveniles: **juvenilecompact.org**

Interstate Compact guide: **www.nicic.org/resources/topics/InterstateCompact.aspx**

National Institute on Drug Abuse: **www.nida.nih.gov**

Smart Recovery: **smartrecovery.org**

Office of Sex Offender Sentencing, Apprehending, Registering, and Tracking: **ojp.usdoj.gov/smart**

Women's Prison Association: **wpaonline.org**

Review Questions

1. What is the single most frequently encountered problem is across P/P populations?
2. Why does cocaine detoxification a serious problem during the early days of abstinence?
3. Why would heroin addicts inject heroin within a few minutes or hours after they complete detoxification?
4. What are the advantages of using methadone to treat heroin addicts?
5. How are drug antagonists used in behavior modification?
6. What are the characteristics of a therapeutic community?
7. How does it differ from a chemical dependency program?
8. What are the essential elements of Alcoholics Anonymous?
9. What are the problems inherent in drug testing?
10. How are legal issues concerning confidentiality of HIV/AIDS a burden for P/P officers?
11. What are the problems for P/P officers supervising sex offenders?
12. What are the difficulties encountered in supervising female offenders?
13. Why are intoxicated drivers such an important category for P/P?
14. What is the focus of restorative justice?
15. How does community justice in P/P differ from traditional supervision?
16. Why is the probation officer a key player in problem-solving courts?
17. What are the features of Project HOPE?
18. What are the purposes of the Interstate Compact for Adult Supervision?

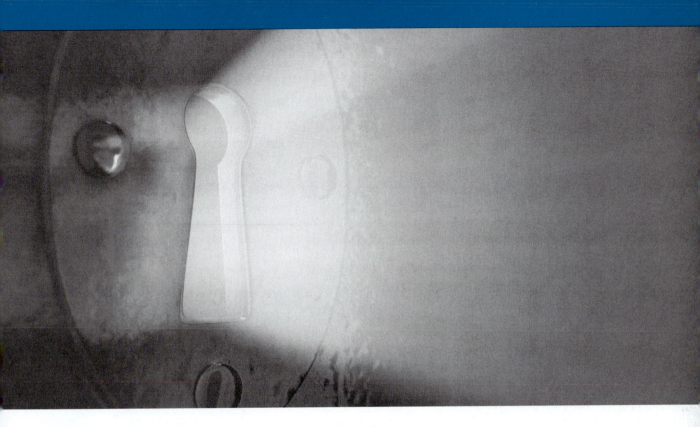

11 Probation and Parole in Juvenile Justice

LEARNING OBJECTIVES

This chapter will enable the student to:

1 *Explain the role of the probation officer (PO) in juvenile justice.*

2 *Discuss the historical development of the juvenile court.*

3 *Understand the legal concept of* parens patriae *as it relates to the juvenile court.*

4 *Appreciate the controversial role of the child-saving movement in establishing the juvenile court.*

5 *Understand the controversy over status offenders.*

6 *Discuss how the juvenile court embodied the positivist view.*

7 *State why a juvenile court should not impose punishment.*

8 *Appreciate the issues in the case of* In re Gault.

9 *State the four types of cases handled by a juvenile court.*

10 *Understand the critical importance of juvenile court intake.*

11 *Explain the use of unofficial probation in juvenile court.*

12 *Appreciate the role of a guardian* ad litem.

13 *Discuss those aspects of the juvenile court process that are parallel to those of the adult criminal court.*

14 *Appreciate how the distinction between the adult criminal court and the juvenile court has blurred.*

15 *Explain why being a judge in juvenile court is more difficult than being judge in adult court.*

16 *State what is meant by the concept of "least restrictive alternative."*

17 *Distinguish between the variety of treatment alternatives for juveniles adjudicated in juvenile court.*

18 *Explain the ways juvenile probation and aftercare is provided in different states.*

In contrast to the secondary role of the probation officer (PO) in adult criminal justice, the PO is at the center of juvenile justice. This chapter will examine the juvenile court, the history and unique qualities of juvenile justice, the PO's role, and pertinent legal decisions.

▶ History of the Juvenile Court

The system of justice used for juveniles in the United States is based on a philosophy radically different from the one on which the adult criminal justice system rests. Before we can examine the services provided by a probation agency to the juvenile court, it is necessary to understand the history and philosophy of this unique institution.

In Europe, from Roman times to the late eighteenth century, children were routinely abandoned by their parents; the classical philosopher Rousseau, for example, boasted of abandoning five of his children to foundling homes (Boswell, 1989). Abandoned children were subjected to extreme levels of deprivation and exploitation. English common law considered children as chattel, and a rather indifferent attitude toward children became characteristic of America, where they became creatures of exploitation. Indeed, the contemporary American concern with the problem of child abuse stands in marked contrast to our earlier history. Child labor remained an important part of economic life into the twentieth century. Children of the poor labored in mines (where their size was an advantage), mills, and factories with unsanitary and unsafe conditions.

The Supreme Court reflected the prevailing belief in *laissez-faire* capitalism and would not intervene—statutes prohibiting children younger than 12 years from employment and those limiting the workday of youngsters older than 12 years to 10 hours were ruled unconstitutional or were routinely disobeyed. Increased immigration, industrialization, and urbanization drastically altered American society. The 10- and 12-hour workday left many children without parental supervision, and family disorganization became widespread. Many children lived in the streets where they encountered the disorder and rampant vice of the urban environment.

In the early days of colonial America, the family remained the mainstay of social control, "although by 1700 the family's inability to accommodate and discipline its young was becoming more apparent" (Mennel, 1973: xxii). Numerous laws began to appear that threatened parents for failing to properly discipline their children. Furthermore, the British practice of transporting wayward young to America for indenture, which often involved neglect, cruelty, and immorality, left many youngsters without supervision as they fled from these onerous circumstances. By the end of the eighteenth century, society began to realize that a "system of social control would have to be developed apart from the family which would discipline homeless, vagrant, and destitute children—the offspring of the poor" (Mennel, 1973: xxvii). This need led to the rise of **houses of refuge**.

▶ Houses of Refuge and Orphan Asylums

In 1817, the Society for the Prevention of Pauperism was established in response to the problem of troubled and troublesome children; and in 1824, it was renamed the Society for the Reformation of Juvenile Delinquency. The society conducted campaigns against the "corrupting" influence of taverns and theaters and opposed the use of jails to house children. Their efforts led to the establishment of houses of refuge, also called houses of reformation or reform schools (Krisberg, 1988).

The first house of refuge opened in New York in 1825 and was quickly followed by one in Boston (1826) and another in Philadelphia (1828). These institutions provided housing and care for troublesome children who might otherwise be left in the streets or, if their behavior brought them into serious conflict with the law, sent to jail or prison. The house of refuge was used "not only for the less serious juvenile criminal, but for runaways, disobedient children or vagrants" (Empey, 1979: 25–26). Orphan asylums were used for abandoned or orphaned children, for the children of women without husbands, or for children whose parents were deemed unfit. Both institutions "were established to inculcate children with the values of hard work, orderliness, and subordination and thereby ensure their future good behavior" (Mennel, 1973: 8). To achieve these ends, however, discipline and punishments were often brutal, and the house of refuge in New York experienced group escapes and inmate uprisings.

Although these institutions were operated by private charities, their public charters included the first statutory definitions of juvenile delinquency and provided the basis for state intervention into the lives of children who were neglected or in need of supervision, in addition to those youngsters who had committed crimes (Walker, 1980). In these charters was embodied a "medieval English doctrine of nebulous origin and meaning" (Schlossman, 1977: 8) known as **parens patriae**, originally referring to the feudal duties of the overlord to his vassals and later the legal duties of the monarch toward his or her subjects who were in need of care, particularly children and the mentally incompetent. In its original form, *parens patriae* provided the Crown with the authority to administer the estates of landed orphans (Sutton, 1988).

"With the independence of the American colonies and the transplanting of the English common-law system, the state in this country has taken the place of the crown as the *parens patriae* of all minors" (Lou, 1972: 4). This concept gave almost complete authority over children to the state—the Bill of Rights simply did not apply to children (*Ex parte Crouse*, 4 Wharton 9, 1838)—and *parens patriae* became the legal basis for the juvenile court. Although this concept has become identified with the rehabilitation of wayward juveniles, it originally applied only to dependent children.

> **Key Fact**
>
> *Parens patriae* provided the legal basis for the juvenile court.

▶ Child-Saving Movement

As immigration, industrialization, and urbanization continued, the fearful image of masses of undisciplined and uneducated children gave rise to the **child-saving movement**. Led by upper-class women of earlier American ancestry, the child savers were influenced by the nativist prejudices of their day as well as by social Darwinism (see Chapter 1). Natural selection resulted in an inferior underclass in need of control but not of aid in the sense of the modern social welfare state. Something had to be done to save these children from an environment that would only lead them into vice and crime—if not rebellion—and cause them to be the progenitors of the same. Reforming juvenile justice became the task of women who "were generally well-educated, widely-traveled, and had access to political and financial resources" (Platt, 1974: 77). The juvenile court was the result of their efforts, although controversy surrounds the interests and motivations of the child savers (Empey, 1979; Platt, 1974).

▶ Emergence of the Juvenile Court

Although juveniles might be sent to a house of refuge, an orphan asylum, or a reformatory—there was confusion over which children should be relegated to which institution—they could be arrested, detained, and tried like any adult accused of a crime. Children older (and sometimes younger) than 14 years of age were routinely prosecuted as adults and punished as adults. Although some modifications of the trial process with respect to juveniles occurred as early as 1869, it was the Illinois Juvenile Court Act of 1899 that established the first law creating a special comprehensive court for juveniles. Consistent with the concept of *parens patriae*, the juvenile court was given jurisdiction over neglected and dependent children in addition to children who were delinquent (e.g., persons younger than 16 years of age who had violated the law) and those whose behavior was troublesome but not criminal (e.g., truants, runaways). Nondelinquents in whom the court was interested because of their behavior became known as **status offenders**.

Within 25 years of the Illinois Juvenile Court Act, every state but one had adopted legislation providing for one or all the features of a juvenile court organization (Lenroot and Lundberg, 1925). A book originally published in 1927, *Juvenile Courts in the United States*, provides insight into the court's prevailing concepts (Lou, 1972: 2):

> These principles upon which the juvenile court acts are radically different from those of the criminal courts. In place of judicial tribunals, restrained by antiquated procedure, saturated in an atmosphere of hostility, trying cases for determining guilt and inflicting punishment according to inflexible rules of law, we have now juvenile courts, in which the relations of the child to his parents or other adults and to the state or society are defined and are adjusted summarily according to the scientific findings about the child and his environments. In place of magistrates, limited by the outgrown custom and compelled to walk in the paths fixed by the law of the realm, we have now socially-minded judges, who hear and adjust cases according not to rigid rules of law but to what the interests of society and the interests of the child or good conscience demand. In the place of juries, prosecutors, and lawyers, trained in the old conception of law and staging dramatically, but often amusingly, legal battles, as the necessary paraphernalia of a criminal court, we have now probation officers, physicians, psychologists, and psychiatrists, who search for the social, physiological, psychological, and mental backgrounds of the child in order to arrive at reasonable and just solutions of individual cases.

Lou's statement clearly embodies the positivist view—or critics might say, positivism run amok—with the child being denied the most basic due process rights. The unstructured and informal system of juvenile justice used in Illinois quickly became the standard as juvenile courts were established throughout the United States. Differences between the adult criminal court and the juvenile court extended even to the terminology used:

Adult Criminal Court	Juvenile Court
Defendant	Respondent
Charges/indictment	Petition
Arraignment	Hearing
Prosecution/trial	Adjudication
Verdict	Finding
Sentence	Disposition
Imprisonment	Commitment
Inmate/prisoner	Resident
Parole	Aftercare

Consistent with the concept of *parens patriae*, the terminology reflects a nonpunitive approach to dealing with troubled and troublesome children (Figure 11.1). Critics often decry the lack of sufficient punishment inflicted in the juvenile court. Such comments indicate a complete misunderstanding of this court, which should *not* punish. Although the concept of *parens patriae* is paternalistic and not inconsistent with the concept of punishment (Weisheit and Alexander, 1988), the use of a punitive approach in juvenile court would make it simply a criminal court for children and, therefore, without grounding as a separate system of justice. Thus, although one could logically argue for abolishing the juvenile court, a juvenile court that imposes punishment has no basis in American history or in logic.

Adoptions: custody hearings, which grant custody to the prospective adoptive parents, and adoption hearings, which grant final adoption

Adjudication: (1) hearing at which the minor enters a plea to one or more allegations of the petition and at which the judge pronounces the child a delinquent minor; (2) contested hearing (trial) at which witnesses testify and evidence is presented at the conclusion of which the judge determines whether or not the child has been found to be a delinquent minor

Advisory: hearing for youth paper-referred to court at which the petition detailing the delinquent allegations is presented, a determination is made whether the minor qualifies for appointed counsel, and a trial review date is selected

Detention: hearing held within 24 hours of the filing of a petition for a detained youth at which counsel is appointed and the court considers whether the minor should be detained or released from custody

Disposition: hearing, analogous to the adult court sentencing, for which the probation officer prepares a comprehensive report of the adjudicated child's background and at which the judge determines what action(s) the court will take

Restitution: hearing at which the judge determines what restitution to a victim the child must pay to satisfy the conditions of probation

Review: review of the child's adherence to probation conditions to consider revising these conditions or terminating the minor from probation

Revocation: hearing to determine if the minor has violated probation by failure to adhere to the conditions of probation or by committing a delinquent act

Transfer: hearing to determine if the juvenile court should retain jurisdiction for the allegations set forth in the petition or whether the matter should be transferred for prosecution to the adult court

Trial review: hearing at which the child requests that the charges be set for a contested adjudication (trial) or at which he/she admits one or more allegations of the pending petition

Source: Pima County, Arizona, Juvenile Court.

FIGURE 11.1   Guide to the Most Common Hearings Held at the Juvenile Court

Because of the noncriminal approach, the usual safeguards of due process that were applicable in criminal courts were absent in juvenile court proceedings: rights to counsel, to confront and cross-examine adverse witnesses, and to avoid self-incrimination. Because the focus of the juvenile court was on providing help, procedures were often informal (if not vague), and the judge, with the assistance of the probation officer, was given broad powers over young persons.

▶ Legal Decisions

The juvenile court continued to operate for many decades without attention or adherence to due process requirements or scrutiny by the judicial branch of government. This ended during the latter half of the 1960s, an era marked by the judicial activism of the Supreme Court with respect to issues involving civil liberties. Because of the central role of the PO in the court, juvenile cases decided by the Supreme Court affected probation services.

In 1966, the Supreme Court reviewed the operations of the juvenile court in *Kent v. United States* (383 U.S. 541). While on probation, Morris Kent, 16 years of age, was convicted in criminal court of raping a woman in her Washington, D.C., apartment and sentenced to a prison term of 30 to 90 years. In juvenile court, he would have faced a maximum term of incarceration until 21 years of age. In accord with existing federal statutes, the case had first been referred to the juvenile court, where over the objections of defense counsel, jurisdiction was waived to the criminal court. On appeal, in a 5–4 decision, the Supreme Court ruled that before a juvenile referred to juvenile court can be tried in criminal court, he or she is entitled to a waiver hearing with counsel, and if jurisdiction is waived the juvenile court judge must state the reasons.

Kent is significant for changing the Supreme Court's hands-off policy that had been in existence since the juvenile court was established in 1899. In its decision, the Court expressed concern over the lack of due process in the juvenile court:

> Although there can be no doubt of the original laudable purpose of juvenile courts, studies and critiques in more recent years raise serious questions as to whether actual performance measures well enough against theoretical purpose to make tolerable the immunity of the process from the reach of constitutional guarantees applicable to adults. There is much evidence that some juvenile courts, including that of the District of Columbia, lack the personnel, facilities, and techniques to perform adequately as representatives of the state in a *parens patriae* capacity, at least with respect to children charged with law violation. There is evidence, in fact, that there may be grounds for concern that the child receives the worst of both worlds, that he gets neither the protections accorded to adults nor the solicitous care and regenerative treatment postulated for children.

The following year, the Supreme Court addressed the issue of due process in the juvenile court (*In re Gault*, 387 U.S. 1, 1967). Gerald Gault, aged 15, had been arrested by the police on the complaint of a female neighbor that he and his friend had made lewd and indecent remarks over the telephone. Gerald's parents were not notified of their son's arrest and did not receive a copy of the juvenile court petition charging him with delinquency. Furthermore, Gerald was not advised of his right to remain silent or his right to counsel. The complainant was not present at the hearing, nor did the judge speak with her on any occasion. Instead, Gerald's mother and two POs appeared before the juvenile court judge in his chambers. No one was sworn, nor was a transcript made of the proceeding.

At a second hearing, a conflict occurred concerning what had transpired at the first hearing. For the second time, the complainant was not present; the judge ruled that her presence was not necessary. Gerald was declared to be a juvenile delinquent and committed to a state training school for a maximum of 6 years, until he turned 21. Had Gerald been an adult (older than 18 years of age), the maximum sentence would have been a fine of not more than $50 or imprisonment for not more than 60 days. Because no appeal in juvenile court cases was permitted under Arizona law, Gerald's parents filed a petition of *habeas corpus* (a legal challenge to custody), which, although it was dismissed by the state courts, was granted (*certiorari*) a hearing by the U.S. Supreme Court.

In its decision, the Supreme Court acknowledged the helping—*noncriminal*—philosophy on which the juvenile court is based. But the decision also revealed a sense of outrage over what had transpired in the case of Gerald Gault: "Under our Constitution, the condition of being a boy does not justify a kangaroo court." The justices held that a child cannot be denied reasonable standards of due process and that he or she is entitled to

- Written notice of the charges
- Right to counsel
- Protection against self-incrimination
- Right to confront and cross-examine witnesses
- Right to have written transcripts and appellate review

Because of the noncriminal nature of the juvenile court, instead of the proof beyond a reasonable doubt standard used in criminal trials, the level of evidence for a finding of delinquency was typically that used in a civil proceeding: preponderance of the evidence. In 1970, in the case of *In re Winship* (397 U.S. 358) the Supreme Court noted: "The reasonable-doubt standard plays a vital role in the American scheme of criminal procedure. It is a prime instrument for reducing the risk of conviction resting on factual error." Accordingly, the Court ruled that "the constitutional safeguard of proof beyond a reasonable doubt is as much required during the adjudicatory stage of a delinquency proceeding as are those constitutional safeguards applied in *Gault*."

The right to an impartial jury in criminal trials is guaranteed by the Sixth Amendment, but the Supreme Court decided against granting this right in juvenile proceedings. In the 1971 decision of *McKeiver v. Pennsylvania* (403 U.S. 528), the Court ruled that a juvenile court proceeding is not a criminal prosecution within the meaning of the Sixth Amendment. Accordingly, the Court held that the "imposition of the jury trial on the juvenile court system would not strengthen greatly, if at all, the fact-finding function." Nevertheless, more than 15 states permit the use of juries in juvenile court.

In 1975, the Supreme Court was faced with the question of double jeopardy—which is prohibited by the Fifth Amendment—with respect to the juvenile court. *Breed v. Jones* (421 U.S. 519) concerned a 17-year-old who was the subject of a juvenile court petition alleging armed robbery. After taking testimony from two prosecution witnesses and the respondent, the juvenile court judge sustained the petition. At a subsequent disposition hearing, the judge ruled that the respondent was not "amenable to the care, treatment and training program available through the facilities of the juvenile court" and ordered that Breed be prosecuted as an adult. The youngster was subsequently found guilty of armed robbery in criminal (superior) court, which led the Supreme Court to rule: "We hold that the prosecution of respondent in Superior Court, after an adjudicatory proceeding in Juvenile Court, violated that Double Jeopardy Clause of the Fifth Amendment, as applied to the States through the Fourteenth Amendment."

In 1984, the Supreme Court (*Schall v. Martin*, 467 U.S. 253), in a strong affirmation of the concept of *parens patriae*, upheld the constitutionality of the preventive detention of juveniles. *Schall* involved a New York statute that authorizes the detention of juveniles arrested for an offense when there is "serious risk" that, before trial, the juvenile may commit an act that, if committed by an adult, would constitute a crime. In this case Gregory Martin, 14 years of age, along with two others, was accused of hitting a youth with a loaded gun and stealing his jacket and sneakers; when arrested, Martin was in possession of the gun. The Court found that juveniles, unlike adults, "are always in some form of custody"; that is, "by definition, [they] are not assumed to have the capacity to take care of themselves [but] are assumed to be subject to the control of their parents, and if parental control falters, the State must play its part as *parens patriae*." The Court stipulated that the detention cannot be for purposes of punishment and must be strictly limited in time; the Court found that the maximum detention under the New York statute, 17 days for serious crimes and 6 days for less serious crimes, was proper.

According to Barry Feld (2003), providing greater due process rights to juveniles has had unintended consequences because it "legitimated the imposition of more punitive sentences." He notes further that once juveniles are given adultlike protections, judges more readily depart from the pure rehabilitative model, which had formed the basis of the juvenile court.

▶ Juvenile Court Procedures

The juvenile court system differs from state to state and even within states. Jurisdiction over juveniles may be located in a separate juvenile court, in a specialized branch of the superior court, or in various types of courts of limited jurisdiction. It is possible that within one state, jurisdiction may be located in two or more different types of courts. The legal age of a juvenile also varies from state to state, ranging from 14 to 18 years of age. Although juveniles are not routinely fingerprinted or photographed by the police, 47 states allow the police to fingerprint and 44 states allow them to photograph certain juveniles. In Texas, for example, all juveniles with alleged delinquent offenses that are crimes punishable by incarceration for adults are fingerprinted and entered into a statewide central repository; their criminal history record may then be accessed by law enforcement and juvenile justice agencies throughout Texas. In Pennsylvania, the records of youth 14 years of age or older are accessible to the public if the offense would have been considered a felony if committed by an adult.

A juvenile's name is not usually printed in the newspapers, and the juvenile court has historically been closed to the public. However, about two-dozen states have open hearings in certain cases. In 1997, New York reversed its long-standing policy of keeping Family Court closed to the public. Although judges still have discretion to close cases, they must have compelling and specific reasons, such as ensuring the privacy of a victim of child sexual abuse (Finder, 1997).

Historically, juvenile court records have been kept confidential, but most states now permit the release of certain juveniles' names and/or photographs, and more and more juvenile records are becoming available to more agencies and the public. In many states, there are provisions for having a juvenile record sealed—not subject to examination except by special court order—and in some jurisdictions expunged; 18 states, however, prohibit the sealing or expunging of juvenile records (Sickmund, Snyder, and Poe-Yamagata, 1997). Until 1992, the Federal Bureau of Investigation (FBI) collected records only of juveniles tried as adults, but in that year new regulations gave the FBI's National Crime Information Center (NCIC) authority to receive juvenile court information. Although states do not have to submit juvenile court records to the FBI, the NCIC can instantly transmit to law enforcement agencies and within days to some employers the juvenile court records formerly kept confidential.

The juvenile court typically handles four types of cases:

1. *Delinquency*. Behavior that, if engaged in by an adult, would constitute a crime.
2. *Status offense*. Behavior that, if engaged in by an adult, would not constitute a crime but (in accord with *parens patriae*) provides the basis for governmental intervention, for example, demonstrating chronic truancy, being beyond the control of parents or guardians, and running away.
3. *Neglect or abuse*. Children who are subjected to neglect or abuse by parents or guardians.
4. *Dependency*. Children who do not have parents or guardians available to provide proper care.

> **Key Fact**
>
> Juvenile courts handle four types of cases: delinquency, status offense, neglect, and dependency.

As part of a status offense or separately under a special addicted category, juveniles may be subject to juvenile court jurisdiction as a result of addiction to alcohol or other drugs.

Instances of delinquency, a status offense, neglect or abuse, or dependency that come to the attention of the authorities are often handled in a manner that does not involve the formal justice apparatus. School officials or the police, for example, may refer such cases directly to public or private social welfare or child protective agencies. Alternatively, the police may make a station adjustment, so the child is allowed to return home with parents or guardians without further action. Those situations that come to the attention of the juvenile court enter by way of the intake section, which is usually staffed by juvenile probation officers. On the eastern end of New York's Long Island, the Suffolk County Probation Department—which supervises adult offenders—is responsible for juvenile intake services at Family Court.

JUVENILE COURT INTAKE

"In many communities, an intake unit within the juvenile court first screens all juvenile matters. The intake unit determines whether the matter should be handled informally (i.e. diverted) or petitioned for formal handling.... In other communities, the juvenile court is not involved in delinquency or status offense matters until another agency (e.g., the prosecutor's office or a social service agency) has first screened the case. In other words, the intake function is performed outside the court, and some matters are diverted to other agencies without the court ever handling them. Status offense cases, in particular, tend to be diverted from court processing in this manner" (Puzzanchera, Adams, and Sickmund, 2011: 1–2).

▶ Intake

Children are referred to the juvenile court by the police, parents, school officials, or other public or private agency personnel (Figure 11.2), although law enforcement agencies are the source of more than 80 percent of delinquency referrals and a little less than half of the status offense referrals that reach the petition stage. In some jurisdictions, all cases are received by a PO assigned to the **intake** or complaint unit; while in others, cases that involve criminal complaints are first sent to the prosecutor's office. The first decision to be made at intake is the custodial status of the youngster: Does the respondent's behavior make him or her a danger to himself or herself or to the safety of others? Will the youngster return to court voluntarily?

Intake in the juvenile court is unique: It permits the court to screen cases not only on jurisdictional and legal grounds but also on social dimensions. The PO interviews the presenting agent, the young person, and the child's parents or guardians. The officer then reviews court files for previous records concerning the child. If the case involves a serious crime or child abuse and has not already been screened by the prosecutor, the PO consults with that office. At this stage, the PO has a dual function: legal and social service.

The **legal function** requires that the PO determine whether the juvenile court has jurisdiction and also requires that the child and parents be advised of the right to counsel

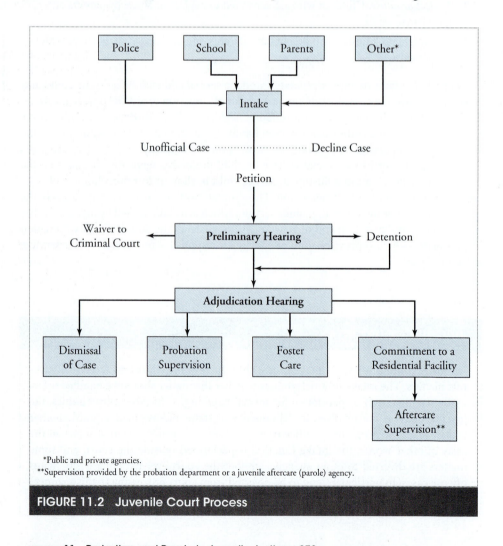

*Public and private agencies.
**Supervision provided by the probation department or a juvenile aftercare (parole) agency.

FIGURE 11.2 Juvenile Court Process

JUVENILE OFFENDERS IN TEXAS

It is 1:15 A.M. in Texarkana. James, 15 years of age, and an adult male have been arrested for aggravated robbery. Police are taking the juvenile to the detention center intake unit at the Bowie County Juvenile Probation Department. Harold Harlston, a probation officer on duty, has just been called to the intake office where he must decide if James will be detained or released. In checking the records, Harlston finds that James has a prior arrest for theft, but the initial police report suggests that this time James was influenced to participate in the robbery by the older man.

Harlston awakens James's parents with a phone call. They are quite upset and head for the center. While continuing to interview James, the PO is interrupted by a call alerting him that the police are bringing in a girl involved in a street fight. She is being charged with assault—again. Harlston anticipates a long, busy night.

The girl being brought in is 14 and goes by her street name, "Decca." Streetwise, she has learned to cover her vulnerability with a defiant attitude and abusive vocabulary. She fidgets nervously as she waits for her intake interview. A file check reveals that Decca lives with her mother and several siblings. The father does not live in the home, and the family has a history of court referrals.

Harlston learns that James's parents have just arrived. He tells them their son will be held until his detention hearing, usually occurring within 48 hours. James's parents express their disappointment; they want to take James home tonight. The PO explains the seriousness of the charges and the state law allowing juveniles to be tried in adult court for offenses as serious as aggravated robbery. If James is transferred to adult court, he could be sentenced to prison. The young man is lucky; his parents express their love and pledge to stand by him. Decca is not so fortunate. When her mother is contacted, she tells the PO, "Do whatever you want with her—I'm tired."

The night is young, and Harlston learns the police are bringing in two more youths. Detention center staff prepare for overcrowding by placing temporary cots in the dining area of the 10-bed facility.

and the right to remain silent during the intake conference. H. Ted Rubin argues that "defense attorney participation at a[n intake] conference is rare, waivers of rights tend to be finessed, and the norm is for parents to encourage the child to discuss his or her participation in the alleged offense with the intake officer" (1980: 304; also Feld, 1988). When defense attorneys are present in juvenile court, tension is inherent in their responsibilities to the client: "a choice between the traditional adversary role (or the procedural model that regulates professional behavior in the criminal court) and the historic treatment or rehabilitative concerns of the family [juvenile] court" (Fabricant, 1983: 41). Barry Feld reports that even when juveniles are represented by counsel, "attorneys may not be capable of or committed to representing their juvenile clients in an effective adversarial manner. Organizational pressures to cooperate, judicial hostility toward adversarial litigants, role ambiguity created by the dual goals of rehabilitation and punishment, reluctance to help juveniles 'beat a case,' or an internalization of a court's treatment philosophy may compromise the role of counsel in juvenile court" (1988: 395). Indeed, he notes that the presence of counsel may actually be disadvantageous to the juvenile—those represented by attorneys tend to receive more severe dispositions. Nevertheless, Feld, a law professor, advocates legislation that mandates counsel and does not permit a waiver of this important constitutional right.

The social services function involves an assessment of the child's situation—home, school, physical, and psychological—and can provide the basis for adjusting the case, that is, handling it informally without the filing of a petition. This happens in about half of the cases reaching juvenile court when the situation is not serious, when the matter can best be handled by the family, and when neither the child nor the public is in any danger. When the child is in conflict with parents or school officials, the PO may serve as a mediator.

If the young person and parents agree to informal processing, the juvenile can be placed under supervision of a PO, usually for a period of 90 days. Although this may save the young person and his or her parents from the trauma of court action, unofficial handling has its critics. Informal processing requires an explicit or tacit admission of guilt. The substantial advantages that accrue from this admission (the avoidance of court action) also act as an incentive to confess. This approach casts doubt on the voluntariness and truthfulness of admissions of guilt. About 20 percent of delinquency cases brought to the juvenile court result in informal or "unofficial probation."

The period of **informal probation** can be a crucial time in the life of a young person. If successful, the youngster may avoid further juvenile court processing; if unsuccessful, the child will face the labyrinth that is the juvenile court process and the serious consequences that can result. No one is more aware of this than the PO who, using all the skills and resources at his or her command, attempts to assist the youngster and the youngster's parent(s) through the crisis. Counseling, group therapy, tutoring, vocational guidance, psychiatric and psychological treatment, and recreational services, if they are available, will be put to use to help the young person. If the intake worker is professionally trained, he or she may provide the counseling, thus avoiding the time-consuming referral process—a family is most effectively aided at the time of crisis. If informal efforts are unsuccessful, the PO can file a petition—a sworn statement containing the specific charges and name(s) of the complaining witness(es), that makes the case an official one.

During the intake process, the PO must determine if the case is to be referred—petitioned—to the court for adjudication. Of the more than 1.5 million delinquency cases received annually by the juvenile court, a little more than half are petitioned. The filing of a petition is made through the prosecutor or directly via the clerk of the court, who sets a date for the first of three types of juvenile court hearing.

Key Fact

Many cases sent to juvenile court intake are handled by informal probation.

A CLOSER LOOK

JUVENILE INTAKE IN TEXAS

In Brazoria County, Texas, an intake officer, taking into consideration the nature of the offense and the juvenile's referral history, evaluates each juvenile referral to the department. If additional contact with the juvenile is required, the intake officer schedules an interview with the family to assist in the evaluation of the juvenile's school performance, behavior, and family situation. Following the assessment, the intake officer makes a recommendation using state-mandated progressive sanction guidelines and pertinent departmental guidelines. In turn, the assistant district attorney considers the officer's recommendation and directs the course of action taken on any charge.

In Harris County (Houston), law enforcement officers may take a juvenile to one of two intake-screening units at the Juvenile Probation Department. Intake screening is responsible for assessing immediate circumstances and deciding where the youth will stay prior to a court hearing. Two 24-hour intake units receive and review incoming cases.

Younger nonviolent offenders may be offered the option of voluntary participation in the Deferred Prosecution Program. This program guides youth through six months of intensive counseling and supervision aimed at diverting them from further contact with the juvenile justice system. When a youth is believed to present a threat to the community or to him- or herself, the youth will be held in detention awaiting a court hearing.

JUVENILE INTAKE IN GRANT COUNTY (MARION), INDIANA

Most cases received by the probation department are referred by school officials and law enforcement officers after receiving and investigating complaints from private citizens. Referring agents complete an intake information form, and on receipt, the probation department orders the child and his or her parent(s)/guardian(s) to report to the probation office for a preliminary inquiry.

The preliminary inquiry is conducted by the intake PO for the purpose of determining whether the child committed a delinquent act and if the interests of society or the child require further action. The PO advises the child and parents of the nature of the inquiry, the alleged offense, and their constitutional rights. If the child and parents choose to discuss the alleged offense and if there is a determination of delinquency, the PO recommends to the court and to the prosecutor's office either that a formal petition alleging delinquency be filed or that the matter be adjusted informally.

If the PO decides during the preliminary inquiry that an informal adjustment should be entered into, parent(s) and child must complete a preliminary investigation form that provides information about the child and the child's family: offense, education, siblings, employment, hobbies, and recreation. An agreement is negotiated, and the child and parent(s) sign an informal agreement form describing the disposition agreed on and the terms of that disposition—for example, driver's license restriction, curfew, sessions with a PO, or referral to a community drug or alcohol treatment program or for psychological treatment. An informal adjustment agreement cannot extend beyond six months. If, at the end of that time, the terms have not been followed or the child commits another offense, the original charges can be filed with the court as a petition. If the PO recommends a petition instead of an informal adjustment, the prosecutor will file it with the court, alleging delinquency.

▶ Preliminary Hearing

Preliminary hearings consider those matters that must be dealt with before the case can proceed further. At the first hearing, the judge (or in some jurisdictions, a referee) informs the parties involved of the charges in the petition and of their rights in the proceeding. If the case involves an abused, neglected, or dependent child, a **guardian** *ad litem* is usually appointed to act as an advocate for the child. Depending on the jurisdiction, this person may be an attorney or trained lay advocate, often a volunteer. If appropriate, the hearing may be used to determine whether an alleged delinquent should remain in detention or a shelter. If the judge determines, usually with the help of the PO, that the respondent's behavior makes him or her a danger to himself or herself or to the safety of others or that he or she will probably not return to court voluntarily, the judge can order that the child remain in or be remanded to custody.

Detention facilities for juveniles have generally been inadequate. In some jurisdictions, they are merely separate sections of an adult jail. The 1974 Juvenile Justice and Delinquency Prevention Act requires **"sight and sound" separation** of juveniles held under juvenile court jurisdiction, but the statute does not apply to youth in adult facilities prosecuted as adults in state court. California outlawed the practice of jailing juveniles in 1986, and Utah makes the practice a misdemeanor.

The Dauphin County (Harrisburg, Pennsylvania) Juvenile Probation Department uses in-home detention, which provides supervision for juveniles who otherwise would be held in a detention facility. The program has two POs who share a caseload that does not exceed 14 youngsters. The clients are visited once or twice a day at their home, school, or place of employment, and a rigidly enforced curfew is set in cooperation with each youngster's parents. In-home detention is limited to 60 continuous days.

> **Key Fact**
>
> "Sight and sound" separation requires juveniles to be housed separately from adult offenders.

GUARDIAN *AD LITEM*

Dependent, neglected, or abused children and status offenders may be placed in foster care or a residential shelter. Under such circumstances, the judge will often appoint a temporary guardian for the child, a guardian *ad litem*, usually a representative of a child welfare agency but sometimes a relative, a friend of the family, or a lay volunteer. Volunteers complete an intensive 40-hour training program and maintain 12 hours of continuing education annually. The judge may also issue an order of protection containing specific restrictions on a potential abuser or assailant, a violation of which allows the penalties for contempt of court—summary imprisonment. In Summit County, Ohio, the juvenile court guardian *ad litem*'s role is to protect the interests of children who have been victimized by their caregivers in cases of abuse, neglect, and dependency throughout the court process. The guardian investigates, advocates, and monitors their cases and submits a written report at all court hearings recommending the findings as to what is in the best interest of the child.

▶ Adjudicatory Hearing

The adjudicatory hearing ("trial") is for the purpose of deciding ("adjudging") whether the child should be made a ward of the juvenile court because he or she is delinquent, abused, neglected, or dependent or is a status offender. If appropriate, the child (respondent) makes a plea, either an admission or a denial, of the allegations contained in petition. The plea process has been the subject of criticism because "much of the country either has not addressed it at all or has not fully developed standards regarding the guilty plea process in juvenile court" (Sanborn, 1992: 142). Thus, pleas are being rendered by juveniles who are incapable of fully understanding the process or to whom the process has not been adequately explained, bringing into question intelligence, voluntariness, and accuracy. This is particularly troubling in view of the move toward a more punitive response in juvenile court (discussed later in this chapter).

> **Key Fact**
>
> An adjudicatory hearing in juvenile court parallels a criminal trial without a jury.

If a denial is made, evidence must be presented to prove "beyond a reasonable doubt" that a delinquent act occurred; in the case of a status offender, it must be proved with a simple "preponderance of evidence" that the child is in need of court supervision. If the allegations are sustained, the judge makes a finding of fact (that the child is delinquent, abused, neglected, or otherwise in need of supervision), sets a date for a dispositional hearing, and orders a social investigation or predisposition report.

▶ Predisposition Report

The goal of the juvenile court is to provide services. To do so on the basis of the best available information, the judge orders a predisposition investigation. The PO who conducts the investigation will present his or her findings in a predisposition report that includes the sociocultural and psychodynamic factors that influenced the juvenile's behavior, providing a social history that is used by the judge to determine a disposition for the case. Because the judge's decision will often be influenced by the contents of the report, it must be factual and objective—a professional statement about the child's family, social and educational history, and any previous involvement with public or private agencies. It also indicates the physical and mental health of the child, as reported by a court psychologist or psychiatrist. The report will typically include the following:

- Review of court records
- Review of school records

- Review of police records
- Interviews with the respondent
- Interviews with family members
- Interviews with teachers and school officials
- Interviews with employers, youth workers, and clergy (whenever appropriate)
- Interviews with complainant, police officer, or witnesses
- Results of any psychological or psychiatric examinations
- Recommendation (including available treatment alternatives)

POs must present their findings with supportive statements as to the actual situation found in the investigation. Other than a recommendation, suppositions or opinions are to be avoided. Sometimes the recommendation of the PO is not included in the report but is transmitted orally to the judge. The completed report should enable the judge to make the best disposition available based on the individual merits of the case and the service needs of the young person. One problem encountered at the disposition stage is the paucity of available alternatives for helping a youngster who will often be placed on probation because of a lack of feasible alternatives.

▶ Disposition Hearing

Traditionally, the disposition stage of the juvenile court process has been based on the concept of *parens patriae*. Distinctions between dispositions were based on the needs of the children and not necessarily the behaviors that brought the cases to the attention of the juvenile court—dispositions were based not on *justice* but on *rehabilitation*. Although the Supreme Court ruled that the juvenile court must adhere to due process, its *raison d'être* as a separate court continued to be as a vehicle for providing social services to children in need. In many jurisdictions, however, the line between the adult criminal court and the juvenile court has become blurred with the adoption of a justice model—what the youngster deserves—rather than a social service model—what the youngster needs. Louise Kiernan (1997: 12) noted that "the concept of *parens patriae* has largely disappeared from the political and public agenda. The delinquency courtrooms now work more like the criminal system that the juvenile court was supposed to counter." The state of Washington provides an example: In 1977, Washington State abrogated the doctrine of *parens patriae* and in its place adopted a new philosophy based on a justice model (Schram et al., 1981):

- Make juvenile offenders accountable for their criminal behavior.
- Provide punishment commensurate with age, crime, and criminal history.

Nowhere is the rehabilitation of the juvenile offender mentioned as a purpose or intent in the law.

As part of this approach, the Washington Division of Juvenile Rehabilitation promulgated "Juvenile Disposition Sentencing Standards" to guide juvenile court judges in making uniform dispositions based not on the needs of the child but on the delinquent behavior—a classical approach. This, of course, reduces the role of the PO in juvenile court. Colorado, Idaho, and New York have mandatory minimum periods of incarceration for juveniles—a clear distortion of the purposes of the juvenile court. However, in Washington and other states that have adopted a hard line on juvenile offenders, statutes enable reconsideration of severe sentences for a variety of mitigating circumstances, including "manifest injustice." In fact, write Patricia Harris and Lisa Graff (1988), the "hard line against juveniles" is often less than what meets the eye: Few of the harsher statutory provisions are mandatory.

Key Fact

The distinction between the adult criminal court and the juvenile court has become less clear as the latter moves away from *parens patriae* and toward a *justice model*.

The state of Washington also relinquished juvenile court jurisdiction over status offenders. Barry Feld (1992: 59) refers to jurisdictional modifications that have narrowed "the scope of juvenile courts at the 'hard' end through the removal of serious juvenile offenders and at the 'soft' end through the removal of noncriminal status offenders."

Contraction of Juvenile Court Jurisdiction

Serious juvenile offenders　　　　　　　　　　　*Status offenders*

To criminal court<—————————————————>To private programs

▶ Status Offenders

As the juvenile court has moved closer to the adult criminal court in both application of legal principles and use of punishment, there has been a corresponding shift away from exercising jurisdiction over status offenders. Official intervention by the legal system in the lives of children who have not been accused of criminal behavior—status offenders—has long been a center of controversy. In 1976, this writer argued: "The juvenile court's continued use of coercion and the stigma it creates are grounds for serious concern. The 'bottom line' of juvenile court authority is the policeman, ready to use his revolver, club and handcuffs to carry out the court's orders. A society that considers preventive detention repulsive has, in some strange way, learned to tolerate the threat or the actual use of force against persons who have not been found guilty of a crime" (Abadinsky, 1976: 458).

Those who support continued jurisdiction of the juvenile court over status offenders—sometimes referred to as minors in need of supervision (MINS), children in need of supervision (CHINS), or persons in need of supervision (PINS)—argue that status offenders are not essentially different from those youngsters committing delinquent acts—they are children in need of services; and without the intervention of the juvenile court, these services would not be forthcoming. Indeed, the youngster may have actually committed a crime that is being treated as a status offense. In Minnesota, in order to avoid having to provide lawyers for youngsters accused of misdemeanors, the legislature decriminalized most common misdemeanors—converted them into status offenses (Feld and Schaeffer, 2010).

Opponents argue that juvenile court intervention does not help youngsters because the services are often inadequate and intervention intensifies existing problems by stigmatizing children. In other words, a juvenile may not be able to discern the subtle differences between the juvenile court and the criminal court—differences that are becoming vague (as in the justice model). Thus, the child, as well as the child's parents, friends, and community, may react to juvenile court intervention as if the child were facing charges in criminal court.

Decades ago, attorney and sociologist Edwin Schur warned that the *labeling* effect of juvenile court can set in motion "a complex process of response and counter-response with an initial act of rule-violation and developing into elaborated delinquent self-conceptions and a full-fledged delinquent career" (1973: 30). However, one research effort found that "the majority of those whose first referral was a status offense did not become more serious delinquents. If anything, they became something considerably less than serious delinquents" (Sheldon, Horvath, and Tracy, 1989: 214). Another study (Brown et al., 1991) also contradicted the labeling argument: Youngsters adjudicated in juvenile court on their first

Key Fact

Status offenders are subject to juvenile court jurisdiction for behavior that would not be of court interest if they were adults (e.g., truancy).

referral were less likely to have criminal records as adults than those whose referrals were delayed until further misbehavior occurred.

Status offense (MINS, CHINS, PINS) petitions are most often filed on behalf of the children's parents, ostensibly because the youngsters are beyond their control. The child's behavior is often merely a symptom of a wider problem. Children frequently become status offenders by running away from pathological family situations or alcoholic and/or abusing parents. Girls are often subjected to juvenile court for sexual behavior that goes unnoticed when committed by boys (Chesney-Lind, 1997). Children who are found to be status offenders are usually warned or placed on probation in their initial encounter with the court. Probation can include placement in a shelter, group home, or foster care. If a youngster fails to cooperate with the treatment program, he or she can be returned to court for further disposition, which can lead to placement in a secure facility, such as a training school. The Juvenile Justice and Delinquency Prevention Act of 1974 requires the deinstitutionalization of status offenders, which has sometimes required litigation to accomplish. In Georgia, in 1998, for example, the state reached an agreement with the U.S. Department of Justice to stop incarcerating an estimated 8,000 status offenders annually (Butterfield, 1998b). While status offenders cannot usually be placed in secure custody at adjudication, they may eventually face incarceration for contempt or violating a valid court order. In 2010, the Board of Trustees of the National Council of Juvenile and Family Court judges voted to support the phase out of the Valid Court Order exception.

▶ Juvenile Court Judges

Central to implementing the helping philosophy of the juvenile court is the juvenile court judge. However, the position presents an anomaly—although most judicial posts require only a knowledge of law and legal procedure, the juvenile court judge, in addition, needs a working knowledge of several disciplines: sociology, psychology, and social work. If persons with such backgrounds were readily available, the relatively low prestige of the juvenile court would make their recruitment difficult. In most states, the juvenile court is located at the bottom of the judicial organizational chart, and the position of juvenile court judge is often seen as the entry level for a future appointment to a more prestigious court. (Exceptions would include Illinois and Arizona, where the juvenile court is a division of the superior court.)

In response to these difficulties, states provide training for juvenile court judges, often by or in conjunction with the National Council of Juvenile Court Judges. The council sponsors a national college located on the campus of the University of Nevada at Reno. The college trains judges and holds periodic sessions throughout the year on topics designed to help juvenile court judges keep abreast of the laws and behavior approaches related to the problems of delinquency, neglect, and child abuse. Other topics include drug and alcohol abuse, juvenile institutions and their alternatives, and waiver of cases to the criminal court. Some jurisdictions use *referees* or *masters*, specialized attorneys who represent the judge and who are empowered to hold certain juvenile court hearings.

▶ Dispositions

Juveniles are sometimes released to the custody of their parents for placement in private boarding schools, military academies, and other private facilities, a disposition most often limited to children from at least middle-income status. Dale Mann notes: "One obvious effect is to guarantee that public institutions for juvenile offenders serve an underclass population" (1976: 12). Jerome Miller (1992: 5) states that a "two-tiered system of residential care has grown up across the country with a dramatic surge in short-term hospitalization in private psychiatric hospitals for recalcitrant, disobedient, or drug-abusing suburban adolescents." He notes that the effect "is to spare these youngsters the correctional diagnosis and the labels which undermine hope—'psychopath,' 'sociopath,' 'unsocialized aggressive.' Such terms apply only to the children of the poor and the racial minorities who populate our youth correctional institutions."

In many states, although a judge can order an adjudicated youth committed to the department having responsibility for institutional care, the judge cannot determine the type of institution to which the youth be confined. In Idaho, for example, youth in the Department of Juvenile Corrections custody go through an observation and assessment process to determine the best placement; a judge may not specify secure confinement or make any recommendations for placement of adjudicated youth.

Basic to dispositions in the juvenile court is the concept of the least restrictive alternative, meaning that a disposition should be no more restrictive than that which will adequately serve the needs of the child; they range from probation supervision, group home, residential treatment center, and secure facility/training school.

▶ Probation Supervision

Probation is appropriate for children who are not seriously delinquent and not in obvious need of intensive services available only in a residential setting. Youngsters with severe behavior problems may be placed on probation, however, not because it is necessarily the most appropriate response but because probation is the only readily available response.

As a condition of probation, juveniles are usually required to obey their parents or guardians, attend school regularly, be home at an early hour in the evening, and avoid disreputable companions or other persons on probation (Figure 11.3). The PO supervising the youngster works toward modifying some of the juvenile's attitudes to help

---

RULES OF PROBATION, LOGAN COUNTY FAMILY COURT

Bellefontaine, Ohio Judge Michael L. Brady and Judge C. Douglas Chamberlain

Name: _____   Date: _____

Offense: _____   Case #: _____

At a hearing held in Juvenile Court you were found delinquent/unruly and placed on probation. You are expected to abide by the following rules:

_____ 1. I shall report to my Probation Officer as directed by him/her. If I am unable to make the assigned time, I will notify the Probation Department. I will follow all instructions of any Court Officer.

_____ 2. I will comply with all STATE, LOCAL LAWS, RULES, AND REGULATIONS.

_____ 3. I will not purchase, possess, own, use or have under my control any firearms, deadly weapons, ammunition, or dangerous ordnance.

_____ 4. I will attend school every day, maintain passing grades, follow all school rules, and treat and address school staff members with respect at all times.

FIGURE 11.3   Rules of Probation, Logan County Family Court

_____ 5. I will conform to the discipline of my parents. I will abide by all house rules. Parents must know my whereabouts at all times and with whom I am associating.

_____ 6. I will not use or engage in the sale of any alcoholic beverage, drug or narcotic or possess any drug paraphernalia, unless use is prescribed by a licensed physician. I will submit to random urinalysis testing. I understand the cost of this test shall be my responsibility and my parents, unless otherwise ordered by the Court. Further, I will not use or possess tobacco products.

_____ 7. Curfew: Sun.-Thurs. _____ Fri.-Sat. _____. Exceptions to these curfew hours are when I am accompanied by my parent or with permission from my P.O. I may leave Logan County if I am with my parents; otherwise I must have prior approval. I will not leave the state of Ohio without prior approval from my P.O.

_____ 8. I will not engage in conduct detrimental to the health, morals, or well-being of myself or others.

_____ 9. I understand that pursuant to Section 2151.411(C)(2)(b) of the Ohio Revised Code, authorized P.O.s engaged within the scope of their supervisory duties or responsibilities may conduct searches during the period of probation if they have reasonable grounds to believe I have not been abiding by the law or otherwise not complying with the conditions of my probation and the search may extend to a motor vehicle, another item of tangible or intangible person, property, or a place of residence or other real property in which a notified parent, guardian, or custodian has a right, title, or interest and that parent, guardian, or custodian expressly or impliedly permits the child to use or occupy or possess.

_____ 10. I will not socialize with other individuals on probation unless otherwise authorized by my P.O.

_____ 11. I shall report any arrest, citation, or any other contact with law enforcement to my P.O.

_____ 12. I will keep my P.O. informed regarding: change in residence, telephone number, employment, school, or use of a vehicle.

_____ Additional rules:

I have read and understand the foregoing rules of probation and will abide by them, realizing if I violate the rules, I may be subject to arrest, prosecution, and/or further appearances in Court.

_____

Juvenile

I/we have read the foregoing rules of probation and agree to help my/our son/daughter abide by them, realizing that if I/we permit my/our son/daughter to violate the rules, I/we may be subject to prosecution for Contributing to the Delinquency of a Minor, or Acting in a Way Tending to Cause the Delinquency of a Minor.

I/we understand it is the parent's responsibility to pay the probation fee as assessed.

I/we also acknowledge that pursuant to O.R.C. Section 3321.38 entitled Failure to Send Child to School, I/we shall make sure that the child under my/our care attends school as provided by law and remains a pupil in school during the term prescribed by law. Failure to do so shall result in a complaint being filed against me/us and an appearance before the Juvenile Court on said charge.

_____   _____
Parent/Guardian   Parent/Guardian

_____ P.O., Logan County Juvenile Court

Figure 11.3 (continued)

JUVENILE PROBATION SUPERVISION, AMARILLO, TEXAS

Barry Gilbert will visit schools this morning to check on 8 youths on his intensive supervision caseload at the Randall County Juvenile Probation Department. He meets with Amarillo High School administrators to check out 4 probationers and is glad to learn their attendance and behavior are good. The PO heads for Fannin Middle School and finds 2 other youths on his caseload are also doing well. As he is leaving, police officers checking a report of a gun on campus ask if he has time to help interview a suspect who is currently on probation. Gilbert values the cooperation his agency receives from the police department and is glad to assist.

Once he completes the investigative interview, the PO visits two other schools, grabs a quick lunch, and returns to his office where he prepares paperwork for residential placement of 2 children on intensive supervision. It takes time to complete the 30-page application required for out-of-home placement of children in Texas. Gilbert seeks drug treatment for one child and a suitable residential placement for the other.

The PO makes curfew checks on 24 of the 32 youngsters on his caseload. In the next few hours, he will make 18 face-to-face meetings with probationers who never know when he will drop by. Gilbert, a former youth pastor and police officer, makes sure they know that intensive supervision is serious business for youngsters in trouble.

> **Key Fact**
>
> Most juvenile court cases result in probation.

the child relate to society in a law-abiding, prosocial manner. At the root of antisocial behavior in many juveniles is a difficulty in relating to authority and authority figures. Parents, school officials, and others who have represented authority to the young person have caused him or her to develop a negative, even hostile, attitude toward authority in general, which leads to rebellion at home and at school or against society in general. The PO must help the young person revise his or her ideas about people in authority by providing a role model as a healthy authority figure or by helping the young person develop healthy attitudes toward others who can provide a desirable role model. These persons may be teachers, athletic coaches, or perhaps a recreation leader in the community.

The probation officer must be able to accept the young person and be able to demonstrate an attitude of respect and concern. At the same time, the PO must be honest and firm with the youngster, setting realistic limits for him or her—something parents are often unable (or unwilling) to do. Misbehavior or antisocial activities cannot be accepted, but the client must be.

In the course of the helping process, the PO will involve the family and meet with the young person on a regular basis. The PO will also work with school officials, sometimes acting as an advocate for the child to secure a public school placement, which is often a difficult task. The youngster has usually exhibited disruptive behavior at school, so officials are understandably resistant to his or her return. If necessary, the officer will seek placement in a foster home for the client (and in some circumstances, adoption).

Many orders of probation require restitution or community service. The term "restitution" refers to the compensation provided by an offender to his or her victim; it can involve financial payments or a service alternative. An increasing interest in restitution as a condition of probation has been spurred by increasing concern for the victims of crime. The service alternative is often imposed on youngsters who are unable to provide financial restitution, although it rarely means direct service to the victim; instead, the juvenile is usually involved in unpaid work for a nonprofit community agency, such as the Salvation Army or the Red Cross.

If the youngster violates any of the conditions of probation, the PO prepares a violation of probation report and the youngster can then be subjected to a motion to revoke probation in favor of a more restrictive setting, such as placement in a secure an institution.

▶ Group Home

The group home may be privately operated under contract with the state (or other level of government), or it can be operated by a public agency. Generally, anywhere from 6 to 15 youngsters live in the home at any one time. The typical home has several bedrooms and baths, as well as a large living room, dining area, and basement recreation area. The interior of the home approximates that of a large single-family dwelling. Group homes are usually located in residential areas that are in proximity to public transportation, public schools, and recreation facilities.

The group home is for youngsters with one or more issues:

- They are in unresolvable conflict with their parents but are not seriously disturbed or psychotic.
- They have inadequate homes and need to develop skills for independent living.
- They need to deal with community social adjustment problems in a therapeutic family environment.
- They need to deal with individual adjustment problems and to learn about themselves in relation to others.
- They need to develop self-confidence through successful experiences.

Each resident has daily chores, such as doing dishes, making beds, or mowing the lawn. Houseparents, usually a married couple with graduate degrees in a therapeutic discipline such as social work or psychology, perform surrogate parent roles by preparing or overseeing the preparation of meals, enforcing a curfew, and helping with homework, as well as doing other tasks usually handled by parents in healthy families. Youngsters attend local schools on a full-time basis, or they have a schedule that incorporates both school and employment.

There are group counseling sessions conducted by group workers geared to help the residents understand and overcome problems that have led to the placement and to define goals consistent with their individual abilities. Individual counseling programs are provided for those youngsters who need help in preparing for independent living and improving their family relationships. Day-by-day counseling and conflict resolution are handled by the houseparents.

> **Key Fact**
>
> The group home is a community residence for nonserious juvenile offenders.

The most difficult aspects of the group home are relationships with the surrounding community—vigorous neighborhood resistance typically exists to placing such a facility in the immediate area. Although both professionals and laypersons generally agree that the group home concept is an excellent one for many youngsters coming to the attention of the juvenile court, this has not translated into widespread acceptance of the reality. Local residents have vigorously and all too often successfully resisted group homes, not only for troubled youngsters but also for persons with mental retardation and other disabilities.

The 1988 Federal Fair Housing Act, which bars discrimination against persons with disabilities, has been interpreted by the courts as outlawing local zoning laws that deny housing to persons with mental retardation, the mentally ill, and drug addicts. In 1995, the Supreme Court ruled that this statute prohibits municipalities from using single-family zoning to bar group homes. In this case, the city of Edmonds, Washington, had attempted to prevent a national organization, Oxford House, from operating a group home for recovering substance abusers (*City of Edmonds v. Oxford House*, 514 U.S. 725).

▶ Residential Treatment Center

The term **residential treatment center (RTC)** is being used to identify private and public institutions that provide residential care for youngsters, with or without intervention of the juvenile court and devoid of coercive elements associated with correctional facilities (e.g., locks, bars, and barbed-wire/razor fences). Generally, the RTC provides a wide variety of enriched services, and the private RTC receives a great deal of public funding. Despite the fact that almost all receive tax money, the private RTC retains the privilege of screening its residents, a luxury not afforded public institutions. One study found, however, that in southern California considerable competition exists for residents between private facilities, and juveniles admitted to private institutions do not significantly differ from those sent to public facilities (Shichor and Bartollas, 1990). Private centers can also mix adjudicated delinquents, status offenders, and voluntary clients in a manner that would not be permissible in a public institution, although the mixing of delinquent and nondelinquent children runs contrary to the prevailing wisdom in the field (Curran, 1988).

> **Key Fact**
>
> Residential treatment centers are nonsecure institutions that offer a wide range of juvenile services.

▶ Secure Facilities/Training School

During the early 1990s, serious juvenile crime rates increased 60 percent, making juvenile crime a national issue. While rates decreased after 1994, by the latter 1990s they were still well above mid-1980s levels. In 1997, juveniles were responsible for 14 percent of all murder and aggravated assault arrests, 37 percent of burglary arrests, and 24 percent of weapons arrests. States responded by adjudicating more children as delinquent, sending more delinquents to correctional facilities, and increasing the number of children tried and imprisoned as adults. By the turn of the twenty-first century, juvenile arrests began to decline; in California, for example, arrests per 100,000 juveniles went from 6,550 in 1994 to 4,228 in 2003, with a corresponding decline in the rate of juvenile incarceration (Turner and Fain, 2005). At the same time, states moved away from placing juvenile delinquents under the adult corrections agency and toward separate juvenile corrections agencies or joint juvenile corrections and a child protection agencies.

The **training school** refers to a public institution that accepts all youngsters committed by the courts. Each is usually set up to handle particular categories of juveniles who may be assigned on the basis of age, aggressiveness, or delinquent history. This is done to avoid mixing older children with younger ones, adjudicated delinquents with status offenders, or more disturbed youngsters with those with less serious problems. The training school usually provides a level of security not available in other types of juvenile institutions (although less than that offered in a correctional facility). Juveniles are committed to training schools based on four criteria:

> **Key Fact**
>
> Training schools are secure public institutions housing juvenile delinquents.

1. A finding of fact occurs indicating that the child has committed an offense that would be punishable by imprisonment if committed by an adult.

2. The parents are unable to control their child or provide for his or her social, emotional, and educational needs.

3. No other child welfare service is sufficient.
4. The child needs the services available at the training school.

The establishment of the Lyman School for Boys in Massachusetts, which opened in 1847 for 400 boys, began an era of providing separate facilities for juvenile offenders. These prejuvenile court facilities—training or reform schools—were patterned after adult prisons. They were regimented with large impersonal dormitories, and each provided some basic medical and dental treatment and limited educational and vocational training. Although the juvenile court "forced a breach in the wall of the criminal justice system," notes Jerome Miller (1992: 8), it did not fully resolve the question of whether to treat or punish, and this dilemma "was complicated by the existence of reform schools, which had been around for most of the century before the juvenile court was invented. Their presence ensured that juvenile offenders would receive the worst the system could offer—punishment labeled as treatment."

Over the years, there has been an increased emphasis on vocational training, remedial education, and rehabilitation through the use of social workers, teachers, psychiatrists, psychologists, and recreation workers. Like a prison or hospital, a training school operates 168 hours per week; this fact, combined with the level of security and services provided, makes the training school an expensive institution in which annual costs can easily run in excess of $40,000 per resident. In Idaho, for example, the estimated annual cost per resident in a Department of Juvenile Corrections facility ranges from $36,000 to $48,000.

The U.S. Department of Justice has brought suit against several state juvenile systems for subjecting children to neglect and abuse. In 2009, the department sent an angry letter to the governor of New York for conditions in several residential juvenile institutions where excessive force—knocked out teeth and fractured bones—was commonplace for such minor offenses as laughing to loudly, getting into fights, and sneaking an extra cookie at snack time ("New York's Disgrace," 2009). In 2010, New York did not have a single full-time psychiatrist to deal with the treatment needs of 800 youngsters in state facilities (Bosman, 2010).

▶ Aftercare/Parole

Aftercare is the planned release of a juvenile from a residential placement (group home, residential treatment center, training school) to supportive services in the community. Each year, about 100,00 juvenile offenders are released from residential facilities (Griffin, 2005). The juvenile may be supervised by a juvenile probation officer, a youth agency parole officer/agent (as in Ohio), or another aftercare worker. Aftercare services are usually provided by the same state agency that administers the juvenile training schools (Hurst and Torbet, 1993). For example, this author worked for the New York State Department of Social Welfare, which used to operate the state training schools. My job title was youth parole worker, and I was responsible for supervising juveniles released from the boys' training schools. In 1978, New York enacted the Juvenile Offender Law, which mandates that youngsters 13 to 19 years of age who commit certain felonies be prosecuted in adult criminal court. If convicted, the youngster can serve a term in a secure facility of the Office of Children and Family Services. During that term, the juvenile becomes subject to the jurisdiction of the New York State Board of Parole for a release decision—parole—and eventual community supervision by a parole officer. Thus, the same agency that supervises adult felons in New York, the Division of Parole, also supervises juveniles convicted of certain violent felonies.

Similarly, in Minnesota, parole agents of the Department of Corrections supervise juveniles who have been sentenced to a correctional facility. In Michigan, youngsters 12 to

> **Key Fact**
>
> Juvenile aftercare or parole supervision may be provided by different agencies, including probation and parole departments.

19 years of age who have been adjudicated delinquent or found to be in need of supervision (status offenders) by the juvenile division of a probate court can be committed to the Department of Social Services for placement in their own home or a foster home, group home, youth camp, diagnostic center, halfway house, residential treatment center, or state training school. In Michigan, status offenders are often committed to the Department of Social Services when the particular juvenile court has insufficient resources available for the youngster. The department offers secure juvenile residential treatment facilities, which may be used as the last resort for the most seriously delinquent youth. Delinquent wards remain under state authority until they are discharged by the Youth Parole and Review Board (YPRB) or reach age 19.

The Colorado Juvenile Parole Board, whose nine members are appointed by the governor, is responsible for release decisions concerning juvenile delinquents who have been committed to the Department of Human Services. Board hearings are usually conducted in panels of two, one of whom is a state agency member. The mandatory 6-month supervision period can be extended by the board to a maximum of 21 months. When considering a youngster for aftercare, a release board will consider the case record, which in some jurisdictions includes a report and recommendation from a juvenile probation officer. In Utah, youngsters committed to any secure facility in the state come under the jurisdiction of the Youth Parole Authority, whose 10 members are appointed by the governor for

---

A CLOSER LOOK

AFTERCARE AUTHORITY

Court Control

Advocates of court-controlled aftercare/reentry services argue that there are natural advantages: knowledge and familiarity with local conditions, enhanced capacity to monitor and respond to a juvenile's everyday behavior, and historical position of leadership in their communities. However, only 4 states—Alabama, Idaho, Iowa, and Pennsylvania—provide for reentry supervision by probation officers working as agents of the courts.

Shared Control

In 15 states, postrelease supervision is a joint responsibility:

- In Mississippi, Nevada, North Carolina, Ohio, Tennessee, and Virginia, state agents provide the supervision, but local courts hear allegations of parole violations and determine whether they merit the offender's return to the commitment institution.

- In Georgia, Kansas, Minnesota, New York, Virginia, and Wisconsin, the state handles juvenile

reentry in some counties, while local courts and probation departments take responsibility in others. In some of these states, such as Kansas and Virginia, juvenile courts also hear and resolve allegations of parole violations, even for state-supervised juveniles.

- In Arkansas, Florida, Indiana, Ohio, and West Virginia, while the state commitment agency generally oversees juvenile parole, the local committing court has the power to inject itself into the reentry process by placing a committed juvenile on postrelease probation—either at the time of the original disposition or at the time of release.

Corrections Control

In the remaining 31 states and the District of Columbia, supervision of juveniles following release from state commitments is entirely the responsibility of the agency that oversees the state's commitment institutions.

Source: Griffin (2005).

terms of four years; they serve part-time. The authority initially establishes a length of stay guideline for each committed youth and reviews his or her progress to determine when parole to the community is appropriate. The authority also conducts violation of parole hearings.

Aftercare supervision is similar (if not identical) to probation supervision and is sometimes provided by a juvenile probation agency. The first responsibility of the aftercare worker is to plan for the release and placement of the young person. Placement plans include where the juvenile will live, whether he or she is to work or attend a school or training program (or both), and what arrangements for supportive services may be needed by the client that are available in the community. The young person may be returned to his or her own home, if this is desirable, or be placed in an alternative setting such as a group home or halfway house. The aftercare worker usually investigates placement alternatives and finalizes a program plan that is submitted to institution officials and those responsible for the release decision.

Once back in the community, the young person will be supervised by an aftercare worker, probation officer, or parole officer and will be required to abide by a set of rules identical to probation rules, the violation of which can cause a return to a "secure setting." The worker will make regular visits to the youngster's residence, school, or place of employment and will involve family and school officials in an effort to facilitate the young person's reintegration and rehabilitation. Unfortunately, juvenile aftercare has typically been underfunded, despite its obvious importance.

▶ Administration of Juvenile Services

The administration of juvenile services is complex, with different levels and branches of government sharing responsibility. Juvenile probation is administered by the juvenile court in most states, although a few have a statewide executive branch agency administering juvenile probation. State institutions for delinquent juveniles are always in the executive branch; however, states vary in the type of executive department in which they choose to place the responsibility for juvenile corrections: the social service department (e.g., Michigan), the corrections department (e.g., Illinois), or separate departments for either family and children's services or youth services (e.g., Idaho).

The 168 juvenile probation agencies in Texas are monitored by the Texas Juvenile Probation Commission (TJPC), which sets standards and provides technical assistance to guarantee uniformity of services. The TJPC also monitors juvenile facilities through audits and unannounced visits to ensure that health and safety conditions are in compliance. State law requires each county to have a juvenile board (some boards govern multiple counties). Each board, consisting of district and county judges, is responsible for overseeing the operation of the juvenile probation system in that county. This includes designating juvenile judges, appointing the chief juvenile probation officer, and setting the policy and budget for the juvenile probation department. TJPC provides funding and technical assistance to juvenile boards.

States without a specialized youth authority/commission typically have their juvenile facilities under the auspices of the same department that is responsible for incarcerating adults. In Illinois, for example, the Juvenile Division of the Department of Corrections receives delinquents adjudicated in juvenile court and those youngsters tried as adults in criminal court. (From 1954 to 1970, these were the responsibilities of the Illinois Youth Commission, which was subsequently abolished.) The Juvenile Division provides secure custody and rehabilitation programs to about 1,500 youths, 13 to 21 years of age, in six centers statewide that range from minimum to maximum security.

► Juveniles in Criminal Court

During the 1970s, there was increasing public concern over juvenile crime and the juvenile justice system, which was frequently attacked as too lenient. Enter Willie Bosket. His first contact with the juvenile system occurred at age 9 when his mother complained to the court that she could not control him. Willie remained in state agency placements for the next several years. At age 15, six months after being released from a maximum security youth facility, he shot and killed two New York City subway passengers. Labeled "the Baby-Faced Butcher," he was subject only to juvenile court jurisdiction—the maximum sentence was a placement with the Division for Youth until he was 21.

In the midst of a tough campaign for reelection, New York's liberal governor called the legislature into special session to pass the "Willie Bosket law," which provides for the automatic transfer of children as young as 13 to criminal court if charged with murder; children as young as 14 would automatically be transferred if charged with various crimes of violence. Many states followed New York's lead, and the jurisdiction of juvenile courts over serious crimes has been cut back in state after state (Klein, 1998). "The pool of cases eligible for criminal court handling has been vastly expanded and critical decision making power in this area has been shifted away from judges and toward prosecutors" (Torbet et al., 2000: 1). It should be noted that the possibility of transfer to adult criminal court is not an invention of the late twentieth century. Since the establishment of the juvenile court, judges have retained the discretion to waive jurisdiction over serious young offenders and allow them to be prosecuted in criminal court. In Cook County, the juvenile court typically waived about 15 boys a year. These were usually juveniles age 16 or older arrested for violent crimes (Klein, 1998).

"All states have transfer laws that allow or require criminal prosecution of some young offenders, even though they fall on the juvenile side of the jurisdictional age" (Griffin et al., 2011: 2). There are three basic mechanisms for accomplishing the transfer of a juvenile to criminal court:

1. *Legislative exclusion.* Some states exclude certain categories of juveniles from juvenile court jurisdiction (Torbet et al., 1996). To mitigate automatic transfer statutes, States may have *reverse waiver* provisions, whereby prosecutors in criminal court can move to have a juvenile case sent back to juvenile court. States also have "once an adult, always an adult" provisions requiring juveniles who have been tried as adults to be subjected to criminal court for any subsequent offenses (Snyder and Sickmund, 2006).

2. *Judicial waiver.* Virtually every state and the federal system permit juvenile court judges to "waive" (transfer) their jurisdiction over certain juvenile offenders.

3. *Prosecutorial discretion.* Some states empower prosecutors to charge juveniles in either juvenile or adult courts.

Researchers have reported a lack of any significant difference in sentence outcome for youngsters adjudicated in juvenile court and those tried in criminal court after statistically controlling for the severity of offense. They point out that "minors are likely to be looked upon as special persons by prosecutors, probation officers, and judges in the criminal courts. They are younger than the main population of defendants before the criminal courts. Even jurors may view the young person in criminal court differently." Thus, in the cases they examined, "there were more findings of 'not guilty' in the criminal court than in the juvenile court. The labeling process may be different in the two courts. While a minor may be looked upon as a hardened criminal in the juvenile court, (s)he may be viewed as a mere innocent youngster in criminal court" (Sagatun, McCollum, and Edwards, 1985: 87). Only about 1.5 percent of petitioned delinquency cases are transferred to criminal court.

A *blended sentence* law in Minnesota created a new category of serious juvenile offender. They are tried as juveniles but given full due process protections, including the right to a jury trial. If convicted, they are given an adult sentence that is applied *only* in the event the juvenile does not satisfactorily complete the juvenile court disposition (Griffin et al., 2011). In some states (e.g., California, Florida), the case is tried in criminal court, which has the authority to impose a juvenile or adult sanction.

There has been a dramatic reversal of "tough on crime" statutes that moved juveniles into the adult criminal court. About half of the states have enacted laws keeping more juveniles in the juvenile system and preventing them from being incarcerated in adult jails and prisons (J. Schwartz, 2013).

Summary

- The probation officer is at the center of juvenile justice.
- Houses of refuge were established as an alternative to jails for homeless and vagrant children.
- The legal concept of *parens patriae* provided the legal basis for the juvenile court.
- The child-saving movement provided the impetus for establishing the juvenile court.
- Nondelinquents over whom the juvenile court was given jurisdiction because of their behavior became known as status offenders.
- The juvenile court embodied the positivist view.
- A juvenile court should not impose punishment.
- Until 1967, youngsters in juvenile court enjoyed no due process protection.
- In the case of *In re Gault* (1967), the Supreme Court established due process requirements for the juvenile court.
- The legal age of a juvenile also varies from state to state, ranging from 14 to 18 years of age.
- The juvenile handles four types of cases: delinquency, status offense, neglect or abuse, and dependency.
- Intake in the juvenile court permits the court to screen cases on jurisdictional and legal grounds, and on social dimensions.
- If the young person and parents agree to informal processing, the juvenile can be placed under supervision of a PO—unofficial probation.
- If the case involves an abused, neglected, or dependent child, a guardian *ad litem* is usually appointed to act as an advocate for the child.
- An adjudicatory hearing in juvenile court parallels a criminal trial without a jury.
- The predisposition report parallels a presentence report in adult criminal court.
- The distinction between the adult criminal court and the juvenile court has blurred because of adoption of a justice model, rather than a social service model.
- Juvenile court jurisdiction over status offenders has been controversial.

- Being a judge in juvenile courts is more difficult than being a judge in adult courts.
- Basic to dispositions in the juvenile court is the concept of the least restrictive alternative.
- A residential treatment center provides care for youngsters, with or without intervention of the juvenile court and devoid of coercive elements associated with correctional facilities.
- A training school is a secure public institution that accepts all youngsters committed by the courts.
- Juvenile aftercare or parole supervision may be provided by different agencies, including probation and parole departments.
- Juvenile probation is administered by the juvenile court in most states.

Key Terms

adjudicatory hearing *274*
aftercare *283*
child-saving movement *264*
guardian *ad litem 273*
houses of refuge *263*
informal probation *272*
justice model *275*

least restrictive alternative *278*
legal function *270*
parens patriae *263*
petition *274*
predisposition report *274*
residential treatment center (RTC) *282*

"sight and sound" separation *273*
social services function *271*
social services model *275*
status offenders *264*
training school *282*

Internet Connections

American Bar Association Juvenile Justice Center: **abanet.org/crimjust/juvjus/home.html**

Council of Juvenile Correctional Administrators: **cjca.net**

National Center for Juvenile Justice: **ncjj.org**

National Council of Juvenile and Family Court Judges: **ncjfcj.org**

National Institute of Corrections: **nicic.org**

Office of Juvenile Justice and Delinquency Prevention: **ojjdp.ncjrs.org**

Review Questions

1. What was the purpose of houses of refuge?
2. What is *parens patriae*?
3. Who were the "child savers" and what was the result of their efforts?
4. What is meant by "status offenders"?
5. Why can the juvenile court be said to embody the positivist view?
6. Why is punishment inappropriate for a juvenile court?
7. What did the Supreme Court determine in the 1967 case of *In re Gault*?
8. What are the four types of cases handled by a juvenile court?
9. What is the purpose of intake in juvenile court?

▼

10. What is informal probation?
11. What is the role of a guardian *ad litem*?
12. How does a preliminary hearing differ from an adjudicatory hearing?
13. What is the purpose of a predisposition report?
14. How does the justice model differ from the social service model?
15. Why is juvenile court jurisdiction over status offenders controversial?
16. Why is being a judge in juvenile courts more difficult than being a judge in adult courts?
17. What is the concept of "least restrictive alternative"?
18. How does a training school differ from a residential treatment center?

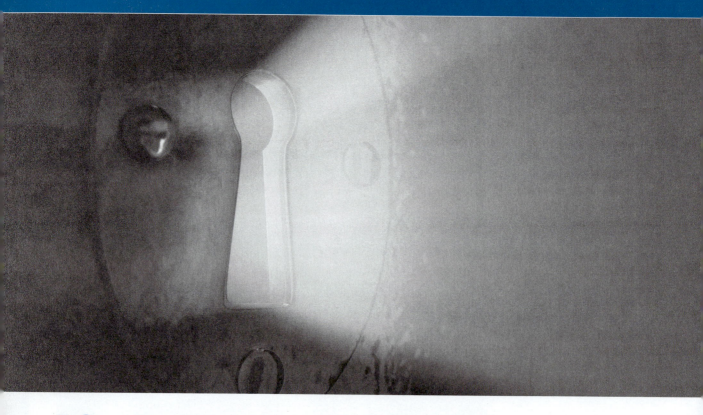

12 Probation and Parole: The Research and the Future

LEARNING OBJECTIVES

This chapter will enable the student to:

1 *Discuss studies of probation and parole (P/P) supervision effectiveness.*

2 *Appreciate that there is no standard to determine if a recidivism rate is high or low.*

3 *Explain why the basic mechanism of P/P supervision is client contact.*

4 *Describe why a focus on providing rehabilitation is more effective than a control/surveillance emphasis.*

5 *Explain evidence-based practice in P/P.*

6 *Appreciate how Politics can interfere with evidence-based practice.*

7 *Understand the difficulty with using data on recidivism as a measure of P/P success.*

8 *State how P/P supervision should be judged a success.*

9 *Understand the practical implications of abolishing parole boards.*

10 *Appreciate why parole was originally established.*

11 *Discuss the use split sentences in the absence of parole.*

12 *Appreciate that the term "treatment" is once again fashionable in corrections.*

This concluding chapter examines the question of success or failure of probation and parole and research related to this issue, followed by an exploration of the direction of probation and parole in the second decade of the twenty-first century.

▶ Probation and Parole: Success or Failure?

The "Gold Standard" for research in the behavioral sciences is the experimental model in which an *experimental group* is exposed to an intervention, community supervision, for example, while a *control group* is not, left unsupervised, To avoid selection bias, members of both groups are assigned randomly. For example, a cohort of offenders is numbered 1 to 100; those with even numbers are assigned to the experimental group and those with odd numbers to the control group, or vice-versa, as determined by a coin toss.

Although a powerful tool for determining program impact, the experimental design is difficult to implement, expensive, and typically requiring considerable time and research expertise. "In addition, there may be resistance to the use of random assignment on the grounds that it is unethical to withhold potentially beneficial services from control group subjects simply for the sake of research" (Przybylski, 2008: 12). In P/P, failure to supervise for the purpose of research entails obvious risks. So research into the impact of supervision typically uses a quasi-experimental approach. Instead of random assignment, program—participants, actively supervised probationers or parolees, are compared to a matched group of offenders who are similar in all relevant ways—for example, age, criminal history—except being supervised (Przybylski, 2008), for example, prisoners who maxed out without any postprison supervision.

And what has research revealed? Is probation/parole (P/P) a success or a failure? In examining the degree to which P/P is successful, the results are often contradictory. The methodology of some research efforts is simply unsound; however, even methodologically sound research has not allowed us to definitively answer the question. For example, one study (Lerner, 1977) found parole supervision in New York reduced the postrelease criminal activity of a group of (conditional) releasees compared with a group of dischargees released from the same institution without supervision. A similar study in Connecticut (Sachs and Logan, 1979) found that parole supervision resulted in only a modest reduction in recidivism. In California, however, no significant difference was found in the recidivism rates of persons released with or without parole supervision (Jackson, 1983; Star, 1979). A study of prisoners released in 1994 in 15 states (Solomon, Kachnowski, and Bhati, 2005) revealed that parole supervision did not have a significant impact on rearrest rates. But a 2006 study in New Jersey revealed that after two years, parole supervision made a significant difference in arrest and conviction rates: 23.6 percent of parolees had been convicted of a new crime, while a control group with similar characteristics and offense histories released without supervision had a two-year conviction rate of 43 percent (Robbins and Ostermann, 2006).

A New Orleans study (Geerken and Hayes, 1993) found that 8 percent of adult arrests for burglary or armed robbery from 1974 to 1986 involved offenders who were on probation; the figure for parolees was less than 2 percent. A study in New York tracked 22,941 conditional releasees (15 percent) and parolees (85 percent) released in 1991 and supervised by parole officers for two years: Fewer than 13 percent were returned to prison for new felony convictions (New York State Division of Parole, 1994). A 1994–1995 study of more than 2,000 felons placed on probation in Arizona in 1989 and 1990 revealed that 61 percent had completed their term of supervision while 25 percent were convicted of new crimes and sentenced to prison; 4 percent absconded (Administrative Office of the Courts, 1996). Annual studies of persons on probation in Minnesota reveal a successful termination—no misdemeanor or felony conviction or technical violation relating to a new criminal offense—rate above 60 percent (Wilks and Nash, 2008).

According to the Marion County, Indiana, Probation Department, in 2002, 63 percent of probationers successfully completed supervision, 13.2 percent had probation revoked for a new offense, and 23.9 percent had probation revoked for a technical violation. A study of parolees in Hawaii (Kassebaum et al., 1999) who were tracked for three years found that 70.7 percent had no criminal convictions, and 11 percent had one or more felony convictions; approximately one-half had their parole revoked, mostly for technical violations. Outcome research in Arkansas revealed that out of a sample of 2,489 probationers, after three years, 248 (10 percent) were reincarcerated for new offenses and 170 (7 percent) for technical violations; of 1,741 parolees, after three years, 149 (8.5 percent) were reincarcerated for new offenses, and 311 (4.8 percent) for technical violations (Department of Community Corrections, 2006). Do these studies indicate success or failure? In order to appreciate the difficulty of providing a definitive answer, we need to consider two issues:

1. What is meant by the term "success" in P/P?
2. What is meant by the term "adequate" supervision in P/P?

▶ What Is Meant by Success?

A major part of the problem is the word success. For example, a researcher for the California Youth Authority candidly portrays his own findings, noting that success depends on which statistics one decides to emphasize:

> Parole behavior in the sample can be made to look quite good, especially considering the high levels of pre–Youth Authority crime, or quite bad. For example, only 13 percent were sent to state prison for parole-period offenses during the 24 months of follow-up, resulting in an 87 percent "success rate" by this criterion. Some correctional jurisdictions who report spectacularly high success rates in fact use such a restricted measure. Alternatively, regarding the same sample we could accurately report that 77 percent of the sample had been arrested or temporarily detained during the 24 months leaving a "success rate" by this criterion of only 23 percent. (Wiederanders, 1983: 4)

According to the Bureau of Justice Statistics (2001), success rates of those under parole supervision have remained relatively stable for more than a decade. About 4 of every 10 persons discharged from parole successfully complete their term of supervision in the community. As might be expected, the success rates for those released by a parole board are higher (54 percent) than those who released under good-time provisions/mandatory release (33 percent).

The success of a P/P system is usually conceived of in terms of **recidivism** (Maltz, 1984: 54): "When recidivism is discussed in a correctional context, its meaning seems fairly clear. The word is derived from the Latin *recidere,* to fall back. A recidivist is one who, after release from custody for having committed a crime, is not rehabilitated. Instead, he or she falls back, relapses, into former behavior patterns and commits more crimes. This conceptual definition of recidivism may seem quite straightforward; however, an operational definition, one that permits measurement, is not so simple."

The 1976 edition of the *Dictionary of Criminal Justice Data Terminology* defines the word *recidivism* as "the repetition of criminal behavior; habitual criminality." However, the 1981 edition avoided providing a definition and noted instead:

> Efforts to arrive at a single standard statistical definition of recidivism have been hampered by the fact that the correct referent of the term is the actual repeated criminal or delinquent behavior of a given person or group, yet the only available statistical indicators of that behavior are records of such system events as rearrests, reconvictions, and probation or parole violations or revocations. It is recognized that these data reflect agency decisions about events and do not closely correspond with actual criminal behavior.

Jay Albanese and his colleagues (1981: 51) point out the following:

- A wide disparity exists in the definition of revocation and recidivism.
- Revocation/recidivism rates without a standardized definition have little comparative value.
- A criterion (or criteria) of "effectiveness" is not well defined.

John Laub and Robert Sampson (2008) ask how should a change from serious criminal acts to less serious be characterized. And what if criminal acts cease but other problem behaviors such as alcohol or drug abuse persist or increase? Gordon Waldo and David Griswold (1979: 230) note that being arrested and convicted for any crime is not sufficient as an operational definition of recidivism. They quote Charles Tittle: "Being arrested for gambling cannot be accepted as evidence of recidivism for a burglar." In addition, the extensive use of plea bargaining means that merely looking at the crime for which a person is convicted does not allow for a determination of whether the person has committed the same crime again, or a less serious or more serious crime. Similarly, with respect to probation recidivism rates, it is necessary to distinguish between those under supervision for misdemeanors and those convicted of felonies because felony probationers have significantly higher rates of recidivism than misdemeanants (Petersilia, 1998b). Then there is the problem of technical violations—do we rate them as recidivism? No consistent definition of recidivism exists, so "one cannot state with any degree of assurance whether a given recidivism rate is high or low; there is no 'normal' recidivism rate as there is a normal body temperature" (Maltz, 1984: 23). Recent efforts to standardize recidivism for statistical purposes refer to imprisonment for a felony within three years of being placed on community supervision.

The Pew Center on the States (2011: 17) points out that recidivism is impacted by sentencing policy:

> States that send comparatively low-risk offenders to prison are likely to see lower rearrest and violation rates compared with states that concentrate prison space on more dangerous offenders. If, for example, a state incarcerates a large proportion of lower-risk offenders, then its recidivism rate might be comparatively low, because such offenders would be, by definition, less of a risk to return to prison. A state with a larger percentage of serious offenders behind bars, on the other hand, might experience higher rates of reincarceration when those offenders return to the community.

Further complicating efforts to determine success is the issue of *selection:* P/P agencies receiving (via judges and parole boards) a greater number of low-risk offenders are more likely to have higher rates of success. A conservative judge/parole board, or perhaps one fearful of an adverse public reaction, will release fewer offenders to supervision, and those who are placed on probation or parole will tend to be the "boy scouts"—correctional term for lower-risk offenders who will probably produce impressive (statistical) measurements of success for the agency. Is a comparison of the results of various P/P agencies any more relevant than one that compares the success rates of doctors treating AIDS and cancer patients with those treating less catastrophic ailments—success rates of oncologists compared to dermatologists. While a senior parole officer, an education official studying community school boards in New York City interviewed me at my office—I was president of one of these boards. In negative terms, he asked about the "success rates" of people on parole. I responded with a question about the "success rates" of inner-city schools and noted "We inherit your failures."

The research literature frequently uses the term "low-risk," but it is often unclear if this means unlikely to commit *any* crime, or if he or she does commit a crime it is likely to be against property, not persons—thus, less likely to gain news coverage and/or become a political issue. Paradoxically, offenders incarcerated for a violent offense are less likely to recidivate than drug or property offenders, although parole boards are more likely to release a property offender than one convicted of a violent crime (Kohl et al., 2008; Rosenfeld, Petersilia, and Visher, 2008). Although anecdotal, I found parolees convicted of violent crimes, such as robbery, to be aggressive in their search for and subsequent success at employment. "Sneaks," such as burglars, tended to be passive during an interview, avoiding eye contact, a trait that negatively impacted securing employment.

Research has identified a number of variables that correlate well with success or failure on probation: age (younger offenders have greater difficulty adhering to probation conditions), employment (those who are employed and financially stable do better), marital status (those who are married are less likely to violate probation), and offense (those on probation for drug- and theft-related crimes have higher recidivism rates—although they are more likely to be placed on probation) (Liberton, Silverman, and Blount, 1990). High-risk offenders lessen the chances of P/P "success." This truism also exists in education and medicine. Inner-city schools with high rates of social disorganization and impoverished families, and hospitals serving these same populations, will have less successful outcomes than their counterparts in middle-class environs. Is crime a symptom, a result, or a causal factor of these conditions? If crime is a dependent variable, what can reasonably be expected of P/P; that is, beyond keeping down the prison population/saving tax dollars.

▶ What Is "Adequate Supervision?"

Joan Petersilia and her colleagues (1985: v), researchers for the Rand Corporation, noted that "over one-third of California's probation population consists of felons convicted in Superior Court—persons who are often quite different from the less serious offenders probation was originally conceived and structured to handle." They found that 51 percent of a sample of California offenders on felony probation who were sentenced in 1980 and tracked for 40 months were reconvicted, 18 percent for violent crimes. They conclude (1985: vi) that "felons granted probation present a serious threat to public safety" and that this threat was not being adequately managed by probation agencies in California and probably elsewhere. In Massachusetts, for example, the number of persons sentenced to probation for crimes against persons increased between 1982 and 1993 by more than 250 percent. As noted in Chapter 1, dramatic increases in probation are often linked to prison overcrowding, which is sometimes exacerbated by abolishing parole.

▼

	California (Percentage)	Missouri (Percentage)	Kentucky (Percentage)
Rearrests	65.0	22.3	22.1
Reconvictions	51.0	12.0	17.7
Violent felonies	18.0	7.1	4.1

Research into felony probation in Missouri and Kentucky revealed a different outcome. Both studies were designed to replicate that of Petersilia and her colleagues in California, that is, to determine whether felony offenders placed on probation in Missouri and Kentucky presented risks similar to those in California. Significant differences were found (McGaha, Fichter, and Hirschburg, 1987):

The results of research into felony probation in New Jersey fell about midway between the findings in California and those in Kentucky and Missouri—four years after those convicted of felonies were sentenced to probation, 40 percent had been rearrested and 35 percent were reconvicted (Whitehead, 1989).

Based on their research, Petersilia et al. (1985: 64) argue that "routine probation, by definition, is *inappropriate for most felons*." What, other than imprisonment, is *appropriate* for most felons? According to Petersilia and her colleagues:

> We believe that the criminal justice system needs an alternative, indeterminate form of punishment for those offenders who are too antisocial for the relative freedom that probation now offers, but not so seriously criminal as to require imprisonment. A sanction is needed that would impose intensive surveillance, coupled with substantial community service and restitution. It should be structured to satisfy public demands that the punishment fit the crime, to show criminals that crime really does not pay, and to control potential recidivists. (1985: ix)

The Rand Corporation researchers recommend a different form of probation supervision:

> In response to changes in the probation population, the system should redefine the role and powers of probation officers. Probation officers cannot deal with felony probationers in the same ways they have dealt with misdemeanants. We certainly do not recommend that they abandon their counseling or rehabilitative roles; however, because the probation population includes a large number of active criminals, we support the growing legal and policy trend toward quasi-policing roles for probation officers, whenever the situation warrants it. Attention should be paid to the recruitment and training of probation officers. Different skills may be required of officers whose primary responsibility is surveillance rather than rehabilitation. (Petersilia et al., 1985: xiii)

This would result in the **combined model**—monitoring/control and social services— discussed in Chapter 8, that involves unannounced home and employment visits; checks for drug use; close working relationships with law enforcement agencies; and attention to client needs, including employment, housing, and counseling, which provides social and psychological support. Just as there are no recognized standards for P/P success, supervision has no generally accepted levels of quality.

"Probation and parole systems have two sets of goals that may appear to be in conflict but are in fact complementary: enabling offenders who have left jail or prison to successfully reintegrate themselves into the community and protecting the community from the risk of further crimes committed by these offenders" (Thigpen, 2004: vii). But in too many states, neither of these goals is relevant. In California, for example, Ryken Grattet and his colleagues (2009: 3) point out that parole agents are so overburdened "that parolees who represent serious threats to public safety are not watched closely, and those who wish to go straight cannot get the help they need."

The basic mechanism of P/P supervision is client contact. Thus, as noted in Chapters 8 and 9, issues of caseload size and increased contacts have been something of a preoccupation in this field. Contacts are easily quantifiable, so little beyond a "numbers game" has been studied. Faye Taxman (2002) notes that the endeavor is essentially atheoretical because other than the contact being seen as some type of control, there has been an absence of interest in the quality of the contact, be it for control or rehabilitation. This issue is of great import because studies of reduced caseload size reveal that "unless the contacts are more than 'check-ins,' it is unlikely that they will impact on offender outcomes" (Taxman, 2002: 17). This is critical because there is research indicating that providing therapy predicts better outcomes—that supervision with a focus on providing rehabilitation services is more effective than a control/surveillance emphasis (Schlager and Robbins, 2008; Taxman, 2002). And research into lower caseload size when combined with evidence-based practice reveals significant reductions in recidivism (Jalbert and Rhodes, 2012).

▶ Evidence-Based Practice

Faced with shrinking budgets, community corrections agencies are taking a cue from the health care field by attempting to implement **evidence-based practice (EBP)**—*not more, but better*. "Evidence-based practice is the objective, balanced, and responsible use of current research and the best available data to guide policy and practice decisions.... An evidence-based approach involves an ongoing, critical review of research literature to determine what information is credible, and what policies and practices would be most effective given the best available evidence" (Crime and Justice Institute, 2009: ix). The focus is on cost-efficient practice proven to reduce risk to the community. "It also involves rigorous quality assurance and evaluation to ensure that evidence-based practices are replicated with fidelity, and that new practices are evaluated to determine their effectiveness" (Crime and Justice Institute, 2009: ix–x).

The core elements of EBP include P/P officers performing assessments to identify risk factors, using these risk factors to predict which offenders are likely to reoffend, and then assigning offenders to different levels of supervision according to assessed risk. "Control and correctional resources are concentrated on the high-risk offenders. The assessment process leads to a case plan designed to address factors—such as use of illegal drugs—that contribute to the risk of reoffending" (Jalbert et al., 201: 4). But risk/needs assessments do not incorporate the media-political implications of violations or violators: How is an offender who has a low-risk score but a high level of potential media/political interest to be rated for purposes of supervision? When I was a parole officer, certain cases were designated "intensive" by the parole board, not because they were necessarily at high risk for recidivism, but because they had the potential subject the board to a great deal of criticism—"intensive" supervision provided the board with some cover for their decisions. At the other end of the spectrum, how is an offender with a high-risk score but a low-"media/political score," a car thief or a shoplifter for example, to be rated/supervised? A low-risk armed robber as contrasted with a high-risk commercial burglar—what are the supervision implications?

Likely case outcome can be predicted by considering two variables: the age of the offender and the neighborhood where he or she will be residing.

P/P officers cannot affect community environment that research has determined is associated with recidivism. Evidence-based practice discounts place of residence, although "the neighborhood where an individual returns for supervision is an important factor in the success of his or her supervision. Offenders who return to neighborhoods that are seen as impoverished and transient have higher failure rates" (Rhodes et al., 2013: 18).

These neighborhoods are likely to be in inner-city environs that are primarily African American or Latino. Will we accept evidence-based practice that is based, directly or indirectly, on race and ethnicity? If EBP concludes that employment has no affect on recidivism, should we discard efforts at helping offenders with employment? Evidence-based practice cannot inform about the right thing to do (Boyes-Watson and Pranis, 2012).

"Justice system practices, unlike many other public service fields, are created as part of an emotional outlet as the public becomes angry with or frightened by particular offenders. Consider the anger and politically charged emotionalism that has fostered many contemporary drug and sex offender laws. Another example of public outrage over justice system issues is the media and political attention given when a parolee or probationer commits a major crime. This emotionalism is not new, but rather is part of the nature of justice policies and practices" (DeMichele and Payne, 2005: 49). If evidence-based practice is to become more than a twenty-first century buzzword, it will need to overcome obstacles presented by pandering politicians and a visceral public reaction to a single ugly incident. Knee-jerk reactions encourage policies, for example, "truth-in-sentencing" (no early release) and "three-strikes-and-your're out" (life imprisonment) that can undermine rational, evidence-based practice.

▶ Goals of Probation and Parole

What are Goals of Probation and Parole the goals of P/P? Success can be measured only against anticipated outcomes. If a P/P agency is based on a social services model, success is measured by the delivery of or referral to services, including education, training, employment, counseling, and client–consumer satisfaction with the level of service. This type of agency will often be affected by variables beyond its control, such as variations in the unemployment rate, particularly for low-skilled workers. A relatively low rate of unemployment makes it easier for ex-offenders to secure employment (Meredith, 2000); the reverse is also true. A jurisdiction with readily available employment will presumably do better at job placement than the same agency in a jurisdiction that has a relatively high rate of unemployment; similarly, an agency located in a community with a variety of available social services will be more likely to show a greater level of success than will one in a community with a paucity of such agencies. The interrelated problems of poverty and the collapse of inner-city families are important issues with which P/P agencies have to contend but are helpless to affect.

If a P/P agency is based on a control model, success is measured according to the agency's ability to hold the offender accountable for his or her behavior. The discovery of supervision violations and/or new crimes by close P/P monitoring, however, could statistically increase recidivism rates by uncovering behavior that might not otherwise be discovered. Recidivism may also be related to unemployment—and to the extent that it is, the success of this type of agency will depend in part on the state of the economy. Recidivism is also related to other practical issues. First, one cannot account for undetected criminality; second, arrest and prosecution are often a measure of the law enforcement activity in a given community. Thus, different levels of law enforcement will produce different levels of official (statistical) recidivism, regardless of P/P agency effectiveness. Indeed, a more effective control model agency may enhance the law enforcement function (e.g., through close cooperation with the police) and will thus help to (statistically) *produce* more recidivism—arrests and convictions of agency clientele. (Ironically, greater police effectiveness increases—statistically—the crime rate.) David Stanley points out what happens if we use recidivism as a measure: "An offender can be unemployed, ignorant, promiscuous, and drunk but still a success as far as the criminal justice system is concerned if he commits no crime" (1976: 173)—or is not arrested for criminal behavior.

Furthermore, how are technical violations of P/P rules to be treated (statistically) with respect to agency goals? More vigorous (i.e., intensive) supervision may *produce* more technical violations (although the research is not clear on this issue), whereas an agency that provides little or no supervision will have few (detected) technical violations—hence, fewer revocations of P/P. The level of individual and agency tolerance for technical violations will also affect the revocation rate, and a higher revocation rate of technical violations may result in a lower number of new convictions—offenders screened out of supervision before they can be arrested for new crimes.

Because neither the social services agency model nor the control model agency need make any claim about rehabilitation, the question of postsupervision arrests and convictions need not be raised. In agencies that include rehabilitation as a (or perhaps *the*) goal, this issue needs to be considered. How long does the agency retain (statistical) responsibility for success or failure of a client who has completed supervision—six months, one year, or life? The implication is that such an agency will succeed in producing a lasting change in client behavior. Is it reasonable to expect a P/P agency—or any other relatively brief intervention—to "correct" a lifetime of problems and problematic behavior? An additional question concerns how to weigh recidivism when the instant offense is a great deal less serious than the original crime. For example, is an armed robber convicted of shoplifting considered a success or a failure?

Perhaps the most difficult agency to evaluate in terms of success or failure is one based on a combined model, and most P/P agencies in the United States fall into this category. In this type of agency, an explicit or implicit claim is usually related to services and rehabilitation *and* control. An agency with such broad purposes—with a plethora of complicated goals—cannot fail, nor can it succeed—it presents no clear-cut basis for measuring anticipated outcome. The claims are too broad, too many, and too dependent on variables beyond agency's control (e.g., the economy, the level of law enforcement in the community, the screening of offenders by judges/parole boards, the availability of resources in the community) for a research effort to analyze in any relevant manner.

Petersilia (1993: 69) urges P/P agencies to "customize their mission statement, methods, and performance indicators so that they reflect local resources and priorities." The mission should be one that can reasonably be expected to be fulfilled and clearly related to the unique services provided by the agency, and performance indicators should be specified: "When public agencies fail to define their mission internally, political influences are more apt to define it for them. And when they fail to articulate how they should be evaluated, outcome measurements such as recidivism rates will likely be imposed upon them" (Petersilia, 1993: 76). Petersilia (1998a, 1998b) also notes that responsibilities of P/P agencies include functions that cannot be measured by recidivism rates, including conducting presentence and executive clemency investigations; collecting fines and fees; monitoring community service, work release, and furloughs; and providing victim services.

One should consider the very reason that P/P exist. As penological history in the United States reveals (Chapters 1, 2, and 4), stripped of the humanistic dynamic, P/P exist for *economic reasons*. In terms of budgetary considerations, if P/P were as costly as or even equal in cost to imprisonment, they would be so severely restricted as to no longer constitute an important issue in criminal justice. Postsupervision behavior is irrelevant to the economic argument. Thus, P/P supervision should be judged a success if it is able to help maintain an offender in the community who would otherwise be in prison. While certainly desirable, adult felony offenders often arrive at P/P with such serious life-long deficits that permanent desistance from criminal behavior is too much to expect from time-limited supervision. Nevertheless, Michael Ostermann (2013: 506) argues, "parole boards must strive to have impacts upon parolees beyond the term of supervision to ensure public safety over the long term." He sees this as conforming to the "underlying theoretical tenets on which parole was originally implemented"—rehabilitation—although a review of the history that led to parole puts this assertion into question.

TOUGH TALK, WEAK POLICY

By exercising discretion, parole boards can single out the more violent and dangerous offenders for longer incarceration. When states abolish parole or reduce the discretion of parole authorities, they replace a rational, controlled system of "earned" release for selected inmates with "automatic" release for nearly all inmates.

No-parole systems sound tough but remove a gatekeeping role that can protect victims and communities.

Parole boards can demand that released inmates receive drug treatment, and research shows that coerced treatment is as successful as voluntary participation. If parole boards also require a plan for the released offender to secure a job and a place to live in the community, the added benefit is to refocus prison staff and corrections budgets on transition planning (Petersilia, 2000b: 5).

As noted in Chapter 1, most serious crimes do not result in an arrest. Of those arrested for felonies, well in excess of 50 percent are not prosecuted for felony crimes; most of those prosecuted for felonies plead guilty, usually the result of negotiations (plea bargaining). Thus, when discussing issues of punishment, *residuals* are involved—but these are sufficiently large, so common sense indicates they cannot all be incarcerated. Even if that were a proper response, enough prison space could not be created expeditiously, nor would taxpayers be willing to pay the required taxes and/or allow the shifting of public resources. However, California is spending as much money on prisons as higher education, and other states are following California's lead (Grattet et al., 2009). While states struggle to deal with the growth and attendant cost of their prison populations, four states achieved significant declines in their prison populations by sentencing more drug offenders to probation and reducing their sentences to make them eligible for early parole: Kansas, Michigan, New Jersey, and New York (Greene and Mauer, 2010). Some states have benefited from a decline in the number of young men in the crime-prone cohort, late adolescence and early adulthood.

Probation offers the first line of defense against prison overcrowding; and if no parole system is in operation, probation becomes *the* method by which prison populations are controlled. As a result, serious felony offenders, for whom probation has historically not been intended, become probation clients. At the other end, mandatory prison releasees typically receive inadequate (if any) supervision because little incentive exists for politicians to expend tax dollars on programs for nondiscretionary-released offenders—an absence of public officials on whom to lay blame in the event a releasee generates public outrage. In any event, relatively few offenders will remain in prison their entire lives—more than 97 percent of all state prison inmates will eventually be released (Schriro, 2000). The Alabama Board of Pardons and Paroles notes that with or without parole, more than 95 percent of incarcerated offenders will walk the streets again. "The real question then is not whether offenders should be released, but rather when should offenders be released and what are the best circumstances for their release?"

The issue remains: Who will make the release decision—judges, prison officials, or parole boards? Will these decisions involve a careful analysis of the case, comparing it to similar cases (issues of equity and reasonable predictions of future behavior), or involve only risk control? Petersilia (2000a) notes that when states abolish parole or reduce the amount of parole board discretion, they effectively replace a rational controlled system of "earned" release for selected inmates with automatic release for nearly all inmates. And what happens after they are released? "Underfunded parole agencies in many jurisdictions have made parole more a legal status than a systematic process of reintegrating returning prisoners" (Travis, 2000: 1). And these releasees can significantly impact neighborhood crime rates: "Parolees in a neighborhood increase the rate of crime," in particular, "aggravated assaults, robberies, and burglaries" (Hipp and Yates, 2009: 644).

> **Key Fact**
>
> The issue is not whether offenders should be released from prison—virtually all will be released—but rather when should they be released and what are the best circumstances for their release?

"The very existence of discretionary release," notes Peggy Burke (2006: 30), "creates an incentive for inmates to engage in activities that will better prepare them for transition to the community." One of the roles of a parole board is to ensure that an inmate is prepared for release, which includes having a residence and some means of support. In the absence of a parole board, release planning may be inadequate or absent, presenting parole officers with supervision challenges that can translate into more parole violations. But these violations can be without consequences, as is seen in Washington, a state without discretionary release but with an overcrowded prison system. In Washington, 83 felons, including high-risk sex offenders and people convicted of violent crimes, who were locked up for violating the terms of their release from state prison were set free for lack of room in King County's two jails (Associated Press, 2007b). And the wheels of criminal justice continue to spin, generating heat but not light.

▶ Where Have We Been? Where Are We Now? Where Are We Going?

When the first edition of this book was published in 1977, the indeterminate sentence and parole were under great scrutiny and pressure, the result of Robert Martinson's article "What Works?" (1974) and publication of the full study (Lipton, Martinson, and Wilks, 1975) the following year (Chapter 4). In the years that followed, about a dozen states adopted determinate sentencing and abolished parole release. By the twenty-first century, most states had either abolished the indeterminate sentence or severely restricted the categories of offenders eligible for parole release—a turn toward classicalism. Although failing to accomplish equal punishment for crimes of equal severity, as per classicalism, determinate sentencing removed a rational vehicle for responding to prison overcrowding. Policymakers and public officials failed to learn the lessons of history reviewed in Chapter 4: The establishment of parole with the onset of the Great Depression was a means of alleviating prison overcrowding—issues of rehabilitation were not a motivating factor.

The rightward movement of politics in the United States swept the criminal justice system into overdrive: "Law and order" rhetoric beget a policy leading to more arrests and more convictions, particularly for drug offenses. States began abolishing the indeterminate sentence and parole or severely restricting their use. In Georgia, for example, all violent offenders and residential burglars serve a minimum of 90 percent of their sentence; offenders convicted of murder, various sex offenses, and armed robbery serve 100 percent of their prison sentence. In New York, violent offenders are not eligible for parole.

A CLOSER LOOK

DÉJÀ VU

The Manhattan grand jury was led to believe that the murders of several policemen were due to an "alleged laxity in the state parole system." According to crime reporter Hickman Powell, "The grand jurors started under the impression, assiduously fostered by J. Edgar Hoover and reactionary policemen, that parole is crooked and incompetent and habitually frees dangerous criminals. They were surprised to discover the murders in question were not to be blamed on parole, and that the parole system was a valuable agency of public protection. In most states, parole continues to be merely a disguise for executive clemency, a means of emptying the prisons and keeping their budgets down. In other states, notably New York, the majority of prisoners continue to be released after a certain time, to live under rigid supervision and to be sent summarily back to prison if they don't behave." Parole judgments are "necessarily fallible, and when the inevitable mistakes are made, the propagandists shout about the inequities of parole" (Powell, 2000 [1939]: 38fn).

These policies were the driving force behind the corrections overload as prison populations reached record levels and the courts began to intervene. Overcrowding and court intervention led to forced releases, and some states passed "one-in/one-out" legislation. This proved insufficient. As pressure built, criminal justice systems increased their use of probation, particularly in those states without parole release. Offenders who would otherwise have been incarcerated (e.g., serious felons who were not candidates for traditional probation) burdened ill-equipped probation agencies.

In 1994, Congress enacted the Violent Crime Control and Law Enforcement Act providing incentive grants to states that adopted truth-in-sentencing (TIS) laws. TIS requires an offender to serve a fixed portion of his or her sentence before being eligible for release. States that require offenders convicted of a federally defined Part 1 violent crime to serve at least 85 percent of their sentences are eligible for federal TIS grants, which can be used to build or expand prisons to house violent offenders or to construct or enhance correctional facilities for nonviolent offenders in order to free up bed space for violent criminals. The TIS money covers bricks and mortar, but not the staggering operating costs associated with prisons. Prison systems throughout the U2nited States are struggling with the problem of recruiting and maintaining an adequate number of correction officers. Alabama, for example, is operating a prison system that is nearly 190 percent of capacity and cannot recruit enough correction officers to replace the 20 to 25 the system loses every month (Kitchen, 2009).

A hurried scramble for ways to deal with the opposing pressures—arrest and incarcerate offenders versus decrease prison populations—ensued. New terminology resulted, with the term "corrections" being displaced by the buzzword of a new era, **intermediate sanctions**. Under this rubric were regurgitated models: From the late nineteenth-century Elmira system sprang boot camps reinvented for the 1990s, the California Special Intensive Parole Unit of the early 1950s was reinvented as intensive probation supervision (IPS), and fondness for technology led penology to adopt electronic monitoring.

New "What Works?" research was critical of these schemes because they failed to control recidivism while having little impact on the central problem of prison overcrowding. Despite decreases in the crime rate, prison overcrowding continued with the enactment of more "get tough" legislation. For example, in 1994, when the state ranked sixth in rates of incarceration, Arizona enacted a TIS law eliminating parole and reducing good time to no more than 15 percent of the sentence. By 2009, to save money, the state was negotiating with private companies to take over its entire prison system. "Three strikes and you're out" became a popular metaphor—life without parole on the third (sometimes the second) felony conviction. As a crime policy, it raises important questions, not the least of which is the cost of turning prisons into expensive geriatric facilities for elderly offenders often convicted of nonviolent crimes. In 2003, for example, California imprisoned more than 300 men whose "third strike" was for petty theft (Greenhouse, 2003). Even the terminology began to change; in 1999, for example, Florida turned back the clock, renaming prison superintendents "wardens."

As the trend toward narrowing or eliminating the discretionary release of prison inmates continues, corrections departments are using special good-time provisions and new schemes are being implemented. In some states without parole, judges impose prison sentences followed by a term of probation supervision; Maricopa County (Phoenix) Arizona has more than 9,000 of these postprison probationers. In New York, judges can place offenders directly on parole or use **split sentences**—prison followed by probation. Connecticut judges are authorized to impose special parole terms on any prison sentence in excess of 2 years; the length of special parole is at the court's discretion but may not exceed 10 years; and in combination with the prison term, it may not exceed the maximum sentence allowable for the crime of conviction. For certain sex offenses, special parole is required. It is easy to see why a governor would find this approach attractive:

▼

It accomplishes the early release and supervision of offenders without the need for action by a politically vulnerable parole board. These schemes fail to promote equity, are devoid of accountability, and abandon both classical and positivist approaches in favor of the gross politicization of our system of justice.

What is the public safety cost of this approach? "No one is more dangerous than a criminal who has no incentive to straighten himself out while in prison and who returns to society without a structured and supervised release plan" (Petersilia, 2003: 18). Petersilia notes that "discretionary parole systems provided a means by which inmates who represent continuing public safety risks can be kept in prison [while focusing] prison staff and corrections budgets on planning for release, not just opening the door at release" (2003: 18).

Traditional P/P still bears the major burden, and some states that had used the determinate sentence reintroduced parole release or split sentencing. At the same time, the law enforcement role and training of P/P officers increased dramatically as the control model became predominant, while some states with determinate sentencing (e.g., Illinois and Virginia), in an effort to save money, have gone to the opposite extreme by virtually ending supervision of offenders released from prison. Some states no longer allow parolees to be returned to prison for technical violations. Illinois, which does not have a parole board, paid the price for its approach. In 1994, after serving 5 years of a 14-year sentence for torture and rape, because the prison system was overcrowded, Paul Runge was released with a recommendation that he be monitored closely in the community. However, there were not enough parole agents to provide monitoring. Runge, who refused to undergo sex offender treatment while in prison, went on a rape and murder spree that did not end until he was arrested in 2001.

In California and other states, there has been a dramatic increase in the number of persons returned to prison for violating the conditions of their release—the result of a form of supervision dominated by control devoid of the social service concerns of an earlier era (Beck, 2000b; Butterfield, 2000b). In the fourth edition of this book, I expressed concern over the movement toward a control model: "This direction brings with it the danger that P/P will become simply offender-monitoring activities devoid of any rehabilitative components" (Abadinsky, 1991: 386). In 1991, I advocated a balanced approach and continue to do so: "A balanced approach to P/P requires that the goal remain protection of the community, but with recognition that this is best accomplished by rehabilitating offenders" (Abadinsky, 1991: 386).

In the second decade of the twenty-first century, there is an opportunity to advance the supervision process. Research reveals that supervision providing treatment and not just control has significantly greater rates of success (Lowenkamp et al., 2006). EBP is an expression of this reality. A proverbial dollar spent in the community saves many dollars that would otherwise need to be spent on incarceration. P/P officers typically reside far from the neighborhoods where clients reside and "therefore lack an understanding of the situational context that geographically oriented supervision could provide" (Solomon, Kachnowski, and Bhati, 2005: 16). Paralleling the success of community-based policing, P/P agencies are stationing P/P officers in neighborhood offices: *place-based supervision*. Instead of the more two-dimensional incarceration or continued supervision response to supervision violations, P/P agencies are using an array of intermediate sanctions ranging from intensive supervision with electronic monitoring to short-term detention.

JUSTICE REINVESTMENT. In a turn toward rehabilitation, in 2008, Congress passed and President George W. Bush signed the Second Chance Act (*Public Law*, 110-199) to promote and support programs that reduce recidivism and provides funding for research to improve the effectiveness of release and revocation decisions. The motivation for this legislation appears to be the cost of imprisonment against the reality of a shortage in tax dollars due to a severe economic downturn. A sense of equilibrium, if not a turning point, can be discerned. The apparent triumph of a "get tough" approach to offender supervision devoid of traditional social work (see Chapter 6) has added to prison overcrowding without a noticeable improvement reducing recidivism. As Michael Ostermann (2009: 141) notes, "the current trend within the criminal justice system has been to reaffirm the rehabilitative ideal by increasing the focus on what works in community corrections." But as William Burrell (2005: 5) notes, "Embracing the rehabilitative model requires a significant role redefinition and organizational change for probation and parole. An entire generation of staff has grown up in the field without exposure to treatment and rehabilitation."

When the Maryland Division of Parole and Probation sought to revamp their system of community supervision by focusing on treatment and rehabilitation—Proactive Community Supervision (PCS)—it was necessary to provide new training for field staff. An emphasis was placed on the quality of the relationship between P/P agents and clients— something fundamental in social casework (discussed in Chapter 6), but often absent in adult P/P for more than three decades. Caseload size was reduced by focusing on high-risk offenders using the Level of Service Inventory-Revised (discussed in Chapter 8), and case plans were established with a "focus on specific behavioral goals and defined behavioral tasks in terms of small, incremental steps that can be taken by those under supervision to improve their situation" (Greene and Ríos, 2009: 20). Outcome measurements of this "new/old" approach revealed significantly less technical violations and a lower rearrest rate: 30 percent for PCS compared with the 40 percent for non-PCS caseloads (Greene and Ríos, 2009). "The results suggest that more productive, goal-centered contact between the offender and agent can have a positive outcome" (Taxman, Yancy, and Bilanin, 2006 :17).

When I entered the field in 1964, a New York State parole officer was sometimes referred to as a "social worker with a gun." The apparent contradiction actually describes an approach to helping offenders while protecting the community that I believe is returning in the second decade of the twenty-first century. Offender monitoring and rehabilitation are not separate approaches, but points along a continuum that will differ from offender to offender. Adequately "armed" with education and training in both treatment and law enforcement, the *Twenty-first Century P/P Officer* has the confidence and flexibility to integrate both in a manner appropriate to the needs of each case aided by tested risk/needs tools.

> **Key Fact**
>
> After being driven underground by the "What works? Nothing!" view that dates back to the 1970s, the term "treatment" is again fashionable in corrections.

Summary

- Studies of probation and parole supervision effectiveness do not use an experimental model.
- Success rates for those released by a parole board are considerably higher than those who released under good-time provisions/mandatory release.
- There is no standard to determine if a recidivism rate is high or low.
- The basic mechanism of P/P supervision is client contact.
- Supervision with a focus on providing rehabilitation services is more effective than a control/surveillance emphasis.
- Evidence-based practice entails the use of current research to guide policy and practice decisions.
- Politics can interfere with evidence-based practice.
- Data on recidivism cannot account for undetected criminality or the law enforcement activity in a given community.
- P/P supervision should be judged a success if it is able to help maintain an offender in the community who otherwise would be in prison.

- Abolishing parole means a rational of release for selected inmates is replaced with automatic release for nearly all inmates.
- Abolishing parole results in an increase in probation.
- In the absence of a parole board, release planning may be inadequate or absent.
- The establishment of parole was a means of alleviating prison overcrowding—issues of rehabilitation were not a motivating factor.
- Some states the abolished parole release use split sentences.
- The term "treatment" is once again fashionable in corrections.

Key Terms

classicalism *300*
combined model *295*
control model *297*
determinate sentence *302*

evidence-based practice *296*
felony probation *294*
indeterminate sentence *300*
intermediate sanctions *301*

recidivism *293*
social services model *297*
split sentences *301*
success *292*

Internet Connections

American Probation and Parole Association: **www.appa-net.org**

Center for Community Corrections: **communitycorrectionsworks.org**

Corrections Connection: **corrections.com**

Review Questions

1. Why don't studies of probation and parole supervision effectiveness use an experimental model?
2. Why is it impossible to provide a definitive answer to the question of P/P supervision effectiveness?
3. Why are success rates for those released by a parole board considerably higher than those who released under good-time provisions/mandatory release?
4. How can parole board policy influence the recidivism rate?
5. What is the basic mechanism of P/P supervision?
6. What is meant by evidence-based practice in P/P?
7. How can politics interfere with evidence-based practice in P/P?
8. How can law enforcement activity impact recidivism?
9. Why shouldn't P/P agencies be judged on the percentage of offenders who permanently discontinue criminal behavior?
10. How does the abolition of parole affect release from prison?
11. How does the abolition of parole affect probation?
12. If issues of rehabilitation were not the reason for parole, what were?
13. How does split sentencing reverse the typical sequence of probation and parole?

Glossary

abandonment The most common legal grounds for termination of parental rights, also a form of child abuse in most states. Sporadic visits, a few phone calls, or birthday cards are not sufficient to maintain parental rights. Fathers who manifest indifference toward a pregnant mother are also viewed as abandoning the child when it is born.

absconder An offender fails to report for probation or parole supervision, is no longer residing at his or her approved residence, and whose whereabouts are unknown.

abuse A term for acts or omissions by a legal caregiver. It encompasses a broad range of acts and usually requires proof of intent.

accomplice A partner in a crime.

acquittal A term for when a defendant is found not guilty.

addiction A preoccupation with the use of psychoactive substances characterized by neurochemical and molecular changes in the brain.

adjournment A delay in trial ordered by the judge, usually at the request of one of the lawyers.

adjudication A judgment or decision.

adjudicatory hearing A trial in juvenile court.

administrative law The body of law created by administrative and regulatory bodies such as a parole board.

adversarial method A system of fact finding used in American trials in which each side is represented by an attorney who acts as an advocate.

affidavit A sworn written statement of facts.

affirm Uphold the decision of a lower court.

affirmative defense A term for when the defendant, without denying the charge, raises extenuating or mitigating circumstances such as insanity, self-defense, or entrapment.

aftercare Outpatient support after the intensive phase of drug or alcohol treatment is concluded; also parole for juveniles.

aggravating factors Elements present in a crime that the judge can take into account at the time of sentencing.

agonist Synthetic substance having a chemical makeup similar to that of another drug.

aid and abet Actively assist another person in the commission of a crime.

Alcoholics Anonymous (AA) Twelve-step mutual self-help organization.

amphetamine Artificially produced central nervous system stimulant.

amyl nitrate Volatile inhalant muscle relaxant.

analgesic Substance that has the ability to reduce feelings of pain without loss of consciousness.

analog Chemical compound that is similar to another drug in its effects but differs slightly in its chemical structure.

anal stage A term used in psychoanalytic theory to refer to the second stage of psychosexual development.

angel dust Phencyclidine (PCP), a stimulant and hallucinogen.

anomie A condition characterized by estrangement from society, the result of being unable to achieve financial success through legitimate avenues.

Antabuse Drug used to treat alcoholism.

antagonist Substance that blocks or counteracts the effects of a drug.

antisocial personality disorder A disorder characterized by psycho- or sociopathic behavior.

appeal A legal challenge to a decision by a lower court.

appellate jurisdiction A court having authority to review and modify the decision of a lower court.

appellate review The consideration of a case by a court of appeals.

appointment system Method of hiring P/P officers that provides a great deal of discretion to appointing officials.

arbitration The submission of a dispute to a nonjudicial third party for binding judgment.

arraignment The early stage in the judicial process when the defendant is informed of the charges and his/her rights and enters a plea of guilty, *nolo contendere*, or not guilty.

arrest The physical taking into custody of a suspected law violator or juvenile.

arrest warrant A document issued by a judicial or administrative officer authorizing the arrest of a specific person.

Ashurst-Sumners Act A 1939 federal statute that effectively ended the prison contract system.

attorney of record The attorney whose name appears on the permanent case files.

Auburn system A fortress-style prison characterized by a factory system exploiting inmate labor.

aversive therapy Form of behavior modification that uses unpleasant responses.

bail Money or other security placed in custody of the court in order to ensure the return of a defendant to stand trial. Bail is forfeited if the defendant fails to return to the court.

bailiff A court officer who keeps order in the courtroom and has custody of the jury.

behavior modification A psychological approach that emphasizes positive and negative reinforcement.

bench trial A trial conducted without benefit of a jury.

bench warrant A court order for a person's arrest for failing to return to court.

best interests of the child The legal doctrine establishing the court as the determiner of the best environment for raising the child.

beyond a reasonable doubt The standard of evidence needed for a criminal conviction.

Big House An Auburn-style prison devoid of a factory system.

bind over Hold for trial or send to grand jury.

blended sentence A combination of juvenile and criminal sanctions given to young offenders.

blood-alcohol level (BAL) The amount of alcohol in the blood: .08 or .10 is the legal standard for determining intoxication, usually measured by a Breathalyzer test.

bond A document signed by a defendant in which he or she agrees to return to court at a subsequent date to stand trial; also personal recognizance or release on recognizance (ROR).

bond hearing An appearance before a judicial officer who determines the conditions of release—bail—pending trial.

booking The process of photographing, fingerprinting, and recording of identifying data subsequent to a suspect's arrest.

boot camp A form of special probation/split sentence that requires offenders, usually between the ages of 16 and 30, to reside in a quasi-military residential program for 90 to 120 days.

brief A report prepared by an attorney and filed in court that sets forth facts and applicable law in support of a case.

"broken windows" supervision An approach that emphasizes strengthening linkages with law enforcement and the community.

broker P/P officer acting to link a client with necessary services.

Bromo-Dragonfly Hallucinogen.

buprenorphine Drug that blocks the action of opiates by occupying their receptor sites.

burden of proof The need to establish a claim or allegation; in a criminal case, the state has the burden of proof.

calendar A list of cases to be heard in a trial court on a specific date, containing the title of the case, the lawyers involved, and the case number.

career criminal A person with a past record of multiple arrests or convictions for serious crimes or with an unusually large number of arrests or convictions for crimes of varying degrees of seriousness.

case law Previous decisions of appellate courts, particularly the Supreme Court.

caseload The number of offenders assigned to the officer or agency on a given date or during a specified time period.

case management Process by which needs and strengths of offenders are matched with selected services and resources in corrections.

casework A system of counseling.

cause Any question/action subject to litigation before a court.

cause of action Facts that give rise to a matter before the court.

certification The process of transferring a minor's case from juvenile to adult (criminal) court.

change of venue The act of moving a trial to a county where the crime did not occur in order to avoid an unfair trial due to pretrial publicity.

charge A formal accusation against the accused that he or she violated a specific criminal law.

cheese heroin Heroin diluted with over-the-counter cold medications containing acetaminophen.

chief judge A judge who has primary responsibility for court administration.

child in need of supervision (CHINS) A status offender.

child-saving movement Activities of middle- and upper-class women of the late nineteenth century to establish the juvenile court.

China White Southeast Asian heroin of high purity.

chipper Occasional user of heroin.

circumstantial evidence Indirect evidence, such as fingerprints, from which an inference can be drawn.

cirrhosis Scarring of the liver, the result of alcohol abuse.

civil protection order A court order according to which an adult suspected of abuse must leave and remain away from the home.

classical conditioning A system of learning in which a primary stimulus that naturally produces a specific response is repeatedly paired with a neutral stimulus. With repeated pairing, the neutral stimulus becomes a conditioned stimulus that can evoke a response similar to that of the primary stimulus.

classicalism An outgrowth of Enlightenment philosophy that stresses free will and equality before law—"all men are created equal"—and provides a basis for determinate sentencing.

classification A procedure in which information is gathered about an offender for law enforcement, correctional, or court agencies, including an offender's behavior patterns, needs, skills, and aptitude, as well as factors related to criminal conduct.

clear and convincing evidence The standard of evidence for certain civil cases that exceeds preponderance of evidence but is lower than beyond a reasonable doubt.

clemency The granting of mercy, such as a pardon, by a chief executive.

clerk of the court An official responsible for managing the flow of cases and maintaining court records.

Clonidine An antihypertension drug used to relieve many of the symptoms of opioid withdrawal, particularly those involving autonomic nervous system hyperactivity.

club drug A term used to characterize psychoactive substances associated with dance parties or *raves*, in particular MDMA, known as ecstasy.

code A compilation of laws arranged by chapters.

cognitive behavior therapy A form of treatment that focuses on helping the client learn and use new thinking skills to modify negative behaviors.

cognitive skills training (CST) A rehabilitation approach that emphasizes the importance of problem-solving skills that can be applied to a variety of problem situations.

cold turkey Slang term for giving up drug use without use of chemicals.

combined model P/P supervision that attempts to balance control and rehabilitation.

commit A court order sending a person to an institution, such as a prison, hospital, or reformatory.

community-based corrections A variety of local, state, or federal activities, in addition to traditional probation and parole, involving punishment and management of offenders within their local communities through such programs as community service, restitution, day reporting centers, drug and alcohol treatment, and electronic monitoring.

community courts A system of courts pioneered in New York City providing speedy adjudication of minor crimes and misdemeanors, as well as restitution and supervision of offenders.

community service A sentence requiring an offender to work a certain number of hours as reparation to the community.

commutation A shortening of sentence provided by a governor or U.S. president as part of the powers of executive clemency.

concurrent jurisdiction The jurisdiction shared by different courts.

concurrent sentences Sentences for more than one time that are served simultaneously.

Conditional Discharge Judicial order releasing offenders from court for a specified period of time during which they must not commit further offense or they will be re-sentenced.

conditional release The release from prison based on the accumulation of time off for good behavior and requiring the releasee to abide by certain regulations.

conflict theory The view that characterizes society by a struggle for power that disadvantages those without financial resources.

consecutive sentence A sentence beginning at the expiration of another.

consensual crime An offense that has no complaining victim but has nevertheless been outlawed, such as the possession of heroin or certain sexual activities.

consolidated model A system in which parole is incorporated into a corrections department.

contempt of court A summary judgment holding that a person has willfully disobeyed a lawful order of the court.

contingency contracting Treatment using a mutually agreed-upon contract providing privileges for compliance and negative contingencies for violations.

continuance A delay in trial granted by the judge at the request of either attorney in a case; an adjournment.

contract system A method for exploiting inmate labor during the Auburn era: Convict labor was sold to private entrepreneurs.

control model A type of probation and parole supervision that emphasizes law enforcement.

corroboration Supplementary evidence that tends to strengthen or confirm other evidence previously introduced.

court of general jurisdiction A trial court that can adjudicate any type of case.

court of last resort The highest appellate court in a jurisdiction.

court of limited jurisdiction A court that can only adjudicate certain minor cases.

court reporter A skilled stenographer who makes a word-by-word record of what is said in court.

crack Smokable form of cocaine.

"crack babies" Abnormalities linked to mothers who use crack during pregnancy.

crank Methamphetamine.

criminal intent A necessary element to be proved in a criminal trial; *mens rea*.

criminal negligence A crime based on someone failing to exercise the necessary degree of care.

criminalistics The science of crime detection, referring to the examination of physical evidence of a crime such as footprints, weapons, and bloodstains.

cross-examination The questioning of a witness by the attorney who did not call the witness; questions aimed at discrediting the courtroom testimony of an opposition witness.

custody The detaining of a person by a lawful authority.

custody theory The obsolete legal view that probationers and parolees are in custody of the courts/prisons and therefore not entitled to due process.

damages The compensation paid by defendants to successful plaintiffs in civil cases.

day deporting center An intermediate punishment requiring attendance at a facility on a daily or otherwise regular basis at specified times for a specific length of time in order to participate in activities, such as substance-abuse counseling, social skills training, or employment training.

death-qualified jury A jury panel whose members do not oppose the death penalty.

defendant A person accused of a crime or against whom the plaintiff brings suit.

deferred sentencing A sentence in which the defendant, after a plea of guilty, is placed under supervision, the successful completion of which can wipe out the conviction.

definite sentence *See* determinate sentence.

delinquent A person found to have violated the law, but whose age prevents defining him or her as a criminal.

delinquent subculture A milieu in which antisocial activity is given high status.

dependent Anyone under the care of someone else. A child ceases to be a dependent when he or she reaches the age of emancipation, which varies by state law; and even then, some states allow for continued treatment as a dependent.

designer drugs Analog of a restricted drug that has psychoactive properties.

desipramine . Antidepressant used to wean cocaine users off the drug.

detainer A warrant placed against a person incarcerated in a correctional facility, notifying the holding authority of the intention of another jurisdiction to take custody of that individual when he or she is released. Under Inter-State Agreement on Detainers, a detainer is a notification filed with an institution in which a prisoner is serving a sentence, advising that he or she is wanted to face pending criminal charges in another jurisdiction.

determinate sentence A sentence having a specific number of years and no provision for discretionary release (parole).

determinism A construct stressing the lack of choice, particularly the belief that one's behavior is "determined" by physiological or environmental variables, devoid of *mens rea*.

detoxification Process of allowing the body to rid itself of a drug while managing the symptoms of withdrawal.

Dextromethorphan (DXM) Active ingredient in many over-the-counter cough medicines that has hallucinogenic properties.

diagnosis Classification of the nature and severity of a medical problem.

Diagnostic and Statistical Manual of Mental Disorders (DSM) American Psychiatric Association publication that classifies mental disorders.

differential association The view of criminal behavior that sees it as being the result of associating with those involved in crime.

diminished expectation of privacy Legal basis for imposing conditions of P/P supervision.

direct evidence Evidence that stands on its own to prove an allegation; usually eyewitness testimony.

direct examination Questions asked of a friendly witness by counsel at trial.

disease model Explanation for drug use based on deficiencies or abnormalities in a person's physical or psychological make-up.

disposition The phase of delinquency proceeding similar to "sentencing" phase of adult trial.

dissociative anesthetics Anesthetics that distort perceptions of sight and sound and produce feelings of detachment.

diversion An alternative to trial decided on at intake to refer a child or adult to counseling or other social services, permitting a person charged with an offense to avoid prosecution in exchange for participation in a rehabilitative or restitution program.

docket The log containing the complete history of each case in the form of a brief chronology.

double jeopardy The act of trying a defendant a second time for the same offense after he or she has already been found not guilty.

drift The view that most juvenile delinquents "drift" out of their antisocial behavior.

drug court A specialized court in which the judge, district attorney, and defense attorney work together in a nonadversarial fashion to help chemically dependent offenders obtain needed treatment and rehabilitation in the hopes of breaking the cycle of crime and addiction.

due process Those procedural guarantees to which every criminal defendant is entitled under the Constitution and its interpretation by the Supreme Court (e.g., the right to remain silent, to a trial by jury).

due process clause A judicial requirement, based on the Fifth and Fourteenth Amendments, that prohibits government from taking life, liberty, or property without due process of law.

ecstasy 3, 4-methylenedioxymethamphetamine (MDMA); designer drug having hallucinogenic and amphetamine-like characteristics.

ego The psyche's contact with reality that maximizes gratification with a minimum of difficulties.

electronic monitoring (EM) The use of surveillance technology, usually by means of a wrist or ankle bracelet, or GPS device to monitor an offender's movements from a central location on a 24-hour basis.

emancipation The independence of a minor from his or her parents before reaching age of majority.

EMIT A commonly used drug test.

entrapment The behavior of an agent of government that encourages the committing of a criminal act by a person who was not predisposed to do so. It constitutes an affirmative defense.

ephedrine Stimulant used in treating allergies and cold symptoms.

equal protection The Fourteenth Amendment clause requiring government to treat similarly situated people the same or have good reason for treating them differently.

evidence (circumstantial) The evidence from which something can be inferred (e.g., fingerprints).

evidence (direct) Eyewitness testimony.

evidence-guided practice Probation and parole practices based on research findings.

exclusionary rule A legal doctrine prohibiting evidence secured in an improper manner from being used at a trial.

executive clemency A pardon, reprieve, or commutation.

expunge To seal or purge records of arrests and criminal or juvenile record information.

extradition The surrender by one jurisdiction to another of a person accused or convicted of an offense committed within the jurisdiction demanding the individual's return.

failure to warn Legal liability resulting from a failure to inform a reasonably foreseeable victim of a possible danger.

family court A court having jurisdiction over juvenile cases, as well as issues such as divorce and custody.

felony The more serious of the two basic types of criminal behavior, usually bearing a possible penalty in excess of 1 year in prison.

fentanyl Potent opiate agonist.

finding The verdict in a juvenile court.

flat sentence See determinate sentence.

formication Sensations caused by cocaine and amphetamine that insects are crawling under the skin (Magnan's syndrome).

foster care Temporary care funded by government and arranged by a child welfare agency.

freebase Cocaine hydrochloride whose crystalline base is separated to enable smoking.

free will A term in classical theory meaning that each person has the opportunity to be law-abiding or criminal (*mens rea*), so the person who opts to commit a crime is deserving of punishment commensurate with the offense.

full faith and credit The constitutional requirement that the official judicial acts of one state will be respected by every other state.

general jurisdiction The ability of a trial court to hear any type of case.

genital stage A term in psychoanalytic theory referring to the third stage of psychosexual development.

GHB (gamma-hydroxybutyrate) Colorless, odorless, virtually tasteless depressant that can produce unconsciousness; used by sexual predators since in addition to rendering victims unconscious, they are often unable to recall what happened.

good-faith exception The exception to the exclusionary rule that allows the admission of evidence based on the officer's reasonable, but mistaken, belief that his or her action was proper.

good time A reduction of the time served in prison as a reward for not violating prison rules; usually one-third to one-half off the maximum sentence.

graduated sanctions A response to technical probation and parole violations that provide a range of alternatives based on factors that are often arranged in the form of a grid.

grand jury A group of citizens, usually numbering 23, who are assembled in secret to hear or investigate allegations of criminal behavior and decide whether enough evidence exists to bring an accused to trial; also to investigate the conduct of public officials.

guardian *ad litem* A Latin term for "for the proceeding," referring to adults, often volunteers, appointed by a court to look after the interests of a minor during the course of a judicial proceeding.

guilty but insane A legal concept according to which a person who is suffering from a mental illness is not relieved of criminal responsibility.

habeas corpus A legal document challenging custody and designed to force authorities holding a prisoner to produce him or her and justify the custody; often used as an alternate method of appealing a conviction.

half-life The time it takes for one-half of a drug to be eliminated from the body.

halfway house A place where offenders work and pay rent while undergoing counseling and job training.

hallucinations Perceiving sounds, odors, tactile sensations, or visual images that arise from within the person, not the environment.

hallucinogens Natural or artificial chemicals that can produce distortions of reality.

hashish More potent form of marijuana.

hearsay A statement by a witness who did not hear or see the incident but heard about it from someone else; a statement whose veracity cannot be subjected to cross-examination and is therefore generally not admissible (although there are many exceptions).

hepatitis C Liver disease spread through sexual intercourse and sharing of hypodermic needles.

herbal stimulants Used as natural "safe" alternatives to illegal drugs.

high risk A supervision level for offenders with high risk/ high need; close supervision with at least two personal contacts per month.

home visit Personal contact by a P/P officer in the client's residence.

house arrest An intermediate punishment that requires an offender to be confined to his or her residence for a period of time unless authorized to leave by the court, parole commission, or supervising officer. House arrest may or may not be accompanied by electronic monitoring.

House of Refuge A prejuvenile court facility for children without adult guardians.

id A term in psychoanalytic theory referring to a primitive human drive.

immunity An exemption from a civil or criminal action.

independent model A system in which the parole board is responsible for release decisions and supervision of those released.

indigent A term referring to someone unable to afford counsel.

infancy A legal age at which a person cannot be held criminally responsible.

informal probation Supervision by a juvenile probation officer without court adjudication.

Information A written accusation by a district attorney that charges one or more defendants with the commission of one or more offenses that serve as a basis for the prosecution.

inhalant Volatile psychoactive chemical produced for nondrug purposes.

inmate subculture Customary behavior formed through the prison socialization process.

innovation A term for sophisticated criminal behavior.

intake A procedure prior to a preliminary hearing in which a probation officer interviews the police officer or other official, parent, and child in order to determine whether the matter is to be handled formally or informally.

intensive supervision A supervision level that focuses on control characterized by a high amount of contacts and unannounced home visits.

intermediate punishments Punishments that are more severe than traditional probation but less severe than prison; also called intermediate sanctions. They encompass community corrections measures, such as day reporting centers and electronic monitoring.

interstate compact An agreement between the states that allows travel by probationers and parolees from one state to another and permits them to reside and be supervised in another state.

jail A local, municipal, or county facility reserved for those awaiting trial, those convicted of a misdemeanor, and those convicted of a felony and awaiting transfer to a prison. Increasingly, jails are used to hold federal and state prisoners awaiting transportation to prison or to another jurisdiction.

judicial conference A body of judges established to provide uniformity of policy and to consider matters of judicial discipline.

judicial review The power of the judicial branch to declare acts of the executive and legislative branches unconstitutional.

jurisdiction The authority to adjudicate a case based on a variety of factors, such as geography, seriousness of the crime, or the value of the amount in dispute.

just deserts The view that punishment should be based exclusively on the seriousness of the offense.

justice model An argument in favor of determinate sentencing devoid of any concern for rehabilitation.

juvenile A person who has not achieved an age set by law.

Korsakoff's syndrome Disease associated with chronic alcoholism characterized by memory loss and psychotic behavior.

labeling The view that a negative identification, a stigma such as ex-convict, can cause a societal reaction that permanently disadvantages the individual and can cause him or her to act in a manner referred to as a "self-fulfilling prophecy."

LAMM Levo-alpha-acetylmethadol; synthetic opiate similar to methadone used in heroin treatment.

latent stage A time (roughly 6 to 13) when there is a lessening of interest in sexual organs and expanded relationships with playmates of the same sex and age.

learning theory The basis for the psychological concept or view (behaviorism) that all behavior is explained or shaped by its consequences.

lease system A system used to exploit inmate labor by "renting" it out to private entrepreneurs.

least restrictive alternative A juvenile court concept for sentencing a youngster to that which restricts liberty the least while meeting the needs of the youngster.

legal aid Legal services provided by an agency to indigent persons.

liberty interest The concept that requires due process procedures whenever any type of freedom is at risk from government action.

limited jurisdiction The jurisdiction of a trial court that can only hear certain types of cases.

LSD Lysergic acid diethylamide; an hallucinogen.

magistrate A judicial officer in a court of limited jurisdiction.

mandatory release The release of an inmate at the end of his or her sentence minus any good time.

mandatory sentence A sentence required by law to be imposed for certain crimes.

maximum The level of offender supervision or the highest range of an indeterminate sentence.

mediation The submission of a dispute to a nonjudicial third party who attempts to get the parties to agree on an outcome.

medical model A metaphor for the system of providing rehabilitative services that parallels the way physicians treat patients.

mens rea A Latin term for "guilty mind," meaning the intent necessary to establish criminal responsibility.

merit system A method for appointing and promoting public employees that avoids political influence.

methadone An artificial opiate used to treat heroin addicts.

methamphetamine Powerful stimulant.

minimum The supervision level for low-risk/low-need offenders. It can be a beginning level or a step down from the maximum and is the lowest of the range in an indeterminate sentence.

misdemeanor An offense less severe than a felony that is normally punished by a fine, a community sanction, or time in a county jail (usually not more than 1 year).

mitigating factors Elements present in the commission of a crime that may be taken into account by the judge to lower a sentence to prison or jail or to select a more appropriate sentence than incarceration.

mock job fair A method for preparing offenders for seeking employment.

motivational interviewing A client-centered approach to counseling that has become prevalent in psychology.

naloxone Short-acting opiate antagonist used to test for opioid dependence and counter opioid overdose.

naltrexone Opiate antagonist used to treat addicts.

Narcan test Use of naloxone to determine opioid dependence.

negative reinforcement The behaviorist concept that the probability of a behavior goes up after the removal of a stimulus.

neglect A parental failure to provide a child with basic necessities when able to do so. It encompasses a variety of forms of abuse that do not require the element of intent.

neoclassicalism The classical approach that encompasses such mitigating factors as age and prior record.

neuroenhancers Use of drugs developed for recognized medical conditions to strengthen ordinary cognition.

neutralization The sociological concept that explains how a person can support conventional values while violating the law.

new offense violation A probation or parole violation that involves an arrest for a new offense.

no true bill A grand jury decision not to indict.

nolle prosequi A decision by the prosecutor declining to prosecute a particular defendant.

nolo contendere The Latin term for a plea of "no contest" to criminal charges. It has the same effect as a plea of guilty but cannot be used as evidence of a criminal conviction at any subsequent civil trial related to the criminal act.

operant conditioning The application of positive and negative reinforcement.

oral stage The earliest stage in psychosexual development.

ordinance A statute enacted by a municipality or county.

organized crime A term that refers to persons involved in ongoing criminal conspiracies whose goals are personal gain and whose actions may persist indefinitely.

overcharging A practice of alleging an excessive number of criminal violations when charging a suspect.

pardon An act of executive clemency that has the effect of releasing an inmate from prison and/or removing certain legal disabilities from persons convicted of crimes.

parens patriae The Latin term for the legal doctrine that refers to the obligation of the state toward persons who are unable to care for themselves, such as children or the mentally ill.

parole The release of a prison inmate prior to the expiration of sentence by a board authorized to make such a decision, followed by a period of supervision by a parole officer.

parole board An administrative body whose members are chosen to review the cases of prisoners eligible for release on parole. The board has the authority to release such persons and to return them to prison for violating the conditions of parole.

parole board guidelines Formal method for determining whether and when an inmate is to be released.

pat-down The act of frisking, placing the hands about the body of a suspect in order to detect any weapons that he or she may be carrying.

PCP Phencyclidine, a dissociative drug.

Pennsylvania system A model used in nineteenth-century prisons and characterized by solitary confinement.

person in need of supervision (PINS) A status offender.

petit jury A trial jury composed of 6 or 12 persons.

petition A formal written request or "prayer" for action; form of complaint used in juvenile proceedings.

plaintiff The person initiating an action in a civil case or on appeal.

plea A criminal defendant's response to the charges.

plea bargain A legal transaction in which a defendant pleads guilty in exchange for some form of leniency.

pleading Written statements of contentions submitted by parties in a legal action, each responding to the other, until the points at issue are sufficiently narrowed to proceed to trial.

plethysmography A method of testing erectile response to erotic stimuli (usually involving children).

positive reinforcement The behaviorist concept that behavior is shaped by rewarding consequences.

positivism The use of the scientific method to study crime and criminals. It denies that crime is simply the result of free will and provides the basis for the indeterminate sentence.

predisposition report A comprehensive report on a juvenile subsequent to a finding of delinquency or status offense.

preliminary hearing The bringing of a juvenile before a magistrate or judge during which charges are formally presented, similar to an arraignment in adult court; also called advisory hearing or initial appearance in some state juvenile justice systems.

Preplea Investigation The process by which probation officers investigate and produce a report as part of a negotiated plea prior to its acceptance by the presiding judge.

preponderance of the evidence The standard used to determine the outcome of a noncriminal action as well as probation and parole revocation.

presentence investigation (PSI) report A document submitted by a probation department to a judge containing information about the offender on which the judge can base his or her sentencing decision.

presumptive sentence A model of sentencing that has decreased use of judicial discretion in individual sentencing cases in an effort to make sentencing more equitable overall.

presumptive waiver A provision according to which certain juvenile offenders must be waived to criminal court unless they can prove that they are amenable to rehabilitation, shifting the burden from the prosecutor to the juvenile.

pretrial release The act of setting free a defendant without requiring bail; also called release on recognizance (ROR).

pretrial services A system of screening services and investigation that may lead to community supervision, including electronic monitoring, for selected individuals who otherwise would be in jail while awaiting trial.

preventive detention The act of holding a defendant in custody pending trial on the belief that he or she is likely to commit further criminal acts.

prison A state-run facility where a person convicted of one or more felonies serves the sentence behind bars. Prisons can vary in security from maximum to medium, minimum, or prerelease.

prisonization Being socialized into the prison process and culture.

probable cause The minimum level of evidence needed to make a lawful arrest or secure certain warrants; a level of information that would lead a prudent person to believe that a crime was being or had been committed by a specific perpetrator.

probable cause hearing A court hearing to determine whether an arrest was justified, that is, whether the officer did have probable cause.

probation A community punishment that requires the offender to comply with certain court-ordered conditions, such as curfew or attendance at a day reporting center, and may subject him or her to various levels of supervision based on public safety and rehabilitative needs.

probation officer A public official authorized to accomplish presentence reports and supervise probationers.

probation subsidy A state grant to encourage the granting of probation.

problem-solving courts Nonadversarial tribunals that focus on helping defendants.

procedural law Specific instructions for invoking substantive law.

professional crime Criminal behavior that exhibits a high degree of skill.

psychoanalytic theory The belief that unconscious material controls conscious behavior.

public defender An attorney employed by government to represent indigent defendants.

public safety exception An exception to the exclusionary rule on the grounds that the action that resulted in securing evidence that would normally be suppressed was necessary to protect the public from some immediate danger.

rave Late-night dance party at which club drugs are often used.

reality therapy (RT) A treatment method whose focus is the present and that stresses the need to adopt conventional behavior.

reasonable doubt The standard of evidence; doubt that a reasonable person could have with respect to the evidence.

recidivism The term used to express the return to criminal activity of persons previously convicted of crimes. Recidivism rate refers to the percentage of those who return to crime once a sentence has been served.

recognizance The obligation to perform some act, usually returning to court to stand trial.

reformatory A penal institution for younger offenders.

reinforcer/reinforcement The behaviorist concept that consequences of a behavior increase the likelihood that it will reoccur.

relapse Reversion to drug use after abstinence and/or treatment.

released on own recognizance (ROR) The release of a defendant without the need to post bail on his/her written promise to appear in court as required.

remand Send back, usually for a new trial or sentencing.

remission Absence of symptoms even though the underlying condition has not been cured.

reprieve A temporary stay of the execution of a sentence to allow more time for judicial review.

residential reentry center Facility that provides a full range of services for released offenders.

residential treatment center (RTC) A private facility for juveniles.

resistance Attitude in response to helping efforts that can include evasive, angry, and uncooperative behaviors.

restitution The act of giving money or services to the victim by the offender, often imposed as a condition of probation.

restorative justice (RJ) An approach to criminal justice in which the victim is at the center and that emphasizes the way in which crimes hurt relationships between people who live in a community.

retainer An advance paid by a client to an attorney in order to engage the attorney's services.

retreatism The response to anomie that refers to substance abuse.

reverse An act of an appellate court setting aside the decision of a trial court.

revocation The administrative or court action that removes a person from either probation or parole status in response to his or her violation of the conditions of probation or parole and that results in imprisonment.

reward Process that reinforces behavior.

risk/needs assessment A classification system that uses the degree to which an offender is likely to recidivate and the amount of help required.

Ritalin (methylphenidate) Stimulant used for treating attention deficit hyperactivity disorder.

Rohypnol A benzodiazepine (sedative) widely prescribed in Europe but not approved for use in the United States. Known to abusers as "roofies" or "rope," it is often ingested with alcohol or marijuana; associated with cases of "date rape."

rules of evidence Standards governing the admission of evidence.

rush How drug users describe a surge of pleasure that follows the intake of a psychoactive substance.

salvia A federally unregulated (illegal in some states) herb that is a member of the mint family and reputed to produce profound introspective states of awareness and visions.

self-incrimination The act of forcing a suspect to provide evidence against himself or herself, which is prohibited by the Fifth Amendment.

sentencing guidelines The system that directs or guides a sentencing judge.

shelter A temporary residential facility for children in need of emergency care.

shock incarceration (SI) A facility that duplicates the military environment; also called boot camp.

shock probation/parole A brief incarceration followed by community supervision.

"sight and sound" separation Requirement that juveniles in custody be kept apart from a adult offenders.

social casework A system for providing assistance based on social work concepts.

social contract The belief that society is tied together by general agreements to conform to law.

social control theory A theory that assumes a person's ties to conventional society determine his or her behavior.

social investigation A study prepared by a probation officer in juvenile court to provide the judge with information on which to base a disposition.

social services model P/P supervision that stresses rehabilitation.

speed Methamphetamine.

Spice Blends of herbs and spices coated with synthetic cannabinoids.

split sentence A sentence of incarceration followed by a period of probation.

spontaneous remission Discontinuing drug use without treatment intervention.

state use system Prison labor that produces products for government.

status offender Youngster who commits a status offense.

status offense An action that would not constitute a crime if the actor were an adult (e.g., truancy) but, in accord with *parens patriae,* can subject the youngster to the juvenile court process.

strain theories Sociological theories that explain criminal behavior as the result of gap between aspirations and ability.

street time The amount of time spent under supervision prior to a finding of a violation.

subcutaneous Ingesting a drug under the skin.

subpoena *ad testificandum* A court order requiring a witness to appear and testify.

subpoena *duces tecum* A term meaning "bring with you," a court order requiring a witness to bring all relevant documents that might affect the outcome of legal proceedings.

superego A psychoanalytic concept referring to a conscious-like mechanism that exerts a sense of morality.

superior court A court that can hold felony trials.

supermax prison A high-security facility that features solitary confinement.

synthetic marijuana Blends of herbs and spices coated with synthetic cannabinoids.

technical violation A probation or parole violation of rules that does not involve a new crime.

termination hearing The process for legally severing the parent–child relationship initiated by the filing of a petition in family court and almost always brought forth by a child welfare agency. It requires a finding of "unfitness" and a determination of the best interests of the child.

theory A building block for scientific knowledge that organizes events, explains past events, and predicts future ones.

therapeutic community (TC) A residential drug treatment program based on Alcoholics Anonymous, emphasizing addicts helping one another to become socially conforming persons.

"three strikes and you're out" A metaphor for life imprisonment upon conviction for a third felony.

token economy A method for employment of positive reinforcement.

tolerance Progressive ability of the body to adapt to the effects of a drug used at regular and frequent intervals, making the drug less effective; higher doses of a drug are required to produce the same effect.

training school A state facility that houses young offenders.

transference Psychoanalytic term referring to the process by which a therapist is viewed by a patient as a parental figure.

truth in sentencing A system that excludes discretionary release and severely limits time off for good behavior.

twelve-step program A method for treating substance abuse, such as Alcoholics Anonymous.

unconscious A psychoanalytic concept referring to "hidden" psychic phenomena that drive conscious behavior.

victim impact statement (VIS) The part of a presentence report that addresses harm to the victim.

victim services A range of activities, usually provided by the prosecutor's office, which attends to the needs of victims and witnesses, coordinates their testimony, and supports them until their case is resolved in the criminal justice system.

waiver of jurisdiction A court action "certifying" the youth as eligible for trial as an adult because it appears rehabilitation is unlikely or the crime was particularly atrocious.

work release A program that permits select inmates to leave incarceration during the day for employment.

yaba Mixture of methamphetamine and caffeine.

youth authority A state agency responsible for the incarceration and supervision of young offenders.

"A Forecast" 2007 *Hampton Roads Daily Press* (April 8): Internet.

Abadinsky, Howard 2014 *Drug Use and Abuse: A Comprehensive Introduction*, 8th ed. Belmont, CA: Wadsworth/Cengage.

Abadinsky, Howard 2013 *Organized Crime*, 10th ed. Belmont, CA: Wadsworth/Cengage.

Abruzzese, George 1999 "Idaho Youth Ranch: A Seamless Continuum of Care for Today's Youth." *Juvenile Justice Magazine* (January/February): Internet.

Adair, David N., and Toby D. Slawsky 1991 "Looking at the Law: Fact-Finding in Sentencing." *Federal Probation* 55 (December): 58–72.

Adams, Benjamin, and Sean Addie 2010 *Delinquency Cases Waived to Criminal Court, 2007*. Washington, DC: Office of Juvenile Justice and Delinquency Prevention

Adams, Benjamin, and Sean Addie 2009 *Delinquency Cases Waived to Criminal Courts, 2005*. Washington, DC: Office of Juvenile Justice and Delinquency Prevention.

Administrative Office of the Courts (AOC) 1996 *Overview and Summary of the Arizona Probation Outcome Study*. Phoenix: Arizona Supreme Court.

Administrative Office of the Courts (AOC) n.d. *Community Service*. Trenton, NJ: AOC.

Advisory Task Force on Female Offenders 2006 *Female Offender Case Planning and Case Management*. St. Paul, MN: Minnesota Department of Corrections.

Agnew, Robert 1992 "Foundation for a General Strain Theory of Crime and Delinquency." *Criminology* 30 (February): 47–87.

Agopian, Michael W. 1990 "The Impact of Intensive Supervision Probation on Gang-Drug Offenders." *Criminal Justice Policy* 4 (3): 214–22.

Aichhorn, August 1963 *Wayward Youth*. New York: Viking Press.

Albanese, Jay S., Bernadette A. Fiore, Jerie H. Powell, and Janet R. Storti 1981 *Is Probation Working?* Washington, DC: University Press of America.

Alexander, Franz, and Hugo Staub 1956 *The Criminal, the Judge, and the Public*. Glencoe, IL: Free Press.

Alexander, Melissa, and Scott VanBenschoten 2008 "The Evolution of Supervision in the Federal Probation System." *Federal Probation* 72 (September): 15–19.

Alexander, Melissa, Scott W. VanBenschoten, and Scott T. Walters 2008 "Motivational Interviewing Training in Criminal Justice: Development of a Model Plan." *Federal Probation* 72 (September): 61–66.

Allen, Fred C., ed. 1926 *Extracts from Penological Reports and Lectures Written by Members of the Management and Staff of the New York State Reformatory, Elmira, N.Y.* Elmira, NY: Summary Press.

Allen, G. Frederick, and Harvey Treger 1994 "Fines and Restitution Orders: Probationers' Perceptions." *Federal Probation* 58 (June): 34–40.

Allen, Harry, Eric Carlson, and Evalyn Parks 1979 *Critical Issues in Probation*. Washington, DC: U.S. Government Printing Office.

Altschuler, David M., and Troy L. Armstrong 1994 *Intensive Aftercare for High-Risk Juveniles*. Washington, DC: Office of Juvenile Justice and Delinquency Prevention.

American Bar Association (ABA) 1970 *Standards Relating to Probation*. Chicago: ABA.

American Correctional Association (ACA) 1981 *Standards for Adult Probation and Parole Field Services*. Rockville, MD: ACA.

American Friends Service Committee 1971 *Struggle for Justice*. New York: Hill and Wang.

American Justice Institute 1981 *Presentence Investigation Report Program*. Sacramento, CA: American Justice Institute.

American Probation and Parole Association (APPA) n.d. [2012] *The Role of Community Corrections in Victim Services*. Lexington, KY: APPA.

American Probation and Parole Association (APPA) n.d. [2011] *Promising Practices in Providing Pretrial Services Functions Within Probation Agencies: A Users Guide*. Lexington, KY: APPA.

American Probation and Parole Association (APPA) 1995 *Abolishing Parole: Why the Emperor Has No Clothes*. Lexington, KY: APPA.

American Psychiatric Association (APA) 1974 *Behavior Therapy in Psychiatry*. New York: Jason Aronson.

Anderson, Elijah 1994 "The Code of the Streets." *Atlantic Monthly* (May): 80–94.

Anderson, James F., Laronistine Dyson, and Tazinski Lee 1997 "A Four Year Tracking Investigation on Boot Camp Participants: A Study of Recidivism Outcome." *Justice Professional* 10 (September): 199–213.

Anderson, Lisa 1998 "Is 'Supermax' Too Much?" *Chicago Tribune* (August 2): 1, 15.

Andreski, Stanislav, ed. 1971 *Herbert Spencer: Structure, Function and Evolution*. New York: Scribners.

Andrews, D. A., Ivan Zinger, Robert D. Hoge, James Bonta, Paul Gendreau, and Francis T. Cullen 1990 "Does Correctional Treatment Work? Clinically Relevant and Psychologically Informed Meta-Analysis." *Criminology* 28 (August): 369–404.

Andrews, Edmund L. 2003 "Economic Inequality Grew in 90's Boom, Fed Reports." *New York Times* (January 23): C1, 7.

Annual Report of the San Francisco Adult Probation Department 1991 San Francisco, CA: San Francisco Adult Probation Department.

Anspach, Donald F., and S. Henry Monsen 1989 "Indeterminate Sentencing, Formal Rationality, and Khadi Justice in Maine: An Application of Weber's Typology." *Journal of Criminal Justice* 17: 471–485.

Aos, Steve, Marna Miller, and Elizabeth Drake 2006 *Evidence-Based Adult Corrections Programs: What Works and What Does Not*. Olympia, WA: Washington State Institute for Public Policy.

Arcaya, Jose 1973 "The Multiple Realities Inherent in Probation Counseling." *Federal Probation* 37 (December): 58–63.

Archibold, Randal C. 2010 "Driven to a Fiscal Brink, A State Throws Open the Doors to Its Prisons." *New York Times* (March 24): 14.

Armstrong, Gaylene S., George Burruss, Marsha Henderson 2007 *An Evaluation of the Cook County Community Based Transitional Services for Female Offenders Program*. Carbondale, IL: Center for the Study of Crime, Delinquency and Corrections, Southern Illinois University.

Arola, Terryl, and Richard Lawrence 1998 "Assaults and Threats against Probation Officers and Some Responses to Officers' Safety Concerns." Paper presented at the annual meeting of the Academy of Criminal Justice Sciences, March 12, Albuquerque, NM.

Ashford, Jose B., and Craig Winston LeCroy 1988 "Predicting Recidivism: An Evaluation of the Wisconsin Juvenile Probation and Aftercare Risk Instrument." *Criminal Justice and Behavior* 15 (June): 141–149.

Associated Press 2009 "Georgia Closes Camp of Sex Offenders." *New York Times* (September 30): 19.

Associated Press 2007a "Philadelphia Jails to Return to Court Oversight." *New York Times* (January 27): 13.

Associated Press 2007b "State Releases 83 Parole Violators, No Room in King County Jails." (February 27): Internet.

Associated Press 2001 "Arkansas Corrections Board Agrees to Release Prisoners Early to Ease Overcrowding." *New Jersey Online* (November 27): Internet.

Associated Press 2000 "Guards Fired over Camp Activities." (January 11): Internet.

Associated Press 1999 "California Has 2.5 Million Unserved Warrants." (June 23): Internet.

Associated Press 1998 "12 Convicted in Prison Plot to Control Drug Gangs." *New York Times* (May 31): 8.

Associated Press 1995 "Sweep of State Prison for Drugs Termed Largest Such Raid Ever." *New York Times* (October 24): 12.

Atherton, Alexine L. 1987 "Journal Retrospective, 1845–1986: 200 Years of Prison Society History as Reflected in the *Prison Journal.*" *Prison Journal* (Spring-Summer): 1–37.

Attica Commission. 1972 *See* New York State Special Commission on Attica.

Auburn Correctional Facility 1998 *Department of Correctional Services Today* (April): Internet.

Auerbach, Barbara J., George E. Sexton, Franklin C. Farrow, and Robert H. Lawson 1988 *Work in American Prisons: The Private Sector Gets Involved.* Washington, DC: U.S. Government Printing Office.

Augustus, John 1972 *John Augustus, First Probation Officer.* Montclair, NJ: Patterson Smith.

Austin, James and Gabrielle Chapman 2009 *The Michigan Department of Corrections Special Alternative Incarceration Program.* Washington, DC: JFA Institute.

Austin, James, and Garry Coventry 2003 "A Second Look at the Private Prison Debate." *The Criminologist* 28 (September/October): 1, 3–9.

Austin, James, and Garry Coventry 2001a *Emerging Issues on Privatized Prisons.* Washington, DC: Bureau of Justice Assistance.

Austin, James, and John Irwin 2001b It's *About Time: America's Imprisonment Binge,* 3rd ed. Belmont, CA: Wadsworth.

Baird, S. Christopher, and Dennis Wagner 1990 "Measuring Diversion: The Florida Community Control Program." *Crime and Delinquency* 36 (January): 112–125.

Baird, S. Christopher, Richard C. Heinz, and Brian J. Bemus 1982 "The Wisconsin Case Classification/Staff Development Project: A Two-Year Follow-Up Report," in *Classification: American Correctional Association Monographs.* College Park, MD: American Correctional Association.

Bakal, Yitzhak 1974 *Closing Correctional Institutions.* Lexington, MA: D.C. Heath.

Baldwin, John D., and Janice I. Baldwin 1998 *Behavior Principles in Everyday Life,* 3rd ed. Upper Saddle River, NJ: Prentice Hall.

Bales, William D., and Linda G. Dees 1992 "Mandatory Minimum Sentences in Florida: Past Trends and Future Implications." *Crime and Delinquency* 38 (July): 309–29.

Ball, Richard A., C. Ronald Huff, and J. Robert Lilly 1988 *House Arrest and Correctional Policy: Doing Time at Home.* Beverly Hills, CA: Sage.

Bandura, Albert 1974 "Behavior Theory and the Models of Man." *American Psychologist* 29 (December): 859–869.

Barnes, Carole Wolff, and Randal S. Franz 1989 "Questionably Adult: Determinants and Effects of the Juvenile Waiver Decision." *Justice Quarterly* 6 (March): 117–135.

Barnes, Geoffrey C. and Jordan M. Hyatt 2012 *Classifying Adult Probationers by Forecasting Future Offending.* Washington DC: U.S. National Institute of Justice.

Baumgartner, Werner A., Virginia Hill, and William H. Blahd 1989 "Hair Analysis for Drugs of Abuse." *Journal of Forensic Sciences* 34 (November): 1433–1453.

Bazelon, Emily 2010 "Arguing Third Strikes." *New York Times Magazine* (May 23): 40–43.

Bazemore, Gordon 1994 "Developing a Victim Orientation for Community Corrections: A Restorative Justice Paradigm and a Balanced Mission." *Perspectives* (special issue): 19–24.

Bazemore, Gordon, and Dennis Maloney 1995 "Rethinking the Sanctioning Function in Juvenile Court: Retributive or Restorative Responses to Youth Crime." *Crime and Delinquency* 41 (July): 296–316.

Bazemore, Gordon, and Dennis Maloney 1994 "Rehabilitating Community Service: Toward Restorative Service Sanctions in a Balanced Justice System." *Federal Probation* 58 (March): 24–35.

Bazemore, Gordon, and Mark S. Umbreit 1994 *Balanced and Restorative Justice: Program Summary.* Washington, DC: Office of Juvenile Justice and Delinquency Prevention.

Beaumont, Gustave de, and Alexis de Tocqueville 1964 *On the Penitentiary System in the United States and Its Application in France.* Carbondale, IL: Southern Illinois University Press. (Originally published in 1833.)

Beck, Allen J. 2000a *Prison and Jail Inmates at Midyear 1999.* Washington, DC: Office of Justice Programs.

Beck, Allen J. 2000b *Prisoners in 1999.* Washington, DC: Office of Justice Programs.

Beck, Allen J., and Jennifer C. Karberg 2001 *Prison and Jail Inmates at Midyear 2000.* Washington, DC: Office of Justice Programs.

Becker, Gary S. 1998 *Behind Bars.* Washington, DC: National Institute of Justice.

Becker, Gary S. 1968 *The Economic Approach to Human Behavior.* Chicago: University of Chicago Press.

Bellis, David J. 1981 *Heroin and Politicians: The Failure of Public Policy to Control Addiction in America.* Westport, CT: Greenwood.

Belluck, Pam 2001 "Desperate for Prison Guards, Some States Even Rob the Cradle." *New York Times* (April 21): 1, 10.

Bennett, Lawrence A. 1988 "Practice in Search of a Theory: The Case of Intensive Supervision—An Extension of an Old Practice." *American Journal of Criminal Justice* 12: 293–310.

Berg, Michael H. 1997 "United States Probation Officers: The Court's Financial Investigators." *Federal Probation* 61 (March): 28–30.

Berk, Richard A., Kenneth J. Lenihan, and Peter Rossi 1980 "Crime and Poverty: Some Experimental Evidence from Ex-Offenders." *American Sociological Review* 45 (October): 766–786.

Bersani, Carl A. 1989 "Reality Therapy: Issues and a Review of Research." In *Correctional Counseling and Treatment,* edited by Peter C. Kratcoski, 2, pages 177–195. Prospect Heights, IL: Waveland Press.

Binder, Arnold, and Gilbert Geis 1983 *Methods of Research in Criminology and Criminal Justice.* New York: McGraw-Hill.

Bishop, Donna M., Charles F. Frazier, and John C. Henretta 1989 "Prosecutorial Waiver: Case Study of a Questionable Reform." *Crime and Delinquency* 35 (April): 179–201.

Bisman, Cynthia D. 2000 "Social Work Assessment: Case Theory Construction." *Families in Society: The Journal of Contemporary Human Services* 80 (May–June): 240–247.

Black, Donald W., with C. Lindon Larson 1999 *Confronting Antisocial Personality Disorder.* New York: Oxford University Press.

Blair, Jayson 2000 "Boot Camps: An Idea Whose Time Came and Went." *New York Times* (January 2): WK 3.

Bloom, Barbara, and Anne McDiarmid 2001 "Gender-Responsive Supervision and Programming for Women Offenders in the Community," in *Responding to Women Offenders in the Community,* pages 11–18. Washington, DC: National Institute of Corrections.

Bloom, Barbara, Barbara Owen, and Stephanie Covington 2003 *Gender-Responsive Strategies Research, Practice, and Guiding Principles for Women Offenders.* Washington, DC: National Institute of Corrections.

Blumberg, Abraham 1970 *Criminal Justice.* Chicago: Quadrangle Books.

Blumenstein, Alfred 1984 "Sentencing Reforms: Impacts and Implications." *Judicature* 68 (October–November).

Bodapati, Madhava R., James W. Marquardt, and Steven J. Cuvelier 1993 "Influence of Race and Gender in Parole Decision Making in Texas: 1980–1991." Paper presented at the annual meeting of the Academy of Criminal Justice Sciences, Kansas City, MO, March 16–20.

Bohlen, Celestine 1989 "Expansion Sought for 'Shock' Prison." *New York Times* (June 8): 14.

Boldt, Richard C. 1998 "Rehabilitative Punishment and the Drug Treatment Court Movement." *Washington University Law Quarterly* 76: 1205–1306.

Bootzin, Richard R. 1975 *Behavior Modification and Therapy: An Introduction.* Cambridge, MA: Winthrop.

Borden, William 2000 "The Relational Paradigm in Contemporary Psychoanalysis: Toward a Psychodynamically Informed Social Work Perspective." *Social Service Review* 74 (September): 352–379.

Bosman, Julie 2010 "For Nearly 800 Youths Jailed by the State, Not One Full-Time Psychiatrist." *New York Times* (February 11): 1, 28.

Boswell, John 1989 *The Kindness of Strangers: The Abandonment of Children in Western Europe from Antiquity to the Renaissance.* New York: Pantheon.

Bowers, Swithun 1950 "The Nature and Definition of Social Casework." In *Principles and Techniques in Social Casework: Selected Articles, 1940–1950,* edited by Cora Kasius, pages 97–127. New York: Family Service Association of America.

Boyes-Watson, Carolyn and Kay Pranis 2012 "Science Cannot Fix This: The Limitations of Evidence-Based Practice." *Contemporary Justice Review* 15 (3): Internet.

Bradsher, Keith 1995a "Gap in Wealth in U.S. Called Widest in West." *New York Times* (April 17): 1, C4.

Bradsher, Keith 1995b "Low Ranking for Poor American Children." *New York Times* (August 14): 7.

Bradsher, Keith 1995c "Widest Gap in Incomes? Research Points to U.S." *New York Times* (October 27): C2.

Breed, Allen F. 1998 "Corrections: A Victim of Situational Ethics." *Crime and Delinquency* 44 (January): 9–18.

Brennan, Thomas P., Amy E. Gedrich, Susan E. Jacoby, Michael J. Tardy, and Katherine B. Tyson 1986 "Forensic Social Work: Practice and Vision." *Social Casework* 67: 340–350.

Brockway, Z. R. 1926 "Character of Reformatory Prisoners." In *Extracts from Penological Reports and Lectures Written by Members of the Management and Staff of the New York State Reformatory, Elmira, N.Y.*, edited by Fred C. Allen, pages 110–18. Elmira, NY: Summary Press.

Broder, John M. 2004 "Dismal California Prisons Hold Juvenile Offenders." *New York Times* (February 15): 18.

Brogue, Bradford and Nandi 2012 *Motivational Interviewing in Corrections: A Comprehensive Guide to Implementing MI in Corrections.* Washington, DC: National Institute of Corrections.

Brooke, James 1997 "Prisons: A Growth Industry for Some." *New York Times* (November 2): 14.

Brown, Allan G. 1986 *Group Work*, 2nd ed. Brookfield, VT: Gower.

Brown, Marjorie 1984 *Executive Summary of Research Findings from the Massachusetts Risk/Need Classification System, Report 5.* Boston: Office of the Commissioner of Probation.

Brown, Waln K., Timothy Miller, Richard L. Jenkins, and Warren A. Rhodes 1991 "The Human Costs of 'Giving the Kid Another Chance.'" *International Journal of Offender Therapy and Comparative Criminology* 35: 296–302.

Buck, Gerald S. 1989 "Effectiveness of the New Intensive Supervision Programs." *Research in Corrections* 2 (September): 64–75.

Bulman, Philip 2013 "Day Reporting Centers in New Jersey: No Evidence of Reduced Recidivism." *Corrections Today* (May/June): 94–95.

Bureau of Justice Statistics 2001 "Forty-Two Percent of State Parole Discharges Were Successful." Press release (October 3).

Burke, Peggy, ed. 2006 *Topics in Community Corrections: Annual Issue 2006: Effectively Managing Violations and Revocations.* Washington, DC: National Institute of Corrections, Community Corrections Division.

Burnett, Walter L. 2007 "Treating Post-Incarceration Offenders with Moral Reconation Therapy: A One-Year Recidivism Study." MBA thesis, University of Phoenix.

Burns, Jerald C. 1993 "Rediscovering That Rehabilitation Works: The Alabama Boot Camp Experience." Paper presented at the annual meeting of the Academy of Criminal Justice Sciences, Kansas City, MO, March 16–20.

Burns, Jerald C., and Gennaro F. Vito 1995 "An Impact Analysis of the Alabama Boot Camp Program." *Federal Probation* 59 (March): 63–67.

Burrell, William D. 2005 *Trends in Probation and Parole in the States.* American Probation and Parole Association Web site.

Burrow, Linda, Jennifer Joseph, and John Whitehead 2001 "A Comparison of Recidivism in Intensive Supervision and Regular Probation: Results from a Southern Jurisdiction." Paper presented at the annual meeting of the Academy of Criminal Justice Sciences, Washington, DC, April 3–7.

Bushway, Shawn 2003 "Reentry and Prison Work Programs." Urban Institute Reentry Roundtable: Internet.

Butterfield, Fox 2004a "Study Tracks Boom in Prisons and Notes Impact on Counties." *New York Times* (April 30): 19.

Butterfield, Fox 2004b "Almost 10% of All Prisoners Are Now Serving Life Terms. *New York Times* (May 12): 17.

Butterfield, Fox 2003a "Inmates Go Free to Reduce Deficits." *New York Times* (December 19): 1, 20.

Butterfield, Fox 2003b "Infections in Newly Released Inmates Are Rising Concern." *New York Times* (January 28): 14.

Butterfield, Fox 2000a "Louisiana Settles Suit, Abandoning Private Youth Prisons." *New York Times* (September 8): 12.

Butterfield, Fox 2000b "Often, Parole Is One Stop on the Way Back to Prison." *New York Times* (November 29): 1, 28.

Butterfield, Fox 1998a "Prisons Replace Hospitals for the Nation's Mentally Ill." *New York Times* (March 5): 1, 18.

Butterfield, Fox 1998b "U.S. and Georgia in Deal to Improve Juvenile Prisons." *New York Times* (March 22): 16.

Butterfield, Fox 1998c "Profits at Juvenile Prisons Earned at a Chilling Cost." *New York Times* (July 15): 1, 14.

Butterfield, Fox 1998d "U.S. Suing Louisiana on Prison Ills." *New York Times* (November 6): 14.

Butterfield, Fox 1995 "Prison-Building Binge in California Casts Shadow on Higher Education." *New York Times* (April 12): 11.

Butts, Jeffrey A., Howard W. Snyder, Terrence A. Finnegan, Anne L. Aughenbaugh, and Rowen S. Poole 1996 *Juvenile Court Statistics 1994.* Washington, DC: Office of Juvenile Justice and Delinquency Prevention.

Byrne, James M 2009 "Social Ecology of Community Corrections— Understanding the Link Between Individual and Community Change." *Criminology and Public Policy* 7 (May): 263–274.

Byrne, James M 1990 "The Future of Intensive Probation Supervision and the New Intermediate Sanction." *Crime and Delinquency* 36 (January): 6–41.

Byrne, James M., Arthur J. Lurigio, and S. Christopher Baird 1989 "The Effectiveness of New Intensive Probation Supervision Programs." *Research in Corrections* 2 (September): 1–48.

Cahalan, Margaret Werner 1986 *Historical Corrections Statistics in the United States, 1850–1984.* Washington, DC: U.S. Government Printing Office.

California Department of Corrections 1981 *Investigation and Surveillance in Parole Supervision: An Evaluation of the High Control Project*, Research Report No. 63. Sacramento: California Department of Corrections.

Campbell, Curtis, Candace McCoy, and Chimezie A. B. Osigweh 1990 "The Influence of Probation Recommendations on Sentencing Decisions and Their Predictive Accuracy." *Federal Probation* 54 (December): 13–21.

Carlson, Eric, and Evalyn Parks 1979 *Critical Issues in Adult Probation: Issues in Probation Management.* Washington, DC: U.S. Government Printing Office.

Carlson, Jill M, 1993 "Restorative Justice: Beyond Crime and Punishment." Master of Science Thesis, Minnesota State University at Mankato.

Carlson, Susan M., and Michael Michalowski 1997 "Crime, Unemployment, and Social Structures of Accumulation: An Inquiry into Historical Contingency." *Justice Quarterly* 14 (June): 209–241.

Carson, E. Ann and Danela Golinelli 2013 *Prisoners in 2012: Advance Counts.* Washington, DC: Bureau of Justice Statistics.

Carter, Madeline M. and Laura Morris 2007 *Enhancing the Management of Adult and Juvenile Sex Offenders: A Handbook for Policymakers and Practitioners.* Silver Spring, MD: Center for Sex Offender Management.

Carter, Robert M. 1966 "It Is Respectfully Recommended …" *Federal Probation* (June): 38–44.

Casius, Cora, ed. 1954 *New Directions in Social Work.* New York: Harper and Row.

Castellano, Thomas C 1997 *Illinois' PreStart Program Revisited: A Further Look at Its Impact on Staff, the Prison System, and Offender Rehabilitation.* Chicago: Illinois Criminal Justice Information Authority.

Center for Sex Offender Management (CSOM) 2008 *The Comprehensive Approach to Sex Offender Management.* Washington, DC: CSOM.

Center for Sex Offender Management (CSOM) 2007 *Managing the Challenges of Sex Offender Reentry.* Washington, DC: CSOM.

Center for Sex Offender Management (CSOM) 2001a "Myths and Facts about Sex Offenders." *Perspectives* 25 (Summer): 34–39.

Center for Sex Offender Management (CSOM) 2001b *Case Studies on the Center for Sex Offender Management's National Resource Sites*, 2nd ed. Silver Spring, MD: CSOM.

Center for Substance Abuse Treatment 2005 *Enhancing Motivation for Change in Substance Abuse Treatment.* Rockville, MD: Substance and Mental Health Services.

Champion, Dean J. 1989 "Private Counsels and Public Defenders: A Look at Weak Cases, Prior Records, and Leniency in Plea Bargaining." *Journal of Criminal Justice* 17: 253–263.

Champion, Dean J. 1988a "Felony Plea Bargaining and Probation: A Growing Judicial and Prosecutorial Dilemma." *Journal of Criminal Justice* 16: 291–301.

Champion, Dean J. 1988b *Felony Probation: Problems and Prospects.* New York: Praeger.

Chapin, Bradley 1983 *Criminal Justice in Colonial America: 1600–1660.* Athens: University of Georgia Press.

Chen, David W. 2000 "Compensation Set on Attica Uprising." *New York Times* (August 29): 1, 25.

Chesney, Steven L. n.d. "The Assessment of Restitution in the Minnesota Probation Services." In *Restitution in Criminal Justice*, edited by Joe Hudson. St. Paul: Minnesota Department of Corrections.

Chesney-Lind, Meda 1997 *The Female Offender: Girls, Women, and Crime.* Thousand Oaks, CA: Sage.

Childress, Anna Rose 1993 "Medications in Drug Abuse Treatment," in *Second Annual Conference on Drug Abuse Research and Practice: An Alliance for the 21st Century*, pages 73–75. Rockville, MD: National Institute on Drug Abuse.

Childress, Anna Rose, A. Thomas McLellan, and Charles P. O'Brien 1985 "Behavioral Therapies for Substance Abuse." *International Journal of the Addictions* 20: 947–969.

Chira, Susan 1994 "Study Confirms Worst Fears on U.S. Children." *New York Times* (April 12): 1, 11.

Chiu, Tina 2010 *It's About Time: Aging Prisoners, Increasing Costs, and Geriatric Release.* New York: Vera Institute of Justice.

Clark, Cherie L., David W. Aziz, and Doris L. MacKenzie 1994 *Shock Incarceration in New York: Focus on Treatment.* Washington, DC: National Institute of Justice.

Clark, Patrick M. 2011 *Cognitive-Behavioral Therapy: An Evidence-Based Intervention for Offenders.* Washington, DC: National Institute of Justice. (Originally published in *Corrections Today*, February/March, 2011.)

Clark, Patrick M. 1991 "Clean and Sober—And Agnostic." *Newsweek* (July 8): 62–63.

Clark, Michael D., Scott Walters, Ray Gingerich, and Melissa Meltzer 2006 "Motivational Interviewing for Probation Officers: Tipping the Balance Toward Change." *Federal Probation* 70 (June): 38–44.

Clear, Todd R., and Edward Latessa 1989 "Intensive Supervision: Surveillance vs. Treatment." Paper presented at the annual meeting of the Academy of Criminal Justice Sciences, Washington, DC, March 30.

Clear, Todd, and Ronald P. Corbett 1998 "Community Corrections of Place." *Perspectives* 23 (Winter): 24–32.

Clear, Todd R., and Patricia R. Hardyman 1990 "The New Intensive Supervision Movement." *Crime and Delinquency* 36 (January): 42–60.

Clear, Todd R., Suzanne Flynn, and Carol Shapiro 1987 "Intensive Supervision in Probation: A Comparison of Three Projects." In *Intermediate Punishments: Intensive Supervision, Home Confinement and Electronic Surveillance*, edited by Belinda R. McCarthy, pages 31–50. Monsey, NY: Criminal Justice Press.

Clem, Constance, Barbara Krauth, and Larry Linke 1998 *A Field Evaluation of the Interstate Compact for Probation and Parole: Findings from an NIC Survey.* Washington, DC: National Institute of Corrections.

Clement, Marshall, Matthew Schwarzfeld, and Michael Thompson 2011 *The National Summit on Justice Reinvestment and Public Safety: Addressing Recidivism, Crime, and Corrections Spending.* New York: Council of State Governments Justice Center

Clemmer, Donald 1958 *The Prison Community.* New York: Holt, Rinehart and Winston.

Clinard, Marshall B., ed. 1964 *Anomie and Deviant Behavior.* New York: Free Press.

Cloninger, Susan C 2013 *Theories of Personality: Understanding Persons*, 6th ed. Upper Saddle River, NJ: Pearson.

Cloward, Richard A., and Lloyd E. Ohlin 1960 *Delinquency and Opportunity.* New York: Free Press.

Cognitive Behavioral Interventions 2001 Raleigh, NC: North Carolina Department of Corrections.

Cohen, Albert K. 1965 *Delinquent Boys.* New York: Free Press.

Cohen, Alvin W. 2007 "Electronic Monitoring: Panacea or Palliative?" *Perspectives* (Summer): 36–41.

Cohen, Lawrence E. 1975 *New Directions in Processing of Juvenile Offenders: The Denver Model.* Washington, DC: U.S. Government Printing Office.

Cohen, Noam S. 1992 "20 Years after Siege Ended in Blood, Attica Is New Prison but Wary Town." *New York Times* (September 1): 15.

Cohn, Alvin W. 2002 "Managing the Correctional Enterprise—The Quest for 'What Works.'" *Federal Probation* 66 (September): 4–9.

Cole, David 2011 *Turning the Corner on Mass Incarceration?* Washington, DC: Georgetown University.

Collier, Walter V. 1980 *Summary of First Year Evaluation of the Special Parole Supervision for Violent Felony Offenders.* Albany: New York State Division of Parole.

Comptroller General of the United States 1979 *Correctional Institutions Can Do More to Improve the Employability of Offenders.* Washington, DC: U.S. Government Printing Office.

Confessore, Nicholas 2009 "New York Finds Extreme Crisis in Youth Prisons." *New York Times* (December 14): 1, 4.

Conly, Catherine 1998 *The Women's Prison Association: Supporting Women Offenders and Their Families.* Washington, DC: National Institute of Justice. Draft.

Conrad, Chris 2009 "Medford Police Sweep Leads to Nine Arrests." *Mail Tribune* (July 29): Internet.

Cook, Philip J., and Maeve E. Gearing 2009 "The Breathalyzer Behind the Wheel." *New York Times* (August 31): 19.

Cooper, Irving Ben 1977 "*United States v. Unterman*: The Role of Counsel at Sentencing." *Criminal Law Bulletin* 13.

Cortes, Katherine and Shawn Rogers 2010 *Reentry Housing Options: The Policymakers' Guide.* New York: Council of State Governments Justice Center.

Council of State Governments Justice Center (CSGJC) 2013 *The Impact of Probation and Parole Populations on Arrests in Four California Cities.* New York: CSGJC.

"Court Orders Trial on Ban of Voting by Felons." 2003 *New York Times* (December 20): 15.

Cox, Stephen M., and Kathleen Bantley 2005 "Evaluation of the Court Support Services Division's Probation Transition Program and Technical Violations Unit: Final Report." Department of Criminology and Criminal Justice, Central Connecticut State University.

Craske, Micehlle G. 2010 *Cognitive-Behavioral Therapy.* Washington, DC: American Psychological Association.

Crawford, Cheryl A. 1994 "Health Care Needs in Corrections: NIJ Responds." *National Institute of Justice Journal* (November): 31–38.

Crawford, William B., Jr. 1988 "Inmates Suing over Gangs Lose Case." *Chicago Tribune* (March 8): Sec. 2: 3.

Crime and Justice Institute 2009 *Implementing Evidence-Based Policy and Practice in Community Corrections.* Washington, DC: National Institute of Corrections.

Cripe, Clair 1997 *Legal Aspects of Corrections Management.* Gaithersburg, MD: Aspen.

Cromwell, Paul F., Jr. 1978 "The Halfway House and Offender Reintegration." In *Corrections in the Community*, 2nd ed., edited by George C. Killinger and Paul F. Cromwell, Jr. St. Paul, MN: West.

Cronin, Roberta C., with Mei Han 1994 *Boot Camp for Adult and Juvenile Offenders: Overview and Update.* Washington, DC: National Institute of Justice.

Crowe, Ann H. 1998 "Restorative Justice and Offender Rehabilitation: A Meeting of the Minds." *Perspectives* 22 (Summer): 28–40.

Crowe, Ann H., Linda Sydney, Pat Bancoft, and Beverly Lawrence 2002 *Offender Supervision with Electronic Technology.* Lexington, KY: American Probation and Parole Association.

Crowley, Jim 1998 "Victim-Offender Mediation: Paradigm Shift or Old Fashioned Accountability?" *Community Links* (Spring): 10.

Cullen, Francis T. 2008 "Prologue" to *Correctional Counseling and Treatment*, edited by Albert R. Roberts, pages vii–xi. Upper Saddle River, NJ: Pearson.

Cullen, Francis T., and Karen E. Gilbert 1982 *Reaffirming Rehabilitation.* Cincinnati, OH: Anderson.

Cullen, Francis T., Nicholas Williams, and John Paul Wright 2002 "Environmental Corrections—A New Paradigm for Effective Probation and Parole Supervision." *Federal Probation* 66 (September): 28–37.

Cullen, Francis T., Nicholas Williams, and John Paul Wright 1997 "Work Conditions and Juvenile Delinquency: Is Youth Employment Criminogenic?" *Criminal Justice Policy Review* 8 (2–3): 119–143.

Curran, Daniel J. 1988 "Destructuring Privatization and the Promise of Juvenile Diversion: Compromising Community-Based Corrections." *Crime and Delinquency* 34 (October): 363–378.

Czajkoski, Eugene H. 1973 "Exposing the Quasi-Judicial Role of the Probation Officer." *Federal Probation* 37 (September): 9–13.

Darrow, Clarence 1975 *Address to the Prisoners in the Cook County Jail, 1902.* Chicago: Charles H. Kerr.

Davey, Monica 2009 "In Michigan, Deficits Defy Years of Cutting." *New York Times* (July 12): 14, 18.

Davey, Monica, and Abby Goodnough 2007a "Doubts Rise as States Hold Sex Offenders after Prison." *New York Times* (March 4): 1, 20.

Davey, Monica, and Abby Goodnough 2007b "A Record of Failure at a Center for Sex Offenders." *New York Times* (March 5): 1, 16.

Davidoff-Kroop, Joy 1983 *An Initial Assessment of the Division of Parole's Employment Services.* Albany: New York State Division of Parole.

Dedel, Kelly 1998 "National Profile of the Organization of State Juvenile Corrections Systems." *Crime and Delinquency* 44 (October): 507–25.

Degler, Carl N. 1991 *In Search of Human Nature: The Decline and Revival of Darwinism in American Social Thought.* New York: Oxford University Press.

Deitch, Michele, Amanda Barstow, Leslie Lukens, and Ryan Reyna 2009 *From Time Out to Hard Time: Young Children in the Adult Criminal Justice System.* Austin, TX: University of Texas.

Delbanco, Andrew, and Thomas Delbanco 1995 "At the Crossroads." *New Yorker* (March 20): 50–63.

del Carmen, Rolando V. 1985 "Legal Issues and Liabilities in Community Corrections." In *Probation, Parole, and Community Corrections: A Reader,* edited by Lawrence F. Travis III, pages 47–70. Prospect Heights, IL: Waveland Press.

del Carmen, Rolando V., and Paul T. Louis 1988 *Civil Liabilities of Parole Personnel for Release, Non-Release, Supervision, and Revocation.* Washington, DC: National Institute of Corrections.

del Carmen, Rolando V., Maldine Beth Barnhill, Gene Bonham, Jr., Lance Hignite, and Todd Jermstad 2001 *Civil Liabilities and Other Legal Issues for Probation/Parole Officers and Supervisors.* Washington, DC: National Institute of Corrections.

De Leon, George 1994 "The Therapeutic Community: Toward a General Theory and Model," in *Therapeutic Community: Advances in Research and Application,* edited by Frank M. Tims, Nancy Jainchill, and George De Leon, pages 16–53. Rockville, MD: National Institute on Drug Abuse.

De Leon, George 1986 "The Therapeutic Community for Substance Abuse: Perspective and Approach," in *Therapeutic Communities for Addictions,* edited by George De Leon and James T. Ziegenfuss, Jr., pages 5–18. Springfield, IL: Charles C Thomas.

DeLong, James V. 1972 "Treatment and Rehabilitation," in *Dealing with Drug Abuse: A Report to the Ford Foundation,* pages 173–254. New York: Praeger.

DeMichele, Matthew, and Brian Payne 2005 *Offender Supervision with Electronic Technology: Community Corrections Resource,* 2nd ed. Washington, DC: Bureau of Justice Statistics.

Denzlinger, Jerry D., and David E. Miller 1991 "The Federal Probation Officer: Life before and after Guideline Sentencing." *Federal Probation* 55 (December): 49–63.

Department of Community Corrections (DCC) 2006 *Recidivism for Probation and Parole.* Little Rock, AK: DCC.

Deschenes, Elizabeth Piper, Susan Turner, and Joan Petersilia 1995 "A Dual Experiment in Intensive Community Supervision: Minnesota's Prison Diversion and Enhanced Supervised Release Programs." *The Prison Journal* 75 (September): 330–356.

Dickey, Walter 1979 "The Lawyer and the Accuracy of the Presentence Report." *Federal Probation* 43 (June): 29–39.

Dietrich, Shelle 1979 "The Probation Officer as Therapist: Examination of Three Major Problem Areas." *Federal Probation* 43 (June): 14–19.

Dighton, Daniel 1997 "States Broaden Scope of Transfer Laws." *The Compiler* 17 (Fall): 11–15.

DiIulio, John J., Jr. 1993 "Rethinking the Criminal Justice System: Toward a New Paradigm." In *Performance Measures for the Criminal Justice System,* pages 1–16. Washington, DC: Bureau of Justice Statistics.

Division of Probation 1974 "The Selective Presentence Investigation." *Federal Probation* 38 (December).

Dobrzynski, Judith H 1997 "For a Summer Getaway, a Model Prison." *New York Times* (July 11): B1.

Doherty, Fiona 2013 "Indeterminate Sentencing Returns: The Invention of Supervised Release." *New York University Law Review* 88: 958–1030.

Dolan, Edward J., Richard Lunden, and Rosemary Barberet 1987 "Prison Behavior and Parole Outcome in Massachusetts." Paper presented at the annual meeting of the American Society of Criminology, Montreal, November 11–14.

Dole, Vincent 1980 "Addictive Behavior." *Scientific American* 243: 138–54.

Donovan, Dennis M. 1988 "Assessment of Addictive Behaviors: Implications for an Emerging Biopsychosocial Model," in *Assessment of Addictive Behaviors,* edited by Dennis M. Donovan and G. Alan Marrlatt, pages 3–48. New York: Guilford.

Dooley, Jim 2011 "Hope Probation Strains Hawaii Criminal Justice System." *Hawaii* (April 28): Internet.

Downing, Hugh 2006 "The Emergence of Global Positioning Satellite (GPS) Systems in Correctional Applications." *Corrections Today* (October): 42–45.

Dressler, David 1951 *Parole Chief.* New York: Viking Press.

National Institute of Justice 1995 *Drug Court Movement.* Washington, DC: National Institute of Justice.

Drumm, Kris 2006 "The Essential Power of Group Work." *Social Work with Groups* 29 (2/3): 17–31.

Dumm, Thomas L. 1987 *Democracy and Punishment: Disciplinary Origins of the United States.* Madison: University of Wisconsin Press.

Dunn, Ashley 1995 "U.S. Inquiry Finds Detention Center Was Poorly Run." *New York Times* (July 22): 1, 8.

DuPont, Robert L., and John P. McGovern 1994 *A Bridge to Recovery: An Introduction to 12-Step Programs.* Washington, DC: American Psychiatric Press.

Duran, Le'Ann, Martha Plotkin, Phoebe Potter, and Henry Rosen 2013 *Integrated Reentry and Employment Strategies: Reducing Recidivism and Promoting Job Readiness.* New York: Council of State Governments Justice Center.

Durham, Alexis M., III 1989a "Origins of Interest in the Privatization of Punishment: The Nineteenth and Twentieth Century American Experience." *Criminology* 27 (February): 107–139.

Durham, Alexis M., III 1989b "Rehabilitation and Correctional Privatization: Observations on the 19th Century Experience and Implications for Modern Corrections." *Federal Probation* 53 (March): 43–52.

Durham, Alexis M., III 1989c "Newgate of Connecticut: Origins and Early Days of an Early American Prison." *Justice Quarterly* 6 (March): 89–116.

Duwe, Grant 2013 "What's Inside the 'Black Box'? The Importance of 'Gray Box' Evaluations for the 'What Works' Movement." *Criminology and Public Policy* 12 (February): 145–152.

Dwyer, Jim 2008 "Less Crime: No Reason to Shut Prisons." *New York Times* (April 12): B1, B6.

Dzur, Albert W., and Alan Wertheimer 2002 "Forgiveness and Public Deliberation: The Practice of Restorative Justice." *Criminal Justice Ethics* 21 (Winter/Spring): 3–21.

Eig, Jonathan 1998 "Deep Hole." *Chicago* (July): 60-64, 87–89.

Eisenkraft, Noah 2001 "Taxation without Representation." *Harvard Political Review* (Winter): Internet.

Eisenstein, James 1978 *Counsel for the United States: U.S. Attorneys in the Political and Legal Systems.* Baltimore, MD: Johns Hopkins University Press.

Eisenberg, Mike, Jason Bryl, and Tony Fabelo 2009 *Validation of the Wisconsin Department of Corrections Risk Assessment Instrument.* New York: Council of State Government Justice Center.

Eisenstein, James, Roy B. Flemming, and Peter F. Nardulli 1988 *The Contours of Justice: Communities and Their Courts.* Boston: Little, Brown.

Electronic Monitoring Reduces Recidivism 2011 Rockville, MD: National Institute of Justice.

"Elmira" 1998 *DOC Today* (October): Internet.

Empey, LaMar T., ed. 1979 *Juvenile Justice: The Progressive Legacy and Current Reforms.* Charlottesville: University Press of Virginia.

Employing Your Mission 2009 New York: Fortune Society and John Jay College.

English, Kim, Suzanne Pullen, and Linda Jones 1997 *Managing Adult Sex Offenders in the Community—A Containment Approach.* Washington, DC: National Institute of Justice.

Erez, Edna 1990 "Victim Participation in Sentencing: Rhetoric and Reality." *Journal of Criminal Justice* 18: 19–31.

Erikkson, Torsten 1976 *The Reformers: An Historical Survey of Pioneer Experiments in the Treatment of Criminals.* New York: Elsevier.

Erwin, Billie S. 1984 *Evaluation of Intensive Supervision in Georgia.* Atlanta: Georgia Department of Offender Rehabilitation.

Erwin, Billie S., and Lawrence A. Bennett 1987 *New Dimensions in Probation: Georgia's Experience with Intensive Probation Supervision.* Washington, DC: National Institute of Justice.

Eskridge, Chris W., and Eric W. Carlson 1979 "The Use of Volunteers in Probation: A National Synthesis." *Journal of Offender Counseling Services and Rehabilitation* 4 (Winter).

Fabelo, Tony, Geraldine Nagy, and Seth Prins 2011 *A Ten-Step Guide to Transforming Probation Departments to Reduce Recidivism.* New York: Council of State Governments Justice Center.

Fabricant, Michael 1983 *Juveniles in the Family Courts.* Lexington, MA: D.C. Heath.

Falcone, David N. 2005 *Dictionary of American Criminal Justice, Criminology, and Criminal Law.* Upper Saddle River, NJ: Prentice Hall.

Falk, Gerhard 1966 "The Psychoanalytic Theories of Crime Causation." *Criminologica* 4 (May).

Fallen, David L., Craig D. Apperson, Joan Hall-Milligan, and Steven Aos 1981 *Intensive Parole Supervision*. Olympia: Washington Department of Social and Health Services.

Feeley, Malcolm M. 1979 *The Process Is Punishment: Handling Cases in a Lower Court*. New York: Russell Sage Foundation.

Feeley, Malcolm M., and Jonathan Simon 1992 "The New Penology: Note on the Emerging Strategy of Corrections and Its Implications." *Criminology* 30 (November): 449–474.

Feld, Barry C. 2003 "The Politics of Race and Juvenile Justice: The 'Due Process Revolution' and the Conservative Reaction." *Justice Quarterly* 20 (December): 765–800.

Feld, Barry C. 1992 "Criminalizing the Juvenile Court: A Research Agenda for the 1990s." In *Juvenile Justice and Public Policy: Toward a National Agenda*, edited by Ira M. Schwartz, pages 59–88. Lexington, MA: Lexington Books.

Feld, Barry C. 1988 "*In Re Gault* Revisited: A Cross-State Comparison of the Right to Counsel in Juvenile Court." *Crime and Delinquency* 34 (October): 393–424.

Feld, Barry C. and Shelly Schaefer 2010 "The Right to Counsel in Juvenile Court: The Conundrum of Attorneys as an Aggravating Factor at Disposition." *Justice Quarterly* 27 (October): 713–741.

Female Offender Resource Center 1979 *Little Sisters and the Law*. Washington, DC: U.S. Government Printing Office.

Finckenauer, James O 2005 "Ruminating About Boot Camps: Panaceas, Paradoxes, and Ideology." *Journal of Offender Rehabilitation* 42: 199–207.

Finckenauer, James O 1984 *Juvenile Delinquency and Corrections: The Gap between Theory and Practice*. New York: Academic Press.

Finder, Alan 1997 "New York's Chief Judge Moves to Assure Family Courts Are Open to Public." *New York Times* (June 19): 18.

Finn, Peter 1997 *Sex Offender Community Notification*. Washington, DC: National Institute of Justice.

Finn, Peter, and Sarah Kuck 2001 *Stress among Probation and Parole Officers and What Can Be Done about It*. Washington, DC: National Institute of Justice.

Finn, Peter, and Sarah Kuck 1998 *The Delaware Department of Corrections Life Skills Program*. Washington, DC: National Institute of Justice.

Finn, Peter, and Dale Parent 1992 *Making the Offender Foot the Bill: A Texas Program*. Washington, DC: National Institute of Justice.

Firestone, David 2001 "Alabama's Packed Jails Draw Ire of Courts, Again." *New York Times* (May 1): 1, 16.

Fisher, George 2000 "Plea Bargaining's Triumph." *Yale Law Review* 109 (March): 857–1086.

Fishman, Nancy 2003 "Briefing Paper: Legal Barriers to Prisoner Reentry in New Jersey." Paper prepared for the New Jersey Reentry Roundtable, April 11.

Foderaro, Lisa W. 1995 "Can Problem Drinkers Really Just Cut Back?" *New York Times* (May 28): 15.

Fogel, David 1984 "The Emergence of Probation as a Profession in the Service of Public Safety: The Next Ten Years." In *Probation and Justice: Reconsideration of Mission*, edited by Patrick D. McAnany, Doug Thompson, and David Fogel. Cambridge, MA: Oelgeschlager, Gunn and Hain.

Fogel, David 1975 *We Are the Living Proof*. Cincinnati, OH: Anderson.

Ford, Daniel, and Annesley K. Schmidt 1985 *Electronically Monitored Home Confinement*. Washington, DC: National Institute of Justice.

Fox, Vernon 1977 *Community-Based Corrections*. Upper Saddle River, NJ: Prentice Hall.

France, Anatole 1927 *The Red Lily*, translated by Winifred Stephens. New York: Dodd, Mead.

Frawley, P. Joseph, and James W. Smith 1990 "Chemical Aversion Therapy in the Treatment of Cocaine Dependence as Part of a Multimodal Treatment Program." *Journal of Substance Abuse Treatment* 7: 21–29.

Freud, Sigmund 1933 *New Introductory Lectures on Psychoanalysis*. New York: W. W. Norton.

Fried, Joseph P. 2006 "Leaving Prison Doors Behind, Some Find New Doors Open." *New York Times* (October 18): B8.

Friedlander, Walter A. 1958 *Concepts and Methods of Social Work*. Upper Saddle River, NJ: Prentice Hall.

Friedman, Lawrence M. 1973 *A History of American Law*. New York: Simon and Schuster.

Fry, Russ 2008 *Why Evidence-Based Practices Matter (Or, Please Pass the Leeches)*: Internet.

"Full-Employment Prisons" 2001 *New York Times* editorial (August 23): 20.

Furhling, Larry 1998 "In Iowa, Some Prisoners Are behind Barns." *Chicago Tribune* (August 7): 10.

Gaes, Gerry 2008 *Cost, Performance Studies Look at Prison Privatization*. Washington, DC: National Institute of Justice.

Galaif, Elisha, and Steve Sussman 1995 "For Whom Does Alcoholics Anonymous Work?" *International Journal of the Addictions* 30 (2): 161–84.

Gaylin, Willard 1974 *Partial Justice: A Study of Bias in Sentencing*. New York: Alfred A. Knopf.

Gebelein, Richard S. 2000 *The Rebirth of Rehabilitation: Promise and Perils of Drug Courts*. Washington, DC: Office of Justice Programs.

Geerken, Michael R., and Hennessey D. Hayes 1993 "Probation and Parole: Public Risk and the Future of Incarceration Alternatives." *Criminology* 31 (November): 549–64.

Gehm, John R. 1998 "Victim-Offender Mediation Programs: An Exploration of Practice and Theoretical Frameworks." *Western Criminology Review* 1 (1): Internet.

Gendreau, Paul, Shelley J. Listwan, and Joseph B. Kuhns 2011 *Managing Prisons Effectively: The Potential of Contingency Management Programs*. Ottawa, Canada: Department of Public Safety.

Gendreau, Paul, and Robert R. Ross 1987 "Revivification of Rehabilitation: Evidence from the 1980s." *Justice Quarterly* 4 (September): 350–407.

Gerstein, Dean R., and Henrick J. Harwood, eds. 1990 *Treating Drug Problems, Vol. I: A Study of the Evolution, Effectiveness, and Financing of Public and Private Drug Treatment Systems*. Washington, DC: National Academy Press.

Gies, Stephen V., Randy Gainey, Marcia I. Cohen, Eoin Healy, Dan Duplantier, Martha Yeide, Alan Bekelman, Amanda Bobnis, Michael Hopps 2012 *Monitoring High-Risk Sex Offenders With GPS Technology: An Evaluation of the California Supervision Program, Final Report*. Bethesda, MD: Deveopment Servies Group, Inc.

Gilligan, Leilah, and Tom Talbot 2000 *Community Supervision of the Sex Offender: An Overview of Current and Promising Practices*. Silver Spring, MD: Center for Sex Offender Management

Gillin, John T. 1931 *Taming the Criminal*. New York: Macmillan.

Gladding, Samuel T. 1999 *Group Work: A Counseling Specialty*. Upper Saddle River, NJ: Prentice Hall.

Glaser, Daniel 1969 *The Effectiveness of a Prison and Parole System*. Indianapolis, IN: Bobbs-Merrill.

Glasser, William 2000 *Reality Therapy in Action*. New York: HarperCollins.

Glasser, William 1980 "Reality Therapy: An Explanation of the Steps of Reality Therapy." In *What Are You Doing? How People Are Helped through Reality Therapy*, edited by Naomi Glasser. New York: Harper and Row.

Glaze, Lauren E. 2003 *Probation and Parole in the United States, 2002*. Washington, DC: Bureau of Justice Statistics.

Glaze, Lauren E., and Thomas P. Bonczar 2006 *Probation and Parole in the United States, 2005*. Washington, DC: Bureau of Justice Statistics.

Glueck, Sheldon, ed. 1933 *Probation and Criminal Justice*. New York: Macmillan.

Goetting, Victor L. 1974 "Some Pragmatic Aspects of Opening a Halfway House." *Federal Probation* 38 (December). 27–29.

Goffman, Erving 1961 *Asylums: Essays on the Social Situation of Mental Patients and Other Inmates*. Garden City, NY: Doubleday.

Goleman, Daniel 1987 "Embattled Giant of Psychology Speaks His Mind." *New York Times* (August 25): 17, 18.

Goodstein, Lynne, and John Hepburn 1985 *Determinate Sentencing and Imprisonment: A Failure of Reform*. Cincinnati, OH: Anderson.

Gottschalk, Marie 2006 *The Prison and the Gallows: The Politics of Mass Incarceration in America*. New York: Cambridge University Press.

Grann, David 2004 "The Brand." *New Yorker* (February 16, 23): 157–171.

Gransky, Laura A., Thomas C. Castellano, and Ernest L. Cowles 1993 "Is There a 'Next Generation' of Shock Incarceration Facilities? The Evolving Nature of Goals, Program Components, and Drug Treatment Services." Paper presented at the annual meeting of the Academy of Criminal Justice Sciences, Kansas City, MO, March 16–20.

Grattet, Ryken, Joan Petersilia, Jeffrey Lin, and Marlene Beckman 2009 "Parole Violations and Revocations in California: Analysis and Suggestions for Action." *Federal Probation* 73 (June): 2–11.

Grattet, Ryken, Joan Petersilia, and Jeffrey Lin 2008 *Parole Violations and Revocations in California*. Washington, D C: U.S. Department of Justice.

Greenberg, David F. 1975 "Problems in Community Corrections." *Issues in Criminology* 10 (Spring): 1–33.

Greenberg, David F., and Drew Humphries 1980 "The Cooptation of Fixed Sentencing Reform." *Crime and Delinquency* 26 (April): 206–225.

Greenberg, Jay R., and Stephen A. Mitchell 1983 *Object Relations in Psychoanalytic Theory*. Cambridge, MA: Harvard University Press.

Greene, Judith, and Marc Mauer 2010 *Downscaling Prisons: Lessons from Four States*. Washington, DC : The Sentencing Project.

Greene, Judith, and Néstor Ríos 2009 *Reducing Recidivism: A Review of Effective State Initiatives*. San Francisco, CA: Tides Center, Inc.

Greenfeld, Lawrence A., and Tracy L. Snell 1999 *Women Offenders*. Washington, DC: Office of Justice Programs.

Greenhouse, Linda 2003 "Justices Uphold Long Prison Terms in Repeat Crimes." *New York Times* (March 6): 1, 26.

Greenhouse, Linda 1997 "Immunity from Suits Is Withheld for Guards in Privately Run Jails." *New York Times* (June 24): 12.

Griffin, Patrick 2005 *Juvenile Court-Controlled Reentry: Three Practice Models*. Pittsburgh, PA: National Center for Juvenile Justice.

Griffin, Patrick, Sean Addie, Benjamin Adams, and Kathy Firestine 2011 *Trying Juveniles as Adults: An Analysis of State Transfer Laws and Reporting*. Washington, DC: Office of Juvenile Justice and Delinquency Prevention.

Griggs, Bertram S., and Gary R. McCune 1972 "Community-Based Correctional Programs: A Survey and Analysis." *Federal Probation* 36 (June).

Grissom, Grant R., and William L. Dubnov 1989 *Without Locks and Bars: Reforming Our Reform Schools*. New York: Praeger.

Grogger, Jeffrey 1989 *Employment and Crime*. Sacramento, CA: Bureau of Criminal Statistics and Special Services.

Gross, Jane 1992 "Collapse of Inner-City Families Creates America's New Orphans." *New York Times* (March 29): 1, 15.

Guggenheim, Ken 1998 "For Ex-Cons, Job Search Tough Obstacle." Associated Press, Nando.net.

Haas, Stephen, and Edward J. Latessa 1995 "Intensive Supervision in a Rural County: Diversion and Outcome," in *Intermediate Sanctions: Sentencing in the 1990s*, edited by John Ortiz Smykla and William Selke, pages 153–169. Cincinnati, OH: Anderson.

Haberman, Clyde 2005 "Only at Grave Does a Barber Get a Break." *New York Times* (November 22): B1.

Haberman, Clyde 2000 "In Turbulent Times, a Prison Boiled Over." *New York Times* (January 5): 23.

Haederle, Michael 2010 "Trouble in Mind: Will the New Neuroscience Undermine Our Legal System?" *Miller-McCune* (March/April): 70–79.

Hagerty, J. E. 1934 *Twentieth Century Crime, Eighteenth Century Methods of Control*. Boston: Stratford.

Hahn, Paul H. 1976 *Community-Based Corrections and the Criminal Justice System*. Santa Cruz, CA: Davis.

Hall, Jerome 1952 *Theft, Law and Society*. Indianapolis, IN: Bobbs-Merrill.

Hall, Trish 1990 "New Way to Treat Alcoholism Discards Spiritualism of A.A." *New York Times* (December 24): 1, 10.

Hallet, Michael 2004 "An Introduction to Prison Privatization," in *Visions for Change: Crime and Justice in the Twenty-First Century*, edited by Roslyn Ruskin and Albert R. Roberts, pages 528–52. Saddle River, NJ: Prentice Hall.

Hamilton, Gordon 1967 *Theory and Practice of Social Work*. New York: Columbia University Press.

Hammett, Theodore M., Lynne Harrold, and Joel Epstein 1994 *Tuberculosis in Correctional Facilities*. Washington, DC: U.S. Government Printing Office.

Hansen, Chris 2008 "Cognitive-Behavioral Interventions: Where They Come From and What They Do." *Federal Probation* 72 (September): 43-49.

Hardman, Dale G 1960 "Constructive Use of Authority." *Crime and Delinquency* 6 (July).

Harper, Robert Francis 1904 *The Code of Hammurabi*. Chicago: University of Chicago Press.

Harris, George A., and David Watkins 1987 *Counseling the Involuntary and Resistant Client*. College Park, MD: American Correctional Association.

Harris, Patricia M., Raymond Gingerich, and Tiffany A. Whittaker 2004 "The 'Effectiveness' of Differential Supervision." *Crime and Delinquency* 50 (April): 235–271.

Harris, Patricia M., and Lisa Graf 1988 "A Critique of Juvenile Sentence Reform." *Federal Probation* 52 (September): 66–71.

Harrison, Mary T. 2006 "True Grit: An Innovative Program for Elderly Inmates. *Corrections Today* (December): 46–49.

Harrison, Paige M., and Allen J. Beck 2003 *Prisoners in 2002*. Washington, DC: U.S. Bureau of Justice Statistics.

Harrison, Paige M, and Jennifer C. Karberg 2004 *Prison and Jail Inmates at Midyear 2003*. Washington, DC: U.S. Bureau of Justice Statistics.

Hartman, Todd 1994 "Suit Targets Neighbors Who Oppose Group Home." *Miami Herald* (November 11): B1, 3.

Hawken, Angela, and Mark Kleiman 2009 *Managing Drug Involved Probationers with Swift and Certain Sanctions: Evaluating Hawaii's HOPE: Executive Summary*. Washington, DC: National Criminal Justice Reference Services.

Hawkins, Dana 2002 "Tests on Trial: Jobs and Reputations Ride on Unproven Drug Screens." *U.S. News & World Report* (August 12): 46–48.

Healy, William, Augusta F. Bronner, and Anna Mae Bowers 1930 *The Structure and Meaning of Psychoanalysis*. New York: Alfred A. Knopf.

Hemmens, Craig, and Rolando del Carmen 1997 "The Exclusionary Rule in Probation and Parole Revocation Proceedings: Does It Apply?" *Federal Probation* 61 (September): 32–39.

Henderson, Marta L. 2004 "Employment and Crime from the Inmate's Perspective," in *Crime and Employment: Critical Issues in Crime Reduction for Corrections*, edited by Jessie L. Krienert and Mark S. Fisher, pages 84–94. Walnut Creek, CA: AltaMira Press.

Henrichson, Christian and Ruth Delaney 2012 *The Price of Prisons: What Incarceration Costs Taxpayers*. New York: Vera Institute of Justice.

Hergenhahn, B. R., and Matthew H. Olson 1999 *An Introduction to Theories of Personality*, 5th ed. Upper Saddle River, NJ: Prentice Hall.

Herman, Ellen 1995 *The Romance of American Psychology: Political Culture in the Age of Experts, 1940–1970*. Berkeley: University of California Press.

Hettema, Jennifer, Julie Steele, and William R. Miller 2005 "Motivational Interviewing." *Annual Review of Clinical Psychology* 1: 91–111.

Hibbert, Christopher 1968 *The Roots of Evil: A Social History of Crime and Punishment*. Boston: Little, Brown.

Hipp, John R., and Daniel K. Yates 2009 "Do Returning Parolees Affect Neighborhood Crime? A Case Study of Sacramento." *Criminology* 47 (August): 619–656.

Hirsch, Adam Jay 1992 *The Rise of the Penitentiary: Prisons and Punishment in Early America*. New Haven, CT: Yale University Press.

Hirschi, Travis 1969 *Causes of Delinquency*. Berkeley: University of California Press.

Hollin, Clive R. 1990 *Cognitive-Behavioral Interventions with Young Offenders*. New York: Pergamon Press.

Hollis, Florence 1950 "The Techniques of Casework," in *Principles and Techniques of Social Casework: Selected Articles, 1940–1950*, edited by Cora Kasius, pages 412–26. New York: Family Service Association of America.

Holloway, Lynette 1995 "Home for Handicapped Still Faces Rough Path." *New York Times* (July 18): 13.

Holmes, Cheryl S. 1997 "AIDS and Supervision." *Federal Probation* 61 (March): 28.

Holsinger, Alexander M., Christopher T. Lowenkamp, and Edward J. Latessa 2006 "Exploring the Validity of the Level Service Inventory-Revised with Native American Offenders." *Journal of Criminal Justice* 34: 331–37.

Holt, Norman 1995 "California's Determinate Sentencing: What Went Wrong?" *Perspectives* (Summer): 19–22.

Holzer, Harry J., Steven Raphael, and Michael A. Stoll 2002 *Prisoner Reentry and the Institutions of Civil Society: Bridges and Barriers to Successful Reintegration*. Washington, DC: The Urban Institute.

Hoover, Kent 2001 "Prison Program May Lose Contracting Monopoly." *BizJournals.com* (June 18): Internet.

Huddleston, West and Douglas B. Marlowe 2011 *Painting the Current Picture: A National Report on Drug Courts and Other Problem-Solving Court Programs in the United States*. Alexandria, VA: National Drug Court Institute.

Hughes, Robert 1987 *The Fatal Shore: The Epic of Australia's Founding*. New York: Alfred A. Knopf.

Hurl, Lorna F., and David J. Tucker 1997 "The Michigan County Agents and the Development of Juvenile Probation." *Journal of Social History* (Summer): 905–35.

Hurst, Hunter, IV, and Patricia McFall Torbet 1993 *Organization and Administration of Juvenile Services: Probation, Aftercare, and State Institutions for Delinquent Youth*. Pittsburgh, PA: National Center for Juvenile Justice.

Hurst, James W. 1950 *The Growth of American Law: The Law Makers*. Boston: Little, Brown.

Husband, Stephen D., and Jerome J. Platt 1993 "The Cognitive Skills Component in Substance Abuse Treatment in Correctional Settings: A Brief Review." *Journal of Drug Issues* 23 (Winter): 31–42.

Hutchinson, Elizabeth D. 1987 "Use of Authority in Direct Social Work Practice with Mandated Clients." *Social Service Review* 61 (December): 581–98.

ICAOS. See Interstate Commission for Adult Offender Supervision.

Ignatieff, Michael 1978 *A Just Measure of Pain: The Penitentiary in the Industrial Revolution*. New York: Pantheon.

Illinois Criminal Justice Authority 1999 "Drug Court Provides Treatment Alternative to Incarceration." *On Good Authority* 2 (April): 1–4.

In Our Backyard: Overcoming Community Resistance to Reentry Housing. 2009. New York: Fortune Society and John Jay College.

International Association of Chiefs of Police (IACP) 2007 *Sex Offenders in the Community*. Alexandria, VA: IACP

Interstate Commission for Adult Offender Supervision (ICAOS) 2012 *Interstate Compact Annual Report, 2012*. Lexington, KY: ICAOS.

Irwin, John 1980 *Prisons in Turmoil*. Boston: Little, Brown.

Irwin, John, and James Austin 1994 *It's About Time: America's Imprisonment Binge*. Belmont, CA: Wadsworth.

It's About Time 2010 New York: Vera Institute of Justice.

Jackson, David, and Cornelia Grumman 1999 "State Puts Kids' Lives on the Block." *Chicago Tribune* (September 26): 1, 18, 19.

Jackson, Patrick G. 1983 "Some Effects of Parole Supervision on Recidivism." *British Journal of Criminology* 23 (January): 17–34.

Jacobs, James B. 1980 "The Prisoners' Rights Movement and Its Impacts, 1960–1980," in *Crime and Justice*, Volume 2, edited by Norval Morris and Michael Tonry, pages 429–70. Chicago: University of Chicago Press.

Jacoby, Joseph, E., Scott A. Desmond, Edna Gree, Lori I. Kepford, Jacinto F. Mendoza, and Monte D. Staton 1994 "Why Bootcamps Fail: Historical; and Theoretical Analysis." Paper presented at the annual meeting of the American Society of Criminology, Miami, Florida, November.

Jalbert, Sarah Kuck, William Rhodes 2012 "Reduced Caseloads Improve Probation Outcomes." *Journal of Crime and Justice* 35 (2): 221–238.

Jalbert, Sarah Kuck, William Rhodes, Christopher Flygare, and Michael Kane 2010 "Testing Probation Outcomes in an Evidence-Based Practice Setting: Reduced Caseload Size and Intensive Supervision Effectiveness." *Journal of Offender Rehabilitation* 49 (4): 233–253.

Jalbert. Sarah Kuck, William Rhodes, Michael Kane, Elyse Clawson, Bradford Bogue, Chris Flygare, Ryan Kling, and Meaghan Guevara 2011 *Multi-Site Evaluation of Reduced Probation Caseload Size in an Evidence-Based Practice Setting*. Cambridge, MA: Abt Associates.

Jannetta, Jesse and Pamela Lachman 2011 *Promoting Partnerships Between Police and Community Supervision Agencies*. Washington, DC: Office of Community Oriented Policing.

Jeffrey, C. Ray 1971 *Crime Prevention through Environmental Design*. Beverly Hills, CA: Sage.

Jenuwine, Michael J., Ronald Simmons, and Edward Swies 2003 "Community Supervision of Sex Offenders—Integrating Probation and Clinical Treatment." *Federal Probation* 67 (December): 20–27.

Jermstad, Todd 2002 "*United States v. Knights* and the Diminished Liberty Interests of Probationers." *Executive Exchange* (Spring): 13–17.

Johnson, Kirk 1994 "Connecticut Closes Boot Camp Built to Assist Troubled Youths." *New York Times* (June 11): 8.

Johnson, Louise C. 1998 *Social Work Practice: A Generalist Approach*. Boston: Allyn and Bacon.

Johnson, Louise C., and Stephen J. Yanca 2007 *Social Work Practice: A Generalist Perspective*, 9th ed. Boston: Allyn and Bacon. 2004 *Social Work Practice: A Generalist Perspective*, 8th ed. Boston: Allyn and Bacon.

Jones, Hendrée E. 2004 "Practical Considerations for the Clinical Use of Buprenorpine." *Perspectives* 2 (August): 4–24.

Jones, Justin, and Carol Robinson 1989 "Keeping the Piece: Probation and Parole Officers' Right to Bear Arms." *Corrections Today* (February): 88, 90.

Jones, Mark, and Darrell L. Ross 1997 "Is Less Better? Boot Camp, Regular Probation and Rearrest in North Carolina." *American Journal of Criminal Justice* 21 (Spring): 147–61.

Johnston, Philip 2001 "Population of Prisons Hits 66,000 Record." *Electric Telegraph* (June 29): Internet.

Judson, Barbara A, and Avram Goldstein 1986 "Uses of Naloxone in the Diagnosis and Treatment of Heroin Addiction." In *Research on the Treatment of Narcotic Addiction: State of the Art,* edited by James R. Cooper, Fred Altman, Barry S. Brown, and Dorynne Czechowicz, pages 1–18. Rockville, MD: National Institute on Drug Abuse.

Justice Reinvestment in Ohio 2011 New York: Council of State Governments Justice Center.

Kachnowski, Vera 2005 *Employment and Prisoner Reentry*. Washington, DC: Urban Institute.

Kanfer, Frederick H., and Arnold P. Goldstein 1975 "Introduction," in *Helping People Change: A Textbook of Methods,* edited by Frederick H. Kanfer and Arnold P. Goldstein, pages 1–14. New York: Pergamon Press.

Kassebaum, Gene, Mel Silverio, Nancy Marker, Paul Perrone, Joseph Allen, and James Richmond 1999 *Survival on Parole: A Study of Post-Prison Adjustment and the Risk of Returning to Prison in the State of Hawaii*. Honolulu: Hawaii Attorney General.

Kaufman, Leslie 2008 "To Save Money, State to Scale Back Drug Abuse Programs for Ex-Convicts." *New York Times* (November 7): 33.

Kelly, William R., and Sheldon Ekland-Olson 1991 "The Response of the Criminal Justice System to Prison Overcrowding: Recidivism Patterns Among Four Successive Parolee Cohorts." *Law and Society Review* 25 (3): 601–20.

Kelman, Mark 1987 *A Guide to Critical Legal Studies*. Cambridge, MA: Harvard University Press.

Kempinen, Cynthia A. 2011 "Pennsylvania's Motivational Boot Camp Program: What Have We Learned Over the Last Seventeen Years? Pennsylvania Commission on Sentencing." *Research Bulletin* 10 (March): 1–6.

Kempinen, Cynthia A., and Megan C. Kurlychek 2003 "An Outcome Evaluation of Pennsylvania's Boot Camp: Does Rehabilitative Programming Within a Disciplinary Setting Reduce Recidivism?" *Crime and Delinquency* 49 (October): 581–602.

Keve, Paul 1979 "No Farewell to Arms." *Crime and Delinquency* 25 (October): 425–435.

Kiernan, Louise 1997 "Trial: At Juvenile Court, an Ongoing Struggle to Mend Broken Lives." *Chicago Tribune Magazine* (January 19): 11–18.

Kilborn, Peter T. 2001 "Rural Towns Turn to Prisons to Reignite Their Economies." *New York Times* (August 1): Internet.

Kim, KiDeuk and Megan Denver 2011 *A Case Study on the Practice of Pretrial Services and Risk Assessment in Three Cities*. Washington, DC: District of Columbia Crime Policy Institute.

King, Ryan Scott, Marc Mauer, and Tracy Huling 2004 "An Analysis of the Economics of Prison Siting in Rural Communities." *Criminology and Public Policy* 3 (July): 453–80.

Kingsnorth, Rodney, and Louis Rizzo 1979 "Decision-Making in the Criminal Court: Continuities and Discontinuities." *Criminology* 17 (May): 3–14.

Kirby, Michael P. 1977 *The Effectiveness of the Point Scale*. Washington, DC: Pretrial Services Resource Center.

Kitchen, Sebastian 2009 "Prisons Underfunded, Understaffed." *Montgomery Advertiser* (August 9): Internet.

Klein, Eric C. 1998 "Dennis the Menace or Billy the Kid: An Analysis of the Role of Transfer to Criminal Court in Juvenile Justice." *American Criminal Law Review* 35 (Winter): 371–401.

Klockars, Carl B., Jr. 1972 "A Theory of Probation Supervision." *Journal of Criminal Law, Criminology and Police Science* 63 (4): 550–57.

Kluger, Jeffrey 2007 "The Paradox of Supermax." *Time* (February 5): 52–53.

Kohl, Rhiana, Hollie Matthews Hoover, Susan M. McDonald, and Amy L. Solomon 2008 *Massachusetts Recidivism Study: A Closer Look at Releases and Returns to Prison*. Washington, DC: Urban Institute.

Kolbert, Elizabeth 1989 "Court Awards $1.3 Million to Inmates Injured at Attica." *New York Times* (October 26): 14.

Konopka, Gisela 1983 *Social Group Work: A Helping Process*, 3rd ed. Upper Saddle River, NJ: Prentice Hall.

Koons-Witt, Barbara A. 2009 "Equal Justice Versus Individualized Justice: Discretion and the Current State of Sentencing Guidelines." *Criminology and Public Policy* 8 (May): 279–283.

Krajick, Kevin 1978 "Parole: Discretion Is Out, Guidelines Are In." *Corrections Magazine* 4 (December).

Kramer, John H. 2008 "Mandatory Sentencing Guidelines: The Framing of Justice." *Criminology and Public Policy* 8 (May): 313–321.

Krause, Kitry 1997 "Borrowed Time: Intensive Probation Offers Kids in Trouble One Last Chance to Stay Out of Jail." *Reader* (January 17): 1, 14, 16, 18–25.

Krauth, Barbara 1987 "Parole: Controversial Component of the Criminal Justice System," in *Observations on Parole: A Collection of Readings from Western Europe, Canada and the United States*, edited by Edward E. Rhine and Ronald W. Jackson, pages 51–57. Washington, DC: U.S. Government Printing Office.

Krienert, Jessie L., and Mark S. Fleisher, eds. 2004 *Crime and Employment: Critical Issues in Crime Reduction for Corrections*. Walnut Creek, CA: AltaMira Press.

Krisberg, Barry 1988 *The Juvenile Court: Reclaiming the Vision*. San Francisco, CA: National Council on Crime and Delinquency.

Krisberg, Barry, Carolina Guzman, and Linh Vuong 2009 *Crime and Economic Hard Times*, Special report by the National Council on Crime and Delinquency: Internet.

Krisberg, Barry, Orlando Rodriguez, Audrey Bakke, Deborah Newenfeldt, and Patricia Steel 1994 *Juvenile Intensive Supervision: An Assessment*. Washington, DC: Office of Juvenile Justice and Delinquency Prevention.

Kupchik, Aaron 2006 "The Decision to Incarcerate in Juvenile and Criminal Courts." *Criminal Justice Review* 31 (December): 309–336.

Kurki, Leena 1999 *Incorporating Restorative and Community Justice into American Sentencing and Corrections*. Washington, DC: National Institute of Justice.

Kurlychek, Megan C., and Brian D. Johnson 2004 "The Juvenile Penalty: A Comparison of Juvenile and Young Adult Sentencing Outcomes in Criminal Court." *Criminology* 42 (May): 485–517.

Kuziemko, Ilyana 2013 "How Should Inmates Be Released From Prison? An Assessment of Parole Versus Fixed-Sentence Regimes." *Quarterly Journal of Economics*: 371–424.

Lab, Steven P., and John T. Cullen 1990 "From 'Nothing Works' to 'The Appropriate Works': The Latest Stop on the Search for the Secular Grail." *Criminology* 28 (August): 405–17.

Langan, Patrick A., and Matthew R. Durose 2003 *Recidivism of Sex Offenders Released from Prison in 1994*. Washington, DC: Bureau of Justice Statistics.

Langevin, Ron, Suzanne Curnoe, Paul Fedoroff, Renee Bennett, Mara Langevin, Cheryl Peever, Rick Pettica, and Shameen Sandhu 2004 "Lifetime Sex Offender Recidivism: A 25-Year Follow-Up Study." *Canadian Journal of Criminology and Criminal Justice* (October): 531–552.

Latessa, Edward J., and Gennaro F. Vito 1988 "The Effects of Intensive Supervision on Shock Probationers." *Journal of Criminal Justice* 16: 319–30.

Latessa, Edward J., Frank T. Cullen, and Paul Gendreau 2002 "Beyond Correctional Quakery—Professionalism and the Possibility of Effective Treatment." *Federal Probation* 66 (September): 40–43.

Latessa, Frank, Richard Lemke, Matthew Makarios, Paula Smith, and Christopher T. Lowenkamp 2010 "The Creation and Validation of the Ohio Risk Assessment System (ORAS)." *Federal Probation* 74 (June): 16–22.

Laub, John H., and Robert J. Sampson 2008 "Dimensions of Desistence." in *Parole, Desistance from Crime, and Community Integration*, pages 19–31. Washington, DC: National Academies Press.

La Vigne, Nancy and Julie Samuels 2012 *The Growth and Increasing Cost of the Federal Prison System: Drivers and Solutions*. Washington, DC: Urban Institute Justice Policy Center.

La Vigne, Nancy, Elizabeth Davies, Tobi Palmer, and Robin Halberstadt 2008 *Release Planning for Successful Reentry*. Washington, DC: Urban Institute.

Law Enforcement Assistance Administration 1973 *Reintegration of the Offender into the Community*. Washington, DC: U.S. Government Printing Office.

Leenhouts, Keith J. 2003 *Misdemeanors and the Miracle of Mentoring*. Davison, MI: Friede Publications.

Lefcourt, Robert, ed. 1971 *Law against the People*. New York: Random House.

Lemert, Edwin M. 1951 *Social Pathology*. New York: McGraw-Hill.

Lemmon, John H. 2006 "The Effects of Maltreatment Recurrence and Child Welfare Services on Dimensions of Delinquency." *Criminal Justice Review* 31 (March): 5–32.

Lenroot, Katherine F., and Emma O. Lundberg 1925 *Juvenile Courts at Work*. Washington, DC: U.S. Government Printing Office.

Leonhardt, David 2000 "As Prison Labor Grows, So Does the Debate." *New York Times* (March 19): 1, 22.

Leone, Peer, and Lois Weinberg 2010 *Addressing the Unmet Needs of Children and Youth in Juvenile Justice and Child Welfare Systems*. Washington, DC: Center for Juvenile Justice Reform, Georgetown University.

Lerner, Mark Jay 1977 "The Effectiveness of a Definite Sentence Parole Program." *Criminology* 15 (August).

Levrant, Sharon, Francis T. Cullen, Betsy Fulton, and John F. Wozniak 1999 "Reconsidering Restorative Justice: The Corruption of Benevolence Revisited?" *Crime and Delinquency* 45 (January): 3–27.

Lewin, Tamar 2001a "Little Sympathy or Remedy for Inmates Who Are Raped." *New York Times* (April 15): 1, 14.

Lewin, Tamar 2001b "3-Strikes Law Is Overrated in California, Study Finds." *New York Times* (August 24): 10.

Lewin, Tamar 1998 "Crime Costs Many Black Men the Vote, Study Says." *New York Times* (October 23): 12.

Lewis, W. David 1965 *From Newgate to Dannemora*. Ithaca, NY: Cornell University Press.

Liberton, Michael, Mitchell Silverman, and William R. Blount 1990 "An Analysis Used to Predict Success of First-Time Offenders While under Probation Supervision." Paper presented at the annual meeting of the Academy of Criminal Justice Sciences, April, Denver, CO; reprinted in 1992 in the *International Journal of Offender Therapy and Comparative Criminology* 36 (4): 335–47.

Lilly, J. Robert, and Richard A. Ball 1987 "A Brief History of House Arrest and Electronic Monitoring." *Northern Kentucky Law Review* 13: 343–74.

Lindner, Charles, and Margaret R. Savarese 1984 "The Evolution of Probation." *Federal Probation* 48 (December).

Lipsey, Mark W., Gabrielle L. Chapman, and Nana A. Landenberger 2001 "Cognitive-Behavioral Programs for Offenders." *Annals* 578 (November): 144–157.

Liptak, Adam 2008 "Inmate Count in U.S. Dwarfs Other Nations." *New York Times* (April 23): 1, 14.

Lipton, Douglas, Robert Martinson, and Judith Wilks 1975 *The Effectiveness of Correctional Treatment: A Survey of Treatment Evaluation Studies*. New York: Praeger.

Logan, Charles H. 1990 *Private Prisons: Cons and Pros*. New York: Oxford University Press.

Lombroso, Cesare 1968 *Crime: Its Causes and Remedies*. Montclair, NJ: Patterson Smith. (Originally published in 1911.)

London, Perry 1964 *The Modes and Morals of Psychotherapy*. New York: Holt, Rinehart and Winston.

Lopez, John S. 2007 "Have Perceptions Changed Among Staff Regarding Parole Officers' Carrying Firearms? A Description of Changes in Safety Perceptions and Supervisory Styles at the Texas Department of Criminal Justice Parole Division." Masters thesis in Public Administration, Texas State University/San Marcos,

Lou, Herbert H. 1972 *Juvenile Courts in the United States*. New York: Arno Press. (Originally published in 1927.)

Lowe, Nathan C. and Matthew DeMichele 2010 *Reentry of Methamphetamine-Using Offenders Into the Community*. Lexington, KY: American Probation and Parole Association.

Lowenkamp, Christopher T., Robert Lemke, and Edward Latessa 2008 "The Development and Validation of a Pretrial Screening Tool." *Federal Probation* (December): 2–9.

Lowenkamp, Christopher T., Brian Lovins, and Edward J. Latessa 2009 "Validating the Level of Service Inventory-Revised and the Level of Service Inventory: Screening Version with a Sample of Probationers." *Prison Journal* 89 (June): 192–204.

Lowenkamp, Christopher T., Jennifer Pealer, Paula Smith, and Edward J. Latessa 2006 "Adhering to the Risk and Need Principles: Does It Matter for Supervision-Based Programs?" *Federal Probation* (December): 3–8.

Lurigio, Arthur J., and Joan Petersilia 1992 "The Emergence of Intensive Probation Supervision Programs in the United States," in *Smart Sentencing: The Emergence of Intermediate Sanctions*, edited by James M. Byrne, Arthur J. Lurigio, and Joan Petersilia, pages 3–17. Newbury Park, CA: Sage.

Lurigio, Arthur J., Marylouise Jones, and Barbara E. Smith 1995 "Child Sexual Abuse: Its Causes, Consequences, and Implications for Probation Practice." *Federal Probation* 69 (September): 69–76.

Luther, Betty 1995 "The Politics of Criminal Justice: A Study of the Impact of Executive Influence on Massachusetts Parole Decisions between 1985 and 1992." Paper presented at the annual meeting of the Academy of Criminal Justice Sciences, Boston, March 7–11.

Lyons, Phillip and Todd Jermstad 2013 *Civil Liabilities and Other Legal Issues for Probation/Parole Officers and Supervisors*. 4th ed. Washington, DC: National Institute of Corrections.

MacKenzie, Doris Layton 2006 *What Works in Corrections: Reducing the Criminal Activities of Offenders*.

MacKenzie, Doris Layton, Robert Brame, David McDowall, and Claire Souryal 1995 "Boot Camp Prisons in Eight States." *Criminology* 33 (August): 327–57.

MacKenzie, Doris Layton, Angela R. Grover, Gaylene Stywe Armstrong, and Ojmarrh Mitchell 2001 *A National Study Comparing the Environments of Boot Camps with Traditional Facilities for Juvenile Offenders*. Washington, DC: National Institute of Justice.

MacKenzie, Doris Layton, and Claire Souryal 1994 *Multisite Evaluation of Shock Incarceration*. Washington, DC: National Institute of Justice.

MacKenzie, Doris Layton, and James W. Shaw 1993 "The Impact of Shock Incarceration on Technical Violations and New Criminal Activities." *Justice Quarterly* 10 (September): 463–87.

MacKenzie, Doris Layton, James W. Shaw, and Claire Souryal 1992 "Characteristics Associated with Successful Adjustment to Supervision: A Comparison of Parolees, Probationers, Shock Participants, and Shock Dropouts." *Criminal Justice and Behavior* 19 (December): 437–54.

MacNamara, Donal E. J. 1977 "The Medical Model in Corrections: Requiescat in Pace." *Criminology* 14 (February): 439–48.

Maestro, Marcello 1973 *Cesare Beccaria and the Origins of Penal Reform*. Philadelphia: Temple University Press.

Magura, Stephen, Sung-Yeon Kang, and Janet L. Shapiro 1995 "Measuring Cocaine Use by Hair Analysis among Criminally-Involved Youth." *Journal of Drug Issues* 25 (Fall): 683–701.

Mahoney, Joe 2007 "Short Arm of the Law." *New York Daily News* (May 8): 6.

Malcolm, Andrew H. 1989a "Florida's Jammed Prisons: More In Means More Out." *New York Times* (July 3): 1, 7.

Maloney, Dennis M., and Mark S. Umbreit 1995 "Managing Change: Toward a Balanced and Restorative Justice Model." *Perspectives* 19 (Spring): 43–46.

Maltz, Michael D. 1984 *Recidivism*. Orlando, FL: Academic Press.

Mander, Anthony M., Martin E. Atrops, Allan R. Barnes, and Roseanne Munafo 1996 *Sex Offender Treatment Program: Initial Recidivism Study*. Executive Summary. Anchorage: Alaska Department of Corrections.

Mangrum, Claude 1972 "The Humanity of Probation Officers." *Federal Probation* 36 (June).

Mann, Arnold 2004 "Successful Trial Caps 25-Year Buprenorphine Development Effort." *NIDA Notes* 19 (3): 7–9.

Mann, Dale 1976 *Intervening with Convicted Serious Juvenile Offenders*. Washington, DC: U.S. Government Printing Office.

"Manufacturers Complain of Prison Work Programs" 1997 *Chicago Tribune* (November 28): 8.

Markel, Howard 2009 "Forcing Sobriety, However Imperfectly." *New York Times* (May 6): F5.

Markland, David, Richard M. Ryan, Vanessa Jayne Tobin, and S. Rollnick 2005 "Motivational Interviewing and Self-Determination Theory." *Journal of Social and Clinical Psychology* 24 (6): 811–831.

Marlowe, Douglas 2006 "When 'What Works' Never Did: Dodging the 'Scarlet M' in Correctional Rehabilitation." *Criminology and Public Policy* 5 (May): 339–46.

Marriott, Michael 1995 "Half Steps vs. 12 Steps." *Newsweek* (March 27): 62.

Marshall, Franklin H. 1989 "Diversion and Probation under the New Sentencing Guidelines: One Officer's Observations." Paper presented at the annual meeting of the Academy of Criminal Justice Sciences, Washington, DC, March 30.

Martin, Andrew 1995 "Few Brains behind Bank Heists." *Chicago Tribune* (June 28): Sec. 2: 1, 4.

Martin, Brian 2008 *Examining the Impact of Ohio's Progressive Sanction Grid, Final Report*. Washington, DC: National Institute of Justice.

Martin, Douglas 1988 "New York Tests Inmates' Boot Camp." *New York Times* (March 4): 15.

Martin, Garry, and Joseph Pear 2011 *Behavior Modification: What It Is and How to Do It*, 4th ed. Upper Saddle River, NJ: Pearson.

Martinson, Robert 1974 "What Works? Questions and Answers about Prison Reform." *The Public Interest* 35 (Spring): 22–54.

Martinson, Robert, and Judith Wilks 1975 "A Static-Descriptive Model of Field Supervision." *Criminology* 13 (May): 3–20.

Maruschak, Laura M. 2006 *HIV in Prisons, 2004*. Washington, DC: Bureau of Justice Statistics.

Marx, Gary 1998 "Panel Uncovers Security Leaks at Juvenile Jail." *Chicago Tribune* (March 2): 1, 12.

Mathias, Rudolf E. S., and James W. Mathews 1991 "The Boot Camp Program for Offenders: Does the Shoe Fit?" *International Journal of Offender Therapy and Comparative Criminology* 35: 322–27.

Matza, David 1964 *Delinquency and Drift*. New York: Wiley.

McCarthy, Belinda Rogers, and Bernard J. McCarthy 1984 *Community-Based Corrections*. Monterey, CA: Brooks/Cole.

McCollum, Sylvia G. 2000 "Mock Job Fairs in Prison: Tracking Participants." *Federal Probation* (June): 13–18.

McCoy, Candace 1993 *Politics and Plea Bargaining: Victim's Rights in California*. Philadelphia: University of Pennsylvania Press.

McDonald, Douglas C. 1988 *Restitution and Community Service*. Washington, DC: National Institute of Justice.

McDowell, Edwin 1991 "Inmates Fill the Front Lines for Tourism." *New York Times* (November 24): 1, 15.

McElrath, Karen 1995 "Alcoholics Anonymous," in the *American Drug Scene: An Anthology*, edited by James A. Inciardi and Karen McElrath, pages 314–37. Los Angeles: Roxbury.

McFadden, Robert D. 1997 "Ex-Attica Inmate Wins $4 Million in Suit over Reprisals after 1971 Uprising." *New York Times* (June 6): 20.

McGaha, Johnny, Michael Fichter, and Peter Hirschburg 1987 "Felony Probation: A Re-Examination of Public Risk." *American Journal of Criminal Justice* 11: 1–9.

McKelvey, Blake 1977 *American Prisons: A History of Good Intentions*. Montclair, NJ: Patterson Smith.

McShane, Marilyn D., and Frank P. Williams III 1989 "The Prison Adjustment of Juvenile Offenders." *Crime and Delinquency* 35 (April): 254–269.

McTavish, Thomas H. 1997 *Performance Audit of the Presentence Invest gation Process*. Lansing: Michigan Office of the Auditor General.

Melossi, Dario, and Massimo Pavarini 1981 *The Prison and the Factory: Origins of the Penitentiary System*. Totowa, NJ: Barnes and Noble.

Mennel, Robert M. 1973 *Thorns and Thistles: Juvenile Delinquents in the United States, 1825–1940*. Hanover, NH: University Press of New England.

Mercado, Cynthia Calkins, Elizabeth Jeglic, Keith Markus, R. Karl Hanson, and Jill Levenson 2013 *Sex Offender Management, Treatment, and Civil Commitment: An Evidence Based Analysis Aimed at Reducing Sexual Violence*. New York: John Jay College of Criminal Justice.

Meredith, Robyn 2000 "Road from Prison to Jobs Gets Smoother." *New York Times* (April 3): 12.

Merlo, Alida V., Peter J. Benekos, and William J. Cook 1997 "Waiver and Juvenile Justice Reform: Widening the Punitive Net." *Criminal Justice Policy Review* 8 (2–3): 145–68.

Merton, Robert K. 1964 "Anomie, Anomia, and Social Interaction." In *Anomie and Deviant Behavior*, edited by Marshall B. Clinard, pages 213–42. New York: Free Press.

Merton, Robert K. 1938 "Social Structure and Anomie." *American Sociological Review* 3: 672–82.

Mieczkowski, Thomas 1995 *Hair Analysis as a Drug Detector*. Washington, DC: National Institute of Justice.

Miley, Karla Krogsrud, Michael O'Melia, and Brenda L. DuBois 2013 *Generalist Social Work Practice: An Empowering Approach*, 7th ed. Upper Saddle River, NJ: Pearson.

Milkman, Harvey and Kenneth Wanberg 2007 *Cognitive-Behavioral Treatment: A Review and Discussion for Corrections Professionals*. Washington, DC: National Institute of Corrections.

Miller, Jerome 1992 *Last One over the Wall: The Massachusetts Experiment in Closing Reform Schools*. Columbus: Ohio State University.

Miller, Walter B. 1958 "Lower Class Culture as a Generating Milieu of Gang Delinquency." *Journal of Social Issues* 14: 5–19.

Miller, William R., and Gary S. Rose 2009 "Toward a Theory of Motivational Interviewing." *American Psychologist* 64 (September): 527–537.

Miller, William R, and Stephen Rollnick 2002 *Motivational Interviewing: Preparing People for Change*, 2nd ed. New York: Guilford Press.

Mills, Jim 1992 "Supervision Fees." *Perspectives* (Fall): 10–12.

Minnesota Department of Corrections (MDOC) 2010 *An Evaluation of the Minnesota Comprehensive Offender Reentry Plan (MCORP): Phase 1 Report*. St. Paul, MN: MDOC.

Mohler, Henry Calvin 1925 "Convict Labor Policies." *Journal of Criminal Law, Criminology and Police Science* 15: 530–597.

Monti, Crostin 1997 "Prison Treatment Program Seeks to Change Sex Offender Behavior." *The Compiler* 17 (Summer): 4–6.

Moore, Kathleen Dean 1989 *Pardons: Justice, Mercy, and the Public Interest*. New York: Oxford University Press.

Moore, Solomon 2009a "The Prison Overcrowding Fix." *New York Times* (February 11): 17.

Morash, Merry, and Lila Rucker 1990 "A Critical Look at the Idea of Boot Camp as a Correctional Reform." *Crime and Delinquency* 36 (April): 204–22.

Morgan, Robert D. and Carrie L. Winterowd 2002 "Interpersonal Process-Oriented Group Psychotherapy." *International Journal of Offender Therapy and Comparative Criminology* 46 (4): 466–482.

Moritz, John 2001 "Prison Population in Texas Declines." *Fort Worth Star Telegram* (July 3): Internet.

Morris, Norval, and Michael Tonry 1990 *Between Prison and Probation: Intermediate Punishments in a Rational Sentencing System*. New York: Oxford University Press.

Moses, Marilyn C. 1996 *Project Re-Enterprise: A Texas Program*. Washington, DC: Office of Justice Programs.

Moses, Marilyn C., and Cindy J. Smith 2008 "Factories Behind Fences: Do Prison 'Real Work' Programs Work?" *NIJ Journal* 257: 33–36.

Mullaney, Fahy G. 1988 *Economic Sanctions in Community Corrections*. Washington, DC: National Institute of Corrections.

Mullen, Joan 1985 "Corrections and the Private Sector." *NIJ Reports* (May).

Mumola, Christopher J., and Thomas P. Bonczar 1998 *Substance Abuse and Treatment of Adults on Probation, 1995*. Washington, DC: Bureau of Justice Statistics.

Murphy, Cait 2001 "Crime and Punishment." *Fortune* 143 (April 30): 126–135.

Mydans, Seth 1995 "Racial Tensions on the Rise in Los Angeles Jail System." *New York Times* (February 6): 8.

Myers, Linnet 1995 "Cultural Divide over Crime and Punishment." *Chicago Tribune* (October 13): 1, 8.

Nasheri, Hedieh 1998 *Betrayal of Due Process: A Comparative Assessment of Plea Bargaining in the United States and Canada*. Lanham, MD: University Press of America.

National Advisory Commission on Criminal Justice Standards and Goals 1975 *A National Strategy to Reduce Crime*. New York: Avon.

National Commission on Law Observance and Law Enforcement 1931 *Report on Penal Institutions*. Washington, DC: U.S. Government Printing Office. National Employment Law Project

National Employment Law Project (NELP) 2012 *Ban the Box: Major Cities and Counties Adopt Fair Hiring Policies to Remove Unfair Barriers to Employment of People with Criminal Records*. New York: NELP.

National League of Cities. n.d. *Cities Pave the Way: Promising Reentry Policies that Promote Local Hiring of People with Criminal Records*. Washington, DC: National League of Cities.

National Governors' Association 1988 *Guide to Executive Clemency among the American States*. Washington, DC: National Institute of Corrections.

National Institute of Corrections (NIC) 2013 *Civil Liabilities and Other Legal Issues for Probation/Parole Officers and Supervisors*, 4th edition. Washington, DC: NIC.

National Research Council 2008 *Parole, Desistance From Crime, and Community Reintegration*. Washington, DC: National Academies Press.

Nelson, E. Kim, Howard Ohmart, and Nora Harlow 1978 *Promising Strategies in Probation and Parole*. Washington, DC: U.S. Government Printing Office.

"Newgate" 1998 *DOC Today* (February): Internet.

New Jersey State Parole Board 2006 State Parole Board Annual Report 2005. Trenton: New Jersey State Parole.

New York State Bar Association 2006 *The Road to Public Safety*. Albany, NY: Special Committee on Collateral Consequences of Criminal Proceedings.

New York State Division of Parole 1994 *1993–1994 Report*. Albany: New York State Division of Parole.

New York State Division of Probation and Correctional Alternatives (NYSDPCA) 2009 *Research Bulletin 3: The Use of the Polygraph in Sex Offender Management*. Albany: NYSDPCA.

New York State Employment Services Vocational Rehabilitation Service 1965 "Vocational Counseling with the Offender" (mimeo). Albany, NY: Vocational Rehabilitation Service.

New York State Special Commission on Attica 1972 *Attica*. New York: Praeger.

"New York State's Disgrace" 2009 *New York Times* (editorial) (August 25): 20.

Niemeyer, Mike, and David Shichor 1996 "A Preliminary Study of a Large Victim/Offender Reconciliation Program." *Federal Probation* 60 (September): 30–34.

Nietzel, Michael T., Douglas A. Bernstein, Geoffrey P. Kramer, and Richard Milich 2003 *Introduction to Clinical Psychology*, 6th ed. Upper Saddle River, NJ: Prentice Hall.

Noonan, Susan B., and Edward J. Latessa 1987 "Intensive Probation: An Examination of Recidivism and Social Adjustment." *American Journal of Criminal Justice* 11: 45–61.

Norman, Michael D., and Robert C. Wadman 2000 "Probation Department Sentencing Recommendations in Two Utah Counties." *Federal Probation* (December): 47–51.

North Carolina Division of Community Corrections (NCDCC) 2005 *Guide to Offender Management: Engaging the Offender in the Change Process*. Raleigh: NCDCC.

Northern, Helen 1988 *Social Work with Groups*, 2nd ed. New York: Columbia University Press.

Office for Victims of Crime 1998 *New Directions from the Field: Victims' Rights and Services for the 21st Century*. Washington, DC: U.S. Department of Justice.

Office of Policy Analysis and Information 1989 *Shock Incarceration: One Year Out*. Albany: New York State Division of Parole.

Ogborne, Alan C., and Frederick B. Glaser 1985 "Evaluating Alcoholics Anonymous," in *Alcoholism and Substance Abuse*, edited by Thomas E. Bratter and Gary G. Forrest, pages 176–192. New York: Free Press.

OJJDP Research 2000. 2001 Washington, DC: Office of Juvenile Justice and Delinquency Prevention.

Old Behind Bars 2012 New York: Human Rights Watch.

O'Leary, K. Daniel, and G. Terrance Wilson 1975 *Behavior Therapy: Application and Outcome*. Upper Saddle River, NJ: Prentice Hall.

Olivares, Kathleen M., Velmer S. Burton, Frances T. Cullen, Debra Oldenettel, and Madeline Wordes 2000 *The Community Assessment Center Concept*. Washington, DC: Office of Juvenile Justice and Delinquency Prevention.

Olivares, Kathleen M., Velmer S. Burton, Frances T. Cullen, Debra Oldenettel, and Madeline Wordes 1996 "The Collateral Consequences of a Felony Conviction: A National Study of State Legal Codes 10 Years Later." *Federal Probation* 60 (September): 10–17.

Olson, Susan M., and Albert W. Dzur 2003 "The Practice of Restorative Justice: Reconstructing Professional Roles in Restorative Justice Programs." *Utah Law Review* 57: Internet.

Oltmanns, Thomas F., and Robert E. Emery 2010 *Abnormal Psychology*, 6th ed. Upper Saddle River, NJ: Pearson.

Omer, Haim, and Perry London 1988 "Metamorphosis in Psychotherapy: End of the Systems Era." *Psychotherapy* 25 (Summer): 171–180.

Opsal, Tara D. 2010 "Women on Parole: Understanding the Impact of Surveillance." *Women and Criminal Justice* 19 (4): 306–328.

Ostermann, Michael 2009 "An Analysis of New Jersey's Day Reporting Center and Halfway Back Programs: Embracing the Rehabilitative Ideal Through Evidence Based Practices." *Journal of Offender Rehabilitation* 48: 139–153.

Ostermann, Michael 2013 "Active Supervision and Its Impact Upon Parolee Recidivism Rates." *Crime and Delinquency* 59: 487–509.

Pace, Eric 1988 "Lois Burnham Wilson, a Founder of Al-Anon Groups, Is Dead at 97." *New York Times* (October 4): 15.

Pager, Devah 2006 "Evidence-Based Policy for Successful Prisoner Reentry." *Criminology and Public Policy* 5 (August): 505–514.

Pager, Devah 2003 "The Mark of a Criminal Record." *American Journal of Sociology* 108 (March): 937–975.

Pager, Devah, and Bruce Western 2009 *Investigating Prisoner Reentry: The Impact of Conviction Status on the Employment Prospects of Young Men*. Washington, DC: U.S. Department of Justice.

Palumbo, Dennis J., and Rebecca D. Peterson 1994 "Shock Incarceration and Intermediate Punishments: Reform or Recycled 'Get Tough' Policy?" Paper presented at the annual meeting of the American Society of Criminology, Miami, FL, November.

Papy, Joseph E. 1997 "Florida's Approach to Probation and Parole Staff Safety," in *Topics in Community Corrections*, pages 23–25. Washington, DC: National Institute of Corrections.

Parent, Dale G. 2003 *Correctional Boot Camps: Lessons from a Decade of Research*. Washington, DC: National Institute of Justice.

Parent, Dale G., Dan Wentworth, Peggy Burke, and Becky Ney 1994 *Responding to Probation and Parole Violations*. Washington, DC: National Institute of Justice.

Parker, William 1975 *Parole*. College Park, MD: American Correctional Association.

Parry, Wayne 2001 "Employers Seeking Workers from Newark Prison Ranks." Associated Press (May 17): Internet.

Parsonage, William H. 1990 *Worker Safety in Probation and Parole*. Longmont, CO: National Institute of Corrections.

Parsonage, William H., and W. Conway Bushey 1989 "The Victimization of Probation and Parole Workers in the Line of Duty: An Exploratory Study." Paper presented at the annual meeting of the Academy of Criminal Justice Sciences, Washington, DC, March.

Parsons, Christi 1998 "Jury Out on Sex-Offender Law." *Chicago Tribune* (June 28): 1, 12.

Payne, Malcolm 1997 *Modern Social Work Theory*, 2nd ed. Chicago: Lyceum.

Peachey, J. E., and H. Lei 1988 "Assessment of Opioid Dependence with Naloxone." *British Journal of Addiction* 83: 93–201.

Pearson, Frank S. 1988 "Evaluation of New Jersey's Intensive Supervision Program." *Crime and Delinquency* 34 (October): 437–48.

Pearson, Frank S., Douglas S. Lipton, Charles M. Cleland, and Dorline S.Yee 2002 "The Effects of Behavioral/Cognitive-Behavioral Programs on Recidivism." *Crime and Delinquency* 48 (July): 476–496.

Peele, Stanton 1985 *The Meaning of Addiction: Compulsive Experience and Its Interpretation*. Lexington, MA: D. C. Heath.

Peréz-Peña, Richard 2003 "New Drug Promises Shift in Treatment." *New York Times* (August 11): 1, B7.

Peréz-Peña, Richard 1998 "Pataki Plan to End Parole Is Tougher Than Others." *New York Times* (January 26): 18.

Perlman, Helen Harris 1971 *Perspectives on Social Casework: A Problem Solving Process*. Chicago: University of Chicago Press.

Peters, Michael, David Thomas, and Christopher Zamberlan 1997 *Boot Camp for Juvenile Offenders: Program Summary*. Washington, DC: Office of Juvenile Justice and Delinquency Prevention.

Petersilia, Joan M. 2006 *Understanding California Corrections*. Berkeley: California Policy Research Center.

Petersilia, Joan, and Elizabeth Piper Deschenes 1994 "What Punishes? Inmates Rank the Severity of Prison vs. Intermediate Sanctions." *Federal Probation* 68 (March): 3–8.

Petersilia, Joan, and Susan Turner 1993 *Evaluating Intensive Supervision Probation/Parole: Results of a Nationwide Experiment*. Washington, DC: National Institute of Justice.

Petersilia, Joan, Susan Turner, and Elizabeth Piper Deschenes 1992 "Intensive Supervision Programs for Drug Offenders," in *Smart Sentencing: The Emergence of Intermediate Sanctions*, edited by James M. Byrne, Arthur J. Lurigio, and Joan Petersilia, pages 18–37. Newbury Park, CA: Sage.

Petersilia, Joan, Susan Turner, James Kahan, and Joyce Peterson 1985 *Granting Felons Probation: Public Risks and Alternatives*. Santa Monica, CA: RAND.

Pew Center on the States (PCS) 2012 *Time Served: The High Cost, Low Return of Longer Prison Terms*. Washington, DC: PCS.

Pickel, Mary Lou 2009 "Homeless Sex Offenders Live in Woods in Cobb County." *Atlanta Constitution* (September 28): Internet.

Pisciotta, Alexander W. 1994 *Benevolent Repression: Social Control and the American Reformatory-Prison Movement*. New York: New York University Press.

Platt, Anthony M. 1974 *The Childsavers: The Invention of Delinquency*. Chicago: University of Chicago Press.

Platt, Jerome J., and Christina Labate 1976 *Heroin Addiction: Research and Treatment*. New York: Wiley.

Polakow, Robert L., and Ronald M. Docktor 1974 "A Behavioral Modification Program for Adult Drug Offenders." *Journal of Research in Crime and Delinquency* 11 (January): 63–69.

Porter, Bruce 1995 "Terror on an Eight-Hour Shift." *New York Times Magazine* (November 26): 42–47, 56, 59, 72, 76, 80, 82.

Powell, Hickman 2000 *Lucky Luciano: The Man Who Organized Crime in America*. New York: Barricade Books. (Originally published in 1939.)

President's Commission on Law Enforcement and Administration of Justice 1972 *The Challenge of Crime in a Free Society*. New York: Avon.

President's Commission on Organized Crime 1986 *The Impact: Organized Crime Today*. Washington, DC: U.S. Government Printing Office.

Prison Association of New York 1936 *The Ninety-First Annual Report*. Albany, NY: J. B. Lyon.

Privacy and Juvenile Justice Records: A Mid-Decade Status Report 1997 Washington, DC: Office of Justice Programs.

Proctor, Jon L. 2000 "Parole as Institutional Control: A Test of Specific Deterrence and Offender Misconduct." *The Prison Journal* 80 (1): 39–55.

Program Services Office 1983 *Probation Classification and Service Delivery Approach*. Los Angeles: County Probation Department.

Przybylski, Roger 2008 *What Works Effective Recidivism Reduction and Risk-Focused Prevention Programs*. Denver: Colorado Department of Public Safety.

Purdy, Matthew 1997 "As AIDS Increases behind Bars, Costs Dim Promise of New Drugs." *New York Times* (May 26): 1, 12.

Puritz, Patricia, and Mary Ann Scali 1998 *Beyond the Walls: Improving Conditions of Confinement for Youth in Custody*. Washington, DC: Office of Juvenile Justice and Delinquency Prevention.

Puzzanchera, Charles M. 2001 *Delinquency Cases Waived to Criminal Court, 1989–1998*. Washington, DC: Office of Justice Programs.

Puzzanchera, Charles, Benjamin Adams, and Melissa Sickmund 2011 *Juvenile Court Statistics*. Pittsburgh, PA: National Center for Juvenile Justice.

Quadagno, Jill S., and Robert J. Antonio 1975 "Labeling Theory as an Oversocialized Conception of Man: The Case of Mental Illness." *Sociology and Social Research* 60 (October): 33–45.

Rachin, Richard 1974 "Reality Therapy: Helping People Help Themselves." *Crime and Delinquency* 20 (January): 45–53.

"Rape Crisis in U.S. Prisons" 2001 *Human Rights Watch* (April 19): Internet.

Re-Entry Policy Council (REPC) 2005 *Report of the Re-Entry Policy Council*. New York: REPC.

Reeves, Bob 2003 "Introduction," in *Misdemeanors and the Miracle of Mentoring*, edited by Keith J. Leenhouts, pages iv–v. Davison, MI: Friede Publications.

Reichel, Phillip L., and Billie D. Sudback 1994 "Differences among Eligibles: Who Gets an ISP Sentence?" *Federal Probation* (58): 51–62.

Reiff, Phillip, ed. 1963 *Freud, Therapy and Techniques*. New York: Crowell-Collier.

Reiman, Jeffrey 1998 *The Rich Get Richer and the Poor Get Prison*, 5th ed. New York: Macmillan.

Reinventing Probation Council (RPC) 2000 *Transforming Probation through Leadership: The "Broken Windows" Model*. New York: Center for Civic Innovation at the Manhattan Institute.

Rhine, Edward E. 2002 "Why 'What Works' Matters under the 'Broken Windows' Model of Supervision." *Federal Probation* 66 (September): 38–42.

Rhine, Edward E., Tina L. Mawhorr, and Evalyn C. Parks 2006 "Implementation: The Bane of Effective Correctional Programs." *Criminology and Public Policy* 5 (May): 347–58.

Rhode, David 2001 "A Health Danger from a Needle Becomes a Scourge behind Bars." *New York Times* (August 6): 1, 14.

Rhodes, William, Christina Dyous, Ryan Kling, Dana Hunt, and Jeremy Luallen 2013 *Recidivism of Offenders on Federal Community Supervision*. Cambridge, MA: Abt Associates.

Richmond, Mary 1917 *Social Diagnosis*. New York: Russell Sage Foundation.

Rimer, Sara 2001 "States Adjust Their Adult Prisons to the Needs of Youth Inmates." *New York Times* (July 25): 1, 13.

Risk/Needs Assessment 101 n.d. Washington, DC: Pew Center on the Courts.

Ritter, Nancy n.d. *New Tools Will Manage Community Corrections … and Beyond*. Washington, DC: National Institute of Justice.

Robbins, Ira P. 1988 *The Legal Dimensions of Private Incarceration*. Washington, DC: American Bar Association.

Robbins, Kelly, and Michael Ostermann 2006 *2004 Recidivism Study: Executive Summary*. Trenton: New Jersey State Division of Parole.

Roberts, Sam 2008 "Census Bureau's Counting of Prisoners Benefits Some Rural Voting Districts." *New York Times* (October 24): 12.

Robertson, John A. 1974 *Rough Justice: Perspectives on Lower Courts*. Boston: Little, Brown.

Robertson, Nan 1988 *Getting Better: Inside Alcoholics Anonymous*. New York: William Morrow.

Robitscher, Jonas 1980 *The Power of Psychiatry*. Boston: Houghton Mifflin.

Rogers, Carl 1951 *Client-Centered Therapy*. Boston: Houghton Mifflin.

Rollnick, Stephen, and Jeff Allison 2004 "Motivational Interviewing." in *The Essential Handbook of Treatment and Prevention of Alcohol Problems*, edited by N. Heather and T. Stockwell, pages 105–115. West Sussex, England: John Wiley and Sons.

Rollnick, Stephen, and William R. Miller 1995 "What is MI?" *Behavioural [sic] and Cognitive Psychotherapy* 23: 325–334.

Roman, John, Michael Kane, Emily Turner, and Beverly Frazier 2006 *Instituting Lasting Reforms for Prisoner Reentry in Philadelphia*. Washington, DC: Urban Institute Justice Policy Center.

Rosenblum, Robert, and Debra Whitcomb 1978 *Montgomery County Work Release/Pre-Release Program*. Washington, DC: U.S. Government Printing Office.

Rosenfeld, Richard 2009 "Recidivism and Its Discontents." *Criminology and Public Policy* 7 (May): 311–318.

Rosenfeld, Richard, Joan Petersilia, and Christy Visher 2008 "The First Days After Release Can Make a Difference." *NIJ Update* reprinted from *Corrections Today* (June): 86–87.

Rosenthal, Mitchell S, 1984 "Therapeutic Communities: A Treatment Alternative for Many But Not All." *Journal of Substance Abuse Treatment* 1: 55–58.

Roshier, Bob 1989 *Controlling Crime: The Classical Perspective in Criminology*. Chicago: Lyceum.

Rothman, David 1971 *The Discovery of the Asylum*. Boston: Little, Brown.

Rottman, David B., Carol R. Flango, Melissa T. Cantrell, Randall Hansen, and Neil LaFountain 2000 *State Court Organization 1998*. Washington, DC: National Institute of Justice.

Rousseau, Jean-Jacques 1954 *The Social Contract*. Chicago: Henry Regnery.

Rubin, H. Ted 1980 "The Emerging Prosecutor Dominance of the Juvenile Court Intake Process." *Crime and Delinquency* 26 (July): 299–318.

Rudes, Danielle S. and Shannon Portillo 2012 "Rules and Power Within Federal Problem Solvong Courtroom Workgroups." *Law and Policy* 34 (October): 402–427.

Russell, Amanda L., Edward J. Latessa, and Lawrence F. Travis III 2005 "Evidence of Professionalism or Quackery: Measuring Practitioner Awareness of Risk/Need Factors and Effective Treatment Strategies." *Federal Probation* (December): 9–14.

Russo, Joe 2006 "Emerging Technologies for Community Corrections." *Corrections Today* (October): 26–28.

Rutgers Center for Behavioral Health Services and Criminal Justice Research 2013 *Halfway from Prison to the Community: From Current Practice to Best Practice*. New Brunswick, NJ: Rutgers University.

Sachs, Howard, and Charles Logan 1979 *Does Parole Make a Difference?* West Hartford: University of Connecticut Law School.

Sagatun, Inger, Loretta McCollum, and Michael Edwards 1985 "The Effect of Transfers from Juvenile to Criminal Court: A Loglinear Analysis." *Journal of Crime and Justice* 8: 65–92.

Sanborn, Joseph B., Jr. 1992 "Pleading Guilty in Juvenile Court: Minimal Ado about Something Very Important to Young Defendants." *Justice Quarterly* 9 (March): 127–50.

Schlager, Melinda D., and Kelly Robbins 2008 "Does Parole Work? Revisited: Reaffirming the Discussion of the Impact of Postprison Supervision on Offender Outcome." *The Prison Journal* 88 (June): 234–251.

Schlosser, Eric 1998 "The Prison-Industrial Complex." *Atlantic Monthly* (December): 51–77.

Schlossman, Steven L. 1977 *Love and the American Delinquent: The Theory and Practice of "Progressive" Juvenile Justice, 1825–1920*. Chicago: University of Chicago Press.

Schmideberg, Melitta 1975 "Some Basic Principles of Offender Therapy: Part II." *International Journal of Offender Therapy and Comparative Criminology* 1.

Schmidt, Annesley K. 1989 "Electronic Monitoring of Offenders Increases." *NIJ Reports* (January/February): 2–5.

Schmitt, Kris Warner, and Sarika Gupta 2010 *The High Budgetary Cost of Incarceration*. Washington, DC: Center for Economic and Policy Research.

Schram, Donna D., Jill G. McKelvy, Anne L. Schneider, and David B. Griswold 1981 *Preliminary Findings: Assessment of the Juvenile Code* (mimeo). Washington State.

Schram, Paula J., Barbara A. Koons-Witt, Frank P. William III, and Marilyn D. McShane 2006 "Supervision Strategies and Approaches for Female Parolees: Examining the Link Between Unmet Needs and Parolee Outcome." *Crime and Delinquency* 52 (July): 450–471.

Schriro, Dora 2000 *Correcting Corrections: Missouri's Parallel Universe*. Washington, DC: National Institute of Justice.

Schultz, J. Lawrence 1973 "The Cycle of Juvenile Court History." *Crime and Delinquency* 19 (October): 457–476.

Schuman, Alan M. 1989 "The Cost of Correctional Services: Exploring a Poorly Charted Terrain." *Research in Corrections* 2 (February): 27–33.

Schur, Edwin M. 1973 *Radical Non-Intervention: Rethinking the Delinquency Problem*. Englewood Cliffs, NJ: Prentice Hall.

Schwartz, Richard, and Jerome H. Skolnick 1962 "Two Studies in Legal Stigma." *Social Problems* 10: 133–42.

Scott, Wayne 2008 *Effective Clinical Practices in Treating Clients in the Criminal Justice System*. Washington, DC: National Institute of Corrections.

Scroggins, Jennifer R, and Sara Malley 2010 "Reentry and the (Unmet) Needs of Women." *Journal of Offender Rehabilitation* 49 (2): 146–163.

Scull, Andrew T. 1977 *Decarceration*. Englewood Cliffs, NJ: Prentice Hall.

Sechcrest, Dale K. 1989 "Prison 'Boot Camps' Do Not Measure Up." *Federal Probation* 53 (September): 15–20.

Sechrest, Lee, Susan O. White, and Elizabeth D. Brown 1979 *The Rehabilitation of Criminal Offenders: Problems and Prospects*. Washington, DC: National Academy of Sciences.

Sedlak, Andrea J., and Karla S. McPherson 2010 *Conditions of Confinement: Findings from the Survey of Youth in Residential Placement*. Washington, DC: Office of Justice Programs.

Selcraig, Bruce 2000 "Camp Fear." *Mother Jones* (December): 64–71.

Sellin, Thorston 1967 "A Look at Prison History." *Federal Probation* 31 (September): 18.

Sengupta, Somini 2000 "Felony Costs Voting Rights for a Lifetime in 9 States." *New York Times* (November 3): 18.

Sever, Brian 2000 "County Sales Tax, Crime Rate, and Prison Bed Use in Florida: Implications for the Misuse of Prison Space." *Criminal Justice Policy Review* 11 (June): 91–112.

Sexton, Joe 2006 "After Death of a Boy, Florida Moves to Close Its Boot Camps." *New York Times* (April 27): 18.

Shaffer, John, and M. David Galinsky 1987 *Models of Group Therapy*, 2nd ed. Upper Saddle River, NJ: Prentice Hall.

Sheafor, Bradford W., Charles R. Horejsi, and Gloria A. Horejsi 2000 *Techniques and Guidelines for Social Work Practice*, 5th ed. Boston: Allyn and Bacon.

Shearer, Robert A. 2003 "Identifying the Special Needs of Female Offenders." *Federal Probation* (June): 46–51.

Sheldon, Randall G., John A. Horvath, and Sharon Tracy 1989 "Do Status Offenders Get Worse? Some Clarifications on the Question of Escalation." *Crime and Delinquency* 35 (April): 202–16.

Shichor, David, and Clemens Bartollas 1990 "Private and Public Juvenile Placements: Is There a Difference?" *Crime and Delinquency* 36 (April): 286–99.

Shilton, Mary K. 2000 *Increasing Offender Employment in the Community*. Washington, DC: Center for Community Corrections.

Short, James R., Jr. 1968 *Gang Delinquency and Delinquent Subcultures*. New York: Harper and Row.

Sickmund, Melissa, Howard Snyder, and Eileen Poe-Yamagata 1997 *Juvenile Offenders and Victims: 1997 Update on Violence*. Washington, DC: Office of Juvenile Justice and Delinquency Prevention.

Silverman, Ira J. 2001 *Corrections: Comprehensive View*, 2nd ed. Belmont, CA: Wadsworth.

Silverman, Mitchell 1994 "Ethical Issues in the Field of Probation." *International Journal of Offender Therapy and Comparative Criminology* 37 (1): 85–94.

Simon, Jonathan 1993 *Poor Discipline: Parole and Social Control of the Underclass, 1890–1990*. Chicago: University of Chicago Press.

Simourd, David 2006 *Validation of Risk/Needs Assessments in the Pennsylvania Department of Corrections*. Collingswood, NJ: Volunteers of America-Delaware Valley.

Sinclair, Jim 1994 "APPA's Public Hearings Explore Probation and Parole's Response to Victims of Crime: Speakers Call for a New Approach to Victim Issues." *Perspectives* (Special Issue): 15–17.

Skidmore, Rex A., Milton G. Thackeray, and O. William Farley 1988 *Introduction to Social Work*, 4th ed. Upper Saddle River, NJ: Prentice Hall.

Skinner, B. F. 1972 *Beyond Freedom and Dignity*. New York: Alfred A. Knopf.

Skipp, Catherine, and Arian Campo-Flores 2009 "A Bridge Too Far." *Newsweek* (August 2): 46–51.

Slevin, Peter 2001 "Prison Firms Seek Inmates and Profits." *Washington Post* (February 18): 3.

Sluder, Richard D., and Rolando del Carmen 1990 "Are Probation and Parole Officers Liable for Injuries Caused by Probationers and Parolees?" *Federal Probation* 54 (December): 3–12.

Smart, Frances 1970 *Neuroses and Crime.* New York: Barnes and Noble.

Smith, Carolyn, and Terence C. Thornberry 1995 "The Relationship between Childhood Maltreatment and Adolescent Involvement in Delinquency." *Criminology* 33 (November): 451–77.

Smith, Michael E. 2001 *What Future for "Public Safety" and "Restorative Justice" in Community Corrections?* Washington, DC: National Institute of Justice.

Snyder, Howard N., and Melissa Sickmund 2006 *Juvenile Offenders and Victims: 2006 National Report.* Washington, DC: Office of Justice Programs.

Solomon, Amy 2006 "Does Parole Supervision Work?" *Perspectives* (Spring): 26–37.

Solomon, Amy, Vera Kachnowski, and Avinash Bhati 2005 *Does Parole Work?* Washington, DC: The Urban Institute.

Solomon, Jolie 1998 "Watching Mike." *Newsweek* (March 2): 54–55.

Specht, Harry 1990 "Social Work and the Popular Psychotherapies." *Social Service Review* 64 (September): 345–57.

Spencer, Herbert 1961 *The Study of Sociology.* Ann Arbor: University of Michigan Press. (Originally published in 1871.)

Spencer, Jim 1987 "Knock 'Em Out, Trainee." *Chicago Tribune* (July 26): Sec. 3: 1, 2.

Spitz, Henry I. 1987 "Cocaine Abuse: Therapeutic Group Approaches," in *Cocaine Abuse: New Directions in Treatment and Research*, edited by Henry I. Spitz and Jeffrey S. Rosecan, pages 156–201. New York: Brunner/Mazel.

Stalans, Loretta J. 2004 "Adult Sex Offenders on Community Supervision: A Review of Recent Assessment Strategies and Treatment." *Criminal Justice and Behavior* 31 (October): 564–608.

Stampfl, Thomas G. 1970 "Comment" [on token economies], in *Learning Approaches to Therapeutic Behavior Change*, edited by Donald H. Levis. Chicago: Aldine.

Stanley, David T. 1976 *Prisoners among Us: The Problem of Parole.* Washington, DC: Brookings Institution.

Staples, Brent 2012 "California Horror Stories and the 3-Strikes Law." *New York Times* (November 25): 10.

Star, Deborah 1979 *Summary Parole: A Six and Twelve Month Follow-Up Evaluation.* Sacramento: California Department of Corrections.

Steiner, Benjamin and H. Daniel Butler 2013 "Why Don't They Work? Thoughts on the Application of New Jersey Day Reporting Centers." *Criminology and Public Policy* 12 (February): 153–162.

Steiner, Benjamin, and Emily Wright 2006 "Assessing the Relative Effects of State Direct File Waiver Laws on Violent Juvenile Crime: Deterrence or Irrelevance." *Journal of Criminal Law and Criminology* 96 (Summer): 1451–1478.

Steinhauer, Jennifer 2009 "To Trim Costs, States Relax Hard Line on Prisons." *New York Times* (March 25): 1, 22.

Steinhauer, Jennifer 2007 "California to Address Prison Overcrowding with Giant Building Program." *New York Times* (April 27): 18.

Stephan, James J. *2004 State Prison Expenditures, 2001.* Washington, DC: Bureau of Justice Statistics.

Stevenson, Carol S., Carol S. Larson, Lucy S. Carter, Deanna S. Gomby, Donna L. Terman, and Richard E. Behrman 1996 "The Juvenile Court: Analysis and Recommendations." *The Future of Children* 6 (Winter): 4–28.

Stille, Alexander 2001 "Grounded by an Income Gap." *New York Times* (December 15): 15, 17.

Stolberg, Sheryl Gay 2001 "Behind Bars, New Effort to Care for the Dying." *New York Times* (April 1): 1, 20.

Stolz, Stephanie B., Louis A. Wienckowski, and Bertram S. Brown 1975 "Behavior Modification: A Perspective on Critical Issues." *American Psychologist* 30 (November): 1027–1048.

Storm, John P. 1997 "What United States Probation Officers Do." *Federal Probation* 61 (March): 13–18.

Strong, Ann 1981 *Case Classification Manual, Module One: Technical Aspects of Interviewing.* Austin: Texas Adult Probation Commission.

Sudnow, David 1965 "Normal Crimes: Sociological Features of the Penal Code." *Social Problems* 12 (Winter): 255–64.

Sullivan, John, and Matthew Purdy 1995 "In Corrections Business, Shrewdness Pays." *New York Times* (July 23): 1, 13.

Sulzer, Beth, and G. Roy Mayer 1972 *Behavior Modification Procedures for School Personnel.* Hinsdale, IL: Dryden.

Sutherland, Edwin H. 1973 *Edwin Sutherland: On Analyzing Crime*, edited by Karl Schuessler. Chicago: University of Chicago Press.

Sutton, John R. 1988 *Stubborn Children: Controlling Delinquency in the United States, 1649–1981.* Berkeley: University of California Press.

Swanger, Harry F. 1988 "*Hendrickson v. Griggs*: A Review of the Legal and Policy Implications for Juvenile Justice Policymakers." *Crime and Delinquency* 34 (April): 209–27.

Sydney, Linda M. 2006 *Gender-Responsive Strategies for Women Offenders.* Washington, DC: National Institute of Corrections.

Sykes, Gresham M., and David Matza 1957 "Techniques of Neutralization: A Theory of Delinquency." *American Sociological Review* 22 (December): 664–70.

Takagi, Paul 1975 "The Walnut Street Jail: A Penal Reform to Centralize the Powers of the State." *Federal Probation* 39 (December): 18–26.

Task Force on Corrections 1966 *Task Force Report: Corrections.* Washington, DC: U.S. Government Printing Office.

Taxman, Faye 2007 "Reentry and Supervision: One Is Impossible Without the Other." *Corrections Today* (April): 98–101, 105.

Taxman, Faye S. 2009 "No Illusions: Offender and Organizational Change in Maryland's Proactive Community Supervision Efforts." *Criminology and Public Policy* 7 (May): 275–302.

Taxman, Faye S., Christina Yancy, and Jeanne E. Bilanin 2006 *Proactive Community Supervision in Maryland: Changing Offender Outcomes.* Baltimore, MD: Maryland Division of Parole and Probation.

Taylor, Ian, Paul Walton, and Jock Young 1973 *The New Criminology.* New York: Harper and Row.

Tedford, Daniel 2009 "Probation Officer Shoots at Dog in Duarte." *Pasadena Star News* (August 7): Internet.

Teeters, Negley K. 1970 "The Passing of Cherry Hill: Most Famous Prison in the World." *Prison Journal* 50 (Spring–Summer): 1–12.

Terry, Don 1993 "Town Builds a Prison and Stores Its Hopes There." *New York Times* (January 3): 9.

Tewksbury, Richard, Wesley G. Jennings, Kristen Zgoba 2012 *Sex Offenders: Recidivism and Collateral Consequences.* Washington, DC: National Institute of Justice.

Texas Adult Probation Commission (TAPC) 1988 *A Comparison of Special Program Probationers and Prison Inmates.* Austin: TAPC.

Texas Department of Criminal Justice (TDCJ) 2011 *Evaluation of Offenders Released in Fiscal Year 2007 That Completed Rehabilitation Tier Programs.* Austin: TDCJ.

Thalheimer, Donald J. 1975 *Halfway Houses*, Volume 2. Washington, DC: U.S. Government Printing Office.

Therapeutic Community 2002 National Institute on Drug Abuse Research Report. Washington, DC: U.S. Department of Human Services.

Thorne, Gaylord L., Roland G. Tharp, and Ralph J. Wetzel 1967 "Behavior Modification Techniques: New Tools for Probation Officers." *Federal Probation* 31 (June): 21–27.

Thornton, Robert L. 2003 *New Approaches to Staff Safety.* Washington, DC: National Institute of Corrections.

Thigpen, Morris L. 2004 "Foreword" to *Parole Violations Revisited*, by Peggy B. Burke. Washington, DC: National Institute of Corrections.

Tims, Frank M., Nancy Jainchill, and George De Leon 1994 "Therapeutic Communities and Treatment Research," in *Therapeutic Community: Advances in Research and Application*, pages 1–15. Rockville, MD: National Institute on Drug Abuse.

Toborg, Mary A., Lawrence J. Carter, Raymond H. Milkman, and Dennis W. Davis 1978 *The Transition from Prison to Employment: An Assessment of Community-Based Programs.* Washington, DC: U.S. Government Printing Office.

Tonry, Michael 2006 "Purposes and Functions of Sentencing." *Crime and Justice* 34 (1): Internet.

Torbet, Patricia, Richard Gable, Hunter Hurst IV, Imogene Montgomery, Linda Szymanski, and Douglas Thomas 1996 *State Responses to Serious and Violent*

Juvenile Crime. Washington, DC: Office of Juvenile Justice and Delinquency Prevention.

Torbet, Patricia, Patrick Griffen, Hunter Hurst, Jr., and Lynn Ryan MacKenzie 2000 *Juveniles Facing Criminal Sanctions: Three States That Changed the Rules.* Washington, DC: Office of Juvenile Justice and Delinquency Prevention.

Torgerson, Fernando G. 1962 "Differentiating and Defining Casework and Psychotherapy." *Social Work* 7 (2).

Torres, Sam 1999 "Early Termination: Outdated Concept in an Era of Punitiveness." *Federal Probation* 63 (June): 35–41.

Toseland, Robert W., and Robert F. Rivas 1998 *An Introduction to Group Work Practice,* 4th ed. Boston: Allyn and Bacon.

Travis, Jeremy 2000 *But They All Come Back: Rethinking Prisoner Reentry.* Washington, DC: National Institute of Justice.

Travis, Jeremy, and Joan Petersilia 2001 "Reentry Reconsidered: A New Look at an Old Question." *Crime and Delinquency* 47 (July): 291–313.

Travis, Jeremy and Sarah Lawrence 2002 *Beyond the Prison Gates: The State of Parole in America.* Washington, DC: Urban Institute Justice Policy Center.

Treaster, Joseph B. 1994 "Beyond Probation: Breaking the Cycle of Juvenile Arrests." *New York Times* (December 29): 1, 11.

Tripodi, Stephen J., Johnny S. Kim, and Kimberly Bender 2010 "Is Employment Associated with Reduced Recidivism?" *International Journal of Offender Therapy and Comparative Criminology* 54 (5): 706–720.

Tubman-Carbone, Hether 2009 "An Exploratory Study of New Jersey's Sex Offender Polygraph Policy: Report to the New Jersey State Parole Board," November 13.

Turner, Susan, and Terry Fain 2005 *Accomplishments in Juvenile Probation in California over the Last Decade.* Arlington, VA: RAND.

Turner, Susan, and Joan Petersilia 1996 *Work Release: Recidivism and Corrections Costs in Washington State.* Washington, DC: Office of Justice Programs.

Twentieth Century Fund Task Force on Sentencing 1976 *Fair and Certain Punishment.* New York: McGraw-Hill.

Umbreit, Mark S. 1994 *Victim Meets Offender: The Impact of Restorative Justice and Mediation.* Monsey, NY: Willow Tree Press.

Umbreit, Mark S., and Mark Carey 1995 "Restorative Justice: Implications for Organizational Change." *Federal Probation* 59 (March): 47–54.

Urbina, Ian 2003 "New York's Federal Judges Protest Sentencing Procedures." *New York Times* (December 8): B1, 4.

U.S. Attorney General 1939 *Attorney General's Survey of Release Procedures: Pardon.* Washington, DC: U.S. Government Printing Office.

U.S. Bureau of Justice Assistance 1989 *Electronic Monitoring in Intensive Probation and Parole Programs.* Washington, DC: U.S. Government Printing Office.

Visher, Christy A., and Jeremy Travis 2003 "Transitions from Prison to Community: Understanding Individual Pathways." *Annual Review of Sociology* 29: 89–113.

Vold, George B., and Thomas J. Bernard 1986 *Theoretical Criminology,* 3rd ed. New York: Oxford University Press.

Von Hirsch, Andrew 1976 *Doing Justice: The Choice of Punishments.* New York: Hill and Wang.

Von Hirsch, Andrew, and Kathleen J. Hanrahan 1978 *Abolish Parole?* Washington, DC: U.S. Government Printing Office.

Wagner, Dennis 1989 "An Evaluation of the High Risk Offender Intensive Supervision Project." *Perspectives* 13 (Summer): 22–27.

Wagner, Dennis, and Christopher Baird 1993 *Evaluation of the Florida Community Control Program.* Washington, DC: National Institute of Justice.

Waldo, Gordon, and David Griswold 1979 "Issues in the Measurement of Recidivism," in *The Rehabilitation of Criminal Offenders: Problems and Prospects,* edited by Lee Sechrest, Susan O. White, and Elizabeth D. Brown. Washington, DC: National Academy of Sciences.

Waldorf, Dan 1973 *Careers in Dope.* Englewood Cliffs, NJ: Prentice Hall.

Walker, Samuel 1980 *Popular Justice: A History of American Criminal Justice.* New York: Oxford University Press.

Wallace, Dee and Laura Wyckoff n.d. *Going to Work with a Criminal Record: Lessons from the Fathers at Work Initiative.* Philadelphia: Public/Private Ventures.

Walmsley, Roy 2011 *World Prison Population List.* London, UK: International Centre for Prison Studies.

Walters, Scott T., Amanda M. Vader, Norma Nguyen, T. Robert Harris, and Jennifer Eells 2010 "Motivational Interviewing as a Supervision Strategy in Probation: A Randomized Effectiveness Trial." *Journal of Offender Rehabilitation* 49 (5): 309–323.

Walters, T. Scott, Michael D. Clark, Ray Gingerich, and Melissa L. Meltzer 2007 *Motivating Offenders to Change.* Washington, DC: National Institute of Corrections.

Washington State Institute for Public Policy (WSIPP) 2006 *Evidence-Based Public Policy Options to Reduce Future Prison Construction, Criminal Justice Costs, and Crime Rates.* Olympia, WA: WSIPP.

Weber, Max 1958 *Protestant Ethic and the Spirit of Capitalism.* New York: Scribner's.

Weed, William Speed 2001 "Incubating Disease." *Mother Jones* (July 10): Internet.

Weidlein-Crist, Philisa J., and John P. O'Connor 2008 *Delaware Sex Offenders: Profiles and Criminal Justice Outcomes.* Newark, DE: Office of Management and Budget Statistical Analysis Center.

Weisheit, Ralph H., and Diane M. Alexander 1988 "Juvenile Justice and the Demise of Parens Patriae." *Federal Probation* 52 (December): 56–63.

Weiss, Robert P. 2001 "'Repatriating' Low-Wage Work: The Political Economy of Prison Labor Reprivatization in the Postindustrial United States." *Criminology* 39 (May): 253–291.

Wellisch, Jean, M. Douglas Anglin, and Michael L. Prendergast 1993 "Numbers and Characteristics of Drug-Using Women in the Criminal Justice System: Implications for Treatment." *Journal of Drug Issues* 23 (Winter): 7–30.

West-Smith, Mary, Mark R. Pogrebin, and Eric D. Poole 2000 "Denial of Parole: An Inmate Perspective." *Federal Probation* (December): 3–10.

Whitehead, John T. 1989 "The Effectiveness of Felony Probation: A Replication and Extension of Three Studies." Paper presented at the annual meeting of the American Society of Criminology, Reno, NV, November; reprinted in *Justice Quarterly* 4 (December 1991): 525–543.

Whitehead, John T., Larry T. Miller, and Laura B. Myers 1995 "The Diversionary Effectiveness of Intensive Supervision and Community Corrections Programs," in *Intermediate Sanctions: Sentencing in the 1990s,* edited by John Ortiz Smykla and William Selke, pages 135–151. Cincinnati, OH: Anderson.

Wicker, Tom 1975 *A Time to Die.* New York: Quadrangle.

Widom, Cathy Spatz 1996 "Childhood Sexual Abuse and Its Criminal Consequences." *Society* 33 (May-June): 47–54.

Widom, Cathy S., and Michael G. Maxfield 2001 *An Update on the "Cycle of Violence."* Washington, DC: National Institute of Justice.

Wiebush, Richard G. 1993 "Juvenile Intensive Supervision: The Impact on Felony Offenders Diverted from Institutional Placement." *Crime and Delinquency* 39 (January): 68–89.

Wiebush, Richard G., and Donna M. Hamparian 1991 "Variations in 'Doing' Juvenile Intensive Supervision: Programmatic Issues in Four Ohio Jurisdictions," in *Intensive Interventions with High-Risk Youths in Juvenile Probation and Parole,* edited by Troy L. Armstrong, pages 153–88. Monsey, NY: Criminal Justice Press.

Wiederanders, Mark R. 1983 *Success on Parole.* Sacramento: California Department of Corrections.

Wiggins, Mike 2007 "Couple Charged with Falsely Accusing Parole Officer of Having Sex with Parolees." *Daily Sentinel* (January 25): Internet.

Wilcock, Katherine, Theodore M. Hammett, and Dale G. Parent 1995 *Controlling Tuberculosis in Community Corrections.* Washington, DC: National Institute of Justice.

Wilensky, Harold L., and Charles N. Lebeaux 1958 *Industrial Society and Social Welfare.* New York: Russell Sage Foundation.

Wilks, Dana, and Kris Nash 2008 *Pre-Release Termination and Post-Release Recidivism Rates of Colorado's Probationers: FY 2007 Releasees.* Denver: State Court Administrator's Office.

Wilson, David B., Leana Allen Bouffard, and Doris L. MacKenzie 2005 "A Quantitative Review of Structured, Group-Oriented, Cognitive-Behavioral Programs for Offenders." *Criminal Justice and Behavior* 32 (April): 172–204.

Wilson, James A., and Robert C. Davis 2006 "Good Intentions Meet Hard Realities: An Evaluation of the Project Greenlight Reentry." *Criminology and Public Policy* 5 (May): 303–38.

Wilson, James Q., and George Kelling 1982 "Broken Windows: The Police and Neighborhood Safety." *Atlantic Monthly* (March). 29–38.

Wines, Frederick Howard 1975 *Punishment and Reformation: A Study of the Penitentiary System*. New York: Thomas Y. Crowell.

Wish, Eric n.d. *Drug Testing*. Rockville, MD: National Institute of Justice.

Wolf, Thomas J. 1997 "What United States Pretrial Officers Do." *Federal Probation* 61 (March): 19–24.

Wolpe, Joseph, Andrew Salter, and L. H. Reyna, eds. 1964 *The Conditioning Therapies*. New York: Holt, Rinehart and Winston.

Wren, Christopher S. 1998 "Connecticut Bill Cuts Jail Time for Nonviolent Offenders Who Take Frequent Drug Tests." *New York Times* (May 6): 23.

Wright, Martin 1991 *Justice for Victims and Offenders: A Restorative Response to Crime*. Philadelphia: Open University.

Wright, Ronald F. 1998 *Managing Prison Growth in North Carolina through Structured Sentencing*. Washington, DC: National Institute of Justice.

Wubbolding, Robert E. 2011 *Reality Therapy*. Washington, DC: American Psychological Association.

Yelloly, Margaret 1980 *Social Work Theory and Psychoanalysis*. New York: Van Nostrand Reinhold.

Yeoman, Barry 2000 "Steeltown." *Mother Jones* (May/June): 38-47.

"Youth Justice, Separate and Unequal" 2000 *Chicago Tribune* editorial (November 21): 22.

Zawitz, Marianne W., ed. 1988 *Report to the Nation on Crime and Justice*. Washington, DC: U.S. Government Printing Office.

Zehr, Howard 1990 *Changing Lenses: A New Focus for Crime and Justice*. Schottdale, PA: Herald Press.

Zehr, Howard, and Harry Mika 1998 "Fundamental Concepts of Restorative Justice." *Contemporary Justice Review* 1 (1): 47–55.

Zevitz, Richard G., and Mary Ann Farkas 2000 "The Impact of Sex-Offender Community Notification on Probation/Parole in Wisconsin." *International Journal of Offender Therapy and Comparative Criminology* 44 (1): 8–21.

Zevitz, Richard G., and Susan R. Takata, Kristen, Zgoba, Bonita M. Veysey, and Melissa Dalessandra 2010 "An Analysis of the Effectiveness of Community Notification and Registration: Do the Best Intentions Predict the Best Practices?" *Justice Quarterly* 27 (October): 667–691.

Zielbauer, Paul 2001 "Felons Gain Voting Rights in Connecticut." *New York Times* (May 15): Internet.

Zimring, Franklin E., and Gordon Hawkins 1995 *Incapacitation: Penal Confinement and the Restraint of Crime*. New York: Oxford University Press.

Zweig, Janine, Jennifer Yahner, and Cindy Redcross 2011 "For Whom Does a Transitional Jobs Program Work?" *Criminology and Public Policy* 10 (November): 945–977.

Author Index

Subject Index